LACTATION
Physiology, Nutrition, and Breast-Feeding

LACTATION

Physiology, Nutrition, and Breast-Feeding

Edited by

Margaret C. Neville and
Marianne R. Neifert

University of Colorado School of Medicine
Denver, Colorado

PLENUM PRESS • NEW YORK AND LONDON *1983*

Library of Congress Cataloging in Publication Data

Main entry under title:

Lactation: physiology, nutrition, and breast-feeding.

Bibliography: p.
Includes index.
1. Lactation. 2. Breast-feeding. 3. Infants—Nutrition. I. Neville, Margaret C.,
date-   . II. Neifert, Marianne R.
QP246.L33   1983   612'.664   83-17652
ISBN 0-306-41311-6

©1983 Plenum Press, New York
A Division of Plenum Publishing Corporation
233 Spring Street, New York, N.Y. 10013

Printed in the United States of America

Contributors

Jonathan C. Allen, Ph.D. • Department of Physiology, University of Colorado School of Medicine, Denver, Colorado 80262

Sally E. Berga, Ph.D. • Department of Physiology, University of Colorado School of Medicine, Denver, Colorado 80262

Watson A. Bowes, Jr., M.D. • Department of Obstetrics/Gynecology, University of North Carolina at Chapel Hill, Chapel Hill, North Carolina 27514

Clare E. Casey, Ph.D. • Department of Pediatrics, University of Colorado Health Sciences Center, Denver, Colorado 80262

Janice E. Errick, Ph.D. • Department of MCD Biology, University of Colorado, Boulder, Colorado 80309

Stanley F. Gould, M.D., Ph.D • Departments of Obstetrics and Gynecology and Anatomy, University of Colorado School of Medicine, Denver, Colorado 80262

K. Michael Hambidge, M.D. • Department of Pediatrics, University of Colorado Health Sciences Center, Denver, Colorado 80262

Anthony R. Hayward, M.D. • Department of Pediatrics, University of Colorado School of Medicine, Denver, Colorado 80262

Kathryn B. Horwitz, Ph.D • Departments of Medicine and Biochemistry, Biophysics, and Genetics, University of Colorado Health Sciences Center, Denver, Colorado 80262

James A. McGregor, M.D., C.M., F.A.C.O.G. • Department of Obstetrics and Gynecology, University of Colorado School of Medicine, Denver, Colorado 80262

Mary B. Mockus, Ph.D. • Departments of Medicine and Biochemistry, Biophysics, and Genetics, University of Colorado Health Sciences Center, Denver, Colorado 80262

Marianne R. Neifert, M.D. • Department of Pediatrics, University of Colorado School of Medicine, Denver, Colorado 80262

Margaret C. Neville, Ph.D. • Department of Physiology, University of Colorado School of Medicine, Denver, Colorado 80262

Robert G. Peterson, M.D. • Children's Hospital of Eastern Ontario, Ottawa, Ontario, Canada K1H 8L1

Robin Dee Post, Ph.D. • Department of Psychiatry, University of Colorado School of Medicine, Denver, Colorado 80262

Rhoda Singer, M.D. • Department of Psychiatry, University of Colorado School of Medicine, Denver, Colorado 80262

Tamiko Kano-Sueoka, Ph.D. • Department of MCD Biology, University of Colorado, Boulder, Colorado 80309

Christopher Watters, Ph.D. • Department of Biology, Middlebury College, Middlebury, Vermont 05753

Preface

This book had its genesis in the frustrations of the editors in locating authoritative, up-to-date material for an interdisciplinary graduate course in mammary gland biology, lactation, and breast-feeding. As we turned to the original literature several reasons for the dearth of usable material became clear: (1) In the areas of mammary gland biology and physiology, particularly as they relate to the human, reviews simply have not kept up with current research, which has in the last two decades provided tremendous insight into the mechanisms of milk secretion and its control. (2) The lack of interest in human milk as infant food inhibited researchers until very recently from investigating human lactation. (3) Much of the relevant clinical information remains anecdotal with little scientific basis.

In this book we have tried to present the fundamentals of mammary gland physiology at the organismic and cellular levels in a form readily understood by physicians, scientists, and other professionals. This basic information is accompanied by authoritative reviews of the nutritional and immunological properties of human milk and by clinically relevant chapters designed to help health care professionals deal with the medical problems of the breast-feeding mother and her infant. We have strived in these chapters for up-to-date, authoritative, but readable accounts. In so far as possible we have avoided areas where much of our understanding rests on speculation. In the clinical domain this was not always possible because of a lack of solid, scientific information about breast-feeding.

In dedicating this book to our families, we wish to express our appreciation for their support throughout the seemingly endless task of writing and editing these chapters. We would also like to thank George Tarver, Julie Blish, and Pat Allen for their expert illustrations, Brian, Mike, and Dorothy for manhandling the references, Joy Seacat for helping us get it all together at the end, and Kirk Jensen of Plenum Press for his patient encouragement.

Margaret C. Neville
Marianne R. Neifert

Denver, Colorado

Contents

3. The Mechanisms of Milk Secretion

Margaret C. Neville, Jonathan C. Allen, and Christopher Watters

4. Regulation of Mammary Development and Lactation

Margaret C. Neville

5. Cellular and Molecular Aspects of the Hormonal Control of Mammary Function

Margaret C. Neville and Sally E. Berga

8. The Immunology of Breast Milk

Anthony R. Hayward

IV. Medical Management of Breast-Feeding

9. Routine Management of Breast-Feeding

Marianne R. Neifert

10. Infant Problems in Breast-Feeding

Marianne R. Neifert

11. Maternal Problems in Lactation

James A. McGregor and Marianne R. Neifert

12. Psychological Implications of Breast-Feeding for the Mother

Robin Dee Post and Rhoda Singer

13. Drugs, Toxins, and Environmental Agents in Breast Milk

Robert G. Peterson and Watson A. Bowes, Jr.

14. Lactation and Contraception

James A. McGregor

15. Pregnancy, Lactation, and Breast Cancer

Mary B. Mockus and Kathryn B. Horwitz

LACTATION
Physiology, Nutrition, and Breast-Feeding

I

Introduction

1

An Introduction to Lactation and Breast-Feeding

Margaret C. Neville and Marianne R. Neifert

An essential characteristic of mammals is the capacity of the female to nourish her offspring with milk, the secretion of the mammary glands. This fluid provides not only nutrients for physical growth but also both immune and nonimmune elements for protection against disease and an opportunity for interaction between newborn and mother which may, at least in higher species of mammals, initiate the learning process necessary to the transition to independent living. In this introductory chapter, we will begin by viewing human lactation from an evolutionary standpoint. Two sections will then be devoted to the historical development of our understanding of milk secretion and its hormonal control. Finally, we will consider breast-feeding in its historical context, a discussion which provides a perspective from which to view the controversy over breast milk versus formula in underdeveloped countries.

EVOLUTION AND LACTATION

The most primitive mammary glands appear in the egg-laying mammals, the *monotremes* or protheria.[1,2] In these species, the glands consist of two abdominal lobes, one on each side of the midline. Each lobe consists of a collection of about 100 simple tubular glands or alveoli, each with its own opening onto the abdominal wall. Each opening is associated with a hair follicle from which grows a very stiff hair, an observation which led to the erroneous idea that the young of monotremes lick the mammary secretion from these hairs[1] rather than suckling. More careful observations by Griffiths[3]

Margaret C. Neville • Department of Physiology, University of Colorado School of Medicine, Denver, Colorado 80262. *Marianne R. Neifert* • Department of Pediatrics, University of Colorado School of Medicine, Denver, Colorado 80262.

showed that echidna (or spiny anteaters, a frequently studied monotreme) do indeed suckle[4,5] and that the secretion of milk is probably associated with a milk ejection reflex which can be elicited by oxytocin just as in placental mammals.[2]

Although marsupials or metatheria are often regarded as more primitive than eutherian mammals, recent studies make it quite clear that, at least in so far as lactation is considered, they have attained the most sophisticated development of all mammals.[6] In marsupials, the mammary glands, which possess true teats, are usually situated in a pouch. The number of glands varies from two to as many as 25 in some oppossums. In the kangaroo and its smaller relative, the wallaby, the neonate emerges from the vaginal orifice after about 26 days of gestation and crawls unaided to the pouch where it attaches to one of four teats and begins to suckle continuously, receiving a clear, watery secretion. It remains in the pouch through a period which corresponds roughly to the latter portion of intrauterine gestation in eutherian mammals, e.g., about 200 days in the agile wallaby.[7] The nipple and mammary gland grow along with the suckling young and the composition of the mammary secretion changes markedly with growth.[8] Once the young wallaby has left the pouch, it continues to suckle intermittently and a second neonate is born which enters the pouch and attaches to a different, smaller teat. The two young, at very different developmental stages, continue to suckle on glands which are also at very different stages of development, receiving milks of different compositions. Recent studies[7] suggest that the neural mechanisms which control letdown are highly developed, so that the stimulation provided by the younger sibling brings about a continuous low level of oxytocin release, sufficient to maintain the small mammary gland in a contracted state for continuous delivery of milk. When the older sibling sucks strongly on the larger teat, it is likely that oxytocin is released in a bolus large enough to produce milk ejection from the larger gland. These adaptations to suckle two young with quite different nutritional requirements continue to fascinate scientists interested in lactation. It is likely that further study of these mammals will provide much interesting information about the interplay between the hormonal and local factors involved in the regulation of mammary growth and secretion.

Although eutherian or true placental mammals do not appear to have the subtle control mechanisms which allow kangaroos and wallabies to suckle young of different ages, the mammary secretion is nevertheless of vital importance in the nutrition of the newborn. The external form, number, and position of the mammary glands vary widely between species as does the composition of the milk. It is tempting to draw generalizations about the relationship of milk composition to the metabolic requirements of the young, the stage of lactation or the size of the animal.[4] Such generalizations by and large do not withstand critical scrutiny, each species apparently having developed a milk composition appropriate to the particular needs of its young for growth.[9] There is, however, a general proportionality between the concentrations of protein, calcium, and phosphate if one surveys the milks of many species,[10] probably related to the need to supply these nutrients for the proportional growth of skeletal mass and muscle.

Human lactation has developed several unique features. For example, human milk has the lowest concentration of any milk examined to date of protein, calcium, and phosphate and the highest concentration of lactose[11] perhaps reflecting both the relatively slow postuterine growth and the high glucose requirement of the large human brain. In addition, the human breast has a protuberant form which develops at puberty and persists in the nonpregnant female. Although many breast-feeding advocates point out that the form and location of the breast allows eye-to-eye contact between mother and infant during the nursing process, the association of the breasts with beauty and sexuality throughout literature and art cannot be denied. Even surgeons have waxed eloquent; for example, Sir Astley Cooper wrote in the early 19th century:[12]

> At puberty the mammary glands enlarge, and become prominent and the breasts assume their roundness, intumescence and agreeable form, the beauty of which is heightened by the rosy colour of the nipple and areola, and the meandering of the veins under the firm snowy whiteness of the skin, giving it altogether a marbled appearance.

Although the sexual significance of the breasts may be overemphasized in our culture, it is likely that the role of the breasts in human reproduction is not limited to the provision of nourishment to the infant. Rather the breasts must participate in those mysterious attractions which bring a male and a female together to form the complex web of attachments resulting first, in the conception of an infant and then, under optimal conditions, in the continuation of a familial relationship which provides a propitious environment for the nurture of the offspring.

HISTORICAL PERSPECTIVES ON MILK SECRETION

The anatomy and physiology of the mammary gland were first reviewed by von Haller in 1765[13] who concluded that milk was derived from blood, a view disputed throughout the early 19th century by others who insisted on either a uterine or a lymphatic origin for the mammary secretion. During the first half of the 19th century, much effort was devoted to elucidation of the gross morphology of the mammary gland. This work culminated in the anatomical studies of the English surgeon, Sir Astley Cooper,[12] on the human breast, both normal and diseased. Cooper defined the lobuloalveolar structure of the mammary gland, made detailed dissections of the blood supply and innervation of the gland (Fig. 1) and described such physiological occurances as the "draught" (letdown) and lactogenesis.

Although Cooper subscribed to the theory that milk was derived from the blood, he was not quite willing to give up the idea of a connection between the uterus and the mammary gland, proposing that blood was shunted from the uterus to the mammary gland after birth by anastomoses

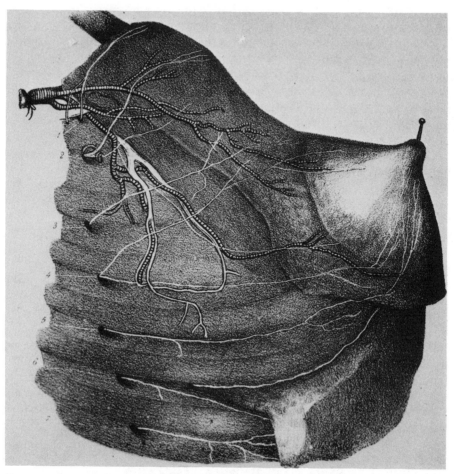

Figure 1. The innervation and blood supply of the areolus. Dissection of the right-hand breast showing that both the fourth and fifth mammary nerves contribute to the innervation of the nipple in the human. (Etching from Sir Astley Cooper, *The Anatomy and Diseases of the Breast*, Lea and Blanchard, Philadelphia, 1845.)

between the epigastric and mammary arteries under the control of the "grand sympathetic nerve." The idea of a connection between the uterus and mammary gland is an old one. Leonardo da Vinci, in a drawing, shows the uterus and mammary gland directly connected by a system of ducts.[14] Cowie[15] pointed out that the theory of the uterine origin of milk persisted much longer than might seem reasonable, possibly because nursing the infant is often associated with uterine cramping, particularly in the early postpartum period. The observation that milk letdown often accompanies orgasm in lactating women probably also contributed to the belief.

In the second half of the 19th century, the light microscope was applied to various preparations of the mammary gland and, with the rise of the cell theory, numerous hypotheses were put forward about the mechanism of secretion.[16] Milk was variously considered to be the product of holocrine secretion (sloughing of entire cells), leukocytic infiltration (e.g., similar to pus formation), apocrine secretion (breaking off of the portion of the cell above the nucleus) or merocrine secretion (no cell destruction). Unfortunately, the level of resolution of the light microscope was not sufficient to resolve the argument which was compounded by the common view that milk was secreted more rapidly during the draught or letdown reflex. This problem was not resolved until the 1930s when Peterson[17] showed by means of pressure measurements in animals that mammary secretion was a continuous process. Further, he and his colleagues were able to make a clear distinction between milk secretion and the ejection of milk into the mammary ducts. Only with the introduction of the electron microscope and the careful tracing of the biochemical pathways involved has it been possible to clearly delineate the cellular mechanisms of milk secretion. Because much of the relevant work has only been completed within the past decade, many 19th century ideas including the confounding of milk secretion and milk ejection and the idea of apocrine secretion have persisted overlong in some of the clinical literature.

HISTORICAL PERSPECTIVES ON THE HORMONAL CONTROL OF LACTATION

The control of lactation has long been of interest to both biologists and clinicians and many theories have been advanced, tested, and withdrawn over past 200 years. Here we will be able to trace the development, and in some cases, the demise of only some of the major concepts. Unlike the mechanisms of milk secretion which are by now reasonably well understood, our knowledge of the mechanisms by which hormones regulate the growth and activities of the mammary gland is still evolving rapidly and major advances in concepts can be expected within the present decade.

It was early recognized[18] that the development of mammary function can be divided into several distinct stages: (1) *mammogenesis*, the growth and differentiation of mammary alveolar tissue, (2) *lactogenesis*, the onset of copious milk secretion around parturition, (3) *lactation*, the continuing production of milk, and (4) *involution*, the return of the mammary gland to a less differentiated state at cessation of lactation. Once the difference between milk secretion and ejection was clarified,[17] the hormonal mechanisms which control lactation itself were quickly elucidated, with prolactin being found to control secretion and oxytocin to mediate letdown. Involution has received relatively little attention. The regulation of both mammogenesis and lactogenesis has been a source of confusion for many decades. The picture which is currently emerging from studies at the cellular and molecular level differs considerably from that often found in current textbooks. The textbook ideas, developed prior to 1960, called for a central role for ovarian steroids in stimulating mammogenesis and for a prolactin surge which stimulated lactogenesis. More recent work suggests that a predominant role should be assigned to lactogenic peptides of pituitary and placental origin in stimulating mammary growth with a postpartal fall in progesterone acting as the trigger to lactogenesis.

Placenta versus Ovary in Mammary Development

It was only near the turn of this century that it became appreciated that the development and function of the mammary glands were under the control of "inner secretions"—as hormones were then termed. In 1905, Halban[18] published a classic set of observations on human pregnancy and lactation from which he drew two extremely important conclusions: (1) Two factors are secreted by the placenta during pregnancy; one stimulates mammary growth; the second is inhibitory to secretion. (2) These placental factors are similar to the ovarian factors which control the growth of the breast at puberty. Had research during the next half-century been directed more toward an understanding of the placental factors rather than the ovarian hormones, an understanding of mammogenesis and lactogenesis might have developed more quickly.

A role for ovarian secretions in mammary growth was suggested by the observation that pseudopregnancy was accompanied by complete mammary development and milk secretion in species like the dog and rabbit where persistance of the corpus luteum follows sterile mating.[19,20] Many studies in the late 1920s, showing that mammary growth was produced by injection of estrogen-containing extracts of ovaries, placentas, or urine,[21] provided further support for this idea. Relatively pure estrogens and progesterone became available for experimental use during the 1930's.[21] By 1932, it was clear in the rabbit, rat, and mouse that only ductile growth was stimulated by estrogen and that both males and females responded to the hormone with mammary growth. Progesterone alone had no effects on mammary growth, but when used in conjunction with estrogens it was possible to obtain full lobuloalveolar development. From these studies, carried out in many species both in America[22] and in England,[21] the inference was made that estrogen and progesterone directly stimulated mammary development in pregnancy and the ovary was given a central role in the regulation of mammary growth.

A Role for the Pituitary Gland

Meanwhile, a pituitary hormone which stimulated lactation was also under investigation. Following the observation by Stricker and Grueter in 1928,[23] that pituitary extracts produced milk secretion in pregnant rabbits, Riddle, Bates, and Dykshorn[24] prepared a purer extract that had the same effect. They designated the active principle in their extract as "prolactin" and showed it to have a separate identity from the other known pituitary hormones. The role of this hormone in the maintenance of lactation was quickly established. However, because injection of prolactin generally did not promote mammary development in virgin animals unless they had been pretreated with estrogen and progesterone, it was not thought to promote mammary growth. Nevertheless, the idea of a "pituitary mammogen" continued to be expressed from time to time. For example, in 1939, Turner[22] suggested that the ovarian hormones exert their effect indirectly, their action being mediated by the pituitary gland. The idea that steroid hormone action could be mediated by pituitary hormones was given considerable support by the work of Reece and Leonard[25] who found that hypophysectomy prevented the stimulation of mammary growth with estrogens and progesterone. However, the injection of pituitary extracts or hormones into hypophysectomized animals gave conflicting results, with many experimenters failing to obtain mammary growth with these preparations.

The Hypothesis of Meites and Turner

The rather confusing observations of the 1930s finally culminated in the hypothesis of Meites and Turner, first proposed in 1942[26] and restated in 1948[27] as follows:

1. In pregnancy, *estrogen and progesterone* promote full mammary growth, the mammary gland is relatively insensitive to prolactin stimulation.
2. In pregnancy, *progesterone* inhibits *estrogen* stimulation of *prolactin* secretion.
3. At parturition, an increase in circulating *prolactin* and *cortisol* and a fall in *estrogen* and progesterone bring about the onset of lactation.

It is now clear that this hypothesis, although partially correct, presented several problems: estrogen and progesterone in the absence of the pituitary do not promote mammary growth, progesterone has little or no effect on prolactin secretion even in the presence of estrogen, and the major trigger to lactogenesis is now thought to be a fall in progesterone (see Chapter 4). However, because this hypothesis served as a guide for much of the research on the hormonal control of lactation for the next two decades, particularly in the United States, it is necessary to discuss each of its tenets in somewhat more detail.

As time passed, evidence began to accumulate that pituitary hormones played a major role in mammary growth and development. For example, estrogens and progesterone did not induce mammary growth in fully hypophysectomized animals[25] and studies of Elias[28] and others[29] in the late 1950s showed that insulin, cortisol, and prolactin were sufficient to maintain differentiation of mammary tissue *in vitro* in the absence of sex steroids. More direct experiments suggesting a positive role for pituitary hormones were provided by Clifton and Furth[30] who implanted a pituitary mammotropic tumor secreting prolactin, growth hormone, and ACTH into adrenogonadectomized rats. They obtained good mammary growth in the complete absence of steroid hormones. Results of this nature finally led Meites to conclude in 1966[31] that "the anterior pituitary hormones are the primary stimulators of mammary growth even in normal 'physiological states.'"

In 1970, with the development of a radioimmunoassay capable of measuring plasma prolactin levels, it finally became possible directly to test the second part of the hypothesis of Meites and Turner. Chen and Meites[32] measured the effect of estrogen on prolactin secretion and found that estrogen at all doses produced a significant increase in plasma prolactin levels over the baseline. Progesterone partially inhibited the estrogen-stimulated prolactin release but in no combination of dosages did progesterone decrease prolactin secretion below the baseline. After these experiments, it was no longer possible to conclude that ovarian steroids inhibited prolactin secretion during pregnancy; on the contrary, the result made it quite clear that a stimulation of prolactin secretion was one effect of increased levels of estrogen and raised the possibility that this phenomenon accounted for the ability of earlier workers to induce mammary development with estrogen injections.

The validity of the third part of the hypothesis was brought into question by an experiment of Kuhn[33] who used the appearance of lactose in the mammary glands of rats as a marker for lactogenesis. He found that progesterone given around the time of parturition in pregnant rats prevented the normally observed increase in lactose content and concluded from these experiments that progesterone during pregnancy prevented secretion of milk by the developing mammary gland. He proposed that the withdrawal of this steroid at parturition brought about the changes associated with lactogenesis. Evidence for this hypothesis is discussed fully in Chapter 4. Because arguments based on the tenets of Meites and Turner persisted well into the past decade, there is still much confusion in the literature about the hormonal control of lactogenesis.

Multiple Hormonal Control

Evidence for multiple hormonal involvement in the induction of mammary growth became available in the 1950s. Lyons[34] carried out extensive experiments injecting replacement hormones into "triply operated" rats (rats from which the ovaries, pituitary, and adrenal gland had been removed) and was able to obtain ductile proliferation with the injection of estrogen, desoxycorticosterone acetate, and growth hormone. Addition of progesterone, prolactin, and prednisolone to this regimen produced the degree of lobuloalveolar development typical of the late pregnant animal. Withdrawal of all hormones except the corticoids and the use of local implants of prolactin led to secretion of milk. Lyons[34] and Cowie[35] obtained similar responses in the goat. These types of ablation and replacement experiments led to pictures of hormonal control like that shown in Fig. 2; almost every hormone known was involved in mammary function with no definitive role assigned to any one of them. Investigators are still working to replace this picture with an

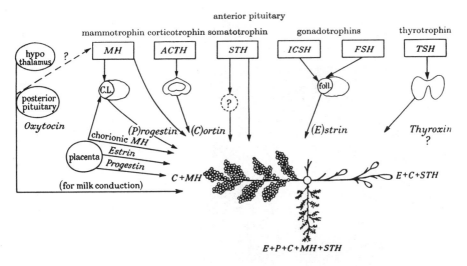

Figure 2. A scheme for the hormonal control of lactation proposed after ablation and replacement experiments performed in the 1950s. (From reference 34. Used by permission.)

understanding of the precise role of each hormone in the regulation of mammary development and function.

The Role of the Placenta

At this point, the story is nearly complete. However, we have neglected the role of the placenta. This is primarily because endocrine function of this organ, postulated by Halban in 1905,[18] was not widely appreciated until the 1960s. An early experiment published in 1945 by Leonard,[36] showing that the placenta was essential for mammary growth in pregnant rats, was followed by a report by Roy *et al.* in 1955[37] that the rat placenta possessed activity similar to that of the pituitary lactogenic hormones. However the importance of this factor was not generally realized until 1962 when Josimovich and Maclaren[38] reported the discovery of a placental lactogen in extracts of human placenta. They characterized this hormone, showing that it had lactogenic activity similar to that of prolactin and that its polypeptide structure was similar to that of both growth hormone and prolactin. Soon, studies from many laboratories[39] showed that a placental lactogen was present in many, but not all, mammalian species and that it was distinct from pituitary prolactin.

These findings set the stage for the elegant studies of hormone action in the last decade which indicate a primary role for lactogenic hormones of placental and pituitary origin in stimulating mammary growth and development with steroids playing a modulatory role. These studies are discussed in detail in Chapters 4, 5, and 6 of this book.

Figure 3. An ancient Grecian nursing flask circa 300 B.C. (From the Mead Johnson Collection of Pediatric Antiques. Used by permission.)

HISTORICAL PERSPECTIVES ON BREAST-FEEDING

Successful lactation has been a requisite for survival of the species among essentially all mammals, the single very recent exception being humans. While the feeding of breast milk substitutes to human newborns has occurred on a large scale for the past 50 years with apparent success, this brief experience represents a tiny fraction of the approximately one million year history of human lactation. This departure in infant feeding probably represents the most important change in dietary habits of the world population in the history of man and should be recognized as a relatively short-term biologic experiment, whose long-term consequences are really unknown.

Historical Alternatives to Breast-Feeding

Although successful bottle feeding is a very recent phenomenon, attempts to escape the biologic necessity to breast-feed date back to ancient times. Since the beginning of recorded history, the search for a substitute to breast-feeding has been documented, either mandated by maternal demise or attempted because women declined for one reason or another to breast-feed. Infant feeding vessels were found at infant burial sites dating as early as 2500 B.C. (Fig. 3).[40-42] Their purpose was deduced by the presence of casein deposits as well as written descriptions of their use in infant feeding. Although accounts exist of women selling their extra breast milk at the market, often animal milk would be used for bottle feeding.

Prior to modern times, the most viable alternative to maternal breast-feeding was wet-nursing, which flourished for many centuries. Hammurabi's Code (2250 B.C.) contains specific laws regulating wet nurses.[41,43] Through the ages, great care was taken in the selection of a wet nurse, since it was common belief that the infant sucked out the qualities of the nurse.[44] Thus, Michelangelo, who was nursed by a stone cutter's wife, is said to have claimed: "With my mother's milk, I sucked in the hammer and chisels I used for my statues."[42] Elaborate descriptions of the ideal wet nurse abounded, such as this one from the Renaissance Period:

> The best wet nurse . . . should be not younger than twenty years and at twenty-five she is at her best. Her own child should be over six weeks old. It is best when she has suckled two or three other children . . . She should be well built; her face healthy in appearance, tanned; and she should have a strong thick neck, strong broad breasts, not too fat and not too thin, but preferably well formed and fleshy and that do not hang down, not too small but average good size. The wet nurse should have praiseworthy habits . . .[43]

Not surprisingly, the ideal wet nurse seldom existed, and when she did, her fees were exorbitant. A conflict often arose because the wet nurse was high in the servant hierarchy but low in social origin and was often linked with immorality and prostitution or was infected with tuberculosis or syphilis. Some wet nurses were known to take far too many infants, few of whom ever returned to their parents.[42,45,46]

A typical outcome of corrupt wet-nursing was the experience of Elizabeth Clinton, the Dowager Countess of Lincoln, who had 18 children, all of whom were wet-nursed, and only one of whom survived. In 1662, she wrote a pamphlet urging other mothers to nurse their children.[41] Physicians also spoke out against mothers who refused to nurse. Among these, Walter Harris (1647–1732), outstanding pediatrician of his century, regretted that so many "Ladies of Quality" do not nurse their babies in order that they may have "more Time to dress, receive and pay Visits, attend public Shews and spend the Night at their beloved Cards."[43]

In the absence of a suitable wet nurse, "dry nursing," the use of nonmilk feedings was in common use in foundling hospitals and "baby farms" during the 17th and 18th centuries, when infant abandonment was widespread. Pap, or panada, was made by mixing flour, rice, and barley or biscuits with water and butter. "Sugar sops," bread soaked in sugar water, and other nonnutritive mixtures were also used. Needless to say, such diets were almost universally fatal, and by the end of the 18th century were generally condemned for infant feeding.[42,43,47,48]

The Decline of Breast-Feeding

While the dramatic decline of breast-feeding is considered to be a 20th century phenomenon, there are reports that breast-feeding by the infant's own mother was rare in several major European cities in the 18th century.[41] Thus, Benjamin Franklin commented in a letter to a friend:

> A Surgeon I met with here excused the Women of Paris by saying, seriously, that they could not give suck ... He ... bade me look at them and observe how flat they were on the Breast; "they have nothing more there," said he, "than I have upon the Back of my hand" ... I have since thought that there might be some Truth in his Observation, and that, possibly, Nature, finding they made no use of Bubbies, has left off giving them any.[49]

The rapid urbanization brought about by the Industrial Revolution after 1850 led to dramatic changes in lifestyle including widespread employment of women in industry, changes in women's status and role, break-down in the traditional extended family support system, and impoverished circumstances of the poorly educated, new urban masses. These factors contributed to progressively increasing artificial feeding, and high infant mortality rates persisted, primarily due to the unreliability of cow's milk. Adulteration of the milk was common, and disease was rampant in cows housed in cities. Without refrigeration and with highly contaminated milk which was unprocessed, "summer diarrhea" resulted in frequent infant death.[50]

A number of major advances occurred within the 40 year period from 1880 to 1920 that made artificial feeding both economically feasible and reasonably safe for infants. Included among these were[51]:

1. Appearance of glass bottles and, more importantly, rubber nipples
2. Availability of evaporated milk capable of shelf storage
3. Provision of sanitary water supplies
4. Demonstration that pasteurization of milk kills pathogenic organisms
5. Introduction of icebox refrigeration
6. Recognition that cod liver oil prevents rickets

By the early 20th century, the cooperation of the cow and ingenuity of man had combined to create an acceptable alternative to breast-feeding. Women's desires for further social, political, and sexual freedom, the increased emphasis on the breast as an erotic organ, and the expanding scientific interest in the regulation of infant feeding combined to promote artificial feeding in the United States and Western Europe.[52]

In 1911, 58% of American infants were still nursing at 1 year of age,[53] whereas by 1946, only 38% of infants were solely breast-fed at the time of hospital discharge. By 1966, this number had fallen to 18%.[54] Diminishing emphasis on breast-feeding was provided in medical training, while formula feeding was elaborated in detail. Despite professional concensus that human milk was superior nutrition, formulas were genuinely believed to be nearly comparable and professionals lacked skills in providing practical advice about breast-feeding. The tight control over infant feeding which formulas provided the medical profession was in keeping with the growing control exhibited in all facets of the hospital-based birthing experience.

A general increase in motivation toward breast-feeding has been evident for over a decade in Northern America, Western Europe, and Australia.

The better-educated, more affluent women who previously were the first to abandon breast-feeding are now leading the trend back to nursing. Meanwhile, the more disadvantaged mothers who lagged behind in the move to bottle feeding now are the least likely to initiate breast-feeding. Breast-feeding among Mexican Americans declined during the 1970s and black mothers are one-third as likely to nurse as white.[55]

Third-World Issues in Breast-Feeding

While the return to breast-feeding in developed countries is gratifying, Third-World nations are witnessing a recent, rapid, and alarming decline in breast-feeding, primarily over the past two decades. Reflecting the past pattern in industrialized nations, "modernized" women in urban areas who are better educated and economically advantaged are least likely to breast-feed. "Transitional" mothers, newly migrated to the urban areas and generally of low income, are demonstrating a decline in breast-feeding, whereas "traditional" mothers in the rural areas are tending to maintain their usual breast-feeding patterns.[52,56–58] Countries where modernization started earlier such as the Phillippines, Mexico, Chile, and Maylasia have generally lower breast-feeding rates than more underdeveloped rural areas, such as Nigeria or Zaire.[58–61]

The cost in economic terms and in human life and morbidity is enormous. One hundred million infants are born in the developing countries each year, 10 million of whom die before their first birthday. Five million of these succumb to diarrhea and dehydration, and one million of the infant deaths have been attributed directly to contaminated infant formula.[62] In broader terms, it is estimated that there are 10 million cases of severe protein–calorie malnutrition in the third world annually, half or more that could be protected wholly or in part by breast-feeding from adequately nourished mothers. Another 5 million are thought to suffer from diarrhea associated with bottle feeding, making approximately 10 million children harmed by inadequate lactation, with an annual medical expenditure of one billion dollars and a potential loss of three million lives.[52]

In the developing countries where poverty is the rule, polluted water sources are ubiquitous and infectious diseases are prevalent, bottle feeding can be a highly dangerous source of infection. Further, formula is often prohibitively expensive so that inadequate amounts are fed. The purchase of formula in adequate amounts to feed a 4-month-old infant would require half or more of the average monthly family income in many impoverished areas.[63,64] Illiteracy precludes accurate knowledge of formula preparation. Stoves, refrigerators, and even clean running water are rare luxuries. Most bottle feeding mothers own a single bottle and nipple, without even a bottle brush. For the majority of infants, formula feeding in underdeveloped countries is synonymous with diluting powdered formula to a fraction of the correct proportion with contaminated water.

While the cause of the decline in breast-feeding has not been adequately studied, a combination of factors are thought to contribute: modernization and urbanization; mothers working away from home; changing cultural attitudes including mimicry of the life-style of the Western world; disruption of extended families reducing the support available to nursing mothers; insufficient knowledge and emphasis by health workers; maternal malnutrition leading to lactation insufficiency; and aggressive marketing of infant formula.[52,57,58]

World Health Organization International Code on Marketing Breast Milk Substitutes

The issue of formula in the Third World has received international attention, beginning in 1974 when British and Swiss activists condemned the advertising practices of the infant-formula industry in a series of public statements. In the United States, the National Council of Churches Interfaith Center on Corporate Responsibility and the Infant Formula Action Coalition (INFACT) mounted an effective public awareness campaign that included a consumer boycott of Nestlé products. Congressional committees held hearings on various aspects of the problem, the most comprehensive being those of the Senate Subcommittee on Health and Scientific Research, chaired by Senator Kennedy in 1978.

An international code for marketing infant formula and other breast milk substitutes, suggested at a joint WHO/UNICEF meeting on Infant and Child Feeding in 1979, received endorsement by the World Health Assembly in 1980. The executive board of WHO recommended a draft code to the 34th World Health Assembly in May, 1981 for adoption. The substance of the Code was: to restrict advertising of breast milk substitutes directly to the public; to forbid personnel paid by manufacturers or distributers of breast milk substitutes from working in the health care system; to prevent samples of infant formula from being given to new mothers unless their infants must be fed on breast milk substitutes for health reasons; to eliminate inducements to health professionals to promote commercial products; to require formula products to contain the necessary information about the appropriate use of the product and the superiority of breast milk; and to promote breast-feeding through adequate information and education.*

The United States cast the sole negative ballot among 119 nations gathered at the United Nations forum in Geneva, leading to a widespread public outcry. By mid-June, both houses of Congress had passed resolutions by lopsided margins condemning the American position. The American Academy of Pediatrics took a neutral stand on the issue, whereas the Ambulatory Pediatric Association supported the Code. Health professionals

---

* The WHO International Code for Marketing of Breastmilk Substitutes is available in a number of languages from: Regional Office for Europe, World Health Organization, Scherfigsvej 8, 2100 Copenhagen, Denmark.

opposing the Code claim that the assumption has not been substantiated that marketing practices for infant formula are a significant factor in the decline of breast-feeding in the Third World or elsewhere.[65,66] They pointed out that breast-feeding is actually increasing in the United States where formula is given free to hospitals and mothers at discharge and infant formula is energetically promoted by its manufacturers. Conversely, in Communist Russia and China, where free enterprise marketing techniques do not exist, breast-feeding is declining.[67] Opponents of the Code feel that the World Health Organization has attacked a single, less important issue in the decline of breast-feeding in the Third World, and that it will do little to foster breast-feeding, while conceivably encouraging the use of more contaminated and less adequate breast milk substitutes.[68,69]

On the other hand, supporters of the Code insist that marketing of formula does influence maternal practice. In 1977, in Papua, New Guinea, promotion of infant formula was banned and feeding bottles could be obtained only by prescription from health workers. Breast-feeding increased from 65% to 88%. Mothers in St. Vincent who recalled advertised brand names were found to be more likely to supplement breast-feeding with commercial infant foods and to wean their infants at an earlier age.[70] A recent randomized controlled clinical trial of the effect of distribution of free samples of formula in newborn nurseries conducted in Montreal showed more women who had received formula samples to have stopped breast-feeding by 1 month postpartum.[71] The Code is viewed by its supporters as addressing a specific factor with a negative impact on breast-feeding, but does not obviate the need for massive social action against poverty, illiteracy, lack of sanitation, and maternal malnutrition.

Future Implications

The widespread publicity received by the Code has been valuable in focusing international attention on the decline of breast-feeding in developing nations. It should not obscure the fact that this is a multifaceted issue. Although different brands of milk powder can be found on the shelf of even the smallest store,[72] all formulas combined constitute only a percentage of breast-milk substitutes used for infant feeding in these nations. If formula disappeared tomorrow, women would still decline to breast-feed and the use of raw animal milk, sugar water, or other undesirable preparations would be increased with continuing disasterous results. What is occurring today appears to be a recurring theme in the story of infant feeding, that a decline in breast-feeding accompanies "modernization." This is not to imply that responsible nations should sit idly by, but that the complex nature of the issue should be recognized. Efforts should be directed at protecting breast-feeding in rural areas where it still predominates, as well as promoting its renewal among the urban economically advantaged and urban poor. Emphasis should be placed on educating health professionals to advise mothers, providing educational materials to school children and mothers which are adapted to the need of individual countries, offering practical information and support in prepartum and postpartum settings and enhancing maternal nutrition.[73,74] Meanwhile, a commitment to the continued promotion of breast-feeding in Western nations which serve as role models for developing countries is likely, in the long run, to be a major factor in a world-wide increase in breast feeding.

REFERENCES

1. Raynaud, A., 1961, Morphogenesis of the mammary gland, in: *Milk: The Mammary Gland and Its Secretion* (S. K. Kon and A. T. Cowie, eds.), Academic Press, New York, pp. 3–46.
2. Cowie, A. T. and Tindall, J. S., 1961, *The Physiology of Lactation*, Edward Arnold, London.
3. Griffiths, M., 1968, *Echidnas*, Pergamon Press, Oxford, England.
4. Blaxter, K. L., 1964, Protein metabolism and requirements in pregnancy and lactation, in: *Mammalian Protein Metabolism*, Volume 2 (H. N. Munro, ed.), Academic Press, New York, pp. 173–223.
5. Griffiths, M., McIntosh, D. L., and Coles, R. E. A., 1969, The mammary gland in the echidna with observations on the incubation of the egg and on the newly hatched young, *J. Zool.* **158**:371–386.
6. Renfree, M. B., 1981, Marsupials: Alternative mammals, *Nature* **293**:100–101.
7. Lincoln, D. W. and Renfree, M. B., 1981, Milk ejection in a marsupial, *Macropus agilis*, *Nature* **289**:504–506.
8. Renfree, M. B., Meier, P., Teng, C., and Battaglia, F. B., 1981, Relationship between amino acid intake and accretion in a marsupial, *Macropus eugenii*, *Biol. Neonat.* **40**:29–37.
9. Jenness, R., 1974, The composition of milk, in: *Lactation*, Volume III (B. L. Larson and V. R. Smith, eds.), Academic Press, New York, pp. 1–107.
10. Jenness, R., 1979, Comparative aspects of milk proteins, *J. Dairy Res.* **46**:197–210.
11. Jenness, R., 1979, The composition of human milk, *Semin. Perinatol.* **3**:225–239.
12. Cooper, A., 1845, Structure of the breast in the human female, in: *The Anatomy and Diseases of the Breast* (A. Cooper. ed.), Lea and Blanchard, Philadelphia, pp. 22–107.
13. von Haller, A., 1778, *Elementa physiologiae corporis humani*, 2nd ed., Volume 7, Part 2, Book 28, Section 1: Mammae, Societas Typographa, Lausanne, Switzerland.
14. O'Malley, C. D. and Saunders, J. B. d. C. M., 1952, *Leonarda da Vinci on the Human Body*, Henry Schuman, New York, p. 461.
15. Cowie, A. T., 1961, The hormonal control of milk secretion, in: *Milk: The Mammary Gland and Its Secretion* (S. K. Kon and A. T. Cowie, eds.), Academic Press, New York, pp. 163–203.
16. Mayer, G. and Klein, M., 1961, Histology and cytology of the Mammary Gland, in: *Milk: The Mammary Gland and Its Secretion* (S. K. Kon and A. T. Cowie, eds.) Academic Press, New York, pp. 47–126.
17. Peterson, W. E., 1944, Lactation, *Physiol. Rev.* **24**:340–371.
18. Halban, J., 1905, Die innere Secretion von Ovarium und Placenta und ihre Bedeutung für die Function der Milchdrüse, *Arch. Gynaek.* **75**:353–441.
19. Hammond, J. and Marshall, F. H. A., 1914, The functional correlation between the ovaries, uterus and the mammary glands in the rabbit, with observations on the oestrous cycle, *Proc. R. Soc. London, Ser. B* **87**:422–440.
20. Marshall, F. H. A. and Halnan, E. T., 1917, On the post-oestrus changes occurring in the generative organs and mammary glands of the non-pregnant dog, *Proc. R. Soc. London, Ser, B,* **89**:546–558.
21. Folley, S. J. and Malpress, F. H., 1948, Hormonal control of lactation, in: *The Hormones* (G. Pincus, ed.) Academic Press, New York, pp. 745–805.
22. Turner, C. W., 1939, The mammary glands, in: *Sex and Internal Secretions*, 2nd ed., (E. Allen, ed.) Williams and Wilkins, Baltimore, pp. 740–803.

23. Stricker, P. and Grueter, F., 1928, Action du lobe antérieur de l'hypophyse sur la montée laiteuse, *C. R. Soc. Biol.* **99:**1978–1980.
24. Riddle, O., Bates, R., and Dykshorn, S. W., 1933, The preparation, identification and assay of prolactin—A hormone of the anterior pituitary, *Am. J. Physiol.* **105:**191–216.
25. Reece, R. P. and Leonard, S. L., 1941, Effect of estrogens, gonadotropins and growth hormone on mammary glands of hypophysectomized rats, *Endocrinology* **29:**297–305.
26. Meites, J. and Turner, C. W., 1942, Studies concerning the mechanism controlling the initiation of lactation at parturition. II. Why lactation is not initiated during pregnancy, *Endocrinology* **30:**719–725.
27. Meites, J. and Turner, C. W., 1948, Studies concerning the induction and maintenance of lactation. I. The mechanism controlling the initiation of lactation at parturition, *Mo. Agric. Expt. Stn. Res. Bull.* **415:**
28. Elias, J. J., 1957 Cultivation of adult mouse mammary gland in hormone-enriched medium, *Science* **126:**842–844.
29. Topper, Y. J. and Freeman, C. S., 1980, Multiple hormone interactions in the developmental biology of the mammary gland, *Physiol. Rev.* **60:**1049–1106.
30. Clifton, K. H. and Furth, J., 1960, Ducto-alveolar growth in mammary glands of adreno-gonadectomized male rats bearing mammotropic pituitary tumors, *Endocrinology* **66:**893–897.
31. Meites, J., 1966, Control of mammary growth and lactation, in *Neuroendocrinology*, Volume 1 (L. Martini and W. F. Ganong, eds.), Academic Press, New York, pp. 669–708.
32. Chen, C. L. and Meites, J., 1970, Effects of estrogen and progesterone on serum and pituitary prolactin levels in ovariectomized rats, *Endocrinology* **86:**503–505.
33. Kuhn, N. J., 1969, Progesterone withdrawal as the lactogenic trigger in the rat, *J. Endocrinol.* **44:**39–54.
34. Lyons, W. R., 1958, Hormonal synergism in mammary growth, *Proc. R. Soc. London, Ser. B,* **149:**303–325.
35. Cowie, A. T. and Tindall, J. S., 1961, The maintenance of lactation in the goat after hypophysectomy, *J. Endocrinol.* **23:**79–96.
36. Leonard, S. L., 1945, The relation of the placenta to the growth of the mammary gland of the rat during the last half of pregnancy, *Anat. Rec.* **91:**65–75.
37. Roy, E. W., Averill, S. C., Lyons, W. R., and Johnson, W. E., 1955, Rat placental hormonal activities corresponding to those of the pituitary mammotropins, *Endocrinology* **56:**359–373.
38. Josimovich, J. B. and MacLaren, J. A., 1962, Presence in the human placenta and term serum of a highly lactogenic substance immunologically related to pituitary growth hormone, *Endocrinology* **71:**209–220.
39. Talamantes, F., 1975, Comparative study of the occurrence of placental prolactin among mammals, *Gen. Comp. Endocrinol.* **27:**115–121.
40. Garrison, F. H., 1965, *Abt-Garrison History of Pediatrics*, (A. F. Abt, ed), W. B. Saunders Company, Philadelphia, p. 16.
41. Phillips, V., 1976, Infant feeding through the ages, *Keeping Abreast Journal* **1:**296–300.
42. Prince, J., 1976, Infant feeding through the ages, *Midwives Chron. Nurs. Notes* **Dec.:**283–885.
43. Davidson, W. D., 1953, A brief history of infant feeding, *J. Pediatr.* **43:**74–87.
44. Wickes, I. G., 1953, A history of infant feeding: Part I. Primitive peoples: Ancient Works: Renaissance writers, *Arch. Dis. Child.* **28:**151–158.
45. Fildes, V., 1978, The Elizabethan wet nurse, *Nurs. Times* **74:**472–473.
46. Wickes, I. G., 1953, A history of infant feeding: Part II. Seventeenth and eighteenth century writers, *Arch. Dis. Child* **28:**232–240.
47. Schmidt, W. M., 1976, Health and welfare of colonial American children, *Am. J. Dis. Child.* **130:**694–701.
48. Wickes, I. G., 1953, A history of infant feeding: Part III. Eighteenth and nineteeth century writers, *Arch. Dis. Child.* **28:**332–340.
49. Pepper, W., 1910, The medical side of Benjamin Franklin, *Univ. Pa. Med. Bull.* **23:**554.
50. Cone, T. E., 1976, *200 Years of Feeding Infants in America*, Ross Laboratories, Columbus, Ohio, pp. 18–19.

51. Foman, S. J., 1974, *Infant Nutrition*, 2nd ed., W. B. Saunders Company, Philadelphia, pp. 2–7.
52. Jelliffe, D. B. and Jelliffe, E. F. P., 1978, *Human Milk in the Modern World*, Oxford University Press, Oxford, pp. 182–210.
53. Woodbury, R. M., 1925, *Causal Factors in Infant Mortality*, Children's Bureau Publication No. 142, U.S. Government Printing Office, Washington, D. C.
54. Meyer, H. F., 1968, Breast feeding in the United States, *Clin. Pediatr.* **7:**708–715.
55. Mayell, M., 1981, Infant formula promotion a domestic threat, too, *Nutrit. Act.* **Aug:**7.
56. Raphael, D. (ed.), 1978, Breastfeeding and weaning among the poor, *The Lactation Review* Volume 3, The Human Lactation Center, Ltd., Westport, Connecticut, pp. 1–6.
57. Raphael, D. (ed.), 1979, *Breastfeeding and Food Policy in a Hungry World, Section Two: Cultural Factors in Infant Feeding Practices*, Academic Press, New York, pp. 37–95.
58. Jelliffe, D. B., 1976, World trends in infant feeding, *Am. J. Clin. Nutr.* **29:**1227–1237.
59. Jelliffe, D. B., 1975, Nutrition and economics in the modern world, *J. Trop. Pediatr. Environ., Child Health* **21:**267–269.
60. Jelliffe, D. B. and Jelliffe, E. F. P., 1975, Human milk, nutrition, and the world resource crisis, *Science* **188:**557–560.
61. Knodel, J., 1977, Breast-feeding and population growth, *Science* **198:**1111–1115.
62. Joseph, S. C., 1981, The anatomy of the infant formula controversy, *Am. J. Dis. Child.* **135:**889–892.
63. World Health Organization, 1981, Marketing and distribution of breast-milk substitutes, in: *Contemporary Patterns of Breastfeeding: Report of the WHO Collaborative Study on Breast-Feeding*, World Health Organization, Geneva, p. 139.
64. Latham, M. C., 1979, International perspectives on weaning foods: The economic and other implications of bottle feeding and the use of manufactured weaning foods, in: *Breastfeeding and Food Policy in a Hungry World* (D. Raphael, ed.), Academic Press, New York, p. 120–121.
65. Lucey, J. F., 1981, Does a vote of 118 to 1 mean that the USA was wrong? *Pediatrics* **68:**431.
66. Graham, G. G., 1981, Comments on the World Health Organization's "International Code" of marketing breastmilk substitutes, *Am. J. Dis. Child.* **135:**892–894.
67. May, C. D., 1981, The "infant formula controversy": A notorious threat to reason in matters of health, *Pediatrics* **68:**428–430.
68. Barness, L. A., 1981 Committee on nutrition and the WHO code of marketing breastmilk substitutes, *Pediatrics* **68:**430–431.
69. McCollough, T., 1979, A perspective on the impact of infant formula in developing nations: Future goals and policies, in: *Breastfeeding and Food Policy in a Hungry World* (D. Raphael, ed.), Academic Press, New York, pp. 129–135.
70. Board of Directors of the Ambulatory Pediatric Association, 1981, The World Health Organization code of marketing of breastmilk substitutes, *Pediatrics* **68:**432–434.
71. Bergevin, Y., Kramer, M. and Dougherty, C., 1981, Do infant formula samples affect the duration of breastfeeding? A randomized controlled trial. Presented at the Annual Meeting of the Ambulatory Pediatric Association, San Francisco, May 1, 1981.
72. Lusty, T., 1981, The child in the third world, *Am. J. Dis. Child.* **135:**462–466.
73. Sosa, R., Klaus, M., and Urrutia, J. J., 1976, Feed the nursing mother, thereby the infant, *J. Pediatr.* **88:**668–670.
74. Carballo, M., 1980, WHO programmes for the promotion of breastfeeding, in: *Human Milk: Its Biological and Social Value* (S. Frier, and A. I. Eidelman, eds.), Excerpta Medica, Amsterdam, International Congress Series 518, pp. 233–235.

II

The Scientific Basis of Lactation

2

Anatomy of the Breast

Stanley F. Gould

The term *breast* includes a variety of anatomical structures lying on the anterior aspect of the thorax. Contained within it is the mammary gland, a highly specialized cutaneous glandular structure, composed of elements involved in the secretion and ejection of milk. This gland is a well-defined dermal structure which has become too large to remain within the skin itself and has, therefore, invaded the underlying subcutaneous and fascial elements. The gland is peculiar to mammals and its development and structure are strikingly similar in even the lowest of this class. In the human, the gland is composed of some 15 to 20 lobules which originate from the nipple and areola, and radiate along the anterior and lateral thoracic wall (Fig. 1).[1] The mammary gland is only one component of the breast; other components include a variable quantity of fat, connective tissue, vessels, nerves, and lymphatics.

ANATOMICAL FEATURES OF THE BREAST

Surface Anatomy, Supporting Structures, and General Relationships

The breast overlies the *pectoralis major, serratus anterior*, and *external oblique* muscles. It extends from the second to the sixth rib and from the sternum to the midaxillary line. The glandular tissue contained within it may stretch beyond the organ itself and extends laterally into the axilla (the axillary tail), superiorly as far as the clavicle, and inferiorly as far as the epigastric fossa.[1] The greatest amount of glandular tissue is found in the superolateral quandrant. Some authors have stated that if inequality of the breast size exists, the right breast is slightly larger than the left.[2] Surrounding and

Stanley F. Gould • Departments of Obstetrics and Gynecology and Anatomy, University of Colorado School of Medicine, Denver, Colorado 80262.

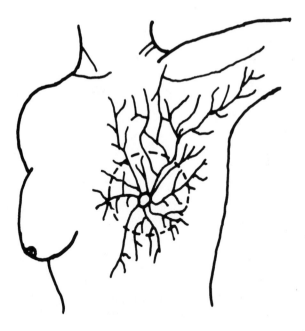

Figure 1. Diagram showing the extent of mammary tissue on the anterior thoracic wall. Note the extension of ductal elements in the axilla and inferiorly along the epigastrium. (Redrawn from reference 1; used with permission.)

overlying the glandular tissue is a variable, often large, amount of adipose tissue.

The gland as a whole lies in the superficial fascia of the thorax and is usually easily dissected from the underlying *pectoralis major* and *serratus anterior* muscles. The base of the breast is semicircular, but its exact surface position is variable. It is firmly attached to the overlying skin in the area of the areola by the connective tissue which surrounds the ducts and by heavy ligamentous brands of connective tissue which traverse and subdivide the adipose tissue and glandular elements. These transverse bands, known as *retinacula cutis*, are particularly well developed in the superior quandrants and form the suspensory ligaments or Ligaments of Cooper.[3] Posterior to the breast is a deep layer of areolar connective tissue known as the retro-mammary space.

The Nipple and Areola

The nipple is a condensation of epithelial tissue which usually, though with great variability, is found at the level of the fourth intercostal space. The lactiferous ducts of the mammary gland empty into it. It is surrounded by specialized pigmented skin, the areola, which contains melanophores and darkens during pregnancy, usually retaining its deepened coloration thereafter. The areola also contains sebaceous glands which hypertrophy and form papillae during pregnancy (Montgomery's follicles), sweat glands, and accessory mammary glands with miniature duct openings through the stratified squamous areolar epithelium. The areola is highly innervated and contains a dense intradermal nerve plexus supplying numerous sensory end organs which include Meissner's corpuscles and Merkel's discs.[4] This plexus also terminates as free nerve endings. This sensory innervation is of great importance during lactation and suckling.

The breast and mammary gland in the male are markedly less well developed than in the postpubertal female. While some cords of glandular elements are present, fat and fibrous tissues are scanty. The nipple and areolar area remain flattened.

Vessels and Nerves

The breast is highly vascularized and derives its blood supply chiefly from the lateral thoracic and internal thoracic arteries. A variable contribution from the anterior intercostal vessels has been reported. The lateral thoracic artery, a direct branch of the axillary artery, often supplies the majority of the blood to the superficial aspects of the organ. The perforating branch of the internal thoracic artery passes through the second intercostal space to supply the deeper portions of the gland, the nipple, areola, and skin of the inner third of the breast.[5] A significant amount of variability exists, however, In general, then, it can be stated that the vascular supply descends from the superior lateral and medial aspects of the thorax to converge around the nipple and areola.

Except for an area deep to the nipple, few if any vascular anastomoses are found within the organ and thus provide little framework for collateral circulation. Care must be exercised in dissections, especially in the superiolateral and superiomedial quadrants as this is likely to interrupt the major portion of the blood supply coming from the internal thoracic artery. Since the areola and nipple derive their blood supply from deeper vessels, circular incisions around the areola do not endanger its circulation. The venous drainage flows medially or mediosuperiorly towards the clavicle.[6]

The breast is innervated chiefly by the intercostal nerves which carry sensory fibers to the skin and autonomic fibers to smooth muscle and blood vessels. The nipple and areolar complex are innervated solely by the interior ramus of the fourth intercostal nerve,[7] a point of considerable importance because interruption of this innervation may interfere with the afferent arm of the letdown reflex. Circular incisions around the lateral aspect of the areola should, for this reason, be avoided.

Lymphatic Drainage

A rich plexus of lymphatic vessels drains the breast and mammary gland. Two major pathways exist which originate in the lobules of the breast and run deep within it. These channels extend both laterally and medially.[8] The chief drainage avenue (more than 75%) is towards the axilla through the pectoral axillary and apical axillary nodes. Most of these lie close to vessels on the anterior surface of the *serratus anterior* muscle. A lesser degree of

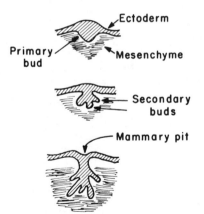

Figure 2. Drawings showing the early development of the mammary gland. (Modified from reference 22; used with permission.)

drainage is afforded by the parasternal (internal mammary) nodes. The chief route of these nodes is from the deeper surface of the gland through the *pectoralis major* muscle. A few efferent vessels follow the lateral perforating branches of the intercostal vessels. The lymphatic drainage from the nipple and areola follows the drainage of the deeper glandular parenchyma and not the adjacent superficial outflow tracts of the skin.

EMBYOLOGICAL DEVELOPMENT

Normal Development

The mammary gland is an ectodermally derived organ which can be definitely identified by 6 weeks postfertilization.[9,10] At this time, a plaque of ectodermal cells can be seen piling up in a line extending from the base of the forelimb (axillary) to the region of the hindlimb (inguinal).[11] This is known as the mammary line or mammary ridge. In lower mammals, the mammary ridge is a discrete entity identifiable because it extends along the entire ventral surface of the embryo. In humans, the line is usually inconspicuous in the abdominal region and regresses shortly after its appearance except in the region of the thorax.

By the end of the sixth week, the ectodermal ridge forms an ectodermal pit and the ectoderm begins to penetrate the underlying mesenchyme, producing the definitive mammary primordium (Fig. 2).[12] By 20 weeks, 16 to 24 primitive, solid, sprouts (the anlage of the lactiferous ducts) have invaded the mesodermal connective tissue. These invading ectodermal sprouts continue to grow deeper and deeper with advancing gestation and begin to arborize. They do not canalize until close to term. Only the main lactiferous ducts are present at birth with the majority of ductal and virtually all of the glandular secretory apparatus awaiting the hormonal events of puberty before making their appearance.

Highly differentiated ectodermal cells develop in direct contact with the developing ducts and mesenchyme. These cells, destined to become myopithelial cells, are localized around and along the developing ductal elements.[13] As gestation advances, the fibrous connective tissue and adipocytes develop from the surrounding mesenchyme. The development of the intralobular alveolar elements awaits the advent of puberty with full development occurring only during pregnancy.

The nipple and areola develop rather late in gestation. At approximately 8 months, the globular surface of the mammary primordium flattens and cornifies. Shortly before birth, this pitlike primordium is transformed into the nipple by a proliferation of the underlying mesenchyme with a resultant eversion of the cornified primordium. The ectoderm and the underlying mesenchyme directly circumferential to the nipple then differentiates into the definitive areola.

Anomalous Development

The most common anomaly of the breast is the occurrence of super-numerary mammary tissue. This may take the form of accessory nipples (hyperthelia or the presence of supernumerary nipples), supernumerary breasts containing all the normal elements, and the condition known as "pseudo-mammae" where the nipple, areola, and fat are present, but in which no glandular parenchyma is represented. Well over 10,000 cases of polymastia and/or hyperthelia have been reported. Absence of the mammary glands (amastia), micromastia, and macromastia occasionally occur as does the development of functional breast tissue in the male (gynecomastia) with the actual secretion of milk.[14] Lesser degrees of gynecomastia actually occur in up to 30% of pubertal boys, caused by an estrogen–testosterone imbalance at that time (see page 152). This type of gynecomastia is different from the true anatomical variety caused by a primary aberation in the control of organogenesis.

The vast majority of supernumerary breasts are found along the original milk line of the embryo with 98.7% of these being found inferior to the normal breast.[15] According to some authors they are more common in the male than the female[16] and have been reported as inferior as the femoral triangle and vulva.

Failure of proper proliferation of the mesenchyme underlying the mammary primordium results in failure of eversion of the nipple. This relatively common phenomenon is known as inversion of the nipple. It may occur bilaterally or unilaterally and, when present, may pose mechanical problems in breast-feeding (see Chapter 9).

STRUCTURE OF THE MAMMARY GLAND

General Features

At puberty, the 15 to 20 primitive embryonic ducts, formed by the invagination of the primordial ectoderm, aborize extensively into separate

Figure 3. Drawing of the ductal system, lactiferous ducts, and nipple of a 21-year-old female. Note how the lactiferous ducts converge on the nipple. Secretory alveoli can be seen along the more peripheral aspects of the intralobular ducts. (From reference 18; used with permission.)

lobes. In the adult female, approximately 10 to 15 of these lobes are functional, the rest appear vestigial. From a functional viewpoint, each of these lobes can be considered as a separate gland embedded within the fatty stroma of the breast itself. These lobes drain towards the nipple through a separate excretory duct, termed the lactiferous duct, which becomes slightly dilated within the nipple to form the lactiferous sinus (Fig. 3). The interlobular ducts receive the secretory products through a complex, tubular pattern of branched intralobular ductal channels (Fig. 4). Through the injection of contrast medium into the lactiferous ducts, Hicken[17] described the full

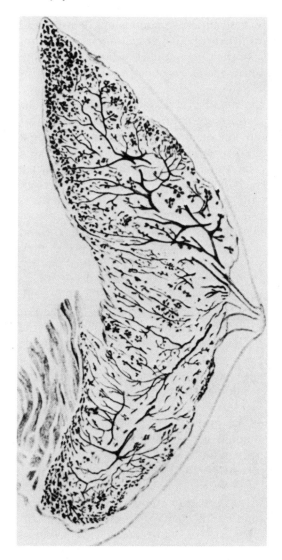

Figure 4. Sagittal section drawing of full extent of ductal ramifications in a 19-year-old nulligravida. Finer and more complex ductal branchings are seen as one moves laterally from the central area of the areola and nipple. (From reference 23; used with permission.)

degree of ductal distribution over the entire anterolateral aspect of the thorax and pioneered what is now known as mammography. Because of its great degree of ductal complexity and multiple branchings, the mammary gland is histologically classified as a compound tubuloalveolar gland.

Each lobe is separated by septa of dense connective tissue which is fibrous and encloses the ductal elements. Blood vessels, lymphatics, and nerves run in these septa and the interlobular septa merge imperceptibly with the fascial coverings suspending the breast from the anterior thoracic wall. These interlobular connective tissue septa further subdivide the lobes into discrete lobules, each with its own excretory duct (the interlobular duct).

The lactiferous duct is lined by a stratified squamous epithelium near the surface of the nipple and by a stratified cuboidal or columnar epithelium at the more distal portions. The cells of the duct lining classically show scanty cytoplasm, centrally placed nuclei, few nucleoli, and marginated heterochromatin.

The basic secretory units of the gland are the alveoli, small saccular evaginations from the alveolar duct, which are composed of a single layer of mammary epithelial cells that are cuboidal or low columnar and rest upon a classic basement membrane. Clustered around a mammary ductule like a bunch of grapes, these alveoli (and the distal portions of the alveolar ducts), produce the secretory product which characterizes the gland. Secretory activity has been reported within the lining of the more terminal ducts themselves. It is these secretory units which show the greatest degree of growth and regression during the different phases of mammary gland development.

Surrounding the alveoli and lying between them and the basal lamina, are highly specialized cells also believed to be derived from ectoderm. These myoepithelial cells are "spiderlike" cells and contain elements of both smooth muscle and epithelial cells; they surround each alveolar unit in a basketlike manner (Fig. 5). They are also found running longitudinally along the interlobular ductal channels (Fig. 6). They are contractile and are responsible for the ejection of milk from the alveoli and alveolar ducts. The presence of these myoepithelial or "basket cells" has been cited as evidence for a morphogenetic relationship between the mammary gland and the cutaneous sweat gland.

Classically, the development of the postpubertal mammary gland has been divided into three major functional stages: (1) an inactive or resting stage seen in the nonlactating, nonpregnant, sexually mature female, (2) a proliferative or active phase during pregnancy, and (3) a lactating or secretory phase during the production of milk. A fourth stage is sometimes characterized as regression and atrophy. This occurs after the cessation of lactation and after the menopause. While some minor changes are thought to occur during the normal menstrual cycle,[18] they have not been extensively studied in the human female.

Inactive or Resting Stage

Prior to pregnancy, the mammary gland from the adult female is in an inactive state which permits easy identification of its parenchymal and stromal organization. As seen in Fig. 7, the lobules consist of tubules or ducts lined with epithelium and embedded in a connective tissue stroma. They are widely separated and connective tissue and adipose tissue are the predominate elements. The interlobular connective tissue is dense, fibrous, and markedly less cellular than the intralobular connective tissue.

At this stage of development, there is only a scanty contribution from the glandular parenchyma. A few budlike sacculations may be seen arising

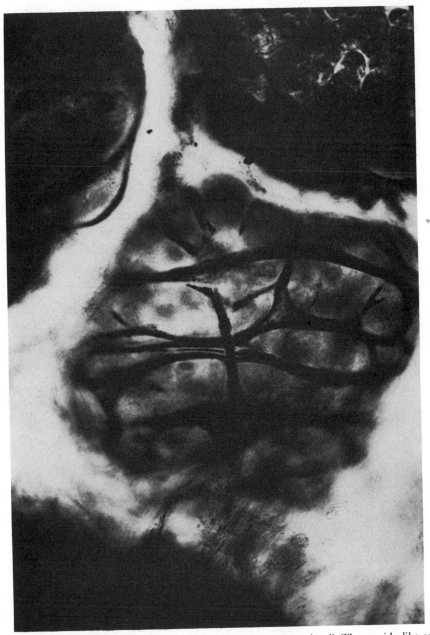

Figure 5. Myoepithelial cells (basket cells) surrounding secretory alveoli. These spiderlike cells contain smooth muscle myofibrils and, upon contracting, propel the intraalveolar contents into the collecting ducts. (From reference 24; used with permission.)

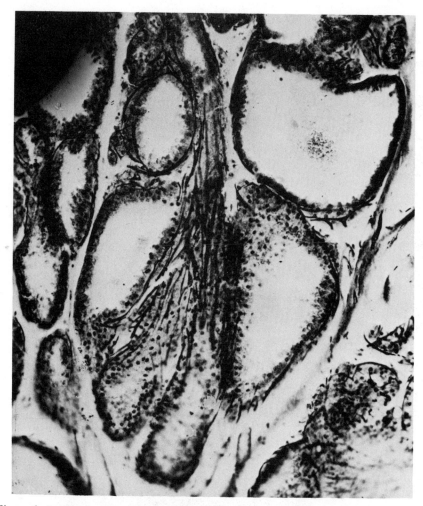

Figure 6. Contractile fibers running longitudinally along the terminal ducts of the mammary gland. In concert with the myoepithelial cells which surround the alveoli, these elements help propel the secretory contents of the alveoli and terminal alveolar ducts towards the nipple. (From reference 24; used with permission.)

from the ducts (Fig. 8), but the gland consists predominantly of lactiferous, interlobar, and interlobular ducts. The larger lactiferous ducts are lined by stratified cuboidal epithelium, except near the nipple where they are lined by stratified squamous epithelium. The smaller ducts display a simple cuboidal epithelium with scanty cytoplasm and centrally placed nuclei. The few alveoli present consist of simple cuboidal epithelial elements without distinctive morphologic features. They are virtually indistinguishable from the epithelium of the smaller ductal channels. Myoepithelial cells have been observed at this stage. The engorgement perceived by many women just

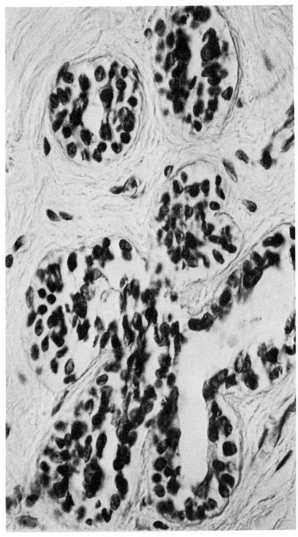

Figure 7. Inactive or resting mammary gland. Note the large connective tissue to parenchyma ratio. Only a few stratified ducts are visible with no evidence of alveolar development. Stained with hematoxylin and eosin. 1200 ×.

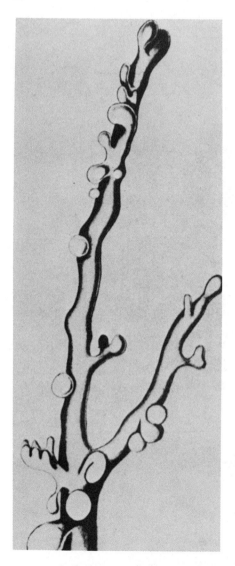

Figure 8. Drawing of duct system of a 15-year-old nulligravida. Note the primitive development of the system with very few secretory alveoli present. (From reference 18; used with permission.)

prior to menses is probably secondary to hyperemia and tissue edema rather than to a significant change in the activity of the glandular parenchyma.

A point of importance, here and in the discussion to follow, is that the glandular parenchyma of the breast apparently does not respond to the hormonal environment in a totally synchronous fashion. Different areas within the same breast may change to greater or lesser degrees. For this reason, a good deal of variability within lobules and between lobules may be seen in random histologic sections.

Proliferative or Active Phase

A modest, though discernable, degree of alveolar development occurs at the time of the menarche (Fig. 9), but with the advent of the hormonal

Figure 9. Drawing of ductal and alveolar development in a 19-year-old nulligravida. With the beginning of cyclic menses, there is a modest amount of development of the ductal and secretory elements. In relation to the breast as a whole, however, this development is scanty compared to the volume of connective and fatty tissue. (From reference 23; used with permission.)

changes of pregnancy, the mammary gland undergoes a spectacular phase of growth and proliferation. Early in pregnancy, this growth is due to a true hyperplasia of the ductal and secretory elements, while in the later trimesters, alveolar cell hypertrophy and secretory activity underlie the changes seen. During the same interval, there appears to be a significant decrease in the supporting stroma with a marked reduction in adipose cells and fibrous connective tissue.

The active phase is characterized by a rapid increase in the number of alveoli. Growth occurs at the terminal portions of the intralobular ducts (Fig.

Figure 10. Drawing of ductal and secretory apparatus in a 21-year-old primigravida at 8 weeks' gestation. Note the development of grape-like clusters of alveoli off the terminal ductal channels. (From reference 23; used with permission.)

10) which branch numerous times to end in alveolar sacculations. In the early trimester, the secretory alveoli are collapsed, but as gestation advances the saccules expand and enlarge, transforming the gland into a classic, tubuloalveolar structure (Fig. 11). Between the alveoli, the connective tissue is thin and compressed.

The epithelium of the alveoli at this stage is composed of simple cuboidal to low columnar cells. Randomly distributed and sparse secretory type microvilli characterize the apical surface of the alveolar epithelium. Relatively large mitochondria and increasing numbers of Golgi are seen. Concommitant to this is an increase in the amount of rough endoplasmic reticulum. As early as the sixth month of pregnancy, lipid droplets can be seen in the alveolar epithelial cells.

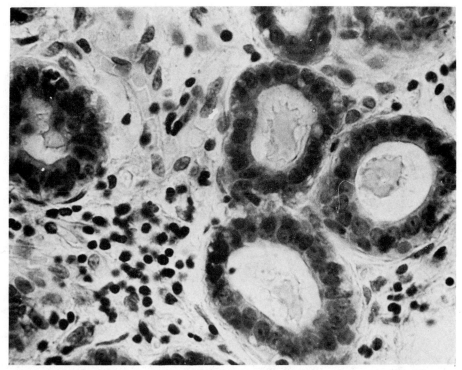

Figure 11. Mammary gland from midtrimester pregnant female. Note the development of secretory alveoli. A marked decrease in the intraalveolar stroma has occurred. A small amount of secretory product is visible within the alveoli. Stained with hematoxylin and eosin. 1200 ×.

Lactation or Secretory Phase

During the first few days after parturtion, a significant change occurs in the secretory elements of the mammary gland. Within the first 12 hr, the cells lining the alveolar sacculations become high cuboidal to columnar and develop the classic cytologic characteristics of an exocrine cell. At the base of the cell (Fig. 12), numerous free ribosomes may be seen within the cytoplasm. These are rapidly replaced by rough endoplasmic reticular membranes which are quite evident by 48 hr postpartum (Fig. 13). The ribosomes, responsible for the basophilia seen at this time, are usually limited to the subnuclear and perinuclear regions of the alveolar cells. Lipid droplets are first seen at the base of the cells, but move towards the apical cytoplasm within 48 hr (Figs. 14 and 15). Extraction of these large, intracytoplasmic inclusions occurs by routine paraffin processing and leaves clear or empty spaces in the apical cytoplasm which have been variously interpreted as the loss of this region of cytoplasm into the adjacent alveolar lumen. By the use of special lipid stains,[19] it appears that some of the lipid inclusions are not homogeneous but rather complex (Fig. 16).

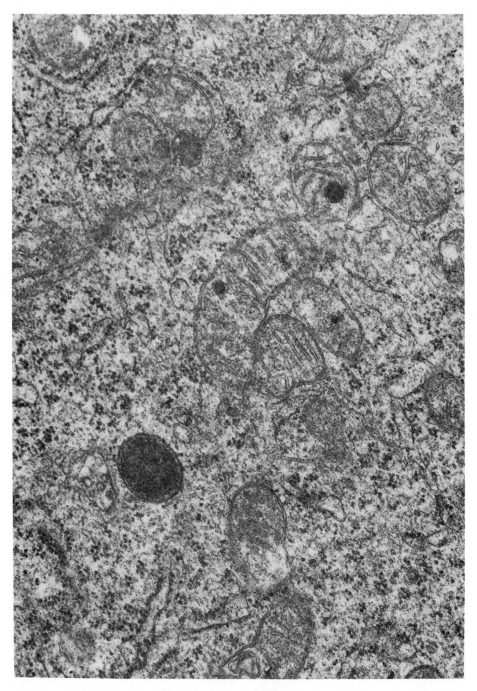

Figure 12. Base of alveolar cell 24 hr after parturition. Note the free ribosomes and large mitochondria. At this stage of lactation, few rough endoplasmic reticula have developed. Stained with uranyl and lead salts. 46,000 ×.

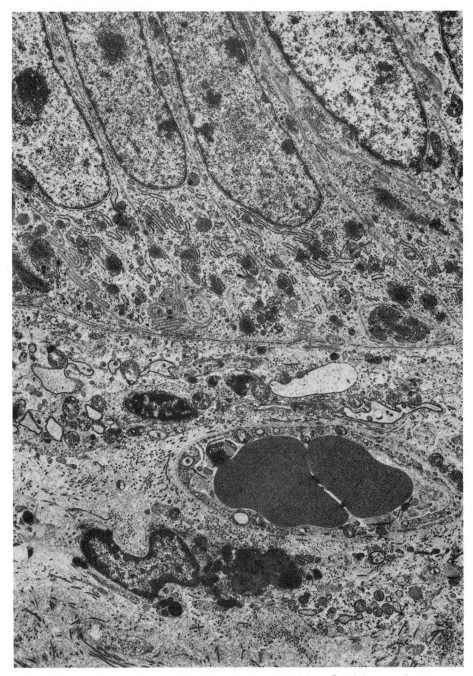

Figure 13. Base of lactating alveoli 48 hr after parturition. Note the development of numerous rough endoplasmic reticula. The nuclei are basal. Numerous proteinaceous secretory granules are seen at the base of the cells. Stained with uranyl and lead salts. 8000 ×.

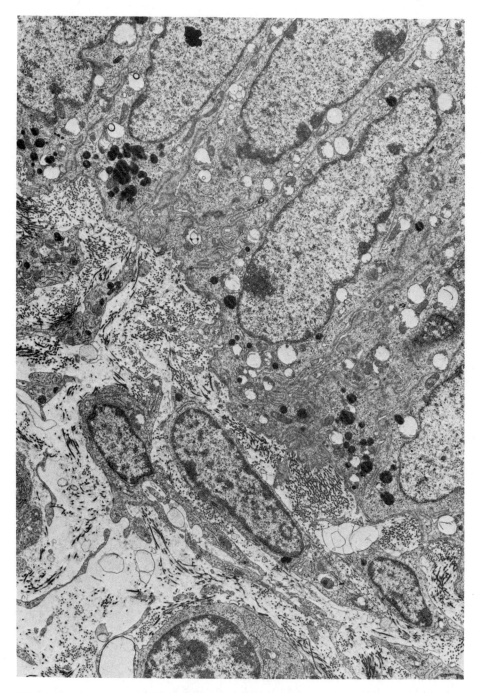

Figure 14. Mammary epithelium from a patient 48 hr postpartum. Lipid droplets are visible after staining with malachite green. In the first 24 to 36 hr, these droplets are seen at the base of the alveolar cells. Within 48 hr after parturition, they will be visible within the apical cytoplasm of the epithelium. Stained with uranyl and lead salts. 8000 ×.

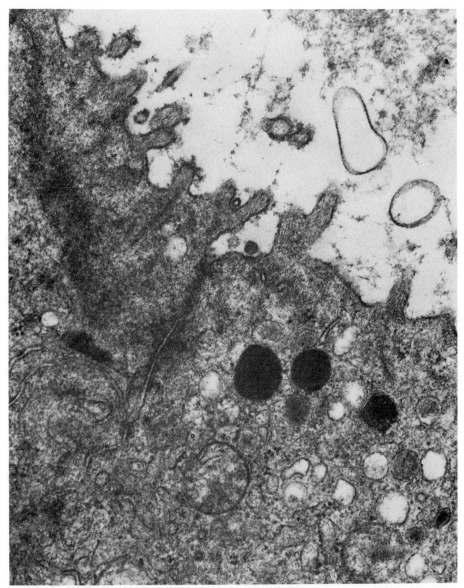

Figure 15. At 48 hr, lipid inclusions are seen in the apical cytoplasm of the lactating mammary gland. These inclusions are not membrane bound. Note the development of secretory-type microvilli on the apical surface. Stained with uranyl and lead salts. 30,000 ×.

Until the advent of electron microscopy, there was a great deal of discussion as to the nature of the secretory process occurring in the lactating cell. The mammary gland was formerly classified as a mixed merocrine and apocrine gland since, in addition to the secretion of lipid, small proteinaceous secretory granules were observed in the apical cytoplasm with the subsequent

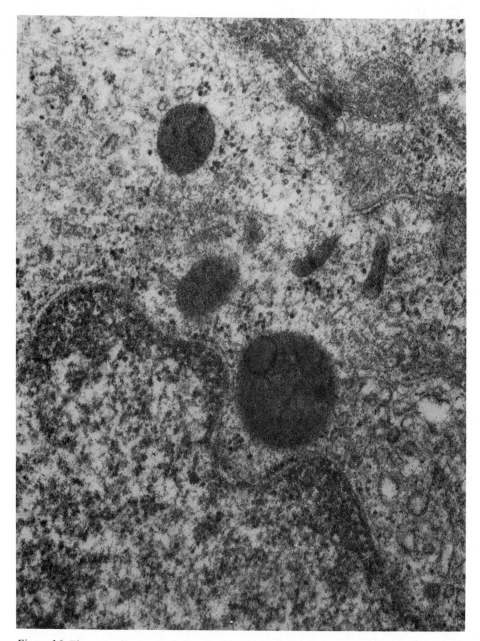

Figure 16. Electron micrograph demonstrating lipid inclusion from tissue fixed in the presence of 0.1% malachite green. Note that the inclusion is complex in nature with lipid and granular material enclosed. Stained with uranyl and lead salts. 50,000 ×.

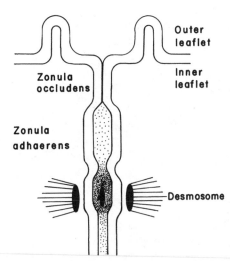

Figure 17. Diagram of the classic tripartite junctional complex. This type of junction is seen in the ducts throughout the mammary cycle, but in the alveolar cells, the desmosome disappears during lactation leaving only the zonula occludens to limit transmigration of extracellular components.

deposition of their contents into the alveolar lumen. Recent studies have indicated that the proteinaceous secretory products are released into the alveolar lumen by classic exocytosis in which secretory material passes out through the cell apex without the loss of cytoplasm; this being due to a fusion of the secretory granule membrane with the apical cytoplasmic membrane. However, the process of release of the lipid droplets results in the loss of some cytoplasm, although far less than was originally deduced from light microscopic studies of paraffin-embedded specimens. Recent fine structure data indicate that only a very fine circumferential ring of specialized cytoplasm accompanies the lipid droplet as it is released into the lumen.

Throughout the proliferative phase of glandular function, the alveolar epithelium displays classic junctional complexes between the apical borders of adjacent cells[20] (Fig. 17). During lactation, the desmosome component of this junction disappears leaving only the zonula occludens to strictly limit the movement of extracellular components into the alveolar lumina. Classic tripartite junctional complexes are found in the ducts, but not between the alevolar cells. Gap junctions have been noted on the lateral cell membranes and are believed to be sites of transport of small molecules between cells. The basal cell membrane is thrown into highly interdigitated basal infoldings which are associated with large numbers of mitochrondia.

Within 48 hr, the alveolar epithelium becomes cuboidal and continuously increases its secretory activity. The alveoli become distended with milk (Fig. 18) and, as they do, the lining epithelium becomes flattened and distorted (Fig. 19). Compression of the intraalveolar connective tissue occurs and, in histological sections, the fully distended alveoli may actually resemble thyroid follicles full of colloid. Contraction of the myoepithelial cells assists in the propulsion of material from the alveolar lumen to the alveolar ducts themselves help propel the secretory product towards the lactiferous ducts and sinuses. A cyclic process of secretory activity, luminal distention, and

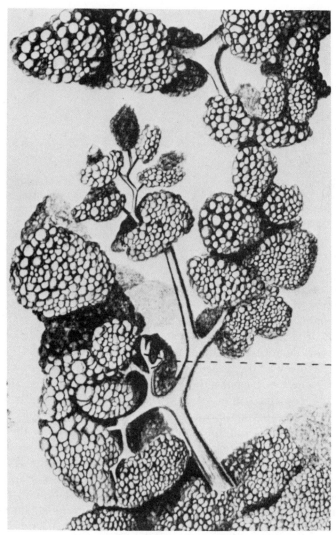

Figure 18. Mammary lobules from a 26-year-old woman 3 weeks postpartum. Note the tremendous distention and development of the secretory alveoli. This woman died 48 hr after last suckling her infant. (From reference 18; used by permission.)

expulsion into the duct system continues throughout lactation, as directed by the suckling of the infant and the letdown reflex.

Regression, Involution, or Atrophy

Regular suckling stimulates the continuation of milk secretion. When this is stopped, the gland quickly ceases its secretory activity and undergoes a relatively rapid phase of regression. Within a few days, the milk remaining in the alveolar lumina and ducts is resorbed. A steady decrease in parenchymal

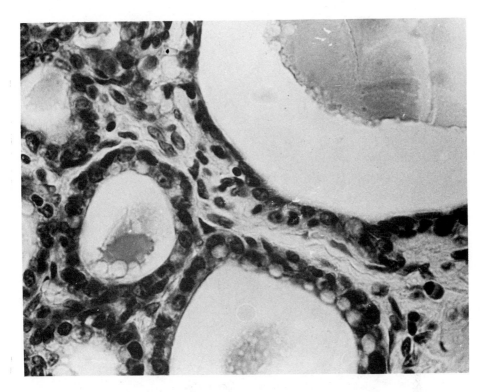

Figure 19. Lactating human mammary gland. Note the extreme distention of the alveolar follicles with the apical secretory products visible in the cytoplasm. With progressive distention, the follicular epithelium becomes flattened. Stained with hematoxylin and eosin. 1200 ×.

elements ensues with the concomitant reappearance of larger amounts of intralobular and interlobar connective tissues. The gland, however, does not regress to its original prepubertal state as many of the alveoli persist (Fig. 20).

Within the alveolar epithelium a great amount of lysosomal and autophagic activity accounts for the initial regression of the epithelium.[21] As this occurs, the cellular debris is removed by macrophages and histiocytes. The gland then remains in a resting condition until the advent of the next pregnancy wherein the developmental cycle of proliferation and secretion commences.

Near the menopause, but usually before the true cessation of cyclic ovarian function, the mammary gland and surrounding breast tissues begin to atrophy. Loss of tissue begins initially in the peripheral aspects of the lobe, but eventually almost all alveolar and intralobular ductal elements are lost. The interstitial connective tissue becomes decidedly less cellular with hyaline change noted as a common occurrence. On random histologic section, only a few scattered ducts may be seen at this time.

Figure 20. Mammary ductal apparatus in a 34-year-old female 5 years after her last birth. Note the degree of regression in the secretory and ductal elements with an increase in the stroma to parenchyma ratio when compared to the lactating gland. (From reference 23; used by permission.)

SUMMARY

The mammary gland is an ectodermally derived organ which forms the major secretory element of the breast and lies within the subcutaneous tissues of the anterior thoracic wall. Prior to pregnancy, the gland is composed primarily of scattered ductal elements which drain into a series of collecting or lactiferous ducts. These ducts drain into the nipple. Upon appropriate hormonal stimulation, the mammary ducts develop numerous secretory alveoli which cyclically produce milk and empty their contents into the ductal system. Upon termination of suckling, a rapid regression occurs in the alveolar and ductal trees with end stage involution occurring after the menopause.

While a great deal of data exists on the nonhuman mammary gland, far too little information is available on the structure and functional morphologic changes seen in the human. For this reason, much of our understanding of the fine structure of the gland is predicated on animal models. It is hoped that future endeavors will address this problem.

ACKNOWLEDGMENT. The author gratefully acknowledges the assistance of Mrs. Wilma Succa in the preparation and editing of this manuscript.

REFERENCES

1. Hicken, N. F., 1940, Mastectomy: A clinical pathologic study demonstrating why most mastectomies result in incomplete removal of the mammary gland, *Arch. Surg.* **40**:6–14.
2. Skerlj, B., 1935, Wieder ein "erblicher" Literaturfehler? *Anthropol. Anz.* **12**:304–306.
3. Hollinshead, W. H., 1971, The thorax, abdomen, and pelvis, in: *Anatomy for Surgeons,* Volume 2, Harper & Row, New York, pp. 11–18.
4. Miller, M. R. and Kasahara, M., 1959, The cutaneous innervation of the human female breast, *Anat. Rec.* **135**:153–167.
5. Maliniak, J. W., 1934, Prevention of necrosis in plastic repair of the breast, *Am. J. Surg.* **26**:292–297.
6. Massopust, L. C. and Gardner, W. D., 1950, Infrared photographic studies of the superficial thoracic veins in the female, *Surg. Gynec. Obstet.* **91**:717–727.
7. Farina, M. A., Newby, B. G., and Alani, H., 1980, Innervation of the nipple-areola complex, *Plast. Reconstruct. Surg.* **66**:497–501.
8. Turner-Warwick, R. T., 1959, The lymphatics of the breast, *Br. J. Surg.* **46**:574–582.
9. Arey, L. B., 1925, Simple formula for estimating the age and size of human embryos, *Anat. Rec.* **30**:289–296.
10. Arey, L. B., 1965, *Developmental Anatomy,* 7th ed., Saunders, Philadelphia, pp. 449–453.
11. Gasser, R. F., 1975, *Atlas of Human Embryos,* Harper, Hagerstown, Maryland.
12. Vorherr, H., 1974, *The Breast: Morphology, Physiology, and Lactation,* Academic Press, New York.
13. Tobon, H. and Salazar, H., 1974, Ultrastructure of the human mammary gland. I. Development of the fetal gland throughout gestation, *J. Clin. Endocrinol. Metab.* **39**:443–456.
14. Haenel, H., 1928, Ein Fall von dauernder Milchsekretion beim Manne, *Muench. Med. Wochenschr.* **1**:261.
15. Speert, H., 1942, Supernumerary mammae, with special reference to the rhesus monkey, *Q. Rev. Biol.* **17**:59–68.
16. Weinshel, L. and Demakopoulos, N., 1943, Supernumerary breasts: With special reference to the pseudomamma type, *Am. J. Surg.* **60**:76–80.
17. Hicken, N., 1937, Mammography: The roentgenographic diagnosis of breast tumors by means of contrast media, *Surg. Gynec. Obstet.* **64**:593–603.
18. Dabelow, A., 1957, Die Milchdrüse, in: *Handbuch der Mikroskopischen Anatomie des Menschen,* Volume III Part 3, Springer-Verlag, Berlin, pp. 277–486.
19. Pourcho, R., Bernstein, M. and Gould, S., 1978, Malachite green: Applications in electron microscopy, *Stain Tech.* **53**:29–35.
20. Pitelka, D., 1978, Cell contacts in the mammary gland, in: *Lactation: A Comprehensive Treastise,* Volume IV, Academic Press, New York, pp. 41–66.
21. Lascelles, A. and Lee, C. S., 1978, Involution of the mammary gland, in: *Lactation: A Comprehensive Treastise,* Volume IV, Academic Press, New York, pp. 115–177.
22. Moore, K. L., 1982, *The Developing Human,* W. B. Saunders Co., Philadelphia.
23. Dabelow, A., 1941, Die postnatale Entwicklung der menschlichen Milchdrüse and ihre Korrelationen, *Morphol. J.* **85**:361–416.
24. Richardson, K. C., 1949, Contractile tissue in the mammary gland with special reference to the myoepithelium in the goat, *Proc. R. Soc. London, Ser. B.* **136**:30–45.

3

The Mechanisms of Milk Secretion

Margaret C. Neville, Jonathan C. Allen, and Christopher Watters

INTRODUCTION AND OVERVIEW

Milk secretion occurs in all mammals, the presence of mammary glands being one of the important criteria distinguishing this class from all others. Although the location and external form of the mammary gland differ from one species to another, the mechanisms of milk production are remarkably similar. Milk is produced by epithelial cells which line the mammary alveoli and is stored in the alveolar lumina adjacent to these cells. During ejection, the milk is forced from the alveoli by contraction of surrounding myoepithelial cells and exits through ductules into ducts which drain several clusters of alveoli. In the human, small ducts coalesce into 15 to 25 larger ducts which dilate into small sinuses as they near the areolus. These ducts open directly on the nipple (see Chapter 2 for a more extensive discussion of the anatomy of the human mammary gland). In other animals, the ducts may empty into a single primary duct or a cistern which in turn is drained by a single teat canal. These structures may provide additional milk storage, particularly in dairy animals.

With the development of electron microscopy and sophisticated tools for probing the biochemical basis of milk secretion, over the past decade five specific pathways for the synthesis and secretion of milk components have been clearly defined. These five pathways, illustrated diagramatically in Fig. 1, operate in parallel to transform precursors derived from the blood into milk constituents and/or transfer them into the alveolar lumina. Although the biochemical processes involved are fundamentally the same in all mammals, differences in their relative rates and, in some cases, in the nature of

Margaret C. Neville and Jonathan C. Allen • Department of Physiology, University of Colorado School of Medicine, Denver, Colorado 80262.   *Christopher Watters* • Department of Biology, Middlebury College, Middlebury, Vermont 05753.

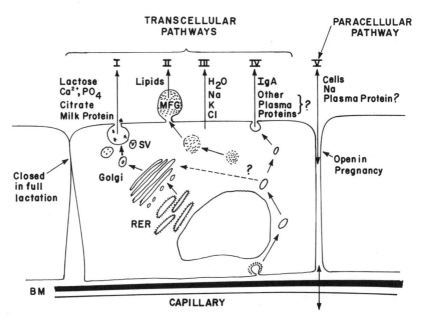

Figure 1. The pathways for milk synthesis and secretion in the mammary alveolus. (I) Exocytosis of milk protein and lactose in Golgi-derived secretory vesicles. (II) Milk fat secretion via the milk fat globule. (III) Secretion of ions and water across the apical membrane. (IV) Pinocytosis-exocytosis of immunoglobulins. (V) The paracellular pathway for plasma components and leukocytes. (Abbreviations: SV, secretory vesicle; RER, rough endoplasmic reticulum; BM, basement membrane; MFG, milk fat globule.)

the products synthesized result in milks whose composition differs widely from species to species. Some of the milk secretion pathways, for example, exocytosis of protein-containing vesicles, are common to many secretory tissues such as pancreas, liver, and salivary gland. In contrast, the mechanism for fat secretion into milk appears to be unique to the mammary gland. Because these five pathways are now well defined, the nineteenth century terms, apocrine, merocrine, and holocrine secretion, occasionally still applied to the mammary gland, no longer add to our understanding of milk secretion and should be abandoned.

    In comparison to related dermal glands such as the salivary and sweat glands, the rate of milk secretion is slow, about 1 to 2 ml of milk per gram of tissue per day.[1] Milk is stored adjacent to the cells which produce it. Histologically, the cells lining the smaller ducts resemble the alveolar cells, even reacting with anticasein antibodies,[2] suggesting that they, like the alveolar cells, secrete milk. Because milk passes through the ducts rapidly during its forced transit from alveolus to nipple, it is unlikely that reabsorptive processes, like those found in the salivary and sweat glands, play a significant role in determining milk composition.

    In this introductory section, the characteristics of the five pathways for milk secretion will be summarized followed by discussions of the changes in composition of the mammary secretion at parturition, the secretion of cellular elements into milk, the mechanism by which the nursing infant removes milk from the breast and finally mammary blood flow. In subsequent sections, the physiology and biochemistry of each of the four transcellular pathways will be considered in greater detail in order to provide the reader with a framework for understanding current developments in mammary physiology. Our current understanding of the hormonal mechanisms which regulate mammary development and function is summarized in the succeeding chapters. Recognizing that there is currently a large gap between our knowledge of the hormones which control mammary function and our understanding of the molecular mechanisms through which they act, in this chapter we have tried to indicate those points in each of the biochemical pathways where regulation is likely to occur.

Cellular Mechanisms for Milk Synthesis and Secretion

To produce milk, four secretory processes are synchronized in the alveolar cell of the mature mammary gland: exocytosis, fat synthesis and secretion, secretion of ions and water, and immunoglobulin transfer from the extracellular space (Fig. 1). These will be summarized briefly, followed by discussions of membrane flow in the alveolar cell and of the role of a fifth process, the paracellular pathway, in determining the composition of the mammary secretion. Most of the concepts in this introductory section will be expanded in later portions of the chapter; for such concepts, detailed references are deferred to the later section.

Exocytosis

Among the major milk components, proteins, lactose, calcium, phosphate, and citrate are packaged into secretory vesicles and secreted by exocytosis. The amino acid sequence of the milk proteins, as coded in the nuclear DNA, is transcribed into messenger RNA (mRNA) which moves to the cytoplasm. Consistent with other secreted proteins, translation of the mRNA occurs on ribosomes bound to the endoplasmic reticulum. As the proteins are synthesized, they are inserted across the endoplasmic reticulum membrane, the *N*-terminal amino acid sequence (the "signal" sequence) is removed, and carbohydrate groups may be added. The sequestered proteins are then transferred to the Golgi system for further processing and sorting.

Calcium, phosphate, and citrate are transported into the Golgi vesicles from the cytoplasm. Within the Golgi vesicles, calcium and phosphate combine with the class of phosphoproteins known as caseins to form large aggregates called micelles. The membrane-bound enzyme, galactosyltransferase, interacts with a soluble protein, α-lactalbumin, within the Golgi system to synthesize the milk sugar, lactose. Because the Golgi membrane is impermeable to lactose, the sugar is osmotically active; as it accumulates, water is drawn into the Golgi vesicles. As they reach the terminal portions of the Golgi system, the casein micelles and other milk proteins, lactose, calcium, phosphate, and citrate are packaged into secretory vesicles. These move toward the apical portion of the cell, fuse with the apical membrane and release their contents into the alveolar lumina (Pathway I, Fig. 1).

Lipid Synthesis and Secretion

Triglycerides, synthesized in the cytoplasm and smooth endoplasmic reticulum of the mammary alveolar cell, coalesce into large droplets which gradually make their way to the apex of the cell. The lipid droplets bulge against and gradually become entirely enveloped in apical plasma membrane, and finally separate from the cell as the milk fat globule. The occasional inclusion of a crescent of cytoplasm within the membrane-bound globule[3] enables any substance contained in the cytoplasm to enter milk (Pathway II, Fig. 1).

Secretion of Monovalent Ions and Water

Sodium, potassium, and water may permeate the Golgi, secretory vesicle, and apical membranes freely.[1,4,4a] Water moves from the cell across these membranes in response to the osmotic gradient set up by lactose. Electrolytes follow water, moving down their electrochemical gradients. The concentrations of potassium and sodium in milk are thought to be regulated by the electrical potential across the apical membrane. Because the chloride in the milk is out of equilibrium with its concentration in the cytoplasm, it is necessary to postulate some sort of active transport for this ion back into the cell. Bicarbonate ion is lower in milk than in plasma. However, nothing is known about its secretion into milk although Linzell and Peaker[5] have postulated $Cl^- - HCO_3$ exchange at the apical membrane (Pathway III, Fig. 1).

Immunoglobulin Secretion

Immunoglobulin A, and perhaps other plasma proteins, combine with a specific receptor on the basolateral membrane of the cell. The receptor and its attached IgA are internalized in endocytotic vesicles and are then transported either to the apical membrane or to the Golgi apparatus for subsequent disgorgement into milk (Pathway IV, Fig.1).[6]

Membrane Flow in the Mammary Alveolar Cell

It is apparent from Fig. 1 that there is considerable traffic between membrane-bound compartments during the synthesis and secretion of milk components. For example, proteins originally sequestered in the rough endoplasmic reticulum must be transferred to the Golgi apparatus for sorting and processing, then further packaged in secretory vesicles. The mechanisms of these transfers and the flow of membranous materials between these compartments are not yet well understood although they are the subject of

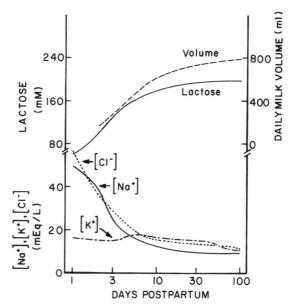

Figure 2. Changes in human milk volume, lactose, and ion content in the puerperium. Data on milk volume compiled from the data in refs. 16 and 17, data on potassium and chloride compiled from refs. 18, 19, 20, and 21, and data on lactose from refs. 17, 21, 22, and 28. Lines represent approximate mean values.

considerable current interest among cell biologists.[7] The chronology and ultrastructural organization of exocytosis and milk fat globule secretion have suggested to some investigators[8] that milk secretion is accompanied by a polarized flow of intracellular membranes. According to this view, membranes, possibly in association with newly synthesized secretory products, move from the Golgi complex to secretory vesicles and then to the apical plasma membrane where they envelope the extruded milk fat globule. In terms of this model, the apical membrane is in constant flux with membrane being added from the secretory vesicle membranes and removed as milk fat globule membrane.[9] Evidence consistent with this scheme is provided by the observation that certain Golgi enzymes, xanthine oxidase, galactosyl transferase, and thiamine pyrophosphatase are also found in the milk fat globule membrane.[10–12] On the other hand, freeze-fracture studies[13,14] indicate that intrinsic membrane particles, presumably proteins, are partially excluded from the milk fat globule membrane, suggesting that there is selection and segregation of the protein components of the apical membrane as it engulfs the milk fat globule.

The mechanism proposed for the receptor-mediated transcellular transport of milk immunoglobulins[6] postulates two additional pathways of membrane flow: (1) A portion of the Golgi membrane containing newly synthesized immunoglobulin-receptor is transported to and fuses with the basolateral plasma membrane of the secretory cell. (2) Following immunoglobulin binding, the immunoglobulin-receptor complex is endocytosed and the resulting membrane vesicle is transported to and fused with the apical membrane. Further elucidation of the pathways through which membranes flow and the mechanisms by which this flow is regulated are likely to provide

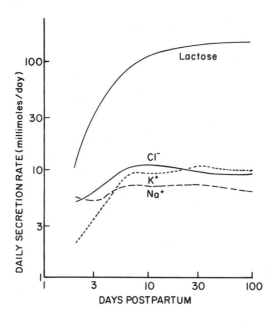

Figure 3. The daily rate of lactose and ion secretion in the puerperium. Data derived by multiplying the average concentrations shown in Fig. 2 by the average volume at each time point.

an exciting chapter in the story of the function of the mammary alveolar cell.

The Role of the Paracellular Pathway in Milk Secretion

The fifth pathway for secretion of substances into milk (Fig. 1) involves passage between the epithelial cells, rather than through them and for this reason is designated the *paracellular pathway.*[1,4] The passage of substances through the spaces between the alveolar cells is normally prevented by the tight junctions (*zonula occludens*) between adjacent alveolar cells. During pregnancy, as well as in mastitic and involuting breasts these junctions become leaky, allowing plasma constituents to pass directly into milk. Under these conditions, the mammary secretion has a high concentration of sodium and chloride and lower concentrations of lactose and potassium than are generally found in milk during full lactation.

Changes in Milk Composition at Parturition

Following parturition in the human, the composition of the mammary secretion changes markedly (Figs. 2 and 4), going from a solution rich in sodium and chloride, immunoglobulins, and lactoferrin to a solution rich in lactose with only moderate protein levels.* A fairly abrupt increase in the synthetic activity of the alveolar cells results in an increase in both the volume of milk secreted and the total output of nutrients (Figs. 3 and 5). The closure of the junctional complexes is largely responsible for the change in the ionic

---

* Casein, the major protein in the milks of most species is not shown in Fig. 4 because longitudinal data on its concentration in human milk are not available. In mature human milk, casein levels are similar to the levels of α-lactalbumin and lactoferrin.[15]

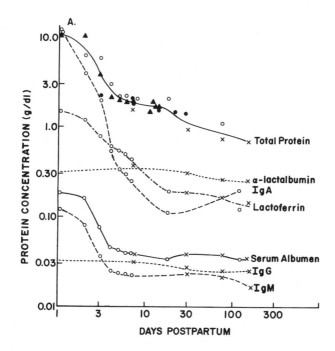

Figure 4. Longitudinal changes in the concentrations of total and individual proteins in human milk. Points represent mean values given by various authors. ●, Gross *et al.*[18]; ▲, Healy *et al.*[22]; ○, McClelland *et al.*[16]; ×, Lönnerdal *et al.*[17]

composition because the direct passage of plasma elements such as sodium and chloride into milk is impeded. During the transition from the secretion of colostrum to the secretion of mature milk, certain aspects of alveolar cell activity also decrease, in particular the secretion of lactoferrin and IgA (Fig. 5). This suggests that the secretory activity of the alveolar cells is regulated in such a way that substances primarily of nutritional significance partially replace those of protective or immunologic significance in the early postpartum period.

A secretion, termed precolostrom, can be obtained from the mammary glands of pregnant women. From midpregnancy to parturition, the composition of precolostrum is rather stable[21] with high concentrations of sodium, chloride, lactoferrin, and immunoglobulins and low levels of lactose. Starting at parturition, the mammary secretion is called colostrum. In general, this term has been used in the human to describe mammary secretions obtained during the first 4 or 5 days postpartum. Secretions obtained during the next 5 days are often referred to as *transitional milk*. As is evident from Figs. 2, 3, and 6, however, the composition of the mammary secretion undergoes a continuous adjustment during the postpartum period, so that particular compositional values cannot be assigned either to colostrum or transitional milk. During mastitis[23,24] and after weaning[25] compositional changes in reverse of those seen during lactogenesis occur.

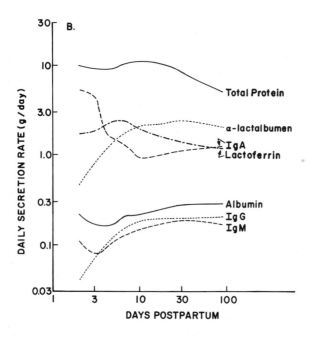

Figure 5. Daily secretion rate of total and individual proteins obtained by multiplying compositional values in Fig. 4 by the mean volumes shown in Fig. 2.

Milk from mothers giving birth to premature infants shows sodium, chloride, and total protein levels higher than milk from mothers of full-term infants (Fig. 6). The lactose level is consistently lower.[18,26,27] It has been postulated that these compositional differences are responsible for the observation that premature infants do better when fed their own mother's milk than when fed banked milk. Whether this is true or not, the data in Fig. 6 make it clear that those changes in the mammary epithelium which lead to the secretion of mature milk are delayed in mothers of preterm

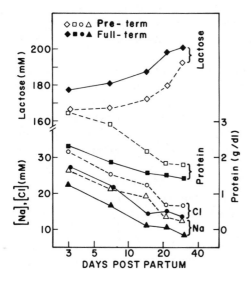

Figure 6. Comparison of milk composition from mothers of preterm infants with that from mothers of full-term infants in the early puerperium. Results plotted from the data of Gross *et al.*[18,26]

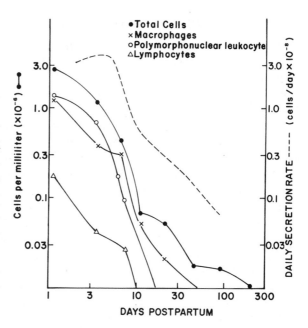

Figure 7. The cellular composition of mammary secretion. Solid lines represent the number of cells per milliliter of milk. After 30 days, more than 50% of the cells were epithelial cells. Data from Ho *et al.*[28] Dotted line is the daily secretion rate for all cellular components obtained by multiplying the total cell concentration by the volumes shown in Fig. 2 for each stage of lactation. Epithelial cells appear to be found at a concentration of 10^4/ml throughout lactation.[29]

infants. The physiological basis of this observation is unclear. The possibility should be investigated that the delay results from incomplete emptying of the breast due to the weak suck of the premature infant or insufficient milk removal with a breast pump in women whose infants are too young to suckle. However, the delayed maturation of the mammary epithelium may also reflect incomplete prepartum development.

The Secretion of Cells into Colostrum and Milk

During the early puerperium, the mammary secretion from the human breast contains about 10^6 cells/ml (Fig. 7), most of which are leukocytes in the form of polymorphonuclear cells, macrophages, and lymphocytes.[28] After the first month, the number of cells secreted is reduced by a factor of at least 100 and the predominant cell type changes from leukocytes to sloughed epithelial cells,[29] which continue to be found in milk throughout lactation at a concentration of about 10^4 cells/ml.

The daily secretion rate of leukocytes into human milk appears to peak about day 5 (Fig. 7) and then falls gradually as the mammary epithelium matures. In electron micrographs,[30] leukocytes can be seen interposed between mammary epithelial cells leading to the postulate that they enter the mammary secretion through the paracellular pathway. Whether they themselves alter the integrity of the junctional complexes or whether they pass through "gaps" in the alveolar epithelium[31,32] is not clear at this time. In any case, the number of leukocytes secreted into milk is highest during early lactation when the junctional complexes are more permeable to small ions and other plasma constituents.

Suckling and the Ejection of Milk from the Breast

Milk removal from the breast is the product of a coordinated interaction between the sucking of the infant and the letdown reflex of the mother. As the infant commences sucking, afferent impulses generated in receptors in the areola travel to the brain where they stimulate the release of oxytocin from the posterior pituitary (see Chapter 4 for a full description of oxytocin release). Oxytocin travels through the blood stream to the breast where it combines with specific receptors on the myoepithelial cells, stimulating them to contract and force milk from the alveoli into the mammary ducts and sinuses. If the infant is nursing correctly, the nipple and much of the areola are drawn well into the mouth so that a long teat reaching nearly to the soft palate is formed.[33,34] The mammary sinuses extend into this teat. Milk is removed not so much by suction as by the stripping motion of the tongue against the hard palate which allows milk to flow from the teat into the baby's mouth. The sinuses refill as the continued acton of oxytocin forces milk from the alveoli into the ducts.

A number of problems can lead to unsatisfactory milk removal. These include the inability of the infant to develop a sufficiently strong suck to stimulate the afferent nerve endings in the areola or completely remove milk from the breast, a severed areolar nerve in a woman who has had breast surgery or an unfavorable emotional state in the mother which interferes with oxytocin secretion.[35] If these problems are not solved (see Chapter 9), it is probable that milk will be retained in the alveolus leading to inhibition of secretion.

Mammary Blood Flow

In all species where it has been measured, mammary blood flow increases markedly at lactogenesis and comprises a fairly substantial proportion of the cardiac output during lactation.[36–41] In the goat and cow,[36] mammary blood flow is closely correlated with milk yield, 400 to 500 liters of blood passing through the mammary gland for each liter of milk produced. Detailed measurements have not been possible in humans, although the prominence of the venous drainage from the breasts during both pregnancy and lactation suggests that breast hyperemia is present in women from an early state of pregnancy.[42] Crude measurements of breast blood flow using skin thermometry[43] indicated that mammary blood flow increased markedly during pregnancy then rose further after parturition. There was some indication of a correlation of blood flow with milk production in this study.

The nature of the factors which control vasomotor tone in the mammary gland has received little investigation. Linzell[36] pointed out that mammary blood vessels show exquisite sensitivity to epinephrine and norepinephrine and that serotonin and $PGF_{2\alpha}$ are vasoconstrictive agents in goats. Adenosine and bradykinin have both been shown to be vasodilators. In concious goats, brief occlusion of the mammary artery resulted in increased mammary blood flow suggesting the accumulation of a vasodilator during a period of reduced tissue perfusion. Bromocriptine infusion in sheep did not prevent the changes in mammary blood flow that accompany parturition in this species[39] suggesting that prolactin is not involved the regulation of mammary blood flow. Finally, a distinct correlation between mammary blood flow and both fasting and mild stress[44,45] has been demonstrated in goats. The mediation of these effects is totally unknown.

In summary, mammary blood flow appears to be closely correlated with the rate of milk secretion and can be regulated by changes in either cardiac output[41] or in local vasomotor tone. The control mechanisms involved have received little attention.

PROTEIN SYNTHESIS, PROCESSING, AND SECRETION IN THE MAMMARY GLAND

The major proteins in human milk are α-lactalbumin (30% of total protein in mature milk), lactoferrin (10 to 20%), casein (40%) and immunoglobulin A (IgA,10%).[46,47] Other major milk proteins include IgG, IgM, lysozyme, and serum albumin. Minor proteins include binding proteins such as corticosterone-binding protein,[48] vitamin-B_{12}-binding protein,[49,50] folate-binding protein,[51] hormones such as prolactin[22] and epidermal growth factor,[52] and the proteins of the milk fat globule membrane,[53,54] to cite a few. In addition, more than 30 enzymes have been identified in human milk.[15,55] The role of these enzymes is by and large unknown except for lactose synthetase and the bile-salt-activated lipase discussed later in this chapter. While some of the enzymes undoubtably arise from the cytoplasmic remnants present in milk, others, like the glycosyl transferases, probably originate with the Golgi vesicles or are cleaved from the milk fat globule membrane.[56]

In this section, we will summarize the properties of the major milk proteins followed by more detailed discussions of the mechanisms of casein and α-lactalbumin synthesis and processing and IgA secretion. Finally, the control of protein synthesis as it is presently understood in the mammary gland will be briefly outlined.

Properties of Milk Proteins

Casein

Casein is the major protein in the milk of most species comprising several families of phosphoproteins of molecular weight (mol. wt.) 26,000 to 45,000. Human milk is exceptional in having a low casein concentration, only about 20% of the total.[15] The α- and β-caseins are linear molecules containing a large proportion of proline residues. One end of these molecules contains a high density of negatively charged carboxyl and phosphate groups which tend to interact with calcium. The other end is largely composed of hydrophobic residues which promote self-association.[57] κ-Casein is a larger molecule, only part of whose structure has been published.[58] In the presence of millimolar concentrations of calcium and phosphate, casein molecules associate to form the casein micelle.[57] This unique protein aggregate, with a diameter about 140 nanometers, contains up to 25,000 monomeric casein molecules. Binding an average of 20 Ca^{2+} and 18 PO_4^{2-} molecules per protein monomer,[59] casein appears to be a highly efficient package for the delivery of protein and salts to the infant. It should be noted that human caseins have not yet been well characterized, nor have the extent of micellular formation and the actual amounts of casein present at various stages of lactation. In fact, it is currently not clear that human milk contains κ-casein at all.[46]

α-Lactalbumin

α-Lactalbumin (mol. wt. 14,081 in humans) appears to be evolutionarily derived from lysozyme; it is present in the milks of all species which secrete lactose.[56] It acts as a cofactor in the synthesis of lactose, a function which is more fully discussed in Section 3 of this chapter. Because human milk has a very low casein content both α-lactalbumin and lactoferrin (below) are nutritionally important fractions of human milk protein.[15]

Lactoferrin

Lactoferrin has variously been called red milk protein, ekkrinosiderophilin and lactotransferrin. It was first found as a red protein in human milk by Sorensen and Sorensen.[60] It is an iron-binding protein, mol. wt. 76,000, closely resembling transferrin. Each molecule binds two ferric ions in conjunction with two bicarbonate anions[61] and may also bind zinc.[62] It is present in high concentration in the colostrum of most species as well as in other exocrine secretions such as saliva and pancreatic fluid.[63] In most species the concentration of lactoferrin falls to very low levels in mature milk (0.2 mg/ml in the cow), but is is found at relatively high levels throughout lactation in the human and guinea pig (2 mg/ml). It is secreted into human milk about 5 to 10% saturated with iron.

Lactoferrin has both bacteriostatic and bacteriocidal activities presumably because its avid binding of iron makes the substance unavailable to bacteria[64] (but see reference 65 for other possible mechanisms of action). Lactoferrin has also been postulated to play a nutritional role in transferring iron to the neonate; however, its low iron saturation, the fact that the iron-saturated form of the protein is resistant to proteolytic hydrolysis, and the observation that breast-fed neonates appear normally to be in negative iron balance argue against such a role.[66] Synthesis of lactoferrin has not been studied in the mammary gland.

β-Lactoglobulin

This protein is present in the milks of ruminants and other species which depend on the transfer of large amounts of immunoglobulin to their young via colostrum.[15] However, its function is unknown and it is not present in the milk of humans, guinea pigs, rats, or mice.

Immunoglobulins

Secretory IgA is present in high concentration the first week after birth, falling to a stable level of about 2 mg/ml in mature milk (Fig. 4). Its possible antiinfective role is discussed in Chapter 7 and the mechanism of IgA secretion is discussed below.

IgG and IgM are only minor components in human milk. In contrast, IgG is the major immunoglobulin in the milk of ruminants and other species in which milk immunoglobulins cross the intestinal mucosa and are important for passive immunity of the newborn. The pathway for secretion of these plasma components into milk is not known.

Serum Albumin

Serum albumin is present at about 2 mg/ml in colostrum falling to 0.5 mg/ml in mature milk (Fig. 4). It is generally presumed to originate from the plasma, perhaps entering milk via the paracellular pathway, although Phillippy and McCarthy[67] have presented evidence which suggests some synthesis of serum albumin within the mammary gland itself.

Proteins of the Milk Fat Globule Membrane

During their secretion, milk fat globules are enveloped by apical plasma membrane that is separated from the core fat globule by a dense proteinaceous coat. Using SDS polyacrylamide gel electrophoresis, Mather and Keenan[54] were able to separate 21 protein components from well-washed bovine milk-fat globule membranes (MFGM) (see also Mather[53]). Similar proteins appear to be present in human MFGM.[68] After removal of membrane and loosely associated proteins, two major proteins are associated with the residual filamentaous material: xanthine oxidase (Band 3 in the terminology of Mather and Keenan,[54] mol. wt ~150,000) and Band 12 protein (mol. wt. 76,000) for which Franke *et al.*,[69] have proposed the name "butyrophilin." This protein has been shown by immunofluorescence to be concentrated at the apical surface of the mammary epithelial cells. It was not found in other epithelial cells or in other cell types in the mammary gland, suggesting to Franke and his colleagues[69] that it is involved in the vectorial discharge of milk fat globules into the alveolar lumina.

Free Amino Acids in Milk

Free amino acids are present in widely varying concentrations in the milks of different species.[70] In most species, the total amounts to 2 to 4 mM.

In the relatively protein-poor human milk, they contribute as much as 25% of the total nitrogen, with higher levels during early lactation.[71] Glutamine and glutamate make up more than half of the total amino acids, being present at concentrations of about 1.4 and 0.3 mM respectively. Taurine is also present at a fairly high level (0.3 mM). The nutritional significance of these observations is not yet clear.

Protein Precursors—The Transport of Amino Acids into Mammary Alveolar Cells

Milk proteins are synthesized from amino acids derived from the blood stream. From measurements of the arterial, venous, and milk concentrations of amino acids as well as mammary blood flow,[72] it is possible to determine what proportion of plasma amino acids are directly utilized in the synthesis of milk proteins. Methionine, histidine, phenylalanine, tryptophan, and tyrosine appear to be quantitatively transferred to milk protein while valine, isoleucine, lysine, threonine, and arginine are partially oxidized within the alveolar cell. The uptake of nonessential amino acids is quite variable and many of these appear to be synthesized within the gland. Whether amino acid supply is a limiting factor in milk synthesis is presently unknown, although as much as 70% of certain essential amino acids (methionine, phenylalanine) have been shown to be extracted from the blood during a single passage through the mammary gland of goats.[73]

The mechanism by which free amino acids enter milk has received no systematic study. The high level of glutamate in human milk as well as the observation, made in the course of a study of monosodium glutamate ingestion in humans, that milk glutamate was not changed when plasma glutamate levels varied from 40 to 310μM,[74] indicate that some mechanism exists for active transport of glutamate into milk. On the other hand, an increase in plasma phenylalanine due to ingestion of a sweetening agent, L-aspartyl-L-phenylalanyl methyl ester, was followed by an increase in phenylalanine levels in milk,[75] suggesting that other amino acids may find their way passively into the milk space.

Synthesis and Processing of Milk-Specific Proteins

Current research on the synthesis and secretion of milk proteins includes some of the most exciting in the field. Within the last decade reconstituted cell-free systems have become available in which the synthesis and processing of specific proteins can be followed under controlled conditions. The application of these techniques to the synthesis of milk proteins[76–80] has shown that the initial product derived from the translation of casein and α-lactalbumin mRNA contains an extra sequence of 16 to 28 primarily hydrophobic amino acids at the N-terminal called a *signal peptide* (Fig. 8). If membrane fractions containing endoplasmic reticulum are included in the synthesizing system, the proteins are "processed" by removal of this signal

SIGNAL PEPTIDES   → AUTHENTIC MILK PROTEINS

β-Casein   Met-Lys-Val-Leu-Ile-Leu-Ala-Cys-Leu-Val-Ala-Leu-Ala-Leu-Ala-   Arg-Gln-Gln-Glu-Glu-Leu-Asn-...

αs1-Casein   Met-Lys-Leu-Leu-Ile-Leu-Thr-Cys-Leu-Val-Ala-Val-Ala-Leu-Ala-   Arg-Pro-Lys-His-Pro-Ile-Lys-...

αs2-Casein   Met-Lys-Val-Leu-Met-Lys-Ala-Cys-Leu-Val-Ala-Val-Ala-Leu-Ala-   Lys- - -Met- - -Val-...

κ-Casein   Met-Arg-Lys-Ser-Ile-Leu / Phe-Phe -Leu-Val-Val-Thr-Ile-Leu-Ala-Leu-Thr-Leu-Pro-Phe-Leu-Ile-Ala-   Gln-Glu-Gln-Asn-Gln-Glu-Gln-...

β-LG   Met-Lys-Cys-Leu-Leu-Leu-Ala-Leu-Gly-Leu-Ala-Leu-Ala-Cys-Gly-Val-Gln-Ala-   Ile-Ile-Val-Thr-Gln-Thr-Met-...

α-LA   Met-Met-Ser-Phe-Val- Ser-Leu-Leu-Val-Gly-Ile-Leu-Phe- -Ala-Thr-Gln-Ala-   Glu-Gln-Leu-Thr-Lys-Cys-Glu-...
             -20 -15 -10 -5 -1 1   5

Figure 8. The amino terminal sequences of the six major proteins in sheep milk including the signal sequence which terminates at the arrow. (Abbreviations: β-LG, β-lactoglobulin; α-LA, α-lactalbumin.) (Redrawn from ref. 80.)

peptide and the authentic molecules are sequestered within the cisternae of the membrane vesicles.[79] This type of observation has been interpreted to mean that the signal sequence triggers the binding of the mRNA/ribosome complex to membranes of the rough endoplasmic reticulum, thereby initiating the vectorial transfer of the nascent protein into the ER cisternae.[81] Because transfer does not occur if the membranes are added after protein synthesis is complete, transport appears to coincide with translation and is called *cotranslational processing*. Since the signal sequence is coded for by nucleotides in the mRNA and complementary bases in the parent DNA, both the fate and the structure of the secreted proteins is under genetic control.

A second type of processing, *N-glycosylation*, or the transfer of a mannose-rich oligosaccharide from a lipid carrier to an arginine residue of the nascent polypeptide (*N*-glycosylation) also takes place in the rough endoplasmic reticulum. Again the reaction appears to occur as the protein crosses the rough endoplasmic reticulum membrane[82,83] and is often called *core glycosylation*. The addition of sugars to milk proteins is specific to particular proteins and is variable between species. κ-Casein is the only casein which contains carbohydrate residues.[47,84] *In vitro* glycosylation has been observed during the cell-free synthesis of α-lactalbumin and casein,[76,78] suggesting that core glycosylation of milk proteins takes place in the rough endoplasmic reticulum.

After sequestration in the rough endoplasmic reticulum, the proteins are rapidly transferred to the Golgi system, possibly by small, smooth-surfaced vesicles located peripherally to the Golgi membranes.[7,85] After transfer of the polypeptide to the Golgi apparatus, additional processing results in the partial removal of mannose residues and addition of other monosaccharides in an *O*-glycosyl linkage between serine or threonine and *N*-acetyl-galactosamine.[86] Other modifications which take place within the Golgi system include phosphorylation and casein micelle formation.

Casein is phosphorylated[87,88] by an enzyme, casein kinase, associated with the Golgi membrane fraction.[89] The reaction is

$$\text{Casein} + \text{ATP} \rightarrow \text{Casein-PO}_4 + \text{ADP} \tag{1}$$

and has been shown to be catalyzed by a cAMP-independent casein kinase obtained from mammary Golgi membranes.[88,90] The amino acid sequence of the first 12 residues of the *N*-terminus of human β-casein is[91]:

$$\overset{5}{} \qquad\qquad \overset{10}{}$$

NH$_2$-Arg-Glu-Thr-Ile-Glu-Ser-Leu-Ser-Ser-Ser-Glu-Glu-   (2)

$$\begin{array}{ccccccc} | & & | & & | & | & | \\ P & & P & & P & P & P \end{array}$$

Phosphate groups appear to be added to threonine and serine residues, two residues to the left of either glutamate or serine.[92] Note that the heavy concentration of glutamic acid and phosphorylated residues gives the amino terminus a strong negative charge which is probably responsible for the calcium binding capacity of the casein micelle. Phosphorylation of human β-casein is heterogeneous and 6 forms of the protein containing 0 to 5 phosphate groups have been identified in human milk.[93] Greenberg *et al.*,[91] showed that the addition of the phosphate residues is nonrandom, occuring in the order 10 or 9, then 8, 6, 3. Residues 3, 6, and 8 are not phosphorylated by casein kinase isolated from bovine mammary glands, suggesting that another kinase or a kinase of different specificity may be responsible for this reaction in the human.

The final step in casein processing is the formation of the casein micelle. Although the physical chemical basis of micelle formation is still a matter of controversy,[57,94] it is clear that both hydrophobic bonds between the casein monomers and electrostatic interactions of Ca^{2+} and PO_4^{2-} with charged residues on the proteins are involved. Waugh and Talbot[95] proposed that κ-casein stabilized the micelle by adsorption to its surface, a postulate in accord with recent data that indicates that the fraction of κ-casein in the micelle is directly proportional to its surface area.[96]

Regulation of Milk Protein Synthesis

Under many *in vivo* conditions, the amount of milk protein in the mammary gland is roughly correlated with the amount of mRNA present.[97,98] This also appears to be the case *in vitro* in short-term explants[99] suggesting that much of the control of milk protein synthesis resides in the control of mRNA levels. In these systems, the accumulation of casein mRNA in the presence of prolactin appears to result from both an increase in the rate of transcription of mRNA and a decrease in its degradation rate.[99,100] Because maximal casein mRNA levels were observed in the absence of casein synthesis just prior to birth in rats, it is likely that translational control mechanisms are also present.[101] Casein itself was found to be degraded in mammary gland explants incubated in the absence of hormone, but not when insulin, prolactin, and cortisol were present, suggesting that protein degradation may be utilized to regulate the proportion of protein actually secreted.[102] It thus appears that hormonal regulation of milk protein synthesis and secretion occurs at several levels including mRNA transcription and degradation as well as protein synthesis and degradation. The mechanism by which these processes are coordinated presents an interesting challenge for future research.

Immunoglobulin Secretion

Although IgG is present in high concentrations in the colostrum of ruminants the predominant immunoglobulin in human milk is polymeric IgA to which a protein known as *secretory component* is attached (see Chapter 7 for a more complete description of this molecule and its function). Current evidence[6,103,104] indicates that IgA synthesized in plasma cells in the interstitial spaces of the mammary glands combines with a large, transmembrane form of secretory component in the basolateral membrane of the mammary alveolar cell. After transport of the complex to the apical membrane, the luminal portion of the complex is cleaved releasing the mature secretory component-IgA complex. It is not clear whether secretory IgA is released directly into the alveolar lumen or whether it first enters the Golgi to be secreted with other milk proteins via exocytosis.

Conclusion

The structure of the major milk proteins in rodents and ruminants and the mechanisms of their synthesis and secretion are well understood at this time. In the near future, we can expect structural comparisons between the milk proteins of various species to provide insight into the details of mammalian evolution. Since the enzymatically active sites of those proteins which also act as enzymes are likely to show great evolutionary stability, interspecific sequence comparisons may allow identification of such sites.[78,79] In addition the availability of well-characterized DNA complementary to the casein, α-lactalbumin and mRNAs of several species[105-109] allows examination of the structure of the milk protein genes and the control of their mRNAs. The stage is thus set for rapid progress toward understanding the genetic mechanisms regulating milk protein synthesis. Finally, there is considerable evidence that the synthesis of the various milk proteins is independently regulated. For example, α-lactalbumin is synthesized in the guinea pig mammary gland at parturition, but casein is not,[101] and cortisol has differential effects on the accumulation of α-lactalbumin and casein in explants from the midpregnant mouse mammary gland.[110] The unravelling of the differential control mechanisms involved should provide fascinating insights into the molecular basis of the regulation of milk protein synthesis and secretion.

THE SYNTHESIS OF MILK SUGARS

The disaccharide lactose, the major sugar in milk, is synthesized within the Golgi secretory vesicle system of the mammary alveolar cell.[56,111] In addition to the female mammary gland, the sugar is synthesized only in a very few plants in low concentrations.[56] Because the Golgi membrane is impermeable to lactose, the disaccharide draws water osmotically into the milk spaces and in most mammals the rate of lactose synthesis serves as the major control of the volume of milk produced. Certain arctic aquatic species secrete very low concentrations of lactose[55]; in such species the major caloric content of milk is provided by lipid (Fig. 9), and milk volume is determined primarily by the rate of secretion of lipid and monovalent ions.

In addition to lactose, human milk contains smaller quantities of both monosaccharides and complex oligosaccharides. The major monosaccharides are glucose and galactose, both present at concentrations of 3 mM or less.[112,113] More than 50 oligosaccharides, containing three to eight or more

Figure 9. Relation between milk lactose content and milk fat content. Representative data from Jenness.[55] 1 hedgehog, 2 water shrew, 3 short-tailed shrew, 4 fringed myotis, 5 long-nosed bat, 6 Mexican free-tailed bat, 7 domestic rabbit, 8 Eastern cottontail, 9 squirrel monkey, 10 green monkey, 11 rhesus monkey, 12 orangutan, 13 chimpanzee, 14 human, 15 Eastern grey squirrel, 16 beaver, 17 hamster, 18 rat, 19 house mouse, 20 guinea pig, 21 dog, 22 wolf, 23 yezo brown bear, 24 otter, 25 cat, 26–32 various types of seal, 33 Indian elephant, 34 horse, 35 zebra, 36 rhinoceros, 37 pig, 38 giraffe, 39 moose, 40 reindeer, 41 cow, 42 goat, 43 sheep, 44 spotted porpoise, 45 blue whale, 46 humpback whale. Circled numbers represent primates, triangles represent rodents, squares represent species living in or near the ocean.

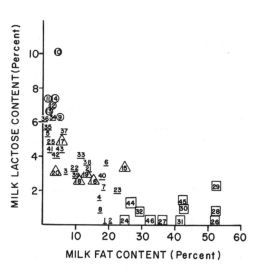

monosacharide subunits have been identified and characterized in human milk.[112,114–117] The components of these oligosaccharides are glucose, galactose, fucose, N-acetylglucoseamine, and sialic acid. Most have a lactose at the reducing end, suggesting that they result from the action of Golgi-associated glycosyl transferases on lactose.[114] The structure of the oligosaccharides in human milk varies with the ABO or Lewis blood type of the individual.[116,118]

In this section, the utilization of glucose by the mammary gland will be reviewed briefly followed by a discussion of lactose synthesis and its regulation. Earlier work has been reviewed by Ebner and Schanbacher,[112] Brew and Hill,[56] and Jones.[119]

Glucose Utilization in the Mammary Gland

In the mammary gland of nonruminants, glucose serves as the major substrate for both lactose and lipid synthesis. In the ruminant, glucose appears to be used only in lactose synthesis and in the pentose phosphate pathway (see below) to provide NADPH for fatty acid synthesis.[120] Acetate supplies most of the carbon atoms for fatty acid synthesis as well as for energy metabolism.

The diagram in Fig. 10 shows the major pathways involved in glucose metabolism. Glucose enters the mammary alveolar cell from the extracellular space utilizing mechanisms that are not yet well defined. A portion of the glucose entering the cell goes directly to the Golgi apparatus where it combines with UDP-galactose to form lactose. The rest is converted to glucose-6-phosphate by hexokinase. Glucose-6-PO$_4$ has three possible fates: conversion to pyruvate via glycolysis, entry into the pentose phosphate

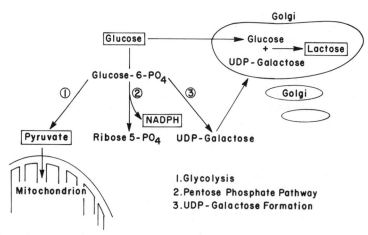

Figure 10. The major pathways of glucose utilization in the mammary alveolar cell.

pathway, and formation of uridine-diphospho-galactose (UDP-galactose). Pyruvate, which can also be formed from lactic acid in the mammary gland[121] enters the mitochondria where it is either oxidized to CO_2 via the tricarboxylic acid cycle or transformed into citrate which passes back into the cytosol and serves as a substrate for fatty acid synthesis.

Synthesis of UDP-Galactose

Three steps are necessary for the conversion of Glucose-6-PO_4 to UDP-galactose:

$$\text{Glucose-6-}PO_4 \leftrightarrow \text{Glucose-1-}PO_4 \tag{3}$$

$$\text{Glucose-1-}PO_4 + \text{UTP} \leftrightarrow \text{UDP-Glucose} + PO_4 \tag{4}$$

$$\text{UDP-Glucose} \leftrightarrow \text{UDP-Galactose} \tag{5}$$

These reactions are catalyzed by phosphoglucomutase, glucose-1-PO_4 uridyltransferase, and UDP-glucose 4-epimerase, respectively. These reactions are thought to be at equilibrium under the conditions prevailing within the cytosol[122] and are, therefore, not considered to be rate limiting for lactose synthesis.

The Pentose Phosphate Pathway

This pathway, in which the 1-carbon of glucose is oxidized to CO_2 with the formation of NADPH from NADP, is highly active in tissues which synthesize fatty acids because the NADPH is necessary to provide reducing equivalents. The ribulose-5-phosphate formed in the pentose phosphate pathway is transformed to ribose-5-phosphate which can be used for nucleotide synthesis or recombined through a complex series of transformations[123] to glucose-6-phosphate which is then reutilized by any of the three pathways.

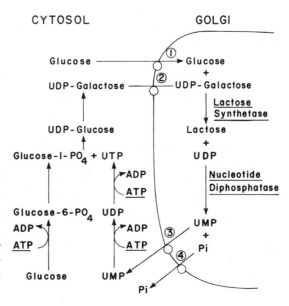

Figure 11. Lactose synthesis and substrate transport across the Golgi membrane. Evidence for the presence of transport mechanisms for glucose,[130] UDP-galactose, and UMP[129] has been obtained by Kuhn and co-workers. Note that the necessity to regenerate UDP from UMP increases the ATP requirement for lactose synthesis to 3 moles/mole lactose.

Lactose Synthesis

The Golgi enzyme complex, *lactose synthetase*, catalyses the formation of lactose using the overall reaction (See Fig. 11):

$$\text{UDP-Galactose} + \text{Glucose} \rightarrow \text{Lactose} + \text{UDP} \tag{6}$$

The complex consists of two components, a membrane-bound enzyme, galactosyl transferase, and a regulatory protein, α-*lactalbumin*. Galactosyl transferase is found in the Golgi membranes of many tissues where it catalyzes the transfer of galactosyl groups from UDP-galactose to carbohydrate groups of glycoproteins. Although it is capable by itself of catalyzing the lactose formation, normally it does not do so because the Michaelis constant (K_m) for glucose is too high ($\sim$ 1 M). The binding of the regulatory protein, α-lactalbumin, to galactosyl transferase increases the affinity of galactosyl-transferase for glucose (to a $K_m \sim$ 1 mM) so that lactose formation can occur under physiological conditions. Galactosyl transferase is found in many tissues; it is the presence of the milk-specific protein, α-lactalbumin, that confers special properties on the mammary enzyme as shown by the observation that galactosyl transferase derived from onion tips can synthesize lactose in the presence of α-lactalbumin.[56]

The molecular mechanism of lactose synthesis has been the object of intense study for over a decade.[56,112,124] The reaction is activated by metal ions which bind to two sites on galactosyl transferase. Mn^{2+} binds with high affinity to metal Site I, stabilizing the active conformation of the enzyme[125]:

$$\text{Enzyme} + Mn^{2+} \rightarrow Mn\cdot\text{Enzyme} \tag{7}$$

Co^{2+}, Zn^{2+}, and Cd^{2+} can all substitute for Mn^{2+} at Site I but Ca^{2+}

cannot.[125,126] A second metal ion, probably Ca^{2+} *in vivo*, and UDP-galactose add to a site at some distance from the first, structural metal site.[126]

$$Mn \cdot Enzyme + Ca^{2+} + UDP\text{-}gal \rightarrow Mn \cdot Enzyme \begin{smallmatrix} \diagup UDP\text{-}gal \\ \diagdown Ca \end{smallmatrix} \tag{8}$$

The calcium probably forms a bridge between the enzyme and the substrate. The K_d for calcium binding at Site II is about 2×10^{-3} M, about equal to the calcium concentration thought to be present within the Golgi vesicles. Mn^{2+} can substitute for Ca^{2+} at this site and is generally used as an activator in *in vitro* studies of galactosyl transferase. However, the affinity for Mn^{2+} at Site II is in the millimolar range[126] suggesting that it is not the ion bound under physiological conditions. In a final step, α-lactalbumin (α-LA) and glucose then add to the enzyme-UDP-galactose complex apparently in random order,[127] each synergistically increasing the affinity of the enzyme for the other.

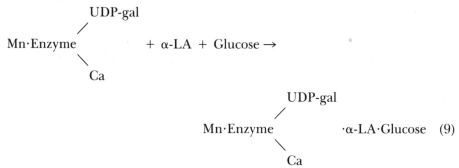

$$Mn \cdot Enzyme \begin{smallmatrix} \diagup UDP\text{-}gal \\ \diagdown Ca \end{smallmatrix} + \alpha\text{-}LA + Glucose \rightarrow$$

$$Mn \cdot Enzyme \begin{smallmatrix} \diagup UDP\text{-}gal \\ \diagdown Ca \end{smallmatrix} \cdot \alpha\text{-}LA \cdot Glucose \tag{9}$$

α-Lactalbumin also contains two metal binding sites that are probably liganded with Ca^{2+} under physiological conditions since their dissociation constants are about 3×10^{-7} mole and 3×10^{-5} M.[124] When all substrates are present on the enzyme, the galactose and glucose are linked in a 1,4 β-glycosidic bond and the lactose thus formed is released from the enzyme followed by release of α-lactalbumin then Ca and UDP:

$$Mn \cdot Enzyme \begin{smallmatrix} \diagup UDP\text{-}gal \\ \diagdown Ca \end{smallmatrix} \cdot \alpha\text{-}LA \cdot Glucose \rightarrow$$

$$Mn \cdot Enzyme + Ca + \alpha\text{-}LA + UDP + Lactose \tag{10}$$

The product UDP is a good inhibitor of the reaction; the mechanism by which it is removed from the Golgi system is discussed below.

The hypothesis of Brew[128] that lactose synthesis takes place within the cisternae of the Golgi apparatus was given firm experimental support by the studies of Kuhn and White[111] in which most of the lactose synthesized in a

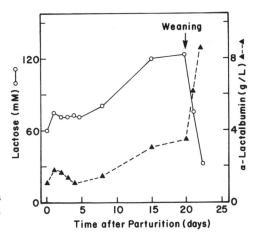

Figure 12. Lactose and α-lactalbumin levels in rat milk during lactation and at weaning. (Redrawn from Nicholas *et al.*[133])

crude "particulate" fraction of rat mammary gland was found to be occluded within membrane vesicles. In later experiments using more purified Golgi membrane fractions, Kuhn and White[129] found that a nucleoside diphosphatase in the vesicles, probably thiamine diphosphatase, hydrolyzes UDP to UMP and P_i. This reaction is thought to perform the dual functions of reducing the concentration of UDP in the Golgi so that it does not inhibit lactose synthesis and converting the impermeant UDP to UMP to which the Golgi membrane is permeable (Fig. 11). The UMP and P_i thus formed return to the cytoplasmic compartment where they are utilized in the resynthesis of UDP-galactose.

Regulation of Lactose Synthesis

Although small quantities of lactose are made within the mammary glands of some species prior to parturition, the onset of copious milk secretion (lactogenesis Stage II, see Chapter 4) is brought about by a rapid increase in lactose synthesis.[131] For this reason and because the regulation of the rate of lactose synthesis must underlie the day-to-day regulation of milk production, the control of lactose synthetase, which performs the rate-limiting step in lactose synthesis, has been a subject of continuing interest. At present, only several possible mechanisms by which lactose synthetase itself may be regulated can be listed. Which of these are of physiological significance, and under what conditions, remains for future investigation.

The lactose and α-lactalbumin contents of milks of various species are generally proportional,[132] suggesting that the concentration of α-lactalbumin in the Golgi may regulate the rate of lactose synthesis. This is supported by the recent observation of Nicholas *et al.*[133] (Fig. 12) that the lactose and α-lactalbumin concentrations of rat milk are correlated throughout the first 20 days of lactation. However, on weaning at 20 days, the concentration of α-lactalbumin increased, while that of lactose dropped precipitously, suggesting that α-lactalbumin is not the only factor controlling lactose synthesis.

Powell and Brew[125] suggested that the calcium concentration in the Golgi vesicles might regulate the rate of lactose synthesis. *In vitro*, galactosyl transferase requires about 4 mM Ca^{2+} for maximum activity. Millimolar concentrations of calcium within the Golgi must be maintained by active transport of calcium from the calcium-poor cytosol presumably by an ATP-dependent calcium transport system.[134] If the activity of the transport system were subject to biological regulation, it could in turn regulate the rate of lactose synthetase through control of the calcium concentration within the Golgi.

The concentration of glucose appears from presently available data to be limiting for lactose synthesis.[135,136] Moreover, in recent experiments in starved goats, the rate of lactose synthesis was directly proportional to the glucose concentration in the milk.[114] Because the milk glucose is thought to be equal to the concentration of glucose in the mammary alveolar cell, this finding suggests that lactose synthesis may be regulated by the intracellular glucose concentration. How the latter is regulated is not yet known.

Conclusion

The biochemical mechanisms of lactose synthesis and their localization within the lumen of the Golgi membranes have been firmly established. Much remains to be learned about the molecular interactions involved in the control of lactose synthetase. Currently, the concentrations of α-lactalbumin, calcium, and glucose within the Golgi system all remain potential candidates for regulation of the rate of lactose synthesis. The possibility that all three interact to determine the rate of lactose synthesis under a given physiological condition should be given serious consideration.

SECRETION OF CALCIUM, PHOSPHATE, AND CITRATE INTO MILK

In the previous sections, we have discussed the secretion of lactose and proteins into milk, both functions mediated by the Golgi secretory vesicle system. There is good evidence that milk calcium, phosphate, and citrate also reach milk via this system.[137,138] How many other substances are secreted via the Golgi system is not known, although it is suspected to be the source of the nucleotides in milk.[139] In this section, we will discuss certain aspects of calcium, phosphate, and citrate secretion followed by a discussion of the possible role of calcium in the regulation of milk secretion. Although magnesium is present in human milk at a concentration of 1.4 mM,[15] nothing is known about the mechanism of its secretion.

Milk has long been known to provide a rich source of dietary calcium and phosphate. However, the mechanisms by which these abundant elements reach milk have received concentrated attention only within the past decade, a time during which the study of calcium metabolism in many types of cells has mushroomed. Both substances exist in two forms in milk, soluble and bound to casein. The latter can be precipitated by ultracentrifugation. Soluble calcium can be further subdivided into free or ionized calcium and calcium complexed with citrate and phosphate ions. In most species, the human being one of few exceptions, the largest proportions of calcium and phosphate are bound to casein. However, human milk has very little casein and only about 40% of the calcium and phosphate in human milk is casein-bound.[15] Human milk also has the lowest total calcium and phosphorus contents of any species whose milk has been analyzed.[140,141] On the other hand, our recent analyses[142] suggest that the ionized calcium in human milk, 3 to 4 mM,[142] is about twice that in bovine milk, (2 mM).[143] Recent longitudinal studies in women[141] show a clear decline in the total calcium and phosphorus content with duration of lactation, a 30 to 40% decrease being reported in women lactating longer than 18 months (see also Jenness[15]). The mechanism and significance of these decrements are unknown.

The Role of the Golgi Secretory Vesicles in Calcium Secretion

The observation that a large proportion of the calcium and phosphate in most milks is bound to the casein micelle suggested that the majority of these substances might be secreted via the exocytotic mechanism responsible for casein secretion. Although it has been inferred that the Golgi membrane is permeable to phosphate (see Fig. 11), no studies of the mechanism of phosphate transport in this system have appeared.

Physiological, morphological, and biochemical evidence support the hypothesis that calcium secretion is mediated by the Golgi system. In physiological experiments in goats, the time course of both calcium and phosphate secretion was shown to be consistent with secretion via exocytosis.[137] The assembly of the casein micelle within the Golgi-derived secretory vesicles was observed with the electron microscope in the early 1970s.[144,145] Because micelle formation requires millimolar concentrations of calcium,[95] it can be inferred that the Golgi system in the mammary gland contains a calcium concentration more than three orders of magnitude higher than that of the cytoplasm, probably less than 1 μM. Biochemical evidence for the existence of an active transport mechanism for calcium which moves calcium up this gradient into Golgi membranes was first obtained by Baumrucker and Keenan[146] in membrane fractions from bovine mammary gland. Subsequent work in other laboratories[134,147] has confirmed the presence of ATP-dependent calcium accumulation in Golgi-derived vesicles from mice and rats. Calcium transport appears to result from the activity of a calcium-activated ATPase which has a K_m for calcium in the micromolar range. Like similar enzymes in both the SR and red cell membranes, the activity depends on the presence of magnesium.[148] The reaction mechanism appears to involve a phosphorylated intermediate with a molecular weight of $\sim$ 100,000.[134]

Possible Regulatory Activities of Calcium in the Mammary Gland

An increase in cytosolic calcium is known to be associated with stimulus-secretion coupling in a wide variety of secretory cells.[149] It is reasonable to postulate that a sustained small increase in cytosolic free calcium accompanies the onset of copious milk secretion at parturition. However, there are no studies of the mammary gland which allow this hypothesis to be evaluated. It is clear that at least two Golgi enzymes, galactosyl transferase and casein kinase, require millimolar concentrations of calcium for activation, raising the possibility that certain aspects of milk synthesis may be regulated by the amount of calcium transported into the Golgi vesicles.

THE SECRETION OF MILK LIPID

The lipids in milk supply essential fatty acids and other fat-soluble factors and make an important contribution to the energy content of milk. The approximately 4% fat content of human milk supplies about 40% of the total calories.[150] Most (98%) of the lipid in milk consists of triglycerides contained in a membrane-bound fat droplet called the *milk fat globule*. Other lipid constituents of milk include cholesterol, phospholipids, vitamin A, vitamin E, vitamin D, and a large number of minor lipids. Most of these are also found in the fat globule. One-half to two-thirds of milk phospholipids are found in the membrane of the milk fat globule; the rest are complexed with proteins present in the skim milk.

Both fatty acids and glycerol for triglyceride synthesis can be obtained from the blood stream or synthesized by the mammary alveolar cell using pathways outlined below. The proportion of fatty acids actually synthesized in the mammary gland is strongly influenced by diet. In women eating a normal western diet in which 40% or more of the calories are taken in as fat, only 20% of the fatty acids of the milk are made in the mammary gland. The remainder are derived from the fatty acids of the diet and their composition reflects that of the dietary fatty acids. With high carbohydrate diets, on the other hand, 40% or more of the milk fatty acids are synthesized in the mammary gland, many of them in the form of the medium chain lauric (C_{12}) and myristic (C_{14}) acids unique to milk. In this section, we will discuss the lipid composition of milk in some detail followed by an outline of the biochemical mechanisms involved in milk synthesis and secretion. For an excellent and comprehensive review of the biochemistry of milk fat synthesis, the reader is referred to Bauman and Davis.[151] More recent findings have been summarized by Dils and co-workers,[152-153] Mayer,[154] Smith,[155] and Hardie.[156]

The Composition of Milk Fat

Milk lipids are a major source of concentrated high energy substrate for the young of most mammals, supplying about 500 kcal/g of milk fat. Because

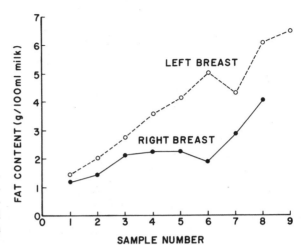

Figure 13. Variation in fat content of human milk during a single feed. Data are successive samples from one woman obtained by breast pump. (Replotted from Hytten.[157])

proteins and carbohydrates must be secreted with sufficient water to render them iso-osmotic with plasma they supply only 30 to 65 kcal/g milk.[55] The proportion of milk fat varies from species to species and an inverse relationship can be seen between the fat and the lactose contents of various milks.[55] In arctic aquatic mammals, a high milk fat content allows transfer of a large amount of energy from mother to pup without the transfer of the quantities of water that would accompany the transfer of these calories in the form of lactose or protein. This is important in a sea water environment where the isotonic body fluids of the mother must be maintained at metabolic expense. On the other hand, it might be argued that the large amount of water necessary for secretion of human milk with its high lactose content represents an adaptation to the high loss of transpired water experienced by infants in the tropical environments where the human species is thought to have originated.

The fat content is the most variable constituent of human milk, changing both within a single feed (Fig. 13) and diurnally.[157] Milk fat is thought to be secreted continuously, but foremilk, obtained early in a feed, has a lower fat content (1 to 2 g/100 ml) than hindmilk, obtained toward the end of the feed (4 g/100 ml). This change in fat content may result from adsorption of fat globules to the walls of the alveoli with displacement only when the gland is nearly empty of milk. The longer term or diurnal variations in milk fat content demonstrated by Hytten[157] may be based on variations in secretion rate. Data exist which suggest that the milk fat content is decreased in poorly nourished mothers, although malnutrition probably has a greater effect on milk volume than composition.[158]

The fatty acid composition of milk lipids varies with both species and diet (Figs. 14 and 15). Given a normal diet in a Western nation, the two most prevalent fatty acids in human milk are palmitic (C_{16}) and oleic (C_{18}) acids.[159,161,162] Elephant and rabbit milks contain a large proportion of

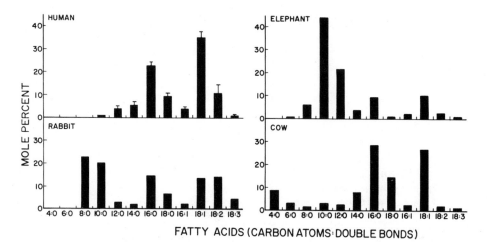

Figure 14. Major fatty acids in the milk fat of several species. Human data is mean ± S.D. from analysis of milk from 60 Australian women, days 40 to 45 of lactation.[159] Data on cow (Holstein) from Breckenridge and Kuksis,[160] data on elephant and rabbit from compilation of Jenness.[55]

medium chain fatty acids (C_8 and C_{10}) and ruminant milk, a significant proportion of short chain fatty acids (C_4 and C_6) to mention only a few examples (Fig. 14). In a series of elegant studies on the goat, Linzell and his colleagues[73] showed that all fatty acids with a carbon chain of 14 atoms or less as well as a portion of the C_{16} fatty acids are synthesized in the mammary gland whereas longer chain fatty acids are derived from the plasma. This appears to be the rule in all species where it has been studied.

Diet affects the fatty acid composition of human milk in three ways (Fig. 15): (1) On high-fat diets, the ratio of saturated to unsaturated fatty acids reflects the ratio of these fatty acids in the diet. For example, a corn oil diet with a high proportion of unsaturated fatty acids leads to an increase in unsaturated fatty acids in the milk compared to a diet high in animal fats.[161,163,164] (2) On low-calorie diets, the fatty acid composition of the milk reflects the composition of the body lipid stores which are mobilized to provide substrate for triglyceride synthesis in the mammary gland.[161] (3) On high carbohydrate, low-fat diets of adequate caloric content, the proportion of medium chain fatty acids in the milk is higher, reflecting increased fatty acid synthesis within the mammary gland and decreased reliance on dietary or body fat as a source of milk triglycerides. The high proportion of medium chain fatty acids in the milk of many malnourished women[165] should be regarded as part of a normal adaptation to a diet low in lipid, rather than a symptom *per se* of an inadequate diet.

It is of some interest that, with the recent increase in the use of corn oil and other sources of polyunsaturated fatty acids in the American diet, the proportion of polyunsaturated fatty acids in milk from women on free choice

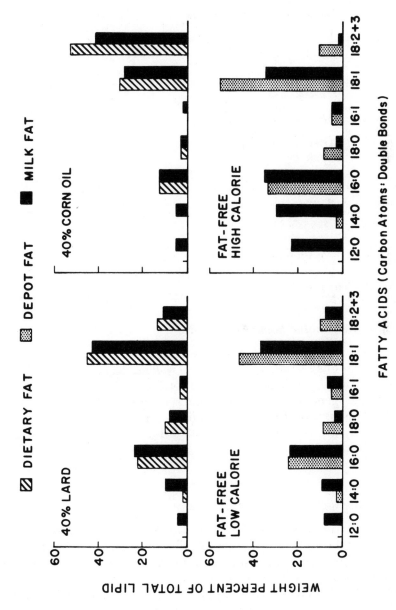

Figure 15. The effect of diet on the lipid composition of human milk. (Data replotted from Insull *et al.*[161])

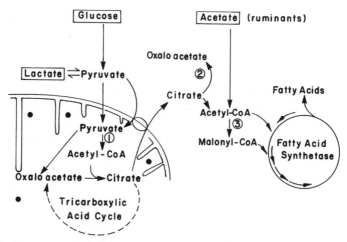

Figure 16. The sources of carbon atoms for fatty acid synthesis. Enzymes: ① Pyruvate dehydrogenase, ② ATP citrate lyase, ③ Acetyl-CoA carboxylase. For details of reactions, see Bauman and Davis.[151]

diets appears to have increased from about 8% in 1959[161] to about 16% in 1977.[164,166] It is not known what, if any, long-range nutritional effects may result from this chronic dietary alteration.

Fatty Acid Synthesis in the Mammary Gland

Fatty acids are synthesized from acetyl-CoA by a series of reactions catalyzed by *acetyl-CoA carboxylase* and *fatty acid synthetase*. The reactions require ATP and reducing equivalents in the form of NADPH. In this section, the pathways which generate acetyl-CoA and NADPH will be summarized followed by a discussion of fatty acid synthesis and the unique thioesterases in the mammary gland which are responsible for the presence of medium chain fatty acids in the milk. Finally, the regulation of fatty acid synthesis will be briefly outlined.

The Sources of Acetyl-CoA for Fatty Acid Synthesis

In most nonruminants, the primary source of carbon atoms for the synthesis of Acetyl-CoA (Fig. 16) is glucose which is transformed to pyruvate by glycolysis or the pentose phosphate pathway. Pyruvate enters the mitochondrion, probably at least partly in exchange for citrate,[167] and is transformed into acetyl-CoA by the complex *pyruvate dehydrogenase.* Because acetyl-CoA itself cannot traverse the mitochondrial membrane, it enters the first step of the tricarboxylic acid cycle forming citrate which enters the cytoplasm to be transformed by the enzyme *ATP citrate lyase* to acetyl-CoA again. Lactate, leucine, and alanine can also be used as sources of carbon atoms.[121,168] In ruminants and certain other species like the rabbit, where portions of the

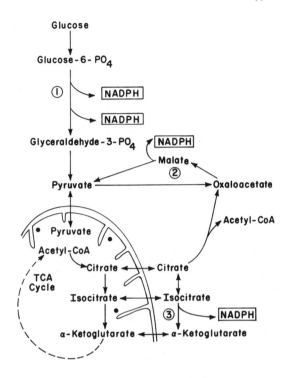

Figure 17. Reactions resulting in the generation of NADPH. ① Pentose phosphate pathway, ② Malate trans-hydrogenase cycle, ③ NADP isocitrate dehydrogenase. For details, see Bauman and Davis.[151]

GI tract are enlarged to allow bacterial fermentation of sugars, acetate is the predominant substrate for fatty acid synthesis, being activated to acetyl-CoA in the cytosol of the mammary epithelial cell.[151]

The Generation of NADPH

Fatty acid synthetase has an absolute requirement for reducing equivalents in the form of NADPH. Three different pathways generate NADPH: the pentose phosphate pathway, the "malate transhydrogenation cycle," and NADP isocitrate dehydrogenase (Fig. 17). In rodent mammary tissue, the first two pathways appear to be most important with the pentose phosphate pathway providing at least half the reducing equivalents necessary for fatty acid synthesis.[168] The NADP$^+$ isocitrate pathway has high activity in species which rely on acetate as a source of carbon atoms for fatty acid synthesis.[151,169]

The time course of citrate entry into milk in goats is similar to the time course of lactose entry, suggesting that this substance is secreted via the Golgi apparatus.[138] A recent demonstration that Golgi membranes are permeable to this anion supports this hypothesis.[130] Studies in goats (cited in Peaker *et al.*[170]) indicate that the citrate concentration in milk is inversely proportional to the rate of mammary synthesis of fatty acids. Since citrate is used to provide reducing equivalents for fatty acid synthesis, the implication of the inverse relationship is that cytosolic citrate levels are higher when NADPH is not being formed and this is reflected in milk citrate levels.

Fatty Acid Synthesis from Acetyl-CoA

Two enzymes, acetyl-CoA carboxylase and fatty acid synthetase, are involved in the conversion of acetyl-CoA to fatty acids via the reactions:

$$Acetyl\text{-}CoA + CO_2 + ATP \xrightarrow{\text{Acetyl-CoA carboxylase}} Malonyl\text{-}CoA + ADP + P_i \quad (11)$$

$$Acetyl\text{-}CoA + 7Malonyl\text{-}CoA + 14NADPH + 14H^+ \xrightarrow{\text{Fatty acid synthetase}} Palmitic\ acid\ (C_{16}) + 7CO_2 + 8CoA + 14NADP^+ + 6H_2O \quad (12)$$

Acetyl-CoA carboxylase catalyzes the formation of malonyl-CoA from acetyl-CoA and, as such, carries out the first committed step in the synthesis of fatty acids. Fatty acid synthetase catalyzes a sequence of seven or more reactions which together add two carbons, derived from malonyl-CoA, to a fatty acid acyl chain. The reaction is initiated by the binding of acetyl-CoA or butyryl-CoA to the enzyme complex,[171] followed by addition of malonyl-CoA. The chain remains covalently attached to the enzyme at the end of each cycle and is available for the successive addition of two more two-carbon units from malonyl CoA. Each cycle requires two molecules of NADPH. The interested reader is referred to recent work by Dodds and co-workers[172] for molecular details of the reaction.

In liver and adipose tissue, when the fatty acid attains a size of 16 carbons or more, synthesis is terminated by a deacylase, *thioesterase I*. This integral part of the fatty acid synthetase complex terminates synthesis by removing the completed molecule from the enzyme. The cytosol of mammary epithelial cells of rats, mice, and rabbits is unique in containing a medium chain acylthioester hydrolase, *thioesterase II*, which terminates fatty acid synthesis after the addition of 8 to 14 carbons.[152,153] Fatty acid synthetases from ruminants as well as rabbits and guinea pigs also synthesize the short chain fatty acids, butyrate (C_4) and hexanoate (C_6).[173]

Regulation of Fatty Acid Synthesis

Because the synthesis of fatty acids is energetically expensive, it is not surprising that it is subject to several types of regulation. Long-term regulation involves modulation of the amount of enzyme present in the cell. Around parturition, for example, the amounts of key enzymes like pyruvate dehydrogenase, ATP-citrate lyase, acetyl-CoA carboxylase and fatty acid synthetase increase several-fold to meet the lipogenic demands of milk formation.[153] Studies of fatty acid synthetase in explant cultures showed that the hormonal combination of prolactin, cortisol, and insulin not only increased the rate of synthesis of the enzyme but also decreased its degradation rate, suggesting multiple control mechanisms involving both protein synthesis and degradation.[154,174] The various enzymes involved in fatty acid synthesis in the mammary gland appear to be regulated independently. For example, the level of thioesterase II increased dramatically during gestation in the rat, but

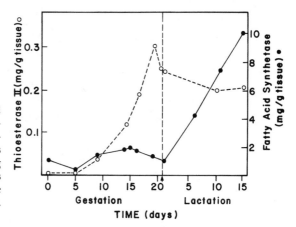

Figure 18. The levels of fatty acid synthetase and thioesterase II during development in the rat mammary gland. Enzyme activity was determined on tissue slices using [^{14}C]-lactate as substrate. Amounts of enzyme present in the tissue correlated with enzyme activity. (Redrawn from Smith.[155])

reached a maximum prior to parturition, whereas levels of fatty acid synthetase began to increase only after parturition (Fig. 18).[175] Elucidation of the difference between the mechanisms regulating the levels of these two enzymes should offer insight into the molecular mechanisms by which hormones regulate protein synthesis during mammary differentiation.

Lipid synthesis in the mammary gland is rapidly decreased by starvation[120,176-178] as well as by changes in the plasma levels of prolactin and insulin. Such short-term regulation likely depends on modulation by both allosteric effectors and phosphorylation–dephosphorylation cycles.[156] Both pyruvate dehydrogenase[177] and acetyl-CoA carboxylase have received considerable attention as possible sites for such regulation. Both have been shown to be inactivated by phosphorylation[156,179] and in the case of pyruvate dehydrogenase, the decreased activity observed after a 24-hr starvation of rats correlated well with the level of phosphorylation of the enzyme.[176] The roles of allosteric regulators and substrate availability in these rapid adaptations have yet to be critically evaluated.

Lipoprotein Lipase and the Extraction of Lipids from Plasma

Plasma triglycerides are the source of as much as 80% of human milk fat. The mechanism by which the fatty acids and glycerol components of these triglycerides are extracted from plasma has received extensive study by Scow and his associates.[180] Lipids are transported through the blood stream primarily in the form of chylomicra (Fig. 19), spherical particles up to 0.5 µm in diameter containing about 92% triglyceride[180] and lesser amounts of cholesterol esters, phospholipids, and cholesterol associated with lipoproteins. After the chylomicra bind to capillary endothelial cells, lipoprotein lipase, an enzyme thought to be localized on the surface of the vascular endothelium, removes the fatty acids from positions 1 and 3 of tri-, di-, and monoglycerides. The free fatty acids either enter the blood stream or diffuse through the subendothelial space into the mammary cell. The diglyceride is further hydrolyzed to 2-monoglyceride and free fatty acid.

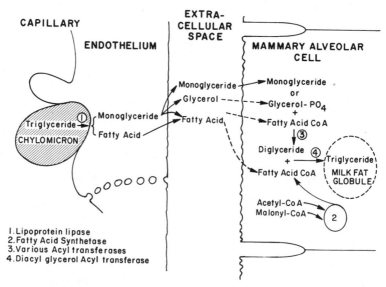

Figure 19. The mechanism of triglyceride transfer from plasma into milk fat.

Both enter the subendothelial space and are taken up by the mammary cell where they are used for the subsequent synthesis of triglycerides.

Lipoprotein lipase is present in large amounts in the mammary glands of lactating rats; its activity decreases rapidly with forced weaning or hypophysectomy.[181] Activity can be restored in hypophysectomized rats with prolactin injections[182] indicating that the enzyme is under hormonal control. There appears to be a reciprocal relation between the lipoprotein lipase activity of the mammary gland and that of adipose tissue in lactating rats[181,183,184] so that adipose tissue loses much of its ability to extract lipids from the plasma during lactation.

Triglyceride Synthesis

The major precursors for triglyceride synthesis are glycerol-3-PO$_4$, monoglycerides, and fatty acyl-CoA.[123] Glycerol-3-PO$_4$ arises either from glycolysis via the reduction of dihydroxyacetone phosphate or from the phosphorylation of glycerol. The first step in triglyceride formation is the acylation of the free hydroxyl groups in glycerol-3-PO$_4$ with two fatty acyl molecules (Fig. 19). The resulting phosphatidic acid is then dephosphorylated to give a diacylglycerol. The diacylglycerol then combines with a third molecule of fatty acyl-CoA to give a triacylglycerol. Monoacylglycerides arising from the partial hydrolysis of triglycerides can be acylated directly without the formation of phosphatidic acid as an intermediate.

Cholesterol Secretion into Milk

Mammary tissue has the capacity for *de novo* synthesis of cholesterol. It is not clear, however, what proportion of milk cholesterol arises from such *de novo* synthesis and what proportion is derived from the plasma. From *in vivo* studies on goats, Long *et al.*[185] concluded that only about 20% of milk cholesterol was synthesized in the gland, the remainder deriving from plasma. On the other hand, experiments in rats[186] suggest that milk cholesterol is largely synthesized in the mammary gland in this species.

Reported values for the cholesterol content of human milk show wide variability from laboratory to laboratory.[187] Further, the literature is contradictory about the dependence of milk cholesterol levels on plasma and dietary cholesterol.[188,189] In rats,[190] both plasma and milk levels of cholesterol were increased on high cholesterol diets. On the other hand, most recent work suggests that the cholesterol content of human milk is relatively constant.[189] A possible exception may be found in the work of Mellies *et al.*[188] who reported a case of a woman with homozygous familial hypercholesterolemia with a 16-fold increase in milk cholesterol. The authors suggest that this represents either an increased extraction of plasma cholesterol or a lack of regulation of mammary cholesterol synthesis. Clearly, reliable values for milk cholesterol under a variety of conditions will be necessary before any conclusions can be drawn about the regulation of milk levels.

The concentration of plant sterols (phytosterols), sterols which are not synthesized in animal tissues, were found by Mellies and co-workers[189] to be correlated with both their dietary intake and plasma level. This observation raises the possibility that mammary cells are able to distinguish between the phytosterols whose milk concentration is highly variable and cholesterol whose secretion appears to be somewhat more constant.

Phospholipids

A major portion of the milk phospholipids are associated with the milk fat globule membrane. These appear to arise from *de novo* synthesis in the mammary gland.[191] The origin of the milk fat globule membrane was discussed in Section 2.

Milk Lipases

Human milk contains substantial amounts of a lipase which is inactive in fresh milk but can be activated by bile salts. Hernell and his co-workers[194] have shown that a *bile-salt-activated lipase*, so far detected only in human and gorilla milks,[193] is responsible for this activity. This lipase, which has a molecular weight of 90,000, may constitute as much as 1% of the protein of human milk. Both its molecular weight and its inhibition by di-isopropyl fluorophosphate identify this enzyme as a lipase distinct from pancreatic lipase and lipoprotein lipase.

Bile-salt-activated lipase is postulated to play an important role in the digestion of lipids in the neonate since its activity is sufficiently high in the presence of bile salts to completely hydrolyze milk fat to free fatty acids and glycerol within 30 min.[194] Activation is thought to occur in the duodenum on interaction with bile salts that also render the enzyme resistant to intestinal proteases. The enzyme is inactivated by pasteurization.

Lipoprotein lipase is also present in human milk at highly variable concentrations.[194,195] It can be distinguished from bile-salt-activated lipase because it is stimulated by serum and inhibited by NaCl and protamine. Nonbile-salt-stimulated lipase was recently found to be present at high concentrations in milk from five women whose infants had breast milk jaundice.[196] The authors postulated that the fatty acids freed by this enzyme in the stomach of the neonate inhibited bilirubin metabolism in the infant's intestine. Insufficient biochemical data is currently available to determine whether this activity represents lipoprotein lipase or some other molecule.

Conclusions

The biochemical pathways involved in lipid synthesis are now well worked out and have been summarized in this section. Both the short- and long-term regulation of milk lipid synthesis are exciting considerable current interest, the former because phosphorylation–dephosphorylation cycles appear to be involved; the latter because the regulation of protein synthesis is a topic of wide interest. Because milk fat content and composition are affected by diet, the elucidation of the regulatory mechanisms involved may have considerable practical value in developing optimal diets for lactating women. Another important aspect of lipid secretion and digestion is the role and regulation of lipases, both in delivery of fatty acids to the mammary cell and in lipid digestion by the infant.

THE SECRETION OF MONOVALENT IONS AND WATER INTO MILK

Since milk is isoosmotic with plasma, the net transfer of water from plasma to the alveolar lumina is directly proportional to the transfer of solute. We have already discussed the secretion of lactose which makes up two-thirds of the osmolarity of human milk and thus accounts for a large proportion of the water transferred into the mammary secretion. Another one-sixth of the osmolarity is contributed by the monovalent ions whose secretion will be discussed in this section and the remainder by proteins and other osmotically active substances such as citrate, magnesium, glucose, and so forth.

Transcellular Ion Transport

Experiments, largely carried out on goats, have shown that disaccharides such as sucrose and lactose[197] as well as the divalent ions calcium and phosphate[137] do not move freely between the plasma and milk spaces. These observations provide strong evidence that, during full lactation, milk formation is a transcellular process. As such it is likely that the secretion of

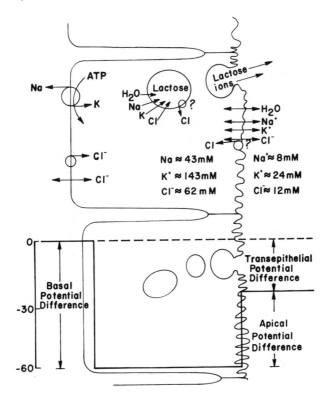

Figure 20. Ion transport and potentials in the mammary alveolar cell. The upper portion shows ion concentrations in the milk and mammary cell as measured in the guinea pig by Linzell and Peaker[198] along with the model for monovalent ion secretion into milk postulated by Peaker.[1,201] The lower portion of the diagram shows that the transepithelial potential, which has been measured to be -16 to -32 mV in the goat, is equal to the difference between the apical and basolateral membrane potentials.

monovalent ions into milk is mediated by the epithelial cells. Careful measurements of the sodium, potassium, and chloride concentrations in the mammary tissues of guinea pigs[198] and other species[4] show that, like most cells, mammary cells have a high intracellular potassium content and lower sodium and chloride (Fig. 20). Although the sodium content of mammary cells appears to be higher than that of most cells,[199] the monovalent cation concentrations appear to be maintained by a Na/K ATPase probably localized in the basolateral membrane of the mammary alveolar cell.[200]

Because ion concentrations in the alveolar cells are quite different from milk (Fig. 20), the secretion of ions into milk is most likely controlled by processes taking place at the Golgi, vesicular, and apical membranes of the alveolar cells. The anatomical structure of the mammary gland makes direct measurement of the transport properties of the apical membrane extremely difficult and studies on monovalent ion transport in Golgi and vesicular membranes are limited.[4a] Our understanding of these processes rests, therefore, largely on inferences drawn from indirect measurements. For example, it can be inferred that the apical membrane is permeable to monovalent ions because isotopic species of these ions, infused up the teat in goats, tend to disappear from the milk space.[197] That these ions can move passively across this membrane has been further inferred from the observation that when isotonic sugar solutions are infused up the teat, again in the goat, ions are drawn down their concentration gradients into the milk space. Because these ion movements appear to be faster than ion secretion during milk formation, it is likely that ions equilibrate across the apical membrane. Finally, an electrical potential of -15 to -40 mV, milk space negative, has been measured between the milk space and the blood in goats[201] and mice (Berga and Neville, unpublished data) indicating that the electrical potentials across the apical and basolateral membranes of the mammary alveolar cell are different as illustrated in the lower portion of Fig. 20. The inference to be drawn is that the ion permeabilities and/or electrogenic pump processes are different in the two membranes.

Peaker[4] has presented a model which suggests that ionic concentrations in milk are achieved as follows: As lactose is synthesized and secreted, water is drawn into the Golgi vesicles and alveolar lumina to maintain isotonicity. Sodium, potassium, and chloride tend to follow down their concentration gradients. However, ionic movement is limited. In the case of cations, the apical electric potential opposes flux into the milk space so that equilibrium is attained with the sodium and potassium concentrations in milk lower than in the cell. A chloride pump in the apical membrane moves chloride from the alveolus back to the cell, maintaining the milk chloride concentration at a low level. This model predicts that the ratio of sodium to potassium in milk is equal to their ratio in the cytoplasm of the mammary alveolar cell, a prediction which appears to be borne out in many species.[1,4]

Further testing of this hypothesis will require the development of model systems in which the apical membrane can be subjected to more direct experimental examination. One such system which shows considerable promise is the culture of mammary cell monolayers on floating collagen gels.[202] Bisbee[203] has been able to make electrical measurements on such systems mounted in a classical Ussing chamber and has obtained potentials between -10 and -25 mV, apical side negative, which responded to prolactin. However, because these cultures did not secrete lactose, it is difficult to relate Bisbee's measurements to the physiological mechanisms of ion secretion into milk. Wicha and his colleagues[203a] have recently developed a culture system for mammary tissue in which a high degree of mammary function, including lactose synthesis, is maintained by culturing mammary alveoli on an extracellular matrix actually derived from the mammary gland itself. This achievement may represent a major breakthrough in our ability to study transepithelial transport in a functioning *in vitro* model system of the mammary epithelium.

Paracellular Ion Transport

As we discussed in the introduction to this chapter, the ionic composition of human colostrum is quite different from that of mature milk, colostrum containing 50 to 60 mM each of sodium and chloride whereas mature milk contains only about 6 mM sodium and 12 mM chloride (Fig. 2). The concentrations of these two ions are inversely related to the lactose concentration (Fig. 2), an observation which has been well documented in the goat and guinea pig.[1,4] Several lines of evidence suggest that transport via paracellular pathways is responsible for the high sodium and chloride contents of colostrum: (1) In goats, the transfer of disaccharides between milk and blood can be measured during pregnancy but not during lactation.[197] (2) No electrical potential difference can be measured between the blood and the milk space during pregnancy in the goat.[201] (3) In the early postpartum period, there is a positive correlation between the rates of potassium and lactose entry into the mammary secretion (see Fig. 3). Peaker[1,4] has shown that such a positive correlation is expected when the junctional complexes are open. Later in lactation, when the junctions are closed, a negative correlation between the concentrations of potassium and lactose is found. (4) During early lactation, high concentrations of the milk-specific protein, α-lactalbumin, were observed in the plasma of women, suggesting that the protein passed from the milk spaces to the blood via the paracellular pathway[204] (Fig. 7, Chapter 5). The plasma concentration of α-lactalbumin fell between days 3 and 10 as the milk composition assumed the characteristics of true milk; this observation is consistent with closure of the junctions at this time. (5) Freeze-fracture studies of the junctional complexes between mouse mammary alveolar cells are consistent with leaky tight junctions during pregnancy and tight junctions during lactation.[205] Thus, the presence of "leaky" tight junctions during pregnancy and the first few days of the puerperium can be regarded as well established.

The mechanisms by which the permeability of the paracellular pathway is controlled are only beginning to be explored. It has been observed in sheep and goats that prepartum milking brings about a change in the composition of the mammary secretion toward that of true milk.[197] Because the hormonal milieu of the mammary gland was unchanged by this process, this observation suggests that some factor in the mammary secretion sequestered within the alveolar lumina maintains leaky tight junctions during pregnancy. This factor may accumulate during mammary infections and when milk is no longer removed from the breast, bringing about a return to a more colostrum-like secretion. The nature of the factor is unknown. It may be physical in nature, for example, flattening of the epithelial cells by sequestered secretion products,[206] or it may be a chemical. Maule Walker[207] found that infusion of a stable prostaglandin into the udder of a parturient goat prevented closure of the junctional complexes and suggested that the function of the rather large amounts of $PGF_{2\alpha}$ secreted in the mammary gland may be to regulate the junctional complexes. Neville and Peaker[208] found that infusion of calcium chelators into the udder of a lactating goat brought about a rapid increase in the permeability of the paracellular pathway, raising the possibility of a regulatory role for calcium as well. Although *in vivo* studies can offer some insight, it is clear that studies in *in vitro* model systems will be necessary for elucidation of the mechanisms involved in the regulation of the permeability of the junctional complexes.

Conclusions

The mechanisms that maintain the ionic composition of mammary secretions present a number of interesting challenges to the investigator. However, the experimental materials available until very recently did not lend themselves to the types of experiment required because none allowed direct investigation of the properties of the apical membrane. If a milk-secreting mammary culture on a substratum such as a collagen gel were available, classical Ussing-type techniques could possibly provide increased insight. On the other hand, more sophisticated microelectrode techniques applied *in vivo* to the glands of species whose mammary glands contain small amounts of connective tissue, such as the mouse, may also allow more definitive studies. It is clear that more advanced techniques will be required for further progress in this area.

TRACE ELEMENT SECRETION INTO MILK

The trace element content of milk is well balanced compared to many foods, making milk a high quality source of these nutrients. Although the mineral content of milk has been repeatedly measured, little attention has been paid to the cellular mechanisms of secretion. Most research interest has been addressed to those elements for which deficiencies have been observed in breast-fed infants or infants fed only milk formulas for extended periods, e.g., iron, copper, and zinc. Iodine has also been studied because the iodine content of milk can become excessive on high dietary intakes. Recent interest in the transfer of selenium to milk in dairy animals has resulted from approval in 1977 of selenium as a feed additive.

Iron

The iron content of human milk is low relative to nutritional require-ments and neonates are thought to draw on the extensive reserves generally present at birth.[66] The iron that is present in human milk is tightly bound to the protein lactoferrin. Binding by other proteins such as casein and transferrin may be quantitatively more important in some species. The high affinity for iron ($K_a = 10^{36}$) and relative unsaturation of lactoferrin means that negligibly low concentrations of free iron can be present in milk.

Although lactoferrin appears to be synthesized in the mammary alveolar cell,[209] the mechanism of iron transfer from serum proteins to milk proteins has not been investigated.

Zinc

Zinc is the most abundant trace element in milk, making it an excellent dietary source of the element. Moreover, the zinc content of human colostrum is eight times higher than that of mature milk.[210] The possibility of zinc deficiency in preterm infants was raised by Dauncey *et al.*[211] who found that such infants fed on pooled human breast milk were in negative balance until the sixtieth day of life.

The study of the milk zinc content was stimulated by the rare genetic disease acrodermatitis enteropathica (AE) in which a deficiency results from the inability of infants to absorb zinc from cows' milk. The symptoms can be alleviated by supplementing the diet with zinc sulfate[212] or human milk. A low molecular weight zinc-binding ligand in human milk appears to increase zinc bioavailability by mimmicking a factor normally secreted in the gut, but is absent in very young infants and patients with AE.[213] The nature of this ligand has been the subject of considerable controversy.[214,215] Cousins and Smith[216] proposed that milk zinc is preferentially bound to high molecular weight proteins that are saturated at the zinc levels present in milk. Excess zinc then binds with lower affinity to various low molecular weight substances. Since the total zinc content of human milk is quite similar to that of bovine milk, the difference in zinc bioavailability may be the result of zinc binding to bovine casein where it may be less available for absorption.

An acrodermatitislike syndrome has been reported for two breast-fed infants whose mothers secreted low-zinc milk.[217] In these mothers, milk zinc did not increase in response to increased dietary zinc, as has been seen in animal studies,[218] although a higher zinc intake did result in increased serum zinc. The impaired zinc transport in the mammary glands of these individuals suggests that a specific zinc transport system exists in the mammary gland. Active transport of zinc from blood to milk is also suggested by comparison of ultrafilterable zinc in the two fluids. Although the serum[219] and milk[210] zinc levels in humans are similar at about 4 months lactation (84 ± 13 and 80 ± 10 µg/dl, respectively), only 2% of plasma zinc is ultrafilterable whereas more than 12% of milk zinc is in this form. However, the mechanism of transport across the mammary epithelium has not been studied.

Iodine

Studies on iodine secretion into milk have stemmed from concerns about concentration of radioactive iodine in milk produced by animals grazing pastures contaminated by radioactive fallout, as well as about excess iodine in milk of animals undergoing treatment for various diseases. Active accumulation of iodide in milk is evident from concentration data. The milk to plasma concentration ratio ranges from 1.8 in cows to 39 in sheep.[220] In man and laboratory animals, the concentration of milk iodine is 20 to 30 times higher than plasma.[221] In plasma, 58% of the iodine is protein bound,[222] whereas only 13% of the iodine in cows milk is protein bound.[223]

The transport of iodine into milk is inhibited by anions which inhibit the iodide pump in the thyroid, such as perchlorate, fluoroborate, and thiourea.[224] Iodide accumulation in milk is not dependent on the continuation of milk secretion,[223] as shown by an experiment in which one-half of a cow's udder was not milked for 24 hrs, stopping milk secretion. Eight hours following an intravenous dose of ^{131}I, total and exchangeable ^{131}I accumulation in milk from the unmilked side was greater than the total in the milk from the normally secreting side. These observations suggest that an iodide pump on the basolateral membrane like that present in the thyroid moves the ion against a concentration gradient into the cell. Iodide would then enter milk by direct transfer across the apical membrane.

In vitro work indicates that iodine binds to tyrosine in milk protein during storage in the udder due to enzymatic oxidation of iodide.[225] Thiouracil-type drugs, which block iodination of tyrosine, do not prevent establishment or maintenance of high milk to plasma iodine ratios,[226] providing evidence that iodination of tyrosine is not important in iodine secretion into milk.

Selenium

The selenium which normally occurs in milk is primarily bound to casein or other proteins, however, its chemical form is, as yet, unknown.[227] Selenium may be added to milk proteins during their synthesis and processing or it may be transported across the mammary alveolar cells with subsequent addition to preformed proteins. Milk proteins will bind a reduced form of selenium (hydrogen selenide) which is presumably similar to the oxidation state of plasma selenium.[228] Selenite anion, a more oxidized selenium compound, does not bind to milk under physiological conditions of temperature and pH.[229] The time course of secretion following an IV dose of labeled selenite is consistent with the hypothesis that the liver rapidly clears selenite from the blood, reduces it, and resecretes it in a form that is taken up by the mammary gland and bound to milk protein in the Golgi and secretory vesicles.[227]

Much of the selenium in plant materials is in the form of the sulfur amino acid analogs, selenocysteine, and selenomethionine. Although the mammary gland is likely to handle these compounds in a manner similar to cysteine and methionine, the low content and uneven distribution of these compounds in milk proteins makes it unlikely that selenoamino acids are the major selenium compounds in milk.

Sulfur

Sulfur may be transported primarily in the amino acid form, although there are other sulfur compounds of importance in milk. Dimethyl sulfide, a catabolite of sulfur amino acids in some organisms, is readily transferred into milk, and is responsible for occasional "off" flavors in bovine milk.[230]

Cobalt

The only known physiological function of cobalt in mammals is as the catalytic center of the vitamin B_{12} coenzyme. Vitamin B_{12} transport into milk appears to be controlled by a specific binding protein which accumulates in the mammary gland prior to lactogenesis, is at high concentration in colostrum and declines and plateaus during later lactation.[49,50] This pattern is parallel to the actual concentration of vitamin B_{12} in milk.

Conclusion

A decline in concentration during the course of lactation (or between colostrum and true milk) has been shown for zinc, copper,[211] manganese,[231] and other trace elements,[232] suggesting that specific or nonspecific protein binding may be important in the mechanism of transport of many of the trace elements into milk. Even those minerals which are partly found in association with milk fat (iron, copper, molybdenum) are likely to be components of proteins in the milk fat globule membrane. Minerals in the aqueous phase of milk are in equilibrium with protein-bound forms and other smaller ligands. Thus, with the possible exception of zinc and iodine, the primary mechanism of transport of trace minerals into milk is likely to be by binding to specific or nonspecific carrier proteins. The mechanisms of transport across the various mammary cell membranes, and the locations at which mineral–protein binding occurs are generally unknown. Considering the importance of minerals in the nutritional quality of milk, more work on this problem is clearly warranted.

MILK SECRETION—QUESTIONS FOR THE FUTURE

The biochemical events responsible for the synthesis and secretion of many of the major components of milk have been firmly established during the last decade. Thus, the enzymes and biochemical pathways by which milk proteins, lipids, and lactose are synthesized are now well understood and have been outlined in this chapter. The current areas of excitement are the genetic control of milk synthesis, the elucidation of the molecular mechanisms through which hormones and other regulatory agents exert their control and the mechanisms by which many of the synthetic products are transferred from one intracellular membrane system to another. Techniques are available to solve most of these problems so that substantial progress can be expected in the next decade.

For the mineral constituents of milk, the situation is much less clear. Without an experimental system that allows direct access to the apical membrane of the mammary alveolar cell, it has been difficult to approach the mechanisms of monovalent ion secretion. Somewhat more is known about calcium and phosphate, but again the approach has largely been indirect. On the other hand, virtually nothing is known about the mechanisms of magnesium and bicarbonate secretion. Advances in this area probably depend on the development of new model systems, a prospect which is now on the immediate horizon.

Finally, when one considers the minor constituents of milk, trace elements, vitamins, hormones, and cofactors, it becomes apparent that even reliable compositional data is often unavailable, although these substances are of great nutritional significance. The first order of business in this area must be good longitudinal studies of the concentrations of minor components throughout the course of human lactation. Once such studies are well underway, it will become important to determine the mechanisms by which these substances are secreted into milk. The practical consequences of such knowledge are great: It will become possible to detect and possibly remedy specific deficiences of minor milk components. Moreover, identification of the pathways through which drugs and environmental pollutants enter milk should become feasible, enabling a rational approach to drug therapy in women who breast-feed. Much more extensive research is necessary if we are to assure that every breast-fed infant receives milk of the highest possible nutritional value.

REFERENCES

1. Peaker, M., 1977, The aqueous phase of milk: Ion and water transport, in: *Comparative Aspects of Lactation* (M. Peaker, ed.), Academic Press, New York, pp. 113–134.
2. Smith, G. H. and Vonderhaar, B. K., 1981, Functional differentiation in mouse mammary gland is attained through DNA synthesis, inconsequent of mitosis, *Dev. Biol.* **88:**167–179.
3. Kurosumi, K., Kobayashi, Y., and Baba, N., 1968, The fine structure of mammary glands of lactating rats, with special reference to the apocrine secretion, *Exp. Cell. Res.* **50:**177–192.
4. Peaker, M., 1978, Ion and water transport in the mammary gland, in: *Lactation: A Comprehensive Treatise* (M. Peaker, ed.), Academic Press, New York, pp. 437–462.
4a. White, M. D., Ward, S., and Kuhn, N. J., 1981, Composition, stability and electrolyte permeability of Golgi membranes from lactating rat mammary gland, *Biochem. J.* **200:**663–669.
5. Linzell, J. L. and Peaker, M., 1975, The distribution and movement of carbon dioxide carbonic acid and bicarbonate between blood and milk in the goat, *J. Physiol. London* **244:**771–782.
6. Mostov, K. E., Kraehenbuhl, J.-P., and Blobel, G., 1980, Receptor-mediated trans-cellular transport of immunoglobulin: Synthesis of secretory component as multiple and larger transmembrane forms, *Proc. Natl. Acad. Sci. U.S.A.* **77:**7257–7261.
7. Rothman, J. E., 1981, The golgi apparatus: Two organelles in tandem, *Science* **213:**1212–1219.
8. Morre, D. J., Kartenbeck, J., and Franke, W. W., 1979, Membrane flow and interconversions among endomembranes, *Biochem. Biophys. Acta* **559:**71.
9. Franke, W. W., Luder, M. R., Kartenbeck, J., Zerban, H., and Keenan, T. W., 1976, Involvement of vesicle coat material in casein secretion and surface regeneration, *J. Cell Biol.* **69:**173–195.

10. Martel, M. B. and Got, R., 1972, Présence d'enzymes marquers des membranes plasmiques de l'appareil du Golgi et du reticulum endoplasmique dans les membranes des globules lipidiques du lait maternel, *FEBS Lett.* **21**:220–222.
11. Briley, M. S. and Eisenthal, R., 1975, Association of xanthine oxidase with the bovine milk-fat-globule membrane, *Biochem. J.* **147**:417–423.
12. Powell, J. T., Jarlfors, U., and Brew, K., 1977, Enzymatic characteristics of fat globule membranes from bovine colostrum and bovine milk, *J. Cell. Biol.* **72**:617–627.
13. Peixoto de Menezes, A. and Pinto da Silva, P., 1978, Freeze-fracture observations of the lactating rat mammary gland, *J. Cell. Biol.* **76**:767–778.
14. Zerban, H. and Franke, W. W., 1978, Milk fat globule membranes devoid of intramembranous particles, *Cell. Biol. Int.,* **2**:87–98.
15. Jenness, R., 1979, The composition of human milk, *Semin. Perinatol.* **3**:225–239.
16. McClelland, D. B. L., McGrath, J., and Samson, R. R., 1978, Antimicrobial factors in human milk. Studies of concentration and transfer to the infant during the early stages of lactation, *Acta Peadiatr. Scand.* **271**(suppl.):1–20.
17. Lönnerdal, B., Forsum, E., and Hambraeus, L., 1976, A longitudinal study of the protein, nitrogen, and lactose contents of human milk from Swedish well-nourished mothers, *Am. J. Clin. Nutr.* **29**:1127–1133.
18. Gross, S. J., David, R. J., Bauman, L., and Tomarelli, R. M., 1980, Nutritional composition of milk produced by mothers delivering preterm, *J. Pediatr.* **96**:641–644.
19. Miyamoto, S., Anan, K., Taki, T., Matsumura, Y., Arai, K., Fujii, K., Hashiguchi, A., and Nagata, I., 1957, On the fluctations of sodium and potassium concentrations in human milk, *Bull. Tokyo Med. Dent. Univ.* **4**:173–177.
20. Kulski, J. K., Hartmann, P. E., Martin, J. D., and Smith, M., 1978, Effects of bromocriptine mesylate on the composition of the mammary secretion in non-breast-feeding women, *Obstet. Gynecol.* **52**:38–42.
21. Kulski, J. K. and Hartmann, P. E., 1981, Changes in human milk composition during the initiation of lactation *Aust. J. Exp. Biol. Med. Sci.* **59**:101–114.
22. Healy, D. L., Rattigan, S., Hartmann, P. E., Herington, A. C., and Burger, H. G., 1980, Prolactin in human milk: Correlation with lactose, total protein and α-lactalbumin levels, *Am. J. Physiol.* **238**:E83–E87.
23. Ramadan, M. A., Salah, M. M., and Eid, S. Z., 1972, Effect of breast infection on the composition of human milk, *Int. J. Biochem.* **3**:543–548.
24. Conner, A. E., 1979, Elevated levels of sodium and chloride in milk from mastitic breast, *Pediatrics* **63**:910–911.
25. Hartmann, P. E. and Kulski, J. K., 1978, Changes in the composition of the mammary secretion of women after abrupt termination of breast feeding, *J. Physiol.* **275**:1–11.
26. Gross, S. J., Buckley, R. H., Wakil, S. S., McAllister, D. C., David, R. J., and Faix, R. G., 1980, Elevated IgA concentration in milk produced by mothers delivered of preterm infants, *J. Pediatr.* **99**:389–393.
27. Schanler, R. J. and Oh, W., 1980, Composition of breast milk obtained from mothers of premature infants as compared to breast milk obtained from donors, *J. Pediatr.* **96**:679–681.
28. Ho, F. C. S., Wong, R. L. C., and Lawton, J. W. M., 1979, Human colostral and breast milk cells, a light and electron microscopic study, *Acta Paediatr. Scand.* **68**:389–396.
29. Brooker, E., 1980, The epithelial cells and cell fragments in human milk, *Cell Tissue Res.* **210**:321–332.
30. Helminen, H. J. and Ericson, J. L. E., 1968, Studies on mammary gland involution *J. Ultrastruct. Res.* **25**:202–239.
31. Seelig, L. L., Jr. and Beer, A. E., 1978, Transepithelial migration of leukocytes in the mammary gland of lactating rats, *Biol. Reprod.* **17**:736–744.
32. Seelig, L. L., Jr. and Beer, A. E., 1981, Intraepithelial leukocytes in the human mammary gland, *Biol. Reprod.* **22**:1157–1163.
33. Ardran, G. M., Kemp, F. H., and Lind, J., 1958, A cineradiographic study of breast feeding, *Br. J. Radiol.* **31**:156–162.

34. Ardran, G. M., Kemp, F. H., and Lind, J., 1958, A cineradiographic study of bottle feeding, *Br. J. Radiol.* **31**:11–22.
35. Newton, M. and Newton, N. R., 1948, The let-down reflex in human lactation, *J. Pediatr.* **33**:698–704.
36. Linzell, J. L., 1974, Mammary blood flow and methods of identifying and measuring precusors of milk, in: *Lactation: A Comprehensive Treatise*, Volume I (B. L. Larson and V. R. Smith, ed.), Academic Press, New York, pp. 143–225.
37. Ota, K. and Peaker, M., 1979, Lactation in the rabbit: Mammary blood flow and cardiac output, *Quart. J. Exp. Physiol.* **64**:225–238.
38. Burd, L. I., Lemons, J. A., Makowski, E. L., Meschia, G., and Niswender, G., 1976, Mammary blood flow and endocrine changes during parturition in the ewe, *Endocrinology* **98**:748–754.
39. Burd, L. I., Ascherman, G., Dowers, S., Scommegna, A., and Auletta, F. J., 1978, The effect of 2-Br-α-ergocryptine on mammary blood flow and endocrine changes at the time of parturition in the ewe, *Endocrinology* **102**:1223–1229.
40. Hanwell, A. and Linzell, J. L., 1973, The effects of engorgement with milk and of suckling on mammary blood flow in the rat, *J. Physiol.* **233**:111–125.
41. Hanwell, A. and Linzell, J. L., 1973, The time cause of cardiovascular changes in lactation in the rat, *J. Physiol.* **233**:93–110.
42. Martin, C., 1980, Physiologic changes during pregnancy: The mother, in: *Fetal and Maternal Medicine* (E. J. Quilligan, ed.), Wiley, New York, pp. 141–179.
43. Pickles, V. R., 1953, Blood-flow estimations as indices of mammary activity, *J. Obs/Gyn Br. Emp.* **60**:301–316.
44. Annison, E. F., Linzell, J. L., and West, C. E., 1968, Mammary and whole animal metabolism of glucose and fatty acid in fasting lactating goats, *J. Physiol.* **197**:445–459.
45. Linzell, J. L., 1960, Mammary-gland blood flow and oxygen, glucose and volatile fatty acid uptake in the concious goat, *J. Physiol.* **153**:492–509.
46. Anderson, N. G., Powers, M. T., and Tollaksen, S. L., 1982, Proteins of human milk. I. Identification of major components, *Clin. Chem. N.Y.* **28**:1045–1055.
47. Bezkorovainy, A., 1977, Human milk and colostrum proteins: A review, *J. Dairy Sci.* **60**:1023–1037.
48. Payne, D. W., Peng, L-H, Pearlman, W. H., and Talbert, L. M., 1976, Corticosteroid-binding proteins in human colostrum and milk and rat milk, *J. Biol. Chem.* **251**:5272–5279.
49. Sandberg, D. P., Begley, J. A., and Hall, C. A., 1981, The content, binding, and forms of vitamin B_{12} in milk, *Am. J. Clin. Nutr.* **34**:1717–1724.
50. Samson, R. R., Mirtle, C., and McClelland, D. B. L., 1980, The effect of digestive enzymes on the binding and bacteriostatic properties of lactoferrin and vitamin B_{12} binder in human milk, *Acta Paediatr. Scand.* **59**:517–523.
51. Waxman, S. and Schreiber, C., 1975, The purification and characterization of the low molecular weight human folate binding protein using affinity chromatography, *Biochemistry* **14**:5422–5428.
52. Carpenter, G., 1980, Epidermal growth factor is a major growth promoting agent in human milk, *Science* **210**:198–199.
53. Mather, I. H., Tamplin, C. B., and Irving, M. G., 1980, Separation of the proteins of bovine milk-fat-globule membrane by electrofocusing with retention of enzymatic and immunological activity, *Eur. J. Biochem.* **110**:327–336.
54. Mather, I. H. and Keenan, T. W., 1975, Studies on the structure of milk fat globule membrane, *J. Membr. Biol.* **21**:65–85.
55. Jenness, R., 1974, The composition of milk, in: *Lactation: A Comprehensive Treatise*, Volume III, (B. L. Larson and V. R. Smith, eds.), Academic Press, New York, pp. 3–107.
56. Brew, K. and Hill, R. L., 1975, Lactose Biosynthesis, *Rev. Physiol. Biochem. Pharmacol.* **72**:103–158.
57. Farrell, H. M., Jr., 1976, Models for casein micelle formation, *J. Dairy Sci.* **56**:1195–1206.
58. Mercier, J.-C., Chobert, J.-M., and Addeo, F., 1976, Comparative study of the amino acid sequences of the caseinomacropeptides from seven species, *FEBS Lett.* **72**:208–214.

59. Jenness, R., 1979, Comparative aspects of milk proteins, *J. Dairy Res.* **46:**197–210.
60. Sorensen, M. and Sorensen, S. P. L., 1939, The proteins in whey, *C. R. Trav. Lab. Carlsberg* **23:**55–99.
61. Ainscough, E. W., Brodie, A. M., Plowman, J. E., Bloor, S. J., Loehr, J. S., and Loehr, T. M., 1980, Studies on human lactoferrin by electron paramagnetic resonance, fluorescence, and resonance raman spectroscopy, *Biochemistry* **19:**4072–4079.
62. Ainscough, E. W., Brodie, A. M., and Plowman, J. E., 1980, Zinc transport by lactoferrin in human milk, *Am. J. Clin. Nutr.* **33:**1314–1315.
63. Masson, P. L., Heremans, J. F., and Dive, C., 1966, An iron-binding protein common to many external secretions, *Clin. Chim. Acta* **14:**735.
64. Weinberg, E. D., 1978, Iron and Infection, *Microbiol. Rev.* **42:**45–66.
65. Arnold, R. R., Brewer, M., and Gauthier, J. J., 1980, Bacteriocidal activity of human lactoferrin: Sensitivity of a variety of microorganisms, *Infect. Immun.* **28:**893–898.
66. Brock, J. H., 1980, Lactoferrin in human milk: Its role in iron absorption and protection against enteric infection in the newborn infant, *Arch. Dis. Child.* **55:**417–421.
67. Phillippy, B. O. and McCarthy, R. D., 1979, Multi-origins of milk serum albumin in the lactating goat, *Biochim. Biophys. Acta* **584:**298–303.
68. Imam, A., Laurence, D. J. R., and Neville, A. M., 1981, Isolation and characterization of a major glycoprotein from milk-fat-globule membrane of human breast milk, *Biochem. J.* **193:**47–54.
69. Franke, W. W., Heid, H. W., Grund, C., Winter, S., Freudenstein, C., Schmid, E., Jarasch, E.-D., and Keenan, T. W., 1981, Antibodies to the major insoluble milk fat globule membrane-associated protein: Specific location in apical regions of lactating epithelial cells, *J. Cell. Biol.* **89:**485–494.
70. Rassin, D. K., Sturman, J. A., and Gaull, G. E., 1978, Taurine and other free amino acids in milk of man and other mammals, *Early Human Dev.* **2:**1–13.
71. Chavalittamrong, B., Suanpan, S., Boonvisut, S., Chatranon, W., and Gershoff, S. N., 1981, Protein and amino acids of breast milk from Thai mothers, *Am. J. Clin. Nutr.* **34:**1126–1130.
72. Mepham, T. B., 1977, Synthesis and secretion of milk proteins, *Symp. Zool. Soc. London* **41:**57–75.
73. Linzell, J. L., 1967, The magnitude and mechanisms of the uptake of milk precursors by the mammary gland, *Nutr. Soc. Symp. Proc.* **27:**44–52.
74. Stegink, L. D., Filer, L. J., and Baker, G. L., 1972, Monosodium glutamate: Effect on plasma and breast milk amino acid levels in lactating women, *Proc. Soc. Exp. Biol. Med.* **140:**836–841.
75. Stegink, L. D., Filer, L. J., Jr., and Baker, G. L., 1979, Plasma erythrocyte and human milk levels of free amino acids in lactating women administered aspartame or lactose, *J. Nutr.* **109:**2173–2181.
76. Lingappa, V. R., Lingappa, J. R., Prasad, R., Ebner, K. E., and Blobel, G., 1978, Coupled cell-free synthesis, segregation and core glycosylation of a secretory protein, *Proc. Natl. Acad. Sci. U.S.A.* **75:**2338–2342.
77. Craig, R. K., Brown, P. A., Harrison, O. S., McIlreavy, D., and Campbell, P. N., 1976, Guinea-pig milk-protein synthesis: Isolation and characterization of messenger ribonucleic acids from lactating mammary gland and identification of caseins and pre-α-lactalbumin as translation products in heterologous cell-free systems, *Biochem. J.* **160:**57–74.
78. Rosen, J. M. and Shields, D., 1980, Post-translational modifications of the rat mammary gland caseins: *In vitro* synthesis, processing, and segregation, in: *Testicular Development, Structure, and Function* (A. Steinberger and E. Steinberger, eds.), Raven Press, New York, pp. 343–349.
79. Mercier, J.-C. and Gaye, P., 1980, Study of secretory lactoproteins: Primary structures of the signals and enzymatic processing, *Ann. N. Y. Acad. Sci.* **343:**232–251.
80. Gaye, P. and Mercier, J.-C., 1979, Study of the precursors of ovine lactoproteins: Primary structures of the "signals" and enzymic processing of prelactoproteins by mammary microsomal membranes, *J. Dairy Res.* **46:**175–180.

81. Blobel, G. and Dobberstein, G., 1975, Transfer of proteins across membranes. I. Presence of proteolytically processed and unprocessed nascent immunoglobulin light chains on membrane-bound microsomes of murine myeloma, *J. Cell. Biol.* **67**:835–851.
82. Struck, D. K. and Lennarz, W. J., 1977, Evidence for the participation of saccharide-lipids in the synthesis of the oligosaccharide chain of ovalbumin, *J. Biol. Chem.* **252**:1007–1013.
83. Vijay, I. K., Perdew, G. H., and Lewis, D. E., 1980, Biosynthesis of mammary glycoproteins, *J. Biol. Chem.* **255**:11210–11220.
84. Jolles, P. and Fiat, A. M., 1979, The carbohydrate portions of milk glycoproteins, *J. Dairy Res.* **46**:187–191.
85. Hollmann, K. H., 1974, Cytology and fine structure of the mammary gland, in: *Lactation: A Comprehensive Treatise,* Volume I (B. L. Larson and V. R. Smith, eds.), Academic Press, New York, pp. 3–95.
86. White, D. A. and Speake, B. K., 1980, The effect of cycloheximide on the glycosylation of lactating-rabbit mammary glycoproteins, *Biochem. J.* **192**:297–301.
87. Turkington, R. W. and Topper, Y. J., 1966, Stimulation of casein synthesis and histological development of the mammary gland by human placental lactogen *in vitro, Endocrinology* **79**:175–181.
88. Bingham, E. W. and Groves, M. L., 1979, Properties of casein kinase from lactating bovine mammary gland, *J. Biol. Chem.* **254**:4510–4515.
89. Bingham, E. W. and Farrell, H. M., 1974, Casein kinase from the Golgi apparatus of lactating mammary gland, *J. Biol. Chem.* **249**:3647–3651.
90. Pascall, J. C., Boulton, A. P., and Craig, R. K., 1981, Characterisation of a membrane-bound serine-specific casein kinase isolated from lactating guinea-pig mammary gland, *Eur. J. Biochem.* **119**:91–99.
91. Greenberg, R., Groves, M. L., and Peterson, R. F., 1976, Amino terminal sequence and location of phosphate groups of the major human casein, *J. Dairy Sci.* **59**:1016–1018.
92. Mercier, J. C., Grosclaude, F., and Ribadeau-Dumas, B., 1972, Primary structure of bovine casein, a review, *Milchwissenschaft* **27**:402.
93. Groves, M. L. and Gordon, W. G., 1970, The major component of human casein; A protein phosphorylated at different levels, *Arch Biochem. Biophys.* **140**:47–51.
94. Thompson, M. D. and Farrell, H., Jr., 1973, Genetic variants of the milk proteins, in: *Lactation. A Comprehensive Treatise* Volume 3, (B. L. Larson and V. R. Smith, eds.), Academic Press, New York, pp. 109–134.
95. Waugh, D. F. and Talbot, B., 1971, Equilibrium casein micelle systems, *Biochemistry* **10**:4153–4162.
96. McGann, T. C. A., Donnelly, W. J., Kearney, R. D., and Buchheim, W., 1980, Composition and size distribution of bovine casein micelles, *Biochim. Biophys. Acta* **630**:261–270.
97. Rosen, J. M., O'Neal, D. L., McHugh, J. E., and Comstock, J. P., 1978, Progesterone-mediated inhibition of casein mRNA and polysomal casein synthesis in the rat mammary gland during pregnancy, *J. Biochem.* **17**:290–297.
98. Nakhasi, H. L. and Qasba, P. K., 1979, Quantitation of milk proteins and their mRNAs in rat mammary gland at various stages of gestation and lactation, *J. Biol. Chem.* **254**:6016–6025.
99. Houdebine L. M., 1980, The control of casein gene expression by prolactin and its modulators, in: *Central and Peripheral Regulation of Prolactin* (R. M. Macloed and U. Scapagnini, eds.), Raven Press, New York, pp. 189–205.
100. Guyette, W. A., Matusik, R. J., and Rosen, J. M., 1979, Prolactin-mediated transcriptional and post-transcriptional control of casein gene expression, *Cell* **17**:1013–1023.
101. Burditt, L. J., Parker, D., Craig, R. K., Getova, T., and Campbell, P. N., 1981, Differential expression of α-lactalbumin and casein genes during the onset of lactation in the guinea-pig mammary gland, *Biochem. J.* **194**:999–1006.
102. Wilde, C. J., Paskin, N., Saxton, J., and Mayer, R. J., 1980, Protein degradation during terminal cytodifferentiation, *Biochem. J.* **192**:311–320.
103. Fisher, M. M., Nagy, B., Bazin, H., and Underdown, B. J., 1979, Biliary transport of IgA: Role of secretory component, *Proc. Nat. Acad. Sci. USA,* **76**:2008–2012.

104. Renston, R. H., Jones, A. L., Christiansen, W. D., Hradek, G. T., and Underdown, B. J., 1980, Evidence for a vesicular transport mechanism in hepatocytes for biliary secretion of immunoglobulin A, *Science* **208**:1276–1278.
105. Richards, D. A., Rodgers, J. R., Supowit, S. C., and Rosen, J. M., 1981, Construction and preliminary characterization of the rat casein and α-lactalbumin cDNA clones, *J. Biol Chem.* **256**:526–532.
106. Richards, D. A., Blackburn, D. E., and Rosen, J. M., 1981, Restriction enzyme mapping and hetero-duplex analysis of the rat milk proteins cDNA clones, *J. Biol. Chem.* **256**:533–538.
107. Craig, R. K., Hall, L., Parker, D., and Campbell, P. N., 1981, The construction, identification and partial characterization of plasmids containing guinea-pig milk protein complementary DNA sequences, *Biochem. J.* **194**:989–998.
108. Hall, L., Davies, M. S., and Craig, R. K., 1981, The construction, identification and characterisation of plasmids containing human α-lactalbumin cDNA sequences, *Nucleic Acids Res.* **9**:65–84.
109. Dandekar, A. M. and Qasba, P. K., 1981, Rat α-lactalbumin has a 17-residue-long COOH-terminal hydrophobic extension as judged by sequence analysis of the cDNA clones, *Proc. Nat. Acad. Sci.* **78**:4853–4857.
110. Ono, M. and Oka, T., 1980, The differential actions of cortisol on the accumulation of α-lactalbumin and casein in midpregnant mouse mammary gland in culture, *Cell* **19**:473-480.
111. Kuhn, N. J. and White, A., 1975, The topography of lactose synthesis, *Biochem. J.* **148**:77–84.
112. Ebner, K. E. and Schanbacher, F. L., 1974, Biochemistry of lactose and related carbohydrates, in: *Lactation*, Volume 2 (B. L. Larson and V. R. Smith, eds.), Academic Press, New York, pp. 77–113.
113. Faulkner, A., Chaiyabutr, N., Peaker, M., Carrick, D. T., and Kuhn, N. J., 1981, Metabolic significance of milk glucose, *J. Dairy Res.* **48**:51–56.
114. Grimmonprez, L. and Montreuil, J., 1975, Isolement et étude des propriétés physico-chimiques d'oligosaccharides du lait de femme, *Biochimie* **57**:695–701.
115. Baer, H. H., 1969, Oligosaccharides, in: *The Amino Sugars*, Volume IA (R. W. Jeanloz, ed.), Academic Press, New York, pp. 267–373.
116. Yamashita, K., Tachibana, Y., and Kobata, A., 1977, Oligosaccharides of human milk, *J. Biol. Chem.* **252**:5408–5411.
117. Kobata, A., Grollman, E. F., and Ginsburg, V., 1968, An enzymatic basis for blood type A in humans, *Arch. Biochem. Biophys.* **124**:608–612.
118. Shen, L., Grollman, E. F., and Ginsburg, V., 1968, An enzymatic basis for secretor status and blood group substance specificity in humans, *Proc. Nat. Acad. Sci.* **59**:224–230.
119. Jones, E. A., 1977, Synthesis and secretion of milk sugars, *Symp. Zool. Soc. London* **41**:77–94.
120. Chaiyabutr, N., Faulkner, A., and Peaker, M., 1980, The utilization of glucose for the synthesis of milk components in the fed and starved lactating goat *in vivo*, *Biochem. J.* **186**:301–308.
121. Robinson, A. M. and Williamson, D. H., 1977, Comparison of glucose metabolism in the lactating mammary gland of the rat *in vivo* and *in vitro*, *Biochem. J.* **164**:153–159.
122. Baldwin, R. Y. and Yang, Y. T., 1974, Enzymatic and metabolic changes in the development of lactation, in: *Lactation*, Volume I (B. L. Larson and V. R. Smith, eds.), Academic Press, New York, pp. 349–413.
123. Lehninger, A. L., 1975, *Biochemistry*, Worth, New York, p. 47.
124. Kronman, M. J., Sinha, S. K., and Brew, K., 1981, Characteristics of the binding of Ca^{2+} and other divalent metal ions to bovine α-lactalbumin, *J. Biol. Chem.* **256**:8582–8587.
125. Powell, J. T. and Brew, K., 1976, Metal ion activation of galactosyltransferase, *J. Biol. Chem.* **251**:3645–3652.
126. O'Keeffe, E. T., Hill, R. L., and Bell, J. E., 1980, Active site of bovine galactosyltransferase: Kinetic and flourescence studies, *Biochemistry* **19**:4954–4962.

127. Powell, J. T. and Brew, K., 1976, A comparison of the interactions of galactosyltransferase with a glycoprotein substrate (ovalbumin) and with α-lactalbumin, *J. Biol. Chem.* **251:**3653–3663.

128. Brew, K., 1969, Secretion of α-lactalbumin into milk and its relevance to the organization and control of lactose synthetase, *Nature* **222:**671–672.

129. Kuhn, N. J. and White, A., 1977, The role of nucleoside diphosphatase in a uridine nucleotide cycle associated with lactose synthesis in rat mammary-gland Golgi apparatus, *Biochem. J.* **168:**423–433.

130. White, M. D., Kuhn, N. J., and Ward, S., 1981, Mannitol and glucose movement across the Golgi membrane of lactating-rat mammary gland, *Biochem. J.* **194:**173–177.

131. Kuhn, N. J. and Lowenstein, J. M., 1967, Lactogenesis in the rat. Changes in metabolic parameters at parturition, *Biochem. J.* **105:**995–2602.

132. Palmiter, R. D., 1969, What regulates lactose content in milk? *Nature* **221:**912–917.

133. Nicholas, K. R., Hartmann, P. E., and McDonald, B. L., 1981, α-Lactalbumin, and lactose concentrations in rat milk during lactation, *Biochem. J.* **194:**149–154.

134. Neville, M. C., Selker, F., Semple, K., and Watters, C., 1981, ATP-dependent calcium transport by a Golgi-enriched membrane fraction from mouse mammary gland, *J. Membr. Biol.* **61:**97–105.

135. Kuhn, N. J., Wooding, F. B. P., and White, A., 1980, Properties of galactosyltransferase-enriched vesicles of Golgi membranes from lactating-rat mammary gland, *Eur. J. Biochem.* **103:**377–385.

136. Wilde, C. J. and Kuhn, N. J., 1981, Lactose synthesis and the utilisation of glucose by rat mammary acini, *Int. J. Biochem.* **13:**311–316.

137. Neville, M. C. and Peaker, M., 1979, The secretion of calcium, and phosphorus into milk, *J. Physiol.* **290:**59–67.

138. Linzell, J. L., Mepham, T. B., and Peaker, M., 1976, The secretion of citrate into milk, *J. Physiol.* **260:**739–750.

139. Johke, T., 1978, Nucleotides of mammary secretion, in: *Lactation: A Comprehensive Treatise,* Volume IV (B. L. Larson, ed.), Academic Press, New York, pp. 513–522.

140. Barltrop, D. and Hillier, R., 1974, Calcium and phosphorus content of transitional and mature human milk, *Acta Paediatr. Scan* **63:**347–350.

141. Vaughan, L. A., Weber, C. W., and Kemberling, S. R., 1979, Longitudinal changes in the mineral content of human milk, *Am. J. Clin. Nutr.* **32:**2301–2306.

142. Allen, J. C., Neville, M. C., and Neifert, M. A., 1982, Ionized calcium in human milk, *Fed. Proc.* **41:**474.

143. Holt, C. and Muir, D. D., 1979, Inorganic constituents of milk: I. Correlation of soluble calcium with citrate in bovine milk, *J. Dairy Res.* **46:**433–439.

144. Carroll, R. J., Thompson, M. P., and Farrell, H. M., Jr., 1970, Formation and structure of casein micelles in lactating mammary tissue, *28th Annual Proceedings Electron Microscopy Society of America,* p. 150.

145. Heald, C. W. and Saacke, R. G., 1972, Cytological comparison of milk protein synthesis of rat mammary tissue *in vivo* and *in vitro, J. Dairy Sci.* **55:**612.

146. Baumrucker, C. R. and Keenan, T. W., 1975, Membranes of the mammary gland. X. ATP-dependent calcium accumulation by Golgi apparatus rich fraction from bovine mammary gland, *Exp. Cell. Res.* **90:**253–260.

147. West, D. W., 1981, Energy-dependent calcium sequestration activity in a Golgi apparatus fraction derived from lactating rat mammary gland, *Biochem. Biophys. Acta,* **673:**374–386.

148. Watters, C. D., 1981, The Golgi apparatus of lactating mammary tissue resembles that of murine skeletal sarcoplasmic reticulum, *J. Cell. Biol.* **91:**262a.

149. Carafoli, E. and Crompton, M., 1978, The regulation of intracellular calcium, *Curr. Topics Membr. Trans.* **10:**151–216.

150. Lemons, J. A., Schreiner, R. L., and Gresham, E. L., 1980, Simple method for determining the caloric and fat content of human milk, *Pediatrics* **66:**626–628.

151. Bauman, D. E. and Davis, C. L., 1974, Biosynthesis of milk fat, in: *Lactation,* Volume 2 (B. L. Larson and V. R. Smith, eds.), Academic Press, New York, pp. 31–75.

152. Dils, R. R., 1977, Mammary glands, in: *Lipid Metabolism in Mammals*, Volume 2 (F. Snyder, ed.), Plenum Press, New York, pp. 131–144.

153. Dils, R., Clark, S., and Knudsen, J., 1977, Comparative aspects of milk fat synthesis, in: *Comparative Aspects of Lactation* (M. Peaker, ed.), Academic Press, New York, pp. 43–55.

154. Mayer, R. J., 1978, Hormonal factors in lipogensis in mammary gland. *Vitam. Horm.* **36**:101–128.

155. Smith, S., 1980, Mechanism of chain length determination in biosynthesis of milk fatty acids, *J. Dairy Sci.* **63**:337–350.

156. Hardie, D. H., 1980, The regulation of fatty acid synthesis by reversible phosphorylation of acetyl CoA carboxylase, in: *Recently Discovered Systems of Enzyme Regulation by Reversible Phosphorylation* (P. Cohen, ed.), Elsevier/North Holland Biomedical Press, Amsterdam, pp. 33–62.

157. Hytten, F. E., 1954, Clinical and chemical studies in human lactation, *Br. Med. J.* **2**:175–182.

158. Whitehead, R. G., 1979, Nutrition and lactation, *Post-Grad. Med. J.* **55**:303–310.

159. Gibson, R. A. and Kneebone, G. M., 1981, Fatty acid composition of human colostrum and mature breast milk, *Am. J. Clin. Nutr.* **34**:252–257.

160. Breckenridge, W. C. and Kuksis, A., 1967, Molecular weight distributions of milk fat triglycerides from seven species, *J. Lipid Res.* **8**:473–478.

161. Insull, W., Jr., Hirsch, J., James, T., and Ahrens, E. H., Jr., 1958, The fatty acids of human milk, Volume II. Alterations produced by manipulation of caloric balance and exchange of dietary fats, *J. Clin. Invest.* **38**:443–450.

162. Jensen, R. G., Clark, R. M., and Ferris, A. M., 1980, Composition of the lipids in human milk: A review, *Lipids* **15**:345–355.

163. Read, W. W. C., Lutz, P. G., and Tashjian, A., 1965, Human milk lipids. II. The influence of dietary carbohydrates and fat on the fatty acids of mature milk. A study in four ethnic groups, *Am. J. Clin. Nutr.* **17**:180–183.

164. Mellies, M. J., Ishikawa, T. T., Gartside, P. S., Burton, K., MacGee, J., Allen, K., Steiner, P. M., Brady, D., and Glueck, C. J., 1979, Effects of varying maternal dietary fatty acids in lactating women and their infants, *Am. J. Clin. Nutr.* **32**:299–303.

165. Crawford, M. A., Laurance, B. M., and Munhambo, A. E., 1977, Breast feeding and human milk composition, *Lancet* **1**:99–100.

166. Guthrie, H. A., Picciano, M. F., and Sheehe, D., 1977, Fatty acid patterns of human milk, *J. Pediatr.* **90**:39–41.

167. Titheridge, M. A. and Coore, H. G., 1977, Preparation and properties of mitochondria from lactating rat mammary gland in particular relation to lipogenesis, *Int. J. Biochem.* **8**:433–436.

168. Katz, J., Wals, P. A., and Van de Velde, R. L., 1974, Lipogenesis by acini from mammary gland of lactating rats, *J. Biol. Chem.* **249**:7348–7357.

169. Crabtree, B., Taylor, D. J., Coombs, J. E., Smith, R. A., Templer, S. P., and Smith, G. H., 1981, The activities and intracellular distributions of enzymes of carbohydrate, lipid and ketone-body metabolism in lactating mammary glands from ruminants and non-ruminants, *Biochem. J.* **196**:747–756.

170. Peaker, M., Faulkner, A., and Blatchford, D. R., 1981, Changes in milk citrate concentration during lactation in the goat, *J. Dairy Res.* **48**:357–361.

171. Knudsen, J. and Grunnet, I., 1980, Primer specificity of mammalian mammary gland fatty acid synthetases, *Biochem. Biophys. Res. Commun.* **95**:1808–1814.

172. Dodds, P. F., Guadalupe, M., Guzman, F., Chalberg, S. C., Anderson, G. J., and Kumar, S., 1981, Acetoacetyl-CoA reductase activity of lactating bovine mammary fatty acid synthase, *J. Biol. Chem.* **256**:6282–6290.

173. Hansen, J. K. and Knudsen, J., 1980, Transacylation as a chain-termination mechanism in fatty acid synthesis by mammalian fatty acid synthetase, *Biochem. J.* **186**:287–294.

174. Speake, B. K., Dils, R., and Mayer, R. J., 1976, Regulation of enzyme turnover during tissue differentiation. Interactions of insulin, prolactin and cortisol in controlling the

turnover of fatty acid synthetase in rabbit mammary gland in organ culture, *Biochem. J.* **154**:359–370.

175. Smith, S. and Ryan, P., 1979, Aschronous appearance of two enzymes concerned with medium chain fatty acid synthesis in developing rat mammary gland, *J. Biol. Chem.* **254**:8932–8936.

176. Baxter, M. A., Goheer, M. A., and Coore, H. G., 1979, Absent pyruvate inhibition of pyruvate dehydrogenase kinase in lactating rat mammary gland following various treatments, *FEBS Lett.* **97**:27–31.

177. Goheer, M. A. and Coore, H. G., 1977, Pyruvate disposal by lactating-rat mammary gland, *Biochem. Soc. Trans.* **5**:834–838.

178. Munday, M. R. and Williamson, D. H., 1981, Role of pyruvate dehydrogenase and insulin in the regulation of lipogenesis in the lactating mammary gland of the rat during the starved-refed transition, *Biochem. J.* **196**:831–837.

179. Coore, H. G. and Field, B., 1974, Properties of pyruvate dehydrogenase of rat mammary tissue and its changes during pregnancy, lactation and weaning, *Biochem. J.* **142**:87–95.

180. Scow, R. O., Blanchette-Mackie, E. J., and Smith, L. C., 1976, A model for lipid transport from blood by lateral diffusion in cell membranes, *Circulation Res.* **39**:149–162.

181. Hamosh, M., Clary, T. R., Chernick, S. S., and Scow, R. O., 1970, Lipoprotein lipase activity of adipose and mammary tissue and plasma triglyceride in pregnant and lactating rats, *Biochim. Biophys. Acta* **210**:473–482.

182. Zinder, O., Hamosh, M., Fleck, T. R. C., and Scow, R. O., 1974, Effect of prolactin on lipoprotein lipase in mammary gland and adipose tissue of rats, *Am. J. Physiol.* **226**:744–748.

183. Scow, R. O., Mendelson, C. R., Zinder, O., Hamosh, M., and Blanchette-Mackie, E. J., 1973, Role of lipoprotein lipase in the delivery of dietary fatty acids to lactating mammary tissue, in: *Dietary Lipids and Postnatal Development* (C. Galli, ed.), Raven Press, New York, pp. 91–114.

184. Steingrimsdottir, L., Brasel, J. A., and Greenwood, M. R. C., 1980, Diet, pregnancy, and lactation: Effects on adipose tissue, lipoprotein lipase, and fat cell size, *Metabolism* **29**:837–841.

185. Long, C. A., Patton, S., and McCarthy, R. D., 1980, Origins of the cholesterol in milk, *Lipids* **15**:853–857.

186. Kris-Etherton, P. M. and Frantz, I. D., Jr., 1980, The contribution of chylomicron cholesterol to milk cholesterol in the rat, *Proc. Soc. Exp. Biol. Med.* **165**:502–507.

187. Gaull, G. E., Jensen, R. E., Rassin, D. K., and Malloy, M. H., 1982, Human milk as food, *Adv. Perinatal Med.* **2**:47–120.

188. Mellies, M. J., Ishikawa, T. T., Gartside, P., Burton, K., MacGee, J., Allen, K., Steiner, P. M., Brady, D., and Glueck, C. J., 1978, Effects of varying maternal dietary cholesterol and phytosterol in lactating women and their infants, *Am. J. Clin. Nutr.* **31**:1347–1354.

189. Mellies, M. J., Burton, K., Larsen, R., Fixler, D., and Glueck, C. J., 1979, Cholesterol, phytosterols and polyunsaturated/saturated fatty acid ratios during the first twelve months of lactation, *Am. J. Clin. Nutr.* **32**:2382–2389.

190. Kris-Etherton, P. M., and Frantz, I. D., Jr., 1978, Inhibition of cholesterol synthesis in mammary tissue, lung and kidney following cholesterol feeding in the lactating rat, *Lipids* **14**:907–912.

191. Easter, D. J., Patton, S., and McCarthy, R. D., 1971, Metabolism of phospholipid in mammary gland: I. The supply of phospholipid for milk synthesis in the rat and goat, *Lipids* **6**:844–849.

192. Blackberg, L. and Hernell, O., 1981, The bile-salt-stimulated lipase in human milk: Purification and characterization, *Eur. J. Biochem.* **116**:221–225.

193. Freudenberg, E., 1966, A lipase in the milk of the gorilla, *Experientia* **22**:317.

194. Hernell, O., Gebre-Medhin, M., and Olivecrona, T., 1977, Breast milk composition in Ethiopian and Swedish mothers. IV. Milk lipases, *Am. J. Clin. Nutr.* **30**:508–511.

195. Jensen, R. G. and Pitas, R. E., 1976, Milk lipoprotein lipases: A review, *J. Dairy Sci.* **59**:1203–1214.

196. Poland, R. L., Schultz, G. E., and Garg, G., 1980, High milk lipase activity associated with breast milk jaundice, *Pediatr. Res.* **14:**1328–1331.
197. Linzell, J. L. and Peaker, M., 1974, Changes in colostrum composition and in the permeability of the mammary epithelium at about the time of parturition in the goat, *J. Physiol.* **243:**129–151.
198. Linzell, J. L. and Peaker, M., 1971, Intracellular concentrations of sodium, potassium and chloride in the lactating mammary gland and their relation to the secretory mechanism, *J. Physiol.* **216:**683–700.
199. Nagy, Zs., Lustyik, G., Zarandi, B., and Bertoni-Freddari, C., 1981, Intracellular Na$^+$:K$^+$ ratios in human cancer cells as revealed by energy dispersive x-ray microanalysis, *J. Cell Biol.* **90:**769–777.
200. Johnson, M. P. and Wooding, F. B. P., 1978, Adenosine triphosphatase distribution in mammary tissue, *Histochem. J.* **10:**171–183.
201. Peaker, M., 1977, Mechanism of milk secretion: Milk composition in relation to potential difference across the mammary epithelium, *J. Physiol.* **270:**489–505.
202. Emerman, J. T. and Pitelka, D. R., 1977, Maintenance and induction of morphological differentiation in dissociated mammary epithelium on floating collagen mambranes, *In Vitro* **13:**316–328.
203. Bisbee, C. A., 1981, Transepithelial electrophysiology of cultured mouse mammary epithelium: Sensitivity to prolactins, *Am. J. Physiol.* **241:**E410–E413.
203a. Wicha, M. S., Lowrie, G., Kohn, E., Bagavandoss, P., and Hann, T., 1982, Extracellular matrix promotes mammary epithelial growth and differentiation *in vitro, Proc. Natl. Acad. Sci. U.S.A.* **79:**3213–3217.
204. Martin, R. H., Glass, M. R., Chapman, C., Wilson, G. D., and Woods, K. L., 1980, Human α-lactalbumin and hormonal factors in pregnancy and lactation, *Clin. Endocrinol.* **13:**223–230.
205. Pitelka, D. R., 1978, Cell contacts in the mammary gland, in: *Lactation: A Comprehensive Treatise* Volume IV, (B. L. Larson, ed.), Academic Press, New York, pp. 41–66.
206. Shannon, O. M. and Pitelka, D. R., 1981, Influences of cell shape on the induction of functional differentiation in mouse mammary cells *in vitro, In Vitro* **17:**1016–1028.
207. Maule Walker, F. M. and Peaker, M., 1980, Local production of prostaglandins in relation to mammary function at the onset of lactation in the goat, *J. Physiol.* **309:**65–79.
208. Neville, M. C. and Peaker, M., 1981, Ionized calcium in milk and integrity of the mammary epithelium in the goat, *J. Physiol.* **313:**561–570.
209. Masson, P. L. and Heremans, J. F., 1971, Lactoferrin in milk from different species, *Comp. Biochem. Physiol.* **39:**119–129.
210. Vuori, E. and Kuitunen, P., 1979, The concentrations of copper and zinc in human milk— A longitudinal study, *Acta Paediatr. Scand.* **68:**33–37.
211. Dauncey, M. J., Shaw, J. C. L., and Urman, J., 1977, The absorption and retention of magnesium, zinc and copper by low birth weight infants fed pasturized human breast milk, *Pediatr. Res.* **11:**1033–1039.
212. Steiner, G. A., 1978, Successful treatment of acrodermatitis enterpathica with zinc sulfate, *Am. J. Hosp. Pharm.* **35:**1535–1538.
213. Duncan, J. R. and Hurley, L. S., 1979, Intestinal absorption of zinc: A role for a binding ligand in milk, *Am. J. Physiol.* **235:**E556–E559.
214. Evans, G. W. and Johnson, P. E., 1980, Characterization and quantitation of a zinc binding ligand in human milk, *Pediatr. Res.* **14:**876–880.
215. Lonnerdal, B., Stanislowski, A. G., and Hurley, L. S., 1980, Isolation of a low molecular weight zinc binding ligand from human milk, *J. Biochem.* **12:**145–158.
216. Cousins, R. J. and Smith, K. T., 1980, Zinc-binding properties of bovine and human milk *in vitro*: Influences on changes in zinc content, *Am. J. Clin. Nutr.* **33:**1083–1087.
217. Zimmerman, A. W. and Hambidge, K. M., 1980, Low zinc in mothers milk and zinc deficiency syndrome in breast fed premature infants, *Am. J. Clin. Nutr.* **33:**951.
218. Neathery, M. W., Miller, W. J., Blackman, D. M., and Gentry, R. P., 1973, Performance and milk zinc from low-zinc intake in Holstein cows, *J. Dairy Sci.* **56:**212–217.

219. Kosman, D. J. and Henkin, R. I., 1979, Plasma and serum zinc concentrations, *Lancet* **1:**1410.
220. Lengemann, F. W., Wentworth, R. A., and Comar, C. L., 1974, Physiological and biochemical aspects of the accumulation of contaminant radionuclides in milk, in: *Lactation: A Comprehensive Treatise,* Volume III (B. L. Larson and V. R. Smith, eds.), Academic Press, New York, pp. 159–215.
221. Brown-Grant, K., 1957, Iodide concentrating mechanism of the mammary gland, *J. Physiol.* **135:**644–654.
222. Swanson, E. W., 1972, Effect of dietary iodine on thyroxine secretion rate of lactating cows, *J. Dairy Sci.* **55:**1763–1767.
223. Miller, J. K. and Swanson, E. W., 1963, Some factors affecting iodine secretion in milk, *J. Dairy Sci.* **46:**927–932.
224. Lengemann, F. W., 1970, Metabolism of radioiodide by lactating goats given [131]iodine for extended periods, *J. Dairy Sci.* **53:**165–175.
225. Potter, G. D. and McIntyre, D. R., 1968, *In vitro* analysis of the binding of ^{131}I-iodide to milk protein, *J. Dairy Sci.* **51:**1177–1181.
226. Brown-Grant, K., 1961, Extrathyroidal iodide concentrating mechanisms, *Physiol. Rev.* **41:**189–213.
227. Allen, J. C. and Miller, W. J., 1981, Transfer of selenium from blood to milk in goats and noninterference of copper with selenium metabolism, *J. Dairy Sci.* **64:**814–821.
228. Gasiewicz, T. A. and Smith, J. C., 1978, The metabolism of selenite by intact rat erythrocytes *in vitro, Chem. Biol. Interact.* **21:**299–313.
229. Allen, J. C. and Miller, W. J., 1980, Selenium binding and distribution in goat and cow milk, *J. Dairy Sci.* **63:**526–531.
230. Clarke, W. A. and Salisbury, R. L., 1980, Dimethyl sulfide in milk of lactating dairy cows fed various sulfur compounds, *J. Dairy Sci.* **63:**375–378.
231. Vuori, E., 1979, Longitudinal study of manganese in human milk, *Acta Paediatr. Scand.* **68:**571–573.
232. Underwood, E. J., 1971, *Trace Elements in Human and Animal Nutrition,* Academic Press, New York.

4

Regulation of Mammary Development and Lactation

Margaret C. Neville

The mammary gland is unique, not only in its secretory products, but in its ability to complete an entire cycle of growth and differentiation each time it is called upon to provide nutrition for a new set of offspring. For this reason, in this chapter, the hormonal control of mammary development and the coordination of mammary function with other events in the female reproductive cycle are considered, along with the regulation of milk secretion and ejection. The focus will be on hormonal controls as they are understood in the human, drawing on animal studies when necessary for clarity or when information from humans is lacking. This chapter is intended to provide an overview of the complex hormonal interactions which regulate mammary function at the organismic level, making the general principles accessible to the nonspecialist. The hormonal control of mammary development will be discussed, followed by a description of prolactin secretion through the female life cycle and the role of oxytocin in milk ejection. Finally, the effects of breast-feeding on fertility and our current understanding of the interaction between nutrition and lactation will be outlined.

We will begin with a brief overview of the developmental cycle of the mammary gland. *Mammogenesis*, or the growth and differentiation of the mammary gland, leads to the development of the lobuloalveolar structure illustrated in Figs. 3 and 4 of Chapter 2. This process begins in the fetus and, after a period of quiescence during childhood, continues with pubertal development of both glandular and stromal elements. Final maturation of the lobuloalveolar elements, sometimes called terminal differentiation, is brought about by the hormonal mileu of pregnancy. In the pregnant woman, limited secretion of milk products commences during the second trimester.[1,2] The onset of copious milk secretion or *lactogenesis* is a gradual process that

---

Margaret C. Neville • Department of Physiology, University of Colorado School of Medicine, Denver, Colorado, 80262.

begins at parturition and continues for 10 to 14 days into established lactation. During the first 5 days of this process, the mammary secretion is known as *colostrum*, a fluid rich in protective substances such as immunoglobulin A, lactoferrin, and leukocytes. From days 5 to 10, the secretion product is known as *transitional milk*. This transitional phase is impeded if milk is not removed from the breast at regular intervals. *Lactation* is maintained as long as the infant continues to suckle regularly. With sufficient suckling, there is a tendency for suppression of the menstrual cycle delaying further pregnancies. After weaning, the mammary epithelium goes through *involution*, gradually returning to a less differentiated state.

Multiple hormonal interactions coordinate each stage. *In vivo* mammogenesis requires sex steroids, a lactogenic hormone (either prolactin or placental lactogen) and probably one or more as yet unknown growth factors. In addition, interactions between the mammary epithelial elements and the stroma in which they are situated are clearly of importance, although poorly understood. Lactogenesis appears to be triggered by the postpartum decline in plasma progesterone levels, but can be blocked by inhibitors of prolactin secretion. The transition to mature milk requires, in addition, removal of milk from the breast at regular intervals. Established lactation is regulated by prolactin, oxytocin, and possibly local factors. Although both prolactin and oxytocin are secreted in response to suckling by the infant, the physiological roles of these two hormones are quite different. Prolactin acts on the mammary epithelial cells to stimulate the production and secretion of milk into the alveolar lumina. Oxytocin acts on the myoepithelial cells, facilitating milk removal from the breast by causing ejection of milk from the alveoli into the ducts and mammary sinuses where it becomes available to the suckling infant. Involution occurs when suckling stimuli are absent or when milk is not removed from the breast.

Our discussion of the regulation of mammary function, a subject of detailed investigation since the turn of the century, must necessarily be somewhat abbreviated. Additional information is available in the recent book by Cowie *et al.*[3] recommended for its clear and detailed discussion, as well as in recent reviews by Topper and Freeman[4] and Rosen *et al.*[5] which provide excellent coverage of more limited aspects of the subject. In this chapter, the mechanisms involved in the regulation of mammary function will be considered from the perspective of the whole organism, focusing, of course, on the human. The cellular actions of the hormones involved will be discussed in the next chapter.

STAGES IN THE DEVELOPMENT OF MAMMARY FUNCTION

Mammogenesis

Mammogenesis begins in early fetal life and is not complete in the woman until after parturition. The exact complement of hormones which stimulate mammary gland development during puberty and pregnancy are not well understood although estrogens, progesterone, and lactogenic hormones all appear to be involved *in vivo*. Nonpuerperal mammary development and lactation can be induced by the regular application of a suckling stimulus, even in nulliparous women and occasionally, in men. While prolactin is thought to mediate this phenomenon, the hormonal accompaniments of induced lactation in humans have received very little attention.

Fetal Development

The fetal mammary gland begins to develop during the second month of gestation as the mammary line, an ectodermal thickening running the length of the ventral body wall. Shortly thereafter, epithelial proliferation in segments of the line leads to formation of mammary buds, the location depending on the eventual position of the mammary gland in that species. The bud consists of a ball of epithelial cells extending into the underlying mesenchyme.[3,4,6,7] During the second trimester, 15 to 25 sprouts branch from this bud to form the precursors of the mammary ducts. Since mammary explants from mouse and rabbit embryos develop sprouts *in vitro* in the absence of added hormones,[6] it is likely that embryonic mammary development is independent of maternal or fetal hormonal influences. However, increasing evidence indicates that specific interactions between the epithelial cells and the underlying stroma are necessary for development and maintenance of functional differentiation.[8] Mammary tissue does acquire the ability to respond to systemic hormones during fetal life. Thus, in the third trimester, high fetal prolactin levels[9] bring about terminal differentiation of the ductile cells so that, at birth, they resemble cells in the lactating gland, often secreting milk. After birth, these cells revert to an undifferentiated state.

Puberty

Following a quiescent period during childhood, the increasing levels of estrogen at puberty directly or indirectly stimulate ductile proliferation and deposition of periglandular adipose tissue leading to breast enlargement. Although ductile proliferation occurs at puberty in most species, the human is virtually the only animal in which the gland enlarges visibly in the absence of pregnancy or lactation. The possible erotic significance of this phenomenon has been noted by a number of authors.[3,10,11] With the establishment of ovulatory menstrual cycles, peaks of ovarian steroids, particularly progesterone, are thought to bring about cyclic changes in breast development and the limited lobuloalveolar growth seen in the nonpregnant woman.

The hormones responsible for growth of the mammary epithelium remain controversial, largely because no entirely satisfactory *in vitro* system for the study of mammary proliferation has been available. In animals, estrogens given *in vivo* bring about ductile proliferation and appear to stimulate secretory activity with very little lobuloalveolar development.[12]

Whether proliferation of mammary cells is the direct result of estrogen stimulation is presently uncertain, since estrogens have generally not been found to promote mammary growth *in vitro*. A number of lines of evidence suggest that factors such as epidermal growth factor[13,14] or a specific mammary growth factor[15] are required for mammary growth. The possibility that estrogens stimulate secretion of these or other factors by extramammary organs was suggested by experiments of Sirbasku[16] in which extracts of uterus, kidney, brain, and platelets from estrogen-treated animals stimulated growth of a mammary tumor line. When progesterone is injected with estrogen, secretion is inhibited and lobuloalveolar development promoted. Because these steroids have no effect in hypophysectomized animals,[17,18] it has been suggested that a pituitary hormone, probably prolactin, bears ultimate responsibility for mammary growth in the estrogen- and progesterone-treated animal.

Pregnancy

During pregnancy, there is a remarkable augmentation of the lobuloalveolar elements of the human breast accompanied by full cytodifferentiation of the epithelial cells, including myoepithelial cells. This process is largely completed in the first half of pregnancy after which lactogenesis is induced by abortion or parturition. Because it is possible to induce mammary growth with either placental lactogen or prolactin in the absence of steroids both *in vivo*[19] and *in vitro* (see Chapter 5), a primary role in the regulation of mammogenesis has been assigned to these lactogenic hormones. In the human, both prolactin and placental lactogen increase continuously during pregnancy, reaching high levels prior to parturition (Fig. 1). However, the available evidence suggests that either hormone may provide a sufficient stimulus for mammogenesis: Thus, mammary development and lactation have been observed in two women with total absence of immunoreactive placental lactogen,[20,21] and in one woman with prolactin levels in the range of nonpregnant women throughout pregnancy and lactation.[22] Although growth hormone appears to be lactogenic in some animals,[3] growth hormone levels do not rise during human pregnancy or lactation[23,24] and normal mammogenesis and lactation have been documented in an ateliotic dwarf.[25] For these reasons, it is unlikely that growth hormone plays a role in human mammogenesis.

The levels of steroid hormones, progesterone, estrogens and cortisol throughout pregnancy are also shown in Fig. 1. In contrast to puberty when estrogens appear directly or indirectly to stimulate breast development, there is no clear role for estrogens in mammary development in pregnancy, although recent reports suggest that estrogens may potentiate prolactin action (see Chapter 5). Estrogen levels are markedly reduced in pregnancies with placental sulfatase deficiency, but lactation has been reported to be normal in two such cases[26,27] suggesting that the high levels of estrogens seen in normal pregnancy are not necessary for mammogenesis. *In vivo*

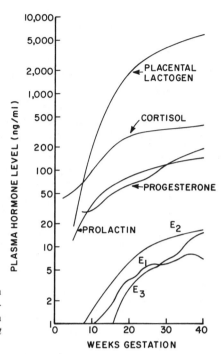

Figure 1. Plasma hormone levels during human pregnancy. Values for progesterone from Tulchinsky et al.,[158] estrogen and placental lactogen from De Hertogh et al.,[159] cortisol from Carr et al.,[57] and prolactin from Rigg et al.[160]

progesterone stimulates lobuloalveolar development while inhibiting secretory activity; its cellular mechanisms of action are not understood although it clearly inhibits the terminal differentiation induced by prolaction in many *in vitro* systems (see Chapter 5). Although cortisol potentiates the actions of prolactin on mammary differentiation, there is little *in vitro* evidence that it is necessary for ductile or alveolar proliferation.[2,3,4,28]

Induced Lactation

Numerous reports in both the anthropological and medical literature attest that mammary gland development and milk secretion can be induced in both nulliparous and parous women[29] and occasionally men[30] by the introduction of a regular suckling stimulus. A similar observation has been made in goats.[31] It seems likely that prolactin is the responsible hormone although this is not yet well documented. In both dairy animals and rodents, mammary growth and milk secretion can be induced by appropriate treatment with estrogen and progesterone. For example, a short (7-day) treatment with estrogen and progesterone in the cow[32] has been shown to stimulate milk secretion in a fairly reproducible manner. Bromocriptine, an inhibitor of prolactin secretion prevented this response to estrogen and progesterone in goats.[33] It is not yet clear whether a similar steroid regime would assist adoptive mothers, for example, to produce sufficient milk to breast-feed their infants.

Summary

Current evidence suggests that estrogens, acting directly or indirectly by stimulating the synthesis of mammary growth factors, render the mammary gland sensitive to growth promoting effects of prolactin and/or placental lactogen. Progesterone induces lobuloalveolar development by mechanisms which are not understood and inhibits milk secretion during pregnancy. Clarification of the cellular mechanisms involved awaits the development of a satisfactory system for the study of mammary proliferation *in vitro*. The progress so far made toward this goal is outlined in Chapter 6. Research in this area is extremely important because insight into the mechanisms that normally control mammary cell proliferation may also contribute to an understanding of the etiology of breast cancer.

Lactogenesis

We shall see below that lactogenesis is sometimes divided into two stages; Stage I occurring prepartum and Stage II occurring around parturition.[34] When the phase is not designated, the usual convention will be adopted; the term *lactogenesis* will be used to mean the onset of copious milk secretion around parturition. Although engorgement and leakage of mammary secretion appears fairly abruptly between the second and fourth days postpartum in the human, the transition from the secretion of colostrum to mature milk is, in fact, a gradual process requiring up to a month as can be seen from Figs. 2 to 7, Chapter 3, which depict longitudinal changes in the composition of human mammary secretion. In most animals, lactogenesis occurs earlier, coinciding with or even preceding parturition.

The hormonal mechanisms which bring about lactogenesis have long been the subject of controversy (Chapter 1). It now seems clear that lactogenesis is triggered by a fall in plasma progesterone levels under conditions where mammary development and plasma prolactin levels are sufficient to promote milk secretion.[35] In this section, we will review the evidence for this statement after a brief description of the stages of lactogenesis.

The Stages of Lactogenesis

Changes in milk composition through pregnancy were studied in detail in the goat by Linzell and his colleagues.[34] Starting about 12 weeks before parturition, there were significant increases in lactose, total proteins, and immunoglobulin and decreases in sodium and chloride. Following a suggestion by Hartmann,[36] these changes were defined as *lactogenesis stage I*. The onset of copious milk secretion at parturition was termed *lactogenesis stage II* and was accompanied by increased blood flow, and O_2 and glucose uptake (not shown). The sharp increase in the citrate concentration at parturition was found to be a reliable marker for lactogenesis stage II (Fig. 2).[37]

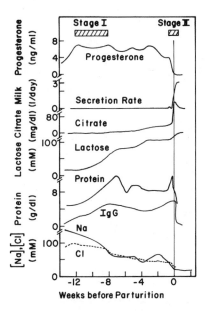

Figure 2. Correlation between plasma progesterone and lactogenesis stages I and II in the goat. Changes in milk composition through pregnancy and parturition in the goat redrawn from the data of Fleet *et al.*[34] and Maule Walker and Peaker.[161] Progesterone for goats carrying twins from Thorburn and Schneider.[162]

In the pregnant woman, the breasts are capable of milk secretion beginning sometime in the midtrimester[38] and the composition of the prepartum secretion appears to be nearly constant from day 120 to parturition.[2] Martin *et al.*[1] found that plasma levels of the milk-specific protein α-lactalbumin* rose at mid-trimester, then stabilized until term, implying that the onset of limited secretion of milk specific products, lactogenesis stage I, occurs during the second trimester (Fig. 3). Lactogenesis stage II occurs 2 to 3 days after parturition in the woman and appears to be marked by a peak of plasma α-lactalbumin (Fig. 4). The transition to the secretion of mature milk is nearly complete by 10 days although further changes in milk

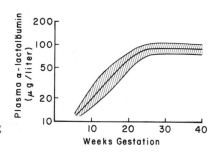

Figure 3. Plasma levels of α-lactalbumin during pregnancy. (Drawn from data of Martin *et al.*[1])

* The presence of this milk-specific protein in plasma during pregnancy probably results from backflux through the junction between the cells which are "leaky" at this stage.

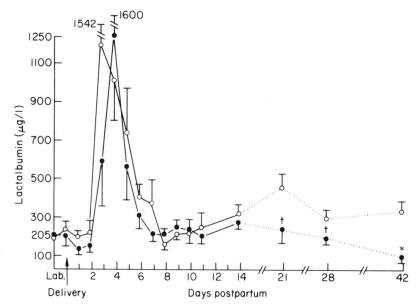

Figure 4. Plasma levels of α-lactalbumin during lactation breast-feeding (solid lines) and non-breast-feeding subjects (dotted lines). (From Martin *et al.*[1] Used with permission.)

composition continue throughout lactation (Figs. 2 and 4, Chapter 3). Lactogenesis and the maturation of the mammary epithelium occur more gradually in women than in many other species as illustrated in Fig. 5 in which the citrate concentration of the human mammary secretion is compared with the similar data from a cow and a goat.[37]

Hormonal Control of Stage II Lactogenesis in the Human

With the delivery of the placenta, the source of the hormones of pregnancy is abruptly removed and their plasma levels begin to fall (Fig. 6).

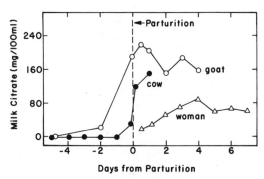

Figure 5. The citrate concentration of the mammary secretion around parturition in a goat, cow, and woman. (Redrawn from Peaker and Linzell.[37])

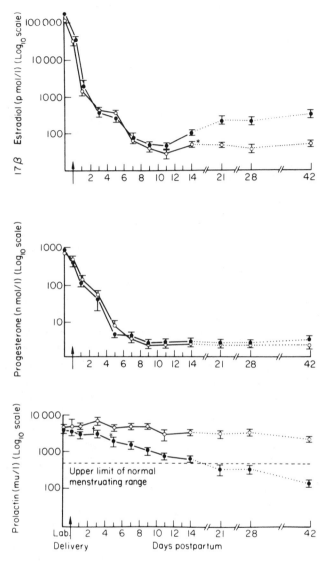

Figure 6. Maternal hormone levels after parturition in breast-feeding and non-breast-feeding women. Breast-feeding subjects (n = 10) (open circles); non-breast-feeding subjects (n = 9) (filled circles); * p < 0.01. (From Martin *et al.*[1] Used by permission.)

Placental lactogen disappears within hours (not shown). Progesterone levels require several days to reach the levels seen in the nonpregnant woman[1] probably because of continued production by the corpus luteum.[39] Estrogens also fall, reaching basal levels in 5 to 6 days. Prolactin falls slowly, requiring 14 days to reach nonpregnant levels in the nonnursing woman.[1] In the nursing woman, the rate of decrease in basal prolactin levels is slower and more variable, depending in part on the amount of suckling.[40] The neonate

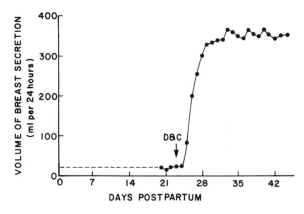

Figure 7. Milk secretion in a woman with placental retention before and after removal of placental fragments by dilatation and curettage (D & C). (From Neifert et al.[44]; used with permission.)

also experiences postnatal declines in prolactin and placental steroids, leading quite often to the appearance of "witches milk" with the same timing as lactogenesis in the mother.[41,42]

As early as 1905, Halban[43] observed that milk secretion did not occur until the placenta was removed from the uterus in many cases of fetal death and suggested that the placenta secreted a substance which inhibited lactogenesis. Further evidence that a placental hormone is responsible for inhibition of lactation in the pregnant woman is found in the observation (Fig. 7) that placental fragments retained after parturition can delay lactogenesis. Overwhelming evidence from animal experiments now indicates that progesterone is the specific inhibitory factor.[35] For example, in sows, the timing of the postpartum decrease in plasma progesterone is highly variable, but the increase in milk lactose concentration accompanying lactogenesis correlates temporally with this decrease.[45] In goats, the rapid prepartum fall in progesterone correlates well with lactogenesis stage II (Fig. 3). Moreover, exogenous progesterone prevents lactose and lipid synthesis after ovariectomy in pregnant rats[46,47] and ewes[48] and progesterone inhibits hormone-stimulated casein and α-lactalbumin synthesis in a variety of *in vitro* systems[50–52] (see Chapter 5). The lack of inhibitory effects of progesterone on established lactation has been a puzzle, possibly explained by the finding[49] that lactating tissues apparently do not contain progesterone binding sites.

The necessity of adequate levels of prolactin for the onset of lactation in humans has been well demonstrated in recent years by the use of bromocriptine, a drug which inhibits prolactin secretion, to suppress lactation in the puerperium.* This drug effectively prevents both engorgement and the appearance of milk when used postpartum, provided it is given over a

---

* Prior to the clinical use of bromocriptine, estrogens were used in the puerperium to suppress milk secretion. These hormones are currently thought to exert their inhibitory effect by acting directly on the mammary gland rather than on the pituitary.[50] Whether they are important in suppressing lactation during pregnancy is unknown, but such a role has been downplayed in recent years because it has not been possible to demonstrate inhibitory effects of estrogens in *in vitro* systems.[51,52]

2- to 3-week interval in doses sufficient to prevent the resurgence of prolactin levels.[53] On the other hand, high levels of prolactin may not be necessary for lactogenesis since milk formation occurs in cows, albeit with a delayed time course, when prolactin secretion is suppressed with bromocriptine.[54] Mammary development and milk secretion have been reported in a woman with low levels of prolactin throughout pregnancy and lactation.[22]

A number of other hormonal stimuli for lactogenesis have been proposed over the years. Although prolactin is probably necessary for normal lactogenesis in the human and most other species, there is little experimental support for the older hypothesis that a prolactin surge at parturition is responsible for the onset of copious milk secretion. A biphase rise in prolactin levels accompanies parturition in the human.[55] However, this rise precedes stage II lactogenesis by 2 to 3 days, by which time basal prolactin levels are already on the decline (Fig. 5). A similar argument can be advanced against the hypothesis that a surge in cortisol is the lactogenic trigger.[56] While an increase in plasma cortisol levels is seen in unanesthetized women at parturition,[57,58] this surge again precedes stage II lactogenesis and is probably associated with the stress of labor.[59] Insulin appears to be necessary for full development of mammary differentiation in most mammary explant systems.[4] Since lactogenesis occurs at parturition in severely diabetic rats, however, insulin probably does not play a regulatory role in this process *in vivo*.[60] Finally, it has been suggested that placental lactogen plays a role in the inhibition of lactation during pregnancy.[61] This role has been discounted by most investigators because human placental lactogen has lactogenic, rather than antilactogenic effects in *in vitro* systems[62–64] and has been found to compete with human prolactin for prolactin receptors on rabbit and other mammary gland membranes.[65] All these lines of evidence against an active role of other hormones add weight to the argument that a decline in plasma progesterone levels is the lactogenic trigger for stage II lactogenesis in humans.

Lactation

By comparison with the hormonal mechanisms which control mammogenesis and lactogenesis, those which regulate lactation are straightforward and fairly well understood. Suckling sets up trains of afferent impulses which travel to the brain via the sensory nerves from the nipple. These impulses are processed at several levels of the central nervous system and eventually bring about the secretion of oxytocin and prolactin. Oxytocin stimulates contraction of the myoepithelial cells leading to milk ejection. Prolactin stimulates the synthesis and secretion of milk into the alveolar spaces. Both these processes are described in detail in later sections of this and the next chapter. Here we need only discuss the present uncertainty about the role of prolactin in the day-to-day regulation of the rate of milk secretion.

Considered over a period of days to weeks, it is clear that the amount of milk secreted is rather carefully matched to the demands of the infant.

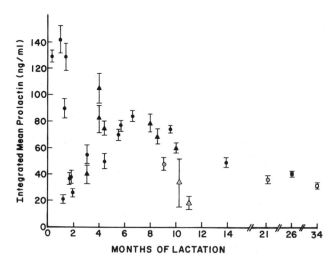

Figure 8. Twelve- or 24-hr integrated mean prolactin levels in breast-feeding women as compiled from several authors. Closed symbols: amenorrheic subjects. Open symbols: menstruating subjects. Circles: Tyson *et al.*[138] Triangles: Gross *et al.*[95] Squares: Madden *et al.*[88]

However, the mechanism is unclear and contradictory evidence exists about the role of prolactin in this process. Since the secretion of prolactin is proportional, at least in a general way, to the amount of suckling in both humans[40] and rats,[66] it seems logical that this hormone might provide the linkage between the amount of milk secreted and the degree of suckling stimulation. A number of observations support this hypothesis. Inhibition of prolactin secretion with bromocriptine inhibits milk production[53] and low milk yields in postpartum women have been associated with decreased prolactin secretion.[67] Increases in plasma prolactin levels brought about by the drug metoclopramide in poorly lactating women with low milk production were accompanied by increases in milk secretion.[68] On the other hand, plasma prolactin levels vary widely in lactating women, even after the same postpartum interval (Fig. 8). Further, in a careful study of the stimulation of prolactin secretion by suckling in the early puerperium, Howie *et al.*[69] and their colleagues were unable to show any relation between plasma prolactin levels and milk yield. As mentioned above, normal lactation was observed in a woman with low (<20 ng/ml) prolactin levels subsequent to pituitary surgery.[22] Finally, plasma prolactin levels are low in late lactation even under conditions where the level of milk secretion in both women[70] and animals[3] is maintained at high levels. These latter observations suggest that some prolactin may be necessary to maintain the functional differentiation of the mammary epithelium but that the actual amount of milk produced may be regulated by some other mechanism, such as the amount of milk remaining in the alveolar spaces after a feeding. The available information on the effects of milk retention in the alveolar spaces is summarized in the next section.

Involution

In their extensive review, Lascelles and Lee[71] described three types of mammary gland involution: *senile involution, initiated involution* which occurs with abrupt weaning, and *gradual involution* which occurs during natural weaning. Senile involution has been described only in women and appears primarily to be a postmenopausal process.[72] Starting about 35 years of age, there is a progressive loss of alveoli and a replacement by stroma and adipose tissue. Postmenopausally, there is also a progressive decrease in adipose tissue with the persistance of ductile structures which often terminate in blind knobs. These may be filled with a serous secretion. The hormonal mechanisms which bring about the senile changes in mammary gland stroma have not been studied. Since they are, in many respects, the inverse of the developmental changes which occur with puberty, it would be of interest to know whether they are reversed by the long-term postmenopausal use of estrogen.

Both initiated and gradual involution after lactation have in common the loss of glandular parenchyma with substitution by interlobular connective tissue, and in humans, adipose cells. Only initiated involution has received much attention in experimental animals although the progressive decline in milk yield during late lactation in dairy animals is of obvious concern to dairy farmers. In the goat, milk secretion stops within 3 days of cessation of milking.[73] The process is much more rapid in the rat, in which formation of new milk stops within 8 to 10 hr of removal of the pups.[74] The morphological changes following removal of the pups have been elegantly described by Helminen and Ericson.[75] Within 24 hr, changes in the rough endoplasmic reticulum, Golgi vesicles, and secretory vesicles can be observed, accompanied by a very marked decline in the activity of enzymes involved with milk synthesis[76–79] and an increase in the activity of free lysosomal enzymes.[80] By 48 hr, there is extensive morphological evidence of autophagic activity by lysosomes within the epithelial cells accompanied by leukocytic infiltration of the tissue[75] and a substantial decrease in both casein mRNA and its transcription.[81] After 3 days, macrophages take over the task of removing fragmented epithelial cells. Myoepithelial cells are largely spared during the early phases of disintegration. It is not clear to what extent these morphological changes in rodents apply to humans in whom the involution process may be much slower.

The composition of human mammary secretion following weaning has been carefully documented by Hartmann and Kulski[82] who observed gradual increases in protein, sodium, and chloride concentrations and decreases in potassium, lactose, and citrate (Fig. 9). Similar changes were found in goat mammary secretion by Fleet and Peaker[73] who suggested the changes resulted from a loss of integrity of the blood-milk barrier allowing entry of plasma constituents into the alveolar lumina. A continuous increase in the concentrations of IgA and lactoferrin suggests in addition that involution involves a change in the activity of the alveolar cells rather than their complete

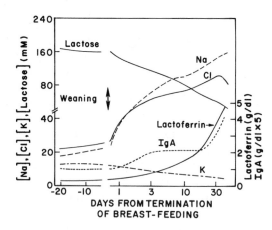

Figure 9. Composition of human milk after weaning. Lines represent mean values from four to six women. The verticle arrow indicates abrupt weaning after 9 or more months of breast feeding. (Redrawn from Hartmann and Kulski.[82])

dissolution. It is of interest that postlactational involution of the mammary gland in humans has a comparatively long time course.[82] The possibility that this is an adaptation which facilitates relactation should be considered.

The cellular mechanisms that control involution have received relatively little study. The decline in activity of the enzymes of milk synthesis observed after removal of the pups from lactating rats resembled the changes observed after hypophysectomy,[76,77] leading to the original postulate that involution was due to withdrawal of lactogenic hormones in the nonsuckled animal. However, when the teats were unilaterally sealed and the young allowed to continue suckling in order to maintain levels of lactogenic hormones, the decline in enzyme activity in the sealed side occurred with the same time course as in nonsuckled animals, suggesting that alveolar distension itself leads to involution.[76-79] In goats, infusion of volumes of isotonic sucrose sufficient to bring the intramammary pressure to the levels seen after cessation of milking brought about a decrease in milk secretion within 6 hr.[83] Mammary blood flow was decreased neither in these animals nor in rats with unilaterally sealed teats,[74] suggesting that distension of the alveoli inhibits mammary secretion directly rather than acting through a decrease in nutrient or hormone access via the mammary blood supply.

Emerman and Pitelka[84] found that the morphological differentiation of cultured mammary cells and their ability to secrete casein was dependent on the use of floating collagen gels on which the alveolar cells could assume a columnar shape. This observation suggests a direct link between mammary cell shape and milk secretion.[84a] If this is the case, the flattening of alveolar cells caused by distension may in some as yet unknown manner reduce their ability to secrete milk. The possibility that an inhibitor of milk secretion was present in retained mammary secretion was suggested by Linzell and Peaker.[85] However, distension with sucrose solutions inhibited milk secretion in goats with the same time course as cessation of milking,[83] indicating that such an inhibitor is not necessary for early changes associated with involution.

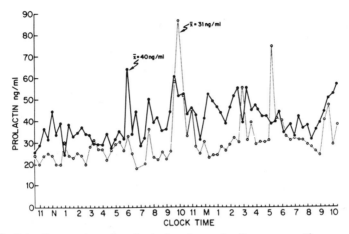

Figure 10. Episodic secretion of prolactin in a breast-feeding woman. Plasma samples were drawn every 20 min for 24 hr and analyzed for prolactin by radioimmunoassay. Closed circles: Lactation duration was 26 months and the woman was amenorrheic. Open circles: Lactation duration was 34 months and menses had resumed. (From Madden *et al.*[88] Used with permission.)

In summary, it is clear that retained mammary secretion inhibits further milk production. Whether a chemical inhibitor of mammary secretion is involved or whether flattening of alveolar cells *per se* is responsible for this inhibition remains for future investigation. In any case, it is likely that this is the mechanism through which poor letdown brings about inadequate lactational performance in women.

PROLACTIN SECRETION THROUGH THE LIFE CYCLE

Since the development of a radioimmunoassay for prolactin in 1971[86], a great deal has been learned about human prolactin levels under both physiological and pathological conditions. In this section, we will review the levels of prolactin found through the life cycle in women. The control of prolactin secretion and its cellular actions on the mammary glands are summarized in the next chapter.

Prolactin is secreted episodically with peaks of up to 75 min in duration that occur 7 to 20 times a day (Fig. 10).[87,88] For this reason, accurate measurement requires frequent sampling intervals, as close as 15 to 20 min.* The prolactin peaks appear to be superimposed upon a continuous background level of secretion whose magnitude depends on the physiological condition. For example, in both men and women background prolactin secretion has a circadian rhythm with a night time increase related to sleep

---

* The apparent half-life of prolactin in a recent study with 15-min sampling intervals was 40 to 60 min in contrast to earlier estimates of 15 to 20 min obtained from studies with less frequent intervals.[89]

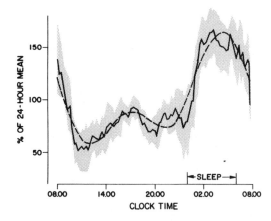

Figure 11. Circadian rhythm in prolactin secretion. Average values for six men. (From Van Cauten *et al.*[87] Used with permission.)

rather than time of day (Fig. 11).[87,89] The background level is higher in postpubertal women than in men and is elevated in pregnancy and lactation.

Prolactin is synthesized in the pituitary starting in the human fetus around 80 days gestation when serum levels of about 20 ng/ml are attained.[9] After 180 days, plasma levels increase sharply to about 150 to 200 ng/ml, similar to maternal plasma levels at this time. After birth, prolactin declines, again paralleling maternal plasma levels (see Fig. 6, non-breast-feeding subjects). After 6 weeks of life, prolactin reaches the prepubertal level of 2 to 8 ng/ml remaining within this range throughout life in males. At puberty in girls, plasma prolactin rises gradually attaining a level after menarche nearly double that of the prepubertal state (8 to 14 ng/ml).[9] Prolactin levels tend to be higher during the luteal phase of the menstrual cycle than during the follicular phase.[89] After the menopause, plasma prolactin returns to the levels seen in prepubertal girls and adult males.[90]

During pregnancy, serum prolactin levels increase steadily (Fig. 1) reaching values of 150 to 200 ng/ml at term. This progressive increase in prolactin levels in pregnant women contrasts sharply with most animals in which prolactin levels remain low during pregnancy and peak rapidly at parturition.[3] In women, prolactin appears to fall 2 to 3 hr prior to parturition and peak again about 2 hr after delivery.[55] After parturition, basal prolactin levels decrease, returning to prepregnancy values at 2 to 3 weeks in the woman who is not breast-feeding[1] (Fig. 6).

In the lactating woman, suckling often leads to a rapid rise in prolactin secretion (Fig. 12).[69,91] This rise is greatest in the immediate postpartum period; it is much less apparent after 6 months (Fig. 13).[70] If the activity of the nerves to the nipple is inhibited by application of xylocaine or surgical intervention, the prolactin rise is abolished[91] and increased serum prolactin levels have been observed after chest wall surgery.[92] These observations provide evidence that receptors in the areolus initiate the prolactin response. The prolactin rise was doubled when two infants were put to the breast simultaneously,[91] suggesting that the amount of prolactin released is related

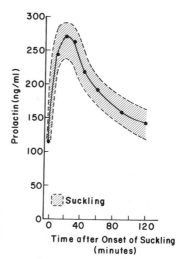

Figure 12. Effect of suckling on serum prolactin levels. Average values from 20 breast-feeding women suckling 10 min on days 5 and 6 of the puerperium. Replotted from data of Howie *et al.*[69] Shaded area indicates one standard error of the mean on either side of the mean.

to the intensity of nipple stimulation.* Considering the reported variability in prolactin levels in lactating women (Fig. 8), it is not surprising that basal prolactin levels in nursing women have been a matter of controversy. In earlier studies,[93] basal prolactin levels similar to nonpregnant, nonlactating women were reported in late lactation. However, Gross *et al.*[94] have recently shown that 24-hr integrated prolactin levels in nursing women are consistently elevated, suggesting that prolactin secretion stays above basal levels for the duration of lactation. A clear correlation between the number of feedings

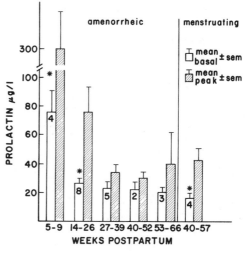

Figure 13. Mean concentration of serum prolactin before (open bars) and after (hatched bars) suckling in amenorrheic and menstruating breast-feeding women. The number of women in each group is indicated by the figure in the open column. A significant difference between the prolactin level before and after suckling is indicated by *. (From Gross and Eastman.[70] Used with permission.)

* Elevated prolactin levels often seen after mastectomy are thought to be the result of inappropriate impulses arising in the terminals of the severed areolar nerve,[92] again illustrating the importance of the sensory input from the areolus in prolactin secretion.

per day and basal prolactin levels is beginning to emerge from recent reports.[40,95]. Further, prolactin levels are elevated in malnourished women[95a] (see below), a finding whose implications are just beginning to be realized. Nevertheless, as discussed above, the role of plasma prolactin in the day-to-day regulation of milk production is presently equivocal. The possible role of the hormone in the regulation of fertility is discussed below.

MILK EJECTION AND OXYTOCIN

As discussed in the previous chapter, milk removal from the breast is accomplished by suckling of the infant in concert with the contraction of the myoepithelial cells whose processes form a basket-like network around the alveoli where milk is stored (Chapter 2). When the infant is suckled, afferent impulses set up in the sensory neurons of the areolus travel to the central nervous system where they promote the release of oxytocin from the posterior pituitary. After entry into the blood stream, the oxytocin is carried to the mammary gland where it interacts with specific receptors on the myoepithelial cells, initiating their contraction and forcing milk from the alveoli into the ducts and sinuses. The passage of milk through the ducts is facilitated by longitudinally arranged myoepithelial processes whose contraction tends to shorten the ducts without constricting them, increasing the milk pressure. This process is called *milk ejection* or *let down*.

The temporal pattern of milk ejection varies markedly from species to species.[96] At one extreme, the rabbit nurses once a day, apparently ejecting about 250 g of milk in 2 to 5 min in response to a single spurt of oxytocin. At the other extreme, the rat nurses her litter, on the average, about half of each hour. Letdown is delayed for at least 15 min after the attachment of the pups to the teats.[97,98] Thereafter, increases in mammary pressure corresponding to oxytocin-induced milk ejection can be measured every 2 to 10 min. Humans fall in between these two extremes. In the woman, ejection can be measured as a rise in pressure sensed with a small catheter placed in a mammary duct or noted subjectively by the mother as a "tingling feeling" in the breast a minute after the onset of suckling.[99–101] The contractions last about 1 min and occur with a frequency of 4 to 10 contractions per 10 min. McNeilly and McNeilly,[102] studying a woman feeding twins, noted that spontaneous letdown occurred even when the infants were not being suckled. At 2 weeks postpartum, letdown was observed at 30 min intervals. The interval increased over the course of lactation being reported to be 4 hr at 4 months postpartum. Letdown was only perceived by the woman when the breasts contained a significant amount of milk suggesting to the authors that the letdown sensation represents ductile distension occurring when milk is transferred from alveoli to ducts.

Mechanisms also exist for preventing unwanted loss of milk from the mammary gland when it is not being suckled.[96] Smooth muscle and elastic fibers form a tight sphincter at the end of the teat in most animals.[72] In addition in rodents, but not in humans,[103] there is evidence for smooth muscle around the larger ducts which may be under sympathetic control.[96] Sympathetic reactions also appear to have a cerebral component which inhibits milk secretion. All these factors probably operate to ensure that effective milk removal is accomplished only by the suckling young under conditions of favorable interaction with the mother.

In addition to its action on the mammary gland, oxytocin causes uterine contractions particularly in the term and postpartum uterus.[99] Women who put their infants to the breast soon after delivery often experience uterine cramping.[104] These oxytocin-induced contractions probably aid in uterine involution. Another reported action of oxytocin comes from recent studies of Pederson and Prange[105] who observed that cerebroventricular injection of oxytocin stimulated maternal behavior in rats. There is as yet no evidence for a similar role of oxytocin in humans.

Oxytocin Synthesis and Release

Oxytocin holds the distinction of being the first naturally-occuring peptide hormone to be synthesized,[106] a feat for which du Vigneaud received the Nobel prize in 1955. More recently, immunostaining techniques have been used to show that oxytocin is synthesized mainly in specialized magnocellular neurons in the supraoptic and paraventricular nucleus of the hypothalamus, separate from the neurons which synthesize vasopressin[107,108] (Fig. 14). Fibers from the paraventricular nucleus course to the level of the supraoptic nucleus where they are joined by fibers from this nucleus as well. Both sets of fibers then travel down the median eminence to the posterior pituitary.

Brownstein *et al.*[109] have made a careful study of the synthesis and processing of oxytocin using pulse labeling in rats to show that the molecule is synthesized as part of a large prohormone with a molecular weight of about 20,000. The prohormone is cleaved within the hypothalamus to smaller molecules with molecular weights (mol. wt.) of 15,000 to 17,000 and packaged in secretory granules. As the granules are transported down the axonal processes of the magnocellular neurons to the posterior pituitary, the prohormone is further cleaved to oxytocin and its binding protein, a neurophysin of about 10,000 mol. wt. (Fig. 14). This process is very rapid; fully formed radioactive oxytocin begins to accumulate in the neurohypophysis $1\frac{1}{2}$ hr after injection of radioactive amino acids into the cerebrospinal fluid. Like the release of neurotransmitters and peptide hormones, oxytocin release involves exocytosis of secretory granules containing both oxytocin and its related neurophysin.[110–112] A burst of electrical activity can be measured in oxytocic neurons 10 to 15 sec prior to milk ejection in rats, providing evidence that nerve depolarization is the ultimate stimulus for oxytocin release.[113]

The neuroendocrine reflex can be conditioned and often occurs in response to the cry of the infant or to other perceptions associated with

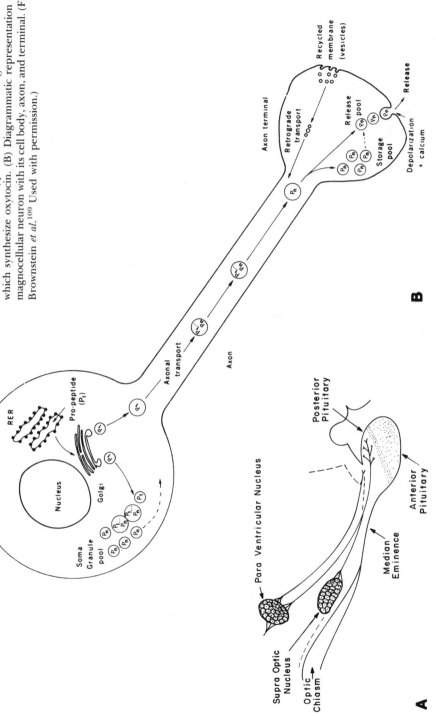

Figure 14. Oxytocin synthesis, processing, and release. (A) Anatomical location in the hypothalamus of the magnocellular neurons which synthesize oxytocin. (B) Diagrammatic representation of a magnocellular neuron with its cell body, axon, and terminal. (From Brownstein *et al.*[109] Used with permission.)

nursing, indicating the involvement of cerebral pathways in the reflex. Newton and Newton[104] showed that painful distraction or emotional reactions interfere with letdown by inhibiting oxytocin release, further evidence of a cerebral component that modulates the reflex.

Although the neural pathways involved in oxytocin release have received intense study, their relation to the emotional and environmental factors which affect letdown is not yet clear. Evidence from the laboratory of Clarke, Lincoln, and their co-workers[114–118] suggests that cholinergic, nicotinic, α-adrenergic, and dopaminergic synapses are all involved at some point in these pathways. For example, intracerebroventricular injection of both norepinephrine and dopamine causes oxytocin release and α-adrenergic blockers, and dopamine antagonists block the milk ejection response[116,119] β-adrenergic agonists and antagonists both block milk ejection.[116,120] All these activities appear to be localized within the central nervous system, since neither the response of the mammary gland to exogenously applied oxytocin nor the release of oxytocin in response to electrical stimulation of the pituitary stalk is affected.

Morphine has been shown to block milk ejection.[121] In a most elegant study in the rat, Clarke and his co-workers[118] showed that morphine did not modify the electrical activity of the hypothalamic oxytocin cells, but did prevent release of oxytocin from the nerve terminals in the posterior pituitary. The authors suggest that β-endorphins of pituitary origin may modulate oxytocin release, acting within the pituitary. Further research will be necessary to determine whether a mechanism of this sort mediates the stress-related inhibition of oxytocin release described above.

Interaction of Oxytocin with Myoepithelial Cells

The processes of the myoepithelial cells lie within the basement membrane of the mammary alveolus and along the interlobular ducts. Autoradiographic studies show that oxytocin binding sites are similarly localized.[122] The nature of the oxytocin receptor has received relatively little study. Sala and Freire[123] observed a correlation between differentiation of myoepithelial cells in the mouse mammary gland during pregnancy (measured by process and myofibril formation) and the development of sensitivity to oxytocin. Soloff *et al.*[124] found a 10-fold increase in the concentration of oxytocin receptors in the mammary gland during pregnancy in rats. The gradual increase in mammary receptor concentration contrasted sharply with the sudden increase in oxytocin receptors in the uterus on the day of parturition. The cellular mechanism of oxytocin action is not understood, although it has been postulated that phosphorylation of myosin is involved in the contraction of the myoepithelial cells.[125] With current advances which allow more pure myoepithelial cells to be obtained for *in vitro* studies,[126] our understanding of the cellular mechanisms of oxytocin action can be expected to increase rapidly.

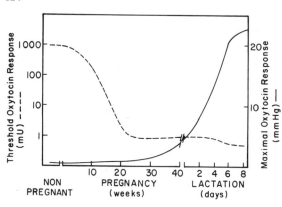

Figure 15. Sensitivity of the human mammary epithelium to oxytocin during pregnancy and lactation. The right-hand scale shows the threshold dose necessary to evoke an increase in intramammary pressure; the left-hand scale shows the maximum intramammary pressure obtained. (Redrawn from data of Caldyro-Barcia.[99])

Some evidence is also available from studies on women. By recording the increase in intramammary pressure obtained with varying doses of oxytocin, administered intravenously, Caldeyro-Barcia[99] was able to show that the amount of oxytocin necessary to evoke threshold responses in women dropped from more than 1000 mU in nonpregnant women to about 1 mU in late pregnancy to 0.5 mU in lactation (Fig. 15). At the same time, the maximum intramammary pressure that could be evoked by oxytocin rose from less than 1mm Hg to 10 mm Hg after 5 days of lactation. These observations suggest that both the sensitivity of the myoepithelial cells to oxytocin and the number of responding units increases during pregnancy. However, *in vitro* studies will be necessary to prove this contention.

The relationship between intramammary pressure and oxytocin release in the nursing woman is currently very confusing. Cobo *et al.*[101] showed that the normal pattern of mammary pressure increases could best be duplicated by intermittent rather than continuous injections of oxytocin. However, more recent measurements of plasma oxytocin levels from two laboratories suggested that plasma oxytocin levels remain elevated during the entire period of suckling.[127,128] These findings were not confirmed in studies using continuous sampling procedures in which the pattern of oxytocin release was found to be pulsatile, highly variable, and poorly correlated with the amount of milk received by the infant.[129] It is to be hoped with the recent development of a new, highly sensitive radioimmunoassay for oxytocin[112] that the relationship between oxytocin release and milk ejection in women will soon be clarified.

Conclusion

Although much practical advice on breast-feeding technique is given in the name of emotional effects on milk letdown, the role of emotional factors in oxytocin release has received little serious study since the pioneering investigations of the Newtons in the 1940s.[104] It is likely that a better understanding of the central neural pathways involved in oxytocin release will eventually allow a more critical examination of emotional and other central factors in lactation failure. In addition, a better understanding of oxytocin–receptor interactions should allow evaluation of the possibility that target organ responsiveness is an element in lactational success in humans.

LACTATION AND POSTPARTUM INFERTILITY

Women are usually infertile for 4 to 8 weeks after the birth of an infant. However, the duration of the infertile period is prolonged by breast-feeding and varies considerably from one society to another, being as short as 2 to 3 months in Western societies[130] and as long as 3 years in the !Kung hunting and gathering society of Botswana and Namibia.[131] Lactational infertility is associated with amenorrhea and clearly results from a suppression of ovarian activity.[132] Most evidence indicates that the high plasma levels of prolactin maintained by frequent suckling are responsible, although it is possible that the suckling stimulus itself may also alter the hypothalamic control of pituitary gonadotropin secretion. The possible mechanisms of prolactin action and the interactions between prolactin levels and gonadotropin secretion are reviewed below. For more detailed information, the reader is referred to two excellent reviews.[130,132]

Relation between Duration of Postpartum Amenorrhea and Breast-Feeding

There is a direct and predictable relationship between the duration of postpartum amenorrhea and the duration of breast-feeding when the phenomenon is considered across a single population.[133,134,135] However, there is a great deal of variation among both societal groups and individual women. Factors which affect the duration of lactational amenorrhea include age at weaning, supplementation with other food, the number of feeds per day or the interfeed interval, maternal age or parity,[130] and maternal nutrition.[135a] The role of the interfeed interval in suppression of the menstrual cycle is receiving increasing attention by investigators. Delvoye and his co-workers[40] were able to show a clear relationship between prolactin levels and the number of feeds per day. With fewer than four feeds per day, prolactin levels fell within the normal range after 6 months of lactation, while with more than 6 feeds per day, mean prolactin levels remained about 50 ng/ml, substantially above the normal range. In the !Kung hunting–gathering people, the average interval between pregnancies was 35 months in bands following the traditional nomadic existence and using no apparent contraceptive measures.[131] In this group, weaning usually occurred about age $3\frac{1}{2}$ and infants were constantly with their mothers for at least the first 2 years. In a careful study of 17 mother–infant pairs ranging from 12 to 139 weeks postpartum, Konner and Worthman[131] showed the mean interval between feeds was 13 minutes during 6 hr of daytime observation, increasing with the age of the infant. By 2 years of age the interfeed interval appeared to be long enough that cyclic hypothalamo–pituitary–ovarian interactions could be restored. Most evidence concerning effects of feeding frequency and supplementation on the duration of postpartum amenorrhea are consistent with an important role for the interfeed interval. However, further studies, particularly on Western women, where feeding schedules vary widely, are needed. In addition, the question of whether the interfeed interval acts through diminished prolactin levels or whether suckling acts directly on pulsatile luteinizing hormone releasing hormone (LHRH) release remains to be resolved.

Reproductive Hormone Levels during Lactation

Rolland *et al.*[136] made twice weekly measurements of the plasma levels of reproductive hormones in a series of breast-feeding women. Figs. 16 and 17 show values obtained from two mothers. In a mother who breast-fed throughout the 90 day period of observation, prolactin declined somewhat over the first 2 weeks, then remained well above basal levels for the next 90 days (Fig. 16). In the first week, high levels of hCG interfered with the luteinizing hormone (LH) assay, thereafter LH levels were below normal. Follicle-stimulating hormone (FSH) rose to levels slightly above normal by the first month. Ovarian steroids remained low. In a second woman who weaned after 60 days (Fig. 17), estradiol levels rose gradually after weaning, and in the subject depicted, ovulation, signified by the peaks of LH and FSH and estrogen, ensued followed by a postovulatory rise in progesterone. These patterns appear to be typical,[137] although the incidence of ovulation prior to the first menses varies from study to study. Because prolactin, like LH and FSH, is secreted in a pulsatile fashion, it is not clear that single samples as obtained in this study are representative. However, Madden and co-workers[88] compared 24-hr secretory patterns of prolactin, LH and FSH in a lactating woman at 26 months postpartum when she was amenorrheic with patterns obtained at 34 months after the onset of menses. Mean prolactin levels were higher (Fig. 10) and LH peaks were attenuated prior to the onset of the menses (not shown).

Although some early studies suggested that basal prolactin levels were near normal in lactating Western women,[24] more recent studies have all shown elevated levels of prolactin, particularly where breast milk forms all or a substantial portion of the infant's diet.[70,137,138] There is a striking effect of nutrition on plasma prolactin levels as shown in Fig. 18. Thus, women in Gambia whose diet is chronically low in calories, showed markedly elevated plasma prolactin levels. When these women received a dietary supplement, calculated to bring their caloric intake to a level similar to that of lactating English women, plasma prolactin levels fell[95a] and the duration of lactational amenorrhea and infertility decreased by 6 months.[135a] These observations strongly suggest that malnutrition suppresses fertility, a response which may be mediated by the plasma prolactin level.

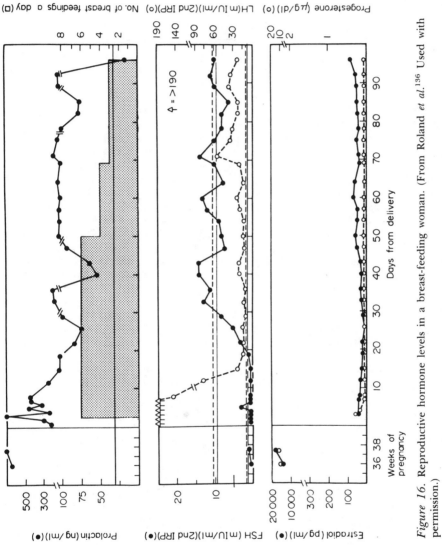

Figure 16. Reproductive hormone levels in a breast-feeding woman. (From Roland *et al.*[136] Used with permission.)

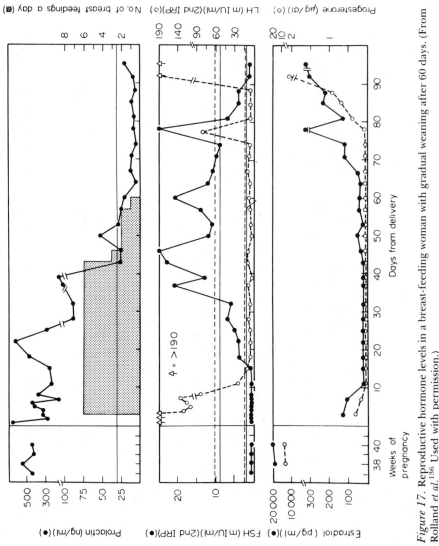

Figure 17. Reproductive hormone levels in a breast-feeding woman with gradual weaning after 60 days. (From Rolland *et al.*[136] Used with permission.)

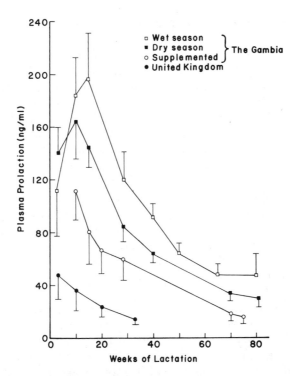

Figure 18. The effect of nutrition on plasma prolactin levels in lactating women. Plasma prolactin levels were measured at intervals in lactating women in the United Kingdom and The Gambia. In the wet season, mean dietary intakes of about 1500 kcal/day were measured whereas during the dry season mean dietary intakes of 1650 kcal/day were observed. In the following season, all women received a dietary supplement which brought the mean intake to 2300 kcal/day, similar to the mean intake of the women in the U.K. Mothers in all groups in The Gambia breast-fed 10 to 16 times per day. (Figure redrawn from Lunn *et al.*[95a] Used with permission.)

The Mechanism of Postpartum Amenorrhea

In the first month postpartum, infertility is probably related to the refractoriness of LH secretion by the pituitary consequent to high levels of progesterone and estrogen during pregnancy.[139] Thereafter, postpartum infertility depends on the duration of lactation and can probably be attributed to high circulating levels of prolactin brought about by suckling,[132] since hyperprolactinemia from other causes is also associated with amenorrhea or menstrual dysfunction in the vast majority of cases.[140] Direct effects of suckling on gonadotrophin secretion cannot be ruled out, however. Lu *et al.*[141] suggested from studies in rats that suckling *per se* rather than high prolactin levels was responsible for suppression of LH and FSH release during the early postpartum period. Similar studies in Rhesus monkeys led Knobil and his colleagues[142,143] to conclude that lactational amenorrhea in the rhesus monkey cannot be accounted for by high circulating levels of prolactin.

Nonetheless, there is sufficient evidence suggesting that high levels of prolactin suppress reproductive function so that possible mechanisms of its action need to be considered. Prolactin appears to act at three levels: (1) suppression of pulsatile LH secretion, (2) suppression of the positive feedback effects of estrogen on the midcycle rise of pituitary gonadotropin secretion, and (3) direct interference with ovarian steroid production. The attenuated levels of LH secretion in lactation already described are most likely due to inhibition of LHRH secretion since exogenous LHRH produces normal rises in FSH and LH after the first two weeks postpartum.[144]

In normally cycling women, estrogen injection induces a 24-hr depression of plasma LH and FSH levels followed by a marked increase in these hormones presumably as part of the positive feedback response to estrogen at ovulation. Baird and colleagues[145] showed that this positive response was missing in lactating women 30 and 100 days postpartum and that the inhibitory phase was prolonged. A similar effect has been observed in pathological hyperprolactinemia[146] and nursing rhesus monkeys,[143] suggesting that prolactin interferes with ovulation by suppressing the ovulatory surge of LH and FSH.

Direct effects of prolactin on steroid synthesis by granulosa cells have been difficult to interpret because prolactin appears, at least in some species, to have both an obligatory permissive role on progesterone secretion and an inhibitory effect on granulosa cell function.[132] Nevertheless, there is mounting evidence that direct inhibitory effects of prolactin do play a role in postpartum amenorrhea. McNatty *et al*,[147] showed that prolactin levels, equivalent to those seen in lactation, inhibited progesterone formation by cultured human granulosa cells. Levels similar to those seen in cycling women (<20 ng/ml) had no effect. High serum levels of prolactin (>100 ng/ml) *in vivo* were found to be associated with decreased FSH levels and a diminished granulosa cell population in ovarian follicles during the follicular phase.[148] Recently, Dorrington and Gore-Langton[149] reported that prolactin interfered with the FSH-stimulated ability of rat ovarian granulosa cells to aromatize testosterone to estrogen suggesting that prolactin directly interferes with ovarian steroidogenesis. On the other hand, there is considerable *in vivo* evidence that the ovaries of breastfeeding women can respond to exogenously administered gonadotropin with steroid hormone secretion.[132] This contradictory evidence suggests that further work is necessary to clarify the role of direct ovarian suppression by prolactin in postpartum amenorrhea.

Conclusion

It is tempting to speculate that prolonged infertility during lactation may be nature's way of assuring a birth interval between infants which is attuned to the food supply. In societies where nutrient supplies are marginal, prolactin levels are increased with the consequence of prolonging postpartum infertility and increasing the birth interval. When food supplies are less restricted, prolactin levels fall, supplementation of the infant's diet may begin

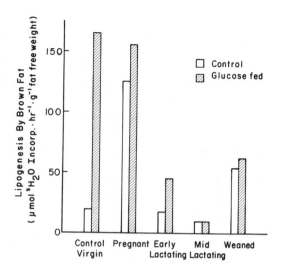

Figure 19. Effect of pregnancy and lactation on the rate of lipogenesis in body adipose tissue (brown fat) in the rat. (Plot of data from Agius and Williamson.[152])

at an earlier age and fertility may increase. As factors other than local food supply become important in limiting family size, contraceptive methods other than lactational amenorrhea must be used. However, current methods are not well adapted for all populations and methodologies based on the mechanisms of lactational amenorrhea should be explored. For this reason, it is of importance to find answers to questions such as: What is the relationship between feeding interval and the duration of postpartum amenorrhea? Are both prolactin levels and suckling *per se* involved in inhibition of ovarian function during lactational amenorrhea? What is the detailed mechanism of action of prolactin? Can drugs which mimic the action of prolactin be developed for contraceptive purposes? An understanding of the answers to these and related questions has profound implications for family planning in both Western and developing societies.

INTERACTIONS BETWEEN FOOD INTAKE AND LACTATION

Two sources of substrate are available for synthesis of milk components—body stores (particularly adipose tissues) and diet. The interactions between these sources and milk production are now beginning to receive serious study in a number of laboratories.

During pregnancy, there is a tendency toward an increase in adipose tissue mass in both women[150] and animals.[151] During lactation, these stores are drawn upon to provide substrate for milk synthesis. This point is well illustrated by experiments in rats in which synthesis of brown fat was measured as a function of the stage of reproduction[152] (Fig. 19). Fatty acid synthesis in adipose tissue was increased during pregnancy and decreased during lactation. The response to a glucose load, normally an increase in lipid synthesis, was strikingly blunted in lactating rats. This experiment demonstrates the shunting of nutrients from adipose tissue to the mammary gland during lactation. Data obtained by Flint and co-workers[153] suggest that a decrease in both insulin receptors and lipoprotein lipase levels in adipose tissues after parturition may be responsible.

It has become clear from studies in developing nations that severe caloric deficiencies during lactation can lead to a depression in milk output in women[150,154] with less profound changes in milk composition. However, aside from the effects of the lipid composition of the diet, discussed in detail in the previous chapter, little is known about the mechanisms of dietary effects on milk production in the human. Studies in rats and goats support the existence of a close regulatory link between nutrient intake and milk production. Food deprivation has three types of documented effect on the mammary gland: (1) Acute and chronic malnutrition reduce the volume of milk secreted presumably by reducing protein and lactose synthesis.[155,156] (2) Acute malnutrition decreases fatty acid synthesis by the mammary gland leading to utilization of body fat stores in the synthesis of triglycerides. This effect has received extensive study, in both man and animals (see Chapter 3). (3) Malnutrition of pregnant rats markedly reduced growth of mammary parenchymal tissue.[157] The effect of such growth reduction on subsequent lactational performance has not been studied, nor is it known whether human malnutrition affects breast development during pregnancy. For this reason, effects of nutrition on mammary growth cannot be further discussed at this time. Studies of the biochemical and hormonal mechanisms by which malnutrition may affect milk volume and fat content are summarized in Chapters 3 and 5.

A FORWARD LOOK

Tremendous progress has been made in the last decade in understanding the multiple hormonal interactions that control the development and function of the mammary gland. Three factors have largely been responsible for this progress. In humans, a major impetus has been the increasing popularity of breast-feeding which has removed many of the earlier sexual taboos associated with studies of mammary gland biology. Increased knowledge about the hormonal mechanisms involved is the result of the development of sensitive radioimmunoassays which have allowed careful measurement of plasma hormone levels throughout pregnancy and lactation. Finally, in the last few years, cellular systems and probes of molecular function have become available that are beginning to allow insight into the molecular mechanisms of hormonal control. The state of our knowledge of these mechanisms at the cellular level is discussed in greater detail in the next chapter.

Many problems remain. Among the most important is the nature of the factors that regulate mammary growth and differentiation, important because of its implications for control of breast cancer. Of potential importance in improving breast-feeding performance, particularly in the Western world, are the factors which control postpartum maturation of the mammary epithelium, the mechanisms by which milk production is regulated to meet the demands of the infant and the pathways through which emotional factors alter oxytocin release. Better knowledge of the mechanisms by which lactation influences fertility may lead to improved contraceptive practice. Finally, an understanding of the interactions between nutrition and milk production may have important implications in third world countries where malnutrition is a continuing problem. It is to be hoped that resources for the study of these problems will continue to be available so that the search for solutions will not be unduly prolonged.

REFERENCES

1. Martin, R. H., Glass, M. R., Chapman, C., Wilson, G. D., and Woods, K. L., 1980, Human α-lactalbumin and hormonal factors in pregnancy and lactation, *Clin. Endocrinol.* **13**:223–230.
2. Kulski, J. K. and Hartmann, P. E., 1981, Changes in human milk composition during the initiation of lactation, *Aust. J. Exp. Biol. Med. Sci.* **59**:101–114.
3. Cowie, A. T., Forsyth, I. A., and Hart, I. C., 1980, *Hormonal Control of Lactation.*, Springer-Verlag, Berlin.
4. Topper, Y. J., and Freeman, C. S., 1980, Multiple hormone interactions in the developmental biology of the mammary gland, *Physiol. Rev.* **60**:1049–1106.
5. Rosen, J. M., Matusik, R. J., Richards, D. A., Gupta, P., and Rodgers, J. R., 1980, Multihormonal regulation of casein gene expression at the transcriptional and post transcriptional levels in the mammary gland, *Recent Prog. Horm. Res.* **36**:157–193.
6. Kratochwil, K., 1975, Experimental analysis of the prenatal development of the mammary gland, *Mod. Probl. Paediatr.* **15**:1–15.
7. Anderson, R. R., 1978, Embryonic and fetal development of the mammary apparatus, in: *Lactation*, Volume IV (B. L. Larson, ed.), Academic Press, New York, pp. 3–40.
8. Cunha, G. R., Shannon, J. M., Neubaeur, B. L., Sawyer, L. M., Fujii, H., Taguchi, O., and Chung, L. W. K., 1981, Mesenchymal-epithelial interactions in sex differentiation, *Human genetik* **58**:68–77.
9. Aubert, M. L., Sizonenko, P. C., Kaplan, S. L., and Grumbach, M. M., 1977, The ontogenesis of human prolactin from fetal life to puberty, in: *Prolactin and Human Reproduction.* (P. G. Crosignani and C. Robyn, eds.), Academic Press, London, pp. 9–20.
10. Short, R. V. and Drife, J. O., 1977, The aetiology of mammary cancer in man and animals: *Symp. Zool. Soc. London* **41**:211–230.
11. Lovejoy, C. O., 1981, The origin of man, *Science* **211**:341–350.
12. Cowie, A. T., 1978, Backward glances, in: *Physiology of Mammary Glands* (A. Yokoyama, H. Mizuno, and H. Nagasawa, eds.), University Park Press, Baltimore, pp. 43–56.
13. Tonelli, Q. J. and Sorof, S., 1980, Epidermal growth factor requirement for development of cultured mammary gland, *Nature* **285**:250–252.
14. Yang, J., Guzman, R., Richards, J., Imagawa, W., McCormick, K., and Nandi, S., 1980, Growth factor and cyclic-nucleotide induced proliferation of normal and malignant mammary epithelial cells in primary culture, *Endocrinology* **107**:35–41.
15. Ptashne, K., Hsueh, H. W., and Stockdale, F. E., 1979, Partial purification and characterization of mammary stimulating factor, a protein which promotes proliferation of mammary epithelium, *Biochemistry* **18**:3533–3539.
16. Sirbasku, D. A., 1978, Estrogen induction of growth factors specific for hormone-responsive mammary, pituitary, and kidney tumor cells, *Proc. Natl. Acad. Sci.* **75**:3786–3790.
17. Cowie, A. T., Tindal, J. S., and Yokoyama, A., 1966, The induction of mammary growth in the hypophysectomized goat, *J. Endocrinol.* **34**:185–195.

18. Stoudemire, G. A., Stumpf, W. E., and Sar, M., 1975, Synergism between prolactin and ovarian hormones on DNA synthesis in rat mammary gland, *Proc. Exp. Biol. Med.* **149:**189–192.

19. Talwalker, P. K. and Meites, J., 1961, Mammary lobulo-alveolar growth induced by anterior pituitary hormones in adreno-ovariectomized–hypophysectomized rats, *Proc. Soc. Exp. Biol. Med.* **107:**880–883.

20. Gaede, P., Trolle, D., and Pedersen, H., 1978, Extremely low placental lactogen hormone (hPL) values in an otherwise uneventful pregnancy preceding delivery of a normal baby, *Acta Obstet. Gynecol. Scand.* **57:**203–209.

21. Nielson, P. V., Pederson, H., and Kampmann, E-M., 1979, Absence of placental lactogen in an otherwise uneventful pregnancy, *Am. J. Obstet. Gynecol.* **135:**322–330.

22. Franks, S., Kiwi, R., and Nabarro, J. D. N., 1977, Pregnancy and lactation after pituitary surgery, *Br. Med. J.* **1:**882.

23. Kelly, P. A., Tsushima, T., Shiu, R. P. C., and Friesen, H. G., 1976, Lactogenic and growth hormone-like activities in pregnancy determined by radioreceptor assays, *Endocrinology* **99:**765–774.

24. Varma, S. K., Sonksen, P. H., Varma, K., Soeldner, J. S., Selenkow, H. A., and Emerson, K., 1971, Measurement of human growth hormone in pregnancy and correlation with human placental lactogen, *J. Clin. Endocrinol. Metab.* **32:**328–332.

25. Rimoin, D. L., Holzman, G. B., Merimee, T. J., Rabinowitz, D., Barnes, A. C., Tyson, J. E. A., and McKusick, V. A., 1968, Lactation in the absence of human growth hormone, *J. Clin. Endocrinol. Metab.* **28:**1183–1188.

26. France, J. T., Seddon, R. J., and Liggins, G. C., 1973, A study of a pregnancy with low estrogen production due to placental sulfatase deficiency, *J. Clin. Endocrinol. Metab.* **36:**19.

27. Gip, H., Bailer, P., and Korte, K., 1979, Serumprolaktin und Laktation beim Plazentaren Sulfatasemengel, *Z. Geburtsh. Perinat.* **183:**234–235.

28. Terry, P. M., Banerjee, M. R., and Lui, R. M., 1977, Hormone-inducible casein messenger RNA in a serum-free organ culture of a whole mammary gland, *Proc. Natl. Acad. Sci. USA* **74:**2441–2445.

29. Brown, R. E., 1978, Relactation with reference to application in developing countries, *Clin. Pediatr.* **17:**333–337.

30. Rosner, M. D., 1979, Galactorrhea in men, *JAMA* **1:**1327.

31. Cowie, A. T., Knaggs, J. S., Tindal, J. S., and Turvey, A., 1968, The milking stimulus and mammary growth in the goat, *J. Endocrinol.* **40:**243–252.

32. Smith, K. L. and Schanbacher, F. L., 1973, Hormone induced lactation in the bovine. I. Lactational performance following ingestion of 17β-oestradiol and progesterone, *J. Dairy Sci.* **56:**738–743.

33. Hart, I. C. and Morant, S. V., 1980, Roles of prolactin, growth hormone, insulin and thyroxine in steroid-induced lactation in goats, *J. Endocrinol.* **84:**343–351.

34. Fleet, I. R., Goode, J. A., Hamon, M. H., Laurie, M. S., Linzell, J. L., and Peaker, M., 1975, Secretory activity of goat mammary glands during pregnancy and the onset of lactation, *J. Physiol.* **251:**763–773.

35. Kuhn, N. J., 1977, Lactogenesis: The search for trigger mechanisms in different species, *Symp. Zool. Soc. London* **41:**165–192.

36. Hartmann, P. E., 1973, Changes in the composition and yield of the mammary secretion of cows during the initiation of lactation, *J. Endocrinol.* **59:**231–247.

37. Peaker, M., and Linzell, J. L., 1975, Citrate in milk: A harbinger of lactogenesis, *Nature* **253:**464.

38. Vorherr, H., 1978, Human lactation and breast feeding, in: *Lactation*, Volume IV (B. L. Larson, ed.), Academic Press, New York, p. 181–280.

39. Weiss, G., Facog, E. M. O., Hochman, J. A., Goldsmith, L. T., Rifkin, I., and Steinetz, B. G., 1977, Secretion of progesterone and relaxin by the human corpus luteum at midpregnancy and at term, *Obstet. Gynecol.* **50:**679–681.

40. Delvoye, P., Demaegd, M., Delogne-Desnoeck, J., and Robyn, C., 1977, The influence of the frequency of nursing and of previous lactation experience on serum prolactin in lactating mothers, *J. Biosocial Sci.* **9:**447–451.

41. Hiba, J., Del Pozo, E., Genazzani, A., Pusterla, E., Lancranjan, I., Sidiropoulos, D., and Gunti, J., 1977, Hormonal mechanism of milk secretion in the newborn, *J. Clin. Endocrinol. Metab.* **44:**973–976.
42. Tobon, H. and Salazar, H., 1974, Ultrastructure of the human mammary gland. I. Development of the fetal gland throughout gestation, *J. Clin. Endocrinol. Metab.* **39:**443–456.
43. Halban, J., 1905, Die innere Secretion von Ovarium und Placenta und ihre Bedeutung für die Function der Milchdrüse, *Arch. Gynaekol.* **75:**353–441.
44. Neifert, M. R., McDonough, S. L., and Neville, M. C., 1981, Failure of lactogenesis associated with placental retention, *Am. J. Obstet. Gynecol.* **140:**477–478.
45. Martin, C. E., Hartmann, P. E., and Gooneratne, A., 1979, Progesterone and corticosteroids in the initiation of lactation in the sow, *Aust. J. Biol.* **31:**517–525.
46. Kuhn, N. J., 1969, Progesterone withdrawal as the lactogenic trigger in the rat, *J. Endocrinol.* **44:**39–54.
47. Martyn, P. and Hansen, I. A., 1981, Initiation of lipogenic enzyme activities in rat mammary glands, *Biochem. J.* **198:**187–192.
48. Hartmann, P. E., Trevethan, P., and Shelton, J. N., 1973, Progesterone and oestrogen and the initiation of lactation in ewes, *J. Endocrinol.* **59:**249–259.
49. Haslam, S. Z. and Shyamala, G., 1979, Effect of oestradiol on progesterone receptors in normal mammary glands and its relationship with lactation, *Biochem. J.* **182:**127–131.
50. Bruce, J. O. and Ramirez, V. D., 1970, Site of action of the inhibitory effect of estrogen upon lactation, *Neuroendocrinology* **6:**19–29.
51. Turkington, R. W., Majumder, G. C., Kadohama, N., MacIndoe, J. H., and Frantz, W. L., 1973, Hormonal regulation of gene expression in mammary cells, *Recent Prog. Horm. Res.* **29:**417–455.
52. Rosen, J. M., O'Neal, D. L., McHugh, J. E., and Comstock, J. P., 1978, Progesterone-mediated inhibition of casein mRNA and polysomal casein synthesis in the rat mammary gland during pregnancy, *Biochemistry* **17:**290–297.
53. Brun del Re, R., del Pozo, E., de Grandi, P., Friesen, H., Hinselman, M., and Wyss, H., 1973, Prolactin inhibition and suppression of puerperal lactation by Br-ergo cryptine (CB154). A comparison with estrogen *Obstet. Gynecol.* **41:**884–890.
54. Akers, R. M., Bauman, D. E., Capuco, A. V., Goodman, G. T., and Tucker, H. A., 1981, Prolactin regulation of milk secretion and biochemical differentiation of mammary epithelial cells in periparturient cows, *Endocrinology* **109:**23–30.
55. Rigg, L. A. and Yen, S. S. C., 1977, Multiphasic prolactin secretion during parturition in human subjects, *Am. J. Obstet. Gynecol.* **128:**215.
56. Chadwick, A., 1971, Lactogenesis in pseudopregnant rabbits treated with adrenocorticotrophin and adrenal corticosteroids, *J. Endocrinol.* **49:**1–8.
57. Carr, B. R., Parker, C. R., Jr. Madden, J. D., MacDonald, P. C., and Porter, J. C., 1981, Maternal plasma adrenocorticotropin and cortisol relationships throughout human pregnancy, *Am. J. Obstet. Gynecol.* **139:**416–498.
58. Lederman, R. P., Lederman, E., Work, B. A., and McCann, D. S., 1978, The relationship of maternal anxiety, plasma catecholamines, and plasma cortisol to progress in labor, *Am. J. Obstet. Gynecol.* **132:**495–500.
59. Maltau, J. M., Eilsen, O. V., and Stokke, K. T., 1979, Effect of stress during labor on the concentration of cortisol and estriol in maternal plasma, *Am. J. Obstet. Gynecol.* **134:**681–684.
60. Kyriakou, S. Y. and Kuhn, N. J., 1973, Lactogenesis in the diabetic rat, *J. Endocrinol.* **59:**199–200.
61. Leader, D. P., 1975, Carbohydrate metabolism, placental lactogen and the control of the initiation of lactation, *Biochem. Soc. Trans.* **3:**257–258.
62. Turkington, R. W. and Topper, Y. J., 1966, Stimulation of casein synthesis and histological development of mammary gland by human placental lactogen *in vitro, Endocrinology* **79:**175–181.

63. Peters, J. M., van Marle, J., and Ariens, A. Th., 1979, Hormonal effects on rat mammary gland *in vitro*, *Acta Endocrinol.* **92**(suppl. 228):1–190.
64. Reddy, S. and Watkins, W. B., 1975, Uptake of ^{125}I-labelled human placental lactogen and human placental lactogen by the tissues of normal and lactating rats, *J. Endocrinol.* **65**:183–194.
65. Waters, M. J., McNeilly, A. S., Ohgo, S., and Friesen, H. G., 1980, Prolactin receptor content of rabbit milk, *Endocrinology* **107**:816–821.
66. Grosvenor, C. E. and Mena, F., 1974, Neural and hormonal control of milk secretion and milk ejection, in: *Lactation*, Volume 1 (B. L. Larsen and V. R. Smith, eds.), Academic Press, New York, p. 227–273.
67. Aono, T., Shioji, T., Shoda, T., and Kurachi, K., 1977, The initiation of human lactation and prolactin response to suckling, *J. Clin. Endocrinol. Metab.* **44**:1101–1106.
68. Kauppila, A., Kivinen, S., and Ylikorkala, O., 1981, Metoclopramide increases prolactin release and milk secretion in puerperium without stimulating the secretion of thyrotropin and thyroid hormones, *J. Clin. Endocrinol. Metab.* **52**:436–439.
69. Howie, P. W., McNeilly, A. S., McArdle, T., Smart, L., and Houston, M., 1980 The relationship between suckling induced prolactin response and lactogenesis, *J. Clin. Endocrinol. Metab.* **50**:670–673.
70. Gross, B. A. and Eastman, C. J., 1979, Prolactin secretion during prolonged lactational amenorrhoea, *Aust. N. Z. J. Obstet. Gynaecol.* **19**:95–99.
71. Lascelles, A. K. and Lee, C. S., 1978, Involution of the mammary gland, in: *Lactation* Volume IV, (B. L. Larson, ed.), Academic Press, New York, p. 115–177.
72. Dabelow, A., 1957, Die Milchdrüse, in: *Mikroskopischen Anatomie des Menschen*, Volume III-3 (W. V. Möllendorff, ed.), Springer-Verlag, Berlin, p. 277–458.
73. Fleet, I. R. and Peaker, M., 1978, Mammary function and its control at the cessation of lactation in the goat, *J. Physiol.* **279**:491–507.
74. Hanwell, A. and Linzell, J. L., 1973, The effects of engorgement with milk and of suckling on mammary blood flow in the rat, *J. Physiol.* **233**:111–125.
75. Helminen, H. J. and Ericson, J. L. E., 1968, Studies on mammary gland involution. II. Ultrastructural evidence for auto- and heterophagocytosis, *J. Ultrastruct. Res.* **25**:214–227.
76. Jones, E. A., 1967, Changes in the enzyme pattern of the mammary gland of the lactating rat after hypophysectomy and weaning, *Biochem. J.* **103**:420–427.
77. Jones, E. A., 1968, The relationship between milk accumulation and enzyme activities in the involuting rat mammary gland, *Biochim. Biophys. Acta* **177**:158–160.
78. Levy, R. H., 1963, The effects of weaning and milk on fatty acid synthesis, *Fed. Proc.* **22**:363.
79. Hamosh, M., Clary, T. R., Chernick, S. S., and Scow, R. O., 1970, Lipoprotein lipase activity of adipose and mammary tissue and plasma triglyceride in pregnant and lactating rats, *Biochim. Biophys. Acta* **210**:473–482.
80. Greenbaum, A. L., Slater, T. F., and Wang, D. Y., 1965, Lysosomal enzyme changes in enforced mammary-gland involution, *Biochem. J.* **97**:518–522.
81. Teyssot, B. and Houdebine, L-M, 1981, Role of progesterone and glucocorticoids in the transcription of the β-casein and 28-S ribosomal genes in the rabbit mammary gland, *Eur. J. Biochem.* **114**:597–608.
82. Hartmann, P. E. and Kulski, J. K., 1978, Changes in the composition of the mammary secretion of women after abrupt termination of breast feeding, *J. Physiol.* **275**:1–11.
83. Peaker, M., 1980, The effect of raised intramammary pressure on mammary function in the goat in relation to the cessation of lactation, *J. Physiol.* **301**:415–428.
84. Emerman, J. T. and Pitelka, D. R., 1977, Maintenance and induction of morphological differentiation in dissociated mammary epithelium on floating collagen membranes, *In Vitro* **13**:316–328.
84a. Shannon, J. M., and Pitelka, D. R., 1981, Influence of cell shape on the induction of functional differentiation in mouse mammary cells *in vitro*, *In Vitro* **17**:1016–1025.
85. Linzell, J. L. and Peaker, M., 1971, The effects of milk removal and oxytocin on milk secretion in the goat, *J. Physiol.* **216**:717–734.

86. Hwang, P., Guyda, H. and Friesen, H., 1971, A radioimmunoassay for human prolactin, *Proc. Natl. Acad. Sci. U.S.A.* **68**:1902–1906.
87. Van Cauten, E., L'Hermite, M., Copinschi, G., Refetoff, S., Desir, D., and Robyn, C., 1981, Quantitative analysis of spontaneous variations of plasma prolactin in normal man, *Am. J. Physiol.* **241**:E355–E363.
88. Madden J. D., Boyar, R. M., MacDonald, P. C., and Porter, J. C., 1978, Analysis of secretory patterns of prolactin and gonadotropins during twenty-four hours in a lactating woman before and after resumption of menses, *Am. J. Obstet. Gynecol.* **132**:436–441.
89. Frantz, A. G., 1979, Rhythms in prolactin secretion, in: *Endocrine Rhythms* (D. T. Krieger, ed.), Raven Press, New York pp. 175–185.
90. Del Pozo, E., Hiba, J., Lancranjan, I., and Kunzig, H. J., 1977, Prolactin measurements throughout the life cycle: Endocrine correlations, in: *Prolactin and Human Reproduction*, (P. G. Crosignani and C. Robyn, eds.), Academic Press, London, pp. 61–69.
91. Tyson, J. E., 1977, Nursing and prolactin secretion: Principal determinants in the mediation of puerperal infertility, in: *Prolactin and Human Reproduction*, (P. G. Crosignani and C. Robyn, eds.), Academic Press, New York pp. 97–108.
92. Herman, V., Kalk, W. J., de Moor, N. G., and Levin, J., 1981, Serum prolactin after chest wall surgery: Elevated levels after mastectomy, *J. Clin. Endocrinol. Metab.* **52**:148–151.
93. Tyson, J. E., Hwang, P., Guyda, H., and Friesen, H. G., 1972, Studies of prolactin secretion in human pregnancy, *Am. J. Obstet. Gynecol.* **113**:14–20.
94. Gross, B. A., Eastman, C. J., Bowen, K. M., and McEldruff, A., 1979, Integrated concentrations of prolactin in breast-feeding mothers, *Aust. N. Z. J. Obstet. Gynecol.* **19**:150–153.
95. Gross, B. A., Haynes, S. P., Eastman, C. J., Balderama-Guzmann, V., and del Castillo, L. V., 1980, A cross cultural comparison of prolactin in long term lactation, *Progress Reprod. Biol.* **6**:179–186.
95a. Lunn, P. G., Austin, S., Prentice, A. M., and Whitehead, R. G., 1980, The influence of maternal diet on plasma prolactin levels during lactation, *Lancet*, **1**:623–655.
96. Cross, B. A., 1977, Comparative physiology of milk removal, *Symp. Zool. Soc. London* **41**:193–210.
97. Grosvenor, C. E. and Mena, F., 1979, Alterations in the oxytocin induced intramammary pressure response after mechanical stimulation of the mammary gland of the anesthetized rat, *Endocrinology* **104**:443–447.
98. Voloschin, L. M. and Tramezzani, J. H., 1979, Milk ejection reflex linked to slow wave sleep in nursing rats, *Endocrinology* **105**:1202–1207.
99. Caldeyro-Barcia, R., 1969, Milk ejection in women, in: *Lactogenesis, the Initiation of Milk Secretion at Parturition* (M. Reynolds and S. J. Folley, eds.), University of Pennsylvania Press, Philadelphia, pp. 229–243.
100. Fox, C. A. and Knaggs, G. S., 1969, Milk ejection activity (oxytocin) in peripheral venous blood in man during lactation and in association with coitus, *J. Endocrinol.* **45**:145–146.
101. Cobo, E., DeBernal, M., Gaitan, E., and Quintero, C. A., 1967, Neurohypophyseal hormone release in the human. II. Experimental study during lactation, *Am. J. Obstet. Gynecol.* **97**:519–529.
102. McNeilly, A. S. and McNeilly, J. R., 1978, Spontaneous milk ejection during lactation and its possible relevance to success of breast feeding, *Br. Med. J.* **2**:466–468.
103. Richardson, K. C., 1949, Contracile tissue in the mammary gland, with special reference to the myoepithelium in the goat, *Proc. R. Soc. London, Ser. B.* **136**:30–45.
104. Newton, M. and Newton, N. R., 1948, The let-down reflex in human lactation, *J. Pediatr.* **33**:698–704.
105. Pederson, C. A. and Prange, A. J., 1979, Induction of maternal behavior in virgin rats after intracerebroventricular administration of oxytocin, *Proc. Natl. Acad. Sci.* **76**:6661–6665.
106. du Vigneaud, V., Ressler, C., Swan, J. M., Roberts, C. W., and Katsoyannis, P. G., 1954, The synthesis of oxytocin, *J. Am. Chem. Soc.* **76**:3115–3121.

107. Zimmerman, E. A. and Defendini, R., 1977, Hypothalamic pathways containing oxytocin, vasopressin and associated neurophysins, in: *International Conference on the Neurohypophysis* (A. M. Moses and L. Share, eds.), Karger, New York, pp. 22–29.

108. Morris, J. F., Sokol, H. W., and Valtin, H., 1977, One neuron–one hormone. Recent evidence from Brattleboro rats in: *International Conference on the Neurohypophysis* (A. M. Moses and L. Share, eds.), Karger, New York, pp. 58–66.

109. Brownstein, M. J., Russell, J. T., and Gainer, H. T., 1980, Synthesis, transport and release of posterior pituitary hormones, *Science* **207:**373–378.

110. Theodosin, D. T. and Dreifuss, J. J., 1977, Ultrastructural evidence for exo-endocytosis in the neurohypophysis, in: *International Conference on the Neurohypophysis* (A. M. Moses and L. Share, eds.), Karger, New York, pp. 88–94.

111. Robinson, A. G., Seif, S. M., Huellmantel, A. B., Davis, B. B., and Zenser, T. V., 1977, Physiologic and pathologic secretion of neurphysins in the rat, in: *International Conference on the Neurohypophysis* (A. M. Moses and L. Share, eds.), Karger, New York, pp. 136–143.

112. Amico, J. A., Seif, S. M., and Robinson, A. G., 1981, Oxytocin in human plasma: Correlation with neurophysin and stimulation with estrogen, *J. Clin. Endocrinol. Metab.* **52:**988–993.

113. Poulain, D. A., Wakerley, J. B., and Dyball, R. E. J., 1977, Electrophysiological differentiation of oxytocin and vasopressin-secreting neurons, *Proc. R. Soc. London, Ser. B,* **196:**367–384.

114. Lincoln, D. W., Clarke, G., Mason, C. A., and Dreifuss, J. J., 1977, Physiological mechanisms determining the release of oxytocin in milk ejection and labour, in: *International Conference on the Neurohypophysis* (A. M. Moses and L. Share, eds.), Karger, New York, pp. 101–109.

115. Clarke, G., Fall, C. H. D., Lincoln, D. W., and Merrick, L. P., 1978, Effects of cholinoceptor antagonists on the suckling induced and experimentally evoked release of oxytocin, *Br. J. Pharmacol.* **63:**519–527.

116. Clarke, G. and Merrick, L. P., 1978, A tentative identification of the synaptic transmitters involved in the neural regulation of oxytocin release, *J. Physiol.* **277:**19–20.

117. Clarke, G., Lincoln, D. W., and Merrick, L. P., 1979, Dopaminergic control of oxytocin release in lactating rats, *J. Endocrinol.* **83:**409–420.

118. Clarke, G., Wood., P., Merrick, L., and Lincoln, D. W., 1979, Opiate inhibition of peptide release from the neurohumoral terminals of hypothalamic neurons, *Nature* **282:**746–748.

119. Barowicz, T., 1978, Inhibitory effect of adrenaline on oxytocin release in the ewe during the milk-ejection reflex, *J. Dairy Res.* **46:**41–46.

120. Moos, F. and Richard, P., 1979, The inhibitory role of β-adrenergic receptors in oxytocin release during suckling, *Brain Res.* **169:**595–599.

121. Haldar, J. and Sawyer, W. H., 1978, Inhibition of oxytocin release by morphine and its analogs, *Proc. Soc. Exp. Biol. Med.* **157:**476–180.

122. Soloff, M. S., Rees, H. D., Sar, M., and Stumpf, W. E., 1975, Autoradiographic localization of radioactivity from [^{3}H]-oxytocin in the rat mammary gland and oviduct, *Endocrinology* **96:**1475–1477.

123. Sala, N. L. and Freire, F., 1974, Relationship between ultrastructure and response to oxytocin of the mammary myoepithelium throughout pregnancy and lactation: Effect of estrogen and progesterone, *Biol. Reprod.* **11:**7–17.

124. Soloff, M. S., Alexandrova, M., and Fernstrom, M. J., 1979, Oxytocin receptors: Triggers for parturition and lactation?, *Science* **204:**1313–1315.

125. Bremel, R. D. and Shaw, M. E., 1978, Actomyosin from mammary myoepithelial cells and phosphorylation by myosin light chain kinase, *J. Dairy Sci.* **61:**1561–1566.

126. Soloff, M. S., Chakraborty, J., Sadhukan, P., Wieder, M., Fernstrom, M. A., and Sweet, P., 1980, Purification and characterization of mammary myoepithelial and secretory cells from the lactating rat, *Endocrinology* **106:**887–897.

127. Weitzman, R. E., Leake, R. D., Rubin, R. T., and Fisher, D. A., 1980, The effect of nursing on neurohypophyseal hormones and prolactin secretion in human subjects, *J. Clin. Endocrinol. Metab.* **51:**836–839.

128. Dawood, M. Y., Khan-Dawood, F. S., Wahi, R. S., and Fuchs, F., 1981, Oxytocin release and plasma anterior pituitary and gonadal hormones in women during lactation, *J. Clin. Endocrinol. Metab.* **52:**678–683.

129. Lucas, A., Drewett, R. B., and Mitchell, M. D., 1980, Breast-feeding and plasma oxytocin concentrations, *Br. Med. J.* **12**:834–835.
130. Simpson-Herbert, M. and Huffman, S. L., 1981, The contraceptive effect of breast-feeding, *Stud. Fam. Plann.* **12**:125–133.
131. Konner, M. and Worthman, C., 1980, Nursing frequency, gonadal function, and birth spacing among !Kung hunter-gatherers, *Science* **207**:788–791.
132. McNeilly, A. S., 1979, Effects of lactation on fertility, *Br. Med. Bull.* **35**:151–154.
133. van Ginneken, J. K., 1977, The chance of conception during lactation, *J. Biosocial Sci.* **4**(Suppl.):41–54.
134. Billewicz, W. Z., 1979, The timing of post-partum menstruation and breast feeding: A simple formula. *J. Biosocial Sci.* **11**:141–151.
135. Bongaarts, J., 1980, Does malnutrition affect fecundity? A summary of evidence, *Science* **208**:564–569.
135a. Lunn, P. G., Watkinson, M., Prentice, A. M., Morrell, P., Austin, S., and Whitehead, R. G., 1981, Maternal nutrition and lactational amenorrhea, *Lancet* **1**:1428–1429.
136. Rolland, R., Lequin, R. M., Schellekens, L. A., and De Jong, F. H., 1975, The role of prolactin in the restoration of ovarian function during the early post-partum period in the human female, *Clin. Endocriol.* **4**:15–25.
137. Delvoye, P., Demaegd, M., Uwayitu-Nyampeta, and Robyn, C., 1978, Serum prolactin, gonadotropins, and estradiol in menstruating and amenorrheic mothers during two years' lactation, *Am. J. Obstet. Gynecol.* **130**:635–639.
138. Tyson, J. E., Carter, J. N., Andreassen, B., Huth, J., and Smith, B., 1978, Nursing-mediated prolactin and luteinizing hormone secretion during puerperal lactation, *Fertil. Steril.* **30**:154–162.
139. Andreassen, B. and Tyson, J. E., 1976, Role of the hypothalamic-pituitary-ovarian axis in puerperal infertility, *J. Clin. Endocrinol. Metab.* **42**:1114–1122.
140. Thorner, M. O. and Besser, G. M., 1977, Hyperprolactinaemia and gonadal function: Results of bromocryptine treatment, in: *Prolactin and Human Reproduction* (P. G. Crosignani and C. Robyn, eds.), Academic Press, London, p. 285–301.
141. Lu, K. H., Chen, H. T., Huang, H. H., Grandison, L., Marshall, S., and Meites, J., 1976, Relation between gonadotrophin secretion and prolactin in postpartum lactating rats, *J. Endocrinol.* **68**:241–250.
142. Schallenberger, E. and Knobil, E., 1980, Suppression of prolactin secretion and the amenorrhea of lactation in the rhesus monkey, The Endocrine Society 62nd Annual Meeting, Washington, D.C.
143. Plant. T. M., Schallenberger, E., Hess, D. L., McCormack, J. T., Dufy-Barbe, L., and Knobil, E., 1980, Influence of suckling on gonadotropin secretion in the female rhesus monkey (*Macaca mulata*), *Biol. Reprod.* **23**:760–766.
144. Robyn, C., Delvoye, P., Van Exter, C., Vekemans, M., Caufriez, A., de Nayer, P., Delogne-Desnoeck, J., and L'Hermite, M., 1977, Physiological and pharmacological factors influencing prolactin secretion and their relation to human reproduction, in: *Prolactin and Human Reproduction* (P. G. Crosignani and C. Robyn, eds.), Academic Press, London, pp. 71–96.
145. Baird, D. T., McNeilly, A. S., Sawers, R. S., and Sharpe, R. M., 1979, Failure of estrogen-induced discharge of luteinizing hormone in lactating women, *J. Clin. Endocrinol. Metab.* **49**:500–506.
146. Glass, M. R., Shaw, R. W., Butt, W. R., Logan Edwards, R., and London, D. R., 1975, An abnormality of oestrogen feedback in amenorrhoea-galactorrhoea, *Br. Med. J.* **3**:274–275.
147. McNatty, K. P., Sawers, R. S., and McNeilly, A. S., 1974, A possible role for prolactin in control of steroid secretion by the human Graafian follicle, *Nature* **250**:653–655.
148. McNatty, K. P., 1979, Relationship between plasma prolactin and the endocrine microenvironment of the developing human antral follicle, *Fertil. Steril.* **32**:433–438.
149. Dorrington, J. and Gore-Langton, R. E., 1981, Prolactin inhibits oestrogen synthesis in the ovary, *Nature* **290**:600–602.

150. Prentice, A. M., Whitehead, R. G., Roberts, S. B., and Paul, A. A., 1981, Long-term energy balance in child-bearing Gambian women, *Am. J. Clin. Nutr.* **34:**2790–2799.
151. Flint, D. J., Clegg, R. A., and Vernon, R. G., 1981, Prolactin and the regulation of adipose tissue metabolism during lactation in the rat, *Mol. Cell. Endocrinol.* **22:**265–275.
152. Agius, L., and Williamson, D. H., 1980, Lipogenesis in interscapular brown adipose tissue of virgin, pregnant and lactating rats, *Biochem. J.* **190:**477–480.
153. Flint, D. J., Sinnett-Smith, P. A., Clegg, R. A., and Vernon, R. G., 1979, Role of insulin receptors in the changing metabolism of adipose tissue during pregnancy and lactation in the rat, *Biochem. J.* **182:**421–427.
154. Naing, K-H., Oo, T-T., Thein, K., and Hlang, N-N., 1980, Study on lactation performance of Burmese mothers, *Am. J. Clin. Nutr.* **33:**2665–2668.
155. Wilde, C. J. and Kuhn, N. J., 1979, Lactose synthesis in the rat, and the effects of litter size and malnutrition, *Biochem. J.* **182:**287–294.
156. Chaiyabutr, N., Faulkner, A., and Peaker, M., 1980, The utilization of glucose for the synthesis of milk components in the fed and starved lactating goat *in vivo, Biochem. J.* **186:**301–308.
157. Rosso, P., Keyou, G., Bassi, J. A., and Slusser, W. M., 1981, Effect of malnutrition during pregnancy on the development of the mammary glands of rats, *J. Nutr.* **111:**1937–1941.
158. Tulchinsky, D., Hobel, C. J., Yeager, E., and Marshall, J. R., 1972, Plasma estrone, estradiol, progesterone, and 17-hydroxyprogesterone in human pregnancy, *Am. J. Obstet. Gynecol.* **112:**1095–1100.
159. De Hertogh, R., Thomas, K., Bietlot, Y., Vanderheyden, I., and Ferin, J., 1975, Plasma levels of unconjugated estrone, estradiol and estriol and of HCS throughout pregnancy in normal women, *J. Clin. Endocrinol. Metab.* **40:**93–101.
160. Rigg, L. A., Lein, A., and Yen, S. S. C., 1977, Pattern of increase in circulating prolactin levels during human gestation, *Am. J. Obstet. Gynecol.* **129:**454–456.
161. Maule Waulker, F. M. and Peaker, M., 1980, Local production of prostaglandins in relation to mammary function at the onset of lactation in the goat, *J. Physiol.* **309:**65–79.
162. Thorburn, G. D. and Schneider, W., 1972, The progesterone concentration in the plasma of the goat during the oestrus cycle and pregnancy, *J. Endocrinol.* **52:**23–26.

5

Cellular and Molecular Aspects of the Hormonal Control of Mammary Function

Margaret C. Neville and Sally E. Berga

In the previous chapter, the regulation of mammary growth and lactation were discussed from the perspective of the whole organism. In the past decade exciting progress has been made toward understanding the cellular and molecular events underlying these regulatory interactions and it has become clear that lactogenic proteins, particularly prolactin, play the primary role in regulating mammary function, with the sex steroids and cortisol acting as important modulators. In this chapter, we will summarize the current status of our knowledge in this area emphasizing prolactin secretion and action and the regulatory effects of estrogens, progesterone and gluco-corticoids. The effects of insulin, thyroid hormones, prostaglandins, and cyclic AMP (cAMP) will be described more briefly. Because these areas are currently the subject of intensive investigation in many laboratories, the serious reader is urged to regard this chapter only as a starting point for consideration of current information as it appears in the primary literature.

LACTOGENIC HORMONES

The somatomammotropic hormones are a group of single-chain poly-peptides with molecular weights of 21,000 to 23,000 that include two hormones of pituitary origin, prolactin and growth hormone, and one hormone synthesized by the syncytiotrophoblast layers of the placenta,[1] placental lactogen (also known as chorionic somatomammotropin or CS). All three hormones have varying degrees of lactogenic activity, but in general

---

Margaret C. Neville and Sally E. Berga • Department of Physiology, University of Colorado School of Medicine, Denver, Colorado 80262.

prolactin is thought to play the major role in the regulation of mammary function. In nonmammalian species, prolactin has a large diversity of physiological functions; for example, the regulation of salt and water balance in amphibians and initiation of nesting behavior in birds.[2] In mammals, the major role of prolactin is the regulation of the activity of the mammary gland. During lactation, prolactin is secreted in response to suckling by the infant. It combines with receptors on the milk secreting cells of the mammary gland, stimulating milk production and possibly regulating the mother's milk supply to meet the demands of her infant. Prolactin also stimulates mammary growth and differentiation. The role of placental lactogen is less clear in humans. Its primary action may be to promote mammary growth and development or to regulate maternal metabolism during pregnancy. Although human growth hormone has lactogenic effects in cultures of monkey mammary gland[3] and other *in vitro* systems (see Chapter 6), it is not currently thought to play a role in human mammary function (see Chapter 4) and will therefore receive only brief attention here.

Studies of amino acid and copy DNA (cDNA) sequence homology show that human placental lactogen is more closely related to growth hormone than to prolactin. There is only about 26% amino acid homology between human growth hormone and human prolactin, indicating that the genes for these hormones diverged about 400 million years ago during the divergence of fish and tetrapods.[4-6] On the other hand, human placental lactogen shows 85% amino acid homology with growth hormone suggesting that the gene for human placental lactogen arose much later by duplication of the growth hormone gene. Various estimates place this event about 56 million years ago somewhat after the mammalian divergence 75 million years ago[7]; or possibly even as recently as 10 million years ago,[6] if a gene recombination event was involved. Recent studies have shown that the growth hormone and placental lactogen genes are located in chromosome 17 along with another similar gene known as the growth-hormone-like gene.[8] The observation that both the primary and intervening sequences of these three genes are similar is good evidence that they arose by gene reduplication.

In this section, we will discuss prolactin synthesis and release and summarize the extensive literature on prolactin action in the mammary gland. Placental lactogen secretion and action will be described more briefly.

Regulation of Prolactin Synthesis and Release

Like other protein and peptide hormones, prolactin is synthesized on membrane-bound ribosomes, processed in Golgi membranes, stored in secretory granules, and secreted by exocytosis. This process has been particularly well studied in pituitary prolactin cells (mammotrophs) by Farquhar and her co-workers.[9-11] Several factors are involved in the control of prolactin synthesis and release including prolactin inhibitory factor (PIF, probably dopamine), estrogens, thyrotropin releasing hormone (TRH), and endogenous opiates. Evidence for a specific hypothalamic prolactin releasing factor (PRF) is presently equivocal.

Prolactin Inhibitory Factor (PIF)

The control of prolactin release is dominated by PIF, a factor or factors secreted into the pituitary portal blood system by tubuloinfundibular neurons of the hypothalamus.[12] Considerable evidence suggests that dopamine is the major prolactin inhibitory factor and that it suppresses release and synthesis of prolactin by interacting with receptor sites on prolactin cells: Dopamine has been found in hypophyseal portal blood[13,14] in concentrations sufficient to inhibit prolactin secretion and high affinity, saturable, stereospecific dopamine receptors are present on prolactin cells.[15] Drugs such as L-dopa, which is converted to dopamine, and bromocriptine, a dopamine agonist, interfere with prolactin release in both intact and stalk-sectioned animals[16] as well as in *in vitro* preparations of pituitary cells.

The development of cDNA probes specific to prolactin messenger RNA (mRNA) has allowed the investigation of the regulation of prolactin mRNA transcription. Recent studies indicate that the inhibition of prolactin synthesis by dopaminergic compounds is brought about by the inhibition of the transcription of prolactin mRNA.[17,18] Maurer[18] observed that dopamine inhibition was reversed by addition of exogenous cyclic AMP (cAMP) in cultured rat pituitary cells suggesting that dopamine may act by reducing cAMP in the prolactin cell.

Estrogen Stimulation of Prolactin Release

Chronic administration of estrogens increases both pituitary and plasma prolactin levels[19]; maximum levels are obtained after 2 weeks. This appears to be the result of an increase in both the number and activity of pituitary prolactin cells.[20] In culture, long-term treatment with estrogens reverses the inhibitory effects of dopamine agonists on pituitary cells causing hypertrophy, accumulation of prolactin-containing granules,[21,22] and an increase in the transcription of prolactin-specific mRNA.[23] Observing that estrogen decreased the dopamine content of pituitary cells, Gudelsky *et al.*[24] suggested that the steroid acts by altering dopamine receptor processing. This interpretation is consistent with earlier experiments[25] which showed that estrogen treatment decreased the sensitivity of prolactin cells to the inhibitory effects of dopamine. There is also evidence that estrogens augment prolactin release by acting at the level of the hypothalamus.[12,25]

Thyrotropin-Releasing Hormone

Currently, thyrotropin-releasing hormone (TRH) is not thought to play a major physiological role in the control of prolactin release,[26] although TRH infusion provokes a rapid increase in plasma prolactin providing a convenient clinical test of prolactin reserve. Because TRH also stimulates prolactin release in *in vitro* pituitary cell preparations, the peptide is proving useful in elucidating the mechanism of prolactin release. Thus, TRH has been found to induce spontaneous electrical activity in prolactin cells in the presence of extracellular calcium, suggesting calcium-mediated release of secretory granules.[27,28] TRH also increased prolactin synthesis by augmenting mRNA transcription.[29]

Stress and Opiates

Stress has long been known to induce prolactin release,[30] although the adaptive significance and mechanism of this phenomenon have remained obscure. Recent evidence suggests that it may be mediated by the stress-induced release of hypothalamic opiates.[31] Morphine and opiate agonists have been shown to act within the central nervous system to increase prolactin secretion[25] whereas naloxone, a specific opiate antagonist, can be shown under certain circumstances to decrease prolactin secretion[12,32,33] including the prolactin release induced by suckling.[34] The relevance of stress or opiate-induced prolactin release to lactation is unclear, since opiates also appear to inhibit oxytocin release (see Chapter 4), presumably interfering through this pathway with effective lactational performance.

Drugs

A wide variety of drugs has been found to alter prolactin release. Of the dopamine agonists, the ergot derivative, bromocriptine, has been found to be fairly specific for prolactin release[35] and has found clinical application in relief of postpartum engorgement in non-breast-feeding women[36] as well as in the treatment of galactorrhea.[37] Neuraleptic drugs like phenothiazine are well-known stimulators of milk secretion and may act by blocking dopamine synthesis.[12] See Chapter 3 for additional discussion of drugs which affect lactation.

Cellular Actions of Prolactin

Prolactin plays a regulatory role in the growth and development of the mammary gland as well as in the regulation of differentiated function including the increased synthesis of caseins, α-lactalbumin, and other mammary-specific proteins observed at lactogenesis. Although the mechanism by which prolactin exerts these effects is not yet completely understood, rapid progress is currently being made in elucidating the molecular mechanisms involved.[38,39] In this section, the cellular and molecular actions of prolactin on milk protein and lipid synthesis will be discussed followed by summaries of prolactin binding to specific receptors and the current status of our knowledge about the intracellular transduction of the prolactin signal. The role of prolactin in stimulating cell proliferation, insofar as it is understood, is discussed in Chapter 6.

Effects of Prolactin on Milk Protein Synthesis and Secretion

Prolactin treatment of mammary epithelium both *in vivo* and *in vitro*[*] leads to increased casein synthesis[38-43] accompanied by an increase in casein mRNA accumulation as measured both by the activity of casein mRNA in cell-free synthesis systems[44-46] and with the use of specific cDNA hybridization.[47-49] Increased casein mRNA accumulation has been observed as early as 60 min after prolactin treatment.[50] The increased levels of casein mRNA appear to be due both to stimulation of casein mRNA transcription and increased stabilization of the mRNA.[50,51] Prolactin may also act at the level of translation of casein mRNA into protein. Teyssot and Houdebine[52] reported that *in vivo* injections of prolactin and colchicine into pseudopregnant rabbits inhibited casein mRNA accumulation but did not prevent the prolactin-induced synthesis of casein, suggesting that casein synthesis is not always closely coupled to casein mRNA levels.

There is also some evidence for posttranslational effects of prolactin. *In vivo* injection of prolactin into pseudopregnant rabbits induced a rapid and preferential binding of ribosomes and casein mRNA to mammary cell membranes.[53,54] *In vitro* incubation of lactating tissue with prolactin for 15 to 45 min resulted in an increase in the volume of the Golgi system,[55] an increase in casein secretion[55] into the medium and an increase in milk fat secretion.[56] The increase in casein secretion was not abolished by inhibitors of protein synthesis. Wilde *et al.*[57] reported that prolactin decreased the rate of casein degradation in mammary explants from pregnant rabbits. All these experiments suggest that prolactin acts at multiple sites in a coordinate fashion to increase the synthesis and secretion of milk components.[58]

Prolactin action varies with both the hormonal environment and the stage of mammary development. For example, Ways *et al.*[59] reported fluctuations in the sensitivity of the mammary gland to prolactin stimulation of casein synthesis on different days of pregnancy in mouse mammary explants. Prolactin-stimulated increases in casein mRNA levels did not result in increased casein synthesis in the virgin rabbit mammary gland.[60] Prolactin may not be an absolute requirement for α-lactalbumin synthesis and activity in pregnant rat mammary gland cultures, although it is required by virgin cultures.[61,62] All these observations indicate the importance of the stage of mammary development in the prolactin response. The possible roles of steroid hormones in altering the response of the mammary gland to prolactin are discussed in later sections of this chapter.

---

* In the *in vitro* experiments described in this section, the levels of prolactin added (generally about 5 μg/ml) were at least 25 times the prolactin levels observed in lactating animals. Recently, Djiane *et al.*[58] reported a half-maximal effect of prolactin on casein synthesis at 30 to 40 ng/ml, suggesting that the effects observed in *in vitro* systems can be obtained with physiological doses of the hormone.

Effects of Prolactin on Lipid Metabolism

Early work showed that prolactin increased the rate of fatty acid synthesis in mammary gland explants from pregnant mice and rabbits cultured with insulin and cortisol. It also produced a shift to the synthesis of the medium chain fatty acids characteristic of lactating mammary tissue and milk within 24 hr.[63-67] These changes were accompanied by an increase in the amount of fatty acid synthetase,[55,68,69] resulting from both an increased rate of synthesis and a decreased rate of degradation of the protein. Whether the increased protein synthesis was due to an increase in specific mRNA activity has not yet been determined.

Prolactin effects on lipoprotein lipase have also been examined. Mammary lipoprotein lipase activity increased slowly during pregnancy and sharply at parturition.[70] Hypophysectomy of lactating rats rapidly decreased lipoprotein lipase. Normal levels could be restored within 48 hr by administration of prolactin *in vivo*.[71] It is not clear whether the increase in lipoprotein lipase activity was the result of activation of existing enzyme or *de novo* synthesis of lipoprotein lipase.

Prolactin Binding to Mammary Membranes

The initial step in the interaction of a polypeptide hormone with a cell is binding to a specific receptor on the plasma membrane.[72] In keeping with this concept, prolactin binding sites have been identified in the mammary glands of small mammals,[12,73] in mammary tumors from both humans and animals[74,75] and in the milk fat globule membrane.[76] Prolactin receptors have also been found in many other tissues.[73,77] In an extensive characterization of prolactin receptors in rabbit mammary gland membranes, Shiu and Friesen[78,79] found 55.6 fmole of high affinity/low capacity prolactin binding sites per mg microsomal membrane protein. These sites had a dissociation constant (K_d) for prolactin of 3.4×10^{-10} M (about 8 ng/ml) and were specific for prolactin, primate growth hormones and placental lactogens. In a more recent study, Suard *et al.*[80] reported that the affinity constant for dispersed rabbit mammary cells and Triton-X-100 solubilized membranes was enhanced by an order of magnitude over the particulate membranes used by others. The essential role of the prolactin receptor in mediating the biological actions of prolactin was established by showing that an antiserum to the partially purified receptor from rabbit mammary gland competitively inhibited both prolactin binding to receptors in mammary gland explants[81,82] and the biological effects of prolactin in this system.

Regulation of Prolactin Receptors

Changes in the number of prolactin receptors parallel changes in the physiological state of the animal and can be observed after manipulation of either the *in vitro* or *in vivo* hormone environment of the mammary gland.[58,73,83] Prolactin receptors exhibit both "up"- (an increase in the number of receptors) and "down"-regulation (a decrease in receptor number) in response to prolactin itself, as explained below. Characterization of these changes was originally difficult because receptor occupation by varying amounts of endogenous placental lactogen or prolactin[84–87] could reduce the number of prolactin receptors available for measurement. In more recent studies, this artifact has been eliminated by washing the membrane preparations with 4 M $MgCl_2$[88,89] prior to measurement of binding capacity.

In both rats and rabbits, prolactin receptor capacity has been observed to increase during early lactation.[84,86,90,91] This increase could be suppressed by treatment with ergot alkaloids, inhibitors of prolactin secretion, suggesting that the postpartum increase in prolactin receptors may be brought about by the suckling-stimulated release of prolactin itself.[91,92] That prolactin controls "up" regulation is supported by the observation that injection of prolactin over a 48-hr period into a pseudopregnant rabbit induced a substantial increase in the level of prolactin receptors in the mammary gland.[92] Concurrent progesterone administration blocked this response raising the possibility that "up" regulation may be a response to a decrease in the ratio of progesterone to prolactin rather than an action of prolactin *per se.*

Djiane *et al.*[87,93] and Kelly *et al.*[89] reported that large doses of prolactin rapidly decreased the number of receptors, even after $MgCl_2$ treatment. This short-term phenomenon, which has been observed minutes after prolactin treatment *in vivo*, has been termed "down" regulation. It occurs in cultured mammary gland at physiological concentrations of prolactin (half-maximal response at 10 ng/ml[58]) and is blocked by lysosomotropic agents like chloroquine,[89,94] as well as by metabolic inhibitors,[95] suggesting that internalization and degradation of the receptor is involved. Whether such processing is necessary for transduction of the prolactin signal or is simply a mechanism for hormone degradation is not yet known.

Plasma membrane prolactin receptor levels must reflect a balance between their rate of degradation and their rate of synthesis; regulation of receptor capacity can involve the regulation of one or the other or both processes. The up regulation or prolactin receptors by prolactin may be due to an increase in the rate of synthesis of prolactin receptors possibly stimulated by prolactin itself. The more short-term down regulation of prolactin receptors may reflect internalization and processing of the hormone-receptor complex.

Transduction of the Prolactin Signal

While the obligatory role of the prolactin plasma membrane receptor in prolactin action is quite clear, the mechanism by which the binding event is transduced to bring about changes in cellular function is not understood. The prolactin-receptor complex may be internalized and the complex or some portion of the complex may act directly to initiate prolactin cellular actions or a second messenger or intracellular mediator may be involved. In fact, the two modes of signal transduction may not be mutually exclusive.

Prolactin Internalization. There is considerable evidence indicating that prolactin is internalized. For example, immunocytochemical studies suggest that intracellular prolactin is present in many tissues including the alveolar lumina and epithelial cells of the mammary gland in lactating rats.[96-97] Nolin[98] examined endogenous immunoreactive prolactin in the mammary glands of lactating rats and defined a cycle of prolactin incorporation. Flattened "resting" secretory cells did not contain intracellular prolactin although the milk in the lumina of the alveoli lined with such resting cells did. Prolactin immunoreactivity was found in clusters throughout the cytoplasm of columnar "active" cells; approximately one-fourth of these cells showed nuclear prolactin staining. In cuboidal "intermediate" secretory cells, cytoplasmic prolactin was uniformly dispersed. Thus, prolactin staining correlated well with the functional secretory activity of the cell, although in these studies it was not clear that the immunoreactive prolactinlike material was intact prolactin.

Further evidence of prolactin internalization was found in a study of human mammary tumor cell lines[99] in which 25% of the internalized prolactin was intact after 10 hr at 37°C. At the electron microscopic level, Suard *et al.*[80] found that prolactin initially bound to the plasma membrane was subsequently internalized and associated with vesicular elements and the nucleus. Although the prolactin appeared to be intact after 30 min at 37°C, again the functional significance of its internalization was not clear.

Recently, Djiane and colleagues[100] reported that antiserum to a partially purified prolactin receptor from rabbit mammary gland membranes could mimic the actions of prolactin on casein synthesis and casein mRNA accumulation with the same time course of action as prolactin. The effect was blocked by colchicine and amplified by glucocorticoids as is the action of prolactin in explant systems. These results suggest that the internalization of prolactin is not essential for the cellular actions of prolactin.

Role of Intracellular Mediators. The intracellular mediation of prolactin action remains a puzzle. Early reports of mediation by polyamines such as spermidine, as well as cyclic nucleotides, and prostaglandins[101-103] could not be confirmed by later investigators using more sensitive and specific assays.[104] Houdebine and co-workers[105,106] investigated the effects of inhibitors of lysosomal enzymes, microfilament formation, and microtubule formation on the prolactin induction of casein mRNA. Only colchicine which inhibits microtubule functioning inhibited casein synthesis and the accumulation of casein mRNA in response to prolactin. This suggests that microtubules are involved in the transduction of the prolactin signal.

The most promising lead at this point is the report by Teyssot *et al.*[107] who found that isolated mammary membranes incubated with prolactin released a soluble factor which specifically induced casein gene transcription in isolated mammary cell nuclei. Reports on the chemical nature of this factor, which presumably acts as a second messenger for prolactin action, have not yet appeared.

Summary

Prolactin appears to act at multiple sites to stimulate the increased synthesis and secretion of milk components at lactogenesis. Prolactin-specific receptors are involved in these actions but the mechanisms by which prolactin binding is translated into intracellular signals are not yet understood. Ongoing research on prolactin internalization and putative second messengers should lead in the near future to defined roles for both in prolactin action.

Placental Lactogen

The first report of a lactogenic hormone derived from human placenta[108] was soon followed by its purification and the demonstration of lactogenic activity in the pseudopregnant rabbit.[109] Josimovich and MacLaren[109] named the hormone, *placental lactogen*. Noting its structural similarity with growth hormone, Li and co-workers[110] applied the term *human chorionic somatomammotropin* (hCS). In 1975, the IUPAC-IUB commission on biochemical nomenclature recommended *human choriomammotropin*. We will use the term *human placental lactogen* (hPL) here because of its historical significance and simplicity as well as the fact that this term is used for animal lactogenic hormones of placental origin.

Regulation of Placental Lactogen Secretion

Placental lactogen levels rise continuously throughout pregnancy in the human (Fig. 3, Chapter 4). Early workers[109] postulated that placental lactogen levels parallel placental mass, a postulate which is in accord with most recent observations.[111,112] These levels must reflect a continuously high secretion rate because the half-life in plasma is only about 20 min.[113] Other factors than placental mass do alter plasma levels. Vigneri *et al.*[114] found hour-to-hour fluctuations in plasma placental lactogen levels in nine women in the third trimester of pregnancy and suggested that the cause might be fluctuations in placental blood flow. Decreases in plasma glucose produced by fasting or insulin infusion led to a 40% increase in placental lactogen levels.[113,115] Hyperglycemia had little effect, but arginine has been shown to stimulate secretion.[116] Although bromocriptine was found to reduce placental lactogen levels in goats,[117,118] Bigazzi *et al.*[118] found that complete suppression of prolactin secretion by bromocriptine throughout human pregnancy had no effect on plasma levels of hPL. In summary, placental mass and hypoglycemia are the only factors with a proven role in regulating hPL secretion.

Actions of Placental Lactogen

Because placental lactogen is secreted only in pregnancy, its physiological role in mammary function must be limited to the stimulation of mammary growth and differentiation. This role is clear in certain mammals in which, unlike the human, prolactin remains low throughout pregnancy.[112] In humans, it has been postulated[119] that placental lactogen may be more important in the regulation of maternal metabolism than in mammogenesis.

Human placental lactogen and prolactin have very similar lactogenic activities in a variety of *in vitro* systems including both mouse and rat mammary explants[120,121] and both bind with equal affinity to prolactin receptors in the rabbit milk fat globule membrane.[76] McManus and Welsch[122] recently reported that hPL stimulates [^{3}H]-thymidine labeling of human mammary fibroadenoma cells transplanted into nude mice, suggesting a specific action on DNA synthesis in human mammary tissue. All these observations plus the fact that plasma levels of placental lactogen are 100 times that of prolactin during human pregnancy suggest that it normally stimulates mammogenesis. However, more evidence is necessary to prove this point. For example, the relative affinities of the prolactin receptor in human mammary membranes for prolactin and placental lactogen have not been published at this writing and studies of the effects of human placental lactogen on normal human mammary epithelial transplants in nude mice are not yet available. Information from such studies is necessary before a definitive role for human placental lactogen in human mammogenesis can be assigned.

Conclusion

Some of the most exciting work on the cellular and molecular aspects of protein hormone function is currently emerging from investigations of the secretion and action of prolactin. For example, consideration of the control of prolactin synthesis and release leads to the inescapable conclusion that mRNA transcription, protein translation and processing, and prolactin release from the cell are all controlled in a coordinated fashion. Similarly, in the mammary gland, prolactin interaction with the plasma membrane appears 'to set in motion a series of intracellular events which lead to the coordinated synthesis and secretion of all the components of milk. Many fascinating insights can be expected over the next few years as the cellular and molecular mechanisms involved in the coordinate regulation of these events are elucidated.

In this section, we have examined the actions of lactogenic hormones on mammary function largely as if they occured in isolation from other controlling influences. Although this separation was necessary to gain insight into the fundamentals of prolactin action, it is very artificial, because the extent to which lactogenic hormones are able to bring about the coordinated events described above depends first, on the presence of a suitably developed mammary gland and secondly, on a favorable hormonal environment. The steroid hormones are particularly important in this regard. Their role in the regulation of mammary function will be described next.

THE ROLE OF STEROID HORMONES IN THE CONTROL OF MAMMARY FUNCTION

Endocrine ablation and replacement studies in whole animals in the 1950s underscored the importance of the steroid hormones, estrogen, progesterone, and adrenal corticoids in the regulation of mammary function. However, more recent evidence from *in vitro* systems suggests that these hormones act to modulate the effects of lactogenic hormones rather than playing a regulatory role in their own right. In this section, we will review this evidence.

Estrogens

In the intact animal, estrogens stimulate mammary growth and development, and promote prolactin secretion by the anterior pituitary. In addition, they have the paradoxical effect of inhibiting milk secretion by the lactating gland. Estrogen stimulation of prolactin secretion can be observed *in vitro*. For the most part, estrogen stimulation of mammary growth and inhibition of milk secretion have been consistently observed only *in vivo*; for this reason, there is still some question as to whether these are indeed direct effects on the mammary gland.

Estrogens and Proliferation of the Mammary Epithelium

A correlation between mammary growth at puberty and the onset of ovarian function in women was clearly recognized by Halban in 1905.[123] By the 1930s, it was well known that estrogen injections produced mammary development in a variety of mammals.[124] The treatment generally produced only ductile proliferation and was accompanied by the formation of mammary cysts due to the accumulation of secretion products.[125] In both ruminants and rodents, *in vivo* treatment with estrogen and progesterone is almost routinely used to induce mammary development prior to *in vitro* or *in vivo* experiments on lactogenesis.[41,126,127] These observations plus the clear association of estrogen receptors with growth of a significant proportion of human mammary tumors[128,129] has lead to a wide acceptance of the idea that estrogens promote proliferation of mammary epithelium, particularly the ductile portions of the gland.

The mechanism of these effects on mammary growth is controversial. Observations indicating direct mitogenic stimulation of the mammary gland by estrogen are few[130–134] and the extent of the observed stimulation has been limited. Moreover, most of the observed effects of estrogens in whole animals require that the pituitary gland be intact,[135,136,156] suggesting either that the hormone acts indirectly by stimulating secretion of a pituitary growth factor or that a pituitary hormone acts synergistically with the steroid to induce mammary growth.

The *in vitro* evidence that estrogens promote pituitary prolactin secretion has been discussed above. That this estrogen effect occurs under physiological conditions in humans is suggested by the correlation between plasma estradiol-17β levels and the levels of prolactin at puberty,[137] during pregnancy,[138,139] and at the menarch[137] and the observation that estrogen-containing birth control pills increase plasma prolactin.[140] Further, increases in estradiol levels in pubertal boys with gynecomastia were correlated with increases in plasma prolactin levels.[141] Thus, from a physiological standpoint, in humans and most animals (the Rhesus monkey being an apparent exception[142]) increases in plasma estrogen and prolactin levels go hand-in-hand, raising the possibility that estrogen effects on mammary growth are mediated by prolactin.

On the other hand, there is evidence suggesting that estrogens have growth promoting actions of their own in mammary tissue, particularly in the presence of prolactin. Mitogenic activity in the MCF-7 human breast cancer line is stimulated by estradiol-17β *in vitro*.[143] Growth of the human breast cancer cell line ZR-75-1 in serum-free medium is dependent on estrogens and inhibited by the antiestrogen tamoxifen.[144] In ovariectomized mice, prolactin stimulation of mammary cell proliferation was enhanced by estrogen and progesterone.[131] Hyperprolactinemia due to pituitary tumors in human males produces mammary growth (gynecomastia) only when plasma estrogen levels are raised for one reason or another.[145,146] All these observations suggest that estrogens act synergistically with prolactin to produce mammary growth. It is important to note, however, that this synergism could be due either to direct action of estrogens on mammary tissue, or to estrogen-stimulated production of mammary growth factors other than prolactin.[147]

What is now needed are critical tests of the alternative hypotheses that (1) estrogens act as primary mitogens in mammary tissue, (2) estrogens are permissive agents that sensitize mammary tissue to the action of lactogenic hormones, or (3) estrogen action is entirely indirect, being mediated through stimulation of secretion of other hormones and growth factors.[147] Culture systems derived from normal mammary tissue which show substantial proliferative activity have recently been developed[132,148,149,149a] (Chapter 6). These systems should make the appropriate experiments feasible.

Mechanism of Estrogen Action in Mammary Tissue

As in other tissues, in the mammary gland estrogens bind to a cytosolic receptor that is translocated to the nucleus.[150] Because their presence is correlated with tumor susceptibility to hormone therapy, estrogen receptors have received extensive study in breast cancer tissues.[129] There have been fewer studies of normal mammary tissue. In lactating mice, Shyamala and Nandi[150] reported a single class of mammary cytosolic estrogen receptors with a binding constant of 9×10^{-10} M for estradiol-17β. These receptors did not cross-react with corticoids, progesterone, or testosterone and appeared to be similar to the uterine estrogen receptor. It has been inferred from the observation that estrogens have biological effects (e.g., an increase in progesterone receptors in mammary tissue from virgin mice[151]) that mammary estrogen receptors are present prior to pubertal development of the gland. However, they have not received detailed study at this stage. Recently, Haslam and Shyamala[152] demonstrated that estrogen receptors with a K_d of 1.5×10^{-9} M were present in equivalent concentration (~350 fmole mg DNA) in the mammary fat pad as well as the mammary epithelium in virgin mice, raising the possibility that mammary mesenchymal tissues are also a target for estrogen action.

The factors which control estrogen receptor levels in normal mammary tissue are not yet understood. Increasing levels of receptors in rat mammary glands were observed during lactation.[153] Bohnet *et al.*[91] observed that, if the pups were removed at birth or 17α-hydroxyprogesterone was administered, this postpartum receptor increase was abolished. In a number of carcinogen-induced rat mammary tumors as well as mammary glands from CSH mice,[154] the levels of estrogen receptor are stimulated by prolactin.[128] However, Bohnet and co-workers[91] found that inhibition of prolactin secretion by administration of bromocriptine administered to lactating rats had no effect on the level of mammary gland estrogen receptors, and therefore they concluded that prolactin was not an important regulator of estrogen receptor levels.

Some information is available on the biological effects of estrogen binding to mammary tissue. In the MCF-7 cell line, estrogens stimulate proliferation,[143] increase protein, RNA and DNA synthesis as well as regulating thymidine kinase, lactate dehydrogenase, and DNA polymerase activities.[129] In rat mammary tumors as well as the human MCF-7 cell line, estrogen has been demonstrated to exert exact control over the level of progesterone receptors.[155] A similar observation has been made in virgin mouse mammary gland[156] where estrogens also increase glucose oxidation and DNA synthesis.[157] However, although estrogen binding sites are available, these biological effects of estrogens are not observed in lactating mice,[153,157] suggesting that the effects depend on the stage of lactation.

Estrogens and Mammary Gland Differentiation

In humans, hypersecretion of prolactin brings about galactorrhea (abnormal milk secretion) in only a small proportion of males (20% in the series by Antune *et al.*[145]), but a larger proportion of females (60% in the same study), suggesting that ovarian hormones sensitize the mammary gland to prolactin. In accord with this suggestion, injections of estrogen in ovariectomized mice[158] apparently restored the sensitivity of the mammary tissue to prolactin, and estrogen treatment of neonatal mice significantly enhanced the later ability of the tissue to develop differentiated function.[159] However, firm *in vitro* evidence for a physiological role of estrogens in mammary gland differentiation is lacking.

Estrogen Production by the Mammary Gland

Maule Walker and Peaker,[160] using arteriovenous difference techniques in the goat found evidence for estradiol-17β production by the mammary gland around parturition. There is considerable evidence that breast tumors themselves can produce estrogens.[129] The physiological significance of these observations is presently obscure.

Estrogen Inhibition of Lactation

The administration of estrogen derivatives has long been known to suppress lactation in the postpartum period.[161,162] An early idea that estrogens acted by suppressing prolactin secretion had to be revised when it became possible to measure plasma prolactin levels and estrogens were found to stimulate prolactin secretion in rats[163] and humans.[140] The mechanism of the inhibition is not understood although it is widely thought to involve a direct action on the mammary gland. Nolin and Bogdanove[164] showed that estradiol decreased the amount of immunohistochemically visible prolactin in mammary epithelial cells and Bohnet *et al.*,[91] showed that estradiol injections prevented the rise in prolactin receptors occuring 48 hr after parturition in the rat. Both these observations raise the possibility that estrogens suppress lactation by interfering with prolactin binding.

Summary

Estrogens, acting directly or indirectly, sensitize mammary tissue to the proliferative effects of prolactin. They may also potentiate the effects of the pituitary hormone on differentiation and themselves stimulate mammary cell proliferation. Whatever the mechanism, the overall effect of increased plasma levels of estradiol in nonlactating women as well as men is to promote mammary development, particularly of stroma and ductile structures. In general, increases in plasma estradiol are correlated with increases in plasma prolactin and the two hormones may work synergistically to promote mammary growth. Estrogens also appear to have paradoxical inhibitory effects on milk production by the lactating gland. The biological basis of these effects is not understood.

Progesterone

Progesterone, the hormone of pregnancy, is largely responsible for coordinating mammary development with pregnancy and parturition. It has two well-characterized effects during pregnancy: (1) Progesterone appears from *in vivo* studies to synergize with estrogen and prolactin to produce full lobuloalveolar development of the gland; these developmental effects are poorly understood. (2) Both *in vivo* and *in vitro* studies indicate that progesterone inhibits the initiation of milk secretion during pregnancy. Studies in *in vitro* systems indicate that progesterone prevents the accumulation or activation of enzymes involved in terminal differentiation of mammary function without affecting mammary growth. A rather paradoxical observation is that progesterone has no discernable effects on the mammary gland during lactation. In this section, we will summarize the evidence for these statements.

The Role of Progesterone in Lobuloalveolar Development

It has been known since the 1930s that injection of estrogen alone into most mammals produces ductile proliferation only, whereas injection of both estrogen and progesterone in the proper doses produces lobuloalveolar development similar to that observed in pregnancy.[41,124,125] The mechanism of the stimulatory effect of progesterone on alveolar formation is not understood. Stoudemire *et al.*[165] reported that *in vivo* progesterone in combination with prolactin stimulated thymidine incorporation into both ductile and alveolar epithelium of hypophysectomized, ovariectomized rats whereas estrogen and prolactin stimulated only the ductile epithelium. There have been few reports of proliferative effects of progesterone *in vitro* and the problem of whether progesterone acts directly or indirectly to stimulate lobuloalveolar development has not been satisfactorily addressed.

Progesterone and the Inhibition of Lactogenesis

Lactogenesis can be precipitated in pregnant females of all species so far examined[166] by removal of the source of the high progesterone levels of pregnancy. The concomitant administration of progesterone largely prevents the changes associated with lactogenesis from occuring under both *in vitro* and *in vivo* conditions, suggesting that the steroid acts directly on the mammary gland. In a classic experiment, Kuhn[167] showed that progesterone injections prevented the increase in lactose content of the mammary gland observed after ovariectomy of pregnant mice.[168] In *in vitro* studies, Turkington and Hill[169] found that progesterone inhibited the prolactin-induced rise of α-lactalbumin activity in mammary explants from pregnant mice (see also refs. 170 to 173). Progesterone has also been found to decrease the prolactin-induced rise in casein and casein mRNA in mammary explants *in vitro*,[38,48,127,174–176] to prevent the prolactin-stimulated increase in membrane-bound polyribosomes in 12-day pseudopregnant rabbit explants,[170] to inhibit rough endoplasmic reticulum formation in the same system,[177] and to prevent the prolactin induction of prolactin receptors *in vitro*.[92] Progesterone inhibits glucose oxidation and conversion to lipid in isolated rat mammary cells.[178] In short, progesterone given *in vivo* or *in vitro* has been found to prevent those changes that lead to terminal differentiation and milk secretion in the mammary gland. Little or no inhibition of mammary growth has been observed in these experiments.

The mechanism by which progesterone inhibits the full expression of the prolactin effect on mammary differentiation[175,176] is not yet clear. Progesterone and its analog R5020 have been found to bind with a high affinity to glucocorticoid receptors in lactating mammary glands,[179,180] suggesting that progesterone acts by inhibiting cortisol binding, thereby preventing the glucocorticoid potentiation of prolactin action.[181] Against this concept are the recent findings of Teyssot and Houdebine[176] that progesterone modifies ribosomal RNA synthesis and casein mRNA translation but glucocorticoids do not. Moreover, progesterone is not inhibitory to established lactation, although the relevant corticol binding sites are clearly present.[179,180] It therefore seems more likely that progesterone exerts its effects by interacting with the specific progesterone binding sites described below. It is also possible that progesterone may act by increasing cAMP.[182] This regulatory nucleotide has been shown to inhibit many of the enzymes involved in milk secretion.[183] The increasing availability of techniques for probing the molecular basis of hormone action in the mammary gland should lead to rapid progress in determining which, if any, of these mechanisms is correct.

Progesterone Binding Sites in the Mammary Gland

Haslam and Shyamala[156] studied cytosolic progesterone receptors from mouse mammary gland during various reproductive stages. Using the synthetic progestin R5020, they found specific binding to a 4.5S receptor with a binding constant of 2.8×10^{-9} M. There were about 4000 receptor sites per cell, about 10% of the uterine concentration. Dexamethasone, a synthetic glucocorticoid, bound poorly to this receptor but did displace R5020 from a second, lower affinity binding site in the same tissue. The level of the high affinity receptor was high in tissue from virgin mice, and its concentration was increased by estrogen,[151] similar to uterine tissue.[155] The receptor concentration per mg DNA decreased during pregnancy. Progesterone receptors also have been found in the mammary fat pad, but did not appear to be regulated by estrogens or stage of lactation.[152] Shyamala and others[153,179,180,184] have been unable to detect any specific R5020 binding sites in the cytosol of glands from lactating mice and rats,* leading them to postulate that a lack of progesterone binding sites may be responsible for the lack of progesterone effects in lactation.

Few studies of progesterone receptors in normal human mammary gland have appeared, although progesterone receptors are present or can be induced in human mammary tumor lines.[155] Lloyd[185] found significant amounts of a progesterone receptor with a K_d of 1.9 nM in the cytosol of three out of nine samples of normal human mammary tissue taken at mastectomy or autopsy. Until a study appears correlating the amount and morphology of alveolar tissue with the receptor content of human mammary gland, it will be difficult to interpret such variable findings.

---

* Progesterone and R5020 do appear to bind to cortisol-binding sites in tissues from lactating mice with affinities in the same range as the progesterone binding sites.[180,181]

Conclusions

The inhibitory effect of progesterone on terminal differentiation of mammary function during pregnancy is well documented, as is the presence of specific progesterone receptors in the cytosol of mammary glands from several species. The molecular mechanism for the inhibitory effects and the nature of the physiologically relevant progesterone receptors are largely unknown as is the importance of progesterone–cortisol competition. In addition, the question of the mechanism by which progesterone stimulates lobuloalveolar differentiation *in vivo* has not been approached in *in vitro* systems. With the recent development of good *in vitro* systems (see Chapter 6) for the study of both proliferation and differentiation as well as good molecular probes of mammary function, answers to these questions should be forthcoming in the near future.

Glucocorticoids

The observations that adrenalectomized animals fail to initiate or maintain lactation unless given glucocorticoids[186,187] and that glucocorticoids are among the hormones necessary to maintain lactation in hypophysectomized animals[135,188] led to the early recognition that adrenal steroids are important in milk secretion. This concept was reinforced by experiments showing that cortisol was necessary to initiate and maintain the differentiated function of mammary tissue *in vitro*.[189,190] Such studies have left little doubt in the minds of most investigators that glucocorticoids potentiate the effects of more specific lactogenic factors. Work currently is directed toward understanding the molecular and cellular mechanisms by which glucocorticoids exert these permissive effects.

Does a Rise in Glucocorticoids Act as the Lactogenic Trigger?

Because the injection of high doses of glucocorticoids into late pregnant or pseudopregnant rabbits induces precocious milk secretion,[191] a number of authors have proposed that increases in glucocorticoid levels at parturition serve, along with increased prolactin levels, as a major hormonal trigger for lactogenesis.[192,193] Most evidence suggests, however, that this is not the case: the doses of glucocorticoid required to initiate milk secretion are generally in the pharmacological, rather than the physiological range.[166] Further, increases in glucocorticoids at parturition are inconstantly seen in animals[166,167] and humans[194] and physiological doses of corticoids given to late pregnant rats do not bring about the increases in casein or RNA content associated with lactogenesis in this species.[187] Infusion of dexamethasone into fetal lambs brought about an immediate increase in mammary blood flow,[195] similar to that seen during lactogenesis.[196] The same dose of dexamethasone infused into a maternal vein had no effect on mammary blood flow, suggesting that some factor other than cortisol is responsible for the changes accompanying lactogenesis in sheep. Finally, high-dose steroids given during pregnancy as therapy for inflammatory disease do not initiate premature lactogenesis in women (M. Neifert, personal communication). Thus, increases in the plasma levels of cortisol at parturition do not in themselves appear to be responsible for lactogenesis. On the other hand, the concept that progesterone withdrawal at parturition allows cortisol to exert its permissive effects has not been ruled out.

Glucocorticoid Receptors in the Mammary Gland

Shyamala[197] found 14,000 glucocorticoid receptor sites per cell in lactating mouse mammary glands with a binding constant for dexamethasone of 8×10^{-9} M. In specificity studies, compounds with glucocorticoid activity displaced bound dexamethasone most actively, with progesterone, deoxycorticosterone and aldosterone showing moderate displacement. The cortisol receptor is transported to the nucleus after binding glucocorticoids.[198] Progesterone binds to this receptor and prevents the translocation,[199] thus acting as an antagonist of glucocorticoid action.

Cellular Actions of Glucocorticoids

The best evidence that glucocorticoids are not absolutely required for mammary proliferation[41] comes from the whole gland culture system of Banerjee and his co-workers[47] in which lobuloalveolar development could be induced *in vitro* in a whole gland culture with a hormonal combination which does not include an adrenal cortical steroid. Moreover, Klevjer-Anderson[134] found no effect of cortisol on the rate of cellular proliferation in cultures of normal and cancerous mammary cells. On the other hand, many investigators have found that cortisol does *enhance* proliferation of mammary cells in *in vitro* systems.[41,132] It is not clear whether this is a specific effect of glucocorticoid or if corticoids act in a general way to promote the health of the culture systems.

There is currently some disagreement as to the absolute or relative requirement for glucocorticoid in the expression of differentiated function. Some investigators maintain that prolactin-induced differentiation observed in the absence of added cortisol in *in vitro* systems is due to the presence of endogenous cortisol.[201,204] An absolute corticoid requirement for maintenance or development of α-lactalbumin synthesis by long-term cultures of rat mammary tissue was demonstrated by Ray *et al.*[61] Again, it is not clear whether this observation represents a specific effect of cortisol on milk protein synthesis or a general effect on the health of the cultures.

Prolactin-induced differentiation has usually been found to be enhanced by glucocorticoids. For example, cortisol increased the development of rough endoplasmic reticulum,[200] and the accumulation of casein[201] and casein mRNA[41,47,48,176,202] in prolactin-treated mammary explants. In general, little or no effect of cortisol has been observed in the absence of prolactin.[48,49,202] These findings suggest that glucocorticoids play a permissive rather than a regulatory role in mammary differentiation. Whether they do this by regulation of prolactin receptor levels,[203] by amplification of prolactin-activated casein mRNA transcription,[176,204] or by action on a posttranscriptional process[38,51] is a problem on which we can expect substantial progress in the near future.

Cortisol does not appear to affect all aspects of differentiated function in mammary tissue to the same extent. Devinoy and Houdebine[49,202] found that cortisol potentiated *in vivo* prolactin action on casein and casein mRNA accumulation more than prolactin action on lactose synthetase or total RNA and DNA. Ono and Oka[205,206] have shown that dose-response curves for the effects of cortisol on α-lactalbumin and casein synthesis differ markedly in explants of both virgin and midpregnant mice. They found that α-lactabumin synthesis was fully stimulated at cortisol concentrations above 10^{-10} M whereas casein synthesis was stimulated at concentrations of cortisol more or less in the physiological range($<10^{-7}$M). It is also of interest that α-lactalbumin synthesis was totally inhibited at cortisol concentrations above 10^{-6} M. These differential effects of glucocorticoids compound the difficulties in formulating and testing a consistent hypothesis for cortisol action.

The Role of Spermidine in Glucocorticoid Action

The level of ornithine decarboxylase and s-adenosyl methionine decarboxylase, the rate-limiting enzymes in the synthesis of polyamines like spermidine, are elevated in mammary glands from both pregnant and lactating animals.[101,207] This observation has led investigators to postulate a regulatory role for polyamines in both mammary growth and milk secretion. In many systems, spermidine simulates the biological activity of glucocorticoids. This was well-illustrated in the studies of Oka and Perry[101] on explants of mouse mammary gland where hydrocortisone potentiated the effects of prolactin on α-lactalbumin and casein synthesis. Spermidine was found to substitute for cortisol in this system. Moreover, cortisol was found to increase the tissue concentrations of spermidine. This increase as well as the increase in milk protein synthesis was abolished by methylglyoxal *bis*(guanyl hydrazone), a specific inhibitor of spermidine synthesis. The block could be overcome by addition of exogenous spermidine. These observations led Oka and Perry[101] to suggest that cortisol effects were mediated by spermidine.

However, more recent studies in other species are not consistent with this straight-forward picture. In rabbits, induction of milk proteins was reported to be independent of spermidine.[208] In rats, both glucocorticoid and spermidine are required for casein gene expression, but spermidine cannot replace glucocorticoids.[201] The picture is further complicated by observations that both insulin[209] and prolactin[210] appear to increase spermidine levels.[211] With a clearer understanding of the mechanism of glucocorticoids at the molecular level, it may be possible more clearly to define the relationship between the regulatory roles of spermidine and glucocorticoids in the mammary gland.

Conclusions

Although they probably do not initiate mammary cell function, glucocorticoids appear to potentiate prolactin action significantly. At one level, their mode of action is quite clear: they bind to a soluble receptor which undergoes a conformation change to allow nuclear binding. The nature of the molecular events which follow nuclear binding and presumably regulate the transcription of specific proteins has not yet been elucidated. A major problem with many of the *in vitro* experiments presently in the literature is that the concentration of cortisol used ($\cong 10^{-5}$ M) was two orders of magnitude greater than the free cortisol concentration in the plasma ($< 10^{-7}$ M). For this reason, the physiological relevance of many of the reported effects of cortisol is not yet clear.

THE ROLE OF INSULIN IN MAMMARY FUNCTION

The major metabolic role of insulin in mammals is the regulation of nutrient storage and mobilization by liver, adipose tissue, and muscle. In mammary cells, as in adipose tissue, insulin increases glucose utilization for lipid synthesis. Because large doses of insulin have generally been found to be necessary to maintain mammary tissues *in vitro*, a role for this hormone has also been proposed in the regulation of mammary cell development. Nothing is known about insulin receptors in mammary tissue although they have been studied in cultures of rat mammary adenocarcinoma.[212]

The Role of Insulin in Mammary Growth

Insulin has long been known to stimulate the replication of mammary explants[190,213] and is almost universally used in high concentrations (10^{-6} M) to maintain mammary cell integrity and hormone responsiveness in *in vitro* systems even in the presence of 50% homologous serum.[121] On the other hand, there is little evidence for an *in vivo* role for insulin as a regulator of mammogenesis: Insulin levels were found to vary randomly during a course of estrogen and progesterone-induced lactation in goats[214] and alloxan diabetes did not interfere with estrogen-stimulated mammary growth in hypophysectomized male rabbits.[133] Streptozotocin diabetes did not prevent estrogen and progesterone-induced mammary growth in male mice.[41] *In vitro*, Errick and Sueoka (Chapter 6) were able to obtain prolactin stimulation of mammary alveolar cell proliferation in the absence of insulin. The most ready interpretation of these rather confusing data is that insulin may serve as a mammary growth factor in some *in vitro* systems, perhaps by mimicking an insulinlike serum factor, but it is not essential *per se* for mammary growth *in vivo*.

The Role of Insulin in Lactogenesis and Lactation

A deficiency in plasma insulin lasting 24 hr or longer led to decreased milk production in goats[215] and rats.[216,217] However, short-term insulin deficiency did not prevent lactogenesis in rats[218] or decrease established lactation in goats,[219] suggesting that *in vivo* effects of insulin on milk secretion may represent secondary effects due to changes in substrate availability rather than primary effects on mammary tissue.

The response of *in vitro* systems to lactogenic agents is often dependent upon or enhanced by insulin. For example, Topper and Freeman[41] found insulin to be essential for the stimulation of milk protein synthesis by prolactin and cortisol in mammary explants from midpregnant mice. Vonderhaar[171] showed that as little as 0.05 μg insulin/ml, only about ten times normal plasma levels, was effective in the same *in vitro* system. On the other hand, insulin was not required for the induction of casein synthesis by prolactin in explants from pseudopregnant rabbits[220] or for the induction of synthesis of medium chain fatty acids in mouse mammary explants.[65] In a recent report, Ray *et al.*,[61] utilizing long-term primary cultures, showed that insulin slightly enhanced the synthesis of α-lactalbumin in alveolar cell cultures from pregnant rats in the presence of prolactin and cortisol. The hormone had a more significant effect in cultures derived from virgin animals, suggesting that this hormone, or an insulinlike growth factor may be necessary to overcome a block to differentiation as suggested much earlier by Topper and co-workers.[41]

Effects of Insulin on Lipid Synthesis

Unlike adipose tissue and muscle, there is no evidence that insulin regulates the transport of glucose into mammary alveolar cells.[221] Nevertheless, the hormone has clear effects on lipid synthesis in this tissue. In particular, insulin has been shown to reverse the effects of starvation on lipid metabolism although in general supraphysiological doses have been used. Acini isolated from starved rats showed a decrease in glucose uptake and metabolism via the pentose monophosphate shunt as well as decreased lipid formation. Similar effects were seen if acini from fed rats were incubated in the presence of the ketone body, acetoacetic acid.[222] Insulin *in vitro* reversed both the effects of starvation and of acetoacetic acid. *In vivo* restoration of lipogenesis after refeeding of starved animals did not occur if insulin synthesis was abolished with streptozotocin.[222] In an interesting study, Agius *et al.*[223] showed that rats fed a high fat diet consisting in part of chocolate chip cookies and potato chips showed both decreased litter weight gain and decreased lipogenesis in acini removed from the gland. The defect in the isolated acini was corrected by insulin. All these observations are consistent with the hypothesis that increased levels of ketone bodies and decreased plasma insulin concentrations are responsible for the decreased lipid synthesis observed in the mammary glands of starved animals. The availability of glucose or other substrates such as lactate and pyruvate influenced the rate of fatty acid synthesis in mammary gland slices from lactating rats,[224] suggesting that substrate availability may also play a role in regulating synthesis of milk lipids.

One site of insulin action in mammary alveolar cells has been identified by Coore and others[222,225-227] as the mitochondrial enzyme complex, pyruvate dehydrogenase. Starvation increased the phosphorylated form of this complex, which is inactive. As in adipose tissue,[228] insulin had the opposite effect, decreasing the phosphorylated form of the enzyme[226] and increasing the utilization of pyruvate for fatty acid synthesis (see Chapter 3). These observations appeared to be linked to altered activity of pyruvate dehydrogenase kinase.[227] Recent evidence also indicates that insulin regulates the activity of acetyl CoA carboxylase and glycerol phosphate acyltransferase.[229,229a]

Conclusion

The physiological role of insulin in mammary alveolar cell growth and differentiation is presently obscure. Large doses (5 μg/ml) are often used in culture systems to maintain the tissue and to obtain proliferation and differentiation in response to prolactin and cortisol. These doses may be necessary because insulin mimics the effect of a growth factor present in low concentrations in plasma, or simply because much of the added insulin is adsorbed to the culture dishes or degraded by the cultures. Whatever the answer, it seems probable that some insulinlike factor is necessary for initiation or maintenance of the hormonal responsiveness of mammary alveolar cells. Studies with well-defined culture systems should provide some answers in the near future.

As in adipose tissue, insulin stimulates fatty acid synthesis in mammary alveolar cells. In the mammary system, however, the hormone appears to regulate intracellular enzymes involved in glucose metabolism without affecting glucose transport. Much work is necessary both *in vivo* to determine the role of insulin in the response of mammary tissue to starvation and *in vitro* to determine whether insulin regulates the activity of enzymes other than pyruvate dehydrogenase. The well-characterized acinar preparation of Robinson and Williamson[222] or the isolated cell preparation of Sapag-Hagar and Greenbaum[182] should be well-suited for *in vitro* experiments. Here again it will be necessary to ascertain that physiological doses of insulin are effective in altering carbohydrate metabolism.

THYROID HORMONES

Although thyroid hormones appear to promote mammary growth and lactation,[135] they probably play a permissive rather than a regulatory role. Vonderhaar and Greco[230] compared mice maintained in hypothyroid, euthyroid, and hyperthyroid states from weaning and found lobuloalveolar development to be proportional to the plasma level of triiodothyronine (T_3). Thyroid hormone was necessary along with prolactin, growth hormone, and corticoids for the restoration of lactation in hypophysectomized goats[231] and rats.[135] On the other hand, Hart and Morant[214] recently reported that thyroid hormone levels varied randomly during mammary development in goats treated with estrogen and progesterone, consistent with a permissive rather than a regulatory role in mammary function.

In vitro studies of thyroid hormone action have also given equivocal results. In the presence of serum, thyroid hormones were found to have no significant effect on lobuloalveolar development[121] or α-lactalbumin production. Singh and Bern[232] reported that suboptimal doses of prolactin and thyroxine synergized to produce maximum lobuloalveolar development in cultures of whole mouse mammary gland. High levels of thyroxine were inhibitory in this system. Vonderhaar and her colleagues[171,233,234] studied the role of T_3 on α-lactalbumin production in mammary gland explants maintained in serum-free cultures. She found that $10^{-9}M$ T_3 potentiated the prolactin stimulation of α-lactalbumin production,[171] but had no effect on galactosyl transferase. Houdebine *et al.*[235] reported that thyroxine specifically enhanced casein synthesis in explants from pseudopregnant rabbits treated with insulin and prolactin. Because thyroxine did not alter the level of casein mRNA, they interpreted their results to mean that thyroid hormone acts at a posttranscriptional level.

From the sketchy evidence available thyroid hormones appear to be necessary for maximum development and lactational performance of the mammary gland. They probably play a permissive rather than a regulatory role and may be active at the concentrations found in serum supplements to culture media. Although *in vitro* mammary systems sensitive to thyroid hormones are available, they have, as yet, been used in only a limited way to elucidate the mechanism of action of this hormone.

PROSTAGLANDINS

Although they are produced in large quantitites by the mammary gland both *in vitro* and *in vivo*,[236,237] prostaglandins have received relatively little attention as possible regulators of mammary function. Reports that prostaglandin $F_{2\alpha}$ initiates lactogenesis in pregnant humans[238] and rats[239] are probably related to the stimulation of the complex hormonal changes that ultimately lead to parturition and lactogenesis rather than to a direct action on the mammary gland itself.

The most solid evidence for an involvement of prostaglandin in mammary function comes from the work of Maule Walker and Peaker.[237] These investigators found, using goats, that the mammary gland produced large quantities (1 ng/min) of $PGF_{2\alpha}$ prior to parturition. A portion of this $PGF_{2\alpha}$ found its way into milk, giving concentrations about 100 ng/ml. After parturition, there was a 100-fold increase in $PGF_{2\alpha}$ production by the mammary gland, but almost all was immediately metabolized and milk levels fell to about 0.7 ng/ml. These workers suggested that a $PGF_{2\alpha}$ acts as a prepartum inhibitor of milk secretion; after parturition, its prompt metabolism prevents further inhibitory action.

Support for a different inhibitory role for $PGF_{2\alpha}$ was obtained by Vorherr and Vorherr[240] who found that intravenous $PGF_{2\alpha}$ reduced the intramammary pressure response to oxytocin in lactating rats. PGE_1 was without effect in this regard. An inhibitory effect of $PGF_{2\alpha}$ on lactation in women was observed by Fioretti *et al.*[241] and changes in the plasma levels of $PGF_{2\alpha}$ during breast-feeding have been documented by Ylikorkala and Viinikka.[242] How these diverse observations fit into a role for prostaglandins in the regulation of mammary function is an interesting problem for the future.

CYCLIC AMP

There are a number of lines of data which suggest that cAMP may play a role in inhibiting lactogenesis during pregnancy. Sapag-Hagar and Greenbaum[182] observed sharp increases in both adenylate cyclase activity and cAMP levels near the end of pregnancy in rat mammary glands. Both variables decreased again on the first day of lactation and remained low during the period of milk production. In *in vitro* studies, these workers observed that dibutryl cAMP inhibited induction of several enzymes in hormone treated explants from 10-day-old pregnant mice.[183] Speake *et al.*[69] found that dibutryl cAMP and theophylline decreased the stimulation of fatty acid synthetase in explants from midpregnant rabbits and Loizzi and co-workers[243–245] found that dibutryl cAMP or theophylline decreased lactose production by mammary gland slices from lactating guinea pigs. It is not yet clear that these effects of theophylline result from an increase in cAMP, since Wilde and Kuhn[246] found that theophylline strongly inhibited lactose synthesis in rat mammary acini whereas dibutryl cAMP was somewhat inhibitory only at very high concentrations.

From these observations and the finding[182] that progesterone increased cAMP levels in membranes from pregnant but not lactating mice, it is tempting to speculate that increased cAMP levels in the late pregnant mammary gland, perhaps stimulated by progesterone, inhibit the terminal changes of lactogenesis. Further, it is of interest that Yang *et al.*[247] have found that cAMP enhances proliferative activity in primary cultures of mammary cells, raising the possibility that cAMP shifts the balance between growth and differentiation toward the growth state. However, further investigation is necessary before a definitive role can be assigned to cAMP in the regulation of mammary function.

CONCLUSION

From the studies outlined in this chapter, it is now clear that multiple hormonal interactions regulate the pleiotypic responses involved in mammary cell proliferation, differentiation, and milk secretion. From studies of casein synthesis, it has become clear that the control of mRNA turnover is a major point of regulation of milk synthesis. However, there are many other steps at which the potential for regulation exists. These include translation and degradation of enzymes involved in the synthesis of lactose and other milk components, the manufacture of the membrane systems involved in the transport and processing of secretory products and the packaging and export of these substances. Clearly, the synthesis and secretion of milk require the coordinate regulation of all these processes. Whether the hormones that regulate mammary function set up a cascade of reactions that act sequentially or whether parallel transduction systems coordinate these events is one of the more interesting problems under current investigation.

In many respects, the explant system appears to be the best currently available for examination of the coordinate regulation of mammary function. The response of this system to hormones often parallels *in vivo* responses, sufficient material is available for biochemical analyses and the tissue can be maintained in a serum-free medium. On the other hand, the explant system contains multiple cell types whose interactions are not clearly understood. Further, *in vivo* terminal differentiation of the mammary gland appears to occur in two stages (see Chapter 4). In lactogenesis Stage I, the potential for milk secretion is only partially expressed. In lactogenesis Stage II, all the secretory processes are amplified and copious milk secretion results. The explant system does not show two-stage onset of differentiated function. Further, because it accumulates secretory products in the alveolar lumina, it may also be undergoing partial involution. For this reason, caution is indicated in applying results obtained in the explant systems to the *in vivo* function of the mammary gland. With the growing recognition of the role of mammary mesenchymal elements in mammary growth and differentiation, it is likely that a more suitable culture system will soon be available.[149a]

Until recently, the multiple developmental stages of mammary function combined with regulation by several hormones made the mammary gland appear too complex to serve as a model system for investigating cellular control mechanisms. Presently, with the availability of good biochemical information about the mechanisms of milk secretion, the emergence of molecular probes for the study of the control of gene expression, and the increasing availability of suitable culture systems, it seems likely that research on the mammary gland may lead the way in providing a basis for the understanding of complex regulatory systems at the molecular level.

REFERENCES

1. McWilliams, D. and Boime, I., 1980, Cytological localization of placental lactogen messenger ribonucleic acid in syncytiotrophoblast layers of human placenta, *Endocrinology* **107**:761–765.
2. Bern, H. A., 1975, Prolactin and osmoregulation, *Am. Zool.* **15**:937–948.
3. Kleinberg, D. L. and Todd, J., 1980, Evidence that human growth hormone is a potent lactogen in primates, *J. Clin. Endocrinol. Metab.* **51**:1009–1013.

4. Wallis, M., 1975, The molecular evolution of pituitary hormones, *Biol. Rev.* **50**:35–98.
5. Dayhoff, M. O., 1978, *Atlas of Protein Sequence*, Volume 5, Suppl. 3, Washington, D.C.: National Biomedical Research Foundation, Silver Spring, Maryland.
6. Cooke, N. E., Coit, D., Shine, J., Baxter, J. D., and Martial, J. A., 1981, Human prolactin cDNA structural analysis and evolutionary comparisons, *J. Biol. Chem.* **256**:4007–4016.
7. Martial, J. A., Hallewell, R. A., Baxter, J. D., and Goodman, H. M., 1979, Human growth hormone: Complementary DNA cloning and expression in bacteria, *Science* **205**:602–607.
8. Owerbach, D., Rutter, W. J., Martial, J. A., Baxter, J. D., and Shows, T. B., 1980, Genes for growth hormone, chorionic somatomammotropin and growth hormone-like gene are on chromosome 17 in humans, *Science* **209**:289–292.
9. Farquhar, M. G., Reid, J. J., and Daniell, L. W., 1978, Intracellular transport and packaging of prolactin: A quantitative electron microscope autoradiographic study of mammotrophs dissociated from rat pituitaries, *Endocrinology* **102**:296–311.
10. Walker, A. A. and Farquhar, M. G., 1980, Preferential release of newly synthesized prolactin granules is the result of functional heterogeneity among mammotrophs, *Endocrinology* **107**:1095–1104.
11. Salpeter, M. M. and Farquhar, M. G., 1981, High resolution analysis of the secretory pathway in mammotrophs of the rat anterior pituitary, *J. Cell. Biol.* **91**:240–246.
12. del Pozo, E. and Brownell, J., 1979, Prolactin. I. Mechanisms of control, peripheral actions and modification by drugs, *Horm. Res.* **10**:143–172.
13. Ben-Jonathan, N., Neill, M. A., Arbogast, L. A., Peters, L. L., and Hoefer, M. T., 1980, Dopamine in hypophyseal portal blood: Relationship to circulating prolactin in pregnant and lactating rats, *Endocrinology* **107**:690–696.
14. Neill, J. D., Frawley, L. S., Plotsky, P. M., and Tindall, G. T., 1981, Dopamine in hypophysial stalk blood of the rhesus monkey and its role in regulating prolactin secretion, *Endocrinology* **108**:489–494.
15. Goldsmith, P. C., Cronin, M. J., and Weiner, R. I., 1979, Dopamine receptor sites in the anterior pituitary, *J. Histochem. Cytochem.* **27**:1205–1207.
16. Richards, G. F., Holland, F. J., Aubert, M. L., Ganong, W. F., Kaplan, S. L., and Grumbach, M. M., 1980, Regulation of prolactin and growth hormone secretion, *Neuroendocrinology* **30**:139–143.
17. Brocas, H., van Coevorden, A., Seo, H., Refetoff, S., and Vassart, G., 1981, Dopaminergic control of prolactin mRNA accumulation in the pituitary of the male rat, *Mol. Cell. Endocrinol.* **22**:25–30.
18. Maurer, R. A., 1981, Transcriptional regulation of the prolactin gene by ergocryptine and cyclic AMP, *Nature* **294**:94–97.
19. Yen, S. S. C., Ehara, Y., and Siler, T. M., 1974, Augmentation of prolactin secretion by estrogen in hypogonadal women, *J. Clin. Invest.* **53**:652–655.
20. Lloyd, H. M., Meares, J. D., and Jacobi, J., 1975, Effects of oestrogen and bromocryptine on *in vivo* secretion and mitosis in prolactin cells, *Nature* **255**:497–498.
21. Raymond, V., Beaulieu, M., Labrie, F., and Boissier, J., 1978, Potent antidopaminergic activity of estradiol at the pituitary level on prolactin release, *Science* **200**:1173–1175.
22. Antakly, T., Pelletier, G., Zeytinoglu, F., and Labrie, F., 1980, Changes of cell morphology and prolactin secretion induced by 2-Br-α-ergocyptine, estradiol, and thyrotropin-releasing hormone in rat anterior pituitary cells in culture, *J. Cell. Biol.* **86**:377–387.
23. Maurer, R. A., 1982, Estradiol regulates the transcription of the prolactin gene, *J. Biol. Chem.* **257**:2133–2136.
24. Gudelsky, G. A., Nansel, D. D., and Porter, J. C., 1981, Role of estrogen in the dopaminergic control of prolactin secretion, *Endocrinology* **108**:440–444.
25. Labrie, F., Ferland, L., Di Paolo, T., and Veilleux, R., 1980, Modulation of prolactin secretion by sex steroids and thyroid hormones, in: *Central and Peripheral Regulation of Prolactin Function* (R. MacLeod and U. Scapagnini, eds.), Raven Press, New York, pp. 97–113.
26. Wakerley, J. B. and ter Haar, M. B., 1978, Plasma concentration of prolactin and thyrotrophin during suckling: Effects of stimulation of the median eminence, *J. Endocrinol.* **76**:557–558.

27. Sand, O., Haug, E., and Gautvik, K. M., 1980, Effects of thyroliberin and H-aminopyridine in action potentials and prolactin release and synthesis in rat pituitary cells in culture, *Acta Physiol. Scand.* **108**:247–252.

28. Vincent, J. D., Dufy, B., Gourdji, D., and Tixier-Vidal, A., 1980, Electrical correlates of prolactin secretion in cloned pituitary cells, in: *Central and Peripheral Regulation of Prolactin Function* (R. MacLeod and U. Scapagnini, eds.), Raven Press, New York, pp. 141–157.

29. Potter, E., Nicolaisen, A. K., Ong, E. S., Evans, R. M., and Rosenfeld, M. G., 1981, Thyrotropin-releasing hormone exerts rapid nuclear effects to increase production of the primary prolactin mRNA transcript, *Proc. Natl. Acad. Sci. USA* **78**:6662–6666.

30. Nicoll, C. S. and Bern, H. A., 1972, On the actions of prolactin among the vertebrates: Is there a common denominator?, in: *Lactogenic Hormones* (G. E. N. Wolstenholme and J. Knight, eds.) Ciba Foundation Symposium, Churchill Livingstone, Edinburgh, p. 299–317.

31. Rossier, J., French, E., Rivier, C., Shibasaki, T., Guillemin, R., and Bloom, F. E., 1980, Stress-induced release of prolactin: Blockade by dexamethasone and naloxone may indicate β-endorphin mediation, *Proc. Natl. Acad. Sci. USA* **77**:666–669.

32. Blank, M. S., Panerai, A. E., and Friesen, H. G., 1980, Effects of naloxone on luteinizing hormone and prolactin in serum of rats, *J. Endocrinol.* **85**:307–315.

33. Shin, S. H., 1978, Blockage of the ether-induced surge of prolactin by naloxone in male rats, *J. Endocrinol.* **79**:307–398.

34. Ferland, L., Kledyik, G. S., Cuson, L., and Labrie, F., 1978, Evidence for a role of endorphins in stress- and suckling-induced prolactin release in the rat, *Mol. Cell. Endocrinol.* **12**:267–272.

35. Fluckiger, E. W., 1978, Lactation inhibition by ergot drugs, in: *Physiology of Mammmary Gland* (A. Yokoyama, H. Mizuno, and H. Nagasawa, eds.) University Park Press, Baltimore, pp. 71–82.

36. Gezelle, H., Dhont, M., Thiery, M., and Parewyk, W., 1979, Puerperal lactation suppression and prolactin, *Acta. Obstet. Gynecol. Scand.* **58**:469–472.

37. Thorner, M. O. and Besser, G. M., 1977, Hyperprolactinaemia and gonadal function: Results of bromocriptine treatment. in: *Prolactin and Human Reproduction* (P. G. Crosignani and C. Robyn, eds.) Academic Press, London, pp. 285–301.

38. Rosen, J. M., Matusik, R. J., Richards, D. A., Gupta, P., and Rodgers, J. R., 1980, Multihormonal regulation of casein gene expression at the transcriptional and posttranscriptional levels in the mammary gland, *Recent Prog. Horm. Res.* **36**:157–193.

39. Houdebine, L-M., 1980, The control of casein gene expression by prolactin and its modulators, in: *Central and Peripheral Regulation of Prolactin Function* (R. MacLeod and U. Scapagnini, eds.) Raven Press, New York, pp. 180–205.

40. Topper, Y. J., 1970, Multiple hormone interactions in the development of the mammary gland *in vitro, Recent Prog. Horm. Res.* **26**:287–308.

41. Topper, Y. J. and Freeman, C. S., 1980, Multiple hormone interactions in the developmental biology of the mammary gland, *Physiol. Rev.* **60**:1049–1106.

42. Turkington, R. W., Majumder, G. C., Kadohana, N., MacIndoe, J. H., and Frantz, W. L., 1973, Hormonal regulation of gene expression in mammary cells, *Recent Prog. Horm. Res.* **29**:417–455.

43. Shiu, R. P. C. and Friesen, H. G., 1980, Mechanism of action of prolactin in the control of mammary gland function, *Ann. Rev. Physiol.* **42**:83–96.

44. Houdebine, L-M. and Gaye, P., 1975, Regulation of casein synthesis in the rabbit mammary gland, *Mol. Cell. Endocrinol.* **3**:37–55.

45. Terry, P. M., Banerjee, M. R., and Dui, R. M., 1977, Hormone-inducible casein messenger RNA in a serum-free organ culture of whole mammary gland. *Proc. Natl. Acad. Sci. USA* **74**:2441–2445.

46. Rosen, J. M. and Barker, S. W., 1976, Quantitation of casein messenger RNA sequences using a specific complementary DNA hybridization probe, *Biochemistry* **15**:5272–5280.

47. Mehta, N. M., Ganguly, N., Ganguly, R., and Banerjee, M. R., 1980, Hormonal modulation of the casein gene expression in a mammogenesis-lactogenesis culture model of the whole mammary gland of the mouse, *J. Biol. Chem.* **255**:4430–4434.

48. Matusik, R. J. and Rosen, J. M., 1978, Prolactin induction of casein mRNA in organ culture, *J. Biol. Chem.* **253:**2343–2347.
49. Devinoy, E., Houdebine, L-M., and Delouis, C., 1978, Role of prolactin and glucocorticoids in the expression of casein genes in rabbit mammary gland organ culture. Quantification of casein mRNA, *Biochim. Biophys. Acta* **517:**360–366.
50. Guyette, W. A., Matusik, R. J., and Rosen, J. M., 1979, Prolactin-mediated transcriptional and post-transcriptional control of casein gene expression, *Cell* **17:**1013–1023.
51. Teyssot, B. and Houdebine, L-M., 1980, Role of PRL in the transcription of β-casein and 28S ribosomal genes in the rabbit mammary gland, *Eur. J. Biochem.* **110:**236–272.
52. Teyssot, B. and Houdebine, L-M., 1981, Induction of casein synthesis by prolactin and inhibition by progesterone in the pseudopregnant rabbit treated by colchicine without any simultaneous variations of casein mRNA concentration, *Eur. J. Biochem.* **117:**563–568.
53. Gaye, P. and Denamur, R., 1969, Acides ribonucleiques et polyribosomes de la glande mammaire de la lapine au cours de la lactogenese induite par la prolactine, *Biochem. Biophys. Acta* **186:**99–109.
54. Houdebine, L-M., 1977, Distribution of casein mRNA between free and membrane-bound polysomes during induction of lactogenesis in the rabbit, *Mol. Cell. Endocrinol.* **7:**125–135.
55. Ollivier-Bousquet, M., 1978, Early effects of prolactin on lactating rabbit mammary gland, *Cell Tissue Res.* **187:**25–43.
56. Daudet, F., Augeron, C., and Ollivier-Bousquet, M., 1981, Effect rapide *in vitro* de la colchicine, du chlorure d'ammonium et de la prolactine, sur la secretion des lipides du lait dans la glande mammaire, *Eur. J. Cell Biol.* **24:**197–202.
57. Wilde, C. J., Paskin, N., Saxton, J., and Mayer, R. J., 1980, Protein degradation during terminal cytodifferentiation, *Biochem. J.* **192:**311–320.
58. Djiane, J., Houdebine, L-M., Kelly, P. A., 1982, Correlation between prolactin-receptor interaction, down-regulation of receptors, and stimulation of casein and deoxyribonucleic acid biosynthesis in rabbit mammary gland explants. *Endocrinology* **110:**791–795.
59. Ways, J., Markoff, E., Ogren, L., and Talamantes, F., 1979, Lactogenic response of mouse mammary explants from different days of pregnancy to placental lactogen and pituitary prolactin, *In Vitro*, **15:**891–894.
60. Houdebine, L-M., 1979, Role of prolactin in the expression of casein genes in the virgin rabbit, *Cell Differ.* **8:**49–59.
61. Ray, D. B., Horst, I. A., Jansen, R. W., Mills, N. C., and Kowal, J., 1981, Normal mammary cells in long term culture. II. Prolactin, corticosterone, insulin, and triiodothyronine effects on α-lactalbumin production, *Endocrinology* **108:**584–590.
62. Nicholas, K. R. and Topper, Y. J., 1980, Enhancement of α-lactalbumin-like activity in mammary explants from pregnant rats in the absence of exogenous prolactin, *Biochem. Biophys. Res. Comm.* **94:**1424–1431.
63. Wang, D. Y., Hallowes, R. C., Bealing, J., Strong, C. R., and Dils, R., 1972, The effect of prolactin and growth hormone on fatty acid synthesis by pregnant mouse mammary gland in organ culture, *J.Endocrinol.* **53:**311–321.
64. Strong, C. R., Forsyth, I., and Dils, R., 1972, The effects of hormones on milk-fat synthesis in mammary explants from pseudo-pregnant rabbits, *Biochem. J.* **128:**509–519.
65. Forsyth, I. A., Strong, C. R., and Dils, R., 1972, Interactions of insulin, corticosterone and prolactin in promoting milk-fat synthesis by mammary explants from pregnant rabbits, *Biochem. J.* **129:**929–935.
66. Hallowes, R. C., Wang, D. Y., Lewis, D. J., Strong, C. R., and Dils, R., 1973, The stimulation by prolactin and growth hormone of fatty acid synthesis in explants from rat mammary gland, *J. Endocrinol.* **57:**265–276.
67. Cameron, J. A., Rivera, E. M., and Emery, R. S., 1975, Hormone-stimulated lipid synthesis in mammary culture, *Am. Zool.* **15:**285–293.
68. Speake, B. K., Dils, R., and Mayer, R. J., 1975, Regulation of enzyme turnover of fatty acid synthesis in rabbit mammary gland in organ culture, *Biochem. J.* **148:**309–320.
69. Speake, B. K., Dils, R., and Mayer, R. J., 1976, Regulation of enzyme turnover during tissue differentiation. Interactions of insulin, prolactin and cortisol in controlling the

turnover of fatty acid synthetase in rabbit mammary gland in organ culture, *Biochem. J.* **154:**359–370.

70. Hamosh, M., Clary, T. R., Chernick, S. S., and Scow, R. O., 1970, Lipoprotein lipase activity of adipose and mammary tissue and plasma triglyceride in pregnant and lactating rats, *Biochem. Biophys. Acta* **210:**473–482.
71. Zinder, O., Hamosh, M., Fleck, T. R. C., and Scow, R. O., 1974, Effect of prolactin on lipoprotein lipase in mammary gland and adipose tissue of rats, *Am. J. Physiol.* **226:**744–748.
72. Catt, K. J. and Dufau, M. L., 1977, Peptide hormone receptors, *Ann. Rev. Physiol.* **39:**529–557.
73. Nagasawa, H., Sakai, S., and Banerjee, M. R., 1979, Prolactin receptor, *Life Sci.* **24:**193–208.
74. McGuire, W. L., 1977, Prolactin and breast cancer, in: *Prolactin and Human Reproduction* (P. G. Crosignani and C. Robyn, eds.), Academic Press, London, pp. 143–151.
75. McGuire, W. L., Chamness, G. C., Horwitz, K. B., and Zava, D. T., 1978, Hormones and their receptors in breast cancer, in: *Receptors and Hormone Action Volume II* (B. W. O'Malley and L. Birnbaumer, eds.), Academic Press, New York, pp. 401–420.
76. Waters, M. J., McNeilly, A. S., Ohgo, S., and Friesen, H. G., 1980, Prolactin receptor content of rabbit milk, *Endocrinology* **107:**816–821.
77. Posner, B. I., Raquidan, D., Josefsberg, Z., and Bergeron, J. J. M., 1978, Different regulation of insulin receptors in intracellular (golgi) and plasma membranes from livers of obese and lean mice, *Proc. Natl. Acad. Sci. USA* **75:**3302–3306.
78. Shiu, R. P. C. and Friesen, H. G., 1974, Properties of a prolactin receptor from the rabbit mammary gland, *Biochem. J.* **140:**301–311.
79. Shiu, R. P. C. and Friesen, H. G., 1974, Solubilization and purification of a PRL receptor from the rabbit mammary gland, *J. Biol. Chem.* **249:**7902–7911.
80. Suard, Y. M. L., Kraehenbuhl, J.-P., and Aubert, M. L., 1979, Dispersed mammary epithelial cells: Receptors of lactogenic hormones in virgin, pregnant, and lactating rabbits, *J. Biol. Chem.* **254:**10466–10475.
81. Shiu, R. P. C. and Friesen, H. G., 1976, Blockade of prolactin action by an antiserum to its receptors, *Science* **192:**259–261.
82. Shiu, R. P. C. and Friesen, H. G., 1976, Interaction of cell-membrane prolactin receptor with its antibody, *Biochem. J.* **157:**619–626.
83. Waters, M. J., Friesen, H. G., and Bohnet, H. G., 1978, Regulation of PRL receptors by steroid hormones and use of radioligand assays in endocrine research, in: *Receptors and Hormone Action*, Volume III (B. W. O'Malley and L. Birnbaumer, eds.), Academic Press, New York, pp. 457–477.
84. Holcomb, H. H., Costlow, M. E., Buschow, R. A., McGuire, W. L., 1976, Prolactin binding in rat mammary gland during pregnancy and lactation, *Biochim. Biophys. Acta* **428:**104–112.
85. Holdaway, I. M., Deegan, M., and Friesen, H. G., 1977, Influence of infused prolactin on hormone binding to tissue slices, *Can. J. Physiol. Pharmacol.* **55:**193–195.
86. Djiane, J., Durand, P., and Kelly, P. A., 1977, Evolution of prolactin receptors in rabbit mammary gland during pregnancy and lactation, *Endocrinology* **100:**1348–1356.
87. Djiane, J., Clauser, H., and Kelly, P. A., 1979, Rapid down-regulation of prolactin receptors in mammary gland and liver, *Biochem. Biophys. Res. Comm.* **90:**1371–1378.
88. Kelly, P. A., Leblanc, G., and Djiane, J., 1979, Estimation of total prolactin-binding sites after *in vitro* desaturation, *Endocrinology* **104:**1631–1638.
89. Kelly, P. A., Djiane, J., and De Lean, A., 1980, Interaction of prolactin with its receptor: Dissociation and down-regulation, in: *Central and Peripheral Regulation of Prolactin Function* (R. M. MacLeod and U. Scapagnini, eds.), Raven Press, New York, pp. 173–188.
90. McNeilly, A. S., and Friesen, H. G., 1977, Binding of prolactin to the rabbit mammary gland during pregnancy, *J. Endocrinol.* **74:**507–508.
91. Bohnet, H. G., Gomez, F., and Friesen, H. G., 1977, PRL and estrogen binding sites in the mammary gland of the lactating and non-lactating rat, *Endocrinology* **101:**1111–1121.

92. Djiane, J. and Durand, P., 1977, Prolactin-progesterone antagonism in self-regulation of prolactin receptors in the mammary gland, *Nature* **266**:641–643.

93. Djiane, J., Delouis, C., and Kelly, P. A., 1979, Prolactin receptors in organ culture of rabbit mammary gland: Effect of cyclohexamide and prolactin, *Proc. Soc. Exp. Biol. Med.* **162**:342–345.

94. Djiane, J., Kelly, P. A., and Houdebine, L.-M., 1980, Effects of lysosomotropic agents, cytocholasin B and colchicine on the "down-regulation" of prolactin receptors in mammary gland explants, *Mol. Cell. Endocrinol.* **18**:87–98.

95. Costlow, M. E., and Hample, A., 1980, Metabolic inhibitors increase prolactin binding to cultured mammary tumor cells, *Biochem. Biophys. Res. Comm.* **92**:213–220.

96. Nolin, J. M. and Witorsch, R. J., 1976, Detection of endogenous immunoreactive prolactin in rat mammary epthelial cells during lactation, *Endocrinology* **99**:949–958.

97. Nolin, J. M., 1978, Target cell prolactin, in: *Structure and Function of the Gonadotropins* (K. W. McKerns, ed.), Plenum Press, New York, pp. 151–182.

98. Nolin, J. M., 1979, The prolactin incorporation cycle of the milk secretory cell, *J. Histochem. Cytochem.* **27**:1203–1204.

99. Shiu, R. P. C., 1980, Processing of prolactin by human breast cancer cells in long term tissue culture, *J. Biol. Chem.* **255**:4278–4281.

100. Djiane, J., Houdebine, L.-M., and Kelly, P. A., 1981, Prolactin-like activity of anti-prolactin receptor antibodies on casein DNA synthesis in the mammary gland, *Proc. Natl. Acad. Sci. USA* **78**:7445–7448.

101. Oka, T. and Perry, J. W., 1974, Spermidine as a possible mediator of glucocorticoid effect on milk protein synthesis in mouse mammary epithelium *in vitro*, *J. Biol. Chem.* **249**:7647–7652.

102. Oka, T., and Perry, J. W., 1976, Studies on regulatory factors of ornithine decarboxylase activity during development of mouse mammary epithelium *in vitro*, *J. Biol. Chem.* **251**:1738–1744.

103. Rillema, J. A., 1980, Mechanism of prolactin action, *Fed. Proc.* **39**:2593–2598.

104. Matusik, R. J. and Rosen, J. M., 1980, Prolactin regulation of casein gene expression: Possible mediators, *Endocrinology* **106**:252–259.

105. Houdebine, L.-M., Djiane, J., and Clauser, H., 1979, Endocrinologie—rôle des lysosomes, des micro-tubules, et des microfilaments dans le mécanisme de l'action lactogène de la prolactine sur la glande mammaire de lapine, *C. R. Acad. Sci. Ser. D* **289**:679–682.

106. Houdebine, L.-M. and Djiane, J., 1980, Effects of lysomotropic agents, and of microfilament- and microtubule-disrupting drugs on the activation of casein-gene expression by prolactin in the mammary gland, *Mol. Cell. Endocrinol.* **17**:1–15.

107. Teyssot, B., Houdebine L.-M., and Djiane, J., 1981, Prolactin induces release of a factor from membranes capable of stimulating β-casein gene transcription in isolated mammary cell nuclei, *Proc. Natl. Acad. Sci. U.S.A.* **78**:6729–6733.

108. Ito, Y. and Hiyashi, K., 1961, Studies on the prolactin-like substance in human placenta, *Endocrinol. Jpn.* **8**:279–287.

109. Josimovich, J. B. and MacLaren, J. A., 1962, Presence in the human placenta and term serum of a highly lactogenic substance immunologically related to pituitary growth hormone, *Endocrinology* **71**:209–220.

110. Li, C. H., Grumbach, M. M., Kaplan, S. L., Josimovich, J. B., Friesen, H., and Catt, K. J., 1968, Human chorionic somato-mammotropin (HCS), proposed terminology for designation of a placental hormone, *Experientia* **24**:1288.

111. Braunstein, G. D., Rasor, J. L., Engvall, E., and Wade, M. E., 1980, Interrelationships of human chorionic gonadotropin, human placental lactogen, and pregnancy-specific β₁-glycoprotein throughout normal human gestation, *Am. J. Obstet. Gynecol.* **136**:506–509.

112. Cowie, A. T., Forsyth, I. A., and Hart, I. C., 1980, *Hormonal Control of Lactation*, Springer Verlag, Berlin.

113. Beck, P. and Daughaday, W. H., 1967, Human placental lactogen: Studies of its acute metabolic effects and disposition in normal man, *J. Clin. Invest.* **46**:103–110.

114. Vigneri, R., Squatrito, S., Pezzino, V., Cinquerui, E., Proto, S., and Montoneri, C., 1975, Spontaneous fluctuations of human placental lactogen during normal pregnancy, *J. Clin. Endocrinol. Metab.* **40:**506–509.

115. Gaspard, U. J., Luyckx, A. S., George, A. N., and Lefebvre, P. J., 1977, Relationship between plasma free fatty acid levels and human placental lactogen secretion in late pregnancy, *J. Clin. Endocrinol. Metab.* **45:**246–254.

116. Prieto, J. C., Cifventes, I., and Serrano-Rios, M., 1976, hCS regulation during pregnancy, *Obstet. Gynecol.* **48:**297–301.

117. Hayden, T. S., Thomas, C. R., Smith, S. V., and Forsyth, I. A., 1980, Placental lactogen in the goat in relation to stage of gestation, number of fetuses, metabolites, progesterone and time of day, *J. Endocrinol.* **86:**279–280.

118. Bigazzi, M., Ronga, R., Lancranjan, I., Ferraro, S., Branconi, F., Buzzoni, P., Martorana, V., Scarselli, G. F., and Del Pozo, E., 1979, Pregnancy in an acromegalic woman during bromocriptine treatment: Effects on growth hormone and prolactin in the maternal, fetal and amniotic compartments, *J. Clin. Endocrinol. Metab.* **48:**9–12.

119. Grumbach, M. M., Kaplan, S. L., Sciarra, J. J., and Burr, I. M., 1968, Chorionic growth hormone-prolactin (CGP): Secretion, disposition, biologic activity in man, and postulated function as the "growth hormone" of the second half of pregnancy, *Ann. N.Y. Acad. Sci.* **148:**501–531.

120. Turkington, R. W. and Topper, Y. J., 1966, Stimulation of casein synthesis and histological development of mammary gland by human placental lactogen *in vitro*, *Endocrinology* **79:**175–181.

121. Peters, J. M., van Marle, J., and Ariëns, A. Th., 1979, Hormonal effects on rat mammary gland *in vitro*, *Acta Endocrinol.* **92:**(Suppl 228):1–190.

122. McManus, M. J. and Welsch, C. W., 1980, DNA synthesis of benign human breast tumors in the untreated athymic "nude" mouse, *Cancer* **45:**2160–2165.

123. Halban, J., 1905, Die innere Secretion von Ovarium und Placenta und ihre Bedeutug für die function der Milchdrüse, *Arch. Gynaekol.* **75:**353–441.

124. Folley, S. J. and Malpress, F. H., 1948, Hormonal control of lactation, in: *The Hormones* Volume 1 (G. Pincus, ed.), Academic Press, New York, pp. 745–805.

125. Cowie, A. T., 1978, Backward glances, in: *Physiology of Mammary Glands* (A. Yokoyama, H. Mizuno, and H. Nagasawa, eds.) University Park Press, Baltimore, pp. 43–56.

126. Smith, K. L. and Schanbacher, F. L., 1973, Hormone induced lactation in the bovine, I. Lactational performance following ingestion of 17β-oestradiol and progesterone, *J. Dairy Sci.* **56:**738–743.

127. Houdebine, L-M., 1976, Effects of prolactin and progesterone on expression of casein genes, *Eur. J. Biochem.* **68:**219–225.

128. Leclerg, G. and Heuson, J. C., 1979, Physiological and pharmacological effects of estrogens in breast cancer, *Biochem. Biophys. Acta* **560:**427–455.

129. Edwards, D. P., Chamness G. C., and McGuire W. L., 1979, Estrogen and progesterone receptor proteins in breast cancer, *Biochem. Biophys. Acta* **560:**457–486.

130. Jacobsohn, D., 1954, Action of estradiol monobenzoate on the mammary glands of hypophysectomized rabbits, *Acta Physiol. Scand.* **32:**304–313.

131. Traurig, H. H. and Morgan, C. F., 1964, The effect of ovarian and hypophyseal hormones on mammary gland epithelial cell proliferation, *Anat. Rec.* **150:**423–434.

132. Stampfer, M., Hallowes, R. C., and Hackett, A. J., 1980, Growth of normal human mammary cells in culture, *In Vitro* **16:**415–425.

133. Norgren, A., 1968, Modification of mammary development in rabbits injected with ovarian hormones, *Acta. Univ. Lund. Sect. 2* **4:**4–42.

134. Klevjer-Anderson, P. and Buehring, G. C., 1980, Effect of hormones on growth rates of malignant and nonmalignant human mammary epithelia in cell culture, *In Vitro* **16:**491–501.

135. Lyons, W. R., 1958, Hormonal synergism in mammary growth, *Proc. R. Soc. London, Ser. B* **149:**303–325.

136. Meites, J., 1966, Control of mammary growth and lactation, in *Neuroendocrinology, Volume 1* (L. Martin and W. F. Ganong, eds.), Academic Press, New York, pp. 669–701.

137. Robyn, C., Delvoye, P., Van Exter, C., Vekemans, M., Caufriez, A., de Nayer, P., Delogne-Desnoeck, J., and L'Hermite, M., 1977, Physiological and pharmacological factors influencing prolactin secretion and their relation to human reproduction, in: *Prolactin and Human Reproduction* (P. G. Crosignani and C. Robyn, eds.), Academic Press, London, pp. 17–96.

138. Del Pozo, E., Hiba, J., Lancranjan, I. and Kunzig, H. J., 1977, Prolactin measurements throughout the life cycle, in: *Prolactin and Human Reproduction*, (P. G. Crosignani and C Robyn, eds.) Academic Press, London, pp. 61–70.

139. Hertz, J., Andersen, A. N., and Larsen, J. F., 1978, Correlation between prolactin and progesterone, oestradiol 17β and oestriol during early human pregnancy, *Clin. Endocrinol.* **9:**97–100.

140. Lemarchand-Béraud, Th., Reymond, M., Berthier, C., and Rey, I., 1977, Effects of oestrogens on prolactin and TSH A secretion in women, in: *Prolactin and Human Reproduction* (P. G. Crosignani and C. Robyn, eds.), Academic Press, London, pp. 135–142.

141. Large, D. M., Anderson, D. C., and Laing, I., 1980, Twenty-four hour profiles of serum prolactin during male puberty with and without gynecomastia, *Clin. Endocrinol.* **12:**293–302.

142. Frawley, L. S. and Neill, J. D., 1980, Effect of estrogen on serum prolactin levels in Rhesus monkeys after hypophyseal stalk section, *Biol. Reprod.* **22:**1089–1093.

143. Lippman, M., Bolan, G., and Huff, K., 1976, The effects of estrogens and antiestrogen on hormone-responsive human breast cancer in long-term tissue culture, *Cancer Res.* **36:**4595–4601.

144. Allegra, J. C. and Lippman, M. E., 1978, Growth of a human breast cancer cell line in serum-free hormone-supplemented medium, *Cancer Res.* **38:**3823–3828.

145. Antunes, J. L., Housepian, E. M., Frantz, A. G., Holub, D. A., Hui, R. M., Carmel, P. W., and Quest, D. O., 1977, Prolactin-secreting pituitary tumors, *Ann. Neurol.* **2:**148–153.

146. Sultan, C., Descomps, B., Garandeau, P., Bressot, N., and Jean, R., 1979, Pubertal gynecomastia due to an estrogen-producing adrenal tumor, *J. Pediatr.* **95:**744–746.

147. Sirbasku, D. A., 1978, Estrogen induction of growth factors specific for hormone-responsive mammary pituitary and kidney tumor cells, *Proc. Natl. Acad. Sci. U.S.A.* **75:**3786–3790.

148. Tonelli, O. J. and Sorof, S., 1980, Epidermal growth factor requirement for development of cultured mammary gland, *Nature* **285:**250–252.

149. Bennett, D. C., 1980, Morphogenesis of branching tubules in cultures of cloned mammary epithelial cells, *Nature* **285:**657–659.

149a. Wicha, M. S., Lowrie, G., Kohn, E., Bagavandoss, P., and Mann, T., 1982, Extracellular matrix promotes mammary epithelial growth and differentiation *in vitro*, *Proc. Natl. Acad. Sci. U.S.A.* **79:**3213–3217.

150. Shyamala, G. and Nandi, S., 1972, Interactions of 6,7-^{3}H-17β estradiol with the mouse lactating mammary tissue *in vivo* and *in vitro*, *Endocrinology* **91:**861–867.

151. Haslam, S. Z. and Shyamala, G., 1979, Effect of oestradiol on progesterone receptors in normal mammary glands and its relationship with lactation, *Biochem. J.* **182:**127–131.

152. Haslam, S. Z. and Shyamala, G., 1981, Relative distribution of estrogen and progesterone receptors among the epithelial, adipose, and connective tissue components of the normal mammary gland, *Endocrinology* **108:**825–830.

153. Mohla, S., Clem-Jackson, N., and Hunter, J. B., 1981, Estrogen receptors and estrogen-induced gene expression in the rat mammary glands and uteri during pregnancy and lactation: Changes in progesterone receptor and RNA polymerase activity, *J. Steroid Biochem.* **14:**501–508.

154. Muldoon, T. G., 1981, Interplay between estradiol and prolactin in the regulation of steroid hormone receptor levels, nature and functionality in normal mouse mammary tissue, *Endocrinology* **109:**1339–1346.

155. Horwitz, K. B. and McGuire, W. L., 1977, Progesterone and progesterone receptors in experimental breast cancer, *Cancer Res.* **37:**1733–1738.

156. Haslam, S. Z. and Shyamala, G., 1979, Progesterone receptors in normal mammary glands of mice: Characterization and relationship to development, *Endocrinology* **105**:786–795.
157. Shyamala, G. and Ferenczy, A., 1982, The nonresponsiveness of lactating mammary gland to estradiol, *Endocrinology* **110**:1249–1256.
158. Bolander, F. F. and Topper, Y. J., 1980, Stimulation of lactose synthetase activity and casein synthesis in mouse mammary gland explants by estradiol, *Endocrinology* **106**:490–495.
159. Warner, M. R., Yam, L., and Rosen, J. M., 1980, Long term effects of perinatal injection of estrogen and progesterone on the morphological and biochemical development of the mammary gland, *Endocrinology* **106**:823–833.
160. Maule Walker, F. M. and Peaker M., 1978, Production of oestradiol-17β by the goat mammary gland during late pregnancy in relation to lactogenesis, *J. Physiol.* **284**:71P.
161. Muckle, C. W., 1940, The suppression of lactation by stilbesterol, *Am. J. Obstet. Gynecol.* **40**:133–135.
162. Foss, G. L. and Phillips, P., 1938, The suppression of lactation by oral estrogen therapy, *Br. Med. J.* **2**:887–890.
163. Chen, C. L. and Meites, J., 1970, Effects of estrogen and progesterone on serum and pituitary prolactin levels in ovariectomized rats, *Endocrinology* **86**:503–505.
164. Nolin, J. M. and Bogdanove, E. M., 1980, Effects of estrogen on prolactin incorporation by lutein and milk secretory cells and on pituitary prolactin secretion in the post-partum rat: Correlations in target cell responsiveness to prolactin, *Biol. Reprod.* **22**:393–416.
165. Stoudemire, G. A., Stumpf, W. E., and Sar, M., 1975, Synergism between prolactin and ovarian hormones on DNA synthesis in rat mammary gland, *Proc. Soc. Exp. Biol. Med.* **149**:189–192.
166. Kuhn, N. J., 1977, Lactogenesis: The search for trigger mechanisms in different species, in: *Comparative Aspects of Lactation* (M. Peaker, ed.), Academic Press, New York, pp. 165–192.
167. Kuhn, N. J., 1969, Progesterone withdrawal as the lactogenic trigger in the rat, *J. Endocrinol.* **44**:39–54.
168. Yokoyama, A., Shinde, Y., and Ota, K., 1969, Endocrine control of changes in lactose content of the mammary gland in rats shortly before and after parturition, in: *Lactogenesis, the Initiation of Milk Secretion at Parturition*, (M. Reynolds and S. J. Folley, eds.) University of Pennsylvania Press, Philadelphia, pp. 65–70.
169. Turkington, R. W. and Hill, R. L., 1969, Lactose synthetase: progesterone inhibition of the induction of α-lactalbumin, *Science* **163**:1458–1460.
170. Assairi, L., Delouis, C., Gaye, P., Houdebine, L-M., Ollivier-Bousquet, M., and Denamur, R., 1974, Inhibition by progesterone of the lactogenic effect of prolactin in the pseudopregnant rabbit, *Biochem. J.* **144**:245–252.
171. Vonderhaar, B. K., 1977, Studies on the mechanism by which thyroid hormones enhance α-lactalbumin activity in explants from mouse mammary glands, *Endocrinology* **100**:1423–1431.
172. Ip, C. and Dao, T. L., 1978, Effect of estradiol and prolactin on galactosyltransferase and α-lactalbumin activities in rat mammary gland and mammary tumor, *Cancer Res.* **38**:2077–2083.
173. Harigaya, T., Sakai, S., and Kohmoto, K., 1978, Induction of mammary prolactin receptors and lactose synthesis after ovariectomy in the mouse, *Endocrinol. Jpn.* **25**:157–161.
174. Davis, J. W., Wilkman-Coffelt, J., and Eddington, C. L., 1972, The effect of progesterone on biosynthetic pathways in mammary tissue, *Endocrinology* **91**:1011–1019.
175. Rosen, J. M., O'Neal, D. L., McHugh, J. E., and Comstock, J. P., 1978, Progesterone-mediated inhibition of casein mRNA and polysomal casein synthesis in the rat mammary gland during pregnancy, *Biochemistry* **17**:290–297.
176. Teyssot, B. and Houdebine, L-M., 1981, Role of progesterone and glucocorticoids in the transcription of the β-casein and 28-S ribosomal genes in the rabbit mammary gland, *Eur. J. Biochem.* **114**:597–608.

177. Devinoy, E., Houdebine, L-M., and Ollivier-Bousquet, M., 1979, Role of glucocorticoids and progesterone in the development of rough endoplasmic reticulum involved in casein biosynthesis, *Biochimie* **61**:453–461.
178. Greenbaum, A. L., Sochor, M., and McLean, P., 1978, Regulation of mammary gland metabolism, pathways of glucose utilization, metabolic profile and hormone response of a modified mammary gland cell preparation, *Eur. J. Biochem.* **87**:505–516.
179. Maki, M., Hirose, M., and Chiba, H., 1980, Occurence of common binding sites for progestin and glucocorticoid in the lactating mammary gland of the rat, *J. Biochem.* **88**:1845–1854.
180. Shyamala, G. and McBlain, W. A., 1979, Distinction between progestin- and glucocorticoid-binding sites in mammary glands, *Biochem. J.* **178**:345–352.
181. Ganguly, R., Majumder, P. K., Ganguly, N., and Banerjee, M. R., 1982, The mechanism of progesterone-glucocorticoid interaction in regulation of casein gene expression, *J. Biol. Chem.* **257**:2182–2187.
182. Sapag-Hagar, M. and Greenbaum, A. L., 1974, Adenosine 3':5'-monophosphate and hormone interrelationships in the mammary gland of the rat during pregnancy and lactation, *Eur. J. Biochem.* **47**:303–312.
183. Sapag-Hagar, M., Greenbaum, A. L., Lewis, D. J., and Hallowes, R. C., 1974, The effects of di-butryl cAMP on enzymatic and metabolic changes in explants of rat mammary tissue, *Biochem. Biophys. Res. Comm.* **59**:261–268.
184. Haslam S. Z. and Shyamala, G., 1980, Progesterone receptors in normal mammary gland: Receptor modulations in relation to differentiation, *J. Cell. Biol.* **86**:730–737.
185. Lloyd, R. V., 1979, Studies on the progesterone receptor constant and steroid metabolism in normal and pathological human breast tissues, *J. Clin. Endocrinol. Metab.* **48**:585–593.
186. Gaunt, R., 1941, Inability of desoxycorticosterone to maintain lactation, *Proc. Soc. Exp. Biol. Med.* **47**:28–31.
187. Davis, J. W. and Liu, T. M. Y., 1969, The adrenal glands and lactogenesis, *Endocrinology* **85**:155–160.
188. Cowie, A. T. and Lyons, W. R., 1959, Mammogenesis and lactogenesis in hypophysectomized, ovariectomized, adrenalectomized rats, *J. Endocrinol.* **19**:29–32.
189. Elias, J. J., 1957, Cultivation of adult mouse mammary gland in hormone-enriched synthetic medium, *Science* **126**:842–844.
190. Juergens, W. F., Stockdale, F. E., Topper, Y. J., and Elias, J. J., 1965, Hormone-dependent differentiation of mammary gland *in vitro*, *Proc. Natl. Acad. Sci. USA* **54**:629–634.
191. Denamur, R., 1971, Reviews of the progress of dairy science: Hormonal control of lactogenesis, *Dairy Res.* **38**:237–262.
192. Folley, S. J. and Young, F. B., 1941, Prolactin as a specific lactogenic hormone, *Lancet* **1**:380–381.
193. Chadwick, A., 1971, Lactogenesis in pseudopregnant rabbits treated with adrenocortico-trophin and adrenal corticosteroids, *J. Endocrinol.* **49**:1–8.
194. Maltau, J. M., Eielson, O. V., and Stokke, K. T., 1979, Effect of stress during labor on the concentration of cortisol and estriol in maternal plasma, *Am. J. Obstet. Gynecol.* **134**:681–684.
195. Burd, L. I., Lemons, J. A., Makowski, E. L., Battaglia, F. C., and Meschia, G., 1975, Relationship of mammary blood flow to parturition in the ewe, *Am. J. Physiol.* **229**:797–800.
196. Linzell, J. L. and Peaker, M., 1974, Changes in colostrum composition and in the permeability of the mammary epithelium at about the time of parturition in the goat, *J. Physiol.* **243**:129–151.
197. Shyamala, G., 1973, Specific cytoplasmic glucocorticoid hormone receptors in lactating mammary glands, *Biochemistry* **12**:3085–3090.
198. Shyamala, G., 1975, Glucocorticoid receptors in mouse mammary tumors: Specific binding to nuclear components, *Biochemistry* **14**:437–444.
199. Shyamala, G. and Dickson, C., 1976, Relationship between receptor and mammary tumor virus production after stimulation by glucocorticoid, *Nature* **262**:107–111.

200. Mills, E. S. and Topper, Y. J., 1970, Some ultrastructural effects of insulin, hydrocortisone, and prolactin on mammary gland explants, *J. Cell. Biol.* **44:**310–328.
201. Bolander, F. F., Jr and Topper, Y. J., 1979, Relationships between spermidine, glucocorticoid and milk proteins in different mammalian species, *Biochem. Biophys. Res. Comm.* **90:**1131–1135.
202. Devinoy, E. and Houdebine, L-M., 1977, Effects of glucocorticoids on casein gene expression in the rabbit, *Eur. J. Biochem.* **75:**411–416.
203. Sakai, S., Bowman, P. D., Yang, J., McCormick, K., and Nandi, S., 1979, Glucocorticoid regulation of prolactin receptors on mammary cells in culture, *Endocrinology* **104:**1447–1449.
204. Ganguly, R., Ganguly, N., Mehta, N. M., and Banerjee, M. R., 1980, Absolute requirement of glucocorticoid for expression of the casein gene in the presence of prolactin, *Proc. Natl. Acad. Sci. U.S.A.* **77:**6003–6006.
205. Ono, M. and Oka, T., 1980, α-Lactalbumin-casein induction in virgin mouse mammary explants: Dose-dependent differential action of cortisol, *Science* **207:**1367–1369.
206. Ono, M. and Oka, T., 1980, The differential actions of cortisol on the accumulation of α-lactalbumin and casein in midpregnant mouse mammary gland in culture, *Cell* **19:**473–480.
207. Russell, D. H. and McVicker, T. A., 1972, Polyamine biogenesis in the rat mammary gland during pregnancy and lactation, *Biochem. J.*, **130:**71–76.
208. Houdebine, L-M., Devinoy, E., and DeLouis, C., 1978, Role of spermidine in casein gene expression in the rabbit, *Biochimie* **60:**735–741.
209. Sakai, T., Lundgren, D. W., and Oka, T., 1978, Polyamine biosynthesis and DNA synthesis in cultured mammary gland explants from virgin mice, *J. Cell. Physiol.* **95:**259–267.
210. Oka, T., 1974, Spermidine in hormone-dependent differentiation of mammary gland *in vitro*, *Science* **184:**78–80.
211. Brosnan, M. E., Ilic, V., and Williamson, D. H., 1979, Regulation of the activity of ornithine decarboxylase and S-adenosylmethionine decarboxylase in mammary gland and liver of lactating rats, *Biochem. J.* **202:**693–698.
212. Sorge, L. K. and Hilf, R., 1982, Down-regulation of insulin receptors in primary cultures of R323OAC rat mammary adenocarcinoma cells, *Endocrinology* **110:**1155–1163.
213. Friedberg, S. H., Oka, T., and Topper, Y. J., 1970, Development of insulin-sensitivity by mouse mammary gland *in vitro*, *Proc. Natl. Acad. Sci. USA* **67:**1493–1500.
214. Hart, I. C. and Morant, S. V., 1980, Roles of prolactin, growth hormone, insulin and thyroxine in steroid-induced lactation in goats, *J. Endocrinol.* **84:**343–351.
215. Nowak, J. and Dzialoszynski, L., 1967, Effect of experimental alloxan diabetes on the secretion and composition of goat milk, *Acta Physiol. Pol.* **18:**488–497.
216. Walters, E. and McLean, P., 1968, Effect of alloxan-diabetes and treatment with anti-insulin serum on pathways of glucose metabolism in lactating rat mammary gland, *Biochem. J.* **109:**407–417.
217. Martin, R. J., and Baldwin, R. L., 1971, Effects of alloxan diabetes on lactational performance and mammary tissue metabolism in the rat, *Endocrinology* **88:**863–867.
218. Kyriakou, S. Y. and Kuhn, N. J., 1973, Lactogenesis in the diabetic rat, *J. Endocrinol.* **59:**199–200.
219. Hove, K., 1978, Maintenance of lactose secretion during acute insulin deficiency in lactating goats, *Acta Physiol. Scand.* **103:**173–179.
220. DeLouis, C. and Combaud, M. L., 1977, Lack of mitotic effects of insulin during synthesis of casein induced by prolactin in pseudopregnant rabbit mammary gland organ cultures, *J. Endocrinol.* **72:**393–394.
221. Robinson, A. M., Girard, J. R., and Williamson, D. H., 1978, Evidence for a role of insulin in the regulation of lipogenesis in lactating rat mammary gland, *Biochem. J.* **176:**343–346.
222. Robinson, A. M. and Williamson, D. H., 1977, Control of glucose metabolism in isolated acini of the lactating mammary gland of the rat, *Biochem. J.* **168:**465–474.
223. Aguis, L., Rolls, B. J., Rowe, E. A., and Williamson, D. H., 1980, Impaired lipogenesis in mammary glands of lactating rats fed on a cafeteria diet, *Biochem. J.* **186:**1005–1008.

224. Bartley, J. C. and Abraham, S., 1976, The absolute rate of fatty acid synthesis by mammary gland slices from lactating rats, *J. Lipid Res.* **17:**467–477.

225. Field, B. and Coore, H. G., 1976, Control of rat mammary-gland pyruvate dehydrogenase by insulin and prolactin, *Biochem. J.* **156:**333–337.

226. Baxter, M. A. and Coore, H. G., 1978, The mode of regulation of pyruvate dehydrogenase of lactating rat mammary gland. Effects of starvation and lactation, *Biochem. J.* **174:**553–561.

227. Baxter, M. A., Goheer, M. A., and Coore, H. G., 1979, Absent pyruvate inhibition of pyruvate dehydrogenase kinase in lactating rat mammary gland following various treatments, *FEBS Lett.* **97:**27–31.

228. Seals, J. R. and Jarett, L., 1980, Activation of pyruvate dehydrogenase by direct addition of insulin to an isolated plasma membrane/mitochondria mixture: Evidence for generation of insulin's second messenger in a subcellular system, *Proc. Natl. Acad. Sci. U.S.A.* **77:**77–81.

229. Munday, M. R. and Williamson, D. H., 1981, Role of pyruvate dehydrogenase and insulin in the regulation of lipogenesis in the lactating mammary gland of the rat during the starved-refed transition, *Biochem. J.* **196:**831–837.

229a. McNeelie, E. M. and Zammit, V. A., 1982, Regulation of acetyl CoA carboxylase in rat mammary gland, *Biochem. J.* **204:**273–280.

230. Vonderhaar, B. K. and Greco, A. E., 1979, Lobulo-alveolar development of mouse mammary glands is regulated by thyroid hormones, *Endocrinology* **104:**409–418.

231. Cowie, A. T., 1969, General hormonal factors involved in lactogenesis, in: *Lactogenesis, the Initiation of Milk Secretion at Parturition* (M. Reynolds and S. J. Folley, eds.) University of Pennsylvania Press, Philadelphia, pp. 157–169.

232. Singh, D. V. and Bern, H. A., 1969, Interaction between prolactin and thyroxine in mouse mammary gland lobulo-alveolar development *in vitro*, *J. Endocrinol.* **45:**579–583.

233. Vonderhaar, B. K., 1975, A role of thyroid hormones in differentiation of mouse mammary gland *in vitro*, *Biochem. Biophys. Res. Comm.* **67:**1219–1225.

234. Vonderhaar, B. K., 1979, Lactose synthetase activity in mouse mammary glands is controlled by thyroid hormones, *J. Cell Biol.* **82:**675–681.

235. Houdebine, L-M., DeLouis, C., and Devinoy, E., 1978, Post-transcriptional stimulation of casein synthesis by thyroid hormone, *Biochimie* **60:**809–812.

236. To, D., Smith, F. L., and Carpenter, M. P., 1980, Mammary gland prostaglandin synthesis: Effect of dietary lipid and propyl gallate, *Adv. Prostag. Thrombox. Res.* **8:**1807–1812.

237. Maule Walker, F. M. and Peaker, M., 1980, Local production of prostaglandins in relation to mammary function at the onset of lactation in the goat, *J. Physiol.* **309:**65–79.

238. Smith, V. G., Convey, E. M., and Edgerton, L. A., 1972, Bovine serum corticoid response to milking and exteroceptive stimuli, *J. Dairy Sci.* **55:**1170–1173.

239. Bussman, L. E. and Deis, R. P., 1979, Studies concerning the hormonal induction of lactogenesis by $PGF_{2\alpha}$ in pregnant rats, *J. Steroid Biochem.* **11:**1489–1492.

240. Vorherr, H. and Vorherr, U. F., 1979, Effect of prostaglandins ($F_{2\alpha}$, E_1, and E_2) on blood pressure and oxytocin-induced intramammary pressure responses in rats, *Endocrinology* **104:**989–995.

241. Fioretti, P., Nasi, A., Medda, F., de Murtas, M., Melis, G. B., and Caminiti, F., 1977, Inhibitory effect of prostaglandin F2alpha on puerperal lactation, *Acta Europ. Fertil.* **8:**265–271.

242. Ylikorkala, O. and Viinikka, L., 1981, Prostacyclin, thromboxane, and prostaglandin $F_{2\alpha}$ in maternal plasma during breast-feeding, *Am. J. Obstet. Gynecol.* **139:**690–692.

243. Loizzi, R. F., dePont, J. J. H. H. M., and Bonting, S. L., 1975, Inhibition by cyclic AMP of lactose production in lactating guinea pig mammary gland slices, *Biochim. Biophys. Acta* **392:**20–25.

244. Loizzi, R. F., 1978, Cyclic AMP inhibition of mammary gland lactose synthesis: Specificity and potentiation by 1-methyl-3-isobutylxanthine, *Horm. Metab. Res.* **10:**415–419.

245. Loizzi, R. F. and Amato, P. A., 1978, Ultrastructural changes in lactating guinea pig mammary gland slices associated with theophylline inhibition of lactose synthesis, *Cytobios* **22:**47–65.

246. Wilde, C. J. and Kuhn, N. J., 1981, Lactose synthesis and the utilisation of glucose by rat mammary acini, *Int. J. Biochem.* **13:**311–316.
247. Yang, J., Guzman, R., Richards, J., Imagawa, W., McCormick, K., and Nandi, S., 1980, Growth factor- and cyclic nucleotide-induced proliferation of normal and malignant mammary epithelial cells in primary culture, *Endocrinology* **107:**35–41.

6

In Vitro Model Systems for the Study of Hormonal Control of Mammary Gland Growth and Differentiation

Janice E. Errick and Tamiko Kano-Sueoka

INTRODUCTION

In vivo studies of mammary function in whole animals have contributed greatly to our understanding of multihormonal control and differentiated function. Because of the extreme complexity of the hormone environment *in vivo*, however, *in vitro* culture techniques are indispensible if the roles of hormones in mammary cell function are to be fully defined. In particular, animal model systems are very useful for *in vitro* studies because the hormonal background of the animal can be manipulated prior to culture and sufficient material can be readily obtained. Cultures can be monitored for growth (cell division) similar to that occurring during puberty or pregnancy, the appearance of mRNAs specific for milk proteins, the synthesis and secretion of casein, α-lactalbumin, lactose, and triglycerides that constitute lactation, and the metabolic changes that occur during involution. In this way, mammary development can be examined in its various stages and the effects of purified hormones can be tested. A number of techniques have been devised for the study of these aspects of mammary development *in vitro*. The advantages of each and the information so far obtained will be discussed.

The animal systems that are most often used for *in vitro* studies are derived from rats, mice, and rabbits, and tissues can be obtained for culture can be in a number of hormonal states: virgin, pregnant, lactating, pseudopregnant, or hormone treated. Ichinose and Nandi[1] found that hormonal pretreatment of mice was necessary for subsequent *in vitro* differentiation to occur. More recently, investigators have used estrogen and progesterone

Janice E. Errick and Tamiko Kano-Sueoka • Department of MCD Biology, University of Colorado, Boulder, Colorado 80309.

injections[2] and perphenazine treatment[3] to obtain increased amounts of mammary tissue that is more responsive *in vitro*.

It will be apparent from the work described here that *in vitro* studies have so far served primarily to confirm results obtained *in vivo*. This has been a necessary step in the development of systems that accurately reflect physiological processes as well as the demonstration that the purified hormones act directly on mammary tissues. Present and future experiments, for which *in vitro* systems are indispensible, are directed towards an understanding of the molecular mechanisms involved in the hormonal control of gene expression in the mammary gland. In this chapter, we will focus on studies directed toward this goal.

In reading this chapter, several technical points common to most of the experimental systems should be kept in mind. First, the purified lactogenic hormones that most investigators use are ovine and bovine prolactin, human placental lactogen, and occasionally, human growth hormone, prepared for the National Institutes of Health by various laboratories. Although, these hormones do not always cross-react immunologically, in general, they all bind to isolated prolactin receptors and stimulate mammary growth *in vivo*. It is interesting that human growth hormone, unlike growth hormone from other species, has lactogenic activity in rodent mammary cultures. Second, the concentrations of purified hormones used in culture range from near-physiological to pharmacological. Possible reasons for high dosage requirements include: (1) purified hormones may lack cofactors or carrier proteins normally present in serum, (2) the hormones may adsorb to the plastic culture plates, thereby lowering the effective concentration, (3) the added hormones may be substituting for as yet unknown factors present in the blood and thus are required at much higher concentrations, and (4) contaminants in the hormone preparations may actually be responsible for their activity *in vitro*. At present, there is no way to determine which of these reasons are correct. Finally, as mentioned, most *in vitro* studies are carried out in tissues from mouse, rat, and rabbit. Although it is clear that differences in the *in vivo* cause of development exist among these species, it seems likely that, at the cellular level, general principles of hormone action will emerge.

WHOLE GLAND CULTURE

Whole mammary gland culture of mice was used first by Ichinose and Nandi,[1] and is a system that closely approximates the *in vivo* situation. The glands are removed from the skin with their supporting connective, fatty tissue, and spread out on Dacron rafts in serum-free, hormone-supplemented medium, usually a complete medium such as Waymouth's or Medium 199. The teats are left intact. Under these conditions, glands can be cultured for several weeks in various hormone environments then analyzed histologically or biochemically.

Tonelli and Sorof[2] obtained two full cycles of development and regression in whole glands from estrogen and progesterone-primed BALB/c mice. After a first cycle of 9 days in a medium containing insulin, prolactin, aldosterone, and hydrocortisone (each at 5 μg/ml), glands showed extensive lobuloalveolar development. On transfer to a medium containing insulin alone, regression occurred. A second cycle of development was obtained only if epidermal growth factor (EGF) was added to the four-hormone combination (Fig. 1). Hydrocortisone was necessary for development in these cultures.

Terry *et al.*[4] cultured mammary glands from estrogen- and progesterone-primed mice and showed pregnancylike development after 6 days in "growth-promoting" media containing insulin, prolactin, growth hormone, estradiol, and progesterone. After an additional 6 days with a "lactogenic hormone" combination, insulin, prolactin, and cortisol (5 μg/ml each), secretory material appeared in the alveolar lumens and casein messenger RNA (mRNA) could be detected.

In neither of these experiments is the significance of each hormone made clear. Insulin generally appears to be required for maintenance of epithelial cells in culture but its role in mammary gland development *in vivo* remains equivocal. Prolactin and placental lactogen are the most important hormones for mammary development *in vivo* and prolactin is absolutely required for lobuloalveolar development and cellular differentiation in these whole gland cultures. Terry *et al.*[4] did not explain why they added growth hormone, estrogen, and progesterone, although *in vivo* evidence suggests that these hormones are important for ductal and alveolar growth.[5]

Both *in vivo* and *in vitro* work strongly suggests a direct effect of glucocorticoids on the synthesis of milk protein: Tonelli and Sorof[2] found no development in glands cultured in the absence of hydrocortisone and/or aldosterone. Banerjee *et al.*[6] in an *in vivo* study, found that adrenalectomy of lactating mice resulted in the loss of casein mRNA as measured by *in vitro* translation of bulk polyribosomes into casein immunoprecipitable material. Cortisol treatment of these animals resulted in a stimulation of ribosomal and messenger RNA, and an increase in casein mRNA. Thus, both *in vivo* and *in vitro* work strongly suggest a direct effect of glucocorticoids on the synthetic machinery for milk protein. In some systems, aldosterone also appears to be effective.[2] The effect of corticosteroids *in vitro* will be discussed further in a later section.

Summary

The finding that whole mammary glands of mice can be taken through two cycles of development *in vitro* represents a significant advance in this field. Cultured in a relatively simple mixture of appropriate hormones and serum-free medium, these glands make casein and secrete it into luminal spaces, thereby providing a model system for hormone-dependent synthesis of specific cell products.

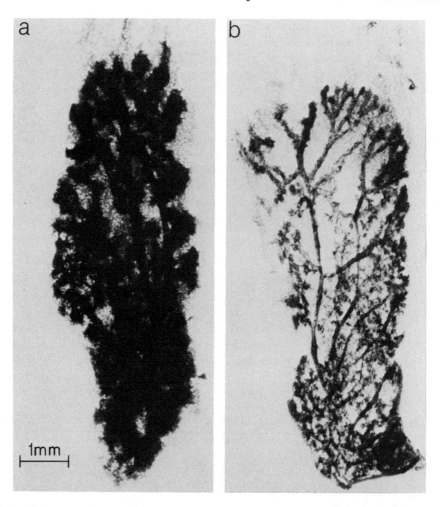

Figure 1. Second lobuloalveolar development of mouse mammary gland in whole organ culture. Glands from hormone-primed female mice (1 µg estradiol and 1 mg progesterone injected daily for 9 days) were cultured in medium containing insulin (I), prolactin (P), aldosterone (A), and hydrocortisone (H) for 9 days followed by exposure to regression medium containing I only (5 µg/ml) for additional 15 days. Glands were subsequently cultured for an additional 9 days in the IPAH medium with or without 10 nM EGF, then fixed and stained. (a) Whole mammary gland showing second-developed lobuloalveoli after incubation in the medium containing EGF. (b) Control glands similarly incubated in the medium without EGF. The epithelial cells are primarily ductal, and alveoli are absent. (From Tonelli and Sorof,[2] used with permission.)

However, the mammary gland consists of various cell types: alveolar and ductal epithelial cells, fat cells, and stromal cells. Therefore, interactions between these cell types may be important for the development of the mammary gland. The mechanism of action of any particular hormone on growth and function of the secretory cell itself cannot be determined with certainty unless indirect effects via stromal cells, for example, are eliminated. Therefore, other culture systems have been devised to eliminate this problem.

EXPLANT CULTURES

The culture of small pieces of mammary tissue containing a mixture of epithelial cells and stromal cells (explant or, formerly, organ culture) is a technique that has been used for several years to study hormone effects in a controlled environment.[7] Investigators such as El-Darwish and Rivera[8] were able to establish the importance of insulin, corticosterone, and prolactin on DNA synthesis and milk production in mammary tissue. In recent years, this technique has been valuable in determining the biochemical events which led to synthesis of milk components and secretion following hormonal stimulation.

In the experiments of El-Darwish and Rivera,[8] cell growth in explants of midpregnant mice was measured in two ways: (1) by increase in DNA content and (2) by incorporation of ^{3}H-thymidine into DNA. Insulin alone (5 μg/ml) caused an increase in DNA on the first day, an effect which was not maintained on subsequent days. Corticosterone (1 μg/ml) alone caused an decrease in DNA content and prolactin alone (5 μg/ml) had a small stimulatory effect which decreased with time. Combinations of the hormones led to synergistic interactions. Insulin and prolactin together caused the greatest increase in DNA content during the first 2 days. Subsequently, only the cultures containing all three hormones had a DNA content greater than the initial values. Incorporation studies showed that the largest increase in the rate of DNA synthesis occurred after 1 day in culture in the presence of any of the hormone combinations and fell sharply by the second day, but less sharply in the presence of all three hormones. These data imply that, whereas any of the combinations cause an initial stimulation of DNA synthesis, only the three together are able to maintain the new cells. Histological examination of the tissue pieces after 5 days in culture showed no loss of alveolar structure and secretory activity only in those explants cultured with the three hormones. Insulin was absolutely necessary to prevent tissue degeneration, and prolactin to maintain secretory activity. The effects of corticosterone were apparent after two days in culture, and seemed to enhance the effects of insulin and prolactin.

Nicholas and Topper[9] used the explant culture technique to study a well-known marker of mammary differentiation, α-lactalbumin, a component of the lactose synthetase enzyme. Tissue from pregnant and virgin rats was cultured in medium containing various combinations of insulin (5 μg/ml), hydrocortisone (1 μg/ml), and prolactin (5 μg/ml). α-Lactalbumin increased steadily over the course of 3 days in the presence of insulin, hydrocortisone, and prolactin; no increase was seen with insulin alone. Unexpectedly, cultures containing only insulin and hydrocortisone expressed α-lactalbumin activity after a lag of about 24 hr. This effect was seen in cultures of midpregnant but not virgin glands, and was not observed with either casein or fatty acid synthesis, both of which were absolutely dependent on the presence of prolactin, in addition to insulin and hydrocortisone. In both the insulin–hydrocortisone and insulin–hydrocortisone–prolactin cultures, development of α-lactalbumin activity was suppressed by progesterone. The authors do not offer an explanation for the appearance of α-lactalbumin activity in the absence of prolactin. However, differential hormonal responses of various milk-specific proteins has been observed by other investigators.[10]

Some investigators have used the explant system to determine more specifically the point of action of hormones on the biochemical processes leading to the production of casein or α-lactalbumin. Devinoy et al.[11] examined both in vivo and in vitro effects of prolactin and glucocorticoids on casein mRNA synthesis in rabbit mammary glands. Explants from pseudopregnant rabbits were cultured for 18 hr in the presence of various combinations of insulin, prolactin, and cortisol, at which time casein was measured by immunoprecipitation and casein mRNA concentration by hybridization to a casein cDNA probe. They found that the rate of casein synthesis was correlated with the amount of specific casein mRNA, implying control at the mRNA level. Prolactin alone brought about an increase in specific casein messenger RNA. Glucocorticoid amplified this response. In the absence of prolactin, neither insulin nor glucocorticoid had any noticeable effect. These effects were similar to in vivo effects of these hormones.

Matusik and Rosen[12] studied the early events following prolactin stimulation of midpregnant rat mammary glands in explant culture. In their system, tissue pieces were cultured for 48 hr in the presence of insulin (5 μg/ml) and hydrocortisone (1 μg/ml). At that time, prolactin (5 μg/ml) was added and, at various intervals, cultures were assayed for casein mRNA by hybridization to a casein cDNA probe. In 13-day pregnant glands, a 1.3-fold increase in casein mRNA in prolactin-stimulated cultures was seen within 1 hr, which reached 13.4-fold in 48 hr. They then calculated that control cultures contained 478 casein mRNA molecules/cell whereas prolactin stimulated cultures contained 6420 molecules/cell. Hydrocortisone, added with prolactin, potentiated the prolactin stimulation of casein mRNA levels. Interestingly, measurable amounts of casein mRNA were found in cultures containing only insulin and hydrocortisone much like the findings of Nicholas and Topper[9] with α-lactalbumin. Matusik and Rosen[12] agree with other investigators[11] that hydrocortisone amplifies the extent of prolactin-induced mRNA but does not itself stimulate casein mRNA synthesis. They found that progesterone inhibited casein mRNA synthesis in a dose-dependent manner.

Another aspect of mammary cell differentiation that has been studied using explant culture is milk fat synthesis. Strong et al.[13] cultured explants from pseudopregnant and lactating rabbits in medium containing various combinations of insulin (5 μg/ml), corticosterone (1 μg/ml), and prolactin (5 μg/ml) in the presence of ^{14}C-acetate or ^{14}C-glucose. Lipids were extracted and the fatty acids separated by chain length. In lactating rabbit mammary explants cultured for 4 days, the pattern of labeled fatty acids approximated most closely the uncultured explants when insulin, corticosterone, and prolactin were present in the medium. In cultures of pseudopregnant glands, the rate of fatty acid synthesis increased about 40-fold in prolactin-containing medium. Well over 65% of the synthesized fatty acids were of the mammary-specific medium chain, compared with 90% for intact lactating gland, and 25% for control cultures lacking prolactin. In the midpregnant rat, essentially similar results were found by Hallowes *et al.*[14]

Wang *et al.*[15] used inhibitors in cultures of midpregnant mouse mammary glands to investigate the nature of the milk-specific fatty acid synthetase. They found that insulin and cortisol caused a considerable stimulation of fatty acid synthesis which was not sensitive to any of the inhibitors. Prolactin and growth hormone each increased fatty acid synthesis another two- to threefold over insulin and cortisol alone. Both DNA and RNA synthesis were required for this increase to occur. Protein synthesis was not required during the final 4 hr of hormonal stimulation, suggesting that the fatty acid synthetase, once induced, is relatively stable, and further or continued protein synthesis is not required.

The control of milk-fat synthesis has been studied by some investigators in terms of the induction of synthetic enzymes for milk fat. Speake and co-workers[16] used antibodies to fatty acid synthetase in rabbit mammary gland in culture to study its synthesis and degradation. They found that insulin, cortisol, and prolactin stimulated the synthesis of fatty acid synthetase, and decreased its rate of degradation in the cells. The amount of enzyme present did not determine the rate of lipogenesis, however, since on removal of hormones from the culture medium, lipid synthesis decreased independently of the decrease in the amount of fatty acid synthetase.

Summary

Explant culture of mammary glands has considerable historical interest as this technique was instrumental in establishing the importance of insulin, glucocorticoids, and especially prolactin in mammary cell growth and differentiation *in vitro*. Cultured glands have been found to respond to prolactin by an increase in specific casein and α-lactalbumin mRNAs and casein synthesis. Glucocorticoids enhance these effects but do not directly bring about these processes. Progesterone appears to inhibit milk secretion during pregnancy in part by an inhibition of casein mRNA synthesis. While most of these conclusions were at least suggested by *in vivo* experiments, the *in vitro* studies have served to confirm the direct effects of specific hormones on the mammary cells.

As discussed earlier, intact glands can be maintained much longer in culture, and, therefore, the development of an entire organ can be followed in a controlled environment. The explants, in contrast, can be kept healthy for only a week to 10 days. However, for quantitative biochemical studies the explant system has the advantage that many cultures can be prepared from one gland. Further, it is not limited to small glands such as those in mice, but may be used with the larger glands of rats and rabbits as well. The drawbacks of the organ culture system still remain, however: (1) heterogeneity of cell types and (2) possible difficulty of nutrient access to all parts of the tissue. In addition, proliferative responses are small and while products of mammary cell differentiation such as casein, α-lactalbumin, and medium-chain fatty acids can be measured in the proper hormonal milieu, their rates of synthesis are much lower than those found in the lactating gland. For these reasons, many laboratories have recently focused on primary culture systems as described in the next section.

PRIMARY CULTURE

Although the cultures described in the preceeding sections are well defined with respect to media and hormone supplements, problems of cell type heterogeneity and possible difficulty in supplying nutrients or hormones to the cells remained. The epithelial components of the tissue can be removed from stromal elements by partial digestion with enzymes. The resulting alveoli and ductal aggregates can be plated onto plastic or specially treated dishes where they attach, spread out, and grow as monolayers. This technique allows one to grow normal mammary epithelial cells for extended periods; subculturing through one or more platings is often possible. Such a system can be used to develop a defined medium for normal mammary cells that allows optimum growth and possibly differentiation.[17,18] Particularly interesting are the studies of mammary cell differentiation of cultures grown on a gelled collagen substrate[19] rather than on plastic. These provide evidence for a relationship between cell shape and function.

In general, primary cultures are prepared by dissecting out the mammary gland, or tumor, and incubating small pieces in medium containing collagenase (1 to 2 mg/ml) and possibly hyaluronidase and DNase. The effect of this treatment is to digest the extracellular matrix causing the release of the stromal cells which can then be eliminated by differential centrifugation of the cell suspension. The epithelial cells, joined together by many cellular junctions, remain as clumps which are the ducts and alveoli. When plated in Medium 199 (M199) + 5% fetal calf serum (FCS), these clumps attach and spread out; after one or two days, two morphologically distinct cell types can be seen in each colony (Fig. 2). In the central area are the secretory epithelial cells, flat and cobblestonelike in appearance. At the periphery of the colony are elongated cells that may be the myoepithelial cells. The effects of hormones and growth factors are monitored in a number of ways: proliferation is usually measured by ^{3}H-thymidine incorporation because of the variability in initial plating density, although changes in DNA or protein content have also been used as indicators of cell growth.[18] Markers for differentiation include casein,[20,21] α-lactalbumin,[22,23] lipid synthesis,[24] and histological appearance.[19]

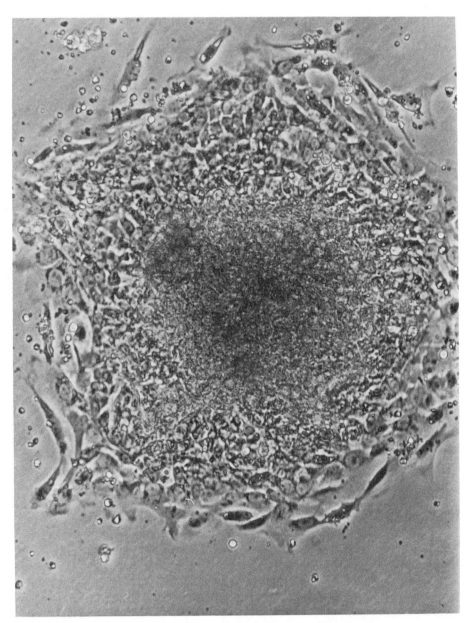

Figure 2. Primary culture of rat mammary epithelial cells 24 hr after plating. Mammary glands from estrogen-primed females were digested overnight at 35°C in M199 + 5% FCS and 2 mg/ml collagenase. Cell clumps were separated from single cells and debris by differential centrifugation and plated in M199 + 5% FCS.

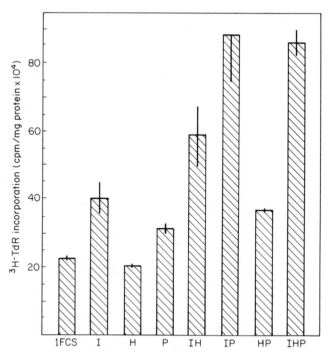

Figure 3. Effect of hormones on ^{3}H-DNA synthesis. Cultures prepared as in Fig. 2. After 48 hr, medium was changed to M199 + 1% FCS and hormones as follows: Insulin (I, 5 μg/ml), hydrocortisone (H, 1 μg/ml), prolactin (P, 5 μg/ml). Twenty-four hr later, ^{3}H-TdR was added (3 μCi/ml, 2.0 Ci/mmole) for 2 hr and trichloroacetic-acid-precipitable radioactivity determined in a liquid scintillation counter. Bars indicate range of duplicates.

The results of experiments in our laboratory and in others[25] have again shown the importance of insulin, corticoids, and prolactin for growth and differentiation. Fig. 3 shows the effects of the three hormones added singly and in combination to primary cultures of mammary cells from estradiol-primed female A × C rats. Of the three hormones added individually, insulin had the most significant effect on the rate of DNA synthesis. When the hormones were added in combinations such that both additive and synergistic effects could be distinguished, hydrocortisone (1 μg/ml) enhanced the stimulatory effect of insulin (5 μg/ml) by 100% but had no effect by itself. The activity of prolactin alone (5 μg/ml) was increased slightly by addition of hydrocortisone. The combination of insulin and prolactin together showed an additive interaction which was seen repeatedly in these cultures. In this particular experiment, the addition of all three hormones did not stimulate the rate of DNA synthesis beyond that seen with insulin and prolactin, although in other cases there was an additional effect.

We further investigated the effects of prolactin alone on DNA synthesis since other laboratories[23,25] have not seen this effect. Fig. 4 shows three representative experiments in which prolactin alone was added to 1% FCS-

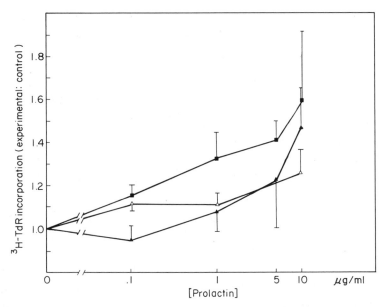

Figure 4. Comparison of prolactin effects on virgin and estradiol-primed rat mammary glands. Cultures in each of three experiments were grown in varying concentrations of prolactin in M199 + 1% FCS. After 24 hrs, ^{3}H-TdR was added for 2 hr and acid precipitable radioactivity determined. Data for each experiment were normalized to 1.0. Symbols: ■, virgin; △, ▲, estrogen-primed.

medium at various concentrations. Virgin and estradiol-primed glands behaved similarly. Although the concentration of prolactin most often used by us and others,[18,25] 5 μg/ml, is higher than physiological, in one case a significant effect was obtained at 1 μg/ml which is close to the level found in pregnant rats. In other experiments (not shown), as little as 10 ng/ml of prolactin was sufficient to enhance the stimulatory effect of insulin.

Using this system, we were able to test a number of hormones and factors for their capacity to initiate DNA synthesis. Ovine growth hormone, estrogen, luteinizing hormone, follicle-stimulating hormone, testosterone, and progesterone had no effect or were inhibitory. Epidermal growth factor had some stimulatory effect alone and in combination with other hormones, and phosphoethanolamine, a factor found to stimulate cell division in a rat mammary cell line[24] enhanced the effects seen in the presence of hormones.

It has been known for a long time that cell shape and substrata are important factors in development. Emerman and Pitelka[19] used this principle to develop a culture system that allowed the mammary cells to assume an organization more like that found *in vivo*. They used a solution of rat tail collagen (Type I) dissolved in weak acid that would gel upon neutralization in the bottom of a Petri dish. This provided a semisolid surface on which cells could be plated. Dissociated mammary epithelial cells from mid- to late-pregnant mice were grown on the collagen gels in medium containing 15%

horse serum, insulin (5 μg/ml), hydrocortisone (1 μg/ml), and prolactin (5 μg/ml). The gels either remained attached to the dishes or were released to float in the medium. Over the course of 1 month, there were remarkable differences in the appearance of cells grown on plastic, attached gels, and floating gels. The latter cultures, which had contracted due to the presence of the sheet of cells on top, had an authentic secretory appearance when viewed in the light and electron microscopes. There were fat droplets, secretory granules, elaborated endoplasmic reticulum, microvilli on the "apical" surface, occluding junctions, and basal nuclei.

The effects of individual hormones on casein synthesis were studied in other experiments.[21] Cells from midpregnant mice were grown in serum-free medium containing either insulin alone or insulin, hydrocortisone and prolactin, and casein was measured by radioimmunoassay at various times up to 10 days. A four- to eightfold increase in intracellular casein was seen in cultures grown with the three hormones on floating collagen gels over those in insulin alone or those grown on plastic, even with the three hormones. Similar results were found when the culture medium was assayed for casein, showing that hormone-stimulated cells grown on floating gels synthesized and secreted casein. Katiyar et al.[20] tested other polypeptide hormones in this system and found that only peptides with lactogenic activity (ovine prolactin, human placental lactogen, human growth hormone) could stimulate casein synthesis in combination with insulin and hydrocortisone. This effect was seen at concentrations of lactogen as low as 10 ng/ml. Hormones that had no effect on casein production were thyroid stimulating hormone, follicle-stimulating hormone, luteinizing hormone, and bovine and ovine growth hormones.

The collagen gel system was used for the study of ion transport by Bisbee et al.[27] The mammary gland is known to transport materials from its basal to its apical surfaces, but actual measurements are difficult to make *in vivo* or in organ culture. A layer of mouse mammary cells on a collagen gel, however, was easily placed in an Ussing chamber and measurements of ion transport made. The results showed that prolactin significantly increased ion transport across the epithelial cells.

These experiments show that morphological and biochemical differentiation are possible *in vitro* using collagen substrates. One drawback of the collagen-gel system, however, is that the cells do not divide once plated on the collagen surface. Therefore, hormonal control of proliferation could not be studied with the floating gel system. Recently, however, Yang et al.[18] have obtained hormone-dependent growth of normal human mammary tissue embedded in collagen gels in medium containing 12% horse serum, 2.3% fetal calf serum, and a mixture of hormones. Under these conditions, the number of cells increased 10- to 30-fold in about 2 weeks, indicating a rate of cell division that was significant but far below that found during pregnancy. The cells could be subcultured by digesting the gel with collagenase. After 2 weeks, the cultures contained sheetlike, cystlike, and ductlike outgrowths. As mentioned, the collagen gels consist of Type I collagen. However, mammary epithelial cells *in vivo* are in contact with Type IV collagen, a component of the basal lamina. Salomon *et al.*[28] found that the ability to synthesize and accumulate Type IV collagen was important for proliferation of rat mammary epithelial cells. Cells grown on plastic or collagen Type I required EGF and glucocorticoids, which promote the accumulation of Type IV, whereas cells grown on a substratum of Type IV did not require these factors for growth.

Another system that shows promise for the culture of normal human mammary cells has been developed by Stampfer *et al.*[17] Primary cultures were grown in plastic dishes in medium containing 5% FCS, a mixture of several hormones, acid extract of blood meal (probably containing somatomedins), and conditioned medium from three human epithelial cell lines. Cells could be subcultured through as many as four passages, although growth potential was considerably reduced. An advantage of this system is that many plates can be generated from tissue from a single individual, so that each sample can be treated as a cell line.

Summary

Primary culture of nearly pure preparations of mammary alveolar and ductal cells is so far the most successful technique for growing normal mammary cells in culture.

Prolactin, insulin, and hydrocortisone are important for some aspects of mammary cell growth, but for continued maintenance of cell differentiation other factors, including proper substrate, need to be considered. In the near future, it is possible that the exact requirements for growth and differentiation at different times during pregnancy and lactation will be known. By studying the interaction between these factors *in vitro*, it should be possible to greatly improve our understanding of the mechanisms involved.

CELL CULTURE

Long-term culture of a homogeneous population of mammary epithelial cells should be a useful tool for the detailed analysis of hormonal effect on growth and differentiation. To date, many breast carcinoma cell lines have been isolated from both human and experimental rodent mammary tumors. However, no normal mammary epithelial cell line that retains the properties of the original mammary tissue is presently available. This is probably because, during the process of establishing cell lines, hormone-responsiveness of the original cells is usually lost; in addition, the cells tend to acquire transformed characteristics. As has been discussed in the previous section, Stampfer *et al.*[17] have succeeded in culturing predominantly epithelial type cells from reduction mammoplasty tissue of humans for 1 to 3 months with up to four subcultures. With consideration of the substratum on which the cells grow[18] and increased knowledge about nutrition of the cells in culture, in the near future, we may be able to obtain cell lines that retain properties of normal breast cells.

Estrogen and prolactin are the two essential hormones that influence the development of the mammary gland *in vivo*. The response of mammary cells to these hormones has been analyzed in culture in some detail using breast cancer cell lines which retain some of the properties of normal mammary epithelial cells. Although estrogen is regarded as a crucial hormone in promoting mammary gland development, it has been very difficult to provide unequivocal proof of a direct effect of estrogen on mammary tissue. Using a human breast cancer cell line, ZR-75-1, grown in a serum-free culture medium, Allegra and Lippman[29] showed that 17 β-estradiol at a concentration of 10^{-8} M stimulated cell division. After 2 weeks, those cultures containing estradiol had more than twice as many cells as those without estradiol. This was the first convincing evidence of a mitogenic effect of estrogen. In these experiments, L-triiodothyronine (10^{-8} M) was also shown to stimulate proliferation of the ZR-75-1 cells.

The mitogenic effect of prolactin on mammary cells in long-term culture has not been demonstrated until recently. Previously, using a human breast cancer cell line MCF-7, Shafie and Brooks[30] demonstrated that prolactin (10 μg/ml, a pharmacological level) along with dibutyryl cAMP stimulated the incorporation of ^{3}H-thymidine into DNA, and Burke and Gaffney[31] showed, using the same cell line, that 5 μg/ml ovine prolactin increased protein synthesis by 50%. However, the stimulation of protein synthesis did not result in an increase in cell number. Recently, in our laboratory, a distinct mitogenic effect of prolactin on rat mammary carcinoma cells has been demonstrated. As shown in Fig. 5, ovine prolactin had growth-promoting activity at a concentration of 100 ng/ml, which is within the physiological range. A possibility that the mitogenic effect of prolactin is due to some contaminant in the prolactin preparation has not yet been entirely excluded. However, since the initial stimulation by prolactin is similar at concentrations of 0.1 μg/ml to 1 μg/ml and the prolactin preparation we used is pure by many criteria, the possibility of a contaminant as the mitogen is rather unlikely, unless it is very potent indeed.

The presence of prolactin receptors in several human breast cancer cell lines was successfully demonstrated by Shiu,[32] who found considerably higher numbers of prolactin receptors, ranging from about 2000 to 26,000 per cell in five cancer cell lines compared to 1700 in a cell line isolated from normal tissue. The functional significance of these differences is unknown. There was only one so-called normal cell line available for this study, and this line had acquired some characteristics of transformed cells during long-term culture. Therefore, this cell line may not be representative of normal mammary cells.

Estrogen receptors have been found in many established breast cancer cell lines including MCF-7. Using this cell line, Shafie and Brooks[30] made the important observations that prolactin is capable of increasing estrogen-binding activity. This prolactin effect had been suggested by some *in vivo*

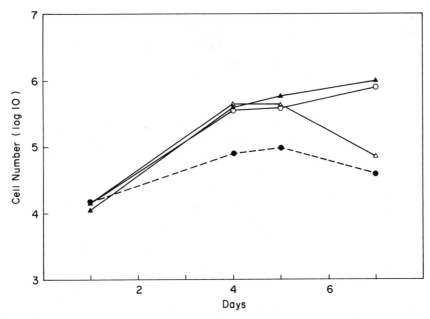

Figure 5. Prolactin-stimulated growth of a rat mammary carcinoma cell line. The cells were plated in a medium consisting of Dulbecco-modified Eagle medium, insulin (5 μg/ml), transferrin (5 μg/ml), triiodothyronine (10^{-10} M), estradiol (10^{-8} M), and bovine serum albumin (1 mg/ml). Varying amounts of ovine prolactin were also added at the time of plating. The cells were grown without changing the medium until they had been harvested and counted. ●——●, no prolactin; △——△, 0.1 μg/ml prolactin; ▲——▲, 0.3 μg/ml prolactin; ○——○, 1 μg/ml prolactin.

and *in vitro* studies. However, this experiment clearly indicated the direct effect of prolactin on estrogen receptors.

In general, the mammary cells maintain for a long time in culture lose the ability to produce milk components in response to hormones. Therefore, even if casein or α-lactalbumin are shown to be present in some mammary cell lines, these are not produced in a hormone-responsive manner or the amount produced is very little. One of the characteristic morphological changes often observed in long-term cultured mammary cells is the formation of domes, which are like blisters formed on the surface of the culture plate. With a cell line isolated from dimethylbenz(a)anthracene-induced rat mammary carcinoma, Dulbecco *et al.*[33] reported that several long-chain saturated fatty acids (C_{13}–C_{16}) are strong dome inducers while a phorbol ester which also has a saturated C_{14} acyl chain is a potent inhibitor for dome formation. These findings suggest that certain lipids may play a role in regulating function of mammary gland.

Cells in culture, particularly in monolayer culture, are under extremely artificial conditions in which the cells neither have proper shapes, possibly proper orientation, nor interactions with surrounding cells (stromal cells, in the case of mammary epithelial cells). Therefore, these cells, which have the potential to respond to hormones to grow or differentiate, may not achieve full differentiation. Irrespective of these limitations, however, cell lines in culture have tremendous potential use since homogenous populations of cells with stable properties can be maintained in a defined environment.

Summary

The maintenance of clonal cell lines of normal and neoplastic mammary cells having the same characteristics of the parent tissues is the goal of many researchers in this field. So far, most of the mammary cell lines that are available, both from human and rodent sources, are from carcinomas that have lost much of the ability to respond to hormones in a normal way. However, with the knowledge that is now being obtained with primary cultures and the cell lines presently available, it may soon be possible to isolate new clonal cell lines with the purpose of preserving their hormone-responsiveness. As pointed out in this section, it is now believed that several factors such as cell shape and cell–cell and cell-substratum interaction play a very important role in mammary cell function. Therefore, a clonal cell line able to exhibit proper function *in vitro* would be extremely useful in studies not only of hormone action, but also the relationship of these factors to mammary function.

GENERAL CONCLUSIONS

In this chapter, we have described several *in vitro* culture techniques and have shown that each system has been useful for investigating certain aspects of mammary development. Thus, in whole gland culture, development is remarkably similar to that *in vivo* but the heterogeneity of the tissue makes analysis of the epithelial cells themselves difficult. On the other hand, the use of long-term cell culture of epithelial cells is advantageous for the biochemical study of mammary cell function, but our present technology is not sufficient to maintain all the functional properties in a defined environment. We are confident that in the near future, an improved *in vitro* culture system will further our knowledge of the total requirements for growth and function of the normal mammary gland and also help in diagnosis and treatment of individuals with breast abnormalities and cancer.

REFERENCES

1. Ichinose, R. and Nandi, S., 1964, Lobuloalveolar differentiation in mouse mammary tissues *in vitro, Science* **145:**496–497.
2. Tonelli, Q. J. and Sorof, S., 1980, Epidermal growth factor requirement for development of cultured mammary gland, *Nature* **285:**250–252.
3. Hallowes, R. C., Rudland, P. S., Hawkins, R. A., Lewis, D. J., Bennett, D., and Durbin, H., 1977, Comparison of the effects of hormones on DNA synthesis in cell cultures of non-neoplastic and neoplastic mammary epithelium from rats, *Cancer Res.* **37:**2492–2504.

4. Terry, P. M., Banerjee, M. R., and Lui, R. M., 1977, Hormone-inducible messenger RNA in a serum-free organ culture of whole mammary gland, *Proc. Natl. Acad. Sci. USA* **74:**2441–2445.
5. Topper, Y. J. and Freeman, C. S., 1980, Multiple hormone interactions in the developmental biology of the mammary gland, *Physiol. Rev.* **60:**1049–1106.
6. Banerjee, M. R., Terry, P. M., Sakai, S., Lin, F. K., and Ganguly, R., 1978, Hormonal regulation of casein messenger RNA (mRNA), *In Vitro* **14:**128–139.
7. Elias, J. J., 1957, Cultivation of adult mouse mammary gland in hormone-enriched synthetic medium, *Science* **126:**842–844.
8. El-Darwish, I. and Rivera, E. M., 1970, Temporal effects of hormones on DNA synthesis in mouse mammary gland *in vitro, J. Exp. Zool.* **173:**285–292.
9. Nicholas, K. R. and Topper, Y. J., 1980, Enhancement of α-lactalbumin-like activity in mammary explants from pregnant rats in the absence of exogenous prolactin, *Biochem. Biophys. Res. Commun.* **94:**1424–1431.
10. Ono, M. and Oka, T., 1980, The differential actions of cortisol on the accumulation of α-lactalbumin and casein in mid-pregnant mouse mammary gland in culture, *Cell* **19:**473–480.
11. Devinoy, E., Houdebine, L-M., and DeLouis, C., 1978, Role of prolactin and glucocorticoids in the expression of casein genes in rabbit mammary glands organ culture: Quantification of casein mRNA, *Biochim. Biophys. Acta* **517:**360–366.
12. Matusik, R. J. and Rosen, J. M., 1978, Prolactin induction of casein mRNA in organ culture, *J. Biol. Chem.* **253:**2343–2347.
13. Strong, C. R., Forsyth, I., and Dils, R., 1972, The effects of hormones on milk-fat synthesis in mammary explants from pseudopregnant rabbits, *Biochem. J.* **128:**509–519.
14. Hallowes, R. C., Wang, D. Y., Lewis, D. J., Strong, C. R., and Dils, R., 1973, The stimulation by prolactin and growth hormone of fatty acid synthesis in explants from rat mammary glands, *J. Endocrinol.* **57:**265–276.
15. Wang, D. Y., Hallowes, R. C., Bealing, J., Strong, C. R., and Dils, R., 1972, The effect of prolactin and growth hormone on fatty acid synthesis by pregnant mouse mammary gland in organ culture, *J. Endocrinol.* **53:**311–321.
16. Speake, B. K., Dils, R., and Mayer, R. J., 1975, Regulation of enzyme turnover during tissue differentiation, *Biochem. J.* **148:**309–320.
17. Stampfer, M., Hallowes, R. C., and Hackett, A. J., 1980, Growth of normal human mammary cells in culture, *In Vitro* **16:**415–425.
18. Yang, J., Guzman, R., Richards, J., Jentoft, V., DeVault, M. R., Wellings, S. R., and Nandi, S., 1980, Primary culture of human mammary epithelial cells embedded in collagen gels, *J. Natl. Cancer Inst.* **65:**337–343.
19. Emerman, J. T. and Pitelka, D. R., 1977, Maintenance and induction of morphological differentiation in dissociated mammary epithelium on floating collagen membranes, *In Vitro* **13:**316–328.
20. Katiyar, V. N., Enami, J., and Nandi, S., 1978, Effect of polypeptide hormones on stimulation of casein secretion by mouse mammary epithelial cells grown on floating collagen gels, *In Vitro* **14:**771–774.
21. Emerman, J. T., Enami, J., Pitelka, D. R., and Nandi, S., 1977, Hormonal effects on intracellular and secreted casein in cultures of mouse mammary epithelial cells on floating collagen membranes, *Proc. Natl. Acad. Sci. USA* **74:**4466–4470.
22. Ray, D. B., Horst, I. A., Jansen, R. W., and Kowal, J., 1981, Normal mammary cells in long-term culture. I. Development of hormone-dependent functional monolayer cultures and assay of α-lactalbumin production, *Endocrinology* **108:**573–583.
23. Ray, D. B., Horst, I. A., Jansen, R. W., Mills, N. C., and Kowal, J., 1981, Normal mammary cells in long-term culture. II. Prolactin, corticosterone, insulin, and triiodothyronine effects on α-lactalbumin production, *Endocrinology* **108:**584–590.
24. Kano-Sueoka, T., Errick, J. E., and Cohen, D. M., 1979, Effects of hormones and a novel mammary growth factor on a rat mammary carcinoma in culture, *Cold Spring Harbor Conf. Cell Prolif.* **6:**499–512.

25. Rudland, P. S., Hallowes, R. C., Durbin, H., and Lewis, D., 1977, Mitogenic activity of pituitary hormones on cell cultures of normal and carcinogenic induced tumor epithelium from rat mammary glands, *J. Cell Biol.* **73:**561–577.

26. Kano-Sueoka, T. and Errick, J. E., 1980, A pituitary-derived growth factor for rat mammary tumor cells: Phosphoethanolamine, in: *Control Mechanisms in Animal Cells* (L. Jimenze de Asua, R. Levi-Montalcini, R. Shields, and S. Iacobelli, eds.), Raven Press, New York, pp. 299–305.

27. Bisbee, C. A., Machen, T. E., and Bern, H. A., 1979, Mouse mammary epithelial cells on floating collagen gels: Transepithelial ion transport and effects of prolactin, *Proc. Natl. Acad. Sci. USA* **76:**536–540.

28. Salomon, D. S., Liotta, L. A., and Kidwell, W. R., 1981, Differential response to growth factors by rat mammary epithelium plated on different collagen substrata in serum-free medium, *Proc. Natl. Acad. Sci. USA* **78:**382–386.

29. Allegra, J. C. and Lippman, M. E., 1978, Growth of a human breast cancer cell line in serum-free hormone-supplemented medium, *Cancer Res.* **38:**3823–3829.

30. Shafie, S. and Brooks, S. C., 1977, Effect of prolactin on growth and the estrogen receptor level of human breast cancer cells (MCF-7), *Cancer Res.* **37:**792–799.

31. Burke, R. E. and Gaffney, E. V., 1978, Prolactin can stimulate general protein synthesis in human breast cancer cells (MCF-7) in long-term culture, *Life Sci.* **23:**901–906.

32. Shiu, R. P. C., 1979, Prolactin receptors in human breast cancer cells in long-term tissue culture, *Cancer Res.* **39:**4381–4386.

33. Dulbecco, R., Bologna, M., and Unger, M., 1980, Control of differentiation of a mammary cell line by lipids, *Proc. Natl. Acad. Sci. USA* **77:**1551–1555.

III

The Nutritional and Immunologic Significance of Mammary Secretions

7

Nutritional Aspects of Human Lactation

Clare E. Casey and K. Michael Hambidge

INTRODUCTION

For many infants, human milk is the sole source of nutrients, including
energy, for up to 1 year and may be a major source of calories and protein
in the diet for 2 years or more. The success of lactation must be judged
ultimately by its adequacy for the growth and health of the breast-fed infant.
The physiological and nutritional demands of lactation on the mother are
high and may last for considerably longer than those of pregnancy. Thus,
the relationship between maternal nutritional status and lactation performance is a public health issue of substantial importance.

In general, lactation performance may be evaluated from: (1) weight
gain of the infant—either by test-weighing immediately before and after a
single feed, or from the weight gain over a longer period of time; (2) yield
of milk—the total amount of milk produced is collected over a specified
period of time, usually 24 hr, and the volume measured; and (3) composition
of milk—milk is collected and analyzed, most commonly for fat and protein
content, or for nutrients of special interest. The total amount of a nutrient
available to the infant may be derived from the yield and composition, and
can be related to his requirements.

Technical Difficulties in the Measurement of Milk Yield

Both the derivation of nutritional requirements and the measurement
of lactation performance require an accurate collection of breast milk from
the lactating mother. Unfortunately, this procedure is fraught with difficulties
some of which may be insurmountable.

Clare E. Casey and K. Michael Hambidge • Department of Pediatrics, University of Colorado
Health Sciences Center, Denver, Colorado 80262.

Measurement of yield by test-weighing of the infant is frequently used in clinical practice. If the baby has emptied the breast, this method may give a reasonably accurate measure of yield over a defined interval since the last feed, or if done at every feed, over 12 to 24 hr. Because the baby may not take all the milk available, milk remaining in the breasts may be removed by expression and measured. This method has obvious disadvantages in that the weight change is small and errors may be large, especially if done by an unskilled person. The expense of the equipment and tediousness of weighing at every feed, particularly with true demand-feeding, generally preclude this technique from use in community surveys and field studies. The greatest disadvantage of test-weighing is the possible upset to the mother–baby interrelationship, particularly if there is a suggestion that her milk is insufficient and the mother feels threatened. Because milk production and letdown are complex processes,[1] involving both hormonal and nervous pathways, partly under emotional control, any interference with the usual pattern may alter either process and thus affect both real and apparent yields.

Expression of milk for measurement of yield may be a more useful method in field studies and is necessary if composition is to be determined also. Milk can be expressed from the breast either manually or with a mechanical device. Total output can be determined over a certain period of time, the most useful being 24 hr. Again the effect of interference with the normal letdown reflex is unknown. Few mothers can condition their letdown to manual or mechanical methods of expression which require a fair degree of willingness and skill. Newer equipment which attempts to mimic the action of the baby at the breast (see Chapter 10) may give a more accurate estimate of yield than manual expression, but to date few studies have utilized such equipment. Collection of a total 24-hr output requires expression of all milk which is then fed back to the baby by bottle. This will usually interfere with normal feeding as times of collection may be restricted. Expression does not, of course, indicate how much a baby will take.

Although results do vary in different studies, in general, greater volumes have been obtained for 24-hr milk yield by expression than by test-weighing.[1] Hytten[2] compared the total milk yields on the sixth and seventh days postpartum using three different techniques. In one series, the mean 24-hr milk yield for 83 mothers on the sixth day was 441 ml by test-weighing with manual expression of residual milk. The mean yield on the seventh day, obtained by the manual expression of all milk at each feed, was 378 ml, a significant reduction. In a second series of 85 mothers, the sixth day yield was again measured by test-weighing and stripping and averaged 420 ml. The seventh day yield was 445 ml, obtained by mechanical expression using an apparatus which mimicked mouth action by the baby. The author felt that this increase on the seventh day was more compatible with the expected trend than was the decrease seen in the first series, and that manual expression was not an effective means of obtaining the total content of the breast.

More recently, Brown *et al.*[3] have compared different methods of measuring milk yield in a careful study of 72 Bangladeshi mothers at 1 to 9 months postpartum. Milk yield was estimated by test-weighing infants at each feed for 6 days before or after 1 day on which the total 24-hr output was obtained by mechanical pumping. From a total of 167 studies, the average yield obtained by pumping was approximately 7% greater than the value obtained by test-weighing, the difference being similar to that in the second series of Hytten.[2] This group also compared test-weighing in a group of infants who were fed with a cup and spoon with the actual amount of milk ingested. The average "recovery" of milk by the test-weighing was about 95% of the amount ingested. Thus, a systematic underestimation by this method may account for most of the differences observed between milk yields obtained by test-weighing compared with mechanical expression. Brown *et al.*[3] also investigated the estimation of milk consumption by infants using indirect methods which would be suitable for field studies. Such methods included comparison of 12-hr milk yield with 24-hr yield and attempts to predict the milk intake of an infant from his age and the frequency and duration of feeding, but they concluded that such methods were not of great value.

Comparison of surveys of nutritional status and different aspects of lactation performance are limited in the first instance by the difficulties of measuring milk yield. The amount of milk collected by expression may be more than the baby would take, particularly if the infant is sickly or premature or unable to suckle well, thus giving a false picture of what the baby is actually obtaining. Apart from some recent Swedish work,[4,5] and one Australian study,[6] most studies of nutrition and lactation performance have been carried out among malnourished women in the Third World.[7] Similar surveys on well-nourished mothers date back 30 to 50 years and included mainly mothers with exceptionally large energy intakes or wet nurses and milk bank donors[8-11] whose outputs were much greater than that required for adequate growth of an average baby. Lastly, a difficulty which cannot be reasonably overcome, successful breast-feeding mothers are a self-chosen group in the Western world and many of the factors involved are not simply biological. Given these limitations, we may now consider the information we do have concerning nutritional aspects of lactation.

COMPOSITION OF HUMAN MILK

The normal composition of human milk may vary with a number of factors such as time of day, time during feed or even breast sampled. Differences also arise among women at the same stage of lactation and in one woman on different days. Although such differences have been reported for lactose,[2,3] protein and trace elements,[12] the most significant variations occur in fat content,[2,12,13] and hence in fat soluble constituents.[14] More subtle variations may also arise from maternal age, parity, pregnancy, oral contraceptives, and diet. However, duration of lactation is probably the most important influence on the nutrient content of milk. Thus, the usefulness of values reported in the literature will depend on whether all these influences are taken into account, as well as the methods used for collection and analysis of milk.

Concentrations of most nutrients fall between certain limits in the milk of healthy, well-nourished mothers. Table I gives representative values for levels in colostrum (1 to 5 days postpartum) and mature milk (more than 30 days) from such women. (It is not intended to be a complete compilation of all nutritional constituents.) The values given are derived from a number of sources but principally from the analytical data of Lönnerdal *et al.*,[4,15,16] and of Macy and Kelly,[17] the recent compilation from the literature by Nayman *et al.*,[18] and a report of the United Kingdom Department of Health and Social Security (DHSS)[19] that included new analytical data as well as reviewing older sources. Substances whose primary function is not nutritional, such as various immunoproteins and environmental contaminants, are discussed elsewhere (Chapters 8 and 13).

Gross Composition

Human colostrum is a yellowish sticky fluid whereas mature milk has a thin bluish appearance. (The yellow color of colostrum may be due to large amounts of β-carotene.)[20] It is a cell-rich fluid with a high content of water in which other substances are dissolved, emulsified, or colloidally dispersed. The caloric value of milk depends mainly on its fat content and is approximately 70 kcal/100 ml for mature milk from well-nourished women,[18] with a slightly lower value for colostrum.[20]

Protein

Earlier analyses of breast milk gave a mean value of about 1.2 g/100 ml for the protein content of mature milk, obtained from total nitrogen analysis by the Kjeldahl method.[17] This method was adapted from that used by the dairy industry and was satisfactory for cow's milk, but does not take into account nonprotein nitrogen (NPN). Hambraeus *et al.*[16] reported that protein comprises only about 75% of total nitrogen in mature milk. In a longitudinal study of lactation in healthy, Swedish mothers, Lönnerdal *et al.*[4] found the true protein content of milk after about 1 month was 0.8 to 0.9 g/100 ml. The method of amino acid analysis that they used does include free amino acids and small peptides, as well as those derived from protein, but these constitute only 3 to 5% of the total nitrogen. Using the same method, DHSS[19] reported a slightly higher mean (1.07 g/100 ml) in milk from English mothers of 2 weeks to 2 months lactation. Of the total protein, about 20% is casein and the three dominant fractions in the 80% whey proteins are α-lactalbumin, lactoferrin, and secretory IgA.[16] Many other proteins are present in low concentrations including other immunoglobulins, enzymes and various gly-

Table I. Composition of Human Colostrum and Mature Breast Milk

Constituent (per 100 ml)		Colostrum 1–5 days	Mature milk >30 days	References
Energy	kcal	58	70	17,19
Total solids	g	12.8	12.0	17,18
Lactose	g	5.3	7.3	15,17,18
Total nitrogen	mg	360	171	16
Protein nitrogen	mg	313	129	16
NPN	mg	47	42	16
Total protein	g	2.3	0.9	4,19,21
Casein	mg	140	187	16,17,20
α-Lactalbumin	mg	218	161	16
Lactoferrin	mg	330	167	16
IgA	mg	364	142	16
Amino acids (total)				
Alanine	mg	—	52	19
Arginine	mg	126	49	17,19
Aspartate	mg	—	110	19
Cystine	mg	—	25	17,19
Glutamate	mg	—	196	17,18,23
Glycine	mg	—	27	17–19
Histidine	mg	57	31	17,19
Isoleucine	mg	121	67	17,19
Leucine	mg	221	110	17,19
Lysine	mg	163	79	17
Methionine	mg	33	19	17,19
Phenylalanine	mg	105	44	17–19,23
Proline	mg	—	89	17,23
Serine	mg	—	54	19
Threonine	mg	148	58	17,19
Tryptophan	mg	52	25	17–19
Tyrosine	mg	—	38	17,19
Valine	mg	169	90	17
Taurine (free)	mg	—	8	23
Urea	mg	10	30	16,17,23
Creatine	mg	—	3.3	17
Total fat	g	2.9	4.2	17–19,24,60
Fatty acids (% total fat)				
12:0 lauric		1.8	5.8	17–19
14:0 myristic		3.8	8.6	17,18
16:0 palmitic		26.2	21.0	17,18
18:0 stearic		8.8	8.0	17–19
18:1 oleic		36.6	35.5	18,19
18:2, n-6 linoleic		6.8	7.2	18,19
18:3, n-3 linolenic		—	1.0	18
C_{20} and C_{22} polyunsaturated		10.2	2.9	17,18
Cholesterol	mg	27	16	14,17,19
Vitamins				
Fat soluble				
Vitamin A (retinol equivalents)	μg	89	47	17,18,32

(continued)

Table I. (Continued)

Constituent (per 100 ml)		Colostrum 1–5 days	Mature milk >30 days	References
β-Carotene	μg	112	23	17,18
Vitamin D	μg	—	0.04	35
Vitamin E (total tocopherols)	μg	1280	315	17–19
Vitamin K$_1$	μg	0.23	0.21	61
Water soluble				
Thiamine	μg	15	16	17,19,40
Riboflavin	μg	25	35	17,19,41
Niacin	μg	75	200	17,19
Folic acid	μg	—	5.2	19
Vitamin B$_6$	μg	12	28	19,44,45
Biotin	μg	0.1	0.6	17,19
Pantothenic acid	μg	183	225	17,19
Vitamin B$_{12}$	ng	200	26	46
Ascorbic acid	mg	4.4	4.0	17,19
Minerals				
Calcium	mg	23	28	18,48,49
Magnesium	mg	3.4	3.0	19,48,49
Sodium	mg	48	15	17,19
Potassium	mg	74	58	17,19
Chlorine	mg	91	40	17,19
Phosphorus	mg	14	15	17,19
Sulphur	mg	22	14	17
Trace elements				
Chromium	ng	—	39	59
Cobalt	μg	—	1	18
Copper	μg	46	35	18,19,48,49,53
Fluorine	μg	—	7	19
Iodine	μg	12	7	17,19,62
Iron	μg	45	40	48,49,52
Manganese	μg	—	0.4,1.5	49,57,58
Nickel	μg	—	2	58
Selenium	μg	—	2.0	18,63
Zinc	μg	540	166	12,17,48,49,53

coproteins.[21] The nitrogen content and major whey proteins are very high in the first few days, decrease rapidly in the first month, then decline more slowly as lactation continues,[4] but may rise again after about a year.[22] There appears to be little change in protein (as total nitrogen) either during one feed or diurnally.[2] Levels of amino acids tend to decrease with time in line with the decrease in total protein. Free amino acids constitute about 5% of the total amino acids, with peptides including another 4 to 5%.[23] The main contributor to the NPN fraction is urea; creatine, creatinine, and uric acid are also present.[16]

Fat

Fat content shows more variation than any other major component of human milk. The sampling protocol is therefore critical and the most satisfactory estimates are obtained from collection of the total 24-hr output. Mean values for the total fat content of mature milk vary from 2.6 to 4.3 g/ 100 ml in published tables with 4.0 g/100 ml being widely accepted.[19,24] In a series of 83 subjects on the seventh day of lactation, Hytten[2] found a variation in 24-hr fat content of 1.6 to 4.75 g/100 ml. Fat concentration increased during a feed, in some cases as much as fivefold, although the increase may be different in each breast. Diurnal variation was generally less marked, being less than twofold. The general trend was of a minimum at the first feed of the day rising steeply to a maximum in mid-morning, then gradually declining. Other workers have reported similar variations.[25–27] The value given in Table I is that reported by the DHSS[19] and obtained from analysis of the total milk output of 10 women over 72 hr (mean and standard deviation: 4.03 ± 0.43 g/100 ml, range: 3.51 to 4.83 g/100 ml). Fat concentration in colostrum is slightly lower than in mature milk. Underwood *et al.*[22] found a trend of increasing fat content with time from 6 to 24 months in Pakistani women, particularly obvious if individuals were considered.

The pattern of individual fatty acids does not vary with time and tends to be similar among women with the same type of dietary intake.[28] The fatty acid composition is, however, very susceptible to dietary manipulation[29] (see subsection on maternal nutrition and lactation performance). The values given in the table are for women on a normal Western-type diet, in whose milk the principal fatty acids are palmitic (16:0) and oleic (18:1) acids with lauric (12:0), myristic (14:0), stearic (18:0), and linoleic (18:2) acids present in smaller quantities. Polyenoic acids represent 2% of the total calories. The cholesterol content of human milk varies widely[14] and has been found to correlate significantly with total lipid content but does not appear to be altered by variations in maternal intake or plasma levels.[30,31]

Lactose

Lactose is the main carbohydrate in human milk although small quantities of other sugars are present particularly as nitrogen-containing compounds. Lönnerdal *et al.*[4] found that levels increased with time over the first month from 5.93 g/100 ml to 7.02 g/100 ml and thereafter rose slowly to 7.64 g/ 100 ml by 6 months. Other workers have also reported a mean concentration of about 7 g/100 ml in mature milk with little variation.[18,19]

Vitamins

Vitamin A and β-carotene concentrations are higher in colostrum and fall with time.[17] A downward trend was also observed in milk collected from Ethiopian women from 1 to 24 months.[32] A mean level of 27 μg/100 ml has been reported for β-carotene in mature milk,[18] although the DHSS survey[19] found none in their samples which were collected in various cities over a period of some months. Levels of β-carotene in cow's milk vary markedly according to the season and this may also apply in human milk.

Vitamin D in human milk has been the subject of much controversy in recent years. Analytical techniques usually involve measurement of the vitamin in the lipid fraction of milk and the concentration reported is generally about 0.05 μg/100 ml.[18] The aqueous portion was thought to contain a water-soluble vitamin D sulfate, however, in a much higher concentration. Lakdawala and Widdowson[33] reported levels of 1.78 μg/100 ml at 3 to 5 days which was significantly higher than the level of 1.00 μg/100 ml at 6 to 8 days. By 1 month, levels were 0.91 μg/100 ml with no change thereafter. Levels of the same order, 0.45 to 1.05 μg/100 ml were reported in another English survey.[19] Sahashi *et al.*[34] found that the vitamin D sulfate in mammalian milks was active in curing and preventing rickets in rats. Conversely, workers in Denmark were not able to obtain significant antirachitic activity from the water-soluble fraction of milk collected from healthy women.[35] At 5 to 8 days postpartum, the level of vitamin D determined by bioassay was 0.04 μg/100 ml of which 80% was in the lipid fraction. In a careful study of vitamin D and its metabolites in human milk, Hollis *et al.*[36] failed to find vitamin D sulfate in the whey. They used a chromatographic technique, unlike the earlier studies[19,33,34] in which less sensitive or specific colorimetric procedures were used. These workers also concluded that the antirachitic properties of human milk are due to the known metabolites of vitamin D and not to D-sulfate.[37]

Vitamin E concentrations, like those of other fat soluble vitamins, tend to be higher in colostrum than mature milk. About 83% of the total is α-tocopherol, with small amounts of β-, γ-, and δ-tocopherols also present.[38]

Water soluble vitamins vary with maternal intake. Levels of thiamine increase with duration to a maximum at 2 to 3 months.[39,40] Riboflavin levels also increase up to about 10 days,[41] but thereafter appear to be constant.[39] A study of folate levels, conducted in 1965, found an increase with time[42] whereas a study done in 1980 reported no change as lactation progressed.[43] (These differences may arise from the analytical method used.) Vitamin B_6 increases markedly from 2 to 14 days,[44] but after 3 weeks, levels tend to be constant with little diurnal variation.[45] Concentrations of vitamin B_{12} show an opposite trend: Samson and McClelland[46] found a range of 40 to 1308 ng/100 ml (median: 202 ng/100 ml) in the first 48 hr, falling rapidly to a mean of 34 ng/100 ml by 3 to 7 days. After about 3 weeks, a steady level of about 26 ng/100 ml was maintained. Macy and Kelly[17] reported that the level of vitamin C in colostrum and mature milk is similar but there may be a slight increase in the "transitional period at 6 to 10 days." Stuart and Connellan[47] found a very wide range of concentrations (0 to 7.1 mg/100 ml) of ascorbic acid in milk from Aborigine mothers, 2 days to 15 months postpartum.

Minerals

Kirksey *et al.*[48] found slight declines in calcium and magnesium in breast milk at intervals of 3 to 14 days, 1 to 3 months, 5 to 7 months, and 1 year, but differences were not significant. Conversely, Vaughan *et al.*[49] reported that calcium levels declined 30% over the first 9 months. In their series, magnesium showed no consistent pattern but any trend may have been masked as there was as much as 75% variation between subjects in 1 month. Both these studies were conducted with healthy, American women whose calcium intake was good. Milk levels were comparable so the differences in trend probably relate to individual values obtained in each study rather than underlying biological differences.

Reported concentrations of both sodium and potassium do not differ much in various groups.[17,19,50] Macy and Kelly[17] found that levels of both minerals declined with time from highest values in colostrum. Keenan *et al.*[51] also found a decline with time in sodium, but not potassium, concentrations. They also reported a diurnal rhythm in sodium levels, reciprocal to potassium, after 11 weeks postpartum.

Trace Elements

Iron concentrations in mature milk show a wide variation among women and on a day-to-day basis in the same woman. Picciano and Guthrie[12] reported a range of < 10 to 160 μg/100 ml with most values being below 70 μg/100 ml (mean and standard deviation; 21 ± 17 μg/100 ml). Levels tended to be lower in the morning compared with evening samples and lower in milk from older women but higher in milk from multipara, allowing for age. Siimes *et al.*[52] reported that iron declines with duration of lactation by 50% from 2 weeks to 9 months. Vaughan *et al.*[49] observed a decline of 20% over 1 year, although no change may be apparent in a short period.

Copper levels also show a decline of 20 to 60% during lactation to a minimum at 4 to 5 months.[49,53] Picciano and Guthrie[12] found a wide range of concentrations in mature milk: 9 to 630 μg/100 ml, with most samples containing less than 40 μg/100 ml. Levels tended to be higher in older and multiparous women.

Zinc concentration is very dependent on the stage of lactation, making comparisons between studies difficult if this is not known. Most of the variation among individuals arises from the stage of lactation.[12] Values as high as 2000 μg/100 ml have been reported for colostrum,[54] but levels are usually about 500 to 700 μg/100 ml. Kirksey *et al.*[48] reported a concentration of 465 μg/100 ml at day 3 declining to 45 μg/100 ml by 1 year, with no diurnal variation. Rajalakshmi and Srikantia[55] found slightly higher levels: 532 μg/100 ml in colostrum declining to 112 μg/100 ml by 7 months, with no significant day-to-day or diurnal variations in mature milk. Vuori and Kuitunen[53] found that the median concentration of 20 samples declined from 400 μg/100 ml at 2 weeks to 130 μg/100 ml at 10 weeks and thereafter fell more slowly to 48 μg/100 ml at 36 weeks. These workers found that, by 9 weeks, all their mothers had a concentration under 300 μg/100 ml which is often quoted as the average value for zinc in human milk. Picciano and Guthrie[12] reported a very wide range of 140 to 395 μg/100 ml in milk at 6 to 12 weeks postpartum, with a fairly even distribution of values. Zinc levels were higher in multiparous and older mothers.

Fluorine, iodine, and selenium show a geographical variation in cow's milk and there is some suggestion that the same occurs in human milk.[19,56]

Other trace elements are difficult to analyze and little work has been done. Values tend to be high unless the utmost care is taken to prevent contamination. Vuori[57] reported that manganese levels declined from 2 weeks to 2 months, then remained steady until 5 to 6 months after which there was a sharp rise. Values in this Finnish study are lower than previous reports probably because of improvements in method. Kirksey *et al.*[48] reported concentrations in American women which were tenfold higher, with a significant rise from day 3 to day 14. Values reported from another American study[49] and from New Zealand[58] were only about threefold the Finnish levels. In a recent study in Finland, Kumpulainen and Vuori[59] have found that the mean chromium concentration of human milk was only 39 ng/100 ml and this did not differ according to stage of lactation. This level is more than an order of magnitude lower than earlier reports and probably reflects improvements in analytical techniques.

NUTRITIONAL REQUIREMENTS FOR LACTATION

Maternal requirements for various nutrients during lactation, in addition to those for maintenance and activity, are based on the amount of the nutrient secreted in the milk. This is generally determined from the yield and composition of milk produced by healthy women with adequate lactation. Both volume and composition tend to change with duration of lactation, but by about 4 weeks postpartum, most constituents have reached a nearly constant level. This discussion of nutritional requirements refers mainly to those needed for production of mature milk.

The requirement for a nutrient is usually more than the amount secreted in the milk because the transfer of energy and nutrients from diet to milk is not 100% efficient. Difficulties frequently arise in the determination of requirements from balance studies because dietary intake at any given time may not be related to output in the milk. In practice, the mother subsidizes lactation from nutrient stores laid down in pregnancy or even by loss of body tissues. Hytten and Thomson[10] suggested an equation, which takes these factors into account, to estimate the requirement for a nutrient during lactation:

$$eR = L = e(D \pm S - M) \tag{1}$$

where

D = dietary intake.

S = contribution to or from body stores (for energy, this is determined by gain or loss in weight).

M = cost of maintenance and activity apart from lactation and can be inferred from the requirement for a healthy nonpregnant, nonlactating women. (For energy, this value may be increased early in lactation as some workers have reported that the basal metabolic rate (BMR) which is elevated in late pregnancy does not return to prepregnancy values until about 2 weeks postpartum.[64,65])

R = requirement.

L = output in milk, one of the more easily determined factors. Since actual milk production by an individual may not correspond to the needs of the baby, a theoretical figure, based on the assessment of the needs of a thriving infant, can be used.

e = efficiency of lactation. This cannot be measured directly but must be inferred from the other components of the equation.

Determination of requirements by the means outlined presupposes that maternal diet prior to and during pregnancy was adequate. (This is particularly the case in discussing energy requirements.) Interpretation of the results of surveys is made difficult by the same token—an apparently inadequate diet, coupled with poor weight gain during pregnancy, may not affect lactation, at least in the early months, as much as might be expected (see section on maternal nutrition and lactation performance). Unfortunately, no study of lactation has taken into account all these terms; indeed, it may never be possible to devise such a study which is practicable. Requirements for energy can be determined from available observations, coupled with reasonable estimates for missing information. There is less information on protein, although recent Swedish work on protein quality and quantity in breast milk[66] has provided newer data. Even less is known about other nutrients including most vitamins and minerals.

Recommended Daily Allowances

The specific requirements during lactation for many nutrients have not been extensively investigated. Recommended daily allowances (RDA) are generally based on the allowance for the nonpregnant, nonlactating woman plus the amount secreted in the milk. The volume of milk used in these calculations is 850 ml, which may be higher than usual even in well-nourished women, but will cover most situations. Experimental evidence suggests that for riboflavin, the efficiency of transfer from diet to milk is 70%.[67] The efficiency is not known for other vitamins or minerals but is assumed to be 100%. Table II gives the RDAs for lactation as presented by the United States National Research Council (US NRC),[68] the United Kingdom DHSS,[69] and the Food and Agriculture Organization/World Health Organization (FAO/WHO).[70] Other national recommendations are usually derived from one or more of these three, which are, for the most part, in agreement. The values given in the table assume a woman is more than 18 years old (i.e., she, herself, is no longer growing), and has a moderately active life-style. An appropriate alteration in the calorie intake, provided a wide choice of

Table II. Recommended Dietary Allowances during Lactation[a]

		U.S. NRC	U.K. DHSS	FAO/WHO
Calories		2500	2750	2750
Protein	g	64	69	46
Vitamin A	μg retinol equivalents	1200	1200	1200
Vitamin D	μg	10	10	10
Vitamin E	mg (α-tocopherol equivalents)	11	—	—
Thiamine	mg	1.5	1.1	1.1
Riboflavin	mg	1.7	1.8	1.7
Niacin	mg (niacin equivalents)	18	21	18
Folacin	μg	500	400	500
Vitamin B_6	mg	2.5	—	—
Vitamin B_{12}	μg	4.0	—	4.5
Ascorbic acid	mg	100	60	30
Calcium	mg	1200	1200	1200
Phosphorus	mg	1200	—	—
Magnesium	mg	450	—	—
Iron	mg	18+	15	14–28+
Zinc	mg	25	—	—
Iodine	μg	200	—	150

[a] Daily allowances; FAO/WHO for first 6 months.

foodstuff is available and used, will generally cover increased needs for most vitamins and minerals. Recommendations for vitamin D and zinc are set higher than can normally be obtained for the diet, and supplementation is recommended, as for iron.

As with all uses of RDA tables, it must be remembered that these values apply to groups of people and should not be used to judge the adequacy of the diet of an individual. Results of surveys are also limited by the method of data collection and analysis; dietary intakes, except under strictly controlled metabolic ward supervision, are notoriously difficult to obtain accurately.[71]

Energy

The energy requirement for lactation depends primarily on the volume of milk produced. The difficulty with using this approach is that the volume of milk varies to some extent with energy intake (see subsection on milk volume in this chapter). Early studies included women with daily intakes of more than 3000 kcal, many of whom produced an average of more than 1 liter of milk per day.[8,72] The official bodies have based their recommendations on a daily output of 850 ml in established lactation, a volume derived mainly from these early studies. The recent studies of Lönnerdal et al.[15] with well-nourished women in Sweden and Ethiopia, of Edozien et al.[73] in Nigeria and of Whitehead et al.[74] in the Gambia, indicate that the daily output of milk is nearer to 750 ml. Using this value, the daily output of energy in human milk, with an average content of 70 kcal/100 ml, is approximately 520 kcal.

Regarded from the point of view of infant growth, a similar figure may be derived. For an average weight gain of about 30 g/day, the daily energy intake of a healthy breast-fed infant is about 115 kcal/kg.[75] By about 2 months of age, the 4.5-kg infant is receiving approximately 520 kcal.

In formulating a dietary requirement for energy two other factors must be considered—the efficiency of milk production and the subsidy by body stores laid down during pregnancy. Although several early investigators suggested that the efficiency of milk production was about 90%,[11] the recommendations by FAO and other bodies in the 1950s used a figure as low as 60%.[76] In 1961, Hytten and Thomson[10] reviewed previous work to derive an efficiency of 80%. In 1970, Thomson *et al.*[77] published the results of a careful study of the energy cost of lactation which they found might be as low as 3%, that is, an efficiency of 97%. These authors felt that an efficiency of energy transfer to milk of 90% was a reasonable estimate, with a lower limit of 80%. Thus, an additional energy supply of approximately 600 kcal/day in the diet should be adequate to support lactation.

The role of body stores is rather difficult to interpret at present. During pregnancy, the well-nourished woman lays down about 5 kg of fat stores.[78] Measurements of weight loss during lactation suggest this store may provide 200 to 300 kcal/day to subsidize milk production. The revised requirement of 500 to 600 kcal/day, calculated above, suggests the subsidy may not be necessary with an adequate diatary intake, unless a woman is producing very large volumes of milk. Unfortunately, few studies have compared the volume of milk produced with weight loss (or gain during pregnancy) and dietary intake.

Recommended dietary allowances for energy (Table II) include an extra 500 to 600 kcal/day for lactation, above the basal allowance for the nonpregnant, nonlactating woman. Differences in the table arise partly from the different basal allowances set by the three recommending committees.[68–70] However, all three estimate 750 kcal/day to be the requirement for lactation (850 ml $\times$ 70 kcal/100 ml $\times$ 80% efficiency) and assume that the well-nourished woman will subsidize lactation from her body fat stores at a rate of 200 to 300 kcal/day. Where the woman is not already well-nourished, the energy required to maintain an adequate milk production is increased. Energy requirements are also increased where utilization is greater, e.g. with a very large output of milk, feeding twins, doing heavy manual work, or growth in a teenage mother.

Dietary surveys indicate that breast-feeding mothers in Western communities tend to increase their energy intake during lactation.[77,79–81] Intakes are generally higher than those of nonpregnant women or of mothers who are not breast-feeding. Naismith and Ritchie[79] reported that lactating mothers in their English study were taking about 2900 kcal/day at 3 months postpartum. Whichelow[80] also reported high energy intakes, 2500 to 2900 kcal/day, by breast-feeding mothers, similar to intakes found in early surveys.[8,11] However, other workers have reported that energy intakes may not achieve recommended levels, even among women of good socioeconomic status.

Surveys in urban Iran,[82] the United States,[83,84] and Australia[6,81] have reported average intakes by lactating mothers to be less than 2500 kcal/day.

The situation among women in poorer communities is more severe. Such women have a lifelong history of inadequate dietary intake and often do not gain weight much during pregnancy.[85] Intakes of 1700 to 1900 kcal/day are frequently reported, but they may be as low as 1300 kcal/day.[9,82,86–90] Generally in poor, rural areas, there is little difference in intake between lactating and nonlactating mothers and milk production is presumably subsidized by weight loss.[86,87] Relationships between lactation performance and dietary intake and weight loss are discussed later in this chapter.

Protein

Determining the requirement for protein in lactation from the amount secreted in the milk is more complex than for energy as there is no direct metabolic relationship. In its first estimates of protein requirements, FAO[91] calculated an extra allowance of 20 g/day, derived from the protein content (1.2 g/100 ml) × average volume of milk (850 ml) and an assumed efficiency of production of 50%. The allowance was later increased to 30 g/day to cover the needs of almost all women, including those with a very large output. Hytten and Thomson[10] suggested that the conversion factor of 50% was too low, and that 80% would be a more reasonable estimate. This gives a requirement of 16 to 17 g/day, for dietary proteins with net protein utilization (NPU) of 75, and this is the figure used in the most recent FAO recommendations.[70] The US NRC[68] assumes a production efficiency of 70%, as for other body proteins, and recommends an extra 20 g/day as a protein of NPU 75. The recommendations from the United Kingdom[69] estimate that an increased daily intake of 15 g mixed protein or 10% of the extra energy requirement is adequate for lactation. The values given in Table II differ mainly because of the differences in the recommendations for nonpregnant, nonlactating women (FAO = 39 g; USA = 44 g; UK = 54 g; all NPU 75).

More recent values for protein content (0.9 g/100 ml) and volume of milk (750 ml), with a conversion rate of 70%, suggest that an extra intake as low as 10 g/day of high quality protein may be adequate. Few studies have investigated protein intakes during lactation, but well-nourished women generally consume far in excess of the recommended levels. In Western diets, protein usually comprises more than 10% of the total energy. Thus, given an adequate energy intake, the lactating women should receive adequate protein. Well-nourished Australian women were found to consume on average 83 g protein/day at 6 to 20 weeks postpartum.[92] The mean daily intake in a group of middle-class American women[83] was 94 g with a range of 50 to 150 g. Intakes by middle-class Iranian women[82] were also reasonably high (82 ± 37 g), but Iranian women from a low socioeconomic group took much less (61 ± 20 g). Other poor groups also have a low protein intake: Deb and Cama[89] reported 41 g/day in poor Indian women; Gopalan and Belavady[85] reported 43 g and 47 g for other groups of women in India.

Among women on a high-carbohydrate diet, as in areas where cassava is the staple foodstuff, protein intake may be very low in spite of an adequate calorie intake. In general, protein in human milk is not related to either the quantity or quality of the mother's protein intake and low protein intakes tend to result in a deterioration of maternal nutritional status, as discussed later in this chapter.

Calcium

Estimation of calcium requirements is complicated by the lack of information regarding adaptation of intestinal absorption to low calcium intakes. Evidence on calcium turnover in the bones during pregnancy and lactation is also inconclusive. Goldsmith and Johnston[93] studied bone mineralization in 2000 well-nourished American women. The poorest mineralization was found in 20- to 59-year-olds who had lactated at some time in life. Compared with nulliparous women, the deficit was only about 3% in white women and was made up after menopause. When compared with parous women who had never breast-fed, the deficit in bone mineralization in lactators was only 1.4% suggesting that pregnancy may be responsible for more bone loss than lactation. Atkinson and West[94] also found a loss of bone mineral in a longitudinal study of lactating women. They estimated a loss of 2.2% over 100 days, equivalent to 250 mg calcium/day. Conversely, radiological surveys of women on very low calcium intakes do not show mineral depletion even after repeated pregnancies and lactations. Paterson[95] concluded, from a review of a number of studies, that there is no indication of bone depletion even with high parity and prolonged lactation. Intakes as low as 150 to 200 mg/day may be sufficient to provide for pregnancy and lactation, with adaptation. On the other hand, balance studies show that even with an intake of 3 g/day, without a long period for adaptation, lactating women may be in negative balance.[94] Indeed, the deciding factor in formulating a dietary recommendation may be the calcium intake to which the individual is accustomed. The status and intake of vitamin D and phosphorus may also alter requirements.

With a milk content of 28 to 34 mg/100 ml,[19] the replacement of calcium lost in the milk requires an intake of about 250 mg/day. Recommendations for total daily intake are 1200 mg (see Table II), based on 500 mg basal + 700 mg for milk production. The three recommending bodies estimate that up to 200 mg calcium is lost daily in the milk and assume that the efficiency of transfer is 40 to 50%.

Intakes by well-nourished women tend to be good, although Sims[83] found that of a group of American women who were not taking dietary supplements, 45% received less than two-thirds of the RDA. The mean intake by healthy Australian women, who generally have a diet high in meat and dairy products, was 1275 mg/day.[92] The traditional Iranian diet includes fewer dairy products as reflected in lower intakes of calcium[82]: middle-class women took about 800 mg/day and poorer women received only 500 mg/

day. Bassir[96] reported intakes as low as 330 to 420 mg/day by Nigerian women on a diet composed mainly of plant foods, and Gopalan and Belavady[85] found even lower intakes (180 to 299 mg) among groups of poor Indian women. Calcium levels in the milk from these mothers were not reduced.

Much more work is required before conclusions can be drawn about calcium requirements during lactation or the adequacy of various dietary intakes. The controlling influence appears to be the intake to which an individual has become accustomed; higher intakes producing higher requirements. At present, few women except those using dairy products appear to be able to obtain the RDA.

Iron

Loss of iron in the milk is about 0.3 mg/day, quite low compared with maternal intake. Since the lactating women, at least for the first 6 months, usually does not lose iron in menstruation, her requirement is not different from that of the nonpregnant, nonlactating female. Nonetheless, recommended allowances (Table II) tend to continue those of pregnancy with the aim of allowing the mother to replenish her iron stores. Allowances during pregnancy are set high and can rarely be achieved without supplementation. The US NRC recommends a continuation of the supplement (30 to 60 mg/day) for 2 to 3 months after parturition.[68] FAO recommends the same intake as the nonpregnant woman (14 to 28 mg/day depending on availability) for women whose intake has always been at this level[70]; otherwise, they recommend continuation of supplementation. The recommendation from the United Kingdom[69] is given on the basis that the average availability of iron from the diet is 10%. It is the experience of many nutritionists that even this intake (15 mg) is not often reached in practice, and the higher recommended intakes may only be achieved by use of iron supplements.

Hitchcock and English[92] found that Australian women received an average of only 11.8 mg iron/day from diets adequate in protein, presumably of mainly animal origin. In well-nourished American women, Sims[83] found that only 11% received more than the RDA of 18 mg from food; the mean of all intakes was 14.4, range: 6.7 to 32.7 mg. In a group of middle-class Iranian women,[82] the average intake was 18 mg iron/day, but less than 10% of the calories were from animal foods. Because of the lower bioavailability of iron from plant sources, the RDA for these women would be 28 mg.[70] The hematocrit and hemoglobin levels of these women were significantly higher than levels in comparison to the low socioeconomic group of Iranian women whose daily iron intake was not significantly lower. Using hemoglobin g/liter of erythrocytes as a measure of iron status, only 18% of the middle-class women, compared with 100% of the lower socioeconomic group, were below normal, suggesting that the intake by the second group of women was not sufficient to meet all the environmental and biological demands including hemorrhage and parasite infestation.

There is still much controversy surrounding the definition of iron requirements for nonpregnant, nonlactating women. Questions include whether or not these can be fulfilled by the women's usual diet, the significance of lower intakes and the need or role of supplementation. Such questions pertain even more to the situation of the lactating mother.

Vitamins

Table II gives RDAs for vitamins during lactation. As with other nutrients, differences in the values arise mainly from different basal recommendations rather than from the additional recommendations for lactation. Thiamine values are higher in the RDA of the United States because this group uses 0.5 mg/1000 kcal as their basic requirement, whereas values of the United Kingdom and FAO are calculated on the basis of 0.3 mg/1000 kcal. This is not the place for discussion of the differing philosophies behind the wide variations in the RDAs for vitamin C. The actual daily requirement is probably no more than 10 mg and the amount secreted in milk would be about 20 mg. Thus, an intake of 30 mg/day should be adequate to cover needs. Levels in the milk of mothers on poor diets can be raised by supplementation with vitamin C.[97] Nevertheless, biochemical parameters of vitamin C status in infants do not always relate to their intake from milk.[47] The practical significance of different dietary intakes by the nursing women with respect to the levels she secretes in her milk is not known.

Very few studies have examined intakes of minor nutrients in lactating women, especially under poor environmental conditions. Gopalan and Belavady[85] reported an intake of only 800 IU/day (240 µg) vitamin A by poor mothers in Hyderabad, who also had low levels in their milk. Mild to severe vitamin A deficiency is endemic in many parts of Southeast Asia, the Middle East and Africa. The FAO suggests that, in these areas in particular, if the diet of the lactating woman is not meeting the RDA, she should receive a supplement as a good intake in breast milk is important in preventing vitamin A deficiency in young children. In their more extensive survey in Iran, Geissler *et al.*[82] found that middle-class, urban women had an average intake of vitamins A, C, B_1, B_2, and B_{12}, which was more than 80% of the RDA of the FAO. Intakes of folic acid, zinc, and vitamin B_6 were low compared with the RDA in the United States. Among low-income women, average intakes of all vitamins except vitamins C and B_1 were lower than recommended, and were significantly lower than the middle-class women for vitamins A, C, B_2, and B_6. This study did not look at differences in milk composition. West and Kirksey[45] examined levels of vitamin B_6 in milk in relation to dietary intake and found that intakes greater than the RDA (2.5 mg) gave significantly higher concentrations of the vitamin in the milk than lower intakes. Sims[83] examined dietary intakes of 61 lactating middle-class women in Indiana and Pennsylvania, using three one-day food records. Eighty percent of these women were taking vitamin/mineral supplements, on general advice rather than for a specific need. Among the women taking supplements, average intakes of all vitamins examined (A, thiamin, ribo-flavin, niacin, and ascorbic acid) exceeded the RDA of the United States; indeed, intakes of thiamin and ascorbic acid from food alone already exceeded the allowance. Of the women who did not take supplements, 50% of individual intakes were less than the RDA, except for ascorbic acid. Of this unsupplemented group, 73% were taking more than 100% of the RDA of the United States for vitamin C, even allowing for the rather high estimate of 100 mg/day. Although this was a small group, the findings raise questions about the need for vitamin/mineral supplementation during lactation, particularly among well-nourished women. Among malnourished women with low intakes, supplementation studies do not show a great difference in lactation performance but levels in milk may be increased (see subsection on vitamins in next section).

MATERNAL NUTRITION AND LACTATION PERFORMANCE

Lactation failure, that is insufficient milk or milk of inadequate composition for the growth and health of the infant, cannot be attributed completely to nutritional causes. Nonetheless, milk yield in particular may be influenced strongly by maternal diet and nutritional status. Lactation performance, as judged by the volume and composition of the milk and the incidence and duration of lactation will be discussed in relation to maternal nutrition.

Volume

In evaluating the data, it must be remembered that reliable information on the volume of milk secreted is difficult to obtain. The technical difficulties involved in an accurate collection have been outlined. Another problem arises in that milk production and secretion are largely supply-and-demand. A large, healthy baby with a vigorous suck will induce and obtain much more milk from its mother than a small, sickly, or premature infant. Thus, differences in yield may not be indicative of a mother's capacity for lactation, and the baby itself may be responsible for "lactation failure due to inadequate milk production."[98] Collection of 24-hr yields is frequently done by asking the mother to express milk at certain set times of the day which may bear little relation to the normal frequency and feeding times of her infant. Egli et al.[99] altered the frequency of suckling over several weeks in one infant. When the child received three feeds/day instead of his usual six, nursing time was reduced by 50% and the amount of milk taken was reduced from 540 ml to 370 ml. When demand feeding was again permitted, the child returned to his usual time and intake. Indeed, Lindblad et al.[100] found that just taking healthy mothers into the hospital to collect samples could decrease their milk yield by 210 ml.

Most reports of 24-hr milk yield in well-nourished women are 20 to 50 years old and frequently difficult to interpret because of differences in sampling and collection techniques. Early estimates of nutritional requirements during lactation were generally based on a daily milk output of 850 ml to 6 months,[91] or 850 ml for 1 to 3 months and 1400 ml for 4 to 6 months.[101] These figures were collated by Morrison[50] from data collected up to 1952 and included studies of a few specially selected women, such as three high-yielding wet nurses in Detroit[11] and a group of mothers with a particularly high food intake in New Zealand.[8] Reinterpretation of these early data led Thomson and Black[102] to conclude that the typical daily yield, once milk is established, is about 600 to 700 ml.

Some recent studies agree with this estimation. In 1975, Lönnerdal *et al.*[103] used test weighing to estimate yield in 53 healthy Swedish mothers. The 24-hr output increased from a mean of 558 ml at 0.5 months to 724 ml at 1 to 5 months and thereafter remained constant at approximately 750 ml for at least 6 months. These values are similar to those obtained by Wallgren[104] in 1945, in a series of 363 healthy Swedish infants, despite differences in detailed technique. Svanberg *et al.*[23] reported a mean intake of 830 ml/day from 2 to 5 months in Swedish infants, similar to the amount, 808 ml, produced by well-nourished Ethiopian women. Picciano *et al.*[105] determined milk production by test-weighing in a series of 26 healthy, fully breast-fed American infants. They found a lower mean intake of 600 ml/day from 1 to 3 months, but the range was very wide (294 to 966 ml at 1 month). An Australian study,[6] using the novel method of test-weighing the mother, reported somewhat higher levels of milk production, 800 to 1200 ml/day from 1 to 15 months. The energy intake of these mothers was not particularly high, being on average 2300 kcal/day, unlike the intakes by the very copious milk producers of Shukers *et al.*[11] and Deem[8] who consumed 3000 to 4000 kcal/day. Although a number of dietary surveys have indicated that breast-feeding mothers consume more energy in the diet than mothers who are not breast-feeding,[77,79–81] very few studies have investigated the relationship of diet or effects of supplementation on the volume of milk produced by well-nourished women. Both Thomson *et al.*[77] and Whichelow[80] reported that the energy intake of successful breast-feeders was 600 to 900 kcal/day greater than that of unsuccessful breast-feeders, "success" being judged by the growth of the breast-fed infant.

More work has been done with regard to milk yield among poorly nourished communities. In rural areas in particular, the general pattern of breast-feeding includes frequent, on-demand feedings. Lactation may last for up to 2 or more years and is usually without supplement until at least 6 months of age.[1] Thus, there are few nonbiological influences on milk yield. Unfortunately, as for Western studies, limitations do exist in interpretation of available data. Most reports do not state when other foods are introduced or if suckling habits have changed as the child grows older. Some reports of very low yields may not take into account night-time feeding. In some areas, particularly at harvest time when the mother cannot be with the baby, more than half the daily intake of calories may be obtained at night.[74]

Estimations of total daily yield have been undertaken in a number of areas in Africa, Asia, and New Guinea. Some workers have found values comparable to those in the West for women who generally appear to be reasonably well-nourished. Edozien *et al.*[73] reported a yield of 750 ml in Nigerian mothers with an adequate caloric but low protein intake. Mean volumes have been recorded at about 6 months of 770 ml in poor Ethiopian women[23] and 680 ml in New Guinea,[106] without corresponding dietary data. Lower outputs have been found among poor Indian women associated with lower dietary intakes. Gopalan and Belavady[85] reported 450 to 500 ml/day up to the end of the first year in women with an intake of about 1800 kcal/day. In some areas of New Guinea, yields as low as 400 ml/day have been measured in women who appeared to be grossly malnourished.[107] (These women subsisted on a carbohydrate diet, did all the heavy labor, and were scantily clothed in a climate that is rainy and often cold.)

There is little information about output during later lactation among Western communities partly because nursing after 6 to 12 months has not been common in recent years. A group of well-nourished Australian mothers who were feeding on demand were still producing over 900 ml/day at 15 months.[6] Surveys in poorer countries also suggest yields may be sustained for 18 to 24 months: Whitehead *et al.*[74] found yields in poorly nourished Gambian women were 790 ml at 3 months and 610 ml at 18 months, similar to outputs measured by Sénécal[108] in another West African community 20 years earlier. Mothers in Papua[107] and New Guinea[106] were found to produce about 590 ml at 18 months, 560 ml at 2 years, and 370 ml at 3 years, with a few women still yielding about 70 ml of milk daily at 4 years. In poor Indian mothers, the yield (450 to 600 ml) is generally sustained for 12 to 18 months, but declines rapidly after that.[7] However, many other factors besides nutritional status may be involved in maintaining yield in prolonged lactation. The age at which other foods are offered to the baby and customs prevailing with respect to weaning behavior will alter the suckling pattern of the infant, which in turn will affect milk production.

In general, volumes of milk produced by mothers in less well-nourished communities are similar to those of many well-nourished mothers and are approximately 500 to 700 ml/day in the first 6 months, 400 to 600 ml at 6 to 12 months, declining to 300 to 500 ml in the second year. The few studies which have been undertaken beyond this period show considerable variation in the third year, 230 to 488 ml/day. Volumes do vary widely but are generally lowest in the poorest communities, such as some rural areas in the New Guinea Highlands or urban Colombo, Sri Lanka.[7] In some parts of the world, daily output may decline with seasonal food shortages.[74]

Because of the importance of adequate sustained lactation in infant nutrition in Third World countries, the effect of supplementing the mother's diet on milk yield has been the subject of a number of studies. Gopalan and Belavady[85] gave a protein supplement, increasing protein intake from 63 g to 91 g/day, to women in southern India; milk yield increased from 420 ml to 540 ml/day. Conversely, Karmarkar *et al.*[88] found no increase in yield in another group of Indian women who were given supplementary fat or protein. These women had an extremely poor diet, receiving only 1300 kcal and 21 g protein daily; even with the supplement the low energy intake may have limited their milk output. Deb and Cama[89] also gave supplementary fat and protein to Indian women with no increase in yield, although these women were slightly better nourished, receiving 1850 kcal and 41 g protein daily. Studies in other countries have also produced conflicting results. Sosa *et al.*[109] demonstrated an increase in milk yield when malnourished Guatemalan women were given an improved diet, particularly with respect to calories and protein. In Western Nigeria, Bassir[96] supplemented the diet of village women with protein (as soy flour) to produce an increase in yield. These women had a diet adequate in calories but low in protein. Edozien *et al.*[73] gave a skim milk supplement to a similar group of Nigerian women and obtained an increase in yield, despite the fact that outputs were already rather high: 740 ml increasing to an average of 870 ml milk per day. Prentice *et al.*[90] carried out an extensive survey in which all nursing mothers in a rural village in The Gambia were supplied with a dietary supplement which increased their mean energy intake from 1568 kcal/day to 2291 kcal/day. The breast milk intake by the infants in this study varied with stage of lactation and season of the year, but did not increase when the mother's diet was supplemented. However, the range of milk volumes produced by the Gambian mothers was already very similar to those of English and Swedish women in the first 3 months. The authors suggest that these may be the physiological norm and that larger quantities should perhaps not have been expected. Indeed, given the variations in methods in the supplementation studies and all the factors other than nutrition which can influence milk production, it is difficult to come to any definite conclusion as to whether "feeding the nursing mother" does in fact "feed the child."

An unexpected, and possibly undesirable, effect of supplementation was observed in the Gambian studies.[110] The improved maternal nutrition appeared to result in a shorter period of postpartum infertility. Before supplementation, 19% of new conceptions occurred before 18 months after the birth of the previous child, whereas after supplementation, the proportion was 33%. A nutrition–fertility interaction has also been reported by Indian workers who found that duration of lactation amenorrhea and interpregnancy interval were inversely related to body weight of a group of low income mothers with similar breast-feeding practices.[111]

Composition

Many factors besides maternal nutrition are known to affect the composition of breast milk, and have been discussed earlier (see previous section on composition of human milk). Only major alterations arising from nutritional factors will be considered in this section. The limitations of sampling apply as much to composition studies as to those examining milk yield; however, some general trends are evident in comparing different groups and communities.

Protein

The direct analysis of amino acid residues gives a lower protein content in mature breast milk than methods based on total nitrogen analysis, so methodology must be taken into account when comparing different surveys. Protein concentration in milk from malnourished mothers does not appear to be different from that of well-nourished, more affluent women,[7] although not all studies are in agreement. Lindblad and Rahimtoola[112] found levels in milk from mothers in a low socioeconomic group in Pakistan were not different from Western values. Similarly, Carniero and de Oliveira[113] reported a range of 0.9 to 1.5 g/100 ml in a low socioeconomic group in Brazil. (Curiously, these workers found slightly lower levels in milk from well-to-do mothers but gave no dietary details.) However, a study in Alexandria found lower protein levels in milk from malnourished women compared to healthy Egyptian mothers.[114]

The effects of protein supplementation on milk protein levels appear more inconsistent. Karmarkar et al.[88] reported an increase in protein concentration with an increase in protein intake in a series of Pakistani women who had an intake of only 21 g/day. Protein levels in milk increased with increasing dietary protein up to a maximum with an intake of 53 to 58 g/day. Other workers[73,89,96] have not found an increase in milk protein with supplementation of diets already providing higher protein intakes. Karmarkar et al.[88] suggested that 34 to 42 g/day provided a critical level above which no influence on protein content of breast milk would be expected. However, Forsum and Lönnerdal[5] produced a significant increase in both total nitrogen and protein concentrations in milk from three healthy, Swedish mothers by increasing their protein intake from 46 g/day to 134 g/day. This finding may arise both from the very high protein supplement and the improved techniques used in this very careful study. In general, most observations suggest that supplementing an inadequate or marginal diet with protein will increase total yield rather than alter protein content of milk.

Very little work has been done on the various protein and NPN fractions. Lönnerdal et al.[15] found little difference in total nitrogen and NPN in milk from well-nourished Swedish and Ethiopian women and poor Ethiopian mothers. The Ethiopian women had high levels of lactoferrin, probably due to extremely high "natural" iron intakes. In the same groups of mothers, Svanberg et al.[23] found that the amino acid composition was identical except that tyrosine was significantly lower in the poor Ethiopian women. Several workers have suggested that protein quality may be impaired in milk from malnourished mothers, and may be improved with protein supplementation.[73,88,112] More casein and less whey is present in such milk and Deb and

Cama[89] obtained an increase in the whey:curd ratio on giving a high protein supplement to their group of poor Indian women.

Fat

The fat content of human milk appears to be subject to more variability than other constituents, and considerably more work has been done examining the effect of maternal diet on fat content and composition.[24] The average fat content in milk from well-nourished mothers is about 4.2 g/100 ml but in less well-nourished women the level is usually lower than 4% and may fall as low as 2%.[7] Nonetheless, even gross malnutrition such as that seen in Karachi may be associated with fat levels greater than 3.5 g/100 ml.[112] Coupled with the lower volume produced by malnourished mothers, this lower fat content may lead to a serious deficit in calories for the growing infant. Deem[8] found that increasing the fat content (but not energy) of the diet increased fat levels in the milk of well-nourished women, whereas Insull *et al.*[115] found no change in the fat content of milk from one mother when her intake of fat comprised 0%, 40%, or 70% of her diet. Karmarkar *et al.*[88] increased the fat content of milk produced by very poor Indian women by supplementing with extra protein and fat their normal daily intake of 1300 kcal and 18 g fat. The authors reported that milk fat concentrations increased from 3.8 g/100 ml up to a maximum of 4.7 g/100 ml which was obtained at an intake of 50 to 55 g fat. This level is less than the dietary intake of most Western and affluent women. Deb and Cama[89] reported that protein supplementation of Indian women taking 1850 kcal/day increased the fat content of their milk, probably by increasing their caloric intake. In parts of Tanzania, where the diet is predominantly carbohydrate, fat may comprise only 7% of the caloric intake,[116] and milk from women in such areas, even when they are receiving adequate calories, may contain less than 2.0 g fat/100 ml. In general, both a low energy intake and an extremely low dietary intake of fat have been associated with a decreased concentration of fat in milk.

The fatty acid composition of milk lipids is very susceptible to dietary manipulation and can be altered by changes in the type and amount of dietary fat, dietary carbohydrate, or total energy intake. Human milk generally contains a good supply of essential fatty acids but the actual content depends to some extent on the source of dietary fat. Read *et al.*[29] compared milk fatty acids with diet in four different ethnic groups. Bedouin women, who had a diet high in fat of mainly animal origin, produced milk with a high stearic acid content and low, but sufficient, levels of linoleic acid. A similar pattern was seen in well-nourished, urban women in Beirut who had a fat intake, including 10% animal fats, which comprised 51% of their total calories. Rural Jordanian women who consumed adequate fat of mainly vegetable origin had high levels of linoleic acid and low stearic acid in their milk. Under conditions of very low fat intake, as in Tanzanian women, they found milk was low in linoleic acid and contained relatively high levels of lauric and myristic acids. Other workers[116,117] have also reported that extremely low intakes of fat cause a replacement by $C_{10}-C_{14}$ fatty acids of the normally predominant $C_{16}-C_{20}$ acids. The mechanism of these changes is discussed in Chapter 3.

Read *et al.*[118] also noted that the fatty acid pattern in the Tanzanian women was closely related to food intake: early in the morning their milk fatty acids were similar to those seen in other groups; levels of lauric and myristic acids were in maximum concentration late at night or 4 to 8 hr after the main meal. They suggested this may be due to the raised blood levels of sugar and fat associated with food intake. Insull *et al.*[115] showed that milk fatty acids resembled dietary fatty acids when the subject is in energy balance. An excess of nonfat calories (as was the case in the Tanzanian women) caused an increase in levels of lauric and myristic acids and a decrease in linoleate, but when calories were deficient milk fat approached the composition of body depot fat, including higher levels of palmitic acid which is derived from extramammary synthesis.

The recent increase in polyunsaturated fatty acids in the American diet has been mirrored in a trend of increasing levels of linoleate in breast milk. The average content in 1953 was 7.8% total fatty acids, increasing to 13.0% by 1967.[28] Wellby *et al.*[119] found that the iodine number (an index of the content of polyunsaturated fats) increased as the index increased in dietary fat. Potter and Nestal[30] also reported a rise in levels of linoleate in milk (from 9.4% to 15.5% of total fatty acids) with an increase in dietary intake, but no increase in total fat content.

The importance of different patterns of fatty acids in human milk in relation to the development of the central nervous system and to cardiovascular disease of adults is as yet unknown. It has been suggested, however, that low levels of polyenoic fatty acids in the milk of malnourished mothers may have ill-consequences for the brain growth and subsequent intellectual development of their infants.[116]

Vitamins

Vitamin A. Vitamin A concentrations are influenced by both the maternal diet during lactation and the size of preexisting stores. Mature milk usually contains more than 40 μg/100 ml which may vary seasonally (as does cow's milk) with the greater supply of fresh vegetables in spring and summer.[17] Particularly high concentrations have been reported in Western Nigeria, probably related to the use of palm oil for cooking in this area.[120] Milk from women in Europe and North America contains more vitamin A than in poor populations in whom serum levels are low.[7] In a comparison of milk from Swedish and Ethiopian mothers, Gebre-Medhin *et al.*[32] found levels of vitamin A were significantly lower in underprivileged Ethiopian women (28 to 33 μg/100 ml), compared with privileged Ethiopian women (36 μg/100 ml), who were in turn lower than Swedish women (40 to 53 μg/100 ml). However, both Ethiopian groups contained much higher levels of β-carotene than the

Swedish mothers, reflecting the higher proportion of plant foods in their diet. Kon and Mawson[121] obtained an increase in vitamin A concentrations in breast milk by supplementing the mother's diet during pregnancy or after parturition. Conversely, Belavady and Gopalan[97] found no increase when Indian women were given 600 μg vitamin A daily for 9 months although levels in both milk and serum were low. The authors felt an increase may not be seen until depleted hepatic stores were replenished.

Thiamine. Thiamine levels in mature milk may respond to dietary supplementation,[17] but in a recent trial in well-nourished American women, no difference was found between supplemented and nonsupplemented groups over the first 6 weeks of lactation.[39] In malnourished women with low thiamine intakes, levels are low and can be increased with supplementation.[122] In areas where diets are based mainly on polished rice unfortified with thiamine, maternal intakes can be so low that infantile beriberi may occur in solely breast-fed infants.[123]

Riboflavin. Riboflavin concentration in milk from well-nourished women is approximately 30 μg/100 ml[19] but levels as low as 17.2 μg/100 ml have been reported in malnourished women in south India.[85] Supplementation of the diet of such women has resulted in increased levels,[122] and even in well-nourished women, levels can be increased by increases in intake,[39] suggesting that concentrations in milk are dependent on dietary intakes.

Vitamin B_6. Vitamin B_6 levels in breast milk appear to be very sensitive to dietary intakes. West and Kirksey[45] found B_6 concentration in milk samples from healthy, American women consuming less than the RDA of 2.5 mg was 129 μg/liter, which was significantly lower than the level (239 μg/liter) in women consuming 2.5 to 5.0 mg B_6 daily. Although intakes greater than 5.0 mg were associated with a higher milk concentration, increases were not significant. There was a diurnal variation in the women who were taking a B_6 supplement, corresponding to the times at which they took the vitamin. Further evidence for a direct relationship between dietary intake and milk levels was obtained in a Swedish study in which blood pyridoxine levels in the infant were found to be influenced by maternal supplementation.[124] Other workers have also produced an increase in milk levels in well-nourished[125] and malnourished[122] women by supplementation with the vitamin. Practical experience has suggested that supplemental B_6 has an antilactogenic effect. Foukas[126] observed that large doses (300 to 600 mg/day) may indeed decrease milk production; supplementation in "ordinary" doses (2 to 6 mg/day) does not appear to do so however.[124]

Folate. Folate levels in milk from healthy mothers do not appear to be increased by increasing dietary intakes,[43] although comparison between different studies is made difficult by differences in analytical technique. Levels in milk from malnourished mothers tend to be lower[127] and may be increased by supplements given either late in pregnancy[128] or during lactation.[122] Osifo and Onifade[128] reported that women with malaria had lower milk levels of folate than healthy women at the same stage of lactation. They concluded that the increased body temperature in malaria may cause a more rapid destruction of folate, and thus possibly increase the requirement for the vitamin.

Vitamin B$_{12}$. Vitamin B$_{12}$ intakes are low among poor, malnourished women whose diet is mainly vegetarian and this is reflected in low concentrations in their breast milk.[127] In various parts of India, solely breast-fed infants may develop a syndrome of tremors ascribed to a deficiency of B$_{12}$ in mothers' milk.[129] Deodhar *et al.*[122] increased milk levels in such mothers with supplementary B$_{12}$ and even in well-nourished mothers, who have normal blood and milk levels, milk B$_{12}$ concentrations could be raised by supplementation of several months.[124]

Vitamin C. Vitamin C concentrations in the milk of well-nourished mothers are above plasma levels and usually in the range of 3.0 to 5.5 mg/ 100 ml, but may vary with the maternal diet particularly with a seasonal intake of fresh fruit.[47] Low levels (1.7 to 2.7 mg/100 ml) have been found in milk from poorly nourished women in Botswana and adaptation to low intakes has been observed in India and the Phillippines.[7] Milk levels may be increased in poorly nourished women by supplementation,[122] but in well-nourished women, whose milk and blood levels were not below normal, no increase was found with a small supplement.[125] However, Gunther was able to raise milk levels to a maximum of 10 mg/100 ml with an intake of 300 mg of vitamin C daily.[131]

Other Nutrients

Lactose. Lactose concentrations do not vary widely and levels in malnourished women are similar to those found in well-nourished groups, although one study from the New Hebrides reported 5.0 g/100 ml[132] compared with the normal mean of about 7 g/100 ml.[19]

Minerals. Minerals have not been studied extensively with respect to maternal diet. Calcium levels do not appear to vary much with intake,[48] concentrations in milk from malnourished mothers being at the lower end of the normal range. One study in Brazil found the opposite in that the mean in poor mothers was 25.7 mg/100 ml compared with 20.8 mg/100 ml in mothers from a higher socioeconomic grouping.[113] There was no nutritional data to suggest an explanation. Magnesium levels in milk from poor Indian women have been reported to be lower than in American samples.[85]

Trace Elements. Trace elements in human milk have excited much interest lately with the recognition of deficiency syndromes in otherwise well-nourished infants. Since concentrations in human milk are generally no higher, and frequently lower, than in cow's milk or formulas, whereas the status of breast-fed infants is usually better, the concept of enhanced bioavailability has assumed much importance.[133] Nonetheless, little is known about the effect of maternal diet on levels of trace elements in milk, partly because of technical difficulties. Previous nutritional status may be as important as present diet, especially in well-nourished women. There appears to be no relationship between dietary intakes and concentrations in the milk for iron, copper, or zinc,[48,134,135] although Vuori *et al.*[135] did find a correlation for manganese at 17 to 22 weeks postpartum. Unlike the mouse or rat,[136] levels of iron were not raised in human milk on supplementation.[12,137] Similarly, supplementary zinc, to give a total intake of more than 25 mg/day, did not increase milk levels in well-nourished American mothers.[48] These trace elements have not been examined extensively in milk from malnourished mothers. Analyses of zinc in milk from women living in areas where populations show chronic zinc deficiency would be of particular interest.

Levels of selenium in milk do not appear to vary much with diet: concentrations in milk from New Zealand mothers, in whom blood levels are markedly lower than elsewhere, were similar to the average level in the United States.[138] However, from a series of analyses from 17 states across the United States, Shearer and Hadjimarkos[63] suggested there was evidence for geographical variation. Possibly, levels in milk are only influenced by dietary intake above a certain minimum.

Incidence and Duration of Lactation

In the past two generations, there have been significant declines in both the incidence and duration of breast-feeding in relatively affluent, Western countries.[139] For example, surveys conducted in the United Kingdom showed that the proportion of infants still being breast-fed at 3 months fell from 60 to 80% in 1929 to 30% in 1955.[77] By 1975, 50% of infants were put to the breast at birth, 20% were still breast-fed at 6 weeks, and only 10% by 6 months of age.[140] Similar trends have been reported in the United States and other European countries, although in the last 5 years, there has been evidence of a reversal particularly among better educated and more well-to-do groups. Observers have noted corresponding declines in developing countries in recent years, associated to some extent with increasing urbanization. The implications for nutrition and health of the infant population in these areas are very serious.

Although it is difficult to draw conclusions, especially where human behavior is concerned, the reasons for not breast-feeding at all or for stopping after a few weeks or months are usually personal and cultural. Nutritional factors have very seldom been implicated directly. Indeed, a high incidence and long duration of lactation is most common among rural poor who are generally the least well-nourished. Among many such groups, breast-feeding for 18 months–2 years is the norm.[1] In some areas, such as the New Guinea Highlands, infants may continue to receive some breast milk for up to 4 years.[106,141] In a recent survey of breast-feeding patterns in 1500 live births in rural Bangladesh, the median duration of breast-feeding was 30 months with 75% of women still feeding at this time.[142] The major reasons for discontinuing breast-feeding were infant death in the first year and pregnancy in the second. Although the customary period may be different in other Third World communities, the reasons for discontinuing breast-feeding tend to be the same.[106,143]

As discussed previously in this chapter, the actual yield of milk in prolonged lactation is variable and is influenced by a number of nonnutritional factors. However, the duration of adequate lactation does depend to some extent on maternal nutritional status. Insufficient milk is frequently cited as a reason for early weaning[140] in Western communities, although this may be subjective and is difficult to judge without infant growth data. Growth rates of solely breast-fed infants fall off earlier in malnourished communities than in groups where mothers have an adequate energy intake (see subsection on the effects of human milk on infant growth). A study conducted in the Sahel during the famine of 1974[144] emphasized the necessity of using infant growth standards which are appropriate to the local community in order to judge lactation performance. Babies born to undernourished mothers during the famine had an average birth weight at the 25th centile using United States standards, but at the 75th centile when compared with weights in a neighboring tribe that was not affected by the famine. By 6 months of age, the exclusively breast-fed infants were still at the 25th centile according to American growth charts, indicating that breast milk had sustained an adequate growth rate.

Women may continue to lactate even with very low calorie intakes. However, severe maternal malnutrition has been implicated in the etiology of early marasmus in the breast-fed infant. This condition, which is seen in a number of Third World situations[145] and may be more common and increasing in urban slums and shanty towns,[1] occurs in the first 9 months and is due primarily to an inadequate food intake. The only evidence for a direct effect of diet on duration of lactation is anecdotal and comes from reports of the seige of Leningrad (1941–1942),[146] and the hunger winter in Holland (1944 to 1945).[147] At the height of the famines, mothers may have been receiving as little as 600 to 900 kcal/day. Their capacity for breast-feeding was maintained but the duration of lactation was apparently considerably shortened.

Influence of Lactation on Maternal Nutritional Status

For adequate lactation, substrates must be available in sufficient quantities from the mother's diet or body stores laid down during pregnancy. If these are insufficient, some degree of subsidy from maternal body tissue may be expected. The simplest evidence of tissue depletion is loss of weight. Well-nourished women tend to lose weight after childbirth whether they are breast-feeding or not, although this does depend to some extent on their caloric intake. Naismith and Ritchie[79] reported the same rate of weight loss up to 3 months postpartum in breast and bottle feeders but the former group consumed on average an extra 900 kcal/day. By 6 months, the lactators were losing weight less rapidly than the other group. Conversely, Dennis and Bytheway[148] reported that breast-feeding mothers had lost 1 kg more than bottle-feeders by 3 months postpartum. (There was no record of intakes in this study.) Among healthy lactating women, Whichelow[80] observed that mothers who were losing weight had an average daily intake of 2509 kcal, whereas women who were not losing weight took 2946 kcal. Some of the weight loss after parturition may be related to energy expenditure; Blackburn and Calloway[84] found, using records, that nonlactating mothers expended more energy (34 kcal/kg per day) than lactating mothers (30 kcal/kg per day) exclusive of milk production, but both groups showed an energy deficit. The increase in BMR which occurs in late pregnancy may extend into early lactation. Venkatachalam and Gopalan[65] observed that nursing women of 2 weeks to 18 months postpartum had a BMR 26% higher than nonpregnant, nonlactating women. In a more recent study, Khan and Belavady[64] found a much lower increase: 12% at 10 days, similar to late pregnancy, falling to 2 to 5% over the next 3 months.

In poorer communities, dietary intakes tend to be similar among lactating and nonlactating women, with the requirements for lactation being met by weight loss and sometimes by curtailment in activity.[86,87,149] Given the lower calorie intakes of such women, weight loss during lactation is not always as severe as might be expected. In a prospective study of 14 lactating women over a period of 90 weeks, Gopalan and Belavady[85] observed that most women did not lose weight and that those who did showed a very slow rate of weight loss (1.8 to 7.3 kg over a year). Women in an impoverished West African rural community also maintained their weight during 23 months lactation.[117] Conversely, declining body weight with duration of lactation has been reported from New Guinea,[87] and from Guatemala, where Schutz *et al.*[86] found that lactating women in rural areas lost weight ten times more rapidly than nonlactating women when both groups had a similar expenditure of 2000 kcal/day, excluding milk production.

Venkatachalam and Gopalan[65] suggested that changes in tissue composition may mask changes in body weight. They found that total body water in 14 poor Indian women at various stages of lactation was 59% of body weight, compared to an average of 51% in healthy European women. The question arises as to whether this high percentage of body water was due to a reduction in body fat or an absolute increase in body water. Harrison *et al.*[87] reported that skinfolds, used as a measure of body fat, did not decrease during one lactation in a New Guinea population, although body weight did. Prentice *et al.*[150] found that triceps skinfold showed a marked seasonal variation in Gambian women but was not affected by stage of lactation. The increase in total body water measured in the Indian women may be an indication of a protein deficiency induced by lactation. A marked increase in the incidence of edema has been observed among lactating women in impoverished areas of Indonesia.[151] Incidence is highest in the first month postpartum and falls with duration of lactation. Decreased levels of serum albumin have been reported to occur during lactation in poor mothers in India[85] and Iran.[82] In malnutrition, the breakdown of plasma albumin is reduced and the half-life is significantly increased. Thus, a reduction in albumin concentration is an indication of a severely deficient protein status.

With regard to loss of calcium from bone during lactation, studies among both well-nourished and poorly nourished women have shown diverse results.[93-95] Atkinson and West[94] suggested that a certain amount of bone depletion may be normal even with an adequate calcium intake. Walker *et al.*[152] found that Bantu women with more than six children had X-ray evidence of bone depletion similar to women with fewer than three, suggesting such losses are not cumulative. Osteomalacia may be precipitated by pregnancy and lactation in malnourished Asian women and particularly in immigrant Indian women in the United Kingdom, where a concurrent deficiency of vitamin D has usually been implicated.[153]

Although it is difficult to separate cause and effect, the general impression from available information is that most women, even when poorly nourished, lactate with unexpectedly little clinically obvious deterioration in their nutritional status. In the long-term, however, the cumulative effect of a number of pregnancies and lactations, coupled with an inadequate diet, may lead to a general maternal depletion. Even among well-nourished women, the higher frequency of complaints of tiredness and minor medical problems in lactating mothers may be due in part to an inadequate energy intake. In much of the Third World, parous women show a prematurely aged appearance and a progressive weight loss with parity and age. More specific deficiencies may also occur with repeated reproductive cycles including osteomalacia, anemia, goiter, and nutritional edema.[1,154]

Other Maternal Factors

Various biological factors, apart from nutritional status, affect lactation performance. Kamal *et al.*[143] reported that later weaning was associated with increasing maternal age and parity among Egyptian women. Becroft[106] found that older mothers had a greater output of milk in her New Guinea study, but Morley[123] reported an opposite effect. Whitehead *et al.*[74] found a decreasing milk yield after 3 months with increasing parity in rural Gambian mothers. In extensive studies of lactation conducted on wellnourished women, Hytten observed that milk yield tended to be lower in older primiparae.[155] This author also reported that output depended on the amount of secretory tissue in the breast and correlated highly with enlargement during pregnancy in primiparae, but not multipara.[156] Two other maternal conditions, pregnancy and oral contraception, may have a significant effect on milk yield and composition, and will be discussed in more detail.

Pregnancy

The effect of pregnancy on lactation performance depends largely on the nutritional status of the mother and on the age of her nursling, i.e., how important a part of his dietary intake breast milk comprises. Both pregnancy and lactation impose their own physiological and nutritional demands but no studies have investigated the requirements or the effect on nutritional status of both occurring simultaneously. The incidence of continued breast-feeding during pregnancy by well-nourished women is not known. In poorer countries, pregnancy is often cited as a reason for discontinuing breast-feeding.[106,143] However, it is not clear whether pregnancy itself causes milk insufficiency and weaning at such a time may be partly customary. In Senegal, 10% of mothers were still nursing when 4 months pregnant and 1.5% during the last month.[102] Similarly in rural Bangladesh, where very prolonged lactation is common, 50% of mothers were still breast-feeding when 6 months pregnant.[142] However, in this same study, of the 18% of women who had insufficient milk, over half were pregnant. A decline in milk output has also been noted in Indian women, with a marked increase in protein concentration during the second and third trimesters of pregnancy.[85] There is certainly a need for more extensive investigation in this area to determine the effects of breast-feeding while pregnant on the well-being of the mother and both her offspring.

Oral Contraception

More work has been done to investigate the effect of oral contraceptives on breast milk output and, in particular, composition.[157–160] The type of contraceptive used appears to have the greatest effect, but duration may also be important with regard to some nutrients.

There is fairly consistent evidence that large-dose mixed estrogen–progestogen tablets have a deleterious effect on lactation. Suppression of milk production occurred in most women studied with decreases in yield ranging between 15 to 80%, although in one study this effect depended to some extent on when contraception was started.[157] The severity of lactation failure was thought to be the cause of growth failure in some infants, leading in extreme cases to "contraceptive marasmus," in Egypt and Tunisia.[1] Combination pills may also decrease the concentrations of protein, fat, lactose, calcium, and phosphorous in milk. Progestogen compounds alone, however, do not appear to inhibit milk secretion and may even enhance yield.[143,157] The effect of progestogens on milk composition has not been clearly defined: milk from women in Cairo had significantly lower levels of protein, fat, and calcium,[161] whereas no such changes were found elsewhere.[44]

It has been noted that use of oral contraceptives by nonlactating women may cause a change in the metabolism of a number of nutrients.[93,162] Serum levels of vitamin A are increased but other vitamins may be lowered. Lewis and King[163] found an initial increase in excretion of thiamin, riboflavin, and pantothenic acid in young women starting oral contraceptives but no eventual difference in status compared with nonusers. Decreased blood levels and increased excretion of vitamin B_6 have been reported. It has been suggested that oral contraceptive users may have an increased requirement for this vitamin, but Bossé and Donald[164] concluded that this apparent increase may arise from the type of analytical method used in such studies. The situation of lactating women with their increased demand is probably more precarious.

Roepke and Kirksey[44] examined the effect of long-term use (more than 30 months) of oral contraceptives on vitamin B_6 status in subsequent reproduction. Results suggested such mothers had lower reserves than nonusers; their blood and milk levels were lower, but not significantly so. Such mothers also had lower levels of manganese in their milk but not of iron, copper, zinc, or calcium.[48] Contraceptive use appears to improve maternal calcium metabolism; users showed better bone remineralization after lactation than nonusers.[93]

With their increasing use in the many areas of the world, the effect of oral contraceptives on lactation requires further study. The present recommendation is that, where necessary, a low-dose progestogen should be used after lactation is established.[159,160,165] On the other hand, some of the extensive research in the field of contraception should be directed at producing an effective contraceptive that does not adversely affect lactation, but, if possible enhances it.

HUMAN MILK IN INFANT NUTRITION

It is not intended to discuss here the relative merits of breast-feeding as opposed to formula feeding. This has been well covered in a number of reviews[1,7,17,20,66,166] covering not only nutritional aspects but also the economic and ecological arguments. This section will consider some of the specific nutritional properties of human milk.

Growth

The most important characteristic of human milk is the provision of nutrients to the growing infant and the ultimate test of the adequacy of lactation in any mother must be the growth and health of her infant. In the first months, the solely breast-fed, full-term infant grows at a rate of approximately 30 g/day.[167] When the lactating mother is well nourished, breast-feeding alone should allow a satisfactory weight gain for 4 to 6 months. After about 6 months, weight gain may begin to fall off unless additional food is given, indicating that breast milk is no longer adequate as a sole source of nutrients. (It must be remembered that these ages are very general; individual children may require supplementary feeding earlier or not until somewhat later than 6 months.)

In developing countries, breast-feeding by less well-nourished mothers should maintain a good growth rate for at least the first 2 months. By 4 months, growth rates in many areas are less than 80% of standards set by the United Kingdom.[168] The situation between 2 and 4 months varies, probably influenced to some extent by the degree of maternal undernutrition. In some countries, volumes of milk produced at this stage may be as much as those of Western mothers (700 to 900 ml),[15,73,90] but where mothers only produce 400 to 600 ml/day, this is probably inadequate to support good growth. The WHO Collaborative Breast-Feeding Study[169] showed that, by 2 to 3 months, from 10 to 50% of mothers in rural areas were giving other foods in addition to breast milk. Waterlow *et al.*[168] made a comparison of longitudinal studies of growth rates of breast-fed infants in a number of Third World populations: by 4 months of age, rates comparable to those in the United Kingdom were found only in Uganda and among Alaskan Eskimos. At 3 months, growth was still good in areas of New Guinea, Tanzania, the Gambia, and South Africa. Infants in some areas showed poor growth rates as early as 2 months, although adequate growth up to 5 months has been reported from Malaysia[1] and the Ivory Coast.[117]

In many rural areas, infants may continue to receive breast milk along with other foods for periods of 2 to 4 years.[139,142] Whitehead *et al.*[74] found that breast milk was still providing a valuable contribution to the caloric intake of Gambian infants at 18 months of age. Becroft[106] reported that children in parts of New Guinea may receive breast milk up to 4 years of age. Children who were exclusively breast-fed at 1 to 2 years in this community did not have a very good weight gain but did not suffer from the malnutrition seen in other areas where prolonged lactation was not satisfactory and weaning foods were mainly starchy roots. The mothers in this series had a very good milk output of 560 ml/day at 2 years. With less copious milk production, prolonged lactation unaccompanied by the introduction of other foods may lead to malnutrition. Gopalan and Belavady[85] reported that infants of malnourished mothers in two different cities in India were still receiving human milk at 18 months to 2 years, but volumes were generally low. Infants in Hyderabad, who were fed exclusively on breast milk, showed a much higher incidence of more severe kwashiorkor and of deficiencies in A and B vitamins than did the infants in Coonor who were receiving supplementary foods.

Early or inappropriate weaning in underdeveloped countries often has disasterous consequences because the introduction of other milk or solid foods brings with it a greatly increased risk of malnutrition from inadequate intakes complicated by infection and diarrhea. Conversely, in technically advanced areas of the world, early weaning may result in overfeeding the infant. This practice, especially before 2 months of age, has been associated with a higher incidence of infantile obesity (weight for age above the 90th centile) with possible ill-consequence later in life.[1]

Biochemical Considerations

Human milk has a low caloric density (67 to 75 kcal/100 ml) and a low protein concentration and, thus is appropriate for a slow growing, continuous contact species like man. In biological terms, man's chief characteristic in his large, complex brain; human milk is rich in those nutrients (e.g., lactose, cystine, cholesterol, thromboplastin) known to be important for brain growth and maturation. Colostrum, which is secreted in varying amounts in the first few days postpartum, differs in many respects from mature milk.[17,170] The protein content is high, up to 7 g/100 ml, half of which may be immuno-globulins. Levels of fat soluble vitamins and minerals are higher, whereas the content of lactose and fat and the total caloric value tend to be lower than in more mature milk. The function of colostrum appears to be mainly antiinfective,[20] but it may also provide a concentrated dose of some nutrients such as zinc and vitamin A.

Protein

The amount of protein obtained from breast milk by an infant with a satisfactory growth rate is approximately 2.4 g/kg per day at 1 month, falling to 1.5 g/kg by 6 months.[171] A higher intake of protein may be associated with greater nitrogen retention but not necessarily with better growth, and also cause a higher incidence of uremia. Kagan *et al.*[172] found that the greater weight gain of infants fed high protein formulas was due to water retention, caused by a concommitant increase in mineral intake, although adding sodium chloride to human milk did not alter weight gain.[173]

Human milk protein is readily digestible and well-absorbed. The low casein:whey ratio[16] (about 20:80 compared with 80:20 in cow's milk) results in a soft, easily digested curd. By the end of the second week, 90% of the ingested nitrogen is absorbed[17]; utilization is also high, suggesting an optimum pattern of amino acids. Human milk protein has a biological value similar to serum proteins with a methionine:cystine ratio which is uniquely low among animal proteins. This has led to the suggestion that cystine may be an essential amino acid for neonates and premature infants, and it has been observed that methionine alone will not maintain plasma levels of sulfur amino acids in neonates on total parenteral nutrition.[174] Similarly, in line with the metabolic capacity of the newborn, human milk has a relatively low content of the aromatic amino acids phenylalanine and tyrosine.[175] The nonprotein amino acid, taurine, is also present in large amounts in breast milk. Taurine, which is present in the brain in a greater concentration at birth than later in life and may function as a neurotransmitter, is not synthesized by the neonate, who is therefore wholly dependent on a dietary supply.[176]

The species specificity of the different types and amounts of amino acids and proteins, including various enzymes, and other nitrogen-containing substances in milk is only now being explored.[177] There are still many questions regarding their significance for the infant's development and health, both immediate and long-term.[66]

Fat

The fat in human milk is the main provider of calories and serves as a vehicle for transfer of fat soluble vitamins and essential fatty acids. Hytten[178] found that lactation failure (early cessation of lactation because of inadequate infant growth) could be related to the total output of fat on the seventh day, and concluded that women who produced less than 10 g of fat daily by this time were unlikely to breast-feed successfully. Human milk fat is very efficiently absorbed by the human infant. This appears to be largely the consequence of two important features: human milk lipases, and the nature of the triglycerides, which are the main components of milk fat.[179] In human milk triglycerides, a high proportion of the palmitic acid is in the 2-position and is absorbed as a 2-monoglyceride. This is in contrast to cow's milk fat in which palmitic acid is mainly in the 1- or 3-position from which it is liberated during digestion as free fatty acid. The free palmitic acid can be precipitated by calcium and excreted as the calcium soap, with loss not only of fat but also of calcium with a risk of causing hypocalcemia.[180]

As discussed earlier in this chapter the pattern of fatty acids will vary somewhat with the mother's diet. The fatty acid composition of the depot fat of infants may resemble that of their dietary intake, particularly in extreme cases. Widdowson *et al.*[181] found that, at 4 months of age, Dutch infants had 33 to 37% linoleic acid in their subcutaneous fat compared with only 3% in English infants, the differences arising from the use of a cow's milk formula in which the fat was replaced by maize oil for the Dutch infants, whereas the British children received relatively unchanged cow's milk. Depot fat of breast-fed infants is different from that of formula-fed infants, in line with the differing composition of milk fats.[182] The high proportion of essential fatty acids, especially linoleic, in human milk may have a significant role in the biochemical development of the brain and central nervous system. Evidence suggests that the newborn may be unable to convert linoleic to arachidonic acid, thus making this structrual lipid an essential dietary requirement at this time of life.[1,183]

The cholesterol content of human milk is generally high but levels are very variable[14] and appear to be unrelated to the maternal intake.[30] An abundant, readily available supply may facilitate myelinization of the central nervous system during the first months of life. In the infant, plasma cholesterol is low at birth, rises gradually during breast-feeding then falls again on weaning.[1] Changes can be induced in plasma cholesterol levels by altering dietary lipid even in breast-fed infants. Formulas with a low level of cholesterol and high levels of polyunsaturated fatty acids have been introduced to reduce the risk of later heart disease. However, it has been argued that high cholesterol during infancy may ensure proper development of enzyme systems for cholesterol metabolism.[184] Several studies have found that, although plasma cholesterol in breast-fed infants is significantly higher than in formula-fed during nursing,[185] by 7 to 12 years[186] or 15 to 19 years[184] plasma levels were not different. More work is needed on the long-term significance of the high levels in breast milk and the consequences of the lower intakes from various formulas.

Lactose

Lactose is a carbohydrate unique to mammalian milk. This sugar is present in human milk in relatively high concentrations[187] and, apart from providing a carbohydrate energy source, is a source of galactose which is required for the development of the central nervous system in the form of galactolipids. Lactose enhances growth of lactobacilli in the intestine along with the bifidus factor. It is less sweet than other sugars which may be of advantage in appetite control and development of taste.[1,20]

Vitamins

Where maternal intakes of vitamins are adequate, particularly of the water soluble ones, the milk supply is sufficient for the infant's needs. In some areas of the Third World, specific vitamin deficiencies, including infantile beriberi due to thiamine deficiency,[123] and vitamin B_{12} deficiency,[129] have been reported in solely breast-fed infants, and are caused by very low milk levels due to low maternal intakes. Vitamin B_{12} nutrition may also be poor in developed countries among otherwise well-nourished infants of strict vegan mothers.[188] Vitamin A nutrition is a public health problem in some parts of the world and breast-fed infants in such areas are also at risk of inadequate intakes.[70] There is no evidence that vitamin supplements are generally required by the solely breast-fed infant, at least for the first 6 months, when the lactating mother is well-nourished. When milk levels are low, supplementation of the mother rather than the infant is probably more appropriate.[85,122]

Vitamin D adequacy in breast milk is a more complex issue. Controversy exists over the amount and biological activity of the vitamin and its metabolites in human milk,[33,35] (see subsection on vitamins in human milk composition). Because of assumed dietary inadequacies, supplemental vitamin D (10 µg/day) is generally recommended for breast-fed infants and lactating mothers.[68,189] Although not as prevalent as among infants receiving unfortified formulas, vitamin-D-deficiency rickets does occur in breast-fed babies. However, environmental factors appear to be largely involved. Most mothers and their infants can obtain sufficient vitamin D from sunlight, but dark skinned people (including Mediterraneans)[190] who have emigrated to cold, cloudy areas, particularly large cities, may not be able to obtain sufficient exposure to meet their requirements. Cases of rickets have been reported in solely breast-fed black children in Michigan[191] and the disease is becoming a problem among Asian children in the United Kingdom.[192] Exposure to sunlight for a half-hour daily should be adequate, but child-care customs (e.g., swaddling) which prevent this may also be an etiological factor in breast-feeding rickets in areas of Turkey and Greece.[193] Thus, although most breast-fed infants do not require extra vitamin D, some specific groups may benefit from supplementation.

Minerals

In general, the varying concentrations of minerals in the milk of different species may be related to the growth rate of their young. The human is a relatively slow growing species and the total inorganic constituents comprise 0.25% of milk compared with, for example, 0.7% of cow's milk.[187] The lower renal solute load is water sparing, making additional feeding of water unnecessary for the healthy fully breast-fed infant even in hot climates.[194] Serum electrolyte levels are lower in breast-fed infants than in those fed formulas,[195] which may also be advantageous in reducing the risk of hypernatremia during episodes of dehydration. In a series of dehydrated infants in Liberia,[196] breast-fed babies were found to be much less at risk of uremia and hypernatremia, with possible consequences of brain damage, than were those fed with cow's milk formulas.

Levels of calcium and phosphorus in human milk are lower than those in some cow's-milk-based formulas. Nonetheless, Lealman *et al.*[197] reported that breast-fed infants had a higher plasma calcium level at 6 days than did groups of infants fed two different formulas. The Ca:P ratio in human milk is high (2:4) compared with cow's milk (1:3) and presumably more optimal for newborn metabolism. The higher absolute and relative intakes of phosphorus with cow's milk preparations cannot be excreted readily by the young kidney, causing a rise in serum phosphorus. The concomittant fall in serum calcium has been associated with a higher incidence of neonatal hypocalcemic tetany in formula-fed infants.[198]

Trace Elements

The concentration of iron in human milk is low and supplies only about 1 mg/day or less to the infant. Absorption from breast milk is very good, at least 50% and may be as high as 70% of the intake.[199] Factors enhancing absorption may include high levels of lactoferrin and vitamin C compared with cow's milk. Nonetheless, this dietary intake will not meet the apparent requirement of about 1 mg/kg per day[68] for growth and maintenance of optimum hemoglobin levels. The full-term infant may make up the difference from liver iron stores and thus should not need supplemental iron until at least 4 to 6 months of age. Indeed, it has been reported that infants fed solely on breast milk for longer periods, up to 18 months, have normal hematological values.[200] Although premature infants may exhaust their liver stores earlier (2 to 3 months), there is no evidence to suggest they need supplemental iron before other foods are added to the diet to meet their increased energy requirements.

Zinc is also much better absorbed from human milk than from formulas.[201] In spite of similar intakes, breast-fed infants have higher levels of zinc in hair and plasma,[202] and the poorer zinc status of some formula-fed infants may be growth limiting.[203] The difference in bioavailability is such that breast milk will prevent the onset of symptoms in acrodermatitis enteropathica, whereas cow's milk will not. (This is an inherited disorder of zinc metabolism, the clinical symptoms of which only appear after weaning from breast milk. Prior to the introduction of zinc therapy, plasma zinc levels and a good clinical status could be maintained by therapeutic use of human milk.)[204]

Dietary Supplementation

Infants who are solely breast-fed by well-nourished mothers who have an established lactation and unimpaired letdown have excellent growth for the first 4 to 6 months of life. For the purpose of recommendations, nutrient requirements are generally estimated from the average amounts supplied by breast milk.[68–70] Recommended dietary allowance tables have built into them safety factors to cover problems of bioavailability of nutrients from animal milks and formulas as well as individual variations in requirement. These RDAs are intended as a basis for planning food supplies and estimating the adequacy of formulas for groups of infants,[69] and it is therefore inappropriate to compare human milk with the RDA and find it wanting. Nonetheless, it is sometimes asserted that human milk supplies inadequate amounts of vitamins C and D, iron, and fluoride.[195] There is no evidence to suggest that vitamin C nutrition is a problem in the breast-fed infant, particularly where the mother's intake is adequate. Similarly, iron intake from breast milk, in conjunction with stores laid down in fetal life, is sufficient for 4 to 6 months or longer. When other foods are introduced, it may be beneficial to use iron-fortified products, in view of the fact that they may inhibit the absorption of iron from breast milk.[205] The need for supplemental fluoride is still open to argument. The American Academy of Pediatrics[206] recommends an intake of 0.25 mg/day from shortly after birth "in expectation that this would have a beneficial effect on mineralization of bone and teeth." In areas where the water contains at least 1 ppm fluoride, milk levels should be adequate but in an area with low levels, intakes from breast milk may be less than 0.1 mg/day. Other factors besides diet complicate assessment of the optimal fluoride intake, including fetal bone stores, maternal supplementation during pregnancy and lactation, and type of feeding. However, supplementation does appear to be beneficial. Hamberg[207] showed that giving fluoride drops, providing 0.5 mg/day, from 3 weeks of age to infants in Stockholm, where the water contained only 0.2 ppm, resulted in 50% fewer cavities at 3 to 6 years whether infants were breast- or bottle-fed. As discussed earlier in this chapter, the adequacy of vitamin D in human milk depends largely on environmental factors. In groups where there is a risk of insufficient exposure to sunlight, a supplemental intake of 10 μg/day is recommended.[68,69]

Premature Infants

Although it is by no means a new argument,[208] there has been growing interest in recent years over possible inadequacies of human milk for feeding the small premature infant.[209,210] One major area of concern has been the limiting effect of protein intake on growth in the premature infant of 1000 to 1500 g and 28 to 32 weeks gestation. Generally, better growth has been achieved with formulas supplying greater amounts of protein (2.5 to 4 g/kg per day) than with lower intakes (1.7 g/kg) from formula or pooled breast milk,[211] although no difference was found in one study which compared growth rates between an isocaloric formula and breast milk.[212] One facet of major importance in these studies is the source of breast milk. Pooled milk in a human milk bank is usually obtained from mothers who have a copious supply and have been lactating for some months. Such milk contains approximately 0.8 g protein/100 ml or 1.2 g/100 kcal, appropriate for an older full-term infant, but clearly inadequate when compared with the requirement for growth of the healthy premature infant. A growth rate the same as that *in utero* from 28 to 32 weeks requires about 2.5 g protein/100 kcal.[211] However, recent studies have shown that milk from the mother of a premature infant contains a higher concentration of protein than that of a full-term mother at the same stage of lactation. Atkinson *et al.*[213] found that during the first 4 weeks after parturition, total nitrogen in milk from preterm mothers (26 to 33 weeks) was higher than full-term mothers (38 to 40 weeks). The relative distribution of nitrogen and the rate of decline with time was the same in both groups. The premature milk also had a higher caloric density, due to a greater fat content, and provided on average 3 g protein/ 100 kcal. Stevens[214] found similar results in milk from mothers with infants whose birth weight was less than 1500 g. He concluded maternal milk was adequate as long as the infants had reached 1500 g by 3 to 4 weeks after birth so they were able to consume a sufficient volume. Of equal concern with protein quantity for growth is the metabolic response to the type of protein. The incidence of metabolic disturbances is much higher in infants receiving higher intakes of protein from formulas compared with human milk.[212,215,216] Azotemia, hyperaminoacidemia, and metabolic acidosis all occur to varying degrees according to the type and amount of protein fed. Conversely, serum albumin has also been observed to be higher in infants fed high protein formula compared with pooled human milk,[212] but such comparisons have not been made using mother-specific milk.

Similar criticisms apply to arguments about the adequacy of other nutrients in human milk. Pooled milk from late lactation may not be adequate to meet requirements for minerals and other major nutrients. However, Atkinson *et al.*[217] found that, in spite of the higher nitrogen content, premature milk did not contain higher levels of calcium, magnesium, sodium, or potassium, nor have differences been found in lactose content.[218] Chan[219] reported that premature milk had a higher level of ionized calcium than full-term milk up to 30 days postpartum but levels of phosphorus and 25-hydroxyvitamin D were not different. Lemons *et al.*[220] also found higher levels of protein and sodium but not calories, and there may also be differences in amino acid pattern between pre- and full-term milks.[221] Such differences suggest some biological adaptation to the needs of the premature infant, although specific problems may arise with certain nutrients under particular conditions. Folate status, as measured by blood levels, was low in a group of low-birth-weight infants on human milk but they did not show hematological symptoms.[222] Extra riboflavin may be required when an infant is treated for hyperbilirubinemia under ultraviolet light as this accelerates the rate of riboflavin breakdown.[223] Supplemental vitamin D may also be required by the small premature infant who may not be exposed to sunlight for several months because of medical care. Hypophosphatemic rickets[224] has been reported in several infants fed mother's milk from 12 days. These infants weighed less than 1000 g at birth and had a low intake of milk and so did not receive enough calcium and phosphorus to support their very rapid growth rate. Premature infants may have an earlier need of supplemental iron than the full-term: fetal stores are laid down mainly in the last 3 months *in utero* and an infant born at 28 weeks may only have enough to last 2 months.

More work is needed to compare both growth and health of the premature infant fed formula with that fed his own mother's milk. The question of suitability of human milk in such cases is as much philosophical as nutritional. Aside from questions of better immunological protection and of mother–infant bonding, issues which must be addressed include whether it is desirable to achieve the growth rates occurring *in utero*, and how much metabolic disturbance can be tolerated. If the infant is healthy and has a birth weight which is more than 1000 g and is appropriate for gestational age, it is probably safer to feed human milk expressed by his own mother until such time as he can obtain it directly.

CONCLUSIONS

Despite the technical difficulties involved and the limitations in data regarding relationships between lactation and nutrition, the available evidence does allow some general conclusions to be drawn.

Mothers who are well-nourished and have laid down adequate nutritional reserves, including fat, during pregnancy and who are well-fed during lactation are able to feed their babies satisfactorily on breast milk for 4 to 6 months or even longer. Full-term, healthy infants of such mothers, with adequate fetal stores, do not require any supplementation during this time. Any additional feeding may be detrimental by interfering with the lactation process or the utilization of nutrients.

While the volume and composition of the milk of poorly nourished mothers is surprisingly good, it may be produced at the expense of maternal tissues and is generally only adequate as a sole food for the infant for 2 to 4 months. Such mothers may produce milk which contains less fat, protein, and vitamins than well-nourished mothers and the yield is frequenlty reduced. Nonetheless, even after other foods are introduced to the infant's diet, breast milk may continue to provide important amounts of high quality protein, fat, calcium, and vitamins. Studies of supplementary feeding suggest that the volume and nutritional quality of breast milk can be improved by additions to the maternal diet, although results of such trials do depend somewhat on the degree and type of undernutrition. Provision of a diet during pregnancy which allows adequate maternal and fetal stores to be laid down may be of equal importance in ensuring both proper nutrition of the breast-fed infant and maintaining maternal health during lactation. The importance of a good supply of human milk of optimum composition is apparent in both public health and economic terms particularly in the Third World.

REFERENCES

1. Jelliffe, D. B. and Jelliffe, E. F. P., 1978, *Human Milk in the Modern World*, Oxford University Press, Oxford.
2. Hytten, F. E., 1954, Clinical and chemical studies in human lactation. Parts I–III, *Br. Med. J.* **1:**175–182.
3. Brown, K. H., Black, R. E., Robertson, A. D., Akhtar, N. A., Ahmed, Md. G., and Becker, S., 1982, Clinical and field studies of human lactation: Methodological considerations, *Am. J. Clin. Nutr.* **35:**745–756.
4. Lönnerdal, B., Forsum, E., and Hambraeus, L., 1976, A longitudinal study of the protein, nitrogen, and lactose contents of human milk from Swedish well-nourished women, *Am. J. Clin. Nutr.* **29:**1127–1133.
5. Forsum, E. and Lönnerdal, B., 1980, Effect of protein intake on protein and nitrogen composition of breast milk, *Am. J. Clin. Nutr.* **33:**1809–1813.
6. Rattigan, S., Ghisalberti, A. V., and Hartmann, P. E., 1981, Breast-milk production in Australian women, *Br. J. Nutr.* **45:**243–249.
7. Jelliffe, D. B. and Jelliffe, E. F. P., 1978, The volume and composition of human milk in poorly nourished communities. A review, *Am. J. Clin. Nutr.* **31:**492–515.
8. Deem, H. E., 1931, Observations on the milk of New Zealand women. Part II. The effect of diet on the secretion of human milk, *Arch. Dis. Child.* **6:**62–70.
9. Macy, I. G., Hunscher, H. A., Donelson, E., and Nims, B., 1930, Human milk flow, *Am. J. Dis. Child.* **39:**1186–1204.
10. Hytten, F. E. and Thomson, A. M., 1961, Nutrition of the lactating women, in: *Milk: The Mammary Gland and its Secretion*, Volume II (S. K. Kon and A. T. Cowie, eds.), Academic Press, New York, pp. 3–46.
11. Shukers, C. F., Macy, I. G., Nims, B., Donelson, E., and Hunscher, H. A., 1932, A quantitative study of the dietary of the human mother with respect to the nutrients secreted into breast milk, *J. Nutr.* **5:**127–139.
12. Picciano, M. F. and Guthrie, H. A., 1976, Copper, iron, and zinc contents of mature human milk, *Am. J. Clin. Nutr.* **29:**242–254.
13. Prentice, A., Prentice, A. M., and Whitehead, R. G., 1981, Breast-milk fat concentrations of rural African women. 1. Short-term variations within individuals, *Br. J. Nutr.* **45:**483–494.
14. Picciano, M. F., Guthrie, H. A., and Sheehe, D. M., 1978, The cholesterol content of human milk, *Clin. Pediatr.* **17:**359–362.
15. Lönnerdal, B., Forsum, E., Gebre-Medhin, M., and Hambraeus, L., 1976, Breast milk composition in Ethiopian and Swedish mothers. II. Lactose, nitrogen, and protein contents, *Am. J. Clin. Nutr.* **29:**1134–1141.
16. Hambraeus, L., Lönnerdal, B., Forsum, E., and Gebre-Medhin, M., 1978, Nitrogen and protein components of human milk, *Acta Paediatr. Scand.* **67:**561–565.
17. Macy, I. G. and Kelly, H. J., 1961, Human milk and cow's milk in infant nutrition, in: *Milk: The Mammary Gland and its Secretion*, Volume II (S. K. Kon and A. T. Cowie, eds.), Academic Press, New York, pp. 265–304.
18. Nayman, R., Thomson, M. E., Scriver, C. R., and Clow, C. L., 1979, Observations on the composition of milk-substitute products for treatment of inborn errors of amino acid metabolism. Comparisons with human milk. A proposal to rationalize nutrient content of treatment products, *Am. J. Clin. Nutr.* **32:**1279–1289.

19. Department of Health and Social Security, Committee on Medical Aspects of Food Policy, 1977, *The Composition of Mature Human Milk*, Her Majesty's Stationery Office, London.
20. Vorherr, H., 1978, Human lactation and breast feeding, in: *Lactation. A Comprehensive Treatise*, Volume IV (B. L. Larson, ed), Academic Press, New York, pp. 182–280.
21. Bezkorovainy, A., 1977, Human milk and colostrum proteins: A review, *J. Dairy Sci.* **60:**1023–1037.
22. Underwood, B. E., Hepner, R., and Abdullah, H., 1970, Protein, lipid, and fatty acids of human milk from Pakistani women during prolonged periods of lactation, *Am. J. Clin. Nutr.* **23:**400–407.
23. Svanberg, U., Gebre-Medhin, M., Ljungquist, B., and Olsson, M., 1977, Breast milk composition in Ethiopian and Swedish mothers. III. Amino acids and other nitrogenous substances, *Am. J. Clin. Nutr.* **30:**499–507.
24. Jensen, R. G., Hagerty, M. M., and McMahon, K. E., 1978, Lipids of human milk and infant formulas: A review, *Am. J. Clin. Nutr.* **31:**990–1016.
25. Nims, B., Macy, I. G., Brown M., and Hunscher, H. A., 1932, Human milk studies IX. Variations in the composition of milk at four hourly intervals during the day and night, *Am. J. Dis. Child.* **43:**828–844.
26. Deem, H. E., 1931, Observations on the milk of New Zealand women. Part I. The diurnal variation of the fat content of human milk, *Arch. Dis. Child.* **6:**53–61.
27. Hall, B., 1979, Uniformity of human milk, *Am. J. Clin. Nutr.* **32:**304–312.
28. Guthrie, H. A., Picciano, M. F., and Sheehe, D., 1977, Fatty acid patterns of human milk, *J. Pediatr.* **90:**39–41.
29. Read, W. C., Lutz, P. G., and Tashjian, A., 1965, Human milk lipids. II. The influence of dietary carbohydrates and fat on the fatty acids of mature milk. A study in four ethnic groups, *Am. J. Clin Nutr.* **17:**180–183.
30. Potter, J. M. and Nestel, P. J., 1976, The effects of dietary fatty acids and cholesterol on the milk lipids of lactating women and the plasma cholesterol of breast-fed infants, *Am. J. Clin. Nutr.* **29:**54–60.
31. Mellies, M. J., Burton, K., Larsen, R., Fixler, D., and Glueck, C. J., 1979, Cholesterol, phytosterols, and polyunsaturated/saturated fatty acid ratios during the first 12 months of lactation, *Am. J. Clin Nutr.* **32:**2383–2389.
32. Gebre-Medhin, M., Vahlquist, A., Hofvander, Y., Uppsäll, L., and Vahlquist, B., 1976, Breast milk composition in Ethiopian and Swedish mothers. I. Vitamin A and β-carotene, *Am. J. Clin. Nutr.* **29:**441–451.
33. Lakdawala, D. R. and Widdowson, E. M., 1977, Vitamin D in human milk, *Lancet* **1:**167–168.
34. Sahashi, Y., Suzuki, T., Higake, M., and Asano, T., 1979, Antirachitic potency of vitamin D sulfate in human milk, *J. Vitaminol.* **15:**78–82.
35. Leerbeck, E. and Søndergaard, H., 1980, The total content of vitamin D in human milk and cow's milk, *Br. J. Nutr.* **44:**7–12.
36. Hollis, B. W., Roos, B. A., Draper, H. H., and Lambert, P. W., 1981, Occurrence of vitamin D sulfate in human milk whey, *J. Nutr.* **111:**384–390.
37. Hollis, B. W., Roos, B. A., and Lambert, P. W., 1981, Vitamin D and its metabolites in human and bovine milk with respect to vitamin D intake, milk fractionation and vitamin D binding protein content, *Fed. Proc.* **40:**898.
38. Kobayashi, H., Kanno, C., Yamauchi, K., and Tsugo, J., 1975, Identification of α-, β-, γ-, and δ-tocopherols and their contents in human milk, *Biochim. Biophys. Acta* **380:**282–290.
39. Nail, P. A., Thomas, M. R., and Eakin, R., 1980, The effect of thiamin and riboflavin supplementation on the level of those vitamins in human breast milk and urine, *Am. J. Clin. Nutr.* **33:**198–204.
40. Roderuck, C., Williams, H. H., and Macy, I. G., 1946, Metabolism of women during the reproductive cycle, VIII. The utilization of thiamine during lactation, *J. Nutr.* **32:**249–265.
41. Roderuck, C., Coryell, M. N., Williams, H. H., and Macy, I. G., 1946, Metabolism of women during the reproductive cycle, IX. The utilization of riboflavin during lactation, *J. Nutr.* **32:**267–283.

42. Ramasastri, B. V., 1965, Folate activity in human milk, *Br. J. Nutr.* **19**:581–586.
43. Tamura, T., Yoshimura, Y., and Arakawa, T., 1980, Human milk folate and the folate status in lactating mothers and their infants, *Am. J. Clin. Nutr.* **33**:193–197.
44. Roepke, J. L. B. and Kirksey, A., 1979, Vitamin B_6 nutriture during pregnancy and lactation. II. The effect of long-term use of oral contraceptives, *Am. J. Clin. Nutr.* **32**:2249–2256.
45. West, K. D. and Kirksey, A., 1976, Influence of vitamin B_6 intake on the content of the vitamin in human milk, *Am. J. Clin. Nutr.* **29**:961–969.
46. Samson, R. R. and McClelland, D. B. L., 1980, Vitamin B_{12} in human colostrum and milk. (Quantitation of the vitamin and its binder and the uptake of bound vitamin B_{12} by intestinal bacteria), *Acta Paediatr. Scand.* **69**:93–99.
47. Stuart, J. E. and Connellan, P., 1973, Ascorbic acid studies in aborigines, *Aust. Paediatr. J.* **9**:159–163.
48. Kirksey, A., Ernst, J. A., Roepke, J. L., and Tsai, T.-L., 1979, Influence of mineral intake and use of oral contraceptives before pregnancy on the mineral content of human colostrum and of more mature milk, *Am. J. Clin. Nutr.* **32**:30–39.
49. Vaughan, L. A., Weber, C. W., and Kemberling, S. R., 1979, Longitudinal changes in the mineral content of human milk, *Am. J. Clin. Nutr.* **32**:2301–2306.
50. Morrison, S. D., 1952, *Human Milk: Yield, Proximate Principles and Inorganic Constituents,* Technical Communication No. 18, Commonwealth Agricultural Bureau, Slough, England.
51. Keenan, B. S., Buzek, S. W., Garza, C., and Nichols, B. L., 1981, Longitudinal and diurnal changes in human milk sodium and potassium, *Fed. Proc.* **40**:931.
52. Siimes, M. A., Vuori, E., and Kuitunen, P., 1979, Breast milk iron—A declining concentration during the course of lactation, *Acta Paediatr. Scand.* **68**:29–31.
53. Vuori, E. and Kuitunen, P., 1979, The concentrations of copper and zinc in human milk. A longitudinal study, *Acta Paediatr. Scand.* **68**:33–37.
54. Berfenstam, R., 1952, Studies on blood zinc. Clinical and experimental investigation into the zinc content of plasma and blood corpuscles with special reference to infancy, *Acta Paediatr. Scand.* **41**(Supplement 87):3–97.
55. Rajalakshmi, K. and Srikantia, S. G., 1980, Copper, zinc and magnesium content of breast milk of Indian women, *Am. J. Clin. Nutr.* **33**:664–669.
56. Underwood, E. J., 1977, *Trace Elements in Human and Animal Nutrition,* 4th ed., Academic Press, New York.
57. Vuori, E., 1979, A longitudinal study of manganese in human milk, *Acta Paediatr. Scand.* **68**:571–573.
58. Casey, C. E., 1977, The content of some trace elements in infant milk foods and supplements available in New Zealand, *N. Z. Med. J.* **85**:275–278.
59. Kumpulainen, J. and Vuori, E., 1980, Longitudinal study of chromium in human milk, *Am. J. Clin. Nutr.* **33**:2299–2302.
60. Jensen, R. G., Clark, R. M., and Ferris, A. M., 1980, Composition of lipids in human milk: A review, *Lipids* **15**:345–355.
61. Haroon, Y., Shearer, M. J., Rahim, S., Gunn, W. G., McEnery, G., and Barkhan, P., 1982, The content of phylloquinone (vitamin K_1) in human milk, cows' milk, and infant formula foods determined by high-performance liquid chromatography, *J. Nutr.* **112**:1105–1117.
62. Man, E. B. and Benotti, J., 1969, Butanol-extractable iodine in human and bovine colostrum and milk, *Clin. Chem.* **15**:1141–1146.
63. Shearer, T. R. and Hadjimarkos, D. M., 1975, Geographic distribution of selenium in human milk, *Arch. Environ. Health* **30**:230–233.
64. Khan, L. and Belavady, B., 1973, Basal metabolism in pregnant and nursing women and children, *Indian J. Med. Res.* **61**:1853–1860.
65. Venkatachalam, P. S. and Gopalan, C., 1960, Basal metabolism and total body water in nursing women, *Indian J. Med. Res.* **48**:507–510.
66. Hambraeus, L., 1977, Proprietary milk versus human breast milk in infant feeding. A critical appraisal from the nutritional point of view, *Pediatr. Clin. N. Am.* **24**(1):17–36.

67. World Health Organization, 1965, *Nutrition in Pregnancy and Lactation*, Technical Report Series No. 302, WHO, Geneva.
68. National Research Council, Food and Nutrition Board, 1980, *Recommended Dietary Allowances*, 9th ed., National Academy of Sciences, Washington, D.C.
69. Department of Health and Social Security, Committee on Medical Aspects of Food Policy, 1979, *Recommended Daily Amounts of Food Energy and Nutrients for Groups of People in the United Kingdom*, Report on Health and Social Subjects No. 15, Her Majesty's Stationery office, London.
70. Food and Agriculture Organization/World Health Organization, 1974, *Handbook on Human Nutritional Requirements*, Nutrition Studies No. 28, FAO, Rome.
71. Adelson, S., 1960, Some problems in collecting dietary data from individuals, *J. Am. Diet. Assoc.* **36:**453–461.
72. Kaucher, M., Moyer, E. Z., Richards, A. J., Williams, H. H., Wertz, A. L., and Macy, I. G., 1945, The diet of lactating women and the collection and preparation of food and human milk for analysis, *Am. J. Dis. Child.* **70:**142–147.
73. Edozien, J. C., Kahn, M. A. R., and Waslien, C. I., 1976, Human protein deficiency: Results of a Nigerian village study, *J. Nutr.* **106:**312–328.
74. Whitehead, R. G., Hutton, M., Müller, E., Rowland, M. G. M., Prentice, A. M., and Paul, A., 1978, Factors influencing lactating performance in rural Gambian mothers, *Lancet* **2:**178–181.
75. Fomon, S. J., Ziegler, E. E., Filer, L. J., Anderson, T. A., Edwards, B. B., and Nelson, S. E., 1978, Growth and serum chemical values of normal breast-fed infants, *Acta Paediatr. Scand.* Supplement 273.
76. Food and Agriculture Organization, 1957, *Report of Second Committee on Calorie Requirements*, Nutrition Studies No. 15, FAO, Rome.
77. Thomson, A. M., Hytten, F. E., and Billewicz, W. Z., 1970, The energy cost of human lactation, *Br. J. Nutr.* **24:**565–572.
78. Appel, J. A. and King, J. C., 1979, Energy needs during pregnancy and lactation, *Fam. Comm. Health,* **1**(4)**:**7–18.
79. Naismith, D. J. and Ritchie, C. D., 1975, The effect of breast-feeding and artificial feeding on body-weights, skinfold measurements and food intakes of forty-two primiparous women, *Proc. Nutr. Soc.* **34:**116A–117A.
80. Whichelow, M. J., 1975, Success and failure of breast-feeding in relation to energy intake, *Proc. Nutr. Soc.* **35:**62A–63A.
81. English, R. M. and Hitchcock, N. E., 1968, Nutrient intakes during pregnancy, lactation and after the cessation of lactation in a group of Australian women, *Br. J. Nutr.* **22:**615–624.
82. Geissler, C., Calloway, D. H., and Margen S., 1978, Lactation and pregnancy in Iran. II. Diet and nutritional status, *Am. J. Clin. Nutr.* **31:**341–354.
83. Sims, L. S., 1978, Dietary status of lactating women. 1. Nutrient intakes from food and from supplements, *J. Am. Diet. Assoc.* **73:**139–146.
84. Blackburn, M. W. and Calloway, D. H., 1976, Energy expenditure and composition of mature, pregnant and lactating women, *J. Am. Diet. Assoc.* **69:**29–37.
85. Gopalan, C. and Belavady, B., 1961, Nutrition and lactation, *Fed. Proc.* **20**(Supplement 7)**:**177–184.
86. Schutz, Y., Lechtig, A., and Bradfield, R. B., 1980, Energy expenditures and food intakes of lactating women in Guatemala, *Am. J. Clin. Nutr.* **33:**892–902.
87. Harrison, G. A., Boyce, A. J., Platt, C. M., and Serjeantson, S., 1975, Body composition changes during lactation in a New Guinea population, *Ann. Human Biol.* **2:**395–398.
88. Karmarkar, M. G., Rajalakshmi, R., and Ramakrishnan, C. V., 1963, Studies on human lactation. I. Effect of dietary protein and fat supplementation on protein, fat and essential amino acid contents of breast milk, *Acta Paediatr. Scand.* **52:**473–480.
89. Deb, A. K. and Cama, H. R., 1962, Studies on human lactation. Dietary nitrogen utilization during lactation, and distribution of nitrogen in mother's milk, *Br. J. Nutr.* **16:**65–73.

90. Prentice, A. M., Whitehead, R. G., Roberts, S. B., Paul, A. A., Watkinson, M., Prentice, A., and Watkinson, A. M., 1980, Dietary supplementation of Gambian nursing mothers and lactational performance, *Lancet* **2**:886–888.

91. Food and Agricultural Organization, 1957, *Report of the Committee on Protein Requirements*, Nutrition Studies No. 16, FAO, Rome.

92. Hitchcock, N. E. and English, R. M., 1966, Nutrient intake during lactation in Australian women, *Br. J. Nutr.* **20**:599–607.

93. Goldsmith, N. F. and Johnston, P. O., 1975, Bone mineral: Effects of oral contraceptives, pregnancy and lactation, *J. Bone Joint Surg.* **57A**:657–668.

94. Atkinson, P. J. and West, R. R., 1970, Loss of skeletal calcium in lactating women, *J. Obstet. Gynaecol. Br. Commonw.* **77**:555–560.

95. Paterson, C. R., 1978, Calcium requirements in man: A review, *Postgrad. Med. J.* **54**:244–248.

96. Bassir, O., 1959, Nutrition studies on breast milk of Nigerian women—Supplementing the maternal diet with a protein-rich plant product, *Trans. R. Soc. Trop. Med. Hyg.* **53**:256–261.

97. Belavady, B. and Gopalan, C., 1960, Effect of dietary supplementation on the composition of breast milk, *Indian J. Med. Res.* **48**:518–523.

98. Davis, D. P., and Evans, T. I., 1976, Failure to thrive at the breast, *Lancet* **2**:1194–1195.

99. Egli, G. E., Egli, N. S., and Newton, M., 1961, The influence of the number of breast feedings on milk production, *Pediatrics* **27**:314–317.

100. Lindblad, B. S., Ljungqvist, A., Gebre-Mehdin, M., and Rahimtoola, R. J., 1977, The composition and yield of human milk in developing countries, in: *Food and Immunology*, Symposia of the Swedish Nutrition Foundation XIII (H. McFarlane, L. Hambraeus, and L. Å. Hanson, eds.), Almquist and Wiksell, Stockholm, pp. 125–132.

101. National Research Council, Food and Nutrition Board, 1958, *Recommended Dietary Allowances*, Publication No. 302, National Academy of Sciences, Washington, D.C.

102. Thomson, A. M. and Black, A. E., 1975, Nutritional aspects of human lactation, *Bull. WHO* **52**:163–177.

103. Lönnerdal, B., Forsum, E., and Hambraeus, L., 1976, The protein content of human milk. 1. A transversal study of Swedish normal material, *Nutr. Rep. Int.* **13**:125–134.

104. Wallgren, A., 1944–1945, Breast milk consumption of healthy full term infants, *Acta Paediatr. Scand.* **32**:778–790.

105. Picciano, M. F., Calkins, E. J., Garrick, J. R., and Deering, R. H., 1981, Milk and mineral intakes of breast fed infants, *Acta Paediatr. Scand.* **70**:189–194.

106. Becroft, T. C., 1967, Child-rearing practices in the highlands of New Guinea: A longitudinal study of breast feeding, *Med. J. Aust.* **2**:598–602.

107. Bailey, K. V., 1965, Quantity and composition of breast milk in some New Guinea populations, *J. Trop. Pediatr.* **11**:35–49.

108. Sénécal, J., 1959, Alimentation de l'enfant dans les pays tropicaux et subtropicaux, *UNESCO Cour.* **9**:1–22.

109. Sosa, R., Klaus, M., and Urrutia, J. J., 1976, Feed the nursing mother: thereby the infant, *J. Pediatr.* **88**:668–670.

110. Lunn, P. G., Watkinson, M., Prentice, A. M., Morrell, P., Austin, S., and Whitehead, R. G., 1981, Maternal nutrition and lactational amenorrhoea, *Lancet* **1**:1428–1429.

111. Prema, K., Nadamuni Naidu, A., Neelakumari, S., and Ramalakshmi, B. A., 1981, Nutrition–fertility interaction in lactating women of low income groups, *Br. J. Nutr.* **45**:461–467.

112. Lindblad, B. S. and Rahimtoola, R. J., 1974, A pilot study of the quality of human milk in a lower socio-economic group in Karachi, Pakistan, *Acta Paediatr. Scand.* **63**:125–128.

113. Carneiro, T. A. and de Oliveira, J. E. D., 1973, Nutritional studies in human lactation in Brazil, *Environ. Child. Health* **19**:384–387.

114. Hanafy, M. M., Morsey, M. R. A., Seddick, Y., Habib, H. A., and el Lozy, M., 1972, Maternal nutrition and lactation performance. A study in urban Alexandria, *J. Trop. Pediatr.* **18**:187–191.

115. Insull, W., Hirsch, J., James, T., and Ahrens, E. H., 1959, The fatty acids of human milk. II. Alterations produced by manipulation of caloric balance and exchange of dietary fats, *J. Clin. Invest.* **38:**443–450.

116. Crawford, M. A., Stevens, P., Msuya, P., and Munhambo, A., 1974, Lipid composition of human milk: Comparative studies on African and European mothers, *Proc. Nutr. Soc.* **33:**50A–51A.

117. Lauber, E. and Reinhardt, M., 1979, Studies on the quality of breast milk during 23 months of lactation in a rural community of the Ivory Coast, *Am. J. Clin. Nutr.* **32:**1159–1173.

118. Read, W. C., Lutz, P. G., and Tashjian, A., 1965, Human milk lipids. III. Short-term effects of dietary carbohydrate and fat, *Am. J. Clin. Nutr.* **17:**184–187.

119. Wellby, M., O'Halloran, M. W., and Wellby, M. L., 1973, Maternal diet and lipid composition of breast milk, *Lancet* **2:**458–459.

120. Naismith, D. J., 1973, Kwashiorkor in Western Nigeria: A study of traditional weaning foods with particular reference to energy and linoleic acid, *Br. J. Nutr.* **30:**567–576.

121. Kon, S. K. and Mawson, E. H., 1960, *Human Milk*, Special Report Series No. 219, Medical Research Council, London.

122. Deodhar, A. D., Rajalakshmi, R., and Ramakrishnan, C. V., 1964, Studies on human lactation, Part III. Effect of dietary vitamin supplementation on vitamin contents of breast milk, *Acta Paediatr. Scand.* **53:**42–48.

123. Morley, D., 1973, *Paediatric Priorities in the Developing World*, Butterworths, London.

124. Ejderhamn, J. and Hamfelt, A., 1980, Pyridoxal phosphate concentration in blood in newborn infants and their mothers compared with the amount of extra pyridoxal taken during pregnancy and breast feeding, *Acta Paediatr. Scand.* **69:**327–330.

125. Thomas, M. R., Kawamoto, J., Sneed, S. M., and Eakin, R., 1979, The effects of vitamin C, vitamin B_6 and vitamin B_{12} supplementation on the breast milk and maternal status of well-nourished women, *Am. J. Clin. Nutr.* **32:**1679–1685.

126. Foukas, M. D., 1973, An antilactogenic effect of pyridoxine, *J. Obstet. Gynaecol. Br. Commonw.* **80:**718.

127. Jathar, V. S., Kamath, S. A., Parikh, M. N., Rege, D. V., and Satoskar, R. S., 1970, Maternal milk and serum vitamin B_{12}, folic acid, and protein levels in Indian subjects, *Arch. Dis. Child.* **45:**236–241.

128. Osifo, B. O. A. and Onifade, A., 1980, Effect of folate supplementation and malaria on the folate content of human milk, *Nutr. Metab.* **24:**176–181.

129. Jahhav, M., Webb, J. K. G., Vaishnava, S., and Baker, S. J., 1962, Vitamin -B_{12} deficiency in Indian infants, *Lancet* **2:**903–907.

130. Tarjan, R., Kramer, M., Szoke, K., Londer, K., Szarvas, T., and Dworschak, E., 1965, The effect of different factors on the composition of human milk. II. The composition of human milk during lactation, *Nutr. Diet.* **7:**136–154.

131. Gunther, M., 1952, Composition of human milk and factors affecting it, *Br. J. Nutr.* **6:**215–220.

132. Peters, F. E., 1953, Chemical composition of New Hebridean milk, *Br. J. Nutr.,* **7:**208–211.

133. Hambidge, K. M., 1977, Trace Elements in pediatric nutrition, *Adv. Pediatr.* **24:**191–231.

134. Murray, M. J., Murray, A. B., Murray, N. J., and Murray, M. B., 1978, The effect of iron status of Nigerian mothers on that of their infants at birth and 6 months, and on the concentration of iron in breast milk, *Br. J. Nutr.* **39:**627–630.

135. Vuori, E., Mäkinen, S. M., Kara, R., and Kuitunen, P., 1980, The effects of the dietary intakes of copper, iron, manganese, and zinc on the trace element content of human milk, *Am. J. Clin. Nutr.* **33:**227–231.

136. Carmichael, D., Hegenauer, J., Lem, M., Ripley, L., Saltman, P., and Hatlen, L., 1977, Iron supplementation of the lactating mouse and suckling neonate, *J. Nutr.* **107:**1377–1384.

137. Henriques, V. and Roche, A., 1929, La teneur en fer du lait peut-elle augmenter sous l'influence d'ingestion ou d'injection de sel de fer? *Bull. Soc. Chim. Biol.* **11:**679–692.

138. Thomson, C. D. and Robinson, M. F., 1980, Selenium in human health and disease with emphasis on those aspects peculiar to New Zealand, *Am. J. Clin. Nutr.* **33**:313–323.

139. Hofvander, Y. and Petros-Barvazian, A., 1978, WHO collaborative study on breast feeding, *Acta Paediatr. Scand.* **67**:556–560.

140. Department of Health and Social Security, Committee on Medical Aspects of Food Policy, 1978, *Breast Feeding*, Office of Population Censuses and Surveys, Her Majesty's Stationery Office, London.

141. Malcolm, L. A., 1970, Growth, malnutrition, and mortality of the infant and toddler in the Asai Valley of the New Guinea Highlands, *Am. J. Clin. Nutr.* **23**:1090–1095.

142. Huffman, S. L., Chowdbury, A. K. M. A., Chakraborty, J., and Simpson, N. K., 1980, Breast-feeding patterns in rural Bangladesh, *Am. J. Clin. Nutr.* **33**:144–154.

143. Kamal, I., Hefnawi, F., Ghoneim, M., Talaat, M., Younis, N., Tagui, A., and Abdalla, M., 1969, Clinical, biochemical, and experimental studies on lactation II. Clinical effects of gestagens on lactation, *Am. J. Obstet. Gynecol.* **105**:324–334.

144. Murray, J. and Murray, A. B., 1979, Breast milk and weights of Nigerian mothers and their infants, *Am. J. Clin. Nutr.* **32**:737.

145. Jelliffe, D. B. and Maddocks, I., 1964, Notes on ecologic malnutrition in the New Guinea highlands, *Clin. Pediatr.* **3**:432–438.

146. Antonov, A. N., 1947, Children born during the Siege of Leningrad in 1942, *J. Pediatr.* **30**:250–259.

147. Smith, C. A., 1947, Effects of maternal undernutrition upon the newborn infant in Holland (1944–1945), *J. Pediatr.* **30**:229–243.

148. Dennis, J. K. and Bytheway, W. R., 1965, Changes in body weight after delivery, *J. Obstet. Gynaecol. Br. Commonw.* **72**:94–102.

149. Norgan, N. G., Ferro-Luzzi, A., and Durnin, J. V. G. A., 1974, The energy and nutrient intake and energy expenditure of 204 New Guinean adults, *Philos. Trans. R. Soc. London, Res. B* **268**:309–348.

150. Prentice, A., Prentice, A. M., and Whitehead, R. G., 1981, Breast-milk fat concentrations of rural African women. 2. Long-term variations within a community, *Br. J. Nutr.* **45**:495–503.

151. Bailey, K. V., 1962, Rural nutrition studies in Indonesia. VI. Field surveys of lactating women, *Trop. Geogr. Med.* **14**:11–19.

152. Walker, A. R. P., Richardson, B., and Walker, F., 1972, The influence of numerous pregnancies and lactations on bone dimensions in South African Bantu and Caucasian mothers, *Clin. Sci.* **42**:189–196.

153. Fairney, A., Naughten, E., and Oppé, T. E., 1977, Vitamin D and human lactation, *Lancet* **2**:739–741.

154. Geissler, C., Margen, S., and Calloway, D. H., 1979, Lactation and pregnancy in Iran. III. Hormonal factors, *Am. J. Clin. Nutr.* **32**:1097–1111.

155. Hytten, F. E., 1954, Clinical and chemical studies in human lactation. VIII. Relationship of the age, physique, and nutritional status of the mother to the yield and composition of her milk, *Br. Med. J.* **2**:844–845.

156. Hytten, F. E., 1954, Clinical and chemical studies in human lactation. VI. The functional capacity of the breast, *Br. Med. J.* **1**:912–915.

157. Rosa, F. W., 1977, Resolving the "Public Health Dilemma" of steroid contraception and its effects on lactation, *Am. J. Pub. Health* **66**:791–792.

158. Koetswang, S., Bhiraleus, P., and Chiemprajert, T., 1972, Effect of oral contraceptives on lactation, *Fertil. Steril.* **23**:24–28.

159. Lönnerdal, B., Forsum, E., and Hambraeus, L., 1980, Effect of oral contraceptives on composition and volume of breast milk, *Am. J. Clin. Nutr.* **33**:816–824.

160. Hull, V. J., 1981, The effects of hormonal contraceptives on lactation: Current findings, methodological considerations, and future priorities, *Stud. Fam. Plan.* **12**:134–155.

161. Kader, M. M. A. and Kamal, I., 1969, Clinical, biochemical, and experimental studies on lactation. III. Biochemical changes induced in milk by gestagens, *Am. J. Obstet. Gynecol.* **105**:978–985.

162. Wynn, V., 1975, Vitamins and oral contraceptive use, *Lancet* **1**:561–564.
163. Lewis, C. M. and King, J. C., 1980, Effect of oral contraceptive agents on thiamin, riboflavin, and pantothenic acid status in young women, *Am. J. Clin. Nutr.* **33**:832–838.
164. Bossé, T. R. and Donald, E. A., 1979, The vitamin B_6 requirement in oral contraceptive users, Parts I and II, *Am. J. Clin. Nutr.* **32**:1015–1032.
165. Chopra, J. G., 1972, Effect of steroid contraceptives in lactation, *Am. J. Clin. Nutr.* **25**:1202–1214.
166. McClelland, D. B. L., McGrath, J., and Samson, R. R., 1978, Microbial factors in human milk, *Acta Paediatr. Scand.* Supplement 271.
167. Ahn, C. H. and MacLean, W. C., 1980, Growth of the exclusively breast-fed infant, *Am. J. Clin. Nutr.* **33**:183–192.
168. Waterlow, J. C., Ashworth, A., and Griffiths, M., 1980, Faltering in infant growth in less-developed countries, *Lancet* **2**:1176–1179.
169. World Health Organization, 1981, *Contemporary Patterns of Breast-Feeding*, WHO, Geneva.
170. Kulski, J. K. and Hartmann, P. E., 1981, Changes in human milk composition during the initiation of lactation, *Aust. J. Exp. Biol. Med. Sci.* **59**:101–114.
171. Fomon, S. J. and May, C. D., 1958, Metabolic studies of normal full-term infants fed pasteurized human milk, *Pediatrics* **22**:101–115.
172. Kagan, B. M., Felix, N., Molander, C. W., Busser, R. J., and Kalman, D., 1963, Body water changes in relation to nutrition of premature infants, *Ann. N. Y. Acad. Sci.* **110**:830–839.
173. Goldman, H. I., Karelitz, S., Acs, H., and Seifter, E., 1962, The relationship of the sodium, potassium and chloride concentration of the feeding to the weight gain of premature infants, *Pediatrics* **30**:909–916.
174. Pohlandt, F., 1974, Cystine: A semi-essential amino acid in the newborn infant, *Acta Paediatr. Scand.* **63**:801–804.
175. Rassin, D. K., Gaull, G. E., Räihä, N. C. R., and Heinonen, K., 1977, Milk protein quantity and quality in low-birth-weight infants. IV. Effects of tyrosine and phenylalanine in plasma and urine, *J. Pediatr.* **90**:356–360.
176. Sturman, J. A., Rassin, D. K., and Gaull, G. E., 1977, Taurine in development, *Life Sci.* **21**:1–22.
177. Shahani, K. M., Kwan, A. J., and Friend, B. A., 1980, Role and significance of enzymes in human milk, *Am. J. Clin. Nutr.* **33**:1861–1868.
178. Hytten, F. E., 1954, Clinical and chemical studies in human lactation. VII. The effect of differences in yield and composition of milk on the infant's weight gain and the duration of breast-feeding, *Br. Med. J.* **1**:1410–1413.
179. Belavady, B., 1978, Lipid and trace element composition of human milk, *Acta Paediatr. Scand.* **67**:566–571.
180. Southgate, D. A. T., Widdowson, E. M., Smits, B. J., Cooke, W. T., Walker, C. H. M., and Mathers, N. P., 1969, Absorption and excretion of calcium and fat by young infants, *Lancet* **1**:487–489.
181. Widdowson, E. M., Dauncey, M. J., Gairdner, D. M. T., Jonxis, J. H. P., and Pelikan-Filipkova, M., 1975, Body fat of British and Dutch infants, *Br. Med. J.* **1**:653–655.
182. Gairdner, D. M. T., 1974, The effect of diet on the development of the adipose organ, *Proc. Nutr. Soc.* **33**:119–121.
183. Crawford, M. A., Laurance, B. M., Hall, B., and Munhambo, A., 1976, Milk lipids and their variabilities, *Curr. Med. Res. Opinion* **4**(Supplement 1):33–43.
184. Friedman, G. and Goldberg, S. J., 1975, Concurrent and subsequent serum cholesterol of breast- and formula-fed infants, *Am. J. Clin. Nutr.* **28**:42–45.
185. Ginsburg, B.-E. and Zetterström, R., 1980, Serum cholesterol concentrations in early infancy, *Acta Paediatr. Scand.* **69**:581–585.
186. Glueck, S. J., Tsang, R., Balestreri, W., and Fallot, R., 1972, Plasma and dietary cholesterol in infancy: Effects of early low and moderate dietary cholesterol intake on subsequent responses to increased dietary cholesterol, *Metabolism* **21**:1181–1192.
187. Jenness, R., 1974, The composition of milk, in: *Lactation: A Comprehensive Treatise*, Volume III, (B. L. Larson and V. R. Smith, eds.), Academic Press, New York, pp. 3–101.

188. Higginbottom, M. C., Sweetman, L., and Nyham, W. L., 1978, A syndrome of methylmalonic aciduria, homocystinuria, megaloblastic anemia and neurologic abnormalities in a Vitamin B_{12}-deficient breast-fed infant of a strict vegetarian, *N. Engl. J. Med.* **299**:317–323.

189. Nelson, W. E., Vaughan, V. C., McKay, R. J., and Behrman, R. E., (eds.), 1979, *Textbook of Pediatrics*, 11th ed., W. B. Saunders, Philadelphia.

190. Widdowson, E. M., 1977, Breast feeding and rickets, *Lancet* **2**:560.

191. O'Connor, P., 1977, Vitamin D deficiency in rickets in two breast-fed infants who were not receiving vitamin D supplementation, *Clin. Pediatr.* **16**:361–363.

192. O'Hara-May, J. and Widdowson, E. M., 1976, Diets and living conditions of Asian boys in Coventry with and without signs of rickets, *Br. J. Nutr.* **36**:23–36.

193. Ozsoylu, S., 1977, Breast feeding and rickets, *Lancet* **2**:560.

194. Almroth, S. G., 1978, Water requirements of breast-fed infants in a hot climate, *Am. J. Clin. Nutr.* **31**:1154–1157.

195. Fomon, S. J., 1974, *Infant Nutrition*, 2nd ed., W. B. Saunders, Philadelphia.

196. Kingston, M. E., 1973, Biochemical disturbances in breast-fed infants with gastroenteritis, *J. Pediatr.* **82**:1073–1079.

197. Lealman, G. T., Logan, R. W., Hutchinson, J. H., Kerr, M. M., Fulton, A. M., and Brown, C. A., 1976, Calcium, phosphorus, and magnesium concentrations in plasma during the first week of life and their relation to type of milk feed, *Arch. Dis. Child.* **51**:377–384.

198. Oppé, T. E. and Redstone, D., 1968, Calcium and phosphorus levels in healthy newborn infants given various types of milk, *Lancet* **1**:1045–1048.

199. Saarinen, U. M., Siimes, M. A., and Dallman, P. R., 1977, Iron absorption in infants: High bioavailability of iron as indicated by the extrinsic tag method of iron absorption and by concentration of serum ferritin, *J. Pediatr.* **91**:36–39.

200. McMillan, J. A., Landaw, S. A., and Oski, F. A., 1976, Iron sufficiency in breast-fed infants and the availability of iron from human milk, *Pediatrics* **58**:686–691.

201. Casey, C. E., Walravens, P. A., and Hambidge, K. M., 1981, Availability of zinc: Loading tests with human milk, cow's milk and infant formulas, *Pediatrics* **68**:394–396.

202. Hambidge, K. M., Walravens, P. A., Casey, C. E., Brown, R. M., and Bender, C., 1979, Plasma zinc concentrations of breast-fed infants, *J. Pediatr.* **94**:607–608.

203. Walravens, P. A. and Hambidge, K. M., 1976, Growth of infants fed a zinc-supplemented formula, *Am. J. Clin. Nutr.* **29**:1114–1121.

204. Hambidge, K. M., Walravens, P. A., and Neldner, K. H., 1978, Zinc and acrodermatitis enteropathica, in: *Zinc and Copper in Clinical Medicine* (K. M. Hambidge and B. Nichols, eds.), Spectrum Publications, New York, pp. 81–98.

205. American Academy of Pediatrics, Committee on Nutrition, 1976, Iron supplementation for infants, *Pediatrics* **58**:765–768.

206. American Academy of Pediatrics, Committee on Nutrition, 1979, Fluoride supplementation: Revised dosage schedule, *Pediatrics* **63**:150–152.

207. Hamberg, L., 1971, Controlled trial of fluoride in vitamin drops for the prevention of caries in children, *Lancet* **1**:441–442.

208. Gordon, H. H., Levine, S. Z., and McNamara, H., 1947, Feeding of premature infants: A comparison of human and cow's milk, *Am. J. Dis. Child.* **73**:442–452.

209. Fomon, S. J., 1977, Human milk in premature infant feeding: Report of a second workshop, *Am. J. Pub. Health* **67**:361–363.

210. American Academy of Pediatrics, Committee on Nutrition, 1977, Nutritional needs of low-birth-weight infants, *Pediatrics* **60**:519–530.

211. Fomon, S. J., Ziegler, E. E., and Vázquez, H. D., 1977, Human milk and the small premature infant, *Am. J. Dis. Child.* **131**:463–467.

212. Räihä, N. C. R., Heinonen, K., Rassin, D. K., and Gaull, G. E., 1976, Milk protein quantity and quality in low-birth-weight infants: 1. Metabolic responses and effects on growth, *Pediatrics* **57**:659–674.

213. Atkinson, S. A., Anderson, G. H., and Bryan, M. H., 1980, Human milk: Comparison of the nitrogen composition in milk from mothers of premature and full-term infants, *Am. J. Clin. Nutr.* **33**:811–815.

214. Stevens, L. H., 1969, The first kilogram: 2. The protein content of breast milk of mothers of babies of low birth weight, *Med. J. Aust.* **2:**555–557.
215. Heird, W. C., 1977, Feeding the premature infant. Human milk or artificial formula? *Am. J. Dis. Child.* **131:**468–469.
216. Schultz, K., Soltész, G., and Mestyán, J., 1980, The metabolic consequences of human milk and formula feeding in premature infants, *Acta Paediatr. Scand.* **69:**647–652.
217. Atkinson, S. A., Bryan, M. H., Radde, I. C., Chance, G. W., and Anderson, G. H., 1977, Effect of premature birth on total N and mineral concentration in human milk, *Proc. Vth Western Hemisphere Nutr. Cong.* (Québec) pp. 46–47.
218. Water, L. A., Olson, A. C., Heldt, G. P., and Perman, J. A., 1979, Changes in lactose content of breast milk during lactation in mothers of premature infants, *Pediatr. Res.* **13:**410.
219. Chan, G. W., 1979, Preterm and term breast milk calcium and vitamin D, *Pediatr. Res.* **13:**396.
220. Lemons, J. A., Hall, D., Benson, J., and Simmons, M. A., 1979, Composition of preterm breast milk, *Pediatr. Res.* **13:**403.
221. Adcock, E. W., Ginsberg, A. K., and Malloy, M. H., 1980, Qualitative differences in amino acid content of human milk from mothers of preterm and term infants, *Pediatr. Res.* **14:**495.
222. Burland, W. L., Simpson, K., and Lord, J., 1971, Response of low birth-weight infants to treatment with folic acid, *Arch. Dis. Child.* **46:**189–194.
223. Hovi, L., Hekali, R., and Siimes, M. A., 1979, Evidence of riboflavin depletion in breast-fed newborns and its further acceleration during treatment of hyperbilibubinemia by phototherapy, *Acta Paediatr. Scand.* **68:**567–570.
224. Rowe, J. C., Wood, D. H., Rowe, D. W., and Raizz, L. G., 1979, Nutritional hypophosphatemic rickets in a premature infant fed breast milk, *N. Engl. J. Med.* **300:**293–296.
224. Rowe, J. C., Wood, D. H., Rowe, D. W., and Raizz, L. G., 1979, Nutritional hypophosphatemic rickets in a premature infant fed breast milk, *N. Engl. J. Med.* **300:**293–296.

Since this chapter was written, a large number of publications has appeared concerning both the volume and composition of human milk in well-nourished women. This is a very active field of research at the present time and thus this chapter should be read as a background to this more recent work.

8

The Immunology of Breast Milk

Anthony R. Hayward

INTRODUCTION

Resistance to infection and protection from allergic disorders (or atopy) are probably the most frequently cited immunologic benefits of breast-feeding. In this chapter, some of the immunologic constituents of breast milk are described and the mechanisms of their possible beneficial effects discussed. In order to provide a background for this discussion, the basic effector mechanisms involved in immune responses are summarized in this section. Special attention has been given to the immune processes occuring at mucosal and secretory surfaces such as the intestinal and mammary epithelium.

There are two types of immunity. The major characteristic of *specific immunity* is an adaptive memory that leads to the production of antibodies and specifically sensitized lymphocytes. *Nonspecific immunity* is mediated by phagocytes and by humoral factors such as complement: it has no intrinsic long-term memory. Specific immune responses usually require the participation of nonspecific mechanisms to eliminate bacteria or viruses from the body. This introduction deals mainly with the mechanisms of specific immune responses.

Antibodies

Antibodies are a class of proteins defined by their specific interaction with the antigen that elicited their production. Antibody activity is restricted to immunoglobulins, serum proteins made by plasma cells that are derived from a special subset of blood lymphocytes called B lymphocytes. There are five main classes of immunoglobulin with different molecular weights and different distributions in the body (Table I). They have in common a basic immunoglobulin structure comprised of two light and two heavy peptide

Anthony R. Hayward • Department of Pediatrics, University of Colorado School of Medicine, Denver, Colorado 80262.

Table I. Characteristics of Human Immunoglobulin Classes

Class	Heavy chain	Molecular weight	Subclasses	Half-life[a]	Distribution	Placental transfer
IgG	γ	150,000	4	25	Plasma and tissue fluids	+
IgA	α	160,000–500,000	2	7	Secretions and plasma	0
IgM	μ	900,000	2	5	Mainly plasma	0
IgD	δ	180,000	1	—	B-cell surface	0
IgE	ε	200,000	1	2.3	Plasma, mast cell	0

[a] Half-life in days in plasma.

chains (Fig. 1) The N terminals of the polypeptide chains contain two binding sites for antigen while the C terminals of the heavy chains have sites for complement activation and for binding to cell surfaces. The specificity of an antibody molecule is determined by the shape and the distribution of charges on the antigen binding site and this in turn depends on the amino acid sequence of the variable (v) region of the heavy and light chains.

Both variable and constant (c) region amino acid sequences of immunoglobulins are, in common with other proteins, determined by a sequence of DNA bases. The variability of sequences needed to give the enormous diversity of antibody specificities is achieved by recombining three or four minigenes from a small library carried in the genome. This library comprises the so called V, D, and J regions of the gene (Fig. 1). At least two gene rearrangements are required for a lymphocyte to acquire the ability to make an IgA antibody. The first is the assembly of a heavy chain variable region by combining the genes for a V, D, and J region. At a pre-B-cell stage, the VDJ sequence is transcribed along with constant region (Cμ) to obtain the messenger RNA for the heavy chain. When the pre-B cell matures to a B cell it selects a light chain V and J region ($V_L J_L$) and joins them to a light

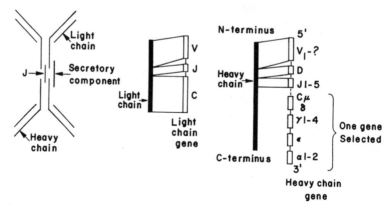

Figure 1. Schematic structure of IgA dimer and the genes that specify the immunoglobulin heavy and light chains. See text for explanation.

chain constant region gene to synthesize the light chain message. Segments are excised from the messenger RNA of both heavy and light chains before translation and assembly of the polypeptide chains into an immunoglobulin molecule of the IgM class.

In order to make IgA, the principal immunoglobulin in breast milk, the cell must switch from IgM to IgA production. In doing so, the original VDJ and V_LJ_L sequences are preserved so that the antibody specificity is unaltered, but the heavy chain VDJ is rearranged to join the $C\alpha$ region and the intervening sequences (which include the μ and γ genes) are deleted. There are two subclasses of IgA: IgA 1 accounts for about 90% of serum IgA and 50% of secreted IgA. The balance is all IgA 2 (reviewed in ref. 1). Ten to fifteen percent of serum IgA has a polymeric form, mostly dimeric.

Different mechanisms mediate the biologic function of antibodies of different classes. IgG and IgM both bind complement so bacteria coated with these antibodies can be opsonized (or prepared) for phagocytosis. IgA antibodies do not activate complement by the classical pathway, although they may do so by an alternative pathway. IgA does not bind to the receptors for IgG and IgM immunoglobulins on phagocytes. IgG and monomeric IgA molecules have two antigen binding sites while the commonly secreted dimer of IgA has four sites; secreted IgA antibodies are therefore effective cross linkers and agglutinators of antigen.

Cellular Aspects of the Specific Immune Response

A specific immune response involves binding of antigen to specific B cells which are stimulated to divide and mature into fully differentiated antibody-producing cells. Effective immune responses require the interaction of several types of lymphocyte and mononuclear phagocytes. All the immunoglobulin made by a given B cell bears the same variable region so each B cell has a predetermined specificity. B cells circulate through blood and lymphoid tissues, carrying samples of the antibody they could make on their plasma membranes. This surface immunoglobulin has a receptor function: antigen binding results in transmission of a maturation signal to the B cell. Antigen stimulated B cells normally leave the circulation and lodge in lymphoid tissue. Most B lymphocytes and particularly those destined to make IgA, require, in addition, a differentiating signal from a T (thymus-derived) lymphocyte in order to mature into an antibody-secreting plasma cell after binding antigen. A minority of B lymphocytes can respond to certain antigens such as bacterial polysaccharides without the help of the T cell.

B lymphocytes at different stages of maturity have surface immunoglobulin receptors of different classes. The least mature have surface IgM (in monomer form) only and these cells are readily tolerized (i.e., rendered incapable of further maturation) by contact with antigen. The predominant type of B lymphocyte in blood is more mature and has a specialized receptor class of surface immunoglobulin called IgD in addition to IgM. When these cells bind antigen and receive an appropriate T-cell signal, they divide; some

Table II. Characteristics of Human Lymphocyte Subpopulations

Subpopulation	Characteristic
B lymphocytes	Cell surface immunoglobulin
	Cell surface Ia antigens
	Proliferate or mature into plasma cells in cultures stimulated with pokeweed mitogen or Cowan strain staphylococci
T lymphocytes	Identified by binding of monoclonal antibodies specific for helper–inducer subset, suppressor–cytotoxic subset, or both
	Rosette with sheep erythrocytes
	Proliferate in cultures stimulated by antigens and by mitogens (phytohemagglutinin, Concanavalin A)

of their progeny mature into plasma cells while others remain in the circulation as memory B cells. One to four percent of adult blood lymphocytes have IgA on their surface. Most of these cells are probably part of the secretory immunoglobulin system described below.

The nature of the T-cell response elicited by a given antigen depends on the condition under which antigens are presented. T lymphocytes recognize antigen through surface receptors. Although these receptors have some features in common with B-lymphocyte receptors, they are not immunoglobulin by conventional criteria. There are several different subsets of T lymphocyte: some help B lymphocytes to mature as described above (helper T cells), some suppress T- or B-lymphocyte responses and others can differentiate into cytotoxic cells. These different effector functions initiate the range of responses conventionally described as *cell-mediated immunity*. T-cell subsets recognize antigen in different ways dependent in part on the association of the antigen with self histocompatability antigens (HLA). Helper T cells preferentially respond to antigens in association with antigens of the HLS DR locus while cytotoxic T cells respond to viral or other antigens in association with HLA A or B histocompatibility antigens. Suppressor T cells appear capable of binding antigens independently of self HLA. Different T-cell subsets have different distributions in the body so there is variability of response to antigen administered by different routes. Some of the characteristics of human T and B cells are summarized in Table II.

Immune responses can be manipulated under experimental conditions to give predominantly antibody- or cell-mediated immunity. Environmental exposure to common antigens probably elicits both and the relative importance of each of the two responses depends on the circumstances. Antibodies alone can protect against the toxins of diptheria and tetanus and they can prevent the binding of viruses to exposed cells. Viruses within cells are protected from antibody. For this reason, cell-mediated immunity appears to be more important for eliminating virus-infected cells. Antibacterial immunity depends mainly on the opsonization (labeling with antibody and complement) of organisms followed by their ingestion and killing by phagocytes.

Phagocytes and Complement

The phagocytic cells in breast milk are neutrophils, macrophages, and monocytes. The ingestion of particles by neutrophils depends mainly on opsonization of the particle by antibody and complement whereas monocytes can, in addition, recognize surfaces which possess foreign polysaccharides. The rate with which opsonized bacteria are killed following ingestion by neutrophils is more rapid than by monocytes but neutrophils only survive for a few days after leaving the marrow. Monocytes are long-lived cells which can differentiate into macrophages in the tissues. They are important for the specific immune response because they ingest and partially catabolize antigens before reexpressing them on their cell surfaces for presentation to lymphocytes.

The complement system comprises a series of serum proteins which, when activated, mediate opsonization and lysis of bacteria. Complement proteins can be readily detected in serum but they are present in very low concentrations in milk. The classical pathway of complement activation is initiated when an IgG of IgM molecule binds to antigen and exposes a binding site for the first component (C1) of complement. Additional components through Component 9 (C9) must then bind before lysis can occur. The alternative pathway by which IgA may activate complement bypasses C1, C4, and C2 to act directly on the third component of complement (C3). Activation of C3 is probably the most important step in the complement pathway for defense against infection because it results in the production of the chemoattractant fragment, C3a, which attracts phagocytes to the opsonized bacteria. The other C3 fragment which is produced, C3b, binds to the C3 receptors on phagocytes and is responsible for opsonization.

The Secretory Immune System

The immune system of secretory tissues like the breast, salivary glands, and bronchial tree has properties different from the system involved in the induction of systemic immunity. Specifically, in the secretory immune system, lymphocytes are sensitized to antigen mainly in the gut or the bronchial tree and they then migrate to mucosal or secretory organs where they secrete antibody independently of local antigen contact (Fig. 2). The discussion which follows is concerned primarily with the breast as a recipient of these cells or their secreted antibody; a more complete review of the entire secretory immune system is given in ref. 1.

Secretory IgA

IgA is the predominant immunoglobulin in breast milk and in other secretions such as those of the prostate, vagina, and gut. Most secreted IgA consists of a dimer of two 7S IgA units attached to a J chain and to secretory component. The J chain is a 15,000 mol. wt. polypeptide made by plasma cells which is added to IgA (and to IgM) polymers shortly before they are

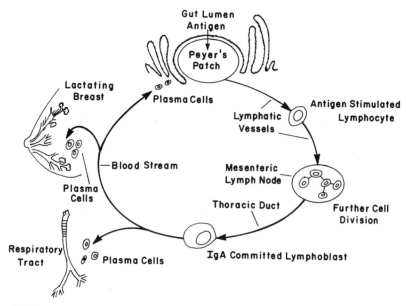

Figure 2. The secretory immune system. Antigen is taken up through the specialized epithelium of the Peyer's patches in the lumen of the gut. The antigen stimulates the division of B lymphocytes which leave the Peyer's patch via the lymphatic vesicles entering the blood system. Some of these cells then "home" to specific organs like the bronchial tree or breast where they settle down and begin to manufacture IgA.

secreted from the cell. Secretory component is a 70,000 mol. wt. polypeptide made by epithelial cells (but not by plasma cells) which binds to IgA and IgM polymers. Secretory component confers resistance to gastrointestinal proteolytic enzymes on IgA dimers; the effectiveness of this protection is illustrated by the recovery of IgA antibodies from the feces of breast-fed infants.[2]

Milk and gastrointestinal secretions contain small amounts of 7S IgA and free secretory component as well as the predominant IgA dimer. IgM is present in small amounts in normal human milk and in gastrointestinal secretions, and in larger amounts in the secretions of IgA deficient patients. There are considerable differences in other species: IgG is the predominant immunoglobulin in cow's milk; IgG 2 predominates in pig colostrum and IgA in pig milk.[3]

The IgA dimers which are secreted in milk may be made by plasma cells in the breast tissue or they may be made at distant sites and transported to the breast via the blood. The existence of a mechanism which transports IgA across the mammary epithelium is documented in mice: labeled IgA dimers were recovered intact from the gut of suckling pups 23 hr after their subcutaneous injection into lactating mothers.[4] A similar transport mechanism for IgA dimer has been demonstrated in the biliary tract.[5] Secretory component is present on the basolateral surface of mammary epithelial cells where it acts as a receptor for IgA dimers present in the serum and extracellular space (see Chapter 3).[6] The relative contributions of serum transport and local production to the IgA which is ultimately secreted in human breast milk is unknown.

Cellular Aspects of IgA Synthesis

The cells which mature into IgA-secreting plasma cells in the gut and breast epithelium enter the circulation from the bone marrow as B lymphocytes. These cells circulate until they are stimulated by antigen and receive maturation signals from T cells. For antibody responses with IgA synthesis, the antigen stimulus comes mainly in the gut or in the bronchial tree. In the gut, most antigen uptake and presentation appears to take place through the specialized dome epithelium of Peyer's patches[7] where the antigen stimulates the division of IgA precursor cells of appropriate specificity (Fig. 2). The progeny of the stimulated cells leave the Peyer's patch in the lymph, at which point they are identifiable by immunofluorescence as IgA plasmablasts, and they enter the circulation via the thoracic duct. Some of the cells from Peyer's patches undergo further division in mesenteric lymph nodes before they enter the circulation. Having entered the circulation, some of the activated plasmablasts settle or "home" to various epithelial tissues like the gut and mammary gland. In rats, there is only a three-day delay between antigen challenge to the gut and the appearance of IgA plasmablasts in the thoracic duct,[8] so the response of the secretory system is fast.

The cell traffic studies in rodents (reviewed below) as well as immunization studies in pigs and mice[3,8] indicate that the optimal route of immunization for mucosal immunity is through the gut. The route of antigen administration that achieves the highest antibody levels in milk is of importance to pig farmers whose piglets often die of coccobacilliosis. Extensive studies by Porter and co-workers (reviewed in ref. 3) showed that milk from sows fed virulent *Escherichia coli* during the 10 days before delivery had the greatest protective effect for the offspring, and that protection was mediated by IgM and IgA antibodies in the milk. Parental immunization with killed organisms was much less effective unless it was preceded by oral feeding with killed *E. coli*. Immunization through the respiratory tract is likely to be important, too, but it is much more difficult to evaluate experimentally.

Factors which influence the homing of IgA plasmablasts to particular epithelial surfaces are not well understood; in many cases, the cells appear to be distributed at random while some less mature cells may tend to return to areas where antigen is present.[10] Cells isolated from the Peyer's patches of rats or mice tend to home to intestinal epithelium. Further, gut-derived lymphocytes are the only cells which can transfer the ability to irradiated recipients to respond to an antigen with IgA secretion.[11] These observations suggest that the majority of B cells in the gut are already committed to IgA antibody and to gut homing. The possibility that antigen may contribute to the gut localization of IgA plasmablasts after they have entered the circulation is not entirely excluded but antigen is unlikely to contribute to the localization of cells to the lactating breast.

There are some uncertainties about the cells which leave Peyer's patches: we do not know if they are programmed by the environment in which they subsequently localize to produce IgA. Most IgA antibody responses are highly T-cell dependent, suggesting that one environmental factor may be the presence of T cells. A role for T cells is consistent with the observation that T-cell-deficient mice have small Peyer's patches without germinal centers and that few IgA plasma cells can be seen in the lamina propria of the intestine.[9]

Plasmablast Localization to the Breast

The localization of IgA plasmablasts to the breast depends on the activity of breast tissue. Virgin mice have few plasma cells in their mammary glands and the number increases during pregnancy in parallel with proliferation of the glandular epithelium.[12] This effect is also seen in experiments in which mouse mesenteric lymph node cells (which include some plasmablasts) preferentially home to lactating as compared with virgin or postlactation mammary glands.[13] The observation that progesterone-, estrogen-, and prolactin-treated virgin mouse mammary glands attract IgA plasmablasts shows that homing is at least partially dependent on hormonal factors. McDermott and co-workers[14] found that the homing of IgA and IgG plasmablasts to mouse cervix and vagina was greatest at estrus and proestrus and least at metaestrus and diestrus, so the breast is not alone in being subject to hormonal influences.

Tolerence to Orally Administered Antigens

Dinitrochlorobenzene (DNCB) applied to the skin is a potent sensitizing agent as judged by the positive delayed hypersensitivity response which follows antigen challenge. In contrast to the immunity which follows skin contact, animals fed DNCB become unresponsive[15] because of the prefer- ential induction of supressor cells.[16] Similar, orally induced tolerance is seen with a range of antigens and provides a marked contrast to the priming for mucosal immunity previously described. It now appears that local IgA production and systemic tolerance can appear simultaneously in mice fed with a foreign protein or with bacteria such as *Streptoccocus mutans*.[17] It is possible to imagine that local secretory IgA immunity is useful in limiting antigen access to the circulation at the same time as systemic tolerance reduces the risk of immune complex disease with IgG antibody to food antigens.

Mucosal Immune Responses in Humans

Although most of the results described in the preceding section derive from animal experiments, there is reason to believe that mucosal immune responses in humans are similar. For example, mothers infected with *Salmonella typhimurium* were shown to secrete antibody to the infecting strain in their milk.[18] Experimental immunization of mothers with nonpathogenic *E. coli* also resulted in the appearance of IgA antibody in breast milk.[19] In the latter experiment, there was little if any antibody response in the serum despite the clearly positive results with milk. It seems reasonable to conclude that one of the functions of the mucosal immune system is to disseminate antibody-making cells to secretory epithelia without requiring local antigen exposure. In humans, as in mice, the homing of antibody-making precursors to the breast appears to be influenced by hormonal conditions.[20] The consequence of the cell traffic for the baby is a supply of secretory antibodies in a form relatively resistant to proteolytic digestion. Epidemiologic studies reviewed later in this chapter suggest that these antibodies confer important resistance to infection.

IMMUNOLOGICALLY ACTIVE CONSTITUENTS OF BREAST MILK

Nonspecific Factors

Lactoferrin

Lactoferrin is an iron-binding protein present in milk and in neutrophil granules. Its concentration in the mammary secretion is between 0.1 and 0.6% and it is mostly unsaturated with iron. Lactoferrin inhibits the *in vitro* growth of a range of organisms including *Staphylococcus aureus, E. coli,* and *Candida* species, probably through the sequestration of iron. The antibacterial effect of lactoferrin is much greater in the presence of antibody and bicarbonate.[21]

Lysozyme

Lysozyme is a cationic protein of low molecular weight which cleaves peptidoglycans off bacterial cell walls.[22] Human breast milk contains 30 to 40 mg% of lysozyme and this material appears to be stable in the gut because activity is recoverable in the feces of breast-fed babies.

Lactoperoxidase

The lactoperoxidase system uses thiocyanate and hydrogen peroxide to kill bacteria including streptococci, *E. coli,* and *Salmonella* sp. The lactoperoxidase concentration of human milk is so low[23] that it is unlikely to be a significant defense. Cows, in contrast, have much higher levels of lactoperoxidases in their milk.

Complement

The classical pathway components C1 to C9 are present in low concentration in human milk.[24] C3 is perhaps the only component that might be

Table III. Cell Numbers in Breast Milk per μl[a]

Time	Total	Macrophages	Neutrophils	Lymphocytes
Antepartum	3430	2140	560	240
Postpartum				
Days				
0–4	2840	1490	1375	250
5–8	450	320	100	27
Weeks				
1–2	69	52	4	1
2–4	51	22	8	1
Months				
1–2	17	4	3	1
2–4	16	5	2	1
4–6	10	1	1	1

[a] Data based on refs. 25, 26, 27, 31.

biologically active in milk through its capacity to opsonize in conjunction with IgA binding to bacteria.

Cells in Milk

There are several reports of the number of cells in human milk throughout lactation.[25–27] From the composite results in Table III it is clear that mononuclear phagocytes predominate and that the number of lymphocytes and neutrophils is small. Interest in the function of breast milk cells arises mainly from uncertainty as to their contribution to the protection of the infant and the protection of the breast from infection. A role for milk T cells in conferring immunity on the suckling infant has also been proposed. For these reasons, the subject is reviewed in detail.

Milk Monocytes and Macrophages

Monocytes prepared from milk ingest latex, adhere to glass, stain positively for nonspecific esterase and kill a variety of microorganisms.[28,29] They also release several lymphokines.[30] Many milk macrophages are distended with lipid droplets, which gives the cells a characteristic foamy appearance. IgA is included in the material macrophages endocytose so that they stain positively for cytoplasmic IgA[31]; Pitt[26] extracted 4 to 5 mg of IgA per 10^6 colostral cells. Slow release of cytoplasmic IgA by breast milk macrophages during *in vitro* culture results in increase in the concentration of IgA in the supernatant: this effect may mimic IgA synthesis.[32]

The importance of breast milk macrophages for protection from infection in the newborn is uncertain. Formula-fed newborn rats who are infected with *Klebsiella* and exposed to hypoxemia develop a form of necrotizing enterocolitis while similarly treated animals fed on breast milk remain healthy.[33] The protective factor in these studies was heat labile and it could possibly have been the phagocytes. We found that milk mononuclear cells could effectively process and present antigens to T lymphocytes.[35] Whether this is important *in vivo* is unknown.

Lymphocyte Subsets in Milk

Only around 10% of colostral or milk mononuclear cells have lymphocyte morphology. Between 37%[34] and 73%[31] of milk mononuclear cells rosette with sheep erthrocytes and 50% stained with an anti-T-cell antibody.[34] Our own results indicate that fewer than 10% of mononuclear cells from colostrum stain with a monoclonal antibody (OKT 3) which binds to all mature T cells and that this small population comprises about equal proportions of inducer (OKT 4[+]) and supressor/cytotoxic (OKT 8[+]) cells.[35] B cells account for 23 to 35% of milk lymphocytes.[34,36] Immunoglobulin class studies suggest that 9% of milk leukocytes possess surface IgA antibodies; 9.5%, surface IgM; and 3.7%, surface IgG.[37] These results should be treated with caution as passive adherence of immunoglobulins to the cell surface can introduce errors.

Functional Responses of Breast Milk Lymphocytes

T-Cell Responses

Breast milk lymphocytes proliferate in phytohemagglutinin (PHA)-stimulated cultures,[24,25] but their response is quantitatively much lower than adult blood lymphocytes. This low response may be due to suppression by monocytes or by soluble factors in the milk[37] or it may result from a deficiency of T cells capable of making lymphocyte growth factors. Parmely and co-workers[39] found that milk lymphocytes proliferated in mixed lymphocyte culture; this suggests that milk T cells can recognize and respond as well as blood lymphocytes to foreign histocompatibility antigens. In a limited study, Parmely *et al.*[40] found that the milk cells which responded in mixed lympho-cyte culture sometimes matured into cytotoxic lymphocytes. Other antigens to which breast milk lymphocytes have been reported to respond include *E. coli* K1[38] and PPD[40], while responses to *Candida* antigens were not found.[40] It seems unlikely that antigen in the breast can be responsible for the appearance in colostrum of T lymphocytes with these specificities, so a gut–bronchial–mammary T-cell circulation similar to that of IgA-B cells has been proposed. The strongest evidence for tissue specific homing by T cells comes from experiments in which intravenously-injected isotopically labeled mes-enteric T-cell blasts were found to home to the small intestine.[41] It is not known whether T cells would also home to the lactating breast.

In humans the presence of *E. coli*, K1-responsive T cells in colostrum but not blood[49] has been presented as evidence for a gut-mammary traffic of T cells; however, others found K1 responsive cells in the blood when these experiments were repeated.[42] Uncertainty as to the subset or specificity of the lymphocytes which proliferated in these cultures cells makes it difficult to make any firm statement as to whether T lymphocytes home to the human mammary gland.

Indirect evidence for the functional maturity of breast milk T lymphocytes also comes from the apparent transfer of cell-mediated immunity from mothers to infants by suckling as described later in this chapter.

B-Cell Response

It is clear from numerous animal studies that oral immunization results in the appearance of antibody in the milk. In humans, most of the milk antibodies are IgA dimers and they have secretory component attached. The antibodies are probably mostly made by plasma cells which are located beneath the mammary epithelium, but some may be synthesized at distant sites and transported via the blood to the breast to be secreted by a secretory component transport mechanism.[6] The extent to which cells in milk may contribute to antibody synthesis is not clearly established. About 9% of colostral lymphocytes have surface IgA,[36] three to four times the proportion in blood. Further, colostral cells have been shown to incorporate radiolabeled amino acids into protein which ço-precipitated with anti-IgA antibodies.[43] However, secretory component was also labeled in these studies which suggests either that the method was not fully specific or that newly synthesized IgA dimers bound free secretory component. Goldblum and co-workers[19] immunized mothers orally with the nonpathogenic *E. coli* 083 and subsequently found antibody to the organism in the breast milk. Testing for production of the antibody by colostral cells they found that 0.1 to 1% of cells apparently made anti-*E. coli* 083 antibodies. Antibody production was prevented by adding puromycin (an inhibitor of protein synthesis) to the cultures, suggesting that the antibody was indeed synthesized by the milk cells. However, the finding that up to 1% of colostral cells made specific antibody in these studies renders this conclusion suspect. Since only 9% of colostral cells are B cells, these figures would suggest that over 10% of colostral B cells were making antibody to a single pathogen. An alternative explanation for the high percentage of antibody-making B cells in Goldblum's study is that antibody was made by plasma cells in the breast, taken up and then slowly released by milk macrophages. This interpretation is consistent with the observation that many milk macrophages contain IgA of both light chain types (κ and λ)[31]; presumably taken up by phagocytosis. Plasma cells and B cells, on the other hand, make only one type of light chain and not both. Since most IgA-containing cells in milk stain for both types of light chain they are more likely to be macrophages than plasma cells.

The Antibody Repertoire of Breast Milk

IgA, and to a lesser extent IgM, antibodies to a wide range of pathogens including viruses, bacteria, and protozoa have been found in breast milk.[44-47] The presence or absence of a particular specificity depends on the recent exposure of the mother; increases in antibody follow both environmental contact with antigens and immunization. Oral immunization elicits antibody in milk and other secretions in the same way as parenteral immunization elicits serum antibodies. Since the immunoglobulin variable region genes that are available to one heavy chain class can be rearranged to another, there are no theoretical reasons to believe that the potential repertoire of milk antibodies differs from that of serum antibodies.

IMMUNOLOGIC CONSEQUENCES OF BREAST-FEEDING FOR THE BABY

Protection from Infection

The strongest evidence for protection from infection comes from retrospective population studies in which the morbidity and mortality of breast-fed babies has been found to be lower than that of formula-fed babies.[45-47] The morbidity differences between breast- and formula-feeding are apparent in studies in the United States, Canada, and the United Kingdom as well as those from less-developed countries such as India and Guatemala. In all populations, breast-feeding appears to protect most effectively against diarrhea, followed by upper respiratory tract infections. The termination of nursery outbreaks of diarrhea in infants by feeding breast milk provides some additional support for a direct protective effect.[48,49] There is, however, little indication as to which of the various protective factors discussed in the section on the immunologically active constituents of breast milk is most important under natural conditions. The possible protective mechanisms are therefore discussed in an arbitrary sequence.

The Gut Flora and Protection from Diarrhea

Factors likely to be important for the prevention of diarrhea are the initial establishment of a nonpathogenic gut flora and the subsequent avoidance of pathogens which might colonize the gut. The gut flora of exclusively breast-fed babies is composed mainly of lactobacilli and bifidobacteria. Their feces have a pH of 5 to 6 due to the fermentation of sugars and the production of acetic acid by the bifidobacteria. Infants fed on formula, either entirely or as a supplement to breast milk, have a higher fecal pH with a predominant flora of *Streptococcus faecalis*, *Bacteroides* sp. and *E. coli*.[50] The low colonic pH of breast-fed babies inhibits the growth of the latter bacteria.[51] In addition, milk contains a carbohydrate growth factor for lactobacilli which may contribute to their predominance.[52]

It seems likely that newborns are exposed to bifidobacteria and lactobacilli during their passage through the birth canal. For these bacterial species to become established, it appears to be necessary that the newborn is fed a milk with a low buffering capacity like human milk.[53] The effect of breast feeding on the infants' gut flora was abolished by cow's milk supplementation. However, in the same study, infants fed on breast milk with supplements of *humanized* cow's milk established a low stool pH and a dominant flora of bifidobacteria with a 2- to 6-week delay.[53] At present, it is not known to what extent supplementation can be practiced without destroying the characteristic intestinal flora of the breast-fed baby.

Avoidance of colonization by pathogens probably depends on preventing the organisms from proliferating in the breast milk or from adhering to the gut wall. Milk is significantly bacteriostatic for *E. coli in vitro*.[54] This effect can be abolished by adding enterochelin, a bacterial iron binding protein made by *E. coli*, or free iron[55] to the cultures. These observations suggest that lactoferrin is the protective agent, and that it acts by preventing the *E. coli* from obtaining essential iron. IgA antibodies contribute to this protection. The lactoferrin-IgA dependent bacteriostasis survives heating to 56°C to 60°C so it is unlikely to involve macrophages. As stated earlier, breast milk macrophages can ingest and kill a range of organisms but whether this is important for the protection of the baby is uncertain.

Antibodies to Enterotoxins

Gram-negative bacilli release enterotoxins which bind to receptors on the small intestine mucosa and trigger a secretory diarrhea. Two reports[56,57] indicate that breast milk contains antibodies to *E. coli* and *Vibrio cholerae* enterotoxins following presumed environmental exposure to these organisms. The antibodies were of IgA class and they neutralized the action of enterotoxin in isolated loops of rabbit ileum. Endotoxin neutralization could explain the anecdotal observation that feeding of breast milk terminated dirrhea in *E. coli*-infected infants before the organism was eliminated from the feces.

Other Antibacterial Actions of Antibody

K 88 and K 99 are plasmid-encoded determinants which enable *E. coli* to synthesize a receptor for adherence to epithelial cells of the gut enterocytes. Antibody to these receptors prevents bacterial binding to pit enterocytes[58] and can prevent infection. Similar effects have been postulated in man. However, Porter *et al.*[3] found that protection of newborn pigs from *E. coli* enteritis did not correlate with the anti-K 88 titer of their mothers' colostrum. Antiadhesion antibodies do not therefore appear to be essential for protection from these organisms which are particularly toxic to baby piglets. Another action of antibacterial antibodies may be to clump organisms together and so facilitate their removal by peristalsis.

Antiviral Immunity

Epidemiologic studies indicate that breast-feeding protects against upper respiratory tract infections and specifically against respiratory syncitial virus infection.[59] Protection against virally caused diarrhea is also likely since a significant proportion of infantile diarrhea is caused by viruses. Protection in both cases probably results from interference with virus adhesion to target cells by IgA antibodies in breast milk. It has been suggested that protection of the respiratory tract may involve regurgitation of milk into upper airways.

Nonspecific factors may protect against certain lipid-coated viruses (flaviviruses, herpes simplex virus, and alphaviruses) through damage to the virus surface by unsaturated fatty acids and monoglycerides which are present in breast milk fat. Other nonspecific factors of undetermined nature neutralize the infectivity of rotaviruses[60] and vesicular stomatitis virus.[61]

Mucosal versus Systemic Protection of the Infant

It is still debated whether the protection against infection conferred by breast milk acts exclusively at the level of the infant's mucosal surfaces or whether antibodies and/or cells in milk also may be absorbed. There are clear species differences in the way milk antibodies are handled by the nursling gut so animal experiments are not particularly helpful in predicting events in humans. The serum IgA levels of infants are not affected by breast-feeding[62] so there is no evidence for the long-term uptake of milk IgA in humans. This does not exclude the possibility that colostral IgA might be absorbed through the infants' intestine for the first 18 to 24 hr of life. Evidence in support of this idea comes from Ogra and co-workers[63] who detected a slight and transient rise in serum IgA in 3 of 7 infants fed with colostrum containing anti-polio virus antibody. The serum IgA of one of these infants had anti-polio activity.

Transfer of Cell-Mediated Immunity

Human newborns are generally unresponsive to the antigens that elicit delayed hypersensitivity skin responses in their mothers. However, Mohr[64] found that the frequency of PPD skin reactivity was much higher in 11 infants who had been breast-fed by their 5 PPD-positive mothers than in nonbreast-fed controls. Two subsequent studies gave comparable results. In each, PPD-positive mothers were identified prior to delivery and their colostral lymphocytes were shown to proliferate in culture with PPD.[63,65] Cord blood lymphocytes from all the infants were unresponsive to PPD but positive responses by their blood lymphocytes were found at 4 or 5 weeks of age. Blood lymphocytes from formula-fed offspring of PPD-positive mothers did not respond to PPD. The possibilities that antigens transferred in breast milk led to priming of the infant or that negative responses by cord blood lymphocytes were due to T-cell suppression are not entirely excluded. However, aside from these objections, the results are suggestive of transfer of cell-mediated immunity through milk. Mechanisms by which this might take place include the direct uptake of live colostral T cells by the baby, or the uptake of informational material from nonviable lymphocytes. In animals, evidence for live lymphocyte uptake derives from experiments in which foster-nursed newborn rats developed graft versus host disease,[66] though these experiments have been refuted by others.[67]

Protection from Allergic Reactions

Epidemiology

Observations suggesting that breast-feeding protects vulnerable infants from allergic reactions have a long history.[68] More recent studies suggest that breast-feeding has to be combined with complete avoidance of cow's milk to reduce the incidence of such reactions. Twenty-one of the 23 exclusively breast-fed infants who were followed by Matthew *et al.*[69] were free of eczema at 6 months' of age, compared with 10 of 19 formula-fed controls who developed eczema. The high incidence of eczema in this study is explained by the selection of participants with a positive family history of allergic reactions. When the infants were re-evaluated at 1 year (after 6 months mixed feeding), the breast-fed babies still had a lower incidence of eczema although some now had positive immediate hypersensitivity skin responses to cow's milk. Infants of either group who developed eczema had the higher serum IgE levels. Protection at 1 year of age from respiratory tract allergy and eczema was found in a large study of babies breast-fed for 6 or more months in Finland.[70] When the same children were reviewed at 3 years of age, a protective effect was still apparent in those with an allergic family history.

While the above observations suggest that avoidance of cows milk antigens for the first few months of life has a protective effect in later years, a follow-up study by the Finnish group did not confirm this. Children who had, or had not, avoided citrus fruits and fish for the first year of life were skin-tested with these at 3 years of age.[71] The percentage of positive immediate hypersensitivity skin responses was similar in both groups; this led the authors to suggest that antigen avoidance during the first year of life deferred rather than prevented the development of allergy. The validity of this view will probably have to await further long-term studies in which the frequency of symptomatic atopy (asthma, eczema) is determined, rather than the frequency of positive skin tests.

Rare infants have become sensitized to allergens in maternal milk.[72] Nineteen infants who had colic between 1 and 4 weeks of age were evaluated following elimination of cow's milk from their diet and 13 improved. Three of the infants who had been exclusively breast-fed continued to have colic while their mothers drank cow's milk: all of these improved when their mothers avoided cow's milk.[73] Milk challenge to the mother was followed by recurrence of colic in 12 babies. One explanation for these findings is that the mothers secreted sufficient cow's milk protein in their own milk to sensitize their babies. This view is supported by the detection of cow's milk antigens in the breast milk of one mother following drinking of cow's milk.

Wheat germ antigens have also been detected in human breast milk.[74] Nevertheless, the sensitization of infants to extraneous antigens carried in maternal milk seems to be unusual. The immunological mechanisms which could account for sensitization in formula- and breast-fed babies are discussed next.

Possible Mechanisms of Protection from Allergic Reactions

The sensitization of infants to cow's milk requires uptake of antigen in the first place. Conceivably, spillage of small amounts of cow's milk onto the skin could suffice but more is probably absorbed intact through the gut. Rothberg[75] found bovine serum albumin (BSA) in the serum of premature infants after 7 days' formula feeding: this was followed by the appearance of IgG and IgM antibodies to BSA in the infants' serum. Other studies have confirmed that normal babies fed formulae of cow's milk make antibodies to cow's milk antigens[76]; these antibodies reach a peak titer at about 3 months' age and their levels subsequently fall. Uptake of dietary antigens may be greatest in prematures and newborns in the first 24 hr of life because of immaturity of the gut.[77] An example of this phenomenon may be the transient appearance of IgA in the serum of breast-fed babies (see subsection on mucosal vs. systemic protection of the infant). Secretory IgA has been shown to reduce antigen uptake across mucosal surfaces[78] so a lack of secretory IgA in the formula-fed newborns may permit more antigen to reach the immune system. Human breast milk usually contains antibody to cow's milk antigens[79] so breast-fed babies may normally be protected from the trace amounts of cow's milk proteins which can be secreted in breast milk. It is tempting to speculate that formula-fed newborns are at a disadvantage because they lack IgA from both internal and maternal sources. The mean age at which IgA normally becomes detectable in infants is 17 days with 90% of saliva samples positive at 4 weeks.[80] Avoidance of highly antigenic feeds for the first 4 weeks of life might therefore reduce the infant susceptibility to sensitization. Some evidence supporting this idea comes from the observation that infants fed hydrolyzed cow's milk for the first 3 months of life have a smaller increase in serum antibodies to cow's milk protein than controls who were fed unmodified cow's milk from birth.[81]

Although antibodies have been discussed first, there is no reason to believe that they are more important than other factors. Genetic predisposition to allergy may be of paramount importance but the immunologic mechanisms involved in determining susceptibility to allergic reactions are poorly understood.[82] Nonspecific factors may also be important. It is, for example, conceivable that antigen uptake through the gut might be greater when the gut pH is higher or when *E. coli* predominates over lactobacilli. Whatever mechanism is involved, the prophylactic effect of breast-feeding appears to be substantial.

Breast-Feeding and Immunization

A number of studies showed that breast-fed infants given vaccine strain polio virus during the first week of life had a lower rate of intestinal colonization with the virus than formula-fed infants.[83,84] This result is to be expected in view of the frequent presence of anti-polio virus antibody in breast milk. However, the results probably do not have any major implications for routine immunization schedules since attenuated polio virus is generally given at 2, 4, and 6 months when the milk antibody titer is lower. This view is supported by a retrospective analysis which showed that serum antibodies to polio virus were similar in breast- and bottle-fed babies.[85]

CONCLUSIONS

The immunological benefits of breast-feeding are sufficiently well established for physicians to urge prospective mothers to breast-feed their babies whenever possible. A question which is now becoming more important is what to feed the infants of mothers who cannot breast-feed. It is disappointing that infants fed on humanized formulae do not develop the predominant bifidobacteria flora unless they are supplemented with human milk, and even then they are slow to establish it. The requirement of the infant for nutrition has to be given first priority in designing formula feeds but modifications which might affect the gut flora should also be taken into account. There are other major areas which still require investigation, including the role of different milks in predisposing to allergic reactions, the extent to which a limited exposure to cow's milk in the newborn nursery may have adverse consequences, and the extent to which breast-fed infants can recieve supplements of formula without alteration of established bifidobacteria after the first month of life. As results of properly controlled trials become available it should be possible to make more securely based recommendations to mothers.

REFERENCES

1. Bienenstock, J., McDermott, M., Befus, D., and O'Neill, M., 1978, A common mucosal immunologic system involving the bronchus, breast and bowel, *Adv. Exp. Med. Biol.* **107**:53–88.
2. Kenny, J. F., Boseman, J. I., and Michaels, R. H., 1967, Bacterial and viral coproantibodies in breast-fed infants, *Pediatrics* **39**:202–213.
3. Porter, P. and Chidlow, J. W., 1979, Response to *E. coli* antigens via local and parenteral routes linking intestinal and mammary immune mechanisms in passive protection against neonatal colibacillosis in the pig, in: *Immunology of Breast Milk* (P. L. Ogra and D. H. Dayton, eds.), Raven Press, New York, pp. 73–80.
4. Halsey, J. F., Johnson, B. H., and Cebra, J. J., 1980, Transport of immunoglobulins from serum into colostrum, *J. Exp. Med.* **151**:767–772.
5. Dive, C. H. and Heremans, J. F., 1974, Nature and origin of the proteins of bile. 1. A comparative analysis of serum and bile proteins in man, *Eur. J. Clin. Invest.* **4**:235–239.

6. Crago, S. S., Kulhavy, R., Prince, S. J., and Mestecky, J., 1978, Secretory component is a surface receptor for polymeric immunoglobulins, *J. Exp. Med.* **147:**1832.
7. Cebra, J. J., Gearhart, P. J., Kamat, R., Robertson, S. M., and Tseng, J., 1976, Origin and differentiation of lymphocytes involved in the secretory IgA response, *Cold Spring Harbor Symp. Quant. Biol.* **41:**201–215.
8. Pierce, N. F. and Gowans, J. L., 1975, Cellular kinetics of the intestinal immune response to cholera toxoid in rats, *J. Exp. Med.* **142:**1550–1563.
9. Husband, A. J. and Gowans, J. L., 1978, The origin and antigen dependent distribution of IgA-containing cells in the intestine, *J. Exp. Med.* **148:**1146–1160.
10. Elson, C. O., Heck, J. A., and Strober, W., 1979, T cell regulation of IgA synthesis, in: *Immunology of Breast Milk* (P. L. Ogra and D. H. Dayton, eds.), Raven Press, New York, pp. 37–44.
11. Cebra, J. J., Emmons, R., Gearhart, P. J., Robertson, S. M., and Tseng, J., 1978, Cellular parameters on the IgA response, in: *Secretory Immunity and Infection, Proceedings of an International Symposium* (J. R. McGhee and J. Mestecky, eds.), Plenum Press, New York, p. 19.
12. Weisz-Carrington, P., Roux, M. E., McWilliams, M., Phillips-Quagliata, J. M., and Lamm, M. E., 1978, Hormonal induction of the secretory immune system in the mammary gland, *Proc. Natl. Acad. Sci. USA* **75:**2928–2932.
13. Roux, M. E., McWilliams, M., Phillips-Quagliata, J. M., Weisz-Carrington, P., and Lamm, M. E., 1977, Origin of IgA secreting plasma cells in the mammary gland, *J. Exp. Med.* **146:**1311–1322.
14. McDermott, M. R., Clark, D. A., and Bienenstock, J., 1980, Evidence for a common mucosal immunologic system. II. Influence of the estrus cycle on B immunoblast migration into genital and intestinal tissues, *J. Immunol.* **124:**2536–2539.
15. Chase, M. W., 1946, Inhibition of experimental drug allergy by prior feeding of the sensitizing agent, *Proc. Soc. Exp. Biol.* **61:**257.
16. Mattingly, J. A. and Waksman, B. H., 1978, Immunologic suppression after oral administration of antigen. I. Specific suppressor cells formed in rat Peyer's patches after oral administration of sheep erythrocytes and their systemic migration, *J. Immunol.* **121:**1878–1883.
17. Challacombe, S. J. and Tomasi, T. B., 1980, Systemic tolerance and secretory immunity after oral immunization, *J. Exp. Med.* **152:**1459–1472.
18. Allardyce, R. A., Shearman, D. J. C., McClelland, D. B. L., Marwick, K., Simpson, A. J., and Laidlaw, R. B., 1974, Appearance of specific colostrum antibodies after clinical infection with *Salmonella typhimurium, Br. Med. J.* **3:**307–309.
19. Goldblum, R. M., Ahlstedt, S., Carlsson, B., Hanson, L. A., Jodal, V., Lidin-Janson, G., and Sohl-Akerlund, A., 1975, Antibody forming cells in human colostrum after oral immunization, *Nature* **257:**797–799.
20. Drife, J. O., McClelland, D. B. L., Pryde, A., Roberts, M. M., and Smith, I. I., 1976, Immunoglobulin synthesis in the resting breast, *Br. Med. J.* **3:**503–506.
21. Bullen, C. L. and Willis, A. T., 1971, Resistance of the breast fed infant to gastroenteritis, *Br. Med. J.* **3:**338–343.
22. Chaudan, R. C., Sahini, K. M., and Holly, R. G., 1974, Lysozyme content of human milk, *Nature* **204:**76.
23. Gothefors, L. and Marklund, S., 1975, Lactoperoxidase activity in human milk and saliva of newborn infants, *Infect. Immun.* **11:**1210–1215.
24. Nakajima, S., Baba, A. S., and Tamura, N., 1977, Complement system in human colostrum, *Int. Arch. Allergy Appl. Immunol.* **54:**428–433.
25. Ogra, S. S. and Ogra, P. L., 1978, Immunologic aspects of human colostrum and milk. II. Characteristics of lymphocyte reactivity and distribution of E-rosette forming cells at different times after onset of lactation, *J. Pediatr.* **92:**550–555.
26. Pitt, J., 1979, The milk mononuclear phagocyte, *Pediatrics* **95:**745–749.
27. Ho, F. C. S., Wong, R. L. C., and Lawton, J. W. M., 1979, Human colostral and breast milk cells, *Acta Paediatr. Scand.* **68:**389–396.

28. Robinson, J. E., Harvey, B. A. M., and Soothill, J. f., 1978, Phagocytosis and killing of bacteria and yeast by human milk cells after opsonization in aqueous phase of milk, *Br. Med. J.* **1:**1443–1445.

29. Johnson, D. F., France, G. L., Marmer, D. J., and Steele, R. W., 1980 Bactericidal mechanisms of human breast milk leukocytes, *Infect. Immun.* **28:**314–318.

30. Mohr, J. A., Leu, R., and Mabry, W., 1970, Colostral leukocytes, *J. Surg. Oncol.* **2:**162–167.

31. Crago, S. S., Prince, S. J., Pretlow, T. G., McGhee, J. R., and Mestecky, J., 1979, Human colostral cells. I. Separation and characterization, *Clin. Exp. Immunol.* **38:**585–597.

32. Pittard, W. B., Polmar, S. H., and Farnaroff, A. A., 1977, The breast milk macrophage: A potential vehicle for immunoglobulin transport, *J. Reticul. Soc.* **22:**597–603.

33. Barlow, B., Santulli, T. V., Heird, W. C., Pitt, J., Blanc, W. A., and Schullinger, J. N., 1974, An experimental study of acute neonatal enterocolitis—The importance of breast milk, *J. Pediatr. Surg.* **9:**587–594.

34. Diaz-Jouanen, E. and Williams, R. C., 1974, T and B lymphocytes in human colostrum, *Clin. Immunol. Immunopathol.* **3:**248–255.

35. Mori, M. and Hayward, A. R., 1982, Phenotype and function of human milk monocytes as antigen presenting cells, *Clin. Immunol. Immunopathol.* **23:**94–99.

36. Bush, J. F. and Beer, A. E., 1979, Analysis of complement receptors on B lymphocytes in human milk, *Am. J. Obstet. Gynecol.* **133:**708–712.

37. Pittard, W., Polmar, S., Fanger, M., and Fanaroff, A., 1976, Identification of immunoglobulin bearing lymphocytes in fresh human breast milk, *Pediatr. Res.* **10:**359 (abstract).

38. Ogra, S. S. and Ogra, P. L., 1979, Components of immunologic reactivity in human colostrum and milk, in: *Immunology of Breast Milk* (P. L. Ogra and D. H. Dayton, eds.), Raven Press, New York, pp. 185–192.

39. Parmely, M. J., Beer, A. E., and Billingham, R. E., 1976, *In vitro* studies on the T lymphocyte population of human milk, *J. Exp. Med.* **144:**358–370.

40. Parmely, M. J. and Williams, S. B., 1979, Selective expression of immunocompetence in human colostrum: Preliminary evidence for the control of cytotoxic T lymphocytes including those specific for paternal antigens, in: *Immunology of Breast Milk* (P. L. Ogra and D. H. Dayton, eds.), Raven Press, New York, pp. 173–180.

41. Rose, M. L., Parrott, D. M. V., and Bruce, R. G., 1976, Migration of lymphoblasts to the small intestine, *Immunology* **31:**723–730.

42. Keller, M. A., Turner, J. L., Stratton, J. A., and Miller, M. E., 1980, Breast milk lymphocyte response to K1 antigen of *E. coli*, *Infect. Immun.* **27:**903–909.

43. Murillo, G. J. and Goldman, A. S., 1970, The cells of human colostrum, *Pediat. Res.* **4:**71–75.

44. Ogra, S. S. and Ogra, P. L., 1978, Immunologic aspects of human colostrum and milk. I. Distribution characteristics and concentrations of immunoglobulins at different times after the onset of lactation, *J. Pediatr.* **92:**546–549.

45. Welsh, J. K. and May, J. T., 1979, Anti-infective properties of breast milk, *J. Pediatr.* **94:**1–9.

46. Cunningham, A. S., 1979, Morbidity in breast-fed and artificially fed infants II, *J. Pediatr.* **95:**685–689.

47. Goldsmith, A. S. and Smith, C. W., 1973, Host resistance factors in human milk, *J. Pediatr.* **82:**1082–1090.

48. Svirsky-Gross, S., 1968, Pathogenic strains of *E. coli* (0:111) among prematures and the use of human milk in controlling the outbreak of diarrhea, *Ann. Pediatr.* **190:**109.

49. Tassovatz, B. and Kotsitch, A., 1961, Le lait de femme et son action de protection contre les infections intestinales chez le nouveau-né, *Sem. Hop.* **37:**1649–1652.

50. Bullen, C. L. and Tearle, P. V., 1976, Bifidobacteria in the intestinal tract of infants: An *in vitro* study, *J. Med. Microbiol.* **9:**335–344.

51. Bullen, C. L., Tearle, P. V., and Willis, A. T., 1976, Bifidobacteria in the intestinal tract of infants: An *in vivo* study, *J. Med. Microbiol.* **9:**325–333.

52. Gyorgy, P., 1971, The uniqueness of human milk. Biochemical aspects. *Am. J. Clin. Nutr.* **24:**970–975.

53. Bullen, C. L., Tearle, P. V., and Stewart, M. G., 1977, The effect of humanized milks and supplemented breast feeding on the faecal flora of infants, *J. Med. Microbiol.* **10**:403–413.
54. Rogers, H. J. and Synge, C., 1978, Bacteriostatic effect of human milk on *E. coli*: The role of IgA, *Immunology* **34**:19–28.
55. Bullen, J. J., Rogers, H. J., and Leigh, L., 1972, Iron binding proteins in milk and resistance to *E. coli* infections in infants, *Br. Med. J.* **1**:69–75.
56. Stolior, O. A., Pelly, R. P., Kaniecki-Green, E., Klaus, M. H., and Carpenter, C. C. J., 1976, Secretory IgA against enterotoxins in breast milk, *Lancet* **1**:1258–1261.
57. Holmgren, J., Hanson, L. A., Carlson, B., Lindblad, B. S., and Rahimtoola, J., 1976, Neutralizing antibodies against *E. coli* and V. cholerae enterotoxins in human milk from a developing country, *Scand. J. Immunol.* **5**:867–871.
58. Williams, R. C. and Gibbons, R. J., 1972, Inhibition of bacterial adherence by secretory immunoglobulin A: A mechanism of antigen disposal, *Science* **177**:697–699.
59. Downham, M. A. P. S., Scott, R., Simms, D. G., Webb, J. K. G., and Gardner, P. S., 1976, Breast feeding protects against respiratory syncitial virus infections, *Br. Med. J.* **2**:274–276.
60. Thouless, M. E., Bryden, A. S., and Flewett, T. H., 1977, Rotavirus neutralization by human milk, *Br. Med. J.* **2**:1390.
61. Matthews, T. H. J., Nair, C. D. G., Lawrence, M. K., and Tyrell, D. A. J., 1976, Antiviral activity of milk of possible clinical significance, *Lancet* **2**:1387–1389.
62. Ammann, A. J. and Stiehm, E. R., 1966, Immune globulin levels in colostrum and breast milk and serum from formula and breast fed newborns, *Proc. Soc. Exp. Biol. Med.* **122**:1098.
63. Ogra, S. S., Weintraub, D., and Ogra, P. L., 1977, Immunologic aspects of human colostrum and milk. III. Fate and absorption of cellular and soluble components in the gastrointestinal tract of the newborn, *J. Immunol.* **119**:245–248.
64. Mohr, J. A., 1973, The possible induction and/or acquisition of cellular hypersensitivity associated with ingestion of colostrum, *J. Pediatr.* **82**:1062–1064.
65. Schlesinger, J. J. and Covelli, H. D., 1977, Evidence for transmission of lymphocyte responses to tuberculin by breast feeding, *Lancet* **2**:529–532.
66. Head, J. R., Beer, A. E., and Billingham, R. E., 1977, Significance of the cellular component of the maternal immunologic endowment in milk, *Transplant. Proc.* **9**:1465–1471.
67. Silvers, W. K. and Poole, T. W., 1975, The influence of foster nursing on the survival and immunologic competence of mice and rats, *J. Immunol.* **115**:1117–1121.
68. Glaser, J. and Johnstone, D. E., 1953 Prophylaxis of allergic disease in newborn, *JAMA* **153**:620–622.
69. Matthew, D. J., Taylor, B., Norman, A. P., Turner, M. W., and Soothill, J. F., 1977, Prevention of eczema, *Lancet* **1**:321–324.
70. Saarinen, V. M., Kajosaari, M., Backman, A., and Siimes, M. A., 1979, Prolonged breast feeding as prophylaxis for atopic disease, *Lancet* **2**:163–166.
71. Saarinen, V. M. and Kajosaari, M., 1980, Does dietary elimination in infancy prevent or only postpone a food allergy? *Lancet* **1**:166–167.
72. Gerrard, J. W., 1979, Allergy in breast fed babies to ingredients in breast milk, *Ann. Allergy* **42**:69–72.
73. Jakobsson, I. and Lindberg, T., 1978, Cows milk as a cause of infantile colic in breast fed infants, *Lancet* **2**:437–439.
74. Hemmings, W. A. and Kulangara, A. C., 1978, Dietary antigens in breast milk, *Lancet* **2**:575.
75. Rothberg, R. M., 1969, Immunoglobulin and specific antibody synthesis during the first weeks of life of premature infants, *J. Pediatr.* **75**:391–399.
76. Kletter, B., Gery, I., Freier, S., and Davies, A. M., 1971, Immune responses of normal infants to cow milk, *Int. Arch. Allergy Appl. Immunol.* **40**:656–674.
77. Walker, A., 1979, Antigen penetration across the immature gut: Effect of immunologic and materational factors in colostrum, in: *Immunology of Breast Milk* (P. L. Ogra and D. H. Dayton, eds.), Raven Press, New York, pp. 227–234.
78. Stokes, C. R., Soothill, J. F., and Turner, M. W., 1975, Immune exclusion is a function of IgA, *Nature* **255**:745–746.

79. Hanson, L. A., Ahlstedt, S., Carlsson, B., and Fallstrom, S. P., 1977, Secretory IgA antibodies against cows milk proteins in human milk and their possible effect in mixed feeding, *Int. Arch. Allergy Appl. Immunol.* **54:**457–462.
80. Selner, J. C., Merrill, D. A., and Claman, H. N., 1968, Salivary immunoglobulin and albumin: Development during the newborn period, *J. Pediatr.* **72:**685–689.
81. Eastham, E. J., Lichauco, T., Grady, M. I., and Walker, W. A., 1978, Antigenicity of infant formulas: Role of immature intestine on protein permeability, *J. Pediatr.* **93:**561–564.
82. Katz, D. H., 1978, The allergic phenotype: Manifestation of allergic breakthrough and imbalance of normal damping of IgE antibody production, *Immunol. Rev.* **41:**77–108.
83. Lepow, M. L., Warren, R. J., Gray, N., Ingram, V. G., and Robbins, F. C., 1961, Sabin type 1 poliovirus vaccine administered by mouth to newborn infants, *New Engl. J. Med.* **264:**1071–1078.
84. Plotkin, S. A., Katz, M., Brown, R. E., and Pagano, J. S., 1966, Oral poliovirus vaccination in newborn African infants, *Am. J. Dis. Child.* **111:**27–30.
85. Deforest, A., Parker, P. B., DiLiberti, J. H., Yates, T., Sibinga, M. S., and Smith, D. S., 1973, The effect of breast feeding on the antibody responses of infants to trivalent oral poliovirus vaccine, *J. Pediatr.* **83:**93–95.

IV

Medical Management of Breast-Feeding

9

Routine Management of Breast-Feeding

Marianne R. Neifert

INTRODUCTION

In recent years, renewed scientific interest in breast-feeding has led to acceptance of human milk as the optimal food for the first several months of life.[1-5] Professional endorsement of natural infant feeding, together with rising consumer demand, have led to an increase in the incidence and duration of breast-feeding throughout the country during the past decade. In 1971, 24.7% of newborns were breast-fed in the hospital, while only 5.5% were still receiving any breast milk at 5 to 6 months of age. By 1979, comparable figures were 51.0% and 23.0%. Currently, the typical breast-feeding mother is a primipara with some college education, in a higher family income group. Her infant is under the care of a pediatrician, and she lives in an urban area within the Mountain region of the United States. However, a trend of increased breast-feeding can be found among all demographic populations surveyed and within each U.S. census region.[6]

Despite the fact that more mothers are electing to breast-feed, most women still experience some difficulties nursing. Many discontinue within the first several months, and nearly half of mothers fail to meet their own breast-feeding goals.[7] Some of the major reasons women discontinue breast-feeding have been identified as lack of milk or fear of lack of milk, maternal fatigue, breast or nipple problems, and health professional recommendations.[8-12] Insufficient technical knowledge, confidence, or emotional support also contribute to the brevity of the nursing experience for many women.[13,14]

While optimal infant nutrition has been defined as exclusive breast-feeding for the first 4 to 6 months of life and continued nursing for a year or more,[2,3] a wide discrepancy between ideal infant feeding recommendations

Marianne R. Neifert • Department of Pediatrics, University of Colorado School of Medicine, Denver, Colorado 80262.

and actual breast-feeding practices exists. Because of a paucity of traditional support systems at the family and community levels, factors which contributed to breast-feeding success in past generations, health professionals increasingly are being asked to counsel breast-feeding mothers. Yet current medical training largely ignores this important aspect of mother–infant care and fails to prepare clinicians adequately to support, promote, and enhance breast-feeding. In addition to theoretical knowledge about the value of human milk, health professionals must also possess the practical information to help the nursing mother maintain lactation for a significant period of time.[15]

Because normal lactation is delegated to the pediatrician while breast problems are referred to the obstetrician, the lactating breast risks falling in the crack between the two specialties. In fact, the effective management of the breast-feeding dyad impinges on many areas of medicine. Clearly, the obstetrician helps to guide the prenatal choice of infant feeding method and plays a role in the preparation and initiation of lactation. In addition, he treats specific complications of the lactating breast such as mastitis. The pediatrician bears primary responsibility for sustaining lactation and assessing the well-being of the infant. The family physician, caring for both members of the nursing dyad, has unique opportunities to influence the full course of lactation. Surgeons who may operate on nursing women or their infants need to be aware of the effects on lactation of separation of mother and baby. Plastic surgeons performing mammoplasties must recognize the importance of the nerve supply to the nipple for subsequent nursing performance. Internists prescribing medications for nursing mothers need to understand the mechanisms of drug excretion in milk and be cognizant of potential effects of drugs on both lactation and the nursing infant. As breast-feeding continues to increase in prevalence, lactation will be found to impact upon more and more medical subspecialties.

PRENATAL PERIOD

Ideally, exposure to breast-feeding should begin at an early age as a natural part of family life, through opportunities to directly observe nursing within the family network. Public schools can offer broad opportunities to introduce children to breast-feeding through sex education classes at the elementary level, or in junior high and high school life education classes which include both boys and girls. The media offers a vast potential for widespread breast-feeding education, but unfortunately infant feeding in public, on television, and in advertising almost exclusively depicts bottle feeding. Furthermore, the breast is typically portrayed in the mass media as an erotic appendage, rather than as an organ with an important nutritional function for the infant.[16]

Role of the Health Professional in Breast-Feeding Education

Because breast-feeding is not generally regarded as a natural adjunct to childbirth in our society, it is often left to physicians and other health care providers to introduce the concept during the prenatal period. Parents should be provided sufficient information to permit an informed decision about infant feeding. As in other areas of health counseling, such as cigarette smoking or the use of car restraints, neutrality on the part of the caretaker (i.e., "breast is best, but formula is just as good") is inappropriate when breast milk clearly provides superior infant nutrition.

Attitudes of the husband should be pursued, as his emotional support can be pivotal to successful breast-feeding. He may have misconceptions about the physical effects of lactation on his wife's breasts, concerns about the sexual role of the lactating breasts, jealousy of the nursing infant, or fears of being left out in the care of the baby. On the other hand, occasionally the husband is overzealous about breast-feeding and may coerce his wife into nursing against her will. Ideally, both partners should have comparable motivation toward nursing. When striking differences exist, this may reflect the couple's problem-solving style in general. Healthy guidelines to decision-making should be encouraged and occasionally referral for marriage counseling will be indicated. When the father is not available, or when other influential relatives are involved, it is wise to explore breast-feeding attitudes of these significant others.

While some fortunate women can nurse successfully without any preparation, breast-feeding is not pure instinct for either mother or infant. Many of the problems women encounter in the course of breast-feeding can be anticipated or avoided by prior knowledge about the art of nursing. Numerous lay books on breast-feeding, covering the advantages of human milk, the physiology of lactation, and practical aspects of breast-feeding are readily available.[17-24] Parents should be encouraged to read at least one of these resources prior to delivery. Childbirth education classes provide another forum in which breast-feeding information can be disseminated.

However, such self-guidance is often insufficient, particularly when negative past experiences color the family's childbearing approaches. Under these circumstances, previous breast-feeding problems should be explored and appropriate reassurance or anticipatory guidance provided. Sometimes it will be evident, for a variety of reasons, that prolonged breast-feeding may not be desirable for a particular woman. Such a woman might be counseled about the value of colostrum and early breast-feeding in the prevention of infant infection. She should be reassured that the success of breast-feeding is not defined by the duration of nursing. When a family decides against breast-feeding altogether, it is important to dispel any guilt associated with their decision and aid the mother with supportive advice about formula preparation and effective techniques of bottle-feeding.

Prenatal Examination

Physical examination of the breasts by the prenatal health care provider is essential to provide assurance when the breasts are normal, to detect the presence of abnormalities when they exist, and to recommend therapy when

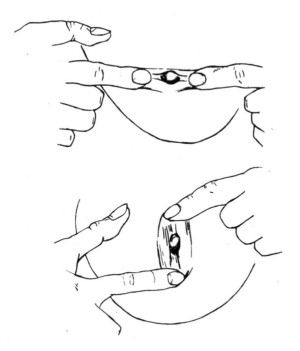

Figure 1. Hoffman's prenatal exercises. The index fingers are placed opposite each other at the sides of the nipple and pulled gradually toward the areolar margins, horizontally, as far as the tissue stretches. Then the fingers are positioned above and below the nipple and the pulling action is repeated vertically.

it is indicated. For example, an inverted nipple which retracts on tactile stimulation can impair proper infant grasp, making nursing difficult or impossible. If detected early, Hoffman exercises, in which the nipple is pulled both vertically and horizontally at the areolar margins, can enhance protractility and break adhesions at the nipple base.[25,26] (Fig. 1). Breast shields, also known as milk cups, are also used to treat inverted nipples. Breast shields are worn over the nipple inside the nursing bra during the latter months of pregnancy to provide slight pressure on the areolae and gentle suction to draw the nipples out[27] (Fig. 2). The wearing of breast shields reportedly corrects inverted nipples during the lactation period.[28] Various commercial brands are available through maternity shops or La Leche League International. If inverted nipples are overlooked prenatally, therapy can still be instituted when breast-feeding commences. Wearing breast shields between feedings will frequently enhance nipple protactility sufficiently for the infant to nurse.

Other abnormalities that can be detected by physical exam include unilateral hypoplastic breast, which may never produce milk normally, or evidence of previous breast surgery. In general, breast augmentation with silicone implantation should not affect the ability to nurse, whereas reduction mammoplasty in which the nipple is autotransplanted will sever afferent nerve pathways and lacteriferous ducts and preclude subsequent breast-feeding. More current reduction techniques which leave the nipple intact should not affect nursing. However, any surgery on the breast, particularly

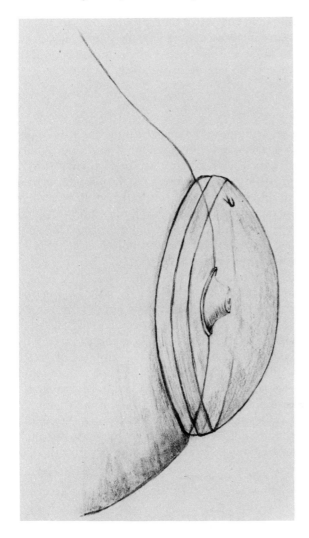

Figure 2. Breast shields, also known as milk cups, provide gentle suction and slight pressure on the areola to draw out a flat or inverted nipple.

in the inferolateral aspect, followed by alteration of sensation in the nipple and areola, likely disrupted the innervation to the nipple–areola complex.[29] Such damage can be expected to interfere with breast-feeding. Following unilateral mastectomy, breast-feeding is still possible with the remaining breast. Maternal vaginal yeast infection during the last trimester should be treated, as it may predispose the infant to oral thrush after delivery[30] and lead to subsequent painful monilia infection of the mother's nipples.

Management Plans

At the time of the prenatal examination, problems which potentially will affect nursing should be aired and appropriate management outlined, for example, twin gestation, chronic maternal drug therapy, the need to return to employment after delivery, or the presence of chronic maternal illness. Expectant parents who desire to nurse will find reassurance in the knowledge that plans have been made to accommodate breast-feeding.

Nipple Preparation

Prenatal nipple preparation techniques to make nipples more supple and condition them for nursing are widely recommended and anecdotally of value. However, there has been little systematic study of their efficacy. Brown and Hurlock found no difference in subsequent nipple tenderness in women who prepared one nipple only.[31] On the other hand, in an earlier study, Waller found the management of breast-feeding on a busy hospital ward to be significantly improved in women who carried out prenatal breast massage.[32] No recent study has controlled for the psychological benefits of becoming accustomed to handling the breasts. Nevertheless, breast preparation likely plays a role in fostering maternal confidence.

Specifically recommended preparation techniques include rolling the nipples between thumb and forefinger, gently tugging the nipples until slight discomfort is felt, exposing the nipples to air by lowering the flaps of a maternity bra, performing Hoffman's exercises described earlier, and daily expressing a few drops of colostrum during the final months of pregnancy.[33,34] Such maneuvers probably condition the nipples for nursing and minimize subsequent nipple tenderness, facilitate infant grasp of the nipple and introduce the technique of manual expression of milk for later use.

More important than all these manipulations is respecting the axiom "First do no harm" by recommending the avoidance of soap, alcohol-containing lotions, and other potentially irritating substances during the last trimester.

Support Groups

La Leche League International is a grass roots, mother-to-mother breast-feeding support group which has been in existence more than 25 years, espousing the motto "Good mothering through breast-feeding." Beginning with seven motivated women in a Chicago suburb who sought one another's help to breast-feed their babies amid a climate of professional apathy and misinformation, La Leche League has grown into a worldwide organization fostering breast-feeding through information, reassurance, and personal mother-to-mother warmth. La Leche League groups meet monthly in the relaxed atmosphere of a member's home and are led by one or more trained League leaders through a series of four topics, one each month: (1) advantages of breast-feeding to the mother and baby, (2) the art of breast-feeding and overcoming difficulties, (3) the baby arrives, and (4) nutrition and weaning. Babies are always welcome at La Leche League meetings and provide an ideal opportunity for prospective mothers to witness nursing in all stages.

At present, La Leche League is active in over 50 countries and provides advice and support to over 100,000 nursing mothers around the world each month. In addition to their manual, *The Womanly Art of Breastfeeding*, La Leche League publishes numerous information sheets, booklets, and reprints. A network of Medical Associates and a Professional Advisory Board are available for consultation and advice.[17]

The League philosophies espoused by all leaders include the concepts of breast-feeding as a form of mothering, exclusive nursing until the infant displays signs of readiness for solids near the middle of the first year, natural weaning guided by signs that the baby has outgrown the need for nursing, and the importance of close maternal–infant contact during the entire nursing period.

While La Leche League fills a great void in the provision of breast-feeding knowledge and support, it is important to acknowledge that the organization and its philosophies will not meet the individual needs of every nursing mother. For example, the mother who elects to return to work early, use supplemental formula routinely, or wean in a highly structured fashion may not receive endorsement for her particular style of nursing.*

INTRAPARTUM PERIOD

Hospital Policies

For most American women, the first breast-feeding experience occurs in a hospital setting under the guidance of one or more influential health professionals. Lip service to breast-feeding is easily overridden by overt messages in hospital protocols and routines which clearly undermine it. Unnecessary separation of mothers and infants, routine bottle supplementation of breast-fed infants, adherence to scheduled feedings, test weighing after feedings, restricted length of feedings and provision of gift packs containing formula to breast-feeding mothers are commonly encountered impediments to the initiation of lactation.

One of the primary aims of the routine postpartum confinement should be the promotion of successful breast-feeding for that majority of women who express a desire to nurse.[35] Protocols that truly support breast-feeding should stem from a commitment to the policy "Breast milk is house formula," and usually require breaking from tradition. Such protocols include early first feeding at the breast,[36–38] demand feedings at frequent intervals (3 hr or closer),[39–41] night nursing,[42] availability of rooming-in of babies with mothers,[43–45] a knowledgeable, supportive nursing staff,[46] and the use of supplementary feeds *only* upon indication.[47]

The common practice of distributing a gift pack containing formula to breast-feeding mothers at the time of hospital discharge has recently been

---

* For more information, contact: La Leche League International, Inc., 9616 Minneapolis Avenue, Franklin Park, IL 60131; (312)-455-7730.

examined in a prospective study. Mothers receiving formula gift packs were more likely to have discontinued breast-feeding by 1 month of age and to have started solids by 2 months of age than breast-feeding mothers who did not receive the formula.[48] Mothers who were ill at the time of discharge and were less educated were more vulnerable to the negative influence of the gift pack. While the giving of formula to nursing mothers remains a fairly uniform nursery procedure, a few hospitals have challenged this tradition by permitting formula distribution to breast-feeding mothers upon prescription only.

The institution of hospital breast-feeding support programs requires commitment and flexibility among personnel. Health professionals may find it easier to monitor infant intake and instruct new mothers to feed by bottle than by breast. Some assume nurseries run smoother within the framework of scheduled feedings and view unstructured demand feedings as chaotic. Optimal newborn care is increasingly recognized as that in which the new parents provide all the care to their infant in the mother's room, with minimal supervision. But this recent move from a highly controlled childbirth and postpartum period to a parent-directed experience requires often painful professional abdication of control and is hindered by the subtle competition among adults for the care of an attractive newborn.

A recent example of a successful effort to modify hospital policies to enhance breast-feeding is an early postpartum educational and support program to foster breast-feeding among inner city mothers at Maricopa County Hospital in Phoenix. La Leche League leaders were hired to contact nursing mothers on the postpartum ward, distribute literature, and man a telephone hotline for both English- and Spanish-speaking patients. In addition, pediatric housestaff at the hospital received 6 hr of breast-feeding education by the counselors. In the first 2 years of the project, mean duration of breast-feeding was increased 54%.[49]

Initiation of Nursing

Current judicious use of obstetrical analgesia and anesthesia has resulted in the decreased incidence of the over-medicated, drowsy, poorly sucking newborn. In the early minutes after birth, the stimulating and almost irresistible state of alertness and responsiveness in the infant, coupled with the heightened sense of awareness in the parents, invite social interaction. The infant's instinctive mouthing movements, the presence of the rooting reflex, and the rapid appearance of bowel sounds make feeding shortly after birth seem appropriate and sensible. It is now well documented that early and frequent suckling in the immediate puerperium enhances subsequent lactational success.[36-38,50]

Every health professional who works with infants and mothers should be skilled in the techniques of breast-feeding, acquired from direct observations of nursing couples during various stages of lactation. To nurse in the sitting position, it is important that the mother be comfortable and have

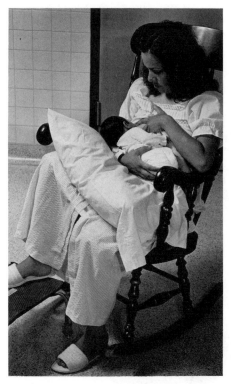

Figure 3. Correct nursing position, depicting the following techniques: Arm supporting infant held tight against mother's body, infant elevated to level of breast, infant's whole body turned to face the breast, nipple protractility enhanced by pinching between first and second fingers.

back support. Because there are 8 to 12 inches between the breast and the lap in the sitting position, it helps initially to elevate the mother's leg on the ipsilateral side with a footstool under her foot or to use a pillow on her lap to bring the baby to the level of the breast. When bottle feeding, one typically holds the arm supporting the infant at an angle to the body. When breast-feeding, however, it is important to keep the supporting arm tight against the body, as if in a sling, in order to align the baby's head with the breast. The mother's arm should support the baby with her hand under the buttocks, so that she can rotate the infant's whole body by turning her arm. The infant should be clearly turned to face the mother's breast, thereby diminishing the tendency for the nipple to become dislodged from the infant's mouth[51] (Fig. 3).

Often a mother expects her new infant instinctively to grasp her relatively soft, flaccid nipple and sufficient areola without assistance, but most infants require some aid in learning to do this. The mother should pinch the nipple with the first and second fingers of the free hand, or cup the breast with the third, fourth and fifth fingers while pinching the nipple between the thumb and index finger, to make it more protractile. This maneuver also serves to depress the breast away from the infant's nostrils as he nurses (Fig. 4). The mother should avoid pushing the baby's cheek toward the nipple, as

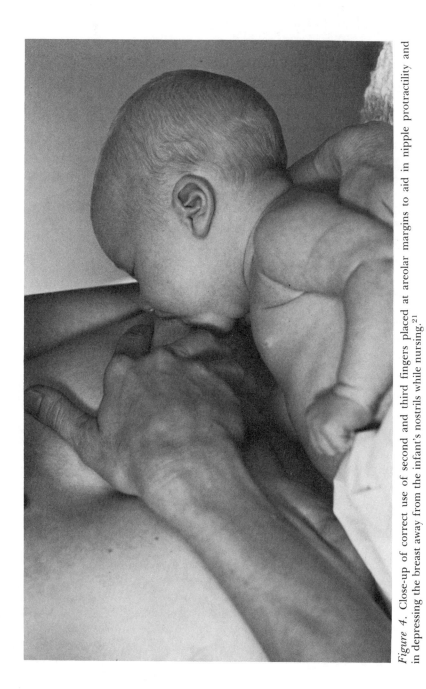

Figure 4. Close-up of correct use of second and third fingers placed at areolar margins to aid in nipple protractility and in depressing the breast away from the infant's nostrils while nursing.[21]

the infant will likely root in the direction of the stimulus. She should stroke the side of the baby's face nearest her nipple, so that the infant will turn toward the breast in response to the rooting reflex. A few drops of expressed colostrum may entice the infant to grasp the nipple.

Most infants will take a few moments to lick, mouth, and play with the nipple before effectively grasping it and suckling. Mothers need reassurance that this exploratory behavior is normal and does not signify a problem in learning to breast-feed. Nursing difficulties often arise during the nursery stay when an infant is either too lethargic or sleepy to nurse or is so agitated that he cries frantically and refuses the nipple altogether. The former infant can be unwrapped and stroked or rocked back and forth in a sitting position to arouse him, while the latter infant should be swaddled and calmed down before being put to the breast.

Commonly accepted recommendations which restrict suckling time at the breast during the first days of nursing ignore basic principles of breast-feeding physiology. If suckling time is interrupted before the initiation of the letdown reflex, the bulk of the feed is unavailable to the infant and breast engorgement is fostered. This contributes to improper grasp of the nipple and associated nipple tenderness. Greatly restricted nursing in the first week may also lead to inadequate milk supply for the infant in later weeks. Reasonable recommendations for initiating nursing are 5 min per breast per feeding the first day, 10 min per breast per feeding the second day, and 15 min or longer per breast per feeding thereafter.[34] An alternative to limiting infant suckling time is to vary the infant's nursing position every 5 min in order to rotate the maximum pressure points on the nipple.

In general, it is best to nurse at both breasts at each feeding, in order to assure adequate infant intake and permit regular stimulation of both breasts. At the beginning of the feeding, the infant gets foremilk of relatively low fat content, which increases as letdown occurs. When the infant is moved to the second breast, some mixing of milk has already occurred, so the initial fat content is higher than the foremilk from the first side. If the infant becomes drowsy after the first breast, he can be burped and stimulated with a diaper change before being offered the second breast. Because the sucking stimulus is usually greatest at the first breast, women are encouraged to initiate feedings on alternate sides. While sucking needs and styles differ greatly among infants, during the first few weeks of nursing, feedings usually last 10 min per breast. Nutritive feeding time was shown to be 15 min or less in 75% of the 100 feeding episodes studied between the fifth and seventh postpartum days.[52] Later, when the letdown reflex is well conditioned and brisk, most infants can effectively empty the breast in approximately 5 min. When terminating a feeding, suction should be broken by inserting a finger in the infant's mouth rather than by pulling him off the nipple.

Common Early Problems

Engorgement

Engorgement, or uncomfortable swelling of the breasts, associated with an increase in milk secretion usually occurs on the second to fourth postpartum day. Lymphatic and vascular congestion, as well as probable interstitial edema, contribute to the swelling and tenderness associated with the sudden surge in milk tension in the ducts. The infant may have difficulty grasping the firm, convex areola and effectively milking the underlying lactiferous sinuses at this time. In addition, nipple tenderness secondary to improper nipple grasp may compound the problem.

Unrelieved engorgement is harmful in two key ways. First, pressure in the duct systems radiates rapidly throughout the breast and can rise sufficiently to ultimately cause pressure atrophy of the glandular secreting and myoepithelial cells, leading to involution of lactation. The role of unrelieved engorgement in involution of the mammary gland is demonstrated by the fact that an unnursed breast ceases lactating despite prolactin stimulation from nursing on the contralateral side. Goat studies, in which isosmotic lactose was injected into the udders after milking, also have demonstrated the inhibitory effect on lactation of mammary distension, despite adequate prolactin stimulation.[53] The fact that unrelieved engorgement is one of the mechanisms by which the bottle-feeding mother dries up is often overlooked in the breast-feeding woman.

Secondly, engorgement of the areolar area may make it difficult for the infant properly to grasp the nipple and areola. The resulting failure to empty the breast can further aggravate engorgement, and the improper grasp can result in nipple trauma and tenderness. If the situation persists, serious deterioration of the breast-feeding relationship between mother and infant can result. For these reasons, interruption of breast-feeding during the first postpartum week, such as frequently occurs with Caesarian delivery, neonatal jaundice, difficulties in nursing technique, or inappropriate feeding schedules can be particularly detrimental to successful nursing.

Engorgement can be minimized by round-the-clock demand feedings of adequate length, beginning shortly after birth. Heat applied to the engorged breasts prior to nursing enhances blood flow and facilitates letdown of milk, while cool compresses between feedings may alleviate further congestion. Compression of the nipple between the first and second fingers may help the infant to grasp sufficient areolar tissue. In the absence of an adequate suckling stimulus, effective relief of engorgement may be accomplished by manual or mechanical expression of milk. Judicious use of oxytocin (Syntocinon®) nasal spray to aid in milk letdown may be indicated.

The engorged bottle-feeding mother may accept intermittent nursing and gradual "drying up" over a week or two as a safe, practical method of managing painful engorgement. While involuting comfortably, she can provide her infant with the immune benefits of colostrum and early milk even though long-term nursing is not desired.

Sore Nipples

Sore nipples are common, transient, and usually mild, but can be alarming to a new mother who had not anticipated any discomfort with nursing. If not managed correctly, soreness can progress to cracking, bleeding, blister formation and pain severe enough to temporarily preclude nursing or lead to early weaning. The primary cause of soreness is improper grasp of the nipple, often secondary to engorgement.[34] Other aggravating factors include (1) failure to keep the nipples dry; (2) the use of irritating agents such as soap, plastic-lined breast pads, or sensitizing creams; (3) improperly breaking suction when removing the infant from the breast; (4) excessive negative pressure exerted on the nipple while an infant sleeps at the breast; (5) the prolonged use of the breast as a pacifier; (6) faulty letdown with associated prolonged vigorous sucking by the infant.

Management of sore nipples should include a careful search for the exacerbating factors and an attempt to alleviate each one, while stressing to the mother the transient nature of the pain. Other treatment includes (1) facilitating proper infant grasp of the nipple; (2) frequent, shorter feedings to avoid engorgement and an overly hungry infant; (3) air-drying the nipples by lowering the flaps on a nursing bra; (4) application of lanolin cream between feedings; (5) varying the position in which the infant is held during the feedings so that he grasps the nipple at different pressure points; (6) starting feedings on the least sore side and then moving the infant to the very painful side after letdown has occurred; and (7) techniques to enhance letdown such as heat, massage, or analgesics. In general, nipple shields should be discouraged in the treatment of sore nipples for the reasons discussed in the following section.

Nipple Confusion

Nipple confusion describes the difficulty an infant may display in grasping his mother's soft, relatively flaccid nipple after repeated, early exposure to the long, stiff artificial nipple offered with a bottle and used as a pacifier. Such an infant will accept a bottle readily, but frets and fusses and seems unwilling to grasp the mother's nipple when put to the breast. The confusion originates from the different tongue and mouth action required for each type of nipple.[34] Once engorgement occurs, the mother's nipple is even more difficult to grasp, and the problem is aggravated further.

Nipple confusion is frustrating to manage and is best prevented by the avoidance of artifical nipples until the infant is nursing effectively. Hospital policies of routine, unnecessary bottle supplementation not only invite nipple confusion, but result in less frequent breast stimulation, expose the infant unnecessarily to cow's milk, undermine maternal confidence, and set up patterns of feeding that vulnerable new mothers are apt to continue at home.

Once nipple confusion is manifest, all artifical nipples, including pacifiers, should be discontinued and attempts made to enhance the protractility of mother's nipple through stimulation, pump suction, a cold wash cloth, or the wearing of breast shields between feedings. Expressing a few drops of colostrum onto the nipple to interest the infant may also help entice him to nurse. Patience and perseverance in working with the baby will usually prove successful within 24 hr. A breast-fed infant who has not yet learned to nurse effectively should not be discharged from the hospital unless close supervision and instruction are available.

Nursing with a nipple shield, or artificial nipple, placed over the mother's nipple should be discouraged in managing nipple confusion, since the practice only serves to reinforce artificial nipples, diminishes direct stimulation of the mother's nipple, and is inconvenient to use with each feeding. If one resorts to the use of a shield, attempts should be made to wean from it as soon as possible. Often the shield can be withdrawn during the feeding after suckling has commenced and the mother's nipple has been drawn out somewhat.

Caesarian Section

With the rising incidence of Caesarian birth, many women find some modifications necessary in the early breast-feeding routines. Whenever mother's condition permits, attempts should be made to introduce the infant to the breast for the first feeding, despite the extra effort required on the part of the staff. When nursing is delayed for several feedings and rubber nipples are introduced, nipple confusion may occur. When sporadic breast-feeding continues for several days, the infant's difficulty in learning to nurse may be compounded by engorgement. Early attempts at the breast may be enhanced by comfortable positioning, perhaps with mother lying down or with a pillow on her lap to protect her suture line. The "football hold," in which the infant is cradled at mother's side with his feet directed toward her back, may be particularly suitable for avoiding discomfort along the incision.

Jaundice

There is conflicting data about the effect of breast-feeding on neonatal hyperbilirubinemia. In one study, no statistical difference in peak bilirubin levels was demonstrated between breast-fed and bottle-fed infants.[54] Other data have revealed a significantly greater incidence of hyperbilirubinemia in the first week of life among breast-fed as compared to bottle-fed infants.[55] Although *in vitro* inhibition of hepatic glucuronyl transferase has been demonstrated in milk samples from Eskimo mothers during the first week postpartum,[56] "exaggerated physiologic jaundice" in breast-fed infants during the first 3 to 5 days of life is most likely related to inappropriate feeding schedules, superimposed dehydration, and inadequate stooling. There is no documentation that supplementing breast-fed infants with glucose water affects peak bilirubin levels.

When jaundice during the first week requires treatment with phototherapy, breast-feeding is usually disrupted significantly by the routine protocol of staggering milk and water feedings every 2 hr. While this regimen may be appropriate to provide extra hydration to a formula-fed infant, nursing every 4 hr is not a physiologic timetable for a breast-fed infant. Nursing every 2 to 3 hr, immediately followed by glucose water supplementation, would seem more rational for breast-fed infants receiving phototherapy. Because the lights predispose infants to lethargy, these babies should be put to the breast at any sign of rooting. If an infant nurses poorly, the mother can be encouraged to pump her breasts to relieve engorgement, and if necessary, her expressed milk can be fed by bottle. When neonatal jaundice delays hospital discharge, attempts should be made to allow the mother to extend her own postpartum stay to be with her infant and remain available for feedings. It is not uncommon for breast-feeding to be permanently disrupted by the treatment of relatively insignificant hyperbilirubinemia. Every clinician treating jaundice in a breast-fed newborn should include the salvage of breast-feeding in his management plan.

THE NORMAL COURSE OF LACTATION

First Two Weeks

Whereas worldwide puerperal customs generally cater to a new mother for many months, the American para is considered fit after 48 hr and "back to normal" after her 6-week check-up. Routine activities take her outside the home almost daily and absent her from her infant for several hours at a time. Her lifestyle does not lend itself to the frequent, ready access to the breast necessary for an infant to receive 8 to 10 feedings each 24 hr during the first month of nursing. While the "all-American baby" is imagined to sleep cooperatively through the night, in fact, night nursing is a normal phenomenon, necessary to foster a generous milk supply. Whereas the bottle-fed infant predictably stools once a day, the breast-fed newborn typically stools with every nursing. The loose yellow movements, while not foul smelling, easily conform to preconceived notions of "diarrhea." Lack of confidence and ignorance about normal feeding routines, coupled with the unrealistic comparison of the breast-fed baby with the bottle-fed infant, lead new mothers to the conclusion that their infant is hungry too often and that their milk is insufficient in either quality or qualtity.

In sharp contrast, among the primitive ¡Kung hunter-gatherers of Botswana and Namibia, infants are always in immediate physical proximity with their mothers until age 2 years or older. Nursing occurs for a few minutes at a time several times each hour throughout the daylight hours and nursing during the night is universal.[57]

Role of the Doula

In a study of over 300 cultures and several animal species, Raphael found that all contained some form of institutionalized emotional and physical support for new mothers. She referred to individuals who "mother the mother" as doulas, those individuals who surround, interact with, and aid the new mother at any time within the perinatal period.[58] The primary task of the doula is to shield the mother from pressures and stress which could interfere with the establishment of lactation, through information, physical help, example, encouragement, praise, and concern. Husband, mother, mother-in-law, sister, friend, visiting health nurse, lay health visitor, La Leche League leader, or other knowledgeable, caring persons can play this supportive role during the critical first postpartum weeks. In the absence of an adequate doula, too many mothers fall victim to fatigue, feelings of incompetence and disorganization, and lack of confidence in their ability to nourish their baby. It is little wonder that a significant percentage of women have abandoned breast-feeding or begun to wean by the routine 2-week pediatric visit.[9,14]

Role of Health Professional

The role of the health professional in establishing successful lactation is multiple. He or she should assure early, close follow-up of breast-fed infants through phone contact within 48 hr of discharge, arrange visiting nurse referral for primiparas or those with difficulties initiating nursing in the hospital, and provide office visits earlier than 2 weeks whenever a problem is suspected. He or she should continue to define "normal" and help parents cope within that framework, rather than scheme to make infants nurse less often or sleep through the night. He or she should guide parents in setting priorities and in minimizing household chores and activities, and should encourage maternal rest throughout the day, rather than urge mothers to "get away" from their babies. Professionals should also endorse the role of the doula and aid parents in enlisting resourse people to serve as doulas.

Two Weeks

Regaining of Birth Weight

The routine 2-week pediatric visit can be very timely in detecting inappropriate feeding regimes, providing encouragement, and elaborating anticipatory guidance. While most infants will have regained their birth weight by 2 weeks, about 10% of healthy breast-fed infants may not have done so.[59] When weight gain is insufficient, a detailed feeding history should indicate areas of intervention. Most common factors include adhering to a 4-hour feeding schedule, nursing too long at the first breast or failing to use both breasts at each feeding, allowing the infant to sleep through the night, inattention to maternal diet, fluids and rest, and physical complaints such as sore nipples which limit feedings or inhibit letdown. When weight gain has been insufficient, appropriate techniques should be suggested and the infant reweighed at frequent intervals to ascertain that no long-term growth problem is present.

Letdown

Part of the early assessment of the success of lactation should include an evaluation of the presence and effectiveness of the milk letdown, or milk ejection reflex. The rapid ejection of milk into the lactiferous ducts, effected by oxytocin, is perceived by the mother as "tightening," "stinging," "burning," "pins-and-needles," or "tingling." The sensation is typically felt circumferentially in each breast and is accompanied by the jetting of milk in several streams from the nipple openings and active infant gulping of milk. While some mothers may nurse without perceiving these sensations, successful breast-feeding mothers are more likely to experience signs of milk letdown.[60] Although letdown occurs via a neurohumeral reflex, it can be conditioned to occur in the absence of nipple stimulation, for example upon seeing the infant or hearing him cry.[61] The reflex can also be inhibited, despite adequate nipple stimulation, by noxious stimuli.[62] Embarrassment, pain, anger, anxiety, and fear can all impair the letdown of milk, thus affecting the quality and quantity of the feeding. Relaxation, gentle breast massage, moderate amounts of alcohol, and nursing rituals such as music or a certain food have all been suggested to aid in conditioning the letdown reflex. Synthetic oxytocin is occasionally prescribed (Syntocinon nasal spray) to enhance and condition the letdown. Spontaneous milk ejection, in addition to suckling induced letdown, has been observed to occur as often as every 30 to 60 min during early lactation.[63]

Appetite Spurts

Appetite spurts, also called growth spurts or frequency days, are typical periods of increased frequency of demand feedings and apparent hunger after nursing. Although they can occur at any time during the first several months, they usually become manifest at 3 weeks, 6 weeks, 3 months, and 6 months. Unless a mother is forewarned about these episodes, most women will respond to the infant's obvious hunger with supplemental feedings of formula or the introduction of solid foods. When weaning foods are started, the usual result is a gradual decline in breast milk supply. When appetite spurts are recognized and managed by increased nursing, as often as every hour or two, breast milk supply increases over several days,[64] and the infant resumes his former nursing schedule. It is presumed that the spurts result from increased requirements by the infant, but it is also possible that a sudden increase in maternal activities diminishes milk supply first.

Two Months

At 2 months, given the successful initiation of lactation, the nutritional needs of essentially all infants can still be met with exclusive breast-feeding. Although the infant sleeps longer, some night nursing is usual. Occasionally, a decline in weight gain occurs when an infant begins to sleep at length through the night. The missed feeding, coupled with decreased breast stimulation, can diminish both infant intake and breast milk supply. The normalcy of night nursings should be emphasized and women reminded to nap during the day. Despite the temptation to start weaning foods in order to lengthen the interval between feedings at night, there is no documentation that rice cereal, for example, has any value for this purpose.

The infant's stooling pattern may begin to change from the frequent, losse stools typical in the first month, to less frequent stooling. Some infants will normally pass a large, loose stool at intervals of several days. Usually, by two months, the letdown is quite well conditioned, and the infant can effectively empty each breast in 4 to 5 min,[65] so the duration of feedings may be shortened.

Caked Breast

At any time during the lactation experience, but especially during the early months, a focal area of breast engorgement, also known as a "clogged duct" or "caked breast" may occur. Obstruction of a milk duct is usually preceded by stasis of milk due to the skipping of feedings or irregular nursing. Obstruction is manifest by a tender lump, and occasionally erythema, along the affected duct system, usually in an outer lobe. Relief may be obtained within 24 hr by instituting the following measures: starting consecutive feeds on the affected side, gently massaging the area, applying heat, taking a warm shower, nursing frequently, hand expressing after feeds, and changing position with each nursing to facilitate emptying of different lobes. Because caked breast is a frequent precursor of mastitis, any area of obstructed milk flow should be relieved promptly.

Four Months

Adding Solids

By 4 months, the majority of infants should still continue to be exclusively breast-fed. One study among American infants documented weight gain at or above the 50% for exclusively breast-fed infants by 6 months of age, and at or above the 25% by 9 months of age.[66] Individual infants will require solid food, or *beikost*, earlier than this, but one should look for signs of readiness, such as interest in adults eating, much hand-to-mouth activity, and loss of the tongue thrust reflex. By preparing first foods such as a mashed overripe banana, mothers can gain appreciation for their own ability to prepare natural, wholesome foods for their infants. Although several hundred varieties of commercially prepared baby foods imply their necessity in infant feeding, these products are an outgrowth of inappropriate early introduction of solids.[67] While some prepared baby foods will make infant feeding more convenient, they need not be used extensively when the introduction of solid foods is deferred until teeth have erupted and necessary motor skills are evident.

When beikost is added to the diet, it should be given only after nursing. If it is not accepted at this time, then the infant is not yet ready for solid foods. Solids should be introduced at the feeding when mother's milk supply is usually lowest, most often in the late afternoon or evening. When solids displace breast milk in the infant's diet, diminished milk supply and insufficient infant weight gain can result.

Working and Nursing

Many nursing mothers are eventually faced with the dilemma of needing to work outside the home. Belying traditional stereotypes, only 7% of American families consist of a working father, nonworking mother, and two children. Women with children under 6 years of age are the fastest growing segment of the female work force, with 42% of these mothers now employed.[68] The long-standing cultural expectations of the exclusive role of mother and the emerging reality of female participation in the labor force are directly contradictory, resulting in guilt, anxiety, and frustration on the part of working mothers.

The impact of maternal employment on incidence and duration of breast-feeding is difficult to ascertain and varies between formal employment in urban areas where infants are separated from their mothers throughout the working day and traditional rural settings where mother–infant proximity is preserved.[69] The Report on the WHO Collaborative Study on Breast-feeding revealed that while mothers themselves did not consider commitments outside the home to be an important factor in determining their feeding behavior, the prevalence of breast-feeding tended to be lower among those mothers resuming paid employment.[70] Certainly, breast-feeding in the presence of maternal employment outside the home requires a high degree of motivation and practical information.

Because of the emotional conflict, ambivalence, and practical dilemmas which accompany the return to work, working–nursing mothers require much support and encouragement from health professionals. Whenever possible, the issue should be discussed prior to the birth of the infant, and the mother should be discouraged from making commitments to return to work at a specified time postpartum. Very few women can accurately predict how they will react to motherhood or when they will feel emotionally or physically capable of employment. In addressing the issue, it is useful to expose all the options that may be available: postponing the return to work; working part-time only; working at home; bringing the infant to the place of employment; utilizing child care near the place of employment, thus permitting contact with the infant throughout the working day; expressing and storing milk to be fed to the infant while separated from him; expressing milk to relieve engorgement and maintain supply, but discarding the milk; and partially weaning the infant, continuing to nurse to a limited degree. A few mothers are even electing to leave their infants with other nursing mothers who wet-nurse the child in his mother's absence.[71] In any case, delaying the return to employment for at least 2 months postpartum to allow lactation to become well established and for mothers to adjust physically and emotionally after delivery will enhance success of her working–nursing endeavor.

Preparation. When accurate, practial information is available, nursing mothers who will be returning to work can begin to prepare early for nursing and working.[72,73] In the early weeks postpartum, when milk supplies are usually generous and engorgement is common, women can be taught to express excess milk and freeze it for future use. Since milk supplies usually decline under the stress of work outside the home, having a "stockpile" of frozen milk can bolster the mother's confidence. Frozen milk can be kept for approximately 2 weeks in the freezer compartment of the refrigerator and for several months in the deep freezer. When more milk is expressed, it can be layered onto the frozen milk after it is first refrigerated for half an hour to chill it.

A mother should practice her method of expression, either hand, manual pump, or electric pump, prior to returning to work, so that the mechanics of expressing milk are well established. She should enlist the support of her husband and baby-sitter who need to appreciate the value of her efforts. She should confront her employer well in advance with her intentions and obtain his approval for her plans, (i.e., arrange to combine two 15-min coffee breaks into one 30-min "lactation break"). In fact, in a recent review of international legislation establishing nursing breaks, the majority of countries surveyed have specific legislation providing lactation breaks for nursing mothers during the working day.[74] Health professionals can be instrumental in conveying to employers the value of breast-feeding and emphasizing the societal compromises necessary to facilitate lactation on a broad scale. Thus, a letter to an employer on appropriate letterhead requesting his cooperation in permitting a nursing employee to maintain lactation may positively influence his response to individual requests. Despite "lip service" to the breast, the cultural climate which objected to a woman firefighter nursing her infant on her "personal time" must be changed before women can escape the "Catch-22" into which a nursing–working mother may be thrust.

Women should not be encouraged to omit feedings prior to the return to employment because the stress, hassle, worry, and fatigue that plague all working mothers usually combine to diminish milk supply, and overabundant milk production is seldom a problem. Rather, women should be encouraged to enjoy nursing at home as long and as normally as possible. It is useful, however, to introduce the infant to an artificial nipple if bottle feedings are to be used. Infants frequently prefer the bottle nipple which most closely resembles the pacifier nipple to which they already are accustomed. Many women select one of the orthodontic nipples, alleged to resemble the breast nipple, thus hoping to avoid a preference for bottle feedings in the infant. The bottle nipple is invariably better accepted from another caretaker than from the mother herself. An infant who will not accept the nipple when he is frantically hungry may cooperate in learning a new method of feeding when he is alert and content. Expressed breast milk can be offered by bottle twice a week after the first several weeks to maintain the infant's acceptance of the rubber nipple. While an infant can be abruptly coerced into bottle feedings with only a few days of unhappy resistance, this "cold turkey" method is particularly difficult for the mother as she returns to work amid many concerns.

Facilities. The ideal nursing–working situation includes child care at the place of employment, with periodic mother–infant contact throughout the workday. Despite scattered successful models in this country, child care provisions, structured lactation breaks, electric pumps, and other specific aids are generally unheard of. Yet, when mothers and infants are separated for long periods during the work day, adequate facilities are necessary to express milk at regular intervals and safely store it for later use. The setting should be private and comfortable and include facilities for cleaning any equipment used and storing milk. Actual settings utilized vary from private offices, to common lounges, to bathroom stalls.

Helpful Hints. Numerous helpful suggestions can be made to the nursing–working mother. She should be encouraged to drink additional fluids at work, as this routine is often neglected. Since many commuters spend considerable time in a car, nutritious snacks, such as nuts, dried fruit, and canned juice should be available while traveling. If the infant is traveling in the car as well, an approved infant car restraint is paramount. The letdown of milk while pumping can be enhanced by keeping a picture of the baby handy, or occasionally using Syntocinon nasal spray. Milk leakage can be managed with the use of breast shields, but milk collected in the shields throughout the day should not be used for feeding the infant. Diminishing milk supplies can be improved by extra night nursing and exclusive nursing on weekends. One should never pump instead of nurse in an attempt to build up milk stores. Nursing will almost always be more effective than any pump in stimulating further milk supply. An insulated container, or small cooler with ice, can be brought each day to keep expressed milk cold if no refrigeration is available. Refrigerated milk can be left at the baby-sitter's at the end of the day for the next day's feeding. Milk expressed at work on Friday should be frozen until Monday.

Women working outside the home still do most of household chores, so housework must assume a lowered priority and the mother should be encouraged to adjust her standards accordingly or obtain outside help. To avoid the inevitable rush each morning and frenetic dash to work, many women choose to set their alarm 20 min early and bring the baby into bed to nurse before arising to get ready. Then the infant can be "topped off" at the sitter's before the mother leaves for work.

Conclusions. In evaluating the success of working and nursing, more emphasis should be placed on the nursing relationship than on the specific quantity of milk produced. Coming home and sitting down to nurse with her feet elevated can be a pleasant wind-down from a mother's hectic day. At every opportunity, health professionals should reinforce the mother's efforts, stress the success of her endeavor and "incise and drain" guilt which plagues nearly all working mothers. Finally, professionals should continue to work toward longer maternity leaves, child care at the place of employment, and lactation breaks during the working day, so that infant feeding recommendations can become feasible for the vast majorty of women and babies.

Further investigation is needed to examine the contribution of employment outside the home to early weaning, the practicality of child care facilities at places of employment, and the effects on young infants of maternal employment.

Six Months

Teething

Although the presence of teeth does not preclude breast-feeding, teething can be a nuisance to the nursing mother and has caused many women to wean. Biting or chewing the nipple often occurs with teething, but can be managed by sharply telling the infant "no" and removing the breast. Biting cannot occur during active nursing, as the tongue overlies the lower teeth. It usually occurs after the bulk of the milk has been obtained and the infant is restless or playful. It is wise during this stage to remove the breast after rhythmic sucking has stopped and move the infant to the second breast. Most infants quickly learn the unacceptability of biting through tone of voice. Smiling or laughing at the cuteness of this antic will only prolong the unpleasant behavior.

Night Nursing

Night nursing is still normal at this age, although some women will be frustrated by continued awakening at night. Other infants who have begun to sleep through the night may begin to awaken at this time as part of normal separation anxiety.

Nursing Strike

Nursing strike is an uncommon phenomenon in which the infant simply refuses to nurse for no apparent reason. It typically occurs at 4 to 7 months of age. The infant may cry whenever put to the breast, arch his back, pull away and essentially reject the breast. Although some women may simply report that their infant "weaned himself at four months," others are alarmed at the prospect of being unable to nurse and seek advice from friends or professionals.

At first appearance, the nursing strike usually occurs suddenly and without cause. Upon more careful examination, however, one or more precipitating factors can almost always be elicited. Some infants begin this unusual behavior during the course of an upper respiratory infection, where nursing creates acute distress because of nasal obstruction. Other infants become aware of a gradually declining milk supply and impaired letdown and become frustrated by the increased effort of nursing. Sometimes the behavior coincides with the onset of teething and apparent discomfort while sucking. Nursing strike seems to be more common when the mother has offered some supplemental bottles and has subtly begun the process of weaning, or has scolded the nursing child for biting, or has hastened feedings because of other activities.

After reviewing the nursing history and determining the presence of exacerbating factors and the level of motivation to return to nursing, the following suggestions can be made. The mother should attempt to nurse the child in his sleep. Most infants will do this, although some may cry upon awakening. Eventually, the infant may awaken and continue to nurse. Some mothers have found they could nurse while walking with the infant. Bottles should be avoided if at all possible. In the presence of an upper respiratory infection, the infant should be nursed after the nasal passages have been cleared with a bulb syringe. When there is a question of diminished milk supply, the mother should express milk or pump her breasts to increase the supply. With reassurance, a commitment to nursing, the temporary abandoning of other methods of infant feeding, and the general approach of nursing the infant in his sleep, most of these infants can be induced to nurse once again.

Nine Months

By 9 months of age, infants' nursing styles vary greatly from the earlier "no nonsense" nursing. Infants may nurse sporadically, or become impatient for the milk to letdown, or become easily distracted and pull the nipple with them as they turn their head to investigate something. Late onset mastitis may occur from the nipple trauma and irregularity of nursing. Nursing becomes exaggerated during minor illnesses, fatigue, and times of stress, and the emotional attachment to the breast becomes stronger for some infants. Others gradually lose interest in nursing and prefer feeding themselves finger foods and sipping from a cup. The gradual transition from nutritional nursing to psychological nursing becomes more obvious at this time. The health professional should continue to provide support to the mother when nursing continues to be enjoyable to both her and the infant. Many women experience various degress of negative feedback from friends and relatives who inquire: "Are you *still* nursing?" Professional assurance that breast milk continues to provide significant nutritional benefits to the infant throughout the first year should be offered.

Twelve Months

By 12 months, many mothers will seek advice about weaning. Weaning should be viewed as a gradual process, dictated by the baby's needs, and the maternal ambivalence frequently accompanying weaning should be recognized and accepted. Initially, as weaning occurs, feedings in which the child holds least interest will be eliminated, and those with special significance, such as before naps and bedtime, will persist. A cup or bottle can be substituted in place of the usual nursing, depending on the age of the infant.

Late Nursing

Nursing can be likened to the use of a pacifier, thumb, comforter, or stuffy that has special meaning to the baby and facilitates his ability to calm himself and ultimately separate from his mother. All children eventually wean themselves, and the history of nursing throughout the ages suggests the normal full course of breast-feeding, with its constantly evolving pattern and mutual interaction, lasts into the third year. Among approximately 50 societies and cultures studied, the mean age for structured weaning was $2\frac{1}{2}$ years.[75,76] The gradual nature of the weaning process is best illustrated by the expression: "You never know when the last nursing has occurred." Days or even weeks may elapse between nursings at the very end. Obviously, the volume of milk is inconsequential at this stage. A nursing may last only a few seconds, as the youngster reassures himself of the mother's presence and love.

Late nursing is increasing among American infants, as more mothers adhere to baby-led weaning. As the clinician assesses the impact of nursing the older baby, he will want to consider the feelings of both parents toward nursing, the child's ability to separate from the mother in other settings, the mother's time spent with the child in other forms of close interaction and play, and the role boredom may play in the extent of nursing. When nursing seems to preoccupy the child and interfere with the parents' own interactions, then structured weaning may be indicated. Distraction techniques, cuddling and hugging without nursing, or periods of separation between mother and child may all be recommended. Abrupt weaning is almost always more difficult for both mother and baby than gradual weaning.

It is important for the clinician to recognize the maternal significance of nursing, the sense of fulfillment, accomplishment, and value she attaches to the nursing relationship. Although weaning is simply one of the many phases of separation between mother and infant, it represents a loss for many women. Untimely weaning, in particular, when an infant stops nursing abruptly or health professionals or circumstances impose weaning on a mother, can linger as an unresolved loss, the significance of which is seldom appreciated by the professional.

Nursing through Pregnancy

As gradual weaning grows in popularity, more women are still nursing when they discover they are pregnant again. Some mothers use conception as an impetus to wean, while others elect to nurse through the pregnancy, and a few even continue to nurse the older child once the new infant is born. The author is aware of one woman who has lactated continuously for 13 years, through six pregnancies. In rural Bangladesh, insufficient milk supply secondary to pregnancy, is a frequently cited reason for premature weaning.[77] No data is available on the quality and quantity of milk produced during pregnancy in Western mothers.

Anecdotal reports from mothers, as well as articulated observations of older babies themselves, suggest that milk volume declines within weeks or months of superimposed pregnancy, and the appearance of milk may more closely resemble colostrum. Some women, however, state that their babies nurse throughout the pregnancy without any indication that their milk has changed.

The onset of exquisite nipple tenderness during pregnancy is commonly reported. This nipple pain, coupled with increasing difficulty positioning a nursing toddler on the gravid abdomen, prompts many women to wean. Although there are no data which specifically contraindicate nursing through a pregnancy, hypothetical effects of oxytocin on an irritable uterus or the presence of the hormones of pregnancy in the milk warrant consideration. In most instances, pregnancy occurs after the older infant has started weaning foods and is no longer solely breast-fed. Failure to thrive in an exclusively breast-fed young infant could result from superimposed pregnancy if breast milk supply indeed declines. For this reason, whenever failure to thrive occurs in a breast-fed infant, one should inquire about possible pregnancy in the mother.

Tandem nursing, or the nursing of two siblings who are not twins, does not occur commonly, but is increasingly encountered. Tandem nursing requires much maternal understanding and patience to prioritize each baby's needs. While postpartum engorgement may be minimized by nursing both the newborn and older sibling, some mothers complain that "after pains" are more severe. When the new infant's suck is weak, the older baby can be effective in stimulating adequate milk production, but care must be exercised to assure that the younger infant has first access to the milk supply. An older baby may be jealous of the new infant and compete for nursing privileges. While tandem nursing is comfortable for many mothers and appears to meet the needs of both babies, the psychological implications of the practice have not yet been studied.

CONCLUSION

As breast-feeding continues to increase in prevalence, and while traditional support systems for new mothers remain generally unavailable, health professionals will be expected to provide appropriate guidance throughout the full course of lactation. Increased access to prenatal information, reexamination of intrapartum hospital practices, and restructuring of infant health maintenance visits will be required in most clinical settings if optimal infant feeding recommendations are to be put into widespread practice. Societal and cultural changes which encourage comfortable exposure to breast-feeding in the media, close maternal–infant contact throughout the nursing period, and more realistic demands upon new mothers will be necessary in order for "token" breast-feeding to give away to "natural" infant feeding and mothering.

Sir Astley Cooper astutely observed the primary causes of unsuccessful breast-feeding in 1845, still identifiable nearly a century and a half later:

> Some women are prevented from suckling by want of milk; some by want of strength; some from a deficiency of the nipple; but too frequently it is the result of caprice, the fear of trouble, the dread of spoiling the figure, and from anxiety to avoid the confinement which it enforces. . . .[78]

To combat maternal misinformation and isolation and in order to facilitate successful breast-feeding, the following guidelines for medical practice are suggested:

1. Provide knowledge and support prenatally, through information and affiliation with support groups.
2. Perform prenatal examination of the breasts to provide reassurance or detect abnormalities and institute therapy.
3. Encourage prenatal nipple preparation and expression of colostrum in the last month of pregnancy to help women become comfortable handling their breasts.
4. Enhance early nursing after delivery, provide easy access to the baby, foster breast-feeding on demand, and avoid unnecessary supplementation in the newborn nursery.
5. Assess the success of nursing at the time of discharge, and either defer discharge if breast-feeding is not adequate or provide close follow-up in the office or home.
6. Provide contact within 48 hr after discharge, and appoint primiparas to the office earlier than 2 weeks.
7. Encourage the establishment of an appropriate feeding schedule that fosters good milk supply in the first weeks postpartum.
8. Increase the frequency of visits for infants of primiparas and whenever any signs of breast-feeding difficulties arise.
9. Offer age-related anticipatory guidance for common breast-feeding questions and concerns.
10. Provide encouragement and practical information for nursing mothers returning to employment outside the home.

Despite the effort involved, numerous health professionals have begun to recognize that the successful management of breast-feeding can be one of the most rewarding aspects of the care of infants and mothers.

REFERENCES

1. American Academy of Pediatrics, Committee on Nutrition, 1976, Commentary on breast-feeding and infant formulas, including proposed standards for formulas, *Pediatrics* **57**:278–285.

2. *Infant Nutrition—A Foundation for Lasting Health?*, 1977, Iowa Infant Nutrition Symposium, Health Learning Systems.
3. American Academy of Pediatrics, Committee on Nutrition, and Canadian Paediatric Society Nutrition Committee, 1978, Breastfeeding, *Pediatrics* **62:**591–601.
4. American Academy of Pediatrics, Task Force on the Promotion of Breast-Feeding, 1982, The promotion of breast-feeding, *Pediatrics* **69:**654–661.
5. American Academy of Pediatrics, Committee on Nutrition, 1980, Encouraging breast-feeding, *Pediatrics* **65:**657–658.
6. Martinez, G. A. and Nalezienski, J. P., 1981, 1980 update: The recent trend in breastfeeding, *Pediatrics* **67:**260–263.
7. Starling, J., Fergusson, D. M., Horwood, L. J., and Taylor, B., 1979, Breast-feeding success and failure, *Aust. Paediatr. J.* **15:**271–274.
8. De Castro, F. J., 1968, Decline of breastfeeding, *Clin. Pediatr.* **7:**703.
9. Bacon, C. J. and Wylie, J. M., 1976, Mothers' attitudes to infant feeding at Newcastle General Hospital in summer 1975, *Br. Med. J.* **1:**308–309.
10. Davies, D. P., 1976, Why do women stop breastfeeding?, *Lancet* **1:**420–421.
11. Cole, J., 1977, Breastfeeding in the Boston suburbs in relation to personal–social factors, *Clin. Pediatr.* **16:**352–356.
12. Coles, E. C., Cotter, S., and Valman, H. B., 1978, Increasing prevalence of breast feeding, *Br. Med. J.* **2:**1122.
13. Ladas, A. K., 1970, How to help mothers breastfeed, *Clin. Pediatr.* **9:**702–705.
14. Eastham, E., Smith, D., Poole, D. and Neligan, G., 1976, Further decline of breast-feeding, *Br. Med. J.* **1:**305–307.
15. Berger, L. R., 1978, Factors influencing breast feeding, *J. Continuing Education Pediatr.* 13–29.
16. Weichert, C., 1975, Breast-feeding: First thoughts, *Pediatrics* **56:**987–990.
17. La Leche League International, Inc., 1981, *The Womanly Art of Breastfeeding*, 3rd ed., Interstate Publishers, Franklin Park, Illinois.
18. Eiger, M. S. and Olds, S. W., 1972, *The Complete Book of Breastfeeding*, Workman Publishing Co., Inc, New York.
19. Pryor, K., 1973, *Nursing Your Baby*, Harper and Row Publishers, Inc., New York.
20. Ewy, D. and Ewy, R., 1975, *Preparation for Breast Feeding*, Doubleday and Co., Inc., New York.
21. Applebaum, R., 1969, *Abreast of the Times*, ICEA Supplies Center, Bellevue, Washington.
22. Gerard, A., 1972, *Please Breast-Feed Your Baby*, New American Library, Inc., New York.
23. Stanway, P. and Stanway, A., 1978, *Breast Is Best*, Pan Original, London.
24. Phillips, V., 1976, *Successful Breast-Feeding*, Nursing Mothers' Association of Australia, Melbourne.
25. Applebaum, R. M., 1975, The obstetrician's approach to the breasts and breastfeeding, *J. Reprod. Med.* **14:**98–116.
26. Hoffman, J. B., 1953, A suggested treatment for inverted nipples, *Am. J. Obstet. Gynecol.* **66:**346–348.
27. Otte, M. J., 1975, Correcting inverted nipples, *Am. J. Nur.* **75:**454–456.
28. Waller, H., 1946, The early failure of breast feeding, *Arch. Dis. Child.* **21:**1–12.
29. Farina, M. A., Newby, B. G., and Alani, H. M., 1980, Innervation of the nipple-areola complex, *Plast. Reconstruct. Surg.* **66:**497–501.
30. Shrand, H., 1961, Thrush in the newborn, *Br. Med. J.* **2:**1530–1533.
31. Brown, M. S. and Hurlock, J. T., 1975, Preparation of the breast for breastfeeding, *Nurs. Res.* **24:**448–451.
32. Waller, H., 1957, *The Breasts and Breast Feeding*, Heinemann Medical Books, London.
33. Newton, M. and Newton, N., 1962, The normal course and management of lactation, *Clin. Obstet. Gynecol.* **5:**44–63.
34. Applebaum, R. M., 1970,The modern management of successful breastfeeding, *Pediatr. Clin. North Am.* **17:**203–225.

35. Winikoff, B. and Baer, E. C., 1980, The obstetrician's opportunity: Translating "breast is best" from theory to practice, *Am. J. Obstet. Gynecol.* **138:**105–117.
36. Lozoff, B., Brittenham, G. M., Trause, M. A., Kennel, J. H., and Klaus, M. H., 1977, The mother–newborn relationship: Limits of adaptability, *J. Pediatr.* **91:**1–12.
37. de Chateau, P., Holmberg, H., Jakobsson, K., and Winberg, J., 1977, A study of factors promoting and inhibiting lactation, *Develop. Med. Child. Neurol.* **19:**575–584.
38. Johnson, N. W., 1976, Breast-feeding at one hour of age, *Am. J. Mat. Child. Nurs.* **1:**12.
39. Aldrich, C. A. and Hewitt, E. S., 1947, Self-regulating feeding program for infants, *JAMA* **135:**340–342.
40. Illingworth, R. S., Stone, D. C. H., Jowett, G. H., and Scott, J. F., 1952, Self-demand feeding in a maternity unit, *Lancet* **1:**683–687.
41. Olmstead, R. W. and Jackson, E. B., 1950, Self-demand feeding in the first week of life, *Pediatrics* **6:**396–401.
42. Beske, E. J. and Garvis, M. S., 1982, Important factors in breast-feeding success, *Am. J. Maternal Child Nurs.* **7:**174–179.
43. Jackson, E. B., Wilkin, L. C., and Auerbach, H., 1956, Statistical report on incidence and duration of breastfeeding in relation to personal social and hospital maternity factors, *Pediatrics* **17:**700–713.
44. Bjerre, J. and Ekelund, H., 1970, Breastfeeding and post-partum care, *Acta. Paediatr. (Uppsala)* **206**(Suppl.):125–126.
45. McBryde, A., 1951, Compulsory rooming-in on the ward and private newborn service at Duke Hospital, *JAMA* **145:**625–628.
46. Sloper, K., McKean, L., and Baum, J. D., 1975, Factors influencing breast feeding, *Arch. Dis. Child.* **50:**165–170.
47. Gillie, L., 1976, Difficulties and discouragements encountered by mothers, *J. Hum. Nutr.* **30:**248–252.
48. Bergevin, Y., Kramer, M., and Dougherty, C., 1981, Do infant formula samples affect the duration of breast-feeding? A randomized controlled trial, Presented at the Annual Meeting of the Ambulatory Pediatric Association, San Francisco, May 1, 1981.
49. Ganelin, R. S., Rapp, E., and Gardner, J., 1981, The effort of an educational and support program for breast feeding among inner city residents, Presented at the Annual Meeting of the Ambulatory Pediatric Association, San Francisco, May 1, 1981.
50. Salariya, E. M., Easton, P. M., and Cater, J. L., 1978, Duration of breast feeding after early initiation and frequent feeding, *Lancet* **2:**1141–1143.
51. Applebaum, R. M., 1975, Techniques of breast-feeding, *J. Trop. Pediatr. Environ. Child. Health* **21:**273–279.
52. Howie, P. W., Houston, M. J., Cook, A., Smart, L., McArdle, T., and McNeilly, A. S., 1981, How long should a breast feed last? *Early Hum. Develop.* **5:**71–77.
53. Fleet, I. R. and Peaker, M., 1978, Mammary function and its control at the cessation of lactation in the goat, *J. Physiol.* **279:**491–507.
54. Dahms, B. B., Krauss, A. N., Gartner, L. M., Klain, D. B., Soodalter, J., and Auld, P. A. M., 1973, Breast-feeding and serum bilirubin values during the first 4 days of life, *J. Pediatr.* **83:**1049–1054.
55. Saul, K. and Warburton, D., 1981, Increased incidence of early onset hyperbilirubinemia in breast fed vs. bottle fed infants, *Clin. Res.* **29:**(1):144A.
56. Fisher, Q., Cohan, M. I., Curda, L., and McNamara, H., 1978, Jaundice and breast-feeding among Alaskan Eskimo newborns, *Am. J. Dis. Child.* **132:**859–861.
57. Konner, M. and Worthman, C., 1980, Nursing frequency, gonadal function, and birth spacing among ¡Kung hunter-gatherers, *Science* **207:**788–791.
58. Raphael, D., 1973, *The Tender Gift: Breastfeeding*, Schocken Books, New York.
59. Foman, S. J., Filer, L. J., Thomas, L. N., and Rogers, R. R., 1970, Growth and serum chemical values of normal breast-fed infants, *Acta. Paediatr. Scand.* **202:**(Suppl.):1–20.
60. Newton, N. R. and Newton, M. A., 1956, Relation of the let-down reflex to the ability to breastfeed, *Pediatrics* **5:**726–733.

61. Caldeyro-Barcia, R., 1969, Milk ejection in women, in: *Lactogenesis, The Initiation of Milk Secretion at Parturition*, University of Pennsylvania Press, Philadelphia, p. 229–243.
62. Newton, M. and Newton, N. R., 1948, The let-down reflex in human lactation, *J. Pediatr.* **33:**698–704.
63. McNeilly, A. S. and McNeilly, J. R., 1978, Spontaneous milk ejection during lactation and its possible relevance to success of breast-feeding, *Br. Med. J.* **2:**466–468.
64. Egli, G. E., Egli, N. S., and Newton, M., 1961, The influence of the number of breast feedings on milk production, *Pediatrics* **27:**314–317.
65. Lucas, A., Lucas, P. J., and Baum, J. D., 1979, Pattern of milk flow in breast-fed infants, *Lancet* **2:**57–58.
66. Ahn, C. H. and MacLean, W. C., 1980, Growth of the exclusively breast-fed infant, *Am. J. Clin. Nutr.* **33:**183–192.
67. Foman, S. J., 1975, What are infants fed in the United States? *Pediatrics* **56:**350–354.
68. Zambrana, R. E., Hurst, M., and Hite, R. L., 1979, The working mother in contemporary perspective: A review of the literature, *Pediatrics* **64:**862–870.
69. Van Esterik, P. and Greiner, T., 1981, Breastfeeding and women's work: Constraints and opportunities, *Stud. Fam. Plann.* **12:**184–197.
70. Report on the WHO Collaborative Study on Breast-Feeding, 1981, *Contemporary Patterns of Breast-Feeding*, WHO, Geneva, p. 150.
71. Krantz, J. Z. and Kupper, N. S., 1981, Cross-nursing: Wet-nursing in a contemporary context, *Pediatrics* **67:**715–717.
72. Christoffel, K. K., Clark, A. V., Esterly, N., Koval, J., Ruiz, B., Chandler, A. B., Doane, B., Chacko, ·D., and Elson, S., 1981, Advice from breast-feeding mothers, *Pediatrics* **68:**141–142.
73. Salomon, M., Schauf, V., and Seiden, A., 1977, Breastfeeding, "natural mothering", and working outside the home, in: *21st Century Obstetrics Now!*, Volume 2 (D. Stewart and L. Stewart, eds.), NAPSAC, Inc., Chapel Hill, p. 475–506.
74. Richardson, J. L., 1975, Review of international legislation establishing nursing breaks, *J. Trop. Pediatr. Environ. Child. Health* **21:**249–258.
75. Ford, C. S., 1945, *A Comparative Study of Human Reproduction*, Publications in Anthropology #32, Yale University Press, New Haven.
76. Whiting, J. W. and Child, I. L., 1953, *Child Training and Personality: A Cross-Cultural Study*, Yale University Press, New Haven.
77. Huffman, S. L., Chowdhury, A. K. M. A., Chakraborty, J., and Simpson, N. K., 1980, Breast-feeding patterns in rural Bangladesh, *Am. J. Clin. Nutr.* **33:**144–154.
78. Cooper, A., 1845, *The Anatomy and Diseases of the Breast with Surgical Papers*, Lea and Blanchard, Philadelphia, p. 94.

10

Infant Problems in Breast-Feeding

Marianne R. Neifert

Empirical contraindications to breast-feeding long antedate modern medicine. In ancient Greek societies, upper-class women were discouraged from nursing if their labor had been particularly difficult, and colostrum was often considered unsuitable for feeding during the first several days of life.[1] Soranus' advice for selecting a wet nurse stressed that the personal characteristics and appearance of the woman, in addition to the appearance of her milk, were major determinants of breast-feeding capabilities.[2] In modern times, employment outside the home, social activities required by the husband's job, any chronic illness in the mother, or the necessity for supplemental formula have been cited as contraindications to nursing.[3] Within the past decade, post partum fever, maternal mastitis,[4] prematurity of the infant, drug therapy in the mother, and even resumption of menstruation, have been suggested, often inappropriately, to contraindicate breast-feeding.

On the other hand, a false notion, current among breast-feeding enthusiasts, is "every woman can nurse." While this philosophy is useful in combating the professional tendency to wean at the slightest obstacle, it appears likely that 1 to 5% of women experience lactation failure on a physiologic basis. Even in the absence of viable infant feeding alternatives, breast-feeding has never enjoyed 100% success. Recognizing that every organ in the human body experiences pathology (i.e., infertility, miscarriage, and birth defects are accepted reproductive risk factors), it is simplistic to assume that there are no physiologic failures of breast-feeding. While attempting to identify the small percentage of women with an organic basis for lactation failure or infants for whom breast-feeding is truly contraindicated, it is equally important to acknowledge that the vast majority of lactation problems are based simply on inappropriate feeding regimes, or inadequate knowledge, support, or confidence. The clinician must, therefore, walk a fine line

Marianne R. Neifert • Department of Pediatrics. University of Colorado School of Medicine, Denver Colorado 80262.

between identifying physiologically based lactation failure in the few, while emphasizing the ability to nurse successfully for the many.

In this chapter, clinical problems of lactation affecting infants will be addressed. Nursing in the face of maternal illness is covered in the chapter that follows. Despite the lack of accurate information about nursing in the presence of clinical problems in the infant, more and more mothers are seeking professional help in establishing and maintaining lactation in unique situations.[5,6] Mothers who have opted for breast-feeding, and especially those who view nursing as a form of mothering, are often reluctant to relinquish breast-feeding when infant health problems are encountered. In such cases, not only may breast milk be important nutritionally, but breast-feeding may also provide a means for fostering attachment to an ill or defective infant. It must be remembered that little solid research is available for many of these issues, so that much of the information presented must, of necessity, be based on clinical experience.

THE PREMATURE OR SICK NEWBORN

Over 100,000 times a year in this country, an infant is born prematurely, often amid his parents' grief and guilt. Not yet prepared for the birth of a child, and having to compete with health professionals for his care and well-being, they feel ignorant and impotent. While premature infants represent the largest group of high-risk newborns, up to 15% of pregnancies are considered "high-risk" and result in some prolongation of mother–infant separation.[7] Disturbances in attachment following early mother–infant separation were first noted by Budin who specialized in premature infant care.[8] An increased incidence of abuse and neglect among infants discharged from an intensive care nursery has recently been reported.[9] Infants whose families had little contact in the nursery were at greater risk for maltreatment. The parents' desire to contribute to their infant's care by providing expressed breast milk for his feedings might help foster attachment and serve as an anchor for immediate tasks and long-range hopes. For this reason, the management of the use of mothers' own milk for feeding premature infants is discussed here in detail.

Advantages of Human Milk in Feeding Preterm Infants

Nutritionally, the use of human milk in feeding preterm infants, particularly those weighing less than 1300 g, remains controversial because breast milk delivers lower levels of many nutrients than those infants would have obtained via the placenta and deemed necessary to achieve postnatal growth at intrauterine rates.[10–13] Specific nutritional deficiencies of protein,[14] sodium,[15] calcium,[16] and phosphate[17–18] have been documented in exclusively breast-fed infants. Several recent studies show that milk expressed by mothers of preterm infants contains higher concentrations of nitrogen,[19] protein, sodium,[20] chloride, and calcium[21] than milk produced by mothers of term infants, although the adequacy of the mother's own milk for feeding the rapidly growing, very-low-birth-weight infant has not been documented. In one recent study of premature infants fed their own mother's milk, the observed growth rate was comparable to that of infants fed 24-calorie-per-ounce formula, while prematures fed mature donor milk grew more slowly.[22] Presumably, breast milk can be supplemented with appropriate nutrients to prevent recognized deficiencies in infants, while retaining the advantages of human milk. In fact, several clinical trials have recently been undertaken in which breast milk was supplemented with human milk protein concentrate[23,24] to prevent hypoproteinemia. Unique differences in breast milk protein quality have been suggested to have metabolic advantages for the premature infant,[25–27] making human-milk-based feedings attractive.

The numerous immunological components of human milk, detailed in Chapter 8 convey several nonnutritional advantages, none of which is offered by proprietary formulas. While their role in protecting the term infant from illness is still being elucidated, it is likely that the preterm infant is an even more appropriate recipient of these factors. Recent data have shown significantly higher concentrations of secretory IgA in milk from mothers delivering preterm infants throughout the first month postpartum.[28] In a controlled prospective study of 62 high-risk, low-birth-weight infants in New Delhi, 5 deaths attributed to infection occurred among 31 infants fed standard formula, while no deaths occurred among the infants fed expressed breast milk, primarily from their own mother.[29] Indeed, a "colostrum cocktail" has been proposed as the first feeding for all prematures.[30] Much interest remains in the possible role of fresh breast milk in protecting against neonatal necrotizing enterocolitis.[31–35] Current evidence suggests, therefore, that there are psychological, nutritional, and immunological advantages favoring the use of an infant's own mother's milk for the feeding of prematures, although it remains likely that supplementation with calcium, phosphorus, sodium, and protein will be necessary during the period of rapid growth of the very small premature.

Initiating Breast-Feeding in the Premature Infant

Despite the advantages cited, breast-feeding the premature should never be urged unless the parents choose to undertake the endeavor. The clinician must be aware of the degree of motivation, time, effort, and external support that will be required and should present the information to the parents without bias. The birth of a premature infant generates a sense of guilt and failure in many women, some of whom are unable to risk failing again so soon by attempting to breast-feed. A fine balance must be struck between giving permission to decline or discontinue efforts when a mother's resources are exhausted, while providing adequate encouragement and practical information when breast-feeding is truly desired. Defining success individually, promoting maternal confidence and preventing long-term feelings of guilt and disappointment should be foremost in mind when counseling a mother.

When the decision to breast-feed is confirmed, practical information for establishing and maintaining a milk supply is required because relatively few women delivering prematurely have any preparation even for routine breast-feeding. Breast stimulation by manual or mechanical expression of milk should begin as soon as the mother can cooperate. Unfortunately, many mothers of premature infants are physically ill in the immediate postpartum period, while others are so emotionally debilitated by the impact of prematurity, that they are unable to focus on the mechanics of milk expression. If efforts are delayed beyond the period of engorgement, significant involution of the mammary epithelium may occur, compromising milk yield. It should be stressed, however, that many women have managed to establish adequate milk supplies despite having been given agents to suppress lactation or having delayed breast stimulation for up to several weeks.[36]

Various methods of disseminating information about expressing and handling milk are in use. Printed information,[37] teaching videotapes,* graduate mothers whose infants were once in the nursery, lactation counselors, patient care coordinators, and premature parenthood groups are all possible means of providing knowledge and support. It is necessary for a successful program that the entire staff view breast-feeding as a high priority and provide parents with prompt information, access to pumping equipment, comfortable and private facilities for expressing milk, and availability of rooming-in during the period of transition from pumping milk to nursing the infant directly.[38]

Methods of Expressing Milk

Mothers should be made aware of the variety of methods available for expressing milk and allow convenience, cost, and personal preference to direct their choice.[38,39] It is desirable to obtain from each mother a history of current and past illnesses, including infectious diseases, and recent medications prior to feeding her milk to the infant. Careful handwashing should preceed any method of expression and gentle breast massage for a few minutes is thought to enhance blood flow, facilitate letdown, and relieve engorged areas.

The oldest and most time-tested method of expressing milk is the manual technique, requiring no special equipment. The Marmet technique is especially effective. With this method, the thumb is placed above and the first two fingers below the nipple, 1 to $1\frac{1}{2}$ inches behind the nipple, so the lactiferous sinuses lie beneath them. Pressure is applied toward the chest wall, and then the thumb and fingers are rolled forward, as if making thumb

---

* "Breast-Feeding Your Premature Newborn," a teaching videotape, Department of Biomedical Communications (A-066), University of Colorado Health Sciences Center, 4200 E. Ninth Avenue, Denver, CO 80262, (303) 394-7342.

and fingerprints at the same time. The procedure should be repeated rhythmically, first positioning the fingers, pushing, then rolling. The thumb and finger positions should be rotated around the breast to milk the other reservoirs.[40] Manual expression is easier to learn if it is practiced in conjunction with a spontaneous letdown reflex. Once mastered, milk should jet from the breast in several streams. When flow tapers to a trickle, the procedure is repeated with the other breast. With all expression techniques, the woman should return to each breast at least once to assure complete emptying. The entire procedure should take from 20 to 30 min to complete. Care should be exercised to assure that milk does not run over the index finger as it flows from the breast. While some women prefer manual expression to the use of mechanical devices, others find the method difficult to use over the long-term.

Bulb type manual breast pumps are readily available and inexpensive, but are generally inefficient. Milk is easily contaminated if it is permitted to enter the bulb. To use these pumps, the funnel is centered over the nipple and the bulb is squeezed to generate suction. To relieve the suction, the finger should be inserted beneath the rim of the funnel to break the seal. Bulb pumps that collect milk into a bottle have fewer risks of contamination, but neither type of pump is optimal for long-term use.

The Loyd-B-Pump by LOPUCO is an effective hand pump that has been widely used. A glass shield, or funnel, fits over the nipple to form a seal and is connected to a glass collecting jar. Suction is supplied by a grip handle which is squeezed three or four times to initiate a vacuum and milk flow. Periodically, the vacuum is released and suction reapplied by squeezing the pump body.*

A newer hand pump, the Japanese-made Kanesan Pump, is distributed in the United States as the Breast Milking and Feeding Unit by Happy Family Products. It is relatively inexpensive, efficient, and easy to clean. The pump is comprised of a larger outer cylinder and a smaller inner cylinder attached to a funnel. The funnel is centered over the nipple and the breast is then milked by rhythmically moving the outer cylinder toward, then away from, the body in a gentle piston-like motion. Milk is collected into the outer cylinder, to which a nipple can be attached for bottle feeding, if desired.†

Several electric breast pumps are available in hospital settings, through rental sites or surgical supply shops. Among the most efficient and comfortable of these are the Medela‡ and Egnell** electric pumps. These simulate the physiologic sucking action of the infant, with a suction phase, a rest phase, and a positive pressure phase. For most women, these two pumps

---

* Loyd-B-Pump available from LOPUCO, Ltd., 1615 Old Annapolis Road, Woodbine, MD 21797, (301) 489-4949.
† Available from Happy Family Products, 12300 Venice Boulevard, Los Angeles, CA 90066, (213) 655–7301.
‡ Available from Medela, Inc., 457 Dartmoor Drive, P.O. Box 386, Crystal Lake, IL 60014, (815) 455-6920.
** Available from Egnell, Inc., 765 Industrial Drive, Cary, IL 60013, (312) 639-2900.

offer the most effective method of emptying the breasts and maintaining a milk supply for many weeks.

Other electric pumps are available, ranging from simple, inexpensive models such as the AXicare Pumps* to the exclusive Whittlestone Breast-milker,† which stimulates both breasts at once. Of course, with all breast pumps, as with manual expression, thorough hand washing and cleanliness of all equipment that will come in contact with milk is of great importance.

Maintaining the Milk Supply

Maintenance of the milk supply is largely dependent upon frequent, regular expression of milk. Women commonly overlook the fact that a newborn nursing on demand would typically feed every $2\frac{1}{2}$ to 3 hr around the clock. It is virtually impossible to adhere to such a frequent pumping schedule. Women who visit the nursery daily may spend much time commuting; fatigue and depression inhibit women from pumping at night; the hassle of cleaning equipment, labeling bags, and properly handling milk prompts women to postpone pumping sessions. The initial period of engorgement and a milk supply that often exceeds the demands of the small, sick infant lure women into expressing milk less frequently. Invariably, after the first week or two, milk production begins to decline, often coinciding with the infant's increased milk requirements, and mothers are easily discouraged from continuing their efforts. A history of pumping routines usually reveals that the mother is expressing her milk only three or four times a day and not at all for 12 or more hr at night. While a few fortunate women can continue to produce adequate volumes of milk on this schedule, the majority will experience a progressively diminishing milk supply. The mother should be counseled that increasing the pumping stimulus and limiting the night interval to 6 or 7 hr will increase the milk supply, and that despite limited milk production with expression techniques, she may still be able to breast-feed once the infant is well enough to nurse directly at the breast. Some women find that visiting and touching their infants prior to pumping in the hospital will increase milk yield. A photograph of the infant or a telephone call to the nursery may accomplish the same effect at home. When stress and the use of mechanical devices impair milk letdown, the temporary use of Syntocinon nasal spray may facilitate milk letdown and allow the mother to condition her reflex to the pump. All nursing mothers experience variations in milk supply, but women who express and carefully measure the milk are more conscious of these fluctuations and vulnerable to their negative effects. In addition, any crisis in the infant's clinical course may abruptly diminish milk production.

* AXicare Pump, available from Neonatal Corporation, One Blue Hill Plaza, Pearl River, NY 10965, (914) 735-5075.
† Available from Whittlestone Breastmilkers Ltd., P.O. Box 710, 475 River Road, Hamilton, New Zealand, 52-308 Telex NZ21691.

Surveillance and Storage of Milk

Contamination with microorganisms is a real threat when milk is expressed and stored.[41] It is crucial that the mother wash her hands prior to handling her breasts or any equipment. A daily shower should suffice for breast hygiene, or the nipples can be wiped with plain water prior to expression. All pumping parts that come into contact with milk should be washed carefully with hot soapy water after each use and sterilized by boiling for 10 to 15 min at home once a day. Equipment used in the hospital setting should be sterilized after each use if it is to be interchanged among mothers, and at least once a day if used by a single mother. Gas sterilization is not recommended for plastic parts unless at least 16 hr are allowed for all parts to de-gas.

In general, expressed breast milk contains 10^3 or more colony-forming units per milliliter (cfu/ml) of normal skin flora, such as *Staphylococcus epidermidis*, α-hemolytic streptococci, and diphtheroids.[42-44] Such milk may be fed to infants without obvious ill effect. However, the presence of potential pathogens or highly contaminated milk may pose a threat to the infant, particularly the sick neonate.[41] Milk containing greater than 10^4 cfu/ml of normal flora or greater than 4×10^3 cfu/ml of *Staphylococcus aureus* suggests a significant problem in collection technique.[44] The presence of pathogens, such as β-hemolytic streptococci, or gram-negative enteric rods, such as *Pseudomonas aeruginosa*, should be considered unacceptable.[44,45] Manual expression, when performed correctly, tends to yield relatively clean milk, with colony counts of 2500 cfu/ml or less, whereas milk collected with manual bulb pumps is notoriously unhygienic, with colony counts of 135,000 cfu/ml or more in one study.[43] "Stripping" the breast, or discarding the first 5 to 10 cm^3 of milk, has been shown to greatly diminish bacterial contamination of expressed samples.[46]

Most hospitals utilize some type of surveillance for bacterial contaminants in breast milk, such as initial screening cultures to evaluate the mother's collection technique, or periodic spot checks of breast milk samples. At each institution, clinicians and microbiologists should jointly adopt the precautions necessary to assure that milk is collected and handled hygienically, without making routine surveillance so cumbersome that it delays the feeding of milk to infants.

The goal of milk storage is to minimize microbial contamination, while maximally preserving labile immune components. Although freshly expressed breast milk collected under optimally clean conditions retains nearly all its immunological properties, it is seldom available for regular feeding. Because of regionalization of perinatal care, infants are often hospitalized at great distances from their families. Typically, milk must be expressed and stored at home and brought to the nursery periodically.

Freshly expressed breast milk can be refrigerated for approximately 24 hr at 1 to 5°C, without increase in bacterial contamination and with retained viability of some of its leukocytes.[42,47] Milk which must be stored for longer periods should be frozen at -18 to $-23°C$, or less, at which temperature it can be kept for approximately 3 months.[47] Milk stored in freezer compartments of refrigerators where the temperature is less stable is empirically kept for only 2 to 3 weeks, whereas milk in a deep freezer at more constant temperatures is commonly stored several months. Milk kept at $-70°C$ has been used after even longer periods of storage. Although freezing does destroy white cells, it is the preferred method of long-term storage, because it preserves the other antimicrobial properties, inhibits bacterial growth, and is not thought to appreciably affect the nutritional content of milk.[48,49] Care must be taken to prevent thawing of frozen milk during transport to the hospital by adequately packing it in ice.

Pasteurization of expressed breast milk is commonly used for pooled donor milk, in organized milk banking, and for samples with elevated colony counts. Various immune constituents of milk are destroyed at progressively higher and prolonged temperatures. Included among these heat-labile properties are secretory IgA, lactoferrin, lysozyme, and vitamin-binding proteins. Holder pasteurization, in which milk is heated to $62.5°C$ for 30 min is the generally preferred method of pasteurizing milk. The majority of samples with original colony counts less than 10^6 will be sterilized, and 70 to 80% of secretory IgA will be preserved, although some lactoferrin and water-soluble vitamins will be destroyed.[47,49,50,51] Pasteurization does decrease the high coefficient of fat absorption of fresh breast milk, probably due to heat inactivation of milk lipase.[52]

Optimally, milk would be collected carefully, stored at less than $5°C$, and fed within 24 hr. Whenever freshly expressed milk is available, it should be fed directly to the infant, with refrigerated milk pumped earlier the same day given next priority. In the mother's absence, and when no refrigerated milk is available, frozen milk should be thawed for the infant's feeding. An attempt should be made to utilize the older milk first, avoiding the dilemma of having "outdated milk."

Milk is frequently stored in sterile, plastic bottle bags. Mothers are instructed to pour into each bag the amount of milk which approximates a single feeding, which is determined by ongoing communication with the baby's nurse. Each bag is properly labeled with the baby's name and the date the milk was expressed. The top of the bag should be tightly sealed with a twist tie or tape. One advantage of the plastic bags is that the retrieval of leukocytes from milk samples stored in plastic results in cell counts much higher than samples incubated in glass.[47] A criticism of bottle bags is their possible permeability to freezer odors and risk of being torn by freezer ice.

Plastic 45-ml "volu-feeders" are also commonly used to store milk. If an infant can nipple, he may be fed directly from the volufeeder.

Thawing milk is an important step in handling frozen expressed breast milk, but frequently is carelessly managed. Milk should be thawed quickly under running water or gradually in the refrigerator at $4°C$.[45] It should not be permitted to stand for hours at room temperature nor subjected to extremely hot water which may damage immunological properties. Immersing bags in a bowl of water risks contamination through the tops of the bags which are not water-tight. Some institutions have used microwave ovens to thaw milk, and while microwave thawing is rapid and avoids contamination, very high temperatures may inadvertently be reached, and no data is available on the safety of microwave thawing of frozen milk.

Transition to the Breast

When an infant is required to master bottle feedings prior to being introduced to the breast, he may not accept the breast nipple easily nor make a smooth transition to effective nursing. For this reason, as soon as the infant is capable of sucking, the mother's nipple should be introduced. If there is concern about the infant's ability to coordinate his suck and swallow, the empty breast can be offered after expression of milk. Numerous attempts may be necessary before the infant learns to grasp the nipple correctly and obtain milk, but the mother will appreciate even holding the infant in the nursing position and letting him lick her nipple. Once the baby has demonstrated his ability to suck and swallow smoothly, he can be introduced to the breast for actual feedings. Although it is generally true that nursing requires more effort on the infant's part than bottle feeding, the milk supply and effectiveness of the letdown reflex greatly influence this factor. In the face of a brisk letdown, very little effort is associated with nursing. Early introduction of the breast nipple not only facilitates learning to nurse, but also conveys to the mother that ultimate breast-feeding is an important goal.

When the infant is willing to nurse, but the milk supply is very low after weeks of pumping milk, the Lact-Aid Nursing Trainer® can be used to supplement the infant's intake while he nurses. This device (Fig. 1) permits supplemental formula to be obtained via a thin flexible tubing which is suckled simultaneously with the breast nipple. Adequate intake can be assured at the same time that the mother's milk supply is stimulated and exposure to rubber nipples is avoided. Cleaning of this device is especially important for the premature infant, and instructions accompanying the kit need to be followed carefully.*[8]

The most common problem during the transition period is simply getting the infant to accept the breast nipple and effectively suckle it. It is important for the infant to be awake and alert at the time of the feeding, even if this means permitting some flexibility in his feeding schedule. Some privacy is important for the mother who may feel she is on display. Positioning the infant is critical, with emphasis on his being elevated to the level of the breast and turned completely to face it. The nipple should be made as protractile as possible and pinched to elongate it. Wearing milk cups between feedings or pump expression prior to nursing may enhance nipple protractility. Positive feedback by medical staff can be very important to the mother's

* Lact-Aid Nursing Trainer, 3885 Forest Street, P.O. Box 6861, Denver, CO 80206, (303) 388-4600.

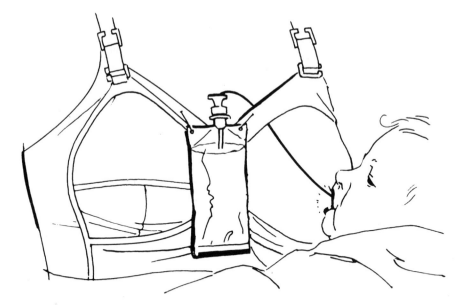

Figure 1. Lact-Aid Nursing Trainer® used to provide supplemental formula simultaneously while breast-feeding. ©Copyright Lact-Aid Service and Supplies Center, reprinted by permission.

confidence. Mothers often feel in competition with the specialized personnel who "mother" their infants, and a word of praise from these "experts" can be very effective.[53]

Follow-Up

Following discharge, some women will have to continue to pump their milk after nursing if the infant's suckling is not effective in emptying the breast. This continued stimulation may be necessary temporarily to assure that the milk supply remains adequate. Close supervision of infant weight will dictate his need for formula supplementation or his ability to nurse more exclusively. A mother should not be forced to make these judgments alone at home. If continued supplementation is required, this should not be viewed as negating the overall success of her efforts. Ongoing support from "graduate moms" can be very helpful during the transition to total breast-feeding.

The broader issue involved in breast-feeding the premature infant lies with the concept that breast-feeding is recommended for many months to a year or more, whereas prematurity is a transient condition. After initial weeks of concerted effort, the mothers of these infants should ultimately enjoy many months of nursing their infants quite naturally. Unfortunately, while many mothers of prematures initiate expression of milk, very few ever nurse at home. Clearly, health professionals need to explore more ways to achieve success for the many women who invest time and effort in this endeavor.

FAILURE TO THRIVE

Among the most frustrating breast-feeding problems facing the clinician is poor weight gain in the infant. Numerous articles and case reports of failure to thrive at the breast have recently appeared,[54–59] implying the increased prevalence of this entity, but little emphasis has been given to identifying etiologies or in maintaining breast-feeding as part of the management of these infants.

Definition

Although failure to thrive in a very young infant is difficult to define within traditional guidelines, the following diagnostic criteria have proved helpful in identifying inadequate weight gain in young breast-fed infants:

1. Failure to regain birth weight by 3 weeks of age
2. Weight loss of greater than 10% of birth weight by 2 weeks of age
3. Deceleration of growth from a previously established pattern of weight gain
4. Evidence of malnutrition on examination, such as minimal subcutaneous fat or wasted buttocks

The clinician should inquire about the course of breast-feeding whenever an infant's rate of weight gain is less than expected. Early diagnosis and institution of a treatment plan are essential if breast-feeding is to be salvaged.

Etiologies of Lactation Failure—Maternal Factors

Lactation failure is most often based on improper interaction between mother and infant either due to inadequate feeding routines or inadequate suckling for some other reason. In these cases, insufficient suckling or poor emptying of the breast leads to impairment of milk supply. Although these problems can often be alleviated with appropriate patient education, other rarer problems are more difficult to diagnose and treat. In this section, maternal factors predisposing to lactation failure are explored, followed by a discussion of infant factors which may lead to failure to thrive on breast milk.

Inadequate Suckling Stimulus Secondary to Inappropriate Feeding Routines

Just as with failure to thrive among bottle-fed infants, the leading cause of poor weight gain among nursing infants is inappropriate feeding technique, often based on inadequate knowledge and inexperience on the part of the mother. In most cases, the suckling stimulus provided by the infant, under the mother's direction, has been insufficient to generate a milk supply adequate to support growth. For example, an uninformed mother may purposely stretch the nursing interval to 4 hr instead of nursing every 2 to 3 hr as recommended for at least the first month. She may temporarily satiate hunger in the infant with sugar water as she was taught in the nursery. She may restrict the duration of feedings due to sore nipples, or else nurse too long on only one breast, after nutritive suckling has ended, bringing an already fatigued infant to the second breast where abundant milk would have awaited him. She may incorrectly expect a newborn to sleep through the night and allow prolonged absences from her infant during the day in the course of her routine activities. Within several weeks, she may note diminished milk letdown, decreased breast fullness, return of her menses, signs of perpetual hunger in her infant, and other evidence that her milk supply is no longer adequate. It is likely that most instances of this common cause of insufficient lactation could be prevented by adequate maternal knowledge and preparation prenatally, the provision of emotional support in the early postpartum weeks, and close medical supervision and follow-up.

Impaired Milk Letdown

Impaired letdown of milk is another frequent cause of inadequate intake by the infant, and shortly leads to accompanying diminished milk supply, due to incomplete emptying of the breast. Normally letdown is perceived by the mother as a "tingling" sensation in the breasts, accompanied by leakage of milk and rapid swallowing by the infant. Newton and Newton documented the role of noxious stimuli in inhibiting milk letdown and limiting the volume of milk delivered to an infant at a feeding,[60] depriving the infant of the higher fat content of hind milk. Furthermore, unrelieved engorgement or poor breast emptying leads to stasis of milk within the alveoli and ultimate atrophy of the mammary epithelium.[61] Frequent causes of impaired letdown are severe or chronic sore nipples and anxiety or stress.

Failure of the Breast to Respond to Appropriate Nursing Stimulus

Less commonly than the above instances, the breast may fail to produce sufficient milk even in the face of an appropriate nursing stimulus. While we are now aware of some of the causes of these cases of "physiologic" lactation failure, the underlying pathology in others has so far eluded the investigator.

Failure of lactogenesis (the onset of copious milk secretion in the early puerperium) has recently been described in a small number of women with retained placental fragments.[62] Presumably, in these cases, the secretion of placental hormones, specifically progesterone, inhibited routine lactogenesis. While the incidence of this phenomenon is unknown, it is possible that the condition is often undiagnosed since nonthriving breast-fed infants are typically managed by initiation of bottle feedings. In the cases reported, normal lactogenesis followed postpartum hemorrhage and removal of the retained placental parts.

Established lactation can be inhibited by high-dose estrogens, or other drugs such as bromocriptine and ergot, and presumably by superimposed pregnancy. Although little is known about the effects of pregnancy on milk volume or composition, a decline in milk supply is anecdotally reported.

Controversy surrounds the question of the inhibitory effects of moderate doses of vitamin B_6, or pyridoxine, on lactation.[63] The drug has been used in clinical trials to suppress postpartum lactation in bottle-feeding mothers.[64] Although the recommended daily allowance (RDA) for lactating women for B_6 is 2.5 mg/day, increased numbers of nutrition-conscious women routinely ingest 25 to 200 mg of B_6 daily. Since there appears to be no biologic advantage to taking 10 to 100 times the RDA for B_6, the possibility of an inhibitory effect on lactation should be considered and a more appropriate intake of this vitamin encouraged.

Although breast surgery for both diagnostic and cosmetic reasons is commonly performed, preservation of the normal innervation of the nipple and areola is not usually emphasized.[65] Disrupted innervation can affect the afferent limb of the neurohumoral reflex arc involved in prolactin and oxytocin secretion. Because prenatal breast examination may have been inadequate, it is important to inquire about previous breast surgery and to examine the breasts and test for nipple sensation whenever insufficient lactation is identified.

Conflicting data exist on the correlation between prolactin response and milk yield in both early and established lactation,[66] but there is evidence that prolactin levels and milk yield are causally related.[67] The possibilities that abnormalities exist in prolactin response to nursing as well as in end organ response to prolactin require thorough scientific investigation.

Abnormalities in Milk Composition

Abnormalities in milk composition are quite rare and continue to be overdiagnosed, most popularly by the misinterpretation of a spot creamatocrit to determine the percentage of milk fat. The creamatocrit can be a reliable reflection of milk fat content when a 24-hr sample or an entire expressed feeding from one or both breasts is used and when the procedure has been standardized by comparison with gravimetric tests of milk fat content;[68,69] but unfortunately it is often performed as an office procedure on a small sample of milk, frequently foremilk, which tends to be low in fat content. The mother is then incorrectly told that her milk "is not rich enough." In fact, although qualitative differences in the fatty acid composition are seen with varying maternal diets, the quantitative content of fat appears to be much less affected by diet.

Abnormalities in vitamin content are well documented with inadequate maternal nutrition. Several case reports of vitamin B_{12} deficiency in infants of strict vegetarian mothers, associated with failure to thrive and central nervous system abnormalities, have recently appeared.[70,71] Supplementation with B_{12} has reversed the clinical symptomatology in the infant.

Elevated sodium content of milk has been described in association with hypernatremic dehydration and failure to thrive in the infants.[72–74] Hartmann demonstated a fourfold increase in milk sodium within days of abrupt weaning, so elevated milk sodium in the presence of low milk supply may imply partial involution of lactation.[75] Elevated sodium and impaired milk production can also be seen in the mastitic breast.[76]

Although probably exceedingly rare, a deficiency in zinc transport into milk has been reported, resulting in failure to thrive and zinc deficiency syndrome in the infant, despite adequate zinc status in the mother.[77] Possibly other defects in the transport of specific elements will be discovered as breast milk composition is more thoroughly investigated.

In the face of higher-than-normal requirements for certain nutrients, normal breast milk may be inadequate for at-risk infants, such as the extremely-low-birth-weight baby. Hypophosphatemic and hypocalcemic rickets with failure to thrive has been reported in very-low-birth-weight infants receiving exclusive diets of breast milk in adequate volumes to meet routine caloric requirements.[16,17]

Etiologies of Lactation Failure—Infant Factors

Insufficient Suckling Stimulus

In many cases of failure to thrive, the infant, for varying reasons, may be providing an inadequate suckling stimulus. Evidence for this may be found in a study by Aono *et al.*, of "good" and "poor" milk producers on the fifth postpartum day. Mothers with poor milk yield demonstrated no prolactin rise when they nursed their babies, while good milk producers showed significant prolactin increases with nursing. Following effective breast stimulation with an electric breast pump, however, consistent increases in prolactin levels were induced in all mothers, independent of milk yield.[78] This data emphasizes the importance of an effective suckling stimulus in effecting prolactin rise and generating milk supply. We have found a "triple prolactin test," to be a useful measure of the infant's suckling effectiveness. In this test, the baseline plasma prolactin level is obtained 4 hr after a nursing. The mother is asked to nurse her infant routinely on both breasts, then a second blood sample is taken for measurement of prolactin. Finally, an effective electric breast pump (such as the Medela or Egnell) is applied to each breast for 10 minutes and a third prolactin level obtained. When the pump induces a far greater prolactin response than the infant, temporarily augmenting the infant's suck with pump stimulation after each feeding is recommended to stimulate further milk supply.

Several reports exist of the "happy to starve," placid breast-fed infant, who despite inadequate intake, fails to complain or to demand more often or to nurse more vigorously.[79,80] Although neurologic impairment should be suspected, sometimes these are normal, "especially good" babies. More often, the insufficient suckling stimulus is the result of borderline prematurity, is associated with hyperbilirubinemia, or is related to cardiac disease causing fatigue with feedings, or neurologic disease impairing suckling effectiveness or appropriate response to hunger.

Physical Abnormalities Impairing Feeding

Physical factors impairing feeding include cleft palate, micrognathia, high arched palate, cyst of the tongue, or other malformation. Careful physical examination should uncover these abnormalities.

Malabsorption or Increased Metabolic Requirements

When the history of feeding routines, before and after feeding weights, pump expression of milk, past breast-feeding success, and other parameters all suggest that milk supply is generous, one must consider the possibility of organic illness in the infant, such as cystic fibrosis, chronic infection, or congestive heart failure.

Evaluation of Failure to Thrive

The following outline can serve as a guide in obtaining subjective and objective data to be used in determining the etiology of failure to thrive (see Table I) and in developing a rational plan for its management. Essential components of the breast-feeding evaluation include a thorough maternal and infant history, physical examination of the mother with emphasis on the breasts, complete physical examination of the infant, and observation of a breast-feeding.

Subjective Data—Maternal Factors

In evaluating maternal factors it is important to assess the degree of maternal motivation toward breast-feeding as well as her knowledge and past experience. The perinatal history should be reviewed for maternal complications of pregnancy, labor, or delivery, often resulting in delays in the initiation of breast-feeding. The nursing pattern established in the postpartum period should be evaluated for use of supplementation, the presence of nipple confusion, the use of nipple shields, and the presence of interruptions in nursing.

The current nursing schedule should be recorded. An inflexible feeding schedule of every 4 to 6 hr often diminishes milk production and prolongs recovery of birth weight,[81] as does limitation of suckling time at a feeding. The presence of physical and emotional stresses placed upon the mother and attitudes of the husband and maternal relatives should be noted, and

Table I. Evaluation of Failure to Thrive Associated with Breast-Feeding

Subjective data	Objective data
Maternal	Physical examination of the infant
Motivation, breast-feeding knowledge, past experience	Growth parameters and growth curves
Pregnancy, labor and delivery history	General appearance and vital signs
Postpartum course: Initiation of nursing, complications	Positive physical findings: neurologic, anomalies
Present feeding routines and function of letdown reflex	Observation of a feeding
Level of activities, stress, and anxiety	Maternal feeding technique, maternal breasts and nipples
Diet, fluids, and rest	Infant suckling effectiveness
Drugs or medications, superimposed pregnancy	Evidence of letdown reflex
Medical factors, chronic illness, surgery, menses	Assessment of milk supply
Infant	Infant weight before and after nursing
Perinatal history and nursery course, early nursing	Milk yield by electric pump
Present feeding routines, frequency, duration	Laboratory data
Past growth parameters	Infant—urinalysis, electrolytes, bilirubin
Review of systems, including voiding and stooling	Mother—prolactin levels
Family history of growth or illness	Milk—fat, sodium, other as indicated

the possible effect of stress on the letdown reflex should be evaluated. A gross indicator of overall effectiveness of the suckling stimulus is the presence of lactation amenorrhea.[82] Early resumption of menses is one suggestion of insufficient nursing.

Maternal diet probably does not have a significant effect on breast-feeding or milk composition in well-nourished women.[83] Similarly, the amount of fluids consumed by the mother probably plays little role in breast milk supply unless significant dehydration occurs.[84] Maternal drug ingestion should be evaluated for possible influence on milk supply or toxic effects on the infant (see Chapter 13). Maternal medical factors which may adversely affect breast-feeding include breast surgery, affecting nipple–areola inner-vation, mastitis, sore nipples, serious illness, or superimposed pregnancy.

Subjective Data—Infant Factors

Because the infant plays a major role in determining his own milk supply, subjective data regarding the infant is of importance. A detailed perinatal history should be designed to uncover factors often associated with poor feeding behavior including borderline prematurity, hyperviscosity, hyperbilirubinemia, or poor apgar scores.

The feeding pattern of the infant may reveal inadequacy of suckling stimulation. A small, weak, or neurologically impaired infant permitted to suck on a pacifier between feedings may be exhausted and nurse less effectively at feeding times. The placid infant who seldom demands, sleeps through the night before a month of age, or falls asleep at the first breast without taking the second side is unlikely to stimulate adequate milk supply.

The previous pattern of growth may be suggestive of etiology. A formerly thriving infant who abruptly fails to gain adequately suggests diminished milk supply or acquired illness, whereas the infant who has never gained well may be more likely to have underlying organic disease.

A thorough review of systems may suggest organic disease in the infant which affects ability to nurse or utilization of nutrients. A history of infrequent voiding is worrisome and suggestive of severe malnutrition and dehydration, since hydration is often still adequate in the absence of caloric sufficiency. Infrequent stooling, while a common pattern in the older breast-fed infant, suggests insufficient intake in the young infant. Family history should be pursued to determine familial growth patterns or identify hereditary conditions such as cystic fibrosis.

Objective Data

Physical Examination. An accurate weight on the same scale which will be used in subsequent appointments is mandatory. Height, weight, and occipital frontal circumference should be plotted and compared to each other. Vital signs and the general appearance of the infant should allow the physician to identify critical malnutrition, an emergency situation, to be distinguished from the stable infant who is underweight, but in no immediate danger. In the former situation, rapid stabilization and attention to fluid intake and caloric adequacy must take precedence over enhancing lactation, whereas in the latter situation, the infant's condition can often be improved by practical feeding suggestions directed toward establishing a more effective breast-feeding relationship.

The physical examination of the infant should focus particularly on underlying medical illness, neurologic deficits affecting nursing, or physical anomalies impairing feeding. The strength and coordination of the suck and root reflex can be ascertained by using a pacifier, mother's breast or the examiner's finger. The presence of thrush should be noted, especially when there is a maternal history of sore nipples.

Observation of a Feeding. If possible, the appointment time should coincide with a feeding. After the mother's breasts are inspected for obvious abnormalities, the infant should be nursed in as normal a fashion as possible. The presence of maternal anxiety, the ability of the infant to grasp the nipple and sufficient areola, the presence of a rhythmic, sustained, effective suck, with pauses for swallowing, and evidence of the letdown reflex should all be noted.

Assessment of Milk Supply. Assessment of milk supply is difficult in the clinic setting, where a single pump expression of milk or infant weights before and after a single feeding may be highly unreliable. An approximate measure of breast milk supply can be obtained in the hospital setting, however, by weighing the clothed infant, before and after feedings over a 24-hr period, being sure not to change the infant's diaper in the interval between weighings. If the infant has been temporarily taken off breast milk, milk yield can be assessed with an efficient electric breast pump. The breasts should be pumped at a usual feeding time, and letdown observed by the streaming of milk into the collection bottle. Ideally, the procedure should be continued for 24 hr if a representative assessment of milk yield is to be obtained.

Laboratory Data. In most cases of failure to thrive, laboratory evaluations not specifically indicated by history or physical examination offer little help in establishing a diagnosis. Because neonatal hypernatremia with breast-feeding failure-to-thrive has been reported, a serum sodium may be indicated. Significant hyperbilirubinemia may also be present in the young infant with caloric deprivation. Urinary tract infection is commonly overlooked as a cause of poor infant suckling. The creamatocrit on the breast milk should only be performed if a representative sample is available and the test has been adequately standardized. Milk sodium might help clarify whether lactation is normally established, or involuting. In general, the analytical procedures used for plasma sodium are also adequate for milk. Baseline, postnursing, and/or postpumping prolactin levels may be useful in selected cases to evaluate the effectiveness of infant suckling or to guide the use of pharmacologic galactogogues which promote pituitary prolactin release.

Assessment and Plan

Once a significant data base has been obtained, an assessment of the etiology of breast-feeding failure can be made and an appropriate plan of management outlined (see Table II). The first concern of the physician should be to improve the infant's weight gain. In many cases, this can be accomplished without sacrificing breast-feeding, although supplementation with formula probably will be required initially.

Before beginning treatment, the clinician should recognize the considerable maternal motivation and professional commitment that successful management will entail. The clinician should act to relieve maternal feelings of inadequacy and guilt that often accompany the situation. The benefits the infant has already derived from breast-feeding and the closeness of the nursing relationship should be stressed; while the volume of milk produced is deemphasized. Permission to institute bottle feedings should be conveyed while options to improve breast-feeding are offered.

Treatment of Low Milk Supply Secondary to Inadequate Suckling Stimulus

When the breast milk supply is only slightly diminished and the problem is short-lived, the infant's condition will usually permit the gradual improvement in milk production that can be afforded by appropriate changes in

Table II. Management of Failure to Thrive Associated with Breast-Feeding

Assessment	Plan[a]
Low milk supply secondary to inadequate suckling stimulus	
Inappropriate feeding routines	Increase frequency of feedings
	Nurse on both sides
	Interrupt long night interval to nurse
	Encourage maternal rest and relaxation
	Provide confidence and support to mother
	Consider trial of galactogogues (Thorazine®, metoclopramide)
Impaired letdown reflex	Rest, relaxation, explanation, conditioning techniques
	Relieve discomfort, such as sore nipples
	Syntocinon nasal spray to condition reflex
Inhibitory factors	Assess for pregnancy
	Remove inhibitory factors, such as medications
	Treat underlying medical condition in mother as indicated
Infant problems	
Insufficient suckling stimulus or malabsorption or increased nutritional needs	Increase frequency of feedings
	Awaken baby to nurse, even at night
	Move infant to second breast 5 min after letdown occurs
	Enhance letdown reflex
	Treat underlying infant condition as warranted
	Augment infant's suck with electric pump stimulation
	Avoid nonnutritive suckling, such as pacifier, water
	Supply formula supplement as indicated by weight gain
Anomalies impairing feeding	Facilitate letdown
	Patiently work with infant and encourage nursing
	Pump and feed expressed milk, temporarily or long term
Rare pathology	
Abnormal milk composition	Supply nutritive supplements or formula
	Enhance maternal diet as indicated
Primary failure of lactation	Bottle feedings of formula, maintain nursing relationship

[a] Always supplement as indicated with formula by bottle after appropriate length of nursing, or with Lact-Aid device while nursing. Taper supplemental formula only as adequate weight gain is achieved and maintained.

feeding routines. In general, increasing the frequency of nursing,[85] using both breasts at each feeding, interrupting the long night interval to nurse, assuring additional maternal rest and relaxation, and the provision of emotional support should gradually increase milk production. Grooming the infant while nursing in a quiet, dark environment has also been purported to elevate prolactin levels and enhance milk supply.[86]

Impaired letdown usually accompanies low milk supply, whether it is primary or secondary. Letdown can be conditioned by developing a relaxing routine before nursing, by breast massage, manual expression, or heat application. Nursing rituals such as listening to music or drinking liquids occasionally help. Synthetic oxytocin, such as Syntocinon nasal spray, can be effective in enhancing the letdown and conditioning the reflex. Letdown will also be facilitated by the removal of noxious stimuli such as anxiety or discomfort.

Any inhibitory factors in the mother such as drugs or illness should be removed whenever possible.

Whenever the breast milk supply is very low, the problem is long-standing, or the infant's condition warrants immediate improvement in nutritional status, *supplementation with formula becomes mandatory*. If the infant does not fatigue easily, he should be nursed 5 to 10 min at each breast before supplement is offered by bottle. The Nuk nipple may be preferred because of its alleged resemblance to the breast nipple, but it requires more effort to extract milk than other nipples so should be used with caution when the infant's suck is weak. As adequate infant weight gain is established and evidence for improved breast milk supply is documented, supplemental formula can be gradually tapered under close supervision.

When the infant is vigorous and correctly grasps the breast nipple, and when bottle supplements are undesired or begin to interfere with breast-feeding, supplementation via the Lact-Aid Nursing Trainer may be ideal.[87] The Lact-Aid permits supplemental formula to be obtained while nursing, thus avoiding bottle supplements and permitting continued breast stimulation to enhance the milk supply (Fig. 1).

Pharmacologic galactogogues, such as chlorpromazine and metoclopramide, are occasionally recommended in the management of lactation failure. Chlorpromazine, in doses of 25 to 100 mg orally three times daily for 7 to 10 days,[88] has been described to induce lactation in healthy nonpregnant women. Metoclopramide has been reported to improve lactation in doses of 10 mg 3 times daily for 7 days or more.[89] Sulpiride is another agent which has been reported to stimulate prolactin secretion by blocking dopamine receptors, and recent clinical trials suggest that 50 mg given orally twice daily in the first 7 days postpartum promotes the initiation of lactation.[99] Extensive clinical trials of these agents are not currently available, however, and we have generally not found them to be effective in severe cases of lactation failure.

Treatment of Infant Factors

Conditions in which the infant is too weak or ill to suck vigorously, or when his nutritional needs are increased, can be managed by: (1) nursing more often, (2) awakening the infant to nurse, (3) introducing an extra nursing at night, (4) using both breasts at each feeding, (5) moving the infant to the second breast after the first 5 min. of nursing,[91,92] and (6) avoiding nonnutritive nursing on pacifiers. Occasionally, it is useful to augment the infant's suck with breast pump stimulation after feedings.

When the infant has a physical abnormality impairing feeding, facilitation of the letdown reflex may help him nurse more effectively. Occasionally, direct nursing is not possible, as with a large cleft palate, and feeding expressed milk by alternative method may be necessary.

Treatment of Rare Pathology

When there is little response to appropriate suckling, such as with severed innervation to the nipple, the infant may need to be bottle-fed with formula. Nevertheless, nursing can be continued for comfort and closeness as long as it continues to be mutually enjoyable. With low serum prolactin levels, a trial of pharmacologic galactogogues may be warranted.

Conclusion

Based on the author's experience, the following conclusions can be drawn about failure to thrive among breast-fed infants:

1. Poor weight gain in breast-fed infants is most often due to low milk supply secondary to inappropriate feeding routines.
2. Abnormalities in breast milk quality are exceedingly rare.
3. The infant plays an important role in generating his own breast milk supply.
4. A small percentage of women have a physiologic basis for lactation failure.
5. A small percentage of breast-fed infants have an organic basis for failure to thrive.

In summary, most cases of failure to thrive among breast-fed infants could be prevented by appropriate anticipatory guidance and most others could be detected earlier if infants of primiparous nursing mothers were given follow-up appointments at closer intervals than is currently routine. Early detection of inadequate weight gain usually allows rapid resumption of appropriate growth simply by making feeding suggestions and offering support. While prevention, early detection, and intervention are time-consuming, it is likely that as breast-feeding becomes the norm, successful lactation will sustain itself through traditional support systems.

CLEFT LIP AND PALATE

Cleft lip and palate are relatively common birth defects, usually necessitating special feeding techniques to permit adequate nutrition and growth. Parents are generally reassured about plans for corrective surgery and simply informed that breast-feeding is not feasible for these infants. For those parents for whom breast-feeding represents more than just a method of infant feeding, the inability to nurse may be viewed as another major loss, further impairing the parents' adjustment to a child with a malformation. In the past, health professionals have been relatively insensitive to this issue.

Women who had planned to nurse should be encouraged to establish milk supplies with regular pump stimulation and to feed their expressed milk to their infants until prognosis and definitive plans for long-range feeding can be made. Third-party coverage should be sought to pay the expense of electric pump rental, and breast milk, when available, should be acknowledged as an important component of the infant's total health care. The infant can be introduced to the breast nipple very early, even if he is unable effectively to obtain milk at first. Regardless of the feeding method, it is important for the infant to room-in with the mother as much as possible and for hospital personnel to involve the mother in feedings and to build her confidence in her ability to care for her baby. Too often, the infant is exposed to multiple feeding techniques by several different nurses, when the mother herself, consistently pursuing her preferred method of feeding, would be more successful.

Nursing Infants with Cleft Lip

Some infants with isolated cleft lip are able to obtain adequate suction to nurse effectively, with feeding proceeding quite normally until the time of repair. Most surgeons prefer that the infant not suck on any object 2 to 6 weeks after repair, so during this period, the mother will need to maintain her milk supply with expression techniques. She can then feed her expressed milk to the infant by cup or syringe until he is allowed to nurse again. A few surgeons are beginning to allow early return to nursing following repair because the comfort provided the infant results in less crying and agitation.

Nursing Infants with Cleft Palate

Nursing in the presence of cleft palate is much more difficult, although several descriptive accounts of women nursing infants with small clefts have appeared. In one such case, a healthy twin aided in stimulating milk supply and generating milk letdown for the affected twin.[93] While the infant is learning to nurse, it is important for the milk supply to be maximally stimulated by augmenting the infant's nursing with an effective breast pump. The infant's intake of breast milk should be accurately assessed and supplementation by cup, syringe, or other method provided, if indicated. The author is aware of one infant who attempted to nurse with a large cleft palate and who arrived moribund for his routine 2-week check-up. The primiparous mother seemingly was unaware that her infant was dangerously malnourished and gravely ill. If supply is adequately stimulated, the infant appropriately supplemented, the letdown conditioned, and breast-feeding patiently encouraged, some infants will ultimately be able to provide sufficient suction to hold the nipple in their mouth and nurse from the breast. This requires a great deal of time and commitment, however, and close attention to the infant's interim nutritional status.

A prosthesis to cover the palatal defect may make nursing quite feasible, but the prosthesis must be kept clean and revised as the infant grows. In addition, fitting and constructing the device require skill and expertise not universally available. Nevertheless, some centers routinely manage cleft palate infants with such devices to facilitate nursing from either bottle or breast. In general, health professionals caring for infants with cleft lip or palate need to be more sensitive to parents' desires to breast-feed these infants.[94] Information, support, options, and follow-up to permit breast-feeding even in a modified fashion should be provided. Some of these infants will still enjoy nursing at the breast, despite the fact that most of their nutrition must be consumed from other sources.

MULTIPLE BIRTHS

Nursing twins is possible, provided the mother is highly motivated and has abundant support. During the early postpartum weeks, fatigue will threaten her success as she finds herself nursing as often as every hour and a half. Budin's records of his wet nurses' milk production clearly document the capacity of the breast to respond to increased feedings with maximized milk supply. Initially, separate feedings will permit individual time with each infant and allow the mother to discover the feeding characteristics of each. Ultimately, feeding the infants simultaneously will be faster and more efficient. If one infant is stronger than the other, he can simultaneously generate the letdown in both breasts, thereby aiding the weaker twin. The advantage of assigning each twin his own breast is that the supply can be adapted to each infant's needs and cross contamination diminished should one infant become ill. On the other hand, rotating sides has the advantage of allowing the stronger twin to alternately stimulate each breast, bilaterally enhancing milk supply. Simply feeding whichever infant is hungry with the fullest breast at that moment will also work.

Positioning the infants for feedings can be awkward. Many women prefer the football hold, in which an infant is held on each arm with his head supported in her hand and his feet directed toward the mother's back. Or, pillows can be positioned on either side of the mother and the infants placed on the pillows, with their heads facing each other in the midline.

While there is little one can do to minimize the initial tremendous expenditure of effort in nursing twins, ultimately breast-feeding them can be easier than bottle-feeding. Encouraging maternal rest and providing emotional support will be more appreciated by motivated mothers than suggesting trial feedings of supplementary formula.

Nursing triplets is also feasible, and numerous accounts of mothers providing total nourishment for all three babies for several months have been documented. Since triplets are usually born prematurely, regular and frequent augmentation of the infants' suckling with electric pump stimulation should be encouraged until the infants are nursing vigorously. If supplementary formula is required, nursing can still continue, perhaps by rotating the infants between breast- and bottle-feedings.

BREAST MILK JAUNDICE

The syndrome of breast milk jaundice is characterized by prolonged *unconjugated* hyperbilirubinemia in an otherwise healthy newborn which is associated with the ingestion of breast milk from certain mothers. Following the first reports of breast milk jaundice in the early 1960s,[95] a progestational steroid, 3-α-20-β-pregnanediol, present in the milk of some mothers, was identified as the offending compound and shown to inhibit bilirubin conjugation *in vitro*.[96] Subsequent studies have failed to confirm these observations, however.[97] More recent data suggest that an abnormal lipase may be responsible for the prolonged hyperbilirubinemia in some breast-fed infants, although lipoprotein lipase activity has been found in fresh milk samples from mothers of asymptomatic infants in the same high range as observed in samples from mothers with jaundiced infants.[98] Inhibitory activity of milk is increased with freezing,[99] which may have implications for storage of breast milk and feeding to low-birth-weight infants.

The incidence of breast milk jaundice has been reported as 2.4% of breast-fed infants,[100] but because there is no clinically available confirmatory laboratory test, the entity is easily overdiagnosed. When one recognizes that breast milk jaundice is a diagnosis of exclusion, it is clear that common and uncommon pathologic causes of jaundice must always be ruled out first. A *conjugated bilirubin* determination is mandatory, since breast milk jaundice is specifically an *unconjugated* hyperbilirubinemia.

Despite the apparent well-being of infants with breast milk jaundice and the absence of documented kernicterus with this entity, there is no evidence that hyperbilirubinemia is any better tolerated in these infants than in infants with jaundice of other etiologies. Until more information is available, traditional guidelines for intervention in hyperbilirubinemia should be followed. The diagnosis of breast milk jaundice can be confirmed by withholding breast milk feedings for 24 to 36 hr while substituting formula feedings. In breast milk jaundice, a dramatic fall in bilirubin level will result from the brief interruption in breast-feeding. The bilirubin may rebound somewhat when breast milk is reintroduced, but it should not reach previous levels. Because disruption of breast-feeding may undermine successful nursing, care must be exercised in assuring that the mother has mastered techniques of expressing milk. She must also be reassured that her milk is causing the jaundice only temporarily, and that long-term breast-feeding is still encouraged.

PHENYLKETONURIA

On a few occasions, zealous women, refusing to abandon nursing in the face of an infant problem which traditionally contraindicated nursing, have ultimately provided insight into the value of breast-feeding in that very situation. Such has been the experience with infants with phenylketonuria (PKU). Due to the strong desire by some mothers of babies with PKU to nurse, even in a limited fashion, supervised attempts to permit some nursing with these infants were explored. Traditionally, the treatment of phenylketonuria involves predominantly feeding Lofenalac® and supplementing the diet with standard formula to prevent hypophenylalaninemia. In the first clinical trials in Denver with feeding breast milk, measured volumes of expressed breast milk were offered by bottle in lieu of regular formula supplement. Because of the significantly lower phenylalanine levels of breast milk than formula, relatively greater amounts of breast milk were permitted while maintaining acceptable serum phenylalanine levels in the infant. Direct nursing at the breast was permitted next, using infant weights before and after nursing to monitor intake. The amount of breast milk permitted was titrated to the infant's phenylalanine levels, and ultimately the infant was significantly breast-fed. In Denver alone, there is experience with over a dozen infants with PKU treated with partial breast-feeding, still under closely monitored conditions at a metabolic center, but the results appear so favorable that the mothers of infants with PKU are being encouraged to breast-feed whenever possible in order to enhance the infants' clinical course. A detailed account of how to manage breast-feeding with infants with PKU is available.[101]

HOSPITALIZATION OF THE INFANT OR MOTHER

Hospitalization of mother or infant should not necessitate weaning. Increased recognition by pediatricians of the importance of unrestricted parental visitation for hospitalized infants and children has relaxed former rigid regulations. Many settings permit round-the-clock presence of parents and some even allow rooming-in arrangements. Illness, diagnostic studies, and new surroundings will make breast-fed infants require the nursing relationship even more strongly. Most mothers appreciate being able to console an uncomfortable baby in this way. When intake needs to be closely monitored, before and after nursing weights will give the clinician a handle on the child's intake. When nothing by mouth is permitted, an electric pump can be used to maintain supply and store milk for later use. Motivated mothers have found ways to nurse babies who are in traction, who are attached to precarious intravenous lines, or who are on oxygen.

Similarly, when maternal hospitalization is necessary, young healthy infants can easily be admitted as "boarders" to room-in with the mother if she can provide all the care or to be admitted to the nursery or infant ward where minimal routine care can be provided by nursing staff. While the cost of boarding an infant is often minimal, unfortunately third-party coverage seldom applies. Sometimes, family members can care for the infant at home and bring him to the mother's room to nurse during the day. When separation must occur or mother is extremely ill, provisions for regular milk expression with help from the nursing staff should be part of the medical orders for the mother.

CONCLUSION

The renewed interest in breast-feeding has not been confined to mothers of healthy infants. Mothers whose infants have unique problems are increasingly voicing their desires to breast-feed their babies too. Recent publicity has been awarded the notion that the birth of an infant with an anomaly or prematurity heralds a grief reaction in the parents over the symbolic death of their "dreamed-about" child. However, little attention has been given to the observation that relinquishment of breast-feeding may represent an additional "loss" for the parents. Increased recognition of the importance of the nursing relationship to mothers and infants is warranted and increased emphasis on practical information for parents to nurse in special situations is indicated.

REFERENCES

1. Garrison, F. H., 1965, History of Pediatrics, in: *Abt–Garrison History of Pediatrics* (A. F. Abt, ed.), W. B. Saunders Company, Philadelphia, pp. 44–45.
2. Wickes, I. G., 1953, A history of infant feeding. Part I. Primitive peoples: Ancient works: Renaissance writers, *Arch. Dis. Child.* **28:**151–158.
3. Handelman, C. C., 1961, Breast feeding, *Pediatr. Clin. North Am.* **8:**7–12.
4. Barnett, H. L. and Einhorn, A. H. (eds.), 1972, *Pediatrics*, Appleton-Century-Crofts, New York, p. 149.
5. Lawrence, R. A., 1980, *Breast-feeding: A Guide for the Medical Profession*, The C. V. Mosby Company, St. Louis.
6. Brewster, D. P., 1979, *You Can Breastfeed Your Baby. . . . Even in Special Situations*, Rondale Press, Emmaus, Pennsylvania.
7. Avery, G. B. (ed.), 1981, *Neonatology*, 2nd ed., J. B. Lippincott Company, Philadelphia, p. 26.
8. Budin, P., 1907, *The Nursling: The Feeding and Hygiene of Premature and Full-Term Infants*, Caxton, London, p. 68.
9. Hunter, R. S., Kilstrom, N., Kraybill, E. N., and Loda, F., 1978, Antecedents of child abuse and neglect in premature infants: A prospective study in newborn intensive care unit, *Pediatrics* **61:**629–635.
10. Fomon, S., Ziegler, E., and Vasquez, H., 1977, Human milk and the small premature infant, *Am. J. Dis. Child.* **131:**463–467.
11. Fomon, S. J., 1978, Milk of the premature infant's mother: Intepretation of the data, *J. Pediatr.* **93:**164.
12. Finberg, L., 1980, One milk for all—Not ever likely and certainly not yet, *J. Pediatr.* **96:**240–241.
13. Forbes, G. B., 1982, Human milk and the small baby, *Am. J. Dis. Child* **136:**577–578.
14. Davies, P., 1977, Adequacy of expressed breast milk for early growth of preterm infants, *Arch. Dis. Child.* **52:**296–301.
15. Kumar, S., 1978, Hyponatremia in very low-birth-weight infants and human milk feedings, *J. Pediatr.* **93:**1026–1027.
16. Greer, F., Steichen, J., and Tsang, R., 1982, Calcium and phosphate supplements in breast milk-related rickets, *Am. J. Dis. Child.* **136:**581–583.

17. Rowe, J. C., Wood, D. H., Rowe, D. W., and Raisz, L. G., 1979, Nutritional hypophosphatemic rickets in a premature infant fed breast milk, *N. Engl. J. Med.* **300:**293–296.
18. Sagy, M., Birenbaum, E., Balin, A., Orda, S., Barzilay, Z., and Brish, M., 1980, Phosphate-depletion syndrome in a premature infant fed human milk, *J. Pediatr.* **96:**683–685.
19. Atkinson, S., Bryan, M. H., and Anderson, G. H., 1978, Human milk: Differences in nitrogen concentration in milk from mothers of term and preterm infants, *J. Pediatr.* **93:**67–69.
20. Gross, S. J., Geller, J., and Tomarelli, R. M., 1981, Composition of breast milk from mothers of preterm infants, *Pediatrics* **68:**490–493.
21. Chan, G. M., 1979, Preterm and term breast milk calcium and vitamin D, *Pediatr. Res.* **13:**396.
22. Atkinson, S. A., Bryan, M. H., and Anderson, G. H., 1981, Human milk feeding in premature infants: Protein, fat, and carbohydrate balances in the first two weeks of life, *J. Pediatr.* **99:**617–624.
23. Ronnholm. K. A. R., Sipila, I., and Siimes, M. A., 1982, Human milk protein supplementation for the prevention of hypoproteinemia without metabolic imbalance in breast milk-fed very low-birth-weight infants, *J. Pediatr.* **101:**243–247.
24. Hagelberg, S., Lindblad, B. S., Lundsjo, A., Carlsson, B., Fonden, R., Fujita, H., Lassfolk, G., and Lindqvist, B., 1982, The protein tolerance of very low birth weight infants fed human milk protein enriched mother's milk, *Acta. Paediatr. Scand.* **71:**597–601.
25. Räihä, N. C. R., Heinonen, K., Rassin, D. K., and Gaull, G. E., 1976, Milk protein quantity and quality in low-birth-weight infants. I. Metabolic responses and effects on growth, *Pediatrics* **57:**659–674.
26. Gaull, G. E., Rassin, D. K., Räihä, N. C. R., and Heinonen, K., 1977, Milk protein quantity and quality in low-birth-weight infants. III. Effects on sulfur amino acids in plasma and urine, *J. Pediatr.* **90:**348–355.
27. Rassin, D., Gaull, G., Räihä, N., and Heinonen, K., 1977, Milk protein quantity and quality in low-birth-weight infants, IV. Effects on tyrosine and phenylalanine in plasma and urine, *J. Pediatr.* **90:**356–360.
28. Gross, S. J., Buckley, R. H., Wakil, S. S., McAllister, D. C., David, R. J., and Faix, R. G., 1981, Elevated IgA concentration in milk produced by mothers delivered of preterm infants, *J. Pediatr.* **99:**389–393.
29. Narayanan, I., Prakash, K., and Gujral, V. V., 1981, The value of human milk in the prevention of infection in the high-risk low-birth-weight infant, *J. Pediatr.* **99:**496–498.
30. Larguia, A. M., Urman, J., Ceriani, J. M., O'Donnell, A., Stoliar, O., Martinez, J. C., Buscaglia, J. C., Weils, S., Quiroga, A., and Irazu, L., 1974, Immunidad local en la recien nacido. Primera experiencia con la administracion de colostro humano a recien nacido pretermino, *Arch. Argent. Pediatr.* **72:**109–125.
31. Barlow, B., Santulli, T. V., Heird, W. C., Pitt, J., Blanc, W. A., and Schullinger, J. N., 1974, An experimental study of acute neonatal enterocolitis: The importance of breast milk, *J. Pediatr. Surg.* **9:**587–595.
32. Kleigman, R. M., Pittard, W. B., and Fanaroff, A. A., 1979, Necrotizing enterocolitis in infants fed human milk, *J. Pediatr.* **95:**450–453.
33. Moriartey, R. R., Finer, N. N., Cox, S. F., Phillips, H. J., Theman, A., Steward, A. R., and Ulan, O. A., 1979, Necrotizing enterocolitis and human milk, *J. Pediatr.* **94:**295–296.
34. Kliegman, R. M., Pittard, W. B., and Fanaroff, A. A., 1980, Human milk feedings and NEC, *J. Pediatr.* **96:**780–781.
35. Gustafson, B., and Kjellman, B., 1981, Use of transpyloric tube feeding with nonpasteurized human milk, *J. Pediatr.* **99:**300–302.
36. Bose, C. L., D'Ercole, J., Lester, A. G., Hunter, R. S., and Barrett, J. R., 1981, Relactation by mothers of sick and premature infants, *Pediatrics* **67:**565–569.
37. Silver, S., 1978, A mother's guide to breastfeeding and mothering the premature or hospitalized sick infant, *Clin. Pediatr.* **17:**425–427.
38. Stewart, D. and Gaires, C., 1978, Supporting lactation when mothers and infants are separated, *Nurs. Clin. North Am.* **13:**47–61.

39. Choi, M. W., 1978, Breast milk for infants who can't breast-feed, *Am. J. Nurs.* **78:**852–855.
40. Marmet, C., 1981, Manual expression of breast milk, Marmet technique, La Leche League, International, Franklin Park, Illinois. Reprint #107.
41. Ryder, R. W., Crosby-Ritchie, A., McDonough, B., and Hall, W. J., 1977, Human milk contaminated with *Salmonella kottbus*, a cause of nosocomial illness in infants, *JAMA* **238:**1533–1534.
42. Hack, M., Boxerbaum, B., and Fanaroff, A., 1975, Fresh human refrigerated milk: Bacterial flora in urban U.S. mothers, *Pediatr. Res.* **9:**304.
43. Liebhaber, M., Lewiston, N., Asquith, M. T., and Sunshine, P., 1978, Comparison of bacterial contamination with two methods of human milk collection, *J. Pediatr.* **92:**236–238.
44. Siimes, M. A., 1978, A perspective on human milk banking, *J. Pediatr.* **94:**173–174.
45. Cash, J. K. and Giacoia, G. P., 1981, Organization and operation of a human breast milk bank, *J. Obstet. Gynocol. Neonat. Nurs.* **10:**434–438.
46. Asquith, M. T. and Harrod, J. R., 1979, Reduction of bacterial contamination in banked human milk, *J. Pediatr.* **95:**993–994.
47. Foman, S. J., 1977, Human milk in premature infant feeding: Report of a second workship, *Am. J. Public Health* **67:**361–363.
48. Pakson, C. L. and Cress, C. C., 1979, Survival of human milk leukocytes, *J. Pediatr.* **93:**61–63.
49. Liebhaber, M., Lewiston, N. J., Asquith, M. T., Olds-Arroyo, L., and Sunshine, P., 1977, Alterations of lymphocytes and of antibody content of human milk after processing, *J. Pediatr.* **91:**897–900.
50. Department of Health and Social Security Panel on Child Nutrition, 1981, The collection and storage of human milk, Working Party report on human milk banks, Reports on Health and Social Subjects 22, *Her Majesty's Stationary Office, London.*
51. Ford, J. E., Law, B. A., Marshall, V. M., and Reiter, B., 1977, Influence of the heat treatment of human milk on some of its protective constituents, *J. Pediatr.* **90:**29–35.
52. Williamson, S., Finucane, E., Ellis, H., and Gamsu, H. R., 1978, Effect of heat treatment of human milk on absorption of nitrogen, fat, sodium, calcium, and phosphorus by preterm infants, *Arch. Dis. Child.* **53:**555–563.
53. Auerbach, K. G., 1979, The role of the nurse in support of breast feeding, *J. Adv. Nurs.* **4:**263–285.
54. Gilmore, H. E. and Rowland, T. W., 1978, Critical malnutrition in breast-fed infants, *Am. J. Dis. Child.* **132:**885–887.
55. Evans, T. and Davies, D. P., 1977, Failure to thrive at the breast: An old problem revisited, *Arch. Dis. Child.* **52:**974–975.
56. Davies, D. P. and Evans, T., 1976, Failure to thrive at the breast, *Lancet* **2:**1194–1195.
57. O'Conner, P., 1978, Failure to thrive with breast feeding, *Clin. Pediatr.* **17:**833–835.
58. Roddey, O. F., Martin, E. S., and Swetenburg, R. L., 1981, Critical weight loss and malnutrition in breast-fed infants, *Am. J. Dis. Child.* **135:**597–599.
59. Davies, D. P., 1979, Is inadequate breast-feeding an important cause of failure to thrive? *Lancet* **1:**541–542.
60. Newton, M. and Newton, N., 1948, The let-down reflex in human lactation, *J. Pediatr.* **33:**698–704.
61. Fleet, I. R. and Peaker, M., 1978, Mammary function and its control at the cessation of lactation in the goat, *J. Physiol.* **279:**491–507.
62. Neifert, M., McDonough, S., and Neville, M. C., 1981, Failure of lactogenesis associated with placental retention, *Am. J. Obstet. Gynecol.* **140:**477–478.
63. Greentree, L. B., 1979, Dangers of Vitamin B_6 in nursing mothers, *N. Engl. J. Med.* **300:**141.
64. Marcus, R., 1975, Suppression of lactation with high doses of pyridoxine, *S. Afr. Med. J.* **49:**2155–2156.
65. Farina, M., Newby, B., and Alani, H., 1980, Innervation of the nipple-areola complex, *Plast. Reconstruct. Surg.* **66:**497–501.

66. Howie, P. W., McNeilly, A. S., McArdle, T., Smart, L., and Houston, M., 1980, The relationship between suckling-induced prolactin response and lactogenesis, *J. Clin. Endocrinol. Metab.* **50:**670–674.
67. Tyson, J. E., Carter, J. N., Andreassen, B., Huth, J., and Smith, B., 1978, Nursing-mediated prolactin and luteinizing hormone secretion during puerperal lactation, *Fertil. Steril.* **30:**154–162.
68. Lucas, A., Gibbs, J. A. H., Lyster, R. L., and Baum, J. D., 1978, Creamatocrit: Simple clinical technique for estimating fat concentration and energy value of human milk, *Br. Med. J.* **1:**1018–1020.
69. Lemons, J. A., Schreiner, R. L., and Gresham, E. L., 1980, Simple method for determining the caloric and fat content of human milk, *Pediatrics* **66:**626–628.
70. Davis, J. R., Goldenring, J., and Lubin, B. H., 1981, Nutritional vitamin B_{12} deficiency in infants, *Am. J. Dis. Child.* **135:**566–567.
71. Higginbottom, M., Sweetman, L., and Nyhan, W., 1978, A syndrome of methylmalonic aciduria, homocystinuria, megaloblastic anemia and neurologic abnormalities in a vitamin B-12 deficient breast fed infant of a strict vegetarian, *N. Engl. J. Med.* **299:**317–323.
72. Rowland, T. W., Zori, R. T., Lafleur, W. R., and Reiter, E. O., 1982, Malnutrition and hypernatremic dehydration in breast-fed infants, *JAMA* **247:**1016–1017.
73. Anand, S. K., Sandborg, C., Robinson, R. G., and Lieberman, E., 1980, Neonatal hypernatremia associated with elevated sodium concentration of breast milk, *J. Pediatr.*, **96:**66–68.
74. Clarke, T. A., Markarian, M., Griswold, W., and Mendoza, S., 1979, Hypernatremic dehydration resulting from inadequate breast-feeding, *Pediatrics* **63:**931–932.
75. Hartmann, P. E. and Kulski, J. K., 1978, Changes in the composition of the mammary secretion of women after abrupt termination of breast feeding, *J. Physiol.* **275:**1–11.
76. Conner, A. E., 1979, Elevated levels of sodium and chloride in milk from mastitis breast, *Pediatrics* **63:**910–911.
77. Zimmerman, A., Hambidge, K., Lepow, M., Greenburg, R., Stover, M., and Casey, C., 1982, Acrodermatitis in breast-fed premature infants: Evidence for a defect in mammary zinc secretion, *Pediatrics* **69:**176–183.
78. Aono, T., Shioji, T., Shoda, T., and Kurachi, K., 1977, The initiation of human lactation and prolactin response to suckling, *J. Clin. Endocrinol. Metab.* **44:**1101–1106.
79. Davies, D. P. and Evans, T., 1978, The starved but contented breast-fed baby, *Arch. Dis. Child.* **53:**763.
80. Rushton, A. R., Lambert, G. P., Katcher, A. L., and Frangakis, D., 1982, Dehydration in a breast-fed infant, *JAMA* **248:**646.
81. Salber, E. G., 1956, The effect of different feeding schedules on the growth of Bantu babies in the first week of life, *J. Trop. Pediatr.* **2:**97–102.
82. Ojofeitimi, E. O., 1982, Effect of duration and frequency of breast-feeding on postpartum amenorrhea, *Pediatrics* **69:**164–168.
83. Hall, B., 1979, Uniformity of human milk, *Am. J. Clin. Nutr.* **32:**304–312.
84. Illingsworth, R. S. and Kilpatrick, B., 1953, Lactation and fluid intake, *Lancet* **2:**1175–1177.
85. Egli, G. E., Egli, N. S., and Newton, M., 1961, The influence of the number of breast feedings on milk production, *Pediatrics* **27:**314–317.
86. Weichert, C. E., 1979, Lactational reflex recovery in breast-feeding failure, *Pediatrics* **63:**799–803.
87. Magnus, P. D., and Frantz, K. D., 1979, Breast-feeding and failure to thrive, *Lancet* **1:**1080–1081.
88. Brown, R. E., 1977, Relactation: An overview, *Pediatrics* **60:**116–120.
89. Kauppila, A., Kivinen, S., and Ylikorkala, O., 1981, Metoclopramide increases prolactin release and milk secretion in puerperium without stimulating the secretion of thyrotropin and thyroid hormones, *J. Clin. Endocrinol. Metab.* **52:**436–439.
90. Aono, T., Shioji, T., Aki, T., Hirota, K., Nomura, A., and Kurachi, K., 1979, Augmentation of puerperal lactation by oral administration of sulpiride, *J. Clin. Endocrinol. Metab.* **48:**478–482.

91. Howie, P. W., Houston, M. J., Cook, A., Smart, L., McArdle, T., and McNeilly, A. S., 1981, How long should a breast feed last?, *Early Hum. Develop.* **5:**71–76.
92. Lucas, A., Lucas, P. J., and Baum, J. D., 1979, Pattern of milk flow in breast-fed infants, *Lancet* **2:**57–58.
93. Grady, E., 1977, Breastfeeding the baby with a cleft of the soft palate, *Clin. Pediatr.* **16:**978–981.
94. Gibbs, J. M., 1973, Cleft palate babies: One mother's experience, *Nurs. Care* **6:**19–23.
95. Newman, A. J., Gross, S., 1963, Hyperbilirubinemia in breast-fed infants, *Pediatrics* **32:**995–1001.
96. Arias, I. M., Gartner, L. M., Seifter, S., and Furman, M., 1964, Prolonged neonatal unconjugated hyperbilirubinemia associated with breast feeding and a steroid, pregnane-3 (alpha), 20 (beta)-diol, in maternal milk that inhibits glucuronide formation *in vitro, J. Clin. Invest.* **43:**2037–2047.
97. Ramos, A., Silverberg, M., and Stern, L., 1966, Pregnane-diols and neonatal hyperbilirubinemia, *Am. J. Dis. Child.* **111:**353–356.
98. Odievre, M. and Luzeau, R., 1978, Lipolytic activity in milk from mothers of unjaundiced infants, *Acta. Paediatr. Scand.* **67;**49–52.
99. Foliot, A., Ploussard, J. P., Housset, E., Christoforov, B., Luzeau, R., and Odievre, M., 1976, Breast milk jaundice: *in Vitro* inhibition of rat liver bilirubin–uridine diphosphate glucuronyltransferase activity and a protein–bromosulfophthalein binding by human breast milk, *Pediatr. Res.* **10:**594–598.
100. Winfield, C. R. and MacFaul, R., 1978, Clinical study of prolonged jaundice in breast- and bottle-fed babies, *Arch. Dis. Child.* **53:**506–507.
101. Ernest, A. E., McCabe, E. R. B., Neifert, M. R., and O'Flynn, M. E., 1980, Guide to breastfeeding the infant with PKU, U. S. Department of Health and Human Services, Publication No. (HSA) 79-5110, U.S. Government Printing Office.

11

Maternal Problems in Lactation

James A. McGregor and Marianne R. Neifert

Until relatively recent times, survival of human newborns depended upon maternal or surrogate human milk. The recognition of possible maternal problems related to lactation now commonly leads to discontinuation of breast-feeding often on inadequate grounds. Maternal complications associated with breast-feeding are diverse and often difficult to manage, frequently because of their interdisciplinary nature. As these problems are more completely understood, it becomes apparent that the majority of mothers may be supported in their decision to nurse. In this chapter, we will consider acute and chronic maternal medical problems in their relation to breast-feeding.

LACTATION AND INFECTIOUS DISEASE

The nutritional importance of milk to all mammalian life should not obscure the point that the microorganisms that surround and endure within us may be spread by breast-feeding. The effects of bacteria, viruses, yeasts, and other microscopic life forms on the mammary gland and the nursling have been better studied in animal husbandry than in human medicine. We will limit our discussion to humans, with the understanding that observations made with other mammalian species may increase awareness of the potentially infective connections between mothers and their nursing babies. Practical recommendations will be given wherever possible, although in many circumstances hard scientific data which would allow firm evaluation of these practices is lacking.

James A. McGregor • Department of Obstetrics and Gynecology, University of Colorado School of Medicine, Denver, Colorado 80262. *Marianne R. Neifert* • Department of Pediatrics, University of Colorado School of Medicine, Denver, Colorado 80262.

Mastitis

Mastitis is a clinical and pathological term which describes a wide range of inflammatory disorders of the breast, beginning with bacterial cellulitis, and proceeding to misadventures with foreign bodies, including silicone, and rapidly advancing "inflammatory" breast cancer.[1-4]

The term *sporadic puerperal mastitis* applies to nonepidemic breast infection in lactating mothers. This common disorder is generally caused by less virulent strains of *Staphylococcus aureus,* or less commonly, other skin or mouth microflora shared between mother and infant.[5,6] Pathologically, puerperal mastitis is a cellulitis of interlobular connective tissue characterized by breast pain, swelling, redness, and fever.[5] It is not clear how infection of connective tissue rather than intraductal or glandular tissue occurs. The disease is often associated with cracked or fissured nipples, which may lead to invasion of bacteria at the areola.

Epidemic puerperal mastitis is mediated by highly virulent strains of *Staphylococcus aureus,* which may spread between mothers and babies as well as hospital personnel.[5] These virulent strains have been responsible for outbreaks of serious disease including sepsis in hospital obstetrical and newborn units, predominantly in the decades subsequent to the introduction of penicillin.[7,8] Nonpuerperal mastitis suggests a ductal abnormality or the local manifestation of a systemic infectious process, such as tuberculosis. Surgical drainage is commonly necessary in nonpuerperal mastitis, whereas lactating women may be treated successfully with appropriate antimicrobial medications.[9]

Sporadic Puerperal Mastitis

Sporadic puerperal mastitis typically presents with chills, fever, malaise, focal erythema, and tenderness in the affected breast.[10,11] The adage "Flu in the breast-feeding mother is mastitis until proven otherwise" should be considered whenever malaise and fever coexist in a nursing mother. The frequency and importance of nonepidemic puerperal mastitis is underestimated because the onset of this infection is typically delayed until after hospital discharge.[12,13] Nonepidemic puerperal mastitis generally occurs before the end of the second postpartum week, with another peak at 5 to 6 weeks postpartum.[11] In the preantibiotic era, the incidence of puerperal mastitis varied between 0.5% and 8%.[12,14] A limited modern study found a 2.5% incidence of mastitis in a large prepaid hospital maternity service with good postpartum care.[6] Abscess formation was diagnosed in 4.6% of all patients with mastitis in this study despite the easy availability of medical care.[6] All of the abscesses occurred in women who had elected to wean, whereas no ill effects were noted in either infants or mothers who continued to nurse.[6]

The actual pathophysiologic mechanisms of mastitis of any kind are ill understood. Apparently, the extraductal breast tissue is colonized by bacteria from the areola, probably shared with baby's oropharynx. Although the microbial population of breast milk is uncertain because samples have always been collected after passing through the exposed areola, several studies suggest that milk from nonmastitic breasts contains low but significant populations of bacteria.[6,7] Microbial constituents similar to skin or mouth flora were found in 97% of samples in a study of expressed milk by Carrol *et al.*[15] Six percent of the samples contained *Staphylococcus aureus*, 7% Enterobacteriacea, and 2% group B streptococci. In a study of women with puerperal mastitis, Marshall *et al.* documented excretion of potential pathogenic bacteria in similar concentrations from both breasts, even when one appeared uninfected.[6] Although not yet reported, examination of mastitic milk for anaerobic microorganisms may be interesting since anaerobes are the most common mouth flora.

Since the site of infection in puerperal mastitis is extraductal, it is thought that continued breast-feeding is not harmful to the infant.[6,11,13,16] Indeed, the infant is probably ingesting bacteria which originated from his own oral flora. Quantitative microbiologic cultures of human milk suggest that normal women may excrete up to 10^8 to 10^9 colony-forming units per milliliter of milk, including *Staphylococcus aureus*, without obvious disease in either the mother or baby.[6,15] One presumption is that the presence of organisms in the breast is associated with secretion of specific IgA antibodies against the involved microflora. Low concentrations of antibiotics are also excreted in breast milk when a mother is treated for mastitis, and this may have some protective value for the infant. Although none of these suppositions is supported by scientific study, empirical observations of relatively large numbers of breast-feeding mothers suggest no untoward effects on the babies when breast-feeding is continued in the presence of nonepidemic puerperal mastitis. A shorter course of illness with decreased abscess formation has been observed in the mother.[6,11,17]

Early institution of antibiotic therapy appears mandatory in the prevention of abscess formation. Because of the preponderance of *Staphylococcus aureus* in mastitic breast milk cultures, either oral dicloxacillin, a cephalosporin, or erythromycin in penicillin-allergic patients, would appear to be optimal therapy. However, treatment with β-lactamase susceptible penicillins is commonly effective, suggesting the possibility that oral anaerobic bacteria such as *Bacteroides melaninogenicus* may play a role in mastitis.

Continued nursing in the presence of sporadic puerperal mastitis, while encouraged, is often hampered by the exquisite pain that can accompany the disease, necessitating appropriate analgesia. Uncomfortable engorgement may be partially due to edema, impairing milk flow from the affected breast. Heat application usually affords temporary relief and may enhance letdown of milk. Feedings should be initiated on the unaffected breast and the infant moved to the affected side only after letdown has occurred. An elevated sodium content of mastitic milk may occasionally lead to an infant's reluctance to nurse on the affected side,[18] so that simultaneous hand expression of milk from the mastitic breast can be performed while the infant nurses on the other side. With severe discomfort, lying on the affected side in a hot tub of water and allowing the breast to float may provide some relief from pain. Milk can be hand expressed directly into the warm water when exquisite pain does not permit emptying of the breast in any other way. Fortunately, symptoms usually subside within 36 to 48 hr of instituting antibiotic therapy. Bedrest, if not self-imposed, is commonly mandated until clinical improvement ensues. Donations to breast milk banks by mastitic mothers are contraindicated, as is the use of communal breast pump facilities because of the possibility of inadequate decontamination procedures.

In some instances, sporadic puerperal mastitis is recurrent, with women experiencing multiple episodes during one lactational period. Recurrence may be attributed to inadequate length or spectrum of antibiotic therapy, to chronic nipple breakdown with cracks and fissures, to ductal abnormalities causing incomplete milk drainage from a particular lobe, as well as the newborn's continued colonization with the original offending organism. Neifert has noted several cases in which vigorous upper arm activity preceded individual episodes of recurrent mastitis. Types of activity included mowing the lawn, vacuuming, jumping rope, raking leaves, and shoveling.

Breast Abscess

Breast abscess formation is a major complication of postpartum mastitis, often associated with abrupt weaning during the illness or with delay in initiation of antibiotics.[6,16] An abscess generally requires hospitalization and surgical drainage with appropriate antimicrobial therapy based on gram stain, culture, and sensitivities.[19-21] While breast-feeding may be continued on the unaffected side, in the face of a draining abscess, the affected breast should be temporarily emptied by manual or gentle pump expression, preferably in conjunction with the letdown reflex.[10]

Epidemic Puerperal Mastitis

Epidemic puerperal mastitis is happily uncommon.[10,11] This infection, often involving both mother and baby, generally occurs as a hospital-acquired infection where virulent organisms may be spread on the hands of medical personnel or from contact with the hospital environment.[5,7,8,12] The possibility of serious complications in both mother and baby has led most authors to proscribe continued lactation.[5,6,7] However, these suggestions for discontinuing breast-feeding were made either in the preantibiotic era or in a time when penicillin-resistant staphylococci were not dealt with easily except by strict isolation techniques. It may be possible that prompt treatment of the mother and baby with appropriate antibiotics, combined with isolation and good antiseptic practices, may cut short a modern outbreak of epidemic mastitis.

Conclusions

A number of problems associated with mastitis demand further investigation, including more exact identification of pathogens by use of aspiration to isolate organisms from the mastitic breast, documentation of effects on the infant of continued nursing through mastitis, evaluation of long-term effects of mastitis on milk production, and examination of factors predisposing to acute and recurrent mastitis. Effective preventive techniques and the optimal cost-effective therapy also require further delineation.[22]

Painful Nipples and Candida albicans

While mild nipple tenderness during the first few days of breast-feeding is common and usually self-limited, nursing is hampered in some women by severe, chronic nipple pain associated with every feeding. Many painful nipples are essentially "chapped" and respond to liberal, almost constant, application of a protective ointment, such as lanolin. Dry heat, provided by a 75-watt light bulb or a hairdryer, may also promote healing. Sometimes a blister, open fissure or other nipple breakdown occurs, with healing being disrupted by the frequency of feeding. Occasionally, the use of Syntocinon® nasal spray to enhance letdown decreases the intensity of nursing or hand expression of milk for 24 to 48 hr rests the affected nipple sufficiently to allow healing to occur. However, none of these measures is likely to be effective in a severe case of infection with the yeast, *Candida albicans*.

Candida albicans grew from 75% of the nipples of a small group of women presenting with chronic nipple pain beginning more than 2 weeks postpartum (J. Parsons and M. Neifert, unpublished data). Typically, the severe burning, stinging pain which radiated throughout the breast persisted long after feedings. None of 18 pain-free controls grew *Candida* from their nipples. Despite the severity of pain in these symptomatic women, the nipples were generally unimpressive upon examination. Positive cultures correlated with maternal prenatal or postpartum monilial vaginitis, recent history of maternal antibiotic therapy, or evidence of thrush in the infant. A high incidence of thrush has been noted in the newborn following vaginal delivery in the presence of untreated maternal monilial vulvovaginitis.[23] *Candida albicans* is passed from the infant's oral pharynx to the mother's nipple which, being a warm, moist, frequently macerated epidermis, is colonized and possibly infected.

In the presence of characteristic and chronic nipple pain or predisposing factors, the nipples should be cultured on blood agar or preferably selective media, such as Sabouraud's or Nickerson's, in order to determine the presence of yeast. Although therapy is still not well defined, suggested treatment includes meticulous air drying of the nipples, topical application of an antifungal agent such as nystatin, clotrimazole, or miconizole, in addition to eradication of infant thrush and maternal genital tract candidiasis. Hopefully, increased recognition of *Candida* infection as a cause of chronic, sore nipples will lead to more effective prevention and management.

In those rare instances when a mother simply cannot tolerate nursing on a severely sore nipple, a simple home-made breast pump can be used to empty the breast, without contact with the nipple, as follows:

> An empty, wide-mouthed jar (i.e., one-quart Ocean Spray® juice jar is ideal) is selected, grasped with protective oven mittens, and filled with hot tap water. After sitting a minute, the jar is emptied and the mouth of the jar is cooled with a cold, wet cloth. The breast is moistened with lukewarm water and then inserted into the mouth of the jar, sealing the top. The mother continues to lean over the jar, maintaining the seal with the breast, while the warm jar is gradually cooled by wiping with a cold, wet cloth. As the heated air in the jar cools, a gentle vacuum is created, and, in conjunction with a letdown reflex, the breast can be emptied without any direct contact with the damaged nipple.[24]

Tuberculosis

Tuberculosis or other granulomatous mastitis is uncommon in the puerperal period.[25,26] Maternal handling of the baby in any way, including breast-feeding, is contraindicated in women with active, possibly communicable tuberculosis. Newborns remain highly susceptible to *Mycobacteria tuberculosis* and prevention of the spread of this disease to the newborn from any family member, including the mother, is of utmost importance. In the past, mothers have been considered to be noninfectious to a newborn after 3 weeks of bactericidal multiple drug antituberculosis therapy. This is an appreciably longer period of time than is considered adequate to prevent communication of tuberculosis from one adult to another. After initiation of multiple drug therapy for this period of time, the mother may handle the baby, but by then breast-feeding may be difficult, unless lactation has been maintained by regular expression of milk (see Chapter 10). We should strive to identify women and other family members with active tuberculosis well before delivery occurs and institute therapy to ensure that they are not infectious to the newborn. Isoniazid prophylaxis in the newborn may be a realistic method of preventing the spread of tuberculosis to the infant and may well replace BCG vaccination. Common sense dictates that use of communal pumps or donations to breast milk banks by mothers with tuberculosis is contraindicated.

Herpes Viruses

Cytomegalovirus

The herpes virus, cytomegalovirus (CMV), remains the commonest intrauterine (1 to 2%) viral infection.[27] Approximately, 5 to 10% of intrauterine infections are symptomatic in the newborn, often causing lifelong multisystem damage. The remainder of congenitally infected individuals are at risk for hearing and visual defects and increased risk of "school failure." Approximately 14% of American women who have been studied have CMV excretion from the cervix during the birth of their infants. The majority of babies that pass through contaminated birth canals become infected with CMV without recognized harm, unless they are immunologically impaired or severely preterm.[27] Vaginal delivery through a CMV-excreting cervix with intrapartum acquisition of CMV is not contraindicated because the newborn generally "handles" the infection without great difficulty.

CMV expression from mammary tissue, as from salivary glands and the cervix, is not uncommon and occurs at least transiently in 27% of seropositive postpartum mothers and at least 18% of all mothers.[27–29] In a well-done study of 17 women excreting detectable CMV in colostrum or milk, but not by the salivary or cervical routes, nine (52%) of the exposed newborns acquired CMV between 3 weeks and 9 months of age.[28] None of these infants developed detectible morbidity after a mean of 2 years of follow-up.

Although it appears that CMV may well be transmitted through breast milk, the normal term newborn is not damaged by this route of infection, suggesting that the benefits of breast-feeding outweigh the small risks of morbidity from CMV-contaminated breast milk. This may not be the case for significantly preterm or immunologically impaired newborns. Breast-feeding of very small newborns by CMV-shedding mothers may reasonably be avoided as might breast milk donations.

Herpes Simplex Virus

Neonatal infection with herpes simplex virus (HSV) is the severest perinatal viral infection.[30] Acquisition of HSV occurs most commonly during passage through the birth canal and less commonly postpartum from hospital or family sources.[30] It is rarely acquired antenatally. Although HSV secretion has been reported to occur asymptomatically from the oropharynx and cervix in as many as 1% of women, there is little data regarding secretion of HSV in breast milk.[30] A single case of neonatal disseminated HSV infection beginning with herpetic vesicles at the newborn's oropharynx has been reported.[31] Examination of the mother revealed no herpetic lesions and medical attendants and family were free of disease. No vesicular lesions were present on either breast, but breast milk 9 days postpartum yielded a positive culture for HSV which corresponded to the virus isolated from the newborn. Transient excretion of HSV from the cervix or other areas cannot be excluded in this case, but it appears possible that HSV excreted from the breast was the cause of the infection.

Herpetic lesions may occur and be infectious on all parts of the body including the breasts. If herpetic lesions are present at the breast, direct contact, and hence breast-feeding, is contraindicated until the lesions are fully healed and are culture-negative. A single case of bilateral areolar herpetic infection with neonatal death has been reported.[32] In this instance, the baby may well have transferred the herpes to the mother's nipples subsequent to an oral infection.

When active genital herpetic lesions are present at onset of labor, caesarean section is indicated to prevent contamination of the infant by vaginal delivery. The infant should be isolated from other infants after birth and his clinical condition carefully monitored, while surface viral cultures are pending. With a well-appearing infant delivered by Caesarean section without premature rupture of membranes, neonatal care can best be accomplished in a rooming-in setting with the mother. Detailed instruction and appropriate supervision should be provided to the mother to assure aseptic care in handling the infant. If breast-feeding is desired, it should be permitted, with care exercised not to contaminate the infant with maternal articles of clothing which have been exposed to the perineum or by breaks in hygiene. A clean cover gown draped over the mother's lap during feedings will serve as a reminder to avoid exposure to maternal undergarments and lochia.

Varicella

Since babies of mothers who develop varicella less than 5 days before birth are unprotected by passive immunization by maternal antibodies transported through the placenta, breast-feeding should be curtailed until the mother is no longer contagious with varicella. In any such instance, the newborn should receive passive immunization with varicella-zoster immunoglobulin promptly at birth.[33]

Rotaviruses

Human rotaviruses are the cause of sporadic and epidemic nonbacterial diarrheal infection in infants and newborns. Some nursery populations show a consistant 40 to 50% of newborns colonized with rotaviruses before discharge.[34] Identification of rotaviruses is made by antigen-detection techniques (ELISA) or direct immunoelectronmicroscopy of stool. Infection of the newborn can occur following transmission of the virus from mother to baby, most likely during birth, or from fecal contamination by infected mothers or hospital personnel.[34,35] Some initial studies showing higher rates of rotavirus excretion by breastfeeding babies are unconfirmed and no rotavirus particles have been identified in limited breast milk samples.[36] Unfortunately, breastfeeding does not appear to protect the infant from rotavirus colonization or infection.

Hepatitis B Virus

Vertical spread of hepatitis B (HBV) or other forms of viral hepatitis from mother to infant should be avoided wherever possible. Hepatitis-B-virus-infected newborns commonly become HBV carriers and may be predisposed to complications of HBV infection as well as being sources of HBV in the community.[36] The neonatal hazards from breast-feeding by an actively HBV-infected or HBV-carrier mother remain a source of concern even though direct proof of Hepatitis B virus transmission to nursing newborns via breast milk is lacking. The breast milk of 60 to 70% of carrier mothers, when examined by radioimmunoassay, and 90% when examined by immunoelectronmicroscopy, has been shown to contain low levels of hepatitis B surface antigen (HBsAg).[37] During breast-feeding, it is thought that some infective HBV virus may enter the infant's mucosal surfaces through an abrasion or by other mechanisms. During lactation, cracked or fissured nipples may even lead to the direct ingestion of HBV infectious maternal serum by the newborn which may be absorbed through a mucosal defect anywhere in the gastrointestinal tract. For these reasons, some authorities recommend against breast-feeding by infected or carrier mothers in situations where human milk substitutes may be safely given.

A contrasting point of view holds that babies at risk for HBV have already been directly exposed to large quantities of maternal blood, antigen-positive amniotic fluid, and vaginal secretions during the birth process, if not an occasional transplacental exposure. Other intimate contacts between mother and baby may expose the newborn to further HBV. Over time, such cumulative exposures may also lead to HBV infection in the newborn, making it unlikely that breast-feeding *per se* can be isolated as a risk factor for vertical transmission of HBV. The multiplicity of possible routes of exposure also serves to underscore the necessity of immunoprophylaxis with hepatitis-B-immune globulin along with possible HBV vaccination promptly after birth in newborns of women who are HBsAg-positive.

Examination of breast milk as a vector of HBV in Taiwan by Beasley[38] suggested that breast-feeding did not alter HBsAg antigenemia in infants born of asymptomatic HBsAg carrier mothers whose infants were examined at 1 year of age. In Taiwan, HBsAg is found in 15 to 20% of mothers, and 40 to 50% of babies born to asymptomatic carriers develop persistent HBsAg antigenemia by radioimmunoassay. Of 92 breast-fed infants followed for 1 year, 49% developed HBsAg antigenemia and a further 4% demonstrated anti-HBsAg, yielding a total infection rate of 53%. Among 55 "similar" bottle-fed infants, 53% developed HBsAg antigenemia and a further 7% demonstrated anti-HBsAg, yielding a total infection rate of 60%, similar to that of the breast-fed infants.[38] Mothers with active disease were not reported. They may provide a greater risk of disease transmission than carriers of HBsAg.

It may well be that breast-feeding by antigen-positive mothers makes little overall difference in geographic areas with endemic HBV because horizontal transmission of HBV after birth obscures any possible disadvantage. In most such areas of the world, breast-feeding should be actively encouraged because of its other advantages in comparison with bottle feeding. However, since less than 1% of North Americans are HBsAg carriers, there is little chance of horizontal transmission of HBV to the newborn. Citing Beasley's work and the availability of immunoprophylaxis, The American Academy of Pediatrics recently altered its recommendations and concluded that breast-feeding is not contraindicated in HBsAg-positive mothers, providing passive hepatitis B immune globulin immunization is accomplished as promptly as possible after birth.[39]

Given these concerns, the following guidelines may be useful in counseling women with viral hepatitis before or during lactation:

1. Breast-feeding is probably permissable in women without active HBV disease and certainly in the uncommon circumstance of an HBsAg-positive newborn. Thus, the majority of mothers with HBV before or during pregnancy may be supported in their decision to breast-feed.
2. Breast-feeding should not be encouraged in women with acute hepatitis, hepatitis B e antigenemia (HBeAg), or other markers of heightened infectivity, such as titers of HBsAg over 1 : 1000.
3. All newborns of mothers with HBV surface antigenemia should receive high titer HBV immunoglobulin 0.5 ml/kg immediately after birth and 1 month later. Active HBV subunit vaccination at birth may prove a useful adjunct to passive immunization when given at a different body site.
4. Mothers with viral hepatitis of any cause and those who are likely or proven HBsAg carriers should be excluded as milk bank donors.

CHRONIC MATERNAL ILLNESS

Psychiatric Illness

Psychiatric illness in the mother is an often cited contraindication to nursing. Yet, if the mother's condition permits custody of the infant, nursing has frequently proved very successful and may actually be safer for the infant than bottle-feeding, provided the mother is motivated in that direction. Although the nature of the underlying psychiatric illness will influence success, in general, a woman should be permitted the opportunity to nurse with close supervision if she strongly desires it. The provision of emotional support and the availability of a doula in the early postpartum weeks are vitally important. Frequent office visits, coupled with public health nurse home visits, should permit adequate supervision of the infant. Maternal self-esteem may be enhanced by carefully explaining to the mother the value of even limited breast-feeding. In many instances, breast-feeding on demand with full breasts as physical reminders of feeding times will be more successful than mixing formula accurately and storing it correctly. However, the effects of maternal drug therapy on the infant and on lactation performance should be considered.

Diabetes Mellitus

Very little is written about nursing in the presence of maternal diabetes mellitus. Because infants of diabetic mothers are frequently born prematurely or encounter neonatal problems, many of these women experience the same initial difficulties faced by mothers of premature infants, necessitating routine pumping of milk until the infant can nurse effectively. Mastitis represents a greater threat to diabetic women, as does monilia infection of the nipples.

Anecdotal data suggest lowered insulin requirements during the actual lactational period for some diabetic women.[40] Clearly, insulin requirements and dietary needs must be closely monitored after delivery and during weaning. Theoretically, the epinephrine response to hypoglycemia may inhibit milk letdown, but no actual data is available. Lactosuria is a normal phenomenon, necessitating specific urine screening for glucose during lactation. Ketones can be excreted in the milk, so ketoacidosis may present a risk to the infant. Despite these cautions, many diabetic mothers have enjoyed nursing their infants when appropriate medical supervision has been available.

Cystic Fibrosis

As the life expectancy for patients with cystic fibrosis has improved, more than 100 women with cystic fibrosis have given birth to infants. Very few reports of breast-feeding among these mothers are available, however. One early report suggested elevated sodium content of a mother's milk,[41] mitigating against breast-feeding of infants born to mothers with cystic fibrosis. A more recent report documented normal milk composition in one mother who successfully nursed for several months.[42] We recently saw an 18-year-old mother with cystic fibrosis who nursed for 3 months with excellent infant growth. The milk had normal electrolyte composition. Because the pulmonary status of the mother deteriorated and she had difficulty maintaining her weight, she elected to wean at 3 months postpartum. An additional concern was the ongoing antibiotic therapy in this woman. Despite the difficulties encountered, the opportunity to nurse was viewed by both parents as a very rewarding experience. Nevertheless, although nursing appears to be feasible in women with cystic fibrosis, close monitoring of their health status and cognizance of potential infant effects of maternal drug therapy are important.

MAMMOPLASTY

Augmentation mammoplasty with silicone implants is commonly performed and generally should not affect the woman's ability to nurse. However, the innervation to the nipple and areola has only recently been defined as being supplied by the lateral cutaneous branch of the fourth intercostal nerve, the lower branch of which pierces the areola at 5 o'clock on the left side and 7 o'clock on the right side.[43] Implants through a periareolar incision which damages this nerve will result in altered nipple sensation postoperatively and will probably interrupt the afferent limb of the neurohumoral reflex involved in prolactin and oxytocin secretion. When unilateral surgery has damaged the reflex arc in one breast only, breast-feeding may proceed fairly normally if feedings are initiated on the unaffected side, thereby stimulating milk letdown in both breasts.

Reduction mammoplasty involving autotransplantation of the nipple severs not only the nerve, but also the lactiferous ducts before they exit at the nipple. Although nerve regrowth may occur, and some ducts may recannalize, normal breast-feeding is never anticipated. It is important that these women not grasp false hopes at the sight of a small amount of milk appearing at the nipple. Nursing can be encouraged, but only if appropriate supplementation is instituted. Reduction techniques in which the lateral cutaneous branch of the fourth intercostal nerve has been carefully identified and preserved should not inhibit breast-feeding. Every surgeon operating on the breast should have knowledge of the anatomy of the innervation to the nipple–areola complex and assure that postoperative sensation and function is preserved.

RELACTATION AND INDUCED LACTATION

There are a number of circumstances in which induction of lactation has occurred in the absence of an immediately preceeding biologic pregnancy or relactation has been established following an interruption in breast-feeding. Many anthropological accounts exist of postmenopausal grand-mothers, or even virginal aunts, who have nursed an infant when necessitated by maternal demise or the birth of twins.[44,45] With premature birth, women who attempt to maintain milk supplies in the absence of a suckling infant often find their volume of milk secretion diminished after the first week. By the time the infant is able to nurse at the breast, the supply often falls very short of his or her nutritional needs. Many women who experience various problems in nursing wean before they had originally anticipated. Some of these women may later obtain new information or support and, regretting their untimely weaning, may elect to relactate. Subsequent infant intolerance of formula may motivate some mothers to return to nursing. Sudden separation of mother and infant through hospitalization of either may cause the milk supply to decline abruptly so that relactation is necessary when the two are reunited. Increasing numbers of adoptive mothers are inquiring about the possibility of nursing their babies, often when they have never experienced a biologic pregnancy. Finally, induced lactation or relactation may have major importance for Third World countries where there is a large infant–protein gap, bottle-feeding is associated with increased morbidity and mortality, and untimely weaning occurs due to ignorance or infant illness and maternal–infant separation.

When counseling a mother who desires to relactate or induce lactation, one must consider several factors: (1) the underlying maternal motivation, (2) the age and needs of the infant, (3) the available support for the endeavor, (4) the history of previous maternal lactation or biologic pregnancy, and (5) the length of time since lactation was interrupted. A woman who has been pregnant, has previously nursed, and is still producing some milk is likely to re-establish a full milk supply. On the other hand, the adoptive mother who has never been pregnant is highly unlikely to fully nurse her infant, although she may make some breast secretion. With this in mind, it is important to stress the significance of the nursing relationship rather than the volume of milk produced.

Although pharmacologic preparations including birth control pills, galactagogues, and synthetic oxytocin have been tried by some women, induced lactation has also been successful in the absence of any pharmacologic priming agents. The essential feature of inducing milk secretion is the provision of an effective, regular suckling stimulus, often coupled with breast massage and nipple stimulation. For adoptive mothers, suckling stimulus can be provided prior to the arrival of the infant by manual or pump stimulation at regular intervals. When possible, enticing the infant to nurse is usually more effective and rewarding for the mother than a mechanical stimulus because of the emotional feelings involved in the act of nursing. The most satisfactory method of encouraging an infant to begin suckling the breast appears to be the Lact-Aid Nursing Trainer® (see Chapter 10), a patented device worn by the mother that allows the infant simultaneously to receive supplemental formula while suckling at the breast, through a flexible plastic tube which lies next to the nipple.[46,47] Prior to arrival of the infant or when the infant suck is weak or ineffective, an electric pump can be used regularly to stimulate milk production at the same time that efforts continue to encourage effective infant suckling at the breast. Galactagogues such as chlorpromazine, metoclopramide and sulpiride, have been advocated to elevate serum prolactin and increase milk production.[48–50] Brown[51] described successful relactation in motivated, healthy women who were provided nutritional support and low-dose chlorpromazine therapy for 1 week. Once milk supply was re-established, each woman provided milk for two young Saigon orphans. Extensive studies of the efficacy of purported galactagogues are not yet available.

In an American study of relactation among 366 mothers, nearly three-quarters of the women nursed beyond 6 months, and 57% were able to eliminate supplements within 4 weeks of the start of relactation. Perhaps more importantly, however, three-quarters of the participants evaluated their relactation experience positively.[47] In a similar study of induced lactation among 240 adoptive mothers, 76% of mothers evaluated adoptive nursing positively although the majority needed to supplement their own milk supply throughout the entire nursing period.[46] Most respondents stressed the maternal–infant relationship and its enhancement through breast-feeding, rather than milk production, as a motivating factor for inducing lactation.

With successfully induced lactation, women report variable degrees of pigment changes in the areola as in routine lactation, as well as secondary amenorrhea, breast engorgement, and letdown sensations. Little data exist on the composition of the milk produced by mothers without biologic pregnancy, but preliminary data indicate the protein composition is similar to that of mature milk, without a colostral phase.[52] Baseline and suckling-stimulated prolactin levels have not been shown to be of value in predicting the likelihood of successful relactation or to correlate with milk production in a small number of women who attempted relactation for sick or premature infants.[53] As might be expected, shorter postpartum intervals and decreased postpartum breast involution correlated with the likelihood of successful relactation and the rapidity of the onset of lactation. A rough estimate of the time needed to establish a full milk supply is about 1 week for each month preceding nonnursing, plus about another week to build up an ample supply.[54] On some occasions, women have overestimated the volume of milk produced, which has inadvertently led to critical malnutrition in their unsupervised infants. Frequent infant weights are necessary as supplemental formula is gradually tapered. By continuing to measure success by the mutual enjoyment of the nursing relationship, rather than by the volume of milk produced, overemphasis on weaning from supplement may be avoided. By 4 to 6 months, when the infant can supplement his diet with solids and sip from a cup, many women find they can discontinue use of the Lact-Aid. The impressive lesson for health professionals is the great effort and expense women will sometimes endure to nurse their infants.[55] Because the situation warrants close monitoring, it behooves professionals to provide the necessary, accurate information, supervision and support.

CONCLUSION

During the recent past decades, bottle-feeding has been substituted for breast-feeding at the merest hint of maternal problems. Only recently have large numbers of women begun to verbalize their wishes to nurse their infants in the face of their own medical problems or special circumstances. Because breast-feeding can often prove advantageous to the infant and fulfilling to the mother, even in unique situations, professionals should be prepared to offer practical information, concrete aids, and emotional support whenever breast-feeding is desired and feasible. The understanding health professional will also be ready with alternative means of emotional support in those, somewhat rare, instances when breast-feeding is inadvisable.

REFERENCES

1. Lang, M., 1977, Mastitis—A melange, *S. Afr. Med. J.* **52:**1–2.
2. Ochsner, A., 1975, Disease of the breast, *Postgrad. Med.* **57:**77–84.
3. Stolz, J. F., Greidman, A. K., and Arger, P. H., 1974, Breast carcinoma mimics acute mastitis, *JAMA* **229:**682–683.
4. Symmers, W. C., 1968, Silicone mastitis in "topless" waitress, *Br. Med. J.* **1:**19–21.
5. Gibberd, G. F., 1953, Sporadic and epidemic puerperal breast infections, *Am. J. Obstet. Gynecol.* **65:**1038–1041.
6. Marshall, B. R., Heppler, J. K., and Zirbel, C. C., 1975, Sporadic puerperal mastitis, an infection that need not interrupt lactation, *JAMA* **233:**1377–79.

7. Leary, W. G., 1948, Acute puerperal mastitis—A review, *Calif. Med.* **68**:147–151.
8. Marsh, F., 1958, Staphyloccocal infection in maternity hospitals, *Lancet* **2**(2):1179–1180.
9. Witten, D. M., 1969, *The Breast*, Yearbook Medical Publishers, Chicago.
10. Devereux, W. P., 1970, Acute puerperal mastitis, *Am. J. Obstet. Gynecol.* **108**:78–81.
11. Niebyl, J. R., Spence, M. R., and Parmley, T. H., 1978, Sporadic (non-epidemic) puerperal mastitis, *J. Reproduct. Med.* **20**:97–100.
12. Moon, A. A. and Gilbert, B., 1935, A study of acute mastitis of the puerperium, *J. Obstet. Gynecol. Br. Emp.* **42**:268–279.
13. Ezrati, J. B. and Gordon, H., 1979, Puerperal mastitis: Its causes, prevention, and management, *J. Nurse—Midwifery* **24**:3–7.
14. Fulton, A. A., 1945, Incidence of puerperal and lactational mastitis in an industrial town of some 43,000 inhabitants, *Br. Med. J.* **2**:693–697.
15. Carrol, L., Davies, D. P., Osman, M., and McNeigh, A. S., 1979. Bacteriologic criteria for feeding raw breast-milk to babies on neonatal units, *Lancet* **2**(2):732–733.
16. Newton, M. and Newton, N. R., 1950, Breast abcess—A result of lactation failure, *Surg. Gynecol. Obstet.* **91**:651–655.
17. Newton, M., 1961, Human lactation, in: *The Mammary Gland and Its Secretions*, Volume 1 (S. K. Kwon and A. T. Cowie, eds.), Academic Press, New York, pp. 281–320.
18. Conner, A. E., 1979, Elevated levels of sodium and chloride in milk from mastitic breasts, *Pediatrics* **63**:910–911.
19. Sherman, A. J., 1956, Puerperal breast abscess, *Obstet. Gynecol.* **7**:268–273.
20. Leach, R. D., Phillips, I., Eykyn, S. J., and Cerrin, B., 1979, Anaerobic subareolar breast abscess, *Lancet* **1**:35–36.
21. Ajao, O. G. and Ajao, A. O., 1979, Breast abscess, *J. Nat. Med. Assoc.* **71**:1197–1198.
22. Brown, M. S. and Hurlock, J. T., 1975, Preparation for breastfeeding, *Nurs. Res.* **24**:448–450.
23. Shrand, H., 1961, Thrush in the newborn, *Br. Med. J.* **2**:1530–1533.
24. Rees, D., 1976, Juice-jar breast pump, *Keeping Abreast J.* **1**:147–148.
25. Cohen, C., 1977, Tuberculosis mastitis, *S. Afr. Med. J.* **52**:12–13.
26. Cohen, C., 1977, Granulomatous mastitis, *S. Afr. Med. J.* **52**:14–15.
27. Handshaw, J., 1975, Cytomegalovirus, in: *Infectious Disease of the Fetus and Newborn Infant*, (J. S. Remington and J. O. Klein, eds.), W. B. Saunders, Philadelphia, pp. 107–156.
28. Stagno, S., Reynolds, D., Pass, R. F., and Alford, C. A., 1980, Breast milk and the risk of cyomegalovirus infection, *N. Engl. J. Med.* **302**:1073–1076.
29. Hayes, K., Danks, D., Gibus, H., and Jack, I., 1975, Cytomegalovirus in human milk, *N. Engl. J. Med.* **287**:176–177.
30. Nahmias, A. J. and Visitine, A. M., 1976, Herpes simplex virus, in: *Infectious Disease of the Fetus and Newborn Infant* (J. S. Remington and J. O. Klein, eds.), W. B. Saunders Philadelphia, pp. 156–190.
31. Dunkle, L. M., Schmidt, R. R., and O'Conner, D. M., 1979, Neonatal herpes simplex infection possibly acquired via maternal breast milk, *Pediatrics* **63**:250–251.
32. Quin, P. T. and Lofberg, J. V., 1978, Maternal herpetic breast infection: Another hazard of neonatal herpes simplex, *Med. J. Aust. N. Z.*, **2**(2):411–412.
33. Young, N. A., 1975, Chickenpox, in: *Infectious Disease of the Fetus and Newborn Infant*, (J. S. Remington and J. O. Klein, eds.), W. B. Saunders, Philadelphia, p. 521–587.
34. Bishop, R. F., Cameron, D. J. S., Venstra, A. A., and Barnes, G. I., 1979, Diarrhea and rotavirus infection associated with differing regimens for postnatal care of newborn babies, *J. Clin. Microbiol.* **9**:525–529.
35. Crewe, E. and Murphy, A. M., 1980, Further studies on neonatal rotovirus infections, *Med. J. Aust. N. Z.* **1**(1):61–62.
36. Crumpacker, C., 1975, Hepatitis, in: *Infectious Disease of the Fetus and Newborn Infant*, (J. S. Remington and J. O. Klein, eds.), W. B. Saunders, Philadelphia, pp. 452–521.
37. Lee, A. D. Y., Ip, H. M. H., and Wong, V. C. W., 1978, Mechanisms of maternal fetal transmission of hepatitis B virus, *J. Infect. Dis.* **138**:668–671.
38. Beasley, R. P., 1980, Breastfeeding and H.B.V. transmission, *Lancet* **2**:740.

39. Klein, J. O., Brunel, P. A., Cherry, J. D., and Fulginiti, V. A., 1982, Report of the Committee on Infectious Disease, Redbook, American Academy of Pediatrics, Evanston, Illinois, pp. 111–114.
40. Miller, D. L., 1976, The diabetic nursing mother, *Keeping Abreast J.* **1:**102–105.
41. Whitelaw, A. and Butterfield, A., 1977, High breast milk sodium in cystic fibrosis, *Lancet* **2:**1288–1289.
42. Welch, M. J., Phelps, D. L., and Osher, A. O., 1981, Breastfeeding by a mother with cystic fibrosis, *Pediatrics* **67:**664–666.
43. Farina, M. A., Newby, B. C., and Alani, H. M., 1980, Innervation of the nipple-areola complex, *Plast. Reconstruct. Surg.* **66:**497–501.
44. Raphael, D., 1973, *The Tender Gift: Breastfeeding,* Schoken Books, New York.
45. Wieschoff, M. A., 1940, Artificial stimulation of lactation in primitive cultures, *Bull. Hist. Med.* **8:**1403–1418.
46. Auerbach, K. G. and Avery, J. L., 1981, Induced lactation, *Am. J. Dis. Child.* **135:**340–343.
47. Auerbach, K. G. and Avery, J. L., 1980, Relactation: A study of 366 cases, *Pediatrics,* **65:**236–242.
48. Weichert, C. E., 1979, Lactational reflex recovery in breastfeeding failures *Pediatrics* **63:**799–803.
49. Kauppila, A., Kivinen, S., and Yikorkala, O., 1981, Metoclopramide increases prolactin release and milk secretion in puerperium without stimulating the secretions of thyrotropin and thyroid hormones, *J. Clin. Endocrinol. Metab.* **52:**436–439.
50. Aono, T., Shiuoji, T., Aki, T., Hirota, K., Nomura, A., and Kurachi, K., 1979, Augmentation of puerperal lactation by oral administration of sulpiride, *J. Clin. Endocrinol. Metab.* **48:**478–482.
51. Brown, R. E., 1977, Relactation: An overview, *Pediatrics* **60:**116–120.
52. Kleinman, R., Jacobson, L., Horman, E., and Walker, A., 1980, Protein values of milk samples from mothers without biologic pregnancies, *J. Pediatr.* **97:**612–615.
53. Bose, C. L., D'Ercele, A. J., Lester, A. G., Hunter, R. S., and Barrett, J. R., 1981, Relactation by mothers of sick and premature infants, *Pediatrics* **67:**567–569.
54. Horman, E., 1976, Relactation, in: *Symposium on Human Lactation* Publication No. (HSA) 79-5107, (L. Waletzky, ed.) Department of Health, Education and Welfare, Washington, D.C., pp. 109–115.
55. Zimmerman, M. A., 1981, Breastfeeding and the adopted newborn, *Pediatr. Nurs.* **7:**9–12.

12

Psychological Implications of Breast-Feeding for the Mother

Robin Dee Post and Rhoda Singer

In this chapter, we explore the psychological factors that confront women as they decide how they will feed their infants, as well as the emotional issues that surround the experience of breast-feeding. We view motherhood as a developmental stage that provides a woman the opportunity to master issues in her own development at the same time that she is nurturing her infant. We will review the research literature on attitudes of breast- and bottle-feeding mothers, mother–infant attachment, and support systems for nursing women, and explore the literature on the interaction of emotion and neurohormonal processes in lactation.

BREAST OR BOTTLE? THE DECISION-MAKING PROCESS

In some non-Western societies, no viable alternative to breast-feeding has existed. With the advent of safe bottle-feeding in Western societies, women can choose between breast and bottle.[1] They frequently make a decision on the basis of limited information. For example, many women today have not had the opportunity to observe other women nursing.

Psychodynamic Factors in the Decision Not to Breast-Feed

The decision to breast- or bottle-feed appears to be multiply determined. Results of a study on infant feeding choice among primiparous women led Brown et al.[2] to suggest that emotional factors and unconscious motivations are of primary importance. Expectant mothers may experience a variety of psychological concerns when they consider nursing. Feelings of incompet-

Robin Dee Post and Rhoda Singer • Department of Psychiatry, University of Colorado School of Medicine, Denver, Colorado 80262.

ence, anxiety about providing the infant with adequate nourishment, and embarrassment about exposing the breasts are concerns that are predictably shared by many expectant mothers.

In addition, each mother is likely to contend with relatively unique psychological issues emerging from her own developmental experiences and personality dynamics. Benedek[3] has described parenthood as a developmental phase. The anticipated birth of an infant revives memories and feelings of the mother's own childhood. Although some aspects of childhood are pleasant to recall, forgotten disappointments and unresolved conflicts also surface. "In parenthood, the volcanic issues from one's past—perhaps quieted, perhaps almost forgotten—begin to rumble and bubble up." (p. 108)[4] As the child progresses through each stage of development, the mother is confronted with unresolved issues from that phase of her own childhood.[3] Parents have the opportunity to rework and ultimately resolve these conflicts.[3]

Parenthood potentially provides the opportunity for psychological growth, increased mastery, and consolidation of an adult self-concept. However, serious unresolved conflicts can also be disruptive. Each individual has her own relatively unique areas of conflict and her own mode of coping with conflicted wishes and feelings. It is possible, nonetheless, to identify several common psychodynamic issues that may lead to negative decisions about breast-feeding or difficulties nursing the infant.

Anxiety about the Sensual/Sexual Aspects of Breast-Feeding

In our society, the women's breasts are strongly associated with sexuality. There is a striking contrast between the infrequent media exposure of women breast-feeding their infants and the steadily increasing exposure of the breasts for purpose of sexual stimulation and financial profit in advertising, magazines, and films.[5-7] The prospect of breast-feeding may be uncomfortable for many women because exposing their breasts and suckling have sexual connotations.

Salber *et al.*[8] found that embarrassment and excessive modesty were a barrier to nursing for the majority of women they surveyed who decided not to nurse. Sears *et al.*[9] reported that mothers who bottle-fed their infants were relatively more uncomfortable about sex than breast-feeding mothers. Nursing mothers were found to have more permissive attitudes with respect to modesty, masturbation, and sex play among children.

Ambivalent Maternal Identification

When a woman rejects her own mother as an adequate model, she may find herself bereft of an effective strategy for nurturing an infant.[10] Becoming a mother may be disruptive if the woman feels threatened by the heightened identification or experience of competition with her own mother. Melges[10] noted ambivalent identification with mother as a prominent characteristic of women with postpartum psychiatric syndromes.

Longings to Be Nurtured

A woman who continues to yearn for nurturance that is not age-appropriate or realistically available may resent the demands of the infant to be fed and nurtured.[4,11] A regressive wish to be taken care of is a relatively common characteristic of postpartum women.[3,11,12] It is not likely to be a problem unless the longings are intense, unremitting, and interfere with the mother's ability to nurture her infant.

Fear of Aggressive Impulses toward the Infant

Caring for an infant occasionally stirs up unconscious feelings of rage and aggressive impulses that are likely to be extremely anxiety-producing.[11] The mother may refuse to nurture the child or otherwise attempt to gain distance to protect herself from acting out destructive impulses. Significant professional skill is required to deal effectively with problems of this nature.

Fear of Engulfment

During the period of symbiotic attachment, some mothers may experience identity diffusion[10] or a blurred sense of boundaries. If a woman already has a shaky sense of self, she may experience the infant as depriving her of a separate identity or devouring and engulfing her. These feelings may be particularly intense if the mother is nursing; the mother may even experience the child's suckling as devouring. Deutsch[11] described a mother who felt compelled to eat while nursing, in order not to be eaten.

Although Deutsch[11] is a proponent of breast-feeding, she strongly advises that the mother be allowed to adopt a workable compromise, that allows her to parent despite intensive conflicts. "Psychic processes cannot be induced by violence, and when they are unconscious, not even by good will." Deutsch advises:

> Very often the situation can be mastered only by means of a compromise. Women whose whole life has assumed certain forms and whose sublimations have become an irrevocable component of their psychic life, can be good and loving mothers only if motherhood does not become a danger to their solidly rooted life values. Such women are no doubt ready to sacrifice for the child everything that can be consciously influenced. But the capacity for nursing, the constant and honest readiness to be there only for the child, cannot be achieved by this method. The task of the psychologic advisor is to give these women permission to compromise and to renounce nursing. (pp. 291–292)[11]

The Influence of Significant Others

Research suggests that the important people in a woman's life exert a modest influence on her choice of infant feeding practice. The husband appears to have the greatest input into the mother's decision,[2,13,14] although typically the final decision is made by the expectant mother.[2] Switzky *et al.*[14]

found that the breast-feeding women in their sample perceived their husbands to be more strongly supportive of their chosen mode of infant feeding than did the bottle-feeding women. The role of friends in the decision-making process is less clear.

Surveys have shown no correlation between the mother's experience of having been breast- or bottle-fed and her subsequent infant feeding preference.[2,14] Although a woman's identification with her own mother has a significant impact on her mothering behavior,[3,10,11,15] the process is a relatively complex one. A woman's response to her own child is not likely to directly mirror her mother's behavior. Instead, the maternal style of a new mother is likely to reflect a creative, partially unconscious process, in which familiar maternal attributes are selected or discarded, modified, and reintegrated into a unique parenting style.

Results of research conducted in the 1950s and 1960s suggest that the influence of physicians and nursing staff was perceived as minimal.[2,13] Only 15% of the women in the study by Brown *et al.*[2] reported that their decision was influenced by contact with a physician, as compared to 68% who were influenced by what they had read. More recent authors suggest that the physician who is enthusiastic about breast-feeding can effectively promote breast-feeding in his or her practice.[16–18]

The most significant determinants of a woman's decision to breast- or bottle-feed appear to be (1) psychodynamic and attitudinal factors unique to each woman and (2) the impact of social trends. The current revival of interest in breast-feeding may be related to the influence of advocacy groups such as La Leche League International, an expanding medical literature on the benefits of breast-feeding, research on mother–infant attachment and increased concern about health and fitness.[1,5,16,18,19]

The Time for Decision

Evidence from several studies suggests that women decide on their mode of infant feeding long before delivery.[13,14] Guthrie and Guthrie[13] found that 93% of the middle-class women they surveyed decided to breast-feed prior to the last trimester of pregnancy, while 36% had already decided to breast-feed before pregnancy. Switzky *et al.*[14] found that complications of pregnancy and delivery did not affect the decision-making process. These authors suggested that once a woman has committed herself to the idea of bottle-feeding, it is useless for medical staff to pressure her to change her mind. In an effort to encourage new mothers to nurse, breast-feeding was made mandatory in the lying-in wards of King's County Hospital. Women who did not wish to breast-feed complied with the hospital's rules as inpatients, but promptly discontinued breast-feeding as soon as they left the hospital.[20]

Newton and Newton[21] investigated impact of the mother's stated desire to breast-feed on her subsequent success. Mothers who were ambivalent or negative about nursing their infants, gave their infants less milk at a fourth day feeding, were more likely to rely on bottle supplementation, and stated more frequently that their infants refused the breast or had difficulty suckling. The findings of Newton and Newton suggest that a mother's reluctance to breast-feed may find expression in nursing difficulties or outright failure.

ATTITUDES AND PERSONALITY CHARACTERISTICS OF BREAST- AND BOTTLE-FEEDING MOTHERS

Many of the studies on characteristics of breast- and bottle-feeding mothers demonstrate a strong pronursing bias. Nursing mothers are portrayed as more altruistic in their mothering efforts, more comfortable with their femininity, and less narcissistic than their bottle-feeding counterparts. The literature on experimenter effects[22] suggests that researcher's biases may influence in subtle ways the results they obtain. When researchers have a strong personal prejudice, they may unintentionally communicate their expectations to the research participant or may be biased by these expectations in interpreting ambiguous data. Another problem is that authors did not consistently consider their findings in the prespective of changing cultural trends. What may be a maverick choice at one time may be socially desirable at another.

In a variety of studies, the expression of positive attitudes toward breast-feeding correlated strongly with successful lactation, whether attitudes were assessed during pregnancy,[23,24] at the time of birth,[21,25] or at 6-weeks postpartum.[14] Newton and Newton[21] found that mothers who expressed a strong desire to breast-feed gave their babies more milk on the fourth day postpartum than mothers who did not wish to breast-feed and reported more frequently that their babies refused to be bottle-fed.

In contrast to mothers who do not want to nurse, mothers who want to breast-feed had a shorter labor period, found childbirth easier,[25] were more pleased at first sight of their babies,[26] and were more positive about women's life experiences.[25] Breast-feeding mothers more frequently chose a rooming-in plan that allowed them to spend more time with their new babies[27] and brought their infants into bed with them at home.[28]

Utilizing an inventory adapted from the Parental Attitude Research Instrument, (PARI),[29] Switzky *et al.*[14] found differences between the attitudes of breast- and bottle-feeding mothers' on only one dimension, acceleration of development. Breast-feeding mothers were mildly opposed to "pushing" the development of children, in contrast to bottle-feeding mothers who tended to favor such statements. Sears *et al.*[9] found that breast-feeding mothers endorsed more sexually permissive attitudes on the PARI than did bottle-feeding mothers. Switzky *et al.*[14] did not replicate this finding.

From their analysis of Rorschach protocols of women in the third trimester of pregnancy, Brown *et al.*[30] suggested that women who wished to breast-feed were more passive, more accepting of a female role, and had greater needs for affection and approval. In comparison, prospective bottle-feeding mothers were more ambitious and concerned with "masculine strivings." Because interpretation of test results such as these is highly subjective, caution is warranted in drawing firm conclusions from these and other studies based on the Rorschach or other projective measures.[30,31]

MOTHER–INFANT ATTACHMENT: THE IMPORTANCE OF THE EARLY POSTPARTUM PERIOD FOR THE MOTHER–INFANT BOND AND THE ESTABLISHMENT OF LACTATION

Hales and co-workers[32] postulate that there is a sensitive period, soon after delivery, that is "optimal" for establishment of a strong affectional bond between mother and infant. Later, social interactions between mother and neonate appear to be influenced by the amount and timing of contact during the first hours and days after the infant's birth. Lozoff *et al.*[33] suggest that the bonding process is an interactive one in which the infant's behavior is as critical as the mother's. Increased infant arousal during the first postpartum hours may be a salient factor in early contact. In the first hour after birth, the neonate tends to be in a heightened state of responsivity and alertness.[34] Infants are also able to initiate suckling more promptly within the first 18 hr than they are 24 hr after birth.[35]

De Chateau and Wiberg[36] investigated the long-term effects of extra contact during the first postpartum hour on mother–infant behavior. After delivery, 22 primiparous mothers were given their infants for 10 to 15 min. of skin-to-skin contact and suckling. At 36 hr, significant differences in mother–infant interactions were noted when the extended contact mothers were compared to a control group of primiparous mothers. The extended contact mothers held their infants more frequently, sat up while nursing, and their infants were less likely to cry. The behavior of extended contact primiparous mothers was comparable to that of a second control group of multiparous mothers.

At a 3-month follow-up, the authors[37] observed mother–infant free play. Mothers in the extended contact group spent more time kissing their infants and in face-to-face contact. These infants smiled more and cried less frequently. A significantly greater proportion of these mothers were still breast-feeding at 3 months. At 36 hr and at 3 months, the influence of extra contact was more pronounced in mother–son pairs than in mother–daughter pairs, suggesting that the opportunity for physical contact between mother and infant immediately after birth may be more critical to the attachment process for male infants.

In a Swedish study, Carlsson *et al.*[38] compared the behavior of mothers who had extended contact with their infants during the first hour postpartum with that of mothers with limited contact. During observation periods on the second and fourth day after parturition, mothers who had 1 hr skin-to-skin contact after the delivery caressed and held their infants more frequently than mothers whose contact was limited to 5 min. They concluded that the separation enforced upon new mothers by traditional delivery procedures interferes, at least temporarily, with emotional bonding between mother and child. Other changes in ward routine permitting more extensive contact between mother and child did not further increase the effects of initial extended contact.

Corroborating evidence was obtained in a study by Hales *et al.*[32] conducted in Guatemala. These authors compared mothers with extended skin-to-skin contact immediately after birth, delayed contact at 12 hr, and a control group. Results drawn from an observation period 36 hr after birth suggest that a delay of even 12 hr results in less proximity-maintaining behavior and fewer face-to-face interactions than were observed with immediate contact mothers. The early contact group was significantly more affectionate with their infants than the control group, with the delayed contact group occupying an intermediate position. Klaus *et al.*[39] found that the positive effects of extra contact during the first hour and subsequent 3 days after parturition persisted for 30 days.

In a review of research on mother–infant bonding, Morgan[40] pointed out a variety of methodological problems in the bonding studies. She expressed concern that some of the studies did not adequately control for factors that might affect the attachment process, such as socioeconomic status of the mother, her anxiety level, history of the pregnancy, as well as the impact of nursing staff attitudes and the special attention that might be offered to mothers who are participating in innovative procedures. Morgan also cited several studies that failed to provide evidence of a sensitive period in the mother–infant bonding process.[41,42] Although Morgan has raised questions about the experimental design and replicability of existing research on mother–infant bonding, the hypothesis that physical contact between mother and infant soon after birth contributes to the attachment process remains an intriguing one, with important implications for hospital policy. Further rigorously designed research is clearly warranted.

PSYCHOLOGICAL AND HORMONAL INTERACTION IN BREAST-FEEDING

Psychological Factors in Milk Secretion

As common sense would suggest, psychological and emotional factors influence the course of lactation. Although the physiological processes involved in lactation have been well delineated in recent years, the mechanisms through which anxiety and other emotions effect lactation are not well understood. Lactation involves two integrated neurohormonal processes: milk production and milk expulsion or "letdown." Although the two processes are regulated by two different hormones, prolactin and oxytocin, the afferent stimulus for both hormones is mediated by sensory nerve endings in the nipple. These neurons carry impulses to the central nervous system in response to suckling by the infant. Prolactin, secreted by the anterior pituitary in response to these impulses, stimulates the alveoli cells in the mammary gland to produce milk and regulates the amount of milk that is produced.

The infant's suckling also stimulates the secretion of oxytocin from the posterior pituitary into the blood stream. This hormone facilitates milk flow into the larger ducts and sinuses of the breast via a "letdown reflex," felt by the mother as a tingling sensation, which typically occurs within a minute or so after the infant begins to suckle.

A variety of psychological factors have an impact on milk flow. The "letdown reflex," for example, can be conditioned to stimuli associated with the infant, so that the cry of the infant in another room or even thoughts about the infant may result in milk dripping from the mother's breast.[43,44] Pain, anxiety, and embarrassment have been reported to inhibit milk letdown. One young woman, otherwise successful at breast-feeding, found that she became anxious and unable to supply milk to her infant when her mother visited.[11] Newton and Newton[43] successfully inhibited milk ejection by painfully pulling the toes of a nursing mother, placing her feet in ice water, or asking her to solve mathematical problems. The infant received a normal amount of milk when oxytocin was injected.

Several authors have proposed physiological mechanisms to account for the inhibiting effects of maternal emotions, especially anxiety, on lactation: (1) Insufficient suckling. Suckling stimulation is essential to the establishment of an adequate milk supply and to the "letdown reflex." A woman who is ambivalent about breast-feeding may allow her baby fewer opportunities to suckle.[25] (2) The reduction of blood flow. Anxiety has been postulated to lead to transitory vasoconstriction in the breast. Call[6] implicated both the central nervous system and the adrenal medulla in this process. Increasing vasoconstrictor tone was thought to reduce the access of circulating oxytocin to the myoepithelial cells, thereby inhibiting milk "letdown" in animal species.[45,46] (3) It is possible that several components of the central nervous system's fight-or-flight response to stress may contribute to the inhibition of milk flow. For example, β-adrenergic agonists, like epinephrine, have been shown to inhibit the milk-ejection reflex when injected into the cerebral ventricles.[47] They may also constrict the smooth muscle around the larger mammary ducts in some animals, preventing milk leakage.[48] This mechanism has not as yet been identified in human females. (4) Stress reactions, in general, are mediated by the anterior and intermediate pituitary lobe hormones, ACTH, and β-endorphins. The recent finding that the morphine analogs, β-endorphins, modulate oxytocin release suggests a specific interaction between stress and milk "letdown."[49] Although it has generally been assumed that stress has an inhibiting effect on the hormones involved in lactation, several authors have recently reported an increase in prolactin levels associated with stress, especially in persons with neurotic disorders.[50,51] Whether stress-induced increases in prolactin are high enough to promote milk secretion is still a question. Further research is necessary to identify the physiological mechanisms by which stress influences breast milk secretion.

Postpartum Blues

During the first postpartum week, many women experience a brief period of labile affect, characterized by rapid mood swings, tearfulness, irritability, insomnia, and oversensitivity to criticism and perceived rejection.[10,12] In the 19th century, postpartum dysphoria was referred to as "milk fever" by Savage[52] because it coincided with lactogenesis. Pitt[53] noted symptoms of "maternity blues" in half of the women randomly selected from the lying-in wards of a London hospital. Yalom *et al.*[12] reported episodic crying in 67% of new mothers at the Palo Alto–Stanford Hospital. Transitory postpartum blues should be differentiated from more serious psychiatric syndromes, which are characterized by persistent, severe impairment of functioning and require psychiatric intervention.[10]

Postulated etiological factors for postpartum dysphoria include: (1) exhaustion resulting from labor and delivery[12]; (2) the effect of a major life transition, which may threaten the mother's basic sense of identity[3,4,54]; (3) intrapsychic conflict about the maternal role[3,15]; and (4) the profound changes in maternal hormone levels following parturition.

There has been much speculation, but limited research, about the etiological significance of hormonal changes in postpartum mood disturbances. Pitt[53] suggested that the rapid decline in estrogen and progesterone levels after delivery may be a precipitant. The symptoms are similar to those observed with premenstrual tension and include irritability and depression,[56] feelings of helplessness, and a yearning for love.[56] Research on premenstrual tension[55] suggests that fluctuations in estrogen level associated with the menstrual cycle predispose some women to anxiety and/or depression. Yalom *et al.*[12] and Melges[10] reported that a previous history of menstrual difficulties (dysmenorrhea and premenstrual tension) correlated with postpartum depression or psychiatric syndromes. These studies suggest that the rapid fluctuations in hormone levels during the postpartum period may contribute to the emotional lability experienced by many women.

The feelings of inadequacy and irritability that are symptomatic of the "blues"[12] may interfere with the milk "letdown" response, so that the woman's labile mood state interferes with successful breast-feeding. Perceived failure in breast-feeding may then lead to increased feelings of depression.[10,53]

The process of unraveling the interwoven strands to separately assess hormonal, environmental, and intrapsychic components of postpartum emotional reactions is a complex one, requiring more extensive research, direct measurement of hormonal activity, and experimental designs that will adequately control for confounding co-variables. Designing and implementing this research will be a challenge.

Sexuality of Breast-Feeding Women

Sexual and Sensual Aspects of Nursing

Breast-feeding has been described repeatedly as stimulating both sensual and sexual feelings in mother and infant.[57–62] Newton[60] views the sensual interaction between mother and infant as an essential component of the mother–infant bond, which helps to maintain nurturing behavior.

A number of parallels between the experience of breast-feeding and sexual activity have been identified, including: (1) stimulation of the nipples and breasts, with subsequent nipple erection[58,60]; (2) skin-to-skin contact; and (3) uterine contractions, as a result of oxytocin release during nursing and intercourse. Breast stimulation alone may induce orgasm in some women.[58] Masters and Johnson[59] found that several of their subjects reported plateau level sexual responses while nursing. Three women reported that they had reached orgasm. Conversely, milk "letdown" may be triggered by sexual excitement before and during orgasm. Campbell and Peterson[62] speculated that the degree of milk ejection from the mother's breasts might be related to the intensity of her sexual response.

Although some mothers may find the erotic aspects of breast-feeding quite pleasurable, others tend to experience considerable guilt about the sexual stimulation. Masters and Johnson[59] mentioned that six of the 24 nursing mothers they interviewed expressed guilt feelings about their sexual arousal during nursing.

Not all professionals share the view that breast-feeding commonly arouses sexual feelings. For example, Eiger and Olds[57] suggested that a loss of sensitivity of the breasts and nipples diminishes the response to stimulation of the breasts during nursing and sexual foreplay. Although Newton[60] and others[58,59] pointed out the parallels between breast-feeding and sexual arousal, there is a need for further systematic investigation of the sexual feelings experienced by nursing women.

Interest in Sexual Relations

Some women report a lower level of interest in sexual relations with their partners the first few months after delivery. Contributing factors may include: (1) fatigue and weakness, (2) vaginal pain, (3) irritative vaginal discharge, (4) fear of permanent physical harm if sex is resumed too early,[59] (5) decreased vaginal lubrication, (6) interruption of love-making by the baby,[61] (7) the mother's absorption in the baby, and (8) difficulty in emotional integration of maternal and sexual roles.

In a sample of 101 mothers interviewed by Masters and Johnson[59] during the postpartum period, 47% reported a lower level of sexual tension than they had experienced prior to their pregnancy. On the other hand, 24 lactating mothers, in this sample, reported significantly higher levels of sexual tension than before pregnancy. They expressed interest in a rapid return to sexual activity with their husbands. Other authors have described no change or declining sexual interest among lactating women in the first postpartum months.[63,64] Breast-feeding itself may be sexually stimulating for some women, while, for others, the chronic vasocongestion and fullness of the breasts associated with lactation may be the cause of the heightened sexual tension. Much research in this area is characterized by deficiencies in both design and sampling techniques. Carefully controlled studies are needed to shed a clearer light on these speculations.

SUPPORT SYSTEMS FOR NURSING WOMEN

Breast-Feeding and Family Life

The birth of a child, especially a first child, precipitates dramatic changes in the parents' marital relationship and family dynamics. There have been few systematic attempts made to assess the relationship between method of infant-feeding and the marital relationship. By using the PARI[24] Switzky *et al.*[14] found that breast-feeding mothers reported significantly less marital conflict than bottle-feeding mothers. Breast-feeding mothers additionally perceived their husbands as more strongly supportive of their infant feeding practice than did bottle-feeding mothers. The authors suggest that women with "better adjusted" marriages may choose to breast-feed.

Other authors have described a variety of negative reactions to nursing on the part of the father. These may include: (1) jealousy of the closeness of wife and baby during nursing, (2) envy because the father does not have a comparable way to be intimate with the baby, (3) feelings of jealousy that his wife's breasts are now shared, and (4) repulsion towards the dripping breasts.[65] Lerner[66] described a family in which the husband was markedly unhappy with his wife's decision to breast-feed.

> His sexual interest in her diminished dramatically and he told her that her breasts, expelling milk during sexual excitement disgusted him and made him feel that he was sleeping with "a mother." (page 347)[66]

The husband's responses to these negative feelings may include withdrawal, hostility, or lack of support.[66]

After the birth of a sibling, an older child may feel displaced and resentful of the new infant. Sibling rivalry, often accompanied by aggressive and regressive feelings and behavior, is a common phenomenon. Esterly[67] suggests that the intimacy of the nursing relationship between mother and infant may intensify the jealousy of the older child. Some mothers may attempt to avoid this by nursing through the pregnancy and tandem nursing both the infant and the toddler.[68,69] Although this might alleviate some of the jealousy, it does not provide a magical cure and may burden the mother with feelings of anger and fatigue. Breast-feeding can in fact have a negative impact, if it is used by the mother in an attempt to avoid grappling with older siblings' feelings of jealousy. In addition to rivalrous feelings, older siblings are likely to feel fascinated and engrossed with the new infant. The opportunity to observe mother breast-feeding her baby may provide children with a model for maternal behavior and a familiarity with breast-feeding.

Medical Support Systems for the Expectant and New Mother

Results of several studies suggest that adequate information and support, during the pregnancy and after the baby is born, contribute significantly to breast-feeding success.[70-72] In traditional societies, female relatives provide the new mother with practical assistance, reassurance, and relief. The geographic mobility of our society leaves many women with no one to turn to when they need help with nursing problems. The responsibility of health care professionals to provide information about nursing has thus become more critical.

The first opportunity to nurse typically occurs in the hospital. Education and support from nursing staff, as well as hospital routines designed to encourage breast-feeding, can have a positive impact on the mother's first nursing experiences. Much criticism has been leveled at traditional nursery routines by Applebaum[18] and other authors[1,33,73] who feel that the practices of the traditional nursery interfere with the establishment of lactation. Problems often include the separation of mother and infant, a 4-hr feeding schedule, and supplementary bottle-feeding. These practices limit opportunities for suckling and milk drainage.

La Leche League International

Since its inception in 1956, La Leche League International (LLL) has served as a support system for women who want to nurse their children. The aim of LLL is to encourage women to breast-feed and to provide, through mutual help groups, the education, advice, and assistance that are likely to promote successful nursing. La Leche League encourages mothers to invest themselves fully in raising their children, to nurse babies on demand, and to respond to the child's needs in determining the frequency of nursing and the time of weaning.

Results of two studies suggest that LLL members tend to come from a more highly educated, Caucasian, middle-class background.[71,74] The renewed interest in breast-feeding has been reported as emerging in this group of women[13,75] and La Leche League appears to have played a key role in re-establishing interest in breast-feeding.

Silverman and Murrow[76] questioned LLL members in the Chicago area about the features of LLL that were most helpful. The members selected the following features: (1) preparation for delivery, labor, and postpartum blues; (2) encouragement to be assertive with physicians and hospital staff; (3) practical information about nursing and advice about specific problems; (4) emotional support during the stressful transition into motherhood; (5) the opportunity to ventilate feelings of anxiety, guilt, and resentment; and (6) the discovery that their problems and negative feelings were shared by other women. Results of three studies suggest that La Leche League has been effective in promoting successful breast-feeding and teaching members a style of intensive, unrestricted breast-feeding.[70,71,74] However, methodological deficiencies in the studies make it difficult to draw firm conclusions and point to the need for additional, carefully designed research on the influence and effectiveness of La Leche League and other mutual support groups.

PSYCHOLOGICAL CONSIDERATIONS IN WEANING AND EXTENDED NURSING

Prevailing philosophies of when to wean a child seem to vary. Members of La Leche League International espouse the principle of child-led weaning.[77,78] Nursing is terminated in response to the infant's or child's wishes to stop suckling. Thus, the mother who feels a genuine commitment to child-led weaning must be willing to continue nursing beyond infancy, if her child so desires. The mother must be attuned to cues from her child that he or she is ready to stop nursing.

In contrast, Esterly[67] suggests that the mother be attuned to her own needs and wean when she is feeling ready, especially if nursing is becoming a chore. Realistically, the decision to wean involves a multitude of considerations, including the other demands on the mother's time, her beliefs about the appropriate time to wean, the attitude of her physician and family members, as well as her perception of her child's wishes. Another pregnancy may crystallize the mother's decision to wean. Newton and Theotokatos[79] reported that 69% of a sample of 503 mothers in La Leche League weaned their children while pregnant. These authors speculate that pregnancy may provide a biological basis for weaning. In the group of mothers who were pregnant and lactating, 74% reported breast and nipple pain, 57% reported feeling restless or irritated with the nursing child, and 64% noted a decrease in milk supply during the first 4 months of the pregnancy. One hundred fifty eight women in their sample did, however, nurse through pregnancy and continued tandem nursing of two children thereafter. Although pregnancy may provide a "gentle nudge" to wean, the mechanism is neither invariable nor automatic.

Advice to mothers on how to wean typically emphasizes gradual reduction in the frequency of nursing, eliminating one feeding at a time.[67,78,80] However, based on their study of infant distress associated with weaning, Sears *et al.*[9] suggest that the transition be made as decisively as possible. The children they studied seemed to be most upset when their mothers were indecisive and prolonged the weaning process.

The most controversial subject, in the literature on weaning, is the extended and, at times, secretive nursing of toddlers and young children, which Avery[77] has referred to as "closet nursing." Consistent with the philosophy of baby-led weaning, members of La Leche League are encouraged to continue nursing until the child is ready to stop. Although nursing is no longer a primary source of food, the toddler may still wish to nurse as a means of obtaining affection, security, and assurance. Avery[77] believes that extended nursing of young children is not acceptable in our culture, although it is traditional in non-Western cultures. Mothers who fear a critical response from other people may decide to keep some aspects of nursing secret. In a survey of 45 La Leche League mothers, Avery[77] found that 60% of these women kept such secrets. Knowledge that the woman was breast-feeding an older child was withheld from physicians, parents and in-laws, preschool teachers, friends and neighbors, and sometimes even the husband.

Since extended nursing is relatively novel in our society and the mother may encounter some negative reactions, it seems that it would be helpful for the nursing mother to evaluate the benefits and liabilities resulting from her decision. Considerations that are relevant include: (1) What impact will continued nursing have on the child's development? Knowledge of the developmental issues that the child is facing may help the mother make this assessment. (2) What benefits are gained by continued nursing? (3) As indicated earlier, each new developmental step in the child has the potential for stimulating conflicts, originating in the parent's childhood, as well as the opportunity for new resolutions and integration. Is the mother using techniques such as breast-feeding, that have proven to be comfortable, to avoid dealing with new issues and conflicts? (4) If nursing must be kept a secret in some situations, what impact will the secrecy have on the child? (5) Can the mother comfortably handle negative reactions from other people? Will criticism affect her self-esteem? (6) Does she have any conflicts about continuing to nurse? These considerations may serve as guidelines to help a nursing mother make a decision that is individually tailored to her situation and her child's age-appropriate needs.

CONCLUSIONS

In our review of the literature on psychological implications of breast-feeding, we were impressed by the recent proliferation of advice and information written for physicians, nurses, and expectant mothers. These clinical articles were strongly supportive of nursing and were potentially quite helpful. The research literature, on the other hand, was relatively inconsistent in quality. Many of the studies we reviewed were limited by methodological deficiencies, including lack of controls, failure to report statistical findings, and small or biased samples. The strong pro-breast-feeding attitudes expressed by many of the researchers caused us to wonder whether some of the experimental findings were biased by the authors' expectations. In addition, the dramatic changes in cultural norms over the last 15 years were not adequately considered by some of the authors. Attempts to isolate personality characteristics of breast- and bottle-feeding women have yielded few significant results. However, research clearly suggests that positive attitudes and a strong commitment to breast-feeding are related to successful outcome.

The most intriguing series of studies we reviewed was on mother–infant bonding. The majority of studies yielded results suggesting that there is a time period immediately after the neonate's birth when mother–infant interaction tends to promote attachment. These authors contend that ex-tended contact soon after birth should lead to more successful nurturing, including breast-feeding. If this research is valid, the results suggest that hospital delivery practices be designed to encourage mother–infant contact in the hours after delivery. Questions reaised by Morgan[40] about the research methodology in these studies and the inconsistent results obtained in several studies point to the need for further, tightly designed research on postpartum mother–infant contact.

Another promising arena for future research is the interaction of maternal emotions and neurohormonal processes and their effects on lactation. A number of intriguing speculations have been offered, however, the specific neurohormonal pathways through which emotions affect milk production and "letdown" need to be identified through the joint efforts of researchers in physiology and psychology.

From a clinical perspective, the most strongly emphasized theme restated by one expert after another, is the importance of information and support for the nursing mother. Mutual support groups, such as La Leche League International, currently fulfill an important function as a source of guidance that in the past was provided by female relatives. However, support groups do not appeal to all women. Thus, it is essential for health professionals to be better informed about lactation so that they can provide guidance and support for their patients.

It is our belief that motherhood is a developmental step that provides a woman the opportunity to enrich the life of her infant and to master issues in her own development. As professionals who assist mothers in the task of nurturing a new infant, it is important that we appreciate the unique needs and choices of each mother and support her best efforts to meet the needs of her child.

ACKNOWLEDGMENTS.The authors would like to thank Debbie Griest and seven other Denver area La Leche League International leaders who shared with us their experiences with LLL.

REFERENCES

1. Jelliffe, D. B., 1976, World trends in infant feeding, *J. Clin. Nutr.* **29:**1227–1237.
2. Brown, F. J., Lieberman, J., Winson, J., and Pleshette, N., 1960, Studies in choice of infant feeding by primiparas. I. Attitudinal factors and extraneous influences, *Psychosom. Med.* **22:**421–429.
3. Benedek, T., 1959, Parenthood as a developmental phase, *J. Am. Psychiatr. Assoc.* **7:**389–417.
4. Galinsky, E., 1981, *Between Generations: The Six Stages of Parenthood,* New York Times Books, New York.
5. Berger, L. R., 1978, Factors influencing breast-feeding, 1978, *Journal of Continuing Education in Pediatr* 13–29.
6. Call, J. D., 1959, Emotional factors favoring successful breast-feeding of infants, *J. Pediatr.* **55:**485–496.
7. Tylden, E., 1976, Psychological and social considerations in breast-feeding, *J. Hum. Nutr.* **30:**239–244.
8. Salber, E. J., Stitt, P. G., and Babbott, J. G., 1959, Patterns of breast-feeding in family health clinics. II. Duration of feeding and reasons for weaning, *N. Engl. J. Med.* **260:**31–35.

9. Sears, R. R., Maccoby, E., and Levin, H., 1957, *Patterns of Child Rearing*, Row Peterson, Evanston, Illinois.
10. Melges, F. T., 1972, Post-partum psychiatric syndromes, in: *Readings on the Psychology of Women* (J. Bardwick, ed.), Harper and Row, New York, pp. 284–292.
11. Deutsch, H., 1945, *The Psychology of Women, Volume Two: Motherhood*, Grune and Stratton, New York.
12. Yalom, I. D., Lunde, D. T., Moos, R. H., and Hamburg, D. A., 1968, Post-partum blues syndrome: A description and related variables, *Arch. Gen. Psychiatry* **18**:16–27.
13. Guthrie, H. A. and Guthrie, G. M., 1966, The resurgence of natural child feeding: A study of 129 middle class mothers in a college community, *Clin. Pediatr.* **5**:481–484.
14. Switzky, L. T., Vietze, P., and Switzky, H. N., 1979, Attitudinal and demographic predictors of breast-feeding and bottle-feeding mothers, *Psychol. Rep.* **45**:3–14.
15. Benedek, T., 1956, Psychobiological aspects of mothering, *J. Orthopsychiatry* **26**:272–278.
16. Applebaum, R. M., 1975, The obstetrician's approach to the breasts and breast-feeding, *J. Reprod. Med.* **14**:98–116.
17. Newton, N. and Newton, M., 1967, Psychological aspects of lactation, *N. Engl. J. Med.* **277**:1179–1188.
18. Applebaum, R. M., 1970, Modern management of successful breast-feeding, *Pediatr. Clin. North Am.* **17**:203–225.
19. Jelliffe, D. B. and Jelliffe, E. F., 1977, Current concepts in nutrition. Breast is best: Modern meanings, *N. Engl. J. Med.* **297**:912–915.
20. Potter, H. W. and Klein, H. R., 1957, On nursing behavior, *Psychiatry* **20**:39–46.
21. Newton, N. and Newton, M., 1950, Relationship of ability to breast-feed and maternal attitudes toward breast-feeding, *Pediatrics* **5**:869–870.
22. Rosenthal, R., 1976, *Experimenter Effects in Behavioral Research*, Irvington Publishers, New York.
23. Maccaig, H. and Smart, J. L., 1980, Infant feeding: Mothers' antenatal attitudes and subsequent practices, *Proc. Nutr. Soc.* **39**:18A.
24. Salber, E. J., Stitt, P. G., and Babbott, J. G., 1958, Patterns of breast-feeding. I. Factors affecting frequency of breast-feeding in newborn period, *N. Engl. J. Med.* **259**:707–713.
25. Newton, N., 1955, *Maternal Emotions: A Study of Womens' Feelings toward Menstruation, Pregnancy, Childbirth, Breast-Feeding, Infant Care, and Other Aspects of Femininity*, Hoeber, New York.
26. Newton, N. and Newton, M., 1962, Mothers' reactions to their newborn babies, *JAMA* **181**:206–210.
27. Newton, N., Paschall, N., Melamed, A., and Ryan, E., 1974, Psychological and behavioral correlates of mothers' choice of post-partum nearness to infant, in: *Proceedings of the 4th International Conference on Psychosomatic Obstetrics and Gynecology* (H. Hirsh, ed.), S. Karger, Basel, Switzerland.
28. Newton, N., Peeler, D., Rawlins, C., 1968, Effects of lactation on maternal behavior in mice with comparable data on humans. *Lying-in, J. Reprod. Med.* **1**:257–262.
29. Schaefer, E. S. and Bell, R. Q., 1958, Development of a parental attitude research instrument, *Child Dev.* **29**:339–361.
30. Brown, F., Chase, J., and Winson, J., 1961, Studies in infant feeding choice of primiparae. II. Comparison of Rorschach determinants of acceptors and rejectors of breast-feeding, *J. Proj. Tech.* **25**:412–421.
31. Adams, A. B., 1959, Choice of infant feeding technique as a function of maternal personality, *J. Consult. Psychol.* **23**:143–146.
32. Hales, D. J., Lozoff, B., Sosa, R., and Kennell, J. H., 1977, Defining the limits of the maternal sensitive period, *Dev. Med. Child Neurol.* **19**:454–461.
33. Lozoff, B., Brittenham, G. M., Trause, M. A., Kennell, J. H., and Klaus, M. H., 1977, The mother–newborn relationship: Limits of adaptability, *J. Pediatr.* **91**:1–12.
34. Saigal, S., Nelson, N. M., Bennett, K. J., and Enkin, M. W., 1981, Observations on the behavioral state of newborn infants during the first hour of life: A comparison of infants delivered by the Le Boyer and conventional methods, *Am. J. Obstet. Gynecol.* **139**:715.

35. Eppink, H., 1969, An experiment to determine a basis for nursing decisions in regard to the initiation of breast-feeding, *Nurs. Res.* **18:**292–299.
36. De Chateau, P. and Weibert, B., 1977, Long-term effect on mother–infant behavior of extra contact during the first hours post-partum. I. First observations at 36 hours, *Acta Paediatr. Scand.* **66:**137–143.
37. De Chateau, P. and Weibert, B., 1977, Long-term effect on mother–infant behavior of extra contact during the first hours post-partum. II. A follow-up at 3 months, *Acta Paediatr. Scand.* **66:**145–151.
38. Carlsson, S. G., Fagerberg, H., Horneman, G., Hwang, C. P., Larsson, K., Rodholm, M., Schaller, J., Danielsson, B., and Gundewall, C., 1978, Effects of amount of contact between mother and child on the mother's nursing behavior, *Dev. Psychobiol.* **11:**143–150.
39. Klaus, M. H., Jerauld, R., Kregers, C., McAlpine, W., Steffa, M., and Kennell, J. H., 1972, Maternal attachment: Importance of the first post-partum days, *N. Engl. J. Med.* **286:**460–463.
40. Morgan, L. J., 1981, Methodological review of research on mother–infant bonding, *Adv. Behav. Pediatr.* **2:**17–31.
41. Carlsson, S. G., Fagerberg, H., Horneman, G., Hwang, C. P., Larsson, K., Rodholm, M., and Schaller, J., 1979, Effects of various amounts of contact between mother and child on the mother's nursing behavior: A follow-up study, *Infant Behav. Dev.* **2:**209–214.
42. Svejda, M., Campos, J. M., and Emde, R., 1979, Mother–infant bonding reconsidered: Some results, Paper presented at the Western Psychological Association meeting, San Diego.
43. Newton, M. and Newton, N., 1948, Let-down reflex in human lactation, *J. Pediatr.* **33:**698–704.
44. Waller, H. as cited in Newton, N. and Newton, M., 1967, Psychological aspects of lactation, *N. Engl. J. Med.* **277:**1179–1188.
45. Cross, B. A., 1955, Neurohormonal mechanisms in emotional inhibition of milk ejection, *J. Endocrinol.* **12:**29–37.
46. Hebb, C. O. and Linzell, J. C., 1951, Some conditions affecting blood flow through the perfused mammary gland with special reference to the action of adrenaline, *Q. J. Exp. Physiol.* **36:**159–175.
47. Clarke, G. and Merrick, L. P., 1978, A tentative identification of the synaptic transmitters involved in the neural regulation of oxytocin release, *J. Physiol.* **277:**19–20.
48. Cross, B. A., 1977, Comparative physiology of milk removal, *Symp. Zool. Soc. London* **41:**193–210.
49. Clarke, G., Wood, P., Merrick, L. P., Lincoln, D. W., 1979, Opiate inhibition of peptide release from the neurohormonal terminals of hypothalamic neurons, *Nature* **282:**746–748.
50. Miyabo, S., Asato, T., and Mizushima, N., 1977, Prolactin and growth hormone responses to psychological stress in normal and neurotic subjects, *J. Clin. Endocrinol. Metab.* **44:**947–951.
51. Noel, G. L., Suh, H. K., Stone, J. G., and Frantz, A. G., 1972, Human prolactin and growth hormone release during surgery and other conditions of stress, *J. Clin. Endocrinol. Metab.* **35:**840–857.
52. Savage, G., 1875, Observations on the insanity of pregnancy and childbirth, *Guy's Hosp. Rep.* **20:**83–117.
53. Pitt, B., 1973, Maternity blues, *Br. J. Psychiatry* **122:**431–433.
54. Thomas, C. L. and Gordon, J. E., 1959, Psychosis after childbirth: Ecological aspects of a single impact stress, *Am. J. Med. Sci.* **238:**363–388.
55. Ivey, M. E. and Bardwick, J. M., 1968, Patterns of affective fluctuation in the menstrual cycle, *Psychosom. Med.* **30:**336–345.
56. Shainess, N., 1961, A re-evaluation of some aspects of femininity through a study of menstruation: A preliminary report, *Compr. Psychiatry* **2:**20–26.
57. Eiger, M. and Olds, S. W., 1972, *The Complete Book of Breast-Feeding*, Bantam Books, New York.
58. Kaufman, I. C., 1970, Biologic considerations of parenthood, in: *Parenthood: Its Psychology and Psychopathology* (E. J. Anthony and T. Benedek, eds.), Little, Brown and Co., Boston.

59. Masters, W. H. and Johnson, V. E., 1966, *Human Sexual Response*, Little, Brown, and Co., Boston.
60. Newton, N., 1973, Interrelationships between sexual responsiveness, birth, and breast-feeding, in: *Contemporary Sexual Behavior: Critical Issues in the 1970's* (J. Zubin and J. Money, eds.), John Hopkins University Press, Baltimore, pp. 77–97.
61. Greenberg, M. and Brenner, P., 1977, The newborn's impact on parents' marital and sexual relationship, *Med. Aspects Hum. Sex.* **110:**16–29.
62. Campbell, B. and Petersen, W. E., 1953, Milk let down and orgasm in the human female, *Hum. Biol.* **25:**165–168.
63. Riordan, J. M. and Rapp, E. T., 1980, Pleasure and purpose: The sensuousness of breast-feeding, *J. Gynecol. Nurs.* **9:**109–112.
64. Kenny, J. A., 1973, Sexuality of pregnant and breast-feeding women, *Arch. Sex. Behav.* **2:**215–229.
65. Waletzky, L. R., 1979, Husband's problems with breast-feeding, *Am. J. Orthopsychiatry* **49:**349–352.
66. Lerner, H. E., 1979, Effects of the nursing mother–infant dyad on the family, *Am. J. Orthopsychiatry* **49:**339–348.
67. Esterly, N. B., 1975, The obstetrician and breast-feeding: Some views of women physicians, *J. Reprod. Med.* **14:**89–97.
68. Horne, A. E., 1973, Observations and reflections on nursing siblings, La Leche League International, Information Sheet #75, Franklin Park, Illinois, pp. 1–3.
69. Lewis, H., 1973, Nursing two, La Leche League International, Information Sheet #75, Franklin Park, Illinois, 3–4.
70. Ladas, A. K., 1970, How to help mothers breast-feed, *Clin. Pediatr.* **9:**702–705.
71. Ladas, A. K., 1972, Breast-feeding: The less available option, *J. Trop. Pediatr. Envir. Child Health,* **25:**317–346.
72. Peterson, J. C. and Bock, W., 1977, Educating nursing mothers, *Perinat. Care* **2:**44–47.
73. Brack, D. C., 1975, Social forces, feminism, and breast-feeding, *Nurs. Outlook* **23:**556–561.
74. Meara, H., 1976, A key to successful breast-feeding in a non-supportive culture, *J. Nurs. Midwife.* **21:**20–26.
75. Meyer, H. F., 1968, Breast-feeding in the United States, *Clin. Pediatr.* **7:**708–715.
76. Silverman, P. R. and Murrow, H. G., 1976, Mutual help during critical role transitions, *J. Appl. Behav. Sci.* **12:**410–418.
77. Avery, J. L., 1977, Closet nursing: A symptom of intolerance and a forerunner of social change, *Keeping Abreast J.* **2:**212–227.
78. *The Womanly Art of Breast-Feeding*, 1963, La Leche League International, Franklin Park, Illinois.
79. Newton, N. and Theotokatos, M., 1979, Breast-feeding during pregnancy in 503 women: Does a psychological weaning mechanism exist in humans?, in: *Proceedings of the 5th International Congress Psychosomatic Obstetics Gynecology* (L. Carenza and L. Zichella, eds.), Academic Press, London, pp. 845–849.
80. Froehlich, E., 1977, Thoughts about weaning, La Leche League International, Information Sheet #125, Franklin Park, Illinois.

13

Drugs, Toxins, and Environmental Agents in Breast Milk

Robert G. Peterson and Watson A. Bowes, Jr.

INTRODUCTION

In this chapter we will discuss the general pharmacologic principles that describe the distribution of drugs and other substances into milk. The quantitative delivery of drugs to neonates who are breast-fed will be discussed in detail with consideration given to fundamental pharmacologic principles and to pharmacokinetics. In two subsequent sections, a practical discussion regarding the use of drugs during lactation will be followed by a review of the drugs that stimulate or inhibit the process of lactation.

It has been known for some time that milk formulas did not have to be strictly sterile in order for the newborn to thrive. Today, we also know something about other contaminants of breast milk in whose presence the newborn still apparently thrives. These include both pharmacologic and environmental agents. Environmental agents, such as oils, detergents, non-biodegradable substances—otherwise categorically termed pollutants—can be found in breast milk. There are quantitative data regarding certain of these environmental agents that allow for their rational discussions in this text; however, there are numerous substances for which our information is inadequate.

Pharmacologic agents can be addressed more directly. Many drugs have been extremely well studied, and we know not only their chemical characteristics, but also their behavior in biologic systems: their absorption, distribution, metabolic transformation, and routes of excretion. However, in general, the literature that documents the excretion of pharmacologic agents in breast milk is anecdotal, typically with one or two case reports that describe

Robert G. Peterson • Children's Hospital of Eastern Ontario, Ottawa, Ontario, Canada K1H 8L1. *Watson A. Bowes, Jr.* • Department of Obstetrics/Gynecology, University of North Carolina at Chapel Hill, Chapel Hill, North Carolina 27514.

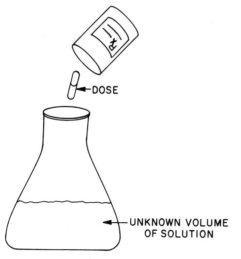

Figure 1. A known dose of medication is added to an unknown volume in the flask. Once mixing occurs, a small sample of the volume is sent for laboratory analysis. The volume in the flask is calculated as:

$$\text{Volume} = \frac{\text{Dose (mg)}}{\text{Concentration (mg/liter)}}$$

a single measurement of a drug in milk with a simultaneous plasma level. As we shall see, in most cases, our knowledge is seriously deficient because dose response characteristics of drugs in milk are generally not available from human studies.

DRUG DISTRIBUTION

Contrary to popular opinion, drugs that are ingested do not move directly from the gastrointestinal tract to the breast. Rather, all substances that enter the body are distributed via the vasculature to various tissues or "compartments" in the body. Breast milk represents one such compartment. In fact, pharmacologically, the elimination of a drug from this compartment represents an additional excretory pathway in the mother. Lipid-soluble substances generally distribute to more hydrophobic sites, e.g., adipose tissues whereas highly polar or charged substances are distributed in body water. Thus, any substance that enters the body is "diluted" into a distribution space in a fashion dependent upon its chemical characteristics, its binding to plasma proteins, its concentration within cells, etc. A substance that is "injected" into the flask shown in Fig. 1 is diluted by the solution in the flask and reaches an equilibrium such that the concentration of the substance is a function of the quantity injected and the volume of solution or distribution volume. In the case of the flask, if one knows the quantity that has been "injected," and if a small sample of the final solution can be sent to an analytical laboratory for concentration analysis, then the volume into which the drug or substance is distributed can be calculated. This is accomplished by:

Volume of distribution (liter/kg) = Dose (mg/kg)/Concentration (mg/liter)   (1)

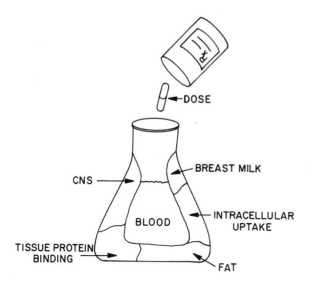

DOSE

CNS

BREAST MILK

BLOOD

INTRACELLULAR UPTAKE

TISSUE PROTEIN BINDING

FAT

Figure 2. A known dose is added to a "body" comprised of numerous compartments which are in equilibrium via the blood. Following distribution of the drug in the various compartments, analysis of its concentration in blood can be used to describe the extent of distribution volume.

The "body" is more complex, but, continuing with the flask analogy in Fig. 2, it can be seen that once the drug has been introduced, it is distributed or diluted into various compartments. This equilibration may take 30 to 60 min following an intravenous injection, and longer if another route of administration is used. Breast milk is just one "compartment" of the body which equilibrates with the remainder of the apparent volume of distribution for the drug. While the concentration of substances in breast milk is often very similar to the concentration of substances in plasma, this is not the case with other body "compartments." The intracellular concentration of substances in various body tissues may be much higher than the concentration in plasma; nevertheless, it is plasma that is readily available from the body for laboratory analysis, not solid tissue, and therefore the distribution of drugs is always related to their concentration in plasma. The apparent volume into which a drug is distributed can be calculated by the pharmacologist as:

$$V_d = \frac{\text{Dose}}{\text{Cp}_0} \qquad (2)$$

where V_d is the apparent volume of distribution, dose is the quantity administered in mg/kg, and Cp_0 is drug concentration in the plasma at zero time.

Cp_0 is a term that requires some explanation. Since the entire body volume is not as accessible as a solution in a flask, there is an equilibration time before complete distribution of the drug throughout the body is achieved. Further, there are also one or more pathways by which the drug is eliminated from this entire volume and this creates a difficulty. When should the concentration of a drug in the plasma be measured in such a dynamic system in order to calculate its distribution space? Fig. 3 depicts the

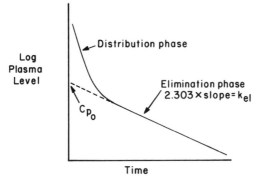

Figure 3. Plot of log of plasma concentration of a hypothetical drug vs. time after administration. Biphasic nature of plot represents early distribution phase followed by elimination phase. Cp_0 is the extrapolated plasma concentration that would occur at time zero if distribution could occur.

problem graphically. A drug injected into the vasculature at time zero reaches relatively high plasma concentrations immediately following the injection. The concentration then falls rapidly as drug is distributed from this central "compartment" to other body spaces. Although there is likely to be some drug elimination occurring during this time, the most substantial contribution to the loss of drug from the plasma is tissue distribution and thus the title, *distribution phase*, issued to describe the initial portion of the biphasic curve. Subsequent to complete distribution, the drug leaves the plasma as a result of metabolic or excretory pathways; the second portion of the curve is titled the *elimination phase*. Since the plasma concentration is continuously changing in this system, the concentration to be used in the calculation of a volume of distribution must be specially selected. The extrapolation of the elimination portion of the curve back to time zero gives the plasma concentration, Cp_0, that would have been observed in plasma had instantaneous distribution of the drug taken place prior to any elimination from the body.

Drug Concentrations in Breast Milk

Since there is good evidence that a drug's concentration in breast milk is often similar to its concentration in plasma,[1-5] the quantity of Cp_0 is useful in estimating the concentration to be expected for drugs in breast milk. Table I lists a number of drugs and several important classes of pharmacologic agents, with their approximate volumes of distribution. In order to estimate the concentration of one of these pharmacologic substances in breast milk, the following calculation can be made:

$$C_b = \frac{\text{Dose}}{V_d} \qquad (3)$$

where C_b is the concentration of drug in breast milk in mg/liter, V_d is the apparent volume of distribution in liter/kg, and dose is the dosage delivered to the systemic circulation in mg/kg.

Table I. Approximate Volumes of Distribution (V_D)

Drug	Volume of distribution (liter/kg)
Acetaminophen	1.0
Amobarbital	1.1
Secobarbital	1.5
Phenobarbital	0.75
Pentobarbital	1.0
Phenytoin	0.75
Amphetamine	0.6
Caffeine	0.6
Salicylate	0.2 (therapeutic doses)
Ethanol	0.6
Furosemide	0.2
Phenothiazines	>30
Theophylline	0.46
Narcotics	>5
Penicillins	0.2–0.3
Digoxin	7.5
Local anesthetics	1.0–1.5
Aminoglycosides	0.3–0.5
Benzodiazepines	>10

As an example, to predict the concentration of digoxin in breast milk following a digitalizing dose of 0.5 mg in a mother who weighs 60 kg the calculation would be:

$$C_b = \frac{0.5 \text{ mg}}{(7.5 \text{ liters/kg})(60 \text{ kg})}$$

$$= \frac{0.5 \text{ mg}}{450 \text{ liters}} \tag{4}$$

$$= 0.0011 \text{ mg/liters}$$

$$= 1.1 \text{ ng/ml}$$

As can be seen, the concentration in breast milk is extremely low. This is because the apparent distribution space for digoxin in this adult body is very large.

The calculation is correct and consistent with the concentrations of digoxin in human breast milk that have been reported.[6] The reason for this large apparent distribution is that this drug achieves high concentration in certain tissues. This demonstrates that the apparent volume of distribution is not a physiologic reality, but rather a pharmacokinetic parameter. Four hundred fifty liters cannot be fit into a 60-kg body (1 liter water = 1 kg)! For comparison, let us consider the distribution of caffeine into breast milk. From Table I, the volume of distribution of caffeine is 0.6 liter/kg. Using this value in the previous equation would give the following predicted caffeine concentration in breast milk (one cup of strong coffee equals 150 mg caffeine):

$$C_b = \frac{150 \text{ mg}}{(0.6 \text{ liter/kg})(60 \text{ kg})} = 4.2 \text{ } \mu\text{g/ml} \tag{5}$$

Both the larger dose and the smaller distribution volume lead to a concentration of caffeine in breast milk almost 4000 times higher than the concentration of digoxin. In spite of this, however, note that while the mother ingested 150 mg of caffeine, the infant will ingest at most a few hundred micrograms of caffeine with a feed.

While the estimation of the concentration of drugs in breast milk appears so far to be straightforward, there are special circumstances that alter the amount of a particular drug that actually reaches the milk. These include plasma protein binding. The concentration of a substance in plasma may be relatively high compared to its concentration in milk due to the fact that a large percentage of the substance in the plasma is bound to albumin or other proteins. An example of this is surosemide where as much as 99% of the drug in plasma is bound to albumin. This binding limits the diffusion or distribution of drug to other compartments of the body, including milk. Other special circumstances must include a consideration of the pKa of the drug, its lipid solubility, its molecular weight, and its possible transport across the mammary alveolar cell. To gain understanding of how these factors will influence drug distribution in milk we must examine more closely the kinetics of transfer of drugs from the vascular compartment to the "milk compartment."

PROPERTIES OF SUBSTANCES THAT AFFECT THEIR DISTRIBUTION INTO MILK

As substances distribute into breast milk, their concentration reaches a maximum dependent upon the maximum concentration in plasma, the main route by which drugs are delivered to the mammary gland. For this reason, substances given by bolus intravenous injection may attain higher concentrations in breast milk than when the same substance and dose is administered orally. As noted in Fig. 3, however, plasma levels of drugs are dynamically changing. During the plasma distribution phase, the concentration of a drug in the breast milk will increase as a fraction of the administered dose reaches the "milk compartment." As noted earlier, substances that are highly protein bound may not distribute rapidly to peripheral compartments. In this case, the peak level attained in plasma is likely to be greater than that attained in milk. It is likely that the same is true for high-molecular-weight substances where diffusion into milk may be slow and plasma elimination may occur at a rate faster than distribution into milk.

Once a drug with a small molecular weight has entered breast milk by equilibration from plasma, where the concentration may be relatively high

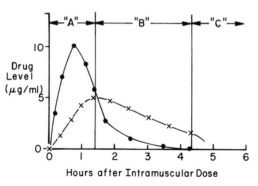

Hours after Intramuscular Dose

Figure 4. Theoretical plot of a low molecular weight drug in plasma (●———●) and breast milk (×———×) following a rapidly absorbed intramuscular dose at time zero. During zone "A," there is distribution of drug from the plasma to milk down a concentration gradient. During zone "B," there is metabolism and elimination of this drug from plasma at a brisk rate. Drug may redistribute from milk into plasma down a reserved concentration gradient. An infant feed occurs during zone "C" with rapid elimination of drug from the breast.

during the distribution phase, a number of factors subsequently affect the concentration of the drug in the breast milk. First, continued dilution of the drug by secreted milk will reduce the concentration, but not the total quantity of drug in the compartment. Of course, expression of milk from the breast either through suckling or by other mechanical means removes the drug permanently from the compartment. But let us consider the case where an infant feeding does not occur for hours following the attainment of peak milk concentration. For those pharmacologic substances where plasma elimination by renal excretion or hepatic metabolism is rapid (that is, when plasma half-times are under 2 hr), the drug may diffuse back from milk into plasma as illustrated in Fig. 4.

There are several considerations for drug diffusion out of milk that relate to the chemical characteristics of the drug molecule. First, highly lipid-soluble substances may be transported on plasma proteins to the mammary gland. Once in milk, however, due to the higher concentration of lipids than present in plasma, the affinity of drug for milk lipid may reduce the quantity of freely diffusable drug to negligible amounts.

A further consideration, widely discussed but of little practical importance from the standpoint of drug *entering* breast milk, is pH and ion-trapping.

Milk, with a pH range from pH 6.8 to pH 7.3 is more acidic than plasma[4] with a normal pH of 7.40. Fig. 5 demonstrates the influence of this lowered milk pH upon the movement of a weakly basic drug (weakly basic due to the presence of a secondary or tertiary amine moiety). The uncharged form of the drug readily crosses the cell boundaries between the plasma compartment and milk; the charged form of the drug is poorly mobile. As a result of the lower pH of milk, a higher percentage of drug is present in the positively charged form in milk than in plasma. The actual percentage of charged drug in a solution compared to total drug depends on both the pH of the solution and also upon the pKa of the drug. When the pH of solution is equal to the drug's pKa, then 50% of the drug in solution at any time will be charged. When the pH is one unit lower than the pKa of the

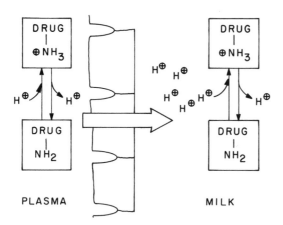

Figure 5. Equilibrium between positively charged and uncharged drug in plasma with movement of uncharged drug into breast milk down a concentration gradient. Relatively higher concentration of hydrogen ions in breast milk favors the charged species.

weak base, then 90% of the drug will be in the charged form. Although this appears to be an overwhelming quantity with only 10% uncharged drug remaining to diffuse back out of milk, in fact this is not the case. The establishment of the ratio between charged and uncharged drugs takes place as an equilibrium influenced by the pH of the solution. However, it is the *ratio* that is dictated by pH, not the absolute quantity of drug that is to bear a charge. As the uncharged drug diffuses back across the cell boundary from milk to plasma late in zone B of Fig. 4, the charged drug remaining in milk will rapidly re-establish the ratio between uncharged and charged fractions. Thus, the amount of total drug falls as uncharged drug moves out of milk, and the quantity of charged drug falls as well. The only stipulation here is that the concentration of uncharged drug in milk determines the concentration gradient between milk and plasma. For example, if the concentration of a drug with a pKa of 8.0 is 5.0 µg/ml in breast milk (pH 7.0), then 90% or 4.5 µg/ml will be charged. The remaining 0.5 µg/ml uncharged drug in solution must then be compared in the uncharged fraction in plasma in assessing the milk–plasma gradient. If early in zone B of Fig. 4 the total concentration in plasma is 2 µg/ml with a plasma pH of 7.4, there will be approximately 0.4 µg/ml in the uncharged form. Since there is a total of 5 µg/ml in milk (pH 7.0) and 0.5 µg/ml uncharged, the drug will slowly move from milk to plasma. Nevertheless, if one were to sample both milk and plasma simultaneously at this time, the drug would be found in milk at a total concentration two and one-half times higher than plasma. This is misleading in that it is only during zone B that milk concentrations are higher. This is due to the fact that drug is cleared from the plasma at a rate that is more rapid than the rate of diffusion out of milk. This back diffusion may be slowed by ion-trapping, but it was never the case that the charge phenomenon led to the $2\frac{1}{2}$-fold concentration of the drug in milk as compared to plasma. The concentration in milk occurred originally by virtue of plasma levels that were high during zone A.

Finally, if the uncharged drug moved rapidly from milk to plasma, then late in zone B, all drugs could have left the milk compartment by continued re-equilibration of charged to uncharged drugs and rapid exit of the uncharged drug. Clearly, single determinations of concentration of the drug in milk and plasma, even when they are simultaneous, do not adequately describe this dynamic state of equilibration.

It is the fact that most pharmacologic weak bases have a pKa between 7.5 and 9.5; since pH of plasma and of milk are both close and rarely fall below 7.0, the ion-trapping phenomenon is probably never as important as considerations of lipid binding, protein binding, or molecular size.

QUANTITATIVE DELIVERY OF PHARMACOLOGIC AGENTS TO THE NEWBORN

The amount of drug delivered to a nursing infant is related both to the concentration of drug in milk and the volume of breast milk that is ingested with each feed. If one assumes that a volume of 200 ml of milk is delivered per kilogram of body weight each 24 hr, then estimation of the "dose" delivered to the infant each day can be made as follows:

$$\text{Dose/24 hr} = C_b \times \text{weight} \times 200 \text{ ml/kg per 24 hr} \tag{6}$$

where C_b is the concentration of drug in milk, weight is neonatal weight in kilograms, and 200 ml/kg per 24 hr is ingested.

Since we have already shown that the approximate concentration of drugs in breast milk can be related to plasma concentrations, values from Table II can be used to estimate the concentration of a therapeutic drug in breast milk.

For example, if one wished to estimate the quantity of digoxin that would be administered to a breast-fed, 4.5-kg infant whose mother was receiving therapeutic doses:

$$\text{Dose/24 hr} = 1.5 \text{ ng/ml} \times 4.5 \text{ kg} \times 200 \text{ ml/kg per 24 hr}$$

$$= 1350 \text{ ng/24 hr} \tag{7}$$

$$= 1.35 \text{ μg/24 hr}$$

In this infant, a therapeutic dose would be 45 to 68 μg/24 hr. Therefore, while the infant would receive digoxin through breast-feeding, the dose would be less than 3% of the dose that would produce therapeutic effects in the neonate, and far below any amount that would produce toxicity.[6]

Table III provides a list of considerations for breast-fed infants whose mothers are receiving therapeutic agents. We will consider each of these questions in turn.

Oral Drug Absorption by the Infant

The consideration of oral drug absorption is important to the breast-fed neonate. For example, the aminoglycoside antibiotics are not well

Table II. Therapeutic Plasma Levels for Selected Drugs[a]

Drug	Plasma level
Acetaminophen (Tylenol)	10–20 μg/ml[b]
Amobarbital (Amytal, Tuinal)	<5 μg/ml
Aprobarbital (Alurate)	<5 μg/ml
Bupivacaine (Marcaine)	<100 ng/ml
Butalbital (Fiorinal)	<5 μg/ml
Carbamazepine (Tegretol)	3–6 μg/ml
Chloramphenicol	15–30 μg/ml
Digoxin (Lanoxin)	0.9–2.4 ng/ml
Ethanol	1000 μg/ml
	("under the influence")
Etchlorvynol (Placidyl)	10 or 20 μg/ml
Ethosuximide (Zarontin)	40–80 μg/ml
Glutethimide (Doriden)	<4 μg/ml
Lidocaine (Xylocaine)	<100 ng/ml (newborn)
	1.5–2.5 μg/ml (adult)
Meprobamate (Equanil, Miltown)	5–20 μg/ml
Methsuximide (Celontin) as the metabolite N-des methsuximide	10–40 μg/ml
Methyprylon (Noludar)	<5 μg/ml
Pentobarbital (Nembutal)	<5 μg/ml
Phenobarbital	15–30 μg/ml
Phensuximide (Milontin)	10–20 μg/ml
Phenytoin (diphenylhydantoin, Dilantin)	10–20 μg/ml
Primidone (Mysoline)	<10 μg/ml
Procainamide (Pronestyl)	4–6 μg/ml
Quinidine	3–5 μg/ml
Salicylate	<350 μg/ml
Secobarbital (Seconal, Tuinal)	5 μg/ml
Sulfisoxazole (Gantrisin)	100 μg/ml
Theophylline	7–20 μg/ml

[a] Therapeutic level or range for drugs which can be routinely analyzed.
[b] Conversions: 1 μg/ml = 1 mg/liter. 1 μg/ml = 0.1 mg/dl.

absorbed orally. Although they are excreted via milk,[4] the aminoglycosides (kanamycin, gentamicin, etc.) will not produce systemic effects in the neonate, nor will they be ototoxic or nephrotoxic, since they remain in the gastrointestinal tract of the infant. There they may have local effects, alteration of bowel flora, diarrhea, or local irritation of rectal mucosa, for example, but they will not have direct systemic toxicity. Table IV lists substances that are excreted in breast milk but which are not effective orally.

Recognizing Drug Toxicity in the Infant

It is always less of a problem to consider maternal therapy with a medication that would, under appropriate medical circumstances, be given directly to the infant. Many pharmacologic agents contemplated for maternal use including narcotics, cardiac glycosides, diuretics, antibiotics, anticonvul-

Table III. Considerations for Breast-Fed Infants Whose Mothers Are under Drug Therapy

1. Is the drug absorbed orally?
2. Is the drug ever given directly to infants for therapeutic reasons?
3. Does the estimated dose delivered by milk approach a therapeutic quantity?
4. Are the effects of the drug easily recognized in the infant?
5. Are there idiosyncratic or allergic reactions to the drug that are not dose related?
6. Are there less toxic alternatives for maternal therapy?
7. Is there a potential for drug accumulation during prolonged therapy?
8. Could sub-therapeutic doses of the drug mask early signs of medical conditions in the infant?

sants, anesthetic agents, and bronchodilators are also used in the neonate or young infant. This implies availability of a certain body of pediatric knowledge relative to effective dose, toxic dose, and other adverse reactions that can be recognized in the infant. In general, it is virtually never the case that therapeutic quantities of pharmacologic substances that are administered to the mother reach the infant as "overdoses." The exceptions to this rule are discussed later.

Toxic effects of pharmacologic agents that are easily recognized in the infant include: sedation, poor feeding, diarrhea, rash, and CNS stimulation. Those effects that are not readily noticed but which can be monitored by routine laboratory analyses include: depressed leukocyte or platelet counts, hepatic injury, acid–base disturbances, and calcium or electrolyte disorders. In addition, using recent analytical methods, the plasma concentrations of many drugs can be determined in the infant using less than 0.1 ml of plasma. Thus, for those pharmacologic agents where toxicities are recognizable, maternal therapy can be undertaken with some impunity.

Idiosyncratic and Allergic Drug Reactions

There are pharmacologic agents where the usual dose–response relationship between quantity delivered and adverse effect does not hold true. This may be the result of idiosyncratic or allergic reactions that are not strictly dose-related; or there can exist a "selective" toxicity in the neonate.

Table IV. Drugs Excreted in Breast Milk That Are
Not Well Absorbed by Infants

Gentamicin, kanamycin, neomycin
Tobramycin
Heparin
Insulin

Table V. Drugs Which Displace Bilirubin from Serum Albumin

Salicylic acid
Sulfonamides
Furosemide
Phenylbutazone

Idiosyncratic reactions include the bone marrow suppression by chloramphenicol that may occur in $1:30,000$ to $1:40,000$ individuals who receive normal, therapeutic quantities of this substance.[7] This appears to be different from the dose-dependent bone marrow suppression that may occur in the neonate as a result of slow chloramphenicol metabolism and subsequent drug accumulation.

Allergic reactions leading to rash, bronchospasm, or acute hypersensitivity are frequently not as related to dose as to frequency of exposure in certain, atopic individuals. The contact dermatitis that may occur on the perineum of infants who are receiving penicillin or its congeners is an example of mild allergy.

Although the dose of penicillin received by the nursing infant via breast milk will be low by therapeutic standards, penicillin is actively secreted by the kidneys into urine, and there may be a prolonged contact to this penicillin in the diapered infant. Such topical exposure should be considered as a potential mechanism for an adverse effect in the infant.

Selective Drug Toxicity in Infants

Selective toxicity of a drug to the neonate, that is, toxicity not usually recognized in adults or older children, is many times more difficult to predict. There are no precise data regarding this occurrence but several theoretical considerations support the necessity for information in this area.

One example of potential selective neonatal toxicity relates to hyperbilirubinemia in the small premature. Since this type of infant typically has a low serum albumin, substances which may displace bilirubin from albumin may prove to be toxic in rather low concentrations. Sulfonamide antibiotics can enter breast milk, are absorbed orally, and are potent displacers of bilirubin from albumin.[8] Kernicterus, a medical condition resulting from bilirubin entering the central nervous system in infants, is a well-recognized cause of mental retardation. There have been no reports of kernicterus resulting from a drug ingested by breast-feeding, and infants who do not have underlying hyperbilirubinemia are not at risk. Nevertheless, there exists the potential for bilirubin displacement by substances listed in Table V and since the objective is not simply to avoid frank kernicterus, but rather any degree of injury from displaced bilirubin, it would be wise to avoid exposure of premature or other susceptible newborn infants to such pharmacologic agents.

Table VI. Substances That May Accumulate in the Neonate

Phenytoin
Barbiturates: Phenobarbital, pentobarbital
Caffeine, theophylline
Diazepam
Phenothiazines: Chlorpromazine, promethazine
Antihistamines: Diphenhydramine, etc.
Local anesthetics: Lidocaine, carboncaine, bupivacaine
Salicylic acid

Neonatal Drug Accumulation

Hepatic metabolism is slow during the first 10 days to 2 weeks in most infants. During this time, many of the substances listed in Table VI are capable of slow, daily accumulation by the neonate. That is, although only fractions of a therapeutic dose may be delivered to the neonate with each day's total breast feedings, this small dose may not be completely eliminated by the infant. This may lead to a gradual accumulation of the substance by the neonate during the first 1 to 2 weeks following delivery. For example, the potential for caffeine accumulation by the neonate does exist at this time since the half-life for caffeine during the first 2 weeks of postnatal existence may be as high as 230 hr.[9] This must be contrasted to a half-life of 3 to 5 hr for older infants, children, and adults. There has not been satisfactory documentation of drug accumulation from breast milk in neonates during early postnatal life. However, plasma half-lives have been well studied for a number of the drugs listed in Table VI following their administration directly to the neonate. The primary difficulty in attempting kinetic studies in infants who are receiving a drug via breast milk is that plasma levels are usually low and therefore difficult to measure precisely. Nonetheless, some drug accumulation during the first 2 weeks of postnatal existence may well occur. Studies to delineate precisely which substances may accumulate in the neonate are necessary to expand our understanding of this potential problem area.

On the other hand, as relates to potential drug accumulation, the volume of breast milk that is available to the infant during the first week of postnatal existence is usually substantially less than the 200 ml/kg per 24 hr that has been used in previous discussions of quantity ingested. It must also be noted that once beyond the initial 2-week period of slow neonatal hepatic metabolism, the infant may be capable of drug metabolism at a rate equal to or faster than adults.[10] In those circumstances, drug accumulation is not an issue.

Potential for Masking Medical Conditions

There may be a potential for the masking of medical conditions in the neonate who is ingesting small quantities of therapeutic agents in breast milk.

Table VII. *Over-the-Counter Drugs in North America*

Analgesics/antipyretics (acetylsalicylic acid, acetaminophen)
Antacids (sodium bicarbonate, aluminum hydroxide)
Cough medications (glyceryl guaicolate, potassium iodide)
Decongestants/antihistamines (phenylpropanolamine, ephredrine, diphenhydramine, methapyrilene)
Iron preparations (ferrous sulfate)
Sedative/sleep preparations (antihistamines, bromides)
Vitamins

Consider the potential of an infant with a urinary tract infection whose mother is receiving ampicillin for another medical problem. Although the quantity of ampicillin that the infant receives via breast-feeding is small, the secretion of this medication into the infant's urine may produce bacteristatic, but not bactericidal, levels of the antibiotic. In this event, when the mother stops her ampicillin, the infection that has been only partially suppressed in the infant may become a severe medical problem. There are no reports in the medical literature which document this type of phenomenon.

OVER-THE-COUNTER MEDICATIONS

Over-the-counter (OTC) agents may well fit into any of the categories of substances in the title: drug, toxin, or environmental agent. Table VII lists the categories of most commonly ingested OTC agents in North America.

There have been no serious difficulties reported for breast-fed infants whose mothers used OTC preparations. This, in part, may be related to the low quantitative delivery of the agents in these preparations to the neonate via milk. However, OTC preparations are usually formulated to make them attractive to the consumer. In so doing, the manufacturer frequently includes flavoring chemicals, dyes, sweeteners, secondary drugs to counteract the side-effects of the primary agents, and various chemicals to keep the drugs in solution while on the shelf. Consider the following hypothetical decongestant preparation:

Diphenhydramine (antihistamine)
Caffeine (methylxanthine)
Alcohol (ethanol)
Red dye
Yellow dye
Saccharin (sweetener)
Aliphatic esters (flavorings)

In this preparation, the primary decongestant is the antihistamine, diphenhydramine. Aside from diminishing the secretions from allergic rhinorrhea, antihistamines frequently produce drowsiness as a side-effect.

Thus, caffeine is included as a mild stimulant with the knowledge that it will exert a slight diuretic effect, perhaps enhancing the "drying" response that is sought. The alcohol is present, 12% by volume (same as wine), to help maintain a clear solution of both the caffeine and diphenhydramine as well as the dyes and flavorings.

The above discussion is not aimed at the toxicities or potential toxicities of any OTC preparation. Rather, we wish to promote the understanding that pharmaceutical formulations designed to be attractive to the general public are usually complex. For this reason, attention must be given not only to the primary drug but also to the other substances that might be considered toxic (ethanol, saccharin) or environmental agents (dyes, esters).

ENVIRONMENTAL AGENTS IN BREAST MILK

Recent concern regarding the quality of the environment has resulted in policies by the federal and state governments that may be effective in reducing the number of deleterious substances entering breast milk. In 1972, the use of DDT was terminated as a pesticide in the United States. This decision by the Environmental Protection Agency (EPA) was based upon animal studies that demonstrated widespread, persistent accumulation of DDT in fat. Unfortunately, DDT does not leave fat and other body stores at any appreciable rate. There are no efficient metabolic pathways for DDT elimination and it is not excreted directly by the kidneys. One major metabolite of DDT, DDE, shares many of the properties of the parent compound and also persists in animals. For humans, this represents a decided problem. As carnivores, the persistence of DDT in animals that are ingested by other animals leads to a potential propagation of the environmental contaminant up the "food-chain" such that the environmental toxin will leave the population of lower, shorter-lived animals first in response to EPA edicts, but will leave humans only after much delay. This delay is clearly longer than the human life span.

As a highly lipid soluble substance with poor metabolic pathways, DDT is similar to the more currently recognized problem agents, polyhalogenated biphenyls, PCB and PBB (polychlorinated biphenyl and polybrominated biphenyl).

These substances persist in fat stores once ingested and can be detected bound to lipids in the plasma. Of concern to this chapter is the appearance of DDT, DDE, PCB, PBB, and other lipophylic toxins in human and cow's milk. In fact, once one has defined a highly lipid soluble substance that is not effectively metabolized in the body, the *major excretory pathway* becomes lactation. Thus, the adult female body burden for PCB can be reduced by lactation but at the expense of the infant who becomes the new reservoir for the substance. At this point it is clear that we must alter our consideration of human milk from that of a highly regarded ideal nutrient, to that of another excretory route from the human body. Major concern and surveillance must be maintained for the future if human milk is to be maintained in its traditional role. At present, it appears that with the exception of individuals who have had long, intensive exposure to such substances, there is no illness in the nursing infant that has been attributed to DDT or PCB. In part, this may be due to the fact that most infants who are breast-fed from mothers with exposure to DDT or PCB were also exposed *in utero* to the same substances. There are no studies in which the body burden of these substances has been assessed in human infants. Extrapolation from animal studies, even monkey investigations, are probably not valid due to differences in body fat, fat content of breast milk, etc.

The major problems for the future relate both to the prevention of environmental contamination by toxic substances as well as the detection of sequelae that are the legacy of the present lax environmental standards. Precisely how to monitor or detect the presence of new contaminants in human milk is decidedly a problem. Infant formulas may be screened by lots in order to assess purity. Human samplings have to be randomized, individual samplings. At present, it is certainly the case that commercial infant formulas are more carefully controlled for the presence of environmental agents than is breast milk.

SUMMARY OF QUANTITATIVE CONSIDERATIONS

The foregoing discussion of the pharmacokinetics of drug excretion in milk suggests the following general principles that can be used by the clinician to manage situations in which drug ingestion by a breast-fed infant is in question:

1. Almost all drugs are excreted to some degree in breast milk.
2. The concentration of the drug in breast milk rarely exceeds the maternal plasma concentration.
3. Even when the breast-milk/maternal-plasma-concentration ratio approaches or exceeds 1.0, the amounts of drug ingested by the infant rarely attain therapeutic levels for a given drug.
4. A short exposure to a drug, as might be expected in the case of analgesics given to relieve postpartum pain, is usually of less concern than a drug given for long periods of time, such as corticosteroids for collagen disease or an anticonvulsant used to treat a seizure disorder. The amount of drug ingested by the infant can, on occasion, be minimized by feeding the infant just prior to or at the time of maternal dosing.
5. In the case of chronic drug therapy, the infant usually will be exposed to lower concentrations of the drug while breast-feeding than it was as a fetus *in utero*. Nevertheless, we do not know in most cases the long-term consequences of chronic exposure to subtherapeutic levels of medications.

6. Recommendations about the breast-feeding infant in a situation where maternal medications are indicated depends upon knowing if small amounts of the drug (subtherapeutic amounts) for even short periods of time might cause idiosyncratic reactions (as in the case of chloramphenicol), interfere with genetically abnormal metabolic pathways (as in the case of nitrofurantoins in patients with glucose-6-phosphate dehydrogenase deficiencies), or act synergistically with drugs the infant is receiving therapeutically (e.g., theobromine in chocolate enhancing an adverse response to theophylline). This requires a reasonable knowledge of pharmacology and therapeutics in the newborn in addition to knowledge of the amount of drug excreted in the breast milk.

A number of review articles and books list information about drug excretion in human breast milk.[1-5,11-17] Most of these reviews have had to rely on data from isolated case reports of drug concentration in breast milk after maternal ingestion of the drug. Many of the case reports are anecdotal and lack sufficient data to adequately assess the dynamics of drug transfer into the breast milk. As noted in the previous discussion of the pharmacokinetics of drug transfer (Fig. 4), an isolated assay of plasma and milk levels of the drug may be quite misleading.[18,19] One would have to know if the assay was done at a time of maternal distribution of the drug, elimination of the drug, or if the drug had reached a steady-state concentration in the mother at the time of sampling. These data have seldom been reported. Therefore, only scanty and sometimes misleading data are available for individual drugs.

The following paragraphs will deal with some of the more common situations in which the breast-fed infant may be exposed to drugs or drug metabolites as a result of either therapeutic or coincidental ingestion of drugs by the mother.

REVIEW OF PHARMACOLOGIC CLASSES OF DRUGS IN BREAST MILK

Antimicrobial Drugs

The most common use of antimicrobial therapy in postpartum infections is the relatively short course of antibiotics used to treat puerperal endometritis. The most commonly used drugs are penicillin or ampicillin combined with an aminoglycoside. Patients with a history of penicillin sensitivity are usually treated with a cephalosporin. Occasionally, anaerobic infections are suspected, in which case, clindamycin, chloramphenicol, or metranidazole will be the most effective drugs. Urinary tract infections are frequent complications of the puerperium, the therapy of which can include ampicillin, sulfonamides, nitrofurantoins, or one of the tetracyclines. Occasionally, long-term antibiotic therapy is necessary to prevent recurrent infection of the urinary tract. Vaginitis due to haemophilus vaginalis may be treated with ampicillin but also responds, as does trichomonas vaginitis, to metranidazole therapy.

Isoniazid therapy for 1 year has been recommended in patients who have positive tuberculin reactions to prevent reactivation of old tuberculosis infection. This therapy is usually postponed until the postpartum period.

Most antimicrobial drugs that have been studied have been found to be excreted in breast milk.[19] The milk:plasma ratio for these drugs is usually found to be less than one, but the data are often derived from only a few cases. For many of the drugs, the amounts ingested by a breast-fed infant will be below therapeutic levels (e.g., penicillin) but might be sufficient to result in idiosyncratic reactions (e.g., chloramphenicol) or cause anemia in a patient with glucose-6-phosphate dehydrogenase deficiency (e.g., nitrofurantoins).

The aminoglycosides are known to be excreted in breast milk when administered intramuscularly to the mother[20]; but because the drugs are poorly absorbed from the gastrointestinal tract, it is unlikely that renal or ototoxicity would occur in the infant.

Clindamycin has been found in breast milk,[21] but its excretion dynamics in lactation have not been reported. Judging from its biochemical characteristics, Brown[19] suggested that clindamycin might have a milk:plasma ratio of 1.14 to 1.69 which does not take into consideration protein binding or active transport.

Chloramphenicol is present in breast milk in sufficient amounts to cause an idiosyncratic bone marrow depression.[22] This serious complication of chloramphenicol therapy has never been reported in a breast-feeding infant, but it is of sufficient theoretical danger that the use of this drug should be avoided in a lactating patient.

Metronidazole has been cited as a drug contraindicated during lactation.[14] This advice is based on reports that the drug is mutagenic in bacteria and carcinogenic in rodents taking the compound throughout their lives.[23] Gray, et al.[24] have demonstrated milk:plasma ratios between 0.72 and 0.87 μg/ml in lactating women treated with therapeutic doses of metronidazole. However, in five of the ten infants in their study, no drug could be found in the plasma and with the other five, the level varied from only 0.05 to 0.4 μg/ml. Specific untoward effects in a nursing infant as a result of metronidazole ingestion have not been reported. Without more direct evidence of the harmful effects in humans of short-term courses of therapy with metronidazole,[25] it seems overly conservative to withhold the drug or discontinue breast-feeding in patients with symptomatic parasitic infections (amebiasis, giardiasis, or trichomoniasis) for which metronidazole may be the treatment of choice. This is particularly true if alternate forms of therapy have failed to cure the infection.

There are theoretical disadvantages to using tetracycline or related broad-spectrum antibiotics because of the potential for delay of bone growth or the staining of decidual teeth. However, Posner et al.[26] found negligible amounts of drug (less than 0.05 μg/ml) in the serum of breast-fed infants whose mothers were being given 500 mg tetracycline every 6 hr and in whom the milk:plasma ratio was 0.6 to 0.8. Moreover, there are no reports of infants with stained decidual teeth or retarded bone growth whose only exposure to tetracycline was from breast milk.

The sulfonamides are excreted in breast milk, though the milk:plasma ratios for each individual drug have not been determined in humans.[27,28] Nitrofurantoin is excreted in amounts that are difficult to detect in the breast milk of women who are being treated with therapeutic amounts of the drug.[29,30] In each case there are theoretical concerns about these drugs causing anemia in an infant with glucose-6-phosphate dehydrogenase deficiency. Consequently, alternative drugs should be used unless the infection (usually a urinary tract infection) is not responding to other therapy. If nitrofurantoins or sulfonamides become the drug of choice, the infant should be observed closely for evidence of anemia.

Isoniazid is excreted in breast milk in amounts that would make toxicity in the nursing infant extraordinarily unlikely, and certainly not in therapeutic amounts that would protect the infant from tuberculosis infection in a setting of familial exposure to the disease.[1]

Analgesics and Psychotherapeutic Drugs

In most peripartum and postpartum situations the need for sedative or analgesic medications is limited to a few hours or, at most, a few days. The amount of the common narcotic analgesics excreted in breast milk is small and should be of no major concern. Even the benzodiazapines, if used as an occasional sedative in the immediate peripartum period, are not contraindicated.

Salicylates, on the other hand, have been shown to be excreted into breast milk in significant quantities. Berlin *et al.*[31] studied salicylate excretion after a single dose of 650 mg of aspirin given to each of ten nursing mothers. Maternal saliva and breast milk salicylate levels were examined at intervals thereafter. Although no salicylate was found in maternal saliva after 12 hr, it could be detected in breast milk at 48 hr in four of the ten patients. The authors estimated that a nursing infant will ingest 9 to 21% of the maternal dose. Infants who nursed 2 hr after maternal ingestion of the aspirin had plasma salicylate levels of 145 to 188 µg/ml. This represents a therapeutic quantity of salicylic acid in the neonate. As discussed earlier (Table I), salicylate has a small volume of distribution in the mother, and therefore, a substantial fraction of the ingested dose may be excreted in milk. Although there may be equivalent anti-inflammatory activities between salicylic acid (measured in these studies) and acetylsalicylic acid, it is the parent drug, acetylsalicylic acid, that is responsible for the acetylation of platelets. In this regard, there exist no data to support a concern for infant bleeding tendencies as a result of acetylsalicylic acid ingestion by the mother of a breast-fed infant. However, given the lack of data regarding acetylsalicylic acid reaching the infant's circulation, it is advisable to use nonsalicylate-containing analgesic medications for the breast-feeding mother if the milk is being provided for a preterm infant who is at risk for intracranial hemorrhage.

Drugs taken over a longer period of time to treat chronic maternal problems may be of greater concern. The most commonly used psychotropic drugs, the benzodiazepines and their metabolites are excreted into breast milk, are poorly metabolized by the neonate, and have been associated with drowsiness in nursing infants.[32-34] Lithium, the drug of choice for certain manic depressive states, has been shown to be excreted in breast milk in quantities sufficient, over a long period of time, to be associated with toxic effects in nursing infants.[35-37] Consequently, the chronic use of either a benzodiazepine or lithium in breast-feeding mothers should be discouraged.

The tricyclic antidepressants have not been systematically studied in lactating women. Although there is evidence of their excretion into breast milk, there are so far no reports of untoward effects of these drugs in breast-fed infants. Their large distribution space in the mother may be responsible for this.

Methylxanthines

This group of compounds are frequently ingested by breast-feeding mothers as either caffeine (1,3,7-trimethylxanthine) in coffee, tea, or many soft drinks; theobromine (3,7-dimethylxanthine) in chocolate and cocoa; or theophylline (1,3-dimethylxanthine) which is the most frequently prescribed drug for the treatment of asthma. The subject of the excretion of methylxanthines into human breast milk has recently been reviewed by Berlin.[38]

For caffeine, the milk:plasma ratio is 0.52 in humans. A hypothetical nursing infant ingesting 90 ml of milk 60 min and 120 min after a maternal dose of 150 mg of caffeine (1 to 2 cups of coffee) would ingest 170 μg or 0.11% of the maternal dose. This is probably an insignificant amount of the drug, but it must be remembered that the half-life of caffeine is 80 hr in the term newborn and 97.5 hr in a premature infant (20 to 30 times that of an adult).[9] Consequently, repeated ingestion of caffeine might lead to accumulation of the drug during the first 2 weeks of postnatal life in the infant. This is yet to be studied.

Theobromine, which is found in chocolate and chocolate products and, in smaller amounts, in coffee and tea, is excreted into breast milk as demonstrated by Resman et al.[39] and Berlin.[38] Milk/serum ratios of the drug vary from 0.60 to 1.06 (mean = 0.82), and a single chocolate bar containing 60 mg of theobromine will result in from 0.44 to 1.68 mg of the drug (0.73 to 2.8% of the maternal dose) being excreted into the breast milk over a 12-hr period.[38] No theobromine has been detectable in breast milk after 15 hr. This amount of drug would have no harmful effect on the infant but, in a woman taking theophylline, drinking strong coffee or tea and consuming chocolate bars, could produce additive effects in the nursing infant.

Theophylline has been found to have a milk:plasma ratio of 0.60 to 0.73 in humans.[40,41] The total amount of theophylline excreted into breast milk is estimated to be not more than 1% of the maternal dose. However, the prolonged half-life of theophylline in preterm infants (30.2 hr),[42] the fact that the infant of an asthmatic patient being treated with therapeutic levels of theophylline will have cord blood levels of the drug of approximately 10 μg/ml,[43] and that caffeine and theobromine may act in additive fashion with theophylline, must all be kept in mind when the mother who desires to breast-feed her infant is being treated for asthma.

The kinetics of drug excretion of other methylxanthines may be quite different from theophylline as illustrated by the recent study of dyphylline, (7-(2,3-dihydroxypropyl)-theophylline)[44] which, unlike theophylline, is subject to renal excretion with little biotransformation. In 20 lactating women given a single dose of 5 mg/kg of dyphylline, the milk : plasma ratio was found to be 2.77 ± 0.77 or about three times that of theophylline. This illustrates that the breast milk kinetics of each new drug introduced for clinical use must be studied before conclusions can be drawn about its effect on a nursing infant. Previous discussion has evaluated the pharmacologic principles that are necessary for such studies to be valid.

Cardiovascular and Diuretic Agents

Chronic hypertension, pregnancy-induced hypertension, and cardiac disorders are intercurrent illnesses that are frequently encountered by obstetricians. The drugs that may be used in the peripartum period are antihypertensive agents (methyldopa, hydralazine, and propranolol), magnesium sulfate, diuretics (furosemide, thiazides, and chlorthalidone), and digitalis.

The excretion of methyldopa and hydralazine in breast milk has not been studied. Propranolol has been detected in the milk of lactating mothers.[45,46] Drug assays of milk in maternal plasma in a patient receiving 40 mg of propranolol four times a day showed a milk : plasma ratio of 0.64 and an estimated drug intake for the infant of 21 μg/24 hr.[47] In a 3000-g infant, this would represent an oral dose of 0.007 mg/kg per day when 0.5 to 5.0 mg/kg per day would be a therapeutic oral infant dose.

Cruikshank *et al.*[48] studied breast milk concentrations of magnesium sulfate in patients who had been treated with this drug in the peripartum period for pregnancy-induced hypertension. Although they could detect increased levels of magnesium in the milk, they estimated that the total amount of magnesium that would be ingested by a nursing infant in excess of the normal amount is 1.5 mg.

There are no reports of furosemide being studied in lactating women, but there is one report of diuretic therapy (bendrofluazide, 5 mg BID) being associated with lactation suppression.[49] This phenomenon has not been confirmed by others. Chlorthiazide was found to be excreted in insignificant quantities in the breast milk of 11 mothers treated with a single dose of 500 mg.[50] However, chlorthalidone given to nursing mothers in doses of 50 mg/day was detected in breast milk at levels that would result in a daily dose of 180 μg for term infants.[51] The authors recommend that this drug not be used in breast-feeding mothers because of the long half-life of the drug in infants (60 hr) and because the effects of the drug in the neonate have not been studied.

Digoxin excretion in breast milk has been studied in several patients.[52–55] Milk:plasma ratios approach 1.0 but, because of the large volume of distribution of digoxin in the body, the total daily excretion of digoxin in mothers with therapeutic serum digoxin levels will not exceed 1 to 2 μg.[52]

Rubella Vaccination

It is common policy on many obstetrical services to immunize in the immediate postpartum period those mothers who are sero-negative when tested for rubella antibodies. There is one report of attenuated rubella virus being isolated from the breast milk of a mother 12 days following vaccination with rubella vaccine (HPV-77 DE_5 strain).[56] Subsequent studies of the infant suggested the child had become immunized by neonatal exposure to the virus in the breast milk. The same authors were unable to isolate virus in the breast milk of women who received RA 27/3 of vaccine in the immediate postpartum period. These findings should not discourage the use of rubella vaccine in the lactating patient during the postpartum period.

Antithyroid Drugs

Hyperthyroidism during pregnancy can be treated either by subtotal thyroidectomy or with antithyroid drugs, the latter being the more common choice in North America. Antithyroid drugs of the thioamide type such as propylthiouracil and methimazole are said to be contraindicated in mothers who are breast-feeding. This advice is based on a single study by Williams *et al.*[57] in 1944 in which the breast milk of two patients who had each received a single dose of 1 g thiouracil was analyzed. Blood and milk samples collected 2 hr after administration of the drug showed that the concentrations of the drug in the milk (12.0 and 9.2 mg%, respectively) were threefold greater than in the corresponding blood samples. As discussed in the earlier theoretical sections, these single-time-point determinations may not be valid. The pharmacologic excretion of propylthiouracil and methimazole in breast milk has not been studied. There have been no reported cases of thyroid suppression in an infant as a result of propylthiouracil or methimazole ingested in breast milk. In fact, White[11] cites a personal communication reporting the treatment of a number of breast-feeding women with propylthiouracil without complications.[11] Clearly, this issue needs further extensive study.

Anticoagulants

Puerperal deep vein thrombophlebitis is not an uncommon complication and requires at least short-term and frequently long-term anticoagulation.

A more infrequent problem is a patient with a prosthetic heart valve who is being treated with long-term anticoagulation. Heparin, administered parenterally, and used for acute short-term therapy in cases of thrombophlebitis, has not been shown to be excreted in breast milk. Moreover, the drug is not effective when ingested orally. The oral anticoagulants, which are frequently used for long-term anticoagulation and are more convenient for the patient, have been said to be contraindicated based on a single report of a nursing infant who developed a hematoma at the site of an inguinal hernia repair.[58] The infant's mother was anticoagulated with phenindione and it was suspected that the infant ingested sufficient drug in the breast milk to develop abnormal hemostasis.

More recent studies using warfarin, the drug most frequently used for oral anticoagulation therapy, showed that breast milk from mothers adequately anticoagulated contained no measurable drug and the nursing infants showed no evidence of anticoagulation or other evidence of the drug in their plasmas.[59]

Anticonvulsants

Mothers treated for a seizure disorder frequently receive phenobarbital and phenytoin. Cordello[60] studying patients taking therapeutic amounts of phenobarbital (60 to 200 mg/day) which resulted in maternal blood concentrations of 10 to 30 μg/ml could not detect phenobarbital in the breast milk. Mirkin[61] studied two mothers treated with phenytoin who were breast-feeding newborn infants. Maternal plasma levels of the drug varied from 2.5 to 8.4 μg/ml (all subtherapeutic). The milk:plasma ratio approached but did not reach 1.0 with breast milk values for phenytoin ranging from 2.2 to 2.6 μg/ml. These amounts of orally ingested anticonvulsants would result in subtherapeutic levels of drug in the neonate. There is a report by Finch and Lorber[62] of a breast-fed infant who developed methemaglobinemia, which the authors attributed to phenytoin ingested in breast milk. The mother was being treated with 6 grains of phenobarbital and 6 grains of phenytoin daily. No blood levels of the drugs were reported in this study; consequently, it is not known if either of the drugs contributed to the infant's morbidity.

Carbamazepine, which is used with increased frequency for selected types of seizures, has been shown to diffuse into breast milk with a milk:plasma ratio of 0.6.[63]

Radio-Pharmaceuticals for Diagnostic Procedures

Radio-pharmaceuticals, used in diagnostic procedures such as brain or lung scans, are occasionally indicated in postpartum women. All diagnostic and therapeutic radioactive substances that have been studied in breast-feeding women have been shown to be excreted in breast milk.[64-69] The question in each case is the duration of radioactivity in the breast milk and the time during which the patient should discontinue nursing. Iodine (^{131}I) may be found in breast milk for up to 2 weeks after the medication is given to the mother. Technetium (99 mTc) has a relatively short half-life and breast milk samples studied 45 hr after the mother has been given diagnostic amounts of this agent are usually free of radioactivity.

Recreational Drugs

Tobacco smoking and alcohol ingestion are the most common and socially acceptable sources of nonmedicinal drug exposure in our society. Because they so frequently occur in the same individual, it is difficult to study their independent effects. Furthermore, increasingly in our society these drugs are used together with other less fashionable and even illicit drugs such as marijuana, cocaine, heroin, and LSD, complicating even further the study of recreational drug effects in the fetus or suckling neonate.

The effects of cigarette (tobacco) smoking on breast-fed infants are not well known. Small amounts of nicotine are known to be excreted in breast milk in women who smoke.[70] Apart from the decreased suckling of infants that is associated with increased maternal smoking,[71] no untoward effects attributable to maternal smoking have been identified.

Redetzki[72] has recently reviewed the available data on alcohol excretion in human breast milk. The milk : plasma ratio for alcohol is 0.9. Assuming a mother to be a habitual drinker (blood alcohol concentration of 100 mg/dl) the maximum blood alcohol concentration of the infant would be under 5 mg/dl, probably an insignificant amount even over a protracted period of time. Moreover, acetaldehyde, the major metabolite of alcohol that contributes to its toxicity has not been detected in breast milk. There is evidence, however, that heavy maternal alcohol use and increased smoking are significantly related to decreased sucking in newborn infants.[71] This has been demonstrated not exclusively in heavy drinkers,[73] but occasionally in women whose drinking habits fall within the realm of "social drinking."[71]

There are no systematic studies on drug or drug metabolite excretion in patients using other recreational or "street drugs." However, drug withdrawal syndromes have been identified in infants of addicted mothers following weaning.[74] This implies that over a long period of time, sufficient amounts of drug may be excreted into breast milk to cause physiological dependence in the infant. An alternative explanation is that "addiction" occurred *in utero* and subsequent exposure to drugs in breast milk simply sustained the physiological dependence.

INSECTICIDES AND POLYCHLORINATED BIPHENYLS (PCBs) IN BREAST MILK

Environmental pollutants that contaminate breast milk, especially organohalides, have been a concern for over 30 years since Laug *et al.*[75] demonstrated dichlorodiphenyl trichloroethane (DDT) in human milk. The subject has recently been reviewed by Rogan *et al.*[76] and Manno.[77] Summarizing a number of reports, these authors point out that there is widespread contamination of human breast milk with DDT and its primary metabolite 1,1 dichloro-2,2-*bis* ethylene (DDE) with mean concentrations in milk samples varying from 120 to 770 parts per billion. It is presumed that this contamination is from ambient rather than occupational exposure. Most other pesticides that have been studied, such as dieldrin, heptachlor epoxide, and oxychlordane have been found in human breast milk.[78] The FDA has set allowable levels for cow's milk and for daily human intake of organohalide compounds.[79] For most of the compounds, the human breast milk concentration and the daily intake of a breast-fed infant exceeds by roughly tenfold the amounts listed by the FDA as "allowable."

Polychlorinatedbiphenyls, widely used as insulators of electric transformers are also found in breast milk of women throughout the United States. The mean level of PCBs found in 1033 samples of breast milk (62.5 parts per billion.[79] A recent study has recommended that women who are suspected of being at risk of exposure to PCBs, e.g., drinking water accidentally contaminated with wastes containing PCBs or eating fish from contaminated waters, should have breast milk samples tested 2 weeks after the beginning of lactation (mature milk).[80] This advice is not particularly practical because test results in many regions are delayed from 2 to 6 weeks, during which lactation would have to be maintained by pumping and breast massage. So far, there have been no reports of illness in infants resulting from ingestion of organohalides in breast milk. However, because of the ubiquitous nature of these compounds in our society, the fact that they are highly fat soluble, that the only route of appreciable excretion in humans is breast milk, and that they therefore accumulate in the body in all age groups, the problem is a major public health concern. Clearly, the earlier that ingestion of such substances occurs, the greater may be the adult body burden. Toxicity may well be delayed for several decades. It is of interest that at least one report has shown that for several organohalides studied, all except PCBs were found to be in substantially lower concentration in breast milk from vegetarian women, whose only source of protein was soy beans and grain, as compared with women at large.[81] This is likely to be more properly related to lipid intake in future investigations since lipids are the primary reservoir for these substances in animals.

SUMMARY OF CLINICAL CONSIDERATIONS

In many situations, a drug in question will not have been studied with respect to its excretion in breast milk. This is particularly true for the many new compounds introduced annually by the pharmaceutical industry. When evaluating the risks and benefits of breast-feeding a newborn of a patient who requires medication, the following guidelines should be considered:

1. The advantage of the nutritional, immunologic, antimicrobial, and emotional benefits of breast-feeding can be sufficiently important that nursing should be discontinued or discouraged only when there is substantial evidence that the drug taken by the mother will be harmful to the infant.

2. Mothers who are nursing should not be given medications unless there is convincing evidence that the drug will benefit the condition for which it is prescribed. In situations in which there are alternative therapies, the drug least likely to be excreted in the breast milk or the drug with the most extensive use without apparent harm to the newborn should be used.

3. Deterioration of the mother's health in either an acute or chronic illness will be more detrimental to breast-feeding than will the effect of most medical (or surgical) treatments of her condition.

4. In the case of a woman who has been taking a medication throughout pregnancy, e.g., corticosteroids for a collagen disease or anticonvulsants for a seizure disorder, the newborn will have been exposed to higher levels of the drug *in utero* than it will be during the breast-feeding period. In many situations, drugs are more quantitatively transported across the placenta than from the mother to the infant in breast milk.

5. The effect on an infant of a drug taken on a chronic basis by the mother may be quite different (and potentially more dangerous) than that of a drug taken for a short time during an acute illness.

6. The pharmacokinetics of most drugs ingested by breast-feeding women are such that administration of the drug as or immediately after the infant nurses will result in the lowest amount of drug in the milk at the subsequent feeding.

7. If a breast-feeding infant of a medicated mother should become ill, and fail to thrive, and the morbidity cannot be explained, one of the following should be done:
   a. Discontinue the drug.
   b. Discontinue breast-feeding. Frequently, this can be accomplished on a temporary basis with the mother pumping her breasts to maintain lactation while the response of the infant is monitored.
   c. Collect maternal plasma, breast milk, and infant plasma samples for drug assay. In situations in which this can be accomplished, it may be possible to incriminate (or exonerate) a drug or one of its metabolites as the source of the morbidity on the basis of the amounts of drug found in the milk or the infant's plasma. As tedious and impractical as this approach may seem, it would eventually lead to the accumulation of a reasonable amount of data from which could be drawn sensible conclusions about the effect of drugs on the breast-fed infant.

DRUGS THAT AFFECT LACTATION

Introduction

The care of maternity patients requires an understanding of the inter-dependence of two individuals, the mother and her fetus or newborn. The simultaneous care of two patients so interrelated is one of the great challenges, and yet one of the great joys, of the science and art of obstetrics. The fetus is grown and nourished through a physiological relationship manifest in the placenta. In our society, that biological relationship is extended into the newborn period by maternal lactation and breast-feeding of the infant. Drugs can be used to alter lactation therapeutically or may be used to treat a maternal disorder coincidental to lactation. This section is intended to provide the physician with some insight into the drugs that may enhance or inhibit lactation.

Normal lactation may be inhibited or enhanced by a number of drugs.[82,83] In some cases, the effect on lactation is inadvertent and coincidental to the therapeutic goal for which the drug is being used. In other situations, drugs may be used therapeutically to inhibit or enhance lactation. For the most part, drugs that influence lactation do so through their effect on the production and release of prolactin from the anterior pituitary which in turn influences the synthesis of milk proteins, lipids, and carbohydrates, in mammary gland epithelial cells. There are only a few drugs that affect milk production indirectly by enhancing or inhibiting milk letdown either by direct stimulation of myoepithelial cells within the breast (oxytocin) or by altering the neurohumeral responses involving the elaboration and release of oxytocin from the posterior pituitary.

Drugs That Inhibit Lactation

Drugs that inhibit prolactin release include: androgens, clomiphene citrate, levodopa, pyridoxine, monoamine oxidase inhibitors, ergot deriva-tives, and metergoline; and, in addition, prostaglandins E and $F_{2\alpha}$.

The effects of the steroid hormones on lactation have been reviewed in Chapter 5 by Neville. Synthetic estrogenlike compounds (diethystilbestrol, quinoestrol and chlorotrinisene) have been widely used in the past to inhibit puerperal lactation. The mechanism of action of lactation suppression by estrogen or estrogenlike compounds is not entirely clear. As noted above by Neville, (Chapter 5), estrogen may interfere with prolactin binding within breast tissue. Progesterone has also been shown to inhibit terminal differ-entiation and milk secretion in the mammary gland (Neville, Chapter 5). Clinically this does not seem to cause a problem in women who are lactating at the time they are being treated with contraceptive medications containing only a progestin.[84,85] It has also been observed that lactating women taking birth control preparations containing combinations of synthetic estrogens and progestins are more likely to have diminished lactation than women being treated with birth control medications containing only progestins.[84,85]

Androgens are known to inhibit lactation. The specific site of action is not known, but serum prolactin levels are suppressed when androgens are given.[86] The most successful hormone regimens for the inhibition of puerperal lactation have been those combining an estrogen with an androgen.[87] Such combinations, while effective in suppressing lactation in the immediate postpartum period, have been associated with a substantial number of patients with breakthrough or rebound lactation when the medication is discontinued.[88] Also reports that synthetic estrogen-like compounds resulted in an increased risk of thromboembolic phenomena have resulted in a decrease in the use of estrogen or estrogen-containing compounds for suppression of postpartum lactation.[89,90]

Clomiphene citrate has been shown to inhibit prolactin release but its effect on puerperal lactation suppression has not been consistent. Zuckerman and Carmel[91] found clomiphene 98% successful in suppressing lactation while Weinstein, *et al.*[86] found it effective in only 50% of patients treated.

L-dopa is an immediate precursor of dopamine which in turn inhibits the production of prolactin. L-dopa has been used to suppress abnormal lactation in nonpregnant patients, but it is not used in the suppression of puerperal lactation.[92]

Pyridoxine, serving as a coenzyme, promotes the conversion of L-dopa to dopamine, thus inhibiting the elaboration of prolactin.[93,94] Large doses of pyridoxine (200 mg TID) have been reported by some authors to suppress postpartum lactation,[95,96] but other studies have failed to demonstrate clinically significant lactation inhibition with pyridoxine.[97,98] It is unlikely that the small doses of pyridoxine found in prenatal vitamin supplements (4 mg) that are often taken by breast-feeding mothers are sufficient to significantly inhibit lactation.

Batta and others[99] reported that prostaglandin $F_{2\alpha}$ given orally will prevent breast engorgement and puerperal lactation but its use was associated with nausea and vomiting in a substantial number of patients. Nasi and co-workers,[100] using oral prostaglandin E_2, 2 mg every 6 hr on the fourth day after delivery, followed by a single 4-mg dose on the fifth day, demonstrated inhibition of lactation and breast engorgement in all of the 20 women so treated. Prolactin levels in plasma were significantly reduced throughout the 7 days of the study. Moreover, there was no rebound lactation during the month following the drug therapy.

Metergoline, a potent serotonin antagonist, given in doses of 4 mg, three times daily for 5 days within 24 to 72 hr after delivery, was effective in suppressing lactation in all of 30 nonnursing parturients.[101] Three of the patients noted rebound lactation when the drug was discontinued. The same study showed that prolactin secretion was significantly inhibited in the women taking the drug. Others have confirmed the effectiveness of metergoline in the suppression of puerperal lactation,[102,103] although these studies suggest that to reduce to a minimum the number of patients with breast swelling and milk secretion, the drug must be given in doses of 4 mg, four times a day for 10 days.[103]

The ergot derivatives block prolactin secretion by activating dopamine receptors in pituitary lactotrophs.[104,105] Ergot derivatives such as ergonovine maleate and methylergonovine are frequently prescribed in the immediate postpartum period for the control of uterine bleeding. In the relatively short courses of therapy used (1 to 3 days), these drugs have not been shown to have an untoward effect on lactation.[106] Other ergot derivatives such as bromocriptine[107–110] and lisuride[111] have been shown to be potent prolactin inhibitors and are effective in suppressing puerperal lactation.

Studies comparing the efficacy of bromocriptine with other pharmacological methods of lactation suppression such as diethystilbestrol,[112] quinoestrol,[113] chlorotrianisene,[114] and pyridoxine[115] have consistently shown bromocriptine to be the superior drug. Bromocriptine in doses of 2.5 mg given twice daily for 14 days is now the preferred method of lactation suppression on most obstetrical services. There are remarkably few complications and side effects of lactation suppression using bromocriptine. Those observed have included headache, hypotension, and occasional rebound lactation. Unlike estrogenlike compounds, there have been no alterations of coagulation with bromocriptine therapy.[112]

The clinician who is faced with the decision about the best approach to puerperal lactation suppression in the patient who for medical or personal reasons will not be breast-feeding has several options. The simplest and perhaps the safest method of lactation suppression is to avoid breast or nipple stimulation. This approach, which depends upon decreasing the milk ejection reflex and the stimulation of prolactin secretion, is associated with breast engorgement, pain, and spontaneous milk secretion for several days in about 50% of patients.[116] However, this treatment is not associated with rebound lactation, abnormal uterine bleeding or abnormal coagulation which are complications of hormonal lactation suppression.

A second alternative is a single injection of testosterone enanthate (90 mg) and estradiol valerate (4 mg) given during labor or immediately after delivery.[117] This therapy is effective, relatively inexpensive, and it is safe if confined to young women (less than 25 years of age) without a history of current complications that would predispose them to thrombophlebitis. It is, however, associated with rebound lactation in 40% of patients.[87]

A third and currently the most popular option is the use of bromocriptine (2.5 mg twice daily for 14 days) which is highly effective, is associated with side effects in only 3% of patients,[110] and avoids problematic changes in blood coagulation. However, the course of therapy is long (2 weeks) and relatively expensive. The interested clinician is advised to read Kochenour's[118] recent review of the current status of puerperal lactation suppression.

Drugs That Enhance Lactation

Many drugs increase prolactin production or release. The lactogenic and mammotropic effect of a number of these compounds including the phenothiazines, thioxanthines, butyrophenones, and reserpine and its derivatives have been extensively reviewed in the monograph by Sulman.[119]

Chlorpromazine, which is a prototype of this group of psychotherapeutic drugs, appears to inhibit the release of prolactin-inhibiting hormone from the hypothalmus by blocking dopamine receptors.[120] The commonly used phenothiazines that have been associated with galactorrhea are: fluphenozine (Prolixin®), perphenazine (Trilifon®), prochlorperazine (Compazine®), thioridazine (Mellaril®), and trifluoperazine (Stelazine®). Thioxanthines including chlorprothixine (Taractan®) and thiothixene (Nabane®) and the butyrophenones, including haloperidol (Haldol®), also promote galactorrhea in a manner and by mechanisms similar to the phenothiazines.

Reserpine and other rauwolfia derivatives antagonize or deplete dopamine in the central nervous system and thus enhance prolactin secretion, but the precise mechanism of action is not entirely clear.[119]

Methyl dopa inhibits dopa-decarboxylase and is said to increase prolactin secretion and lactation in humans.[121] Nevertheless, abnormal lactation is not a frequent complication of methyl-dopa treatment of hypertension.

Sulpiride is a drug which has been used to inhibit gastric secretion in peptic ulcer disease and has been shown, as has metoclopramide, to be a cause of hyperprolactinemia.[122] A prospective study by Aono and coworkers[123] demonstrated that patients treated with 50 mg of oral sulpiride twice a day for the first 7 days of puerperium had significantly greater milk yields than nontreated controls. The authors suggest that the drug stimulates prolactin secretion by blocking dopamine receptors. Metoclopramide, which has been shown to increase serum prolactin levels,[124,125] will also enhance lactation.[126] However, more studies are necessary before this drug can be recommended as an effective and safe therapy for lactation insufficiency.

Hormones that have been reported to enhance prolactin secretion are thyrotropin releasing hormone (TRH),[127,128] estrogen, and insulin.[129] The clinical significance of their effect on lactation is not well established. For example, TRH, like estrogen, may have the paradoxical effect of stimulating prolactin secretion while inhibiting milk yield.

Milk ejection or letdown is a result of contraction of myoepithelial cells in the breast that are stimulated by oxytocin. The natural source of oxytocin is the cells of the paraventricular and supraoptic nuclei of the hypothalamus. The hormone migrates along the axons of these cells to be released from the posterior pituitary in response to suckling. The specific relationship between plasma oxytocin concentrations and lactation is not entirely clear. Lucas *et al.*[130] studied plasma oxytocin concentrations in ten lactating mothers in the first week postpartum. The initiation of lactation did not appear to be related to the release of oxytocin. They also found that in established lactation an oxytocin response did not appear to be essential for adequate milk flow. Nevertheless, the administration of oxytocin by either the intramuscular or intranasal routes results in prompt milk letdown and can be a valuable adjunct to promoting lactation in the early postpartum period.[131,132] This may be particularly helpful in mothers who have delivered prematurely.[133] Oxytocin is most conveniently administered by means of an intranasal spray given 2 to 3 min prior to breast-feeding.[134,135] Several substances have been shown to antagonize the effect of oxytocin. Among the more important are catecholamines and ethanol.

Catecholamines, through stimulation of myopithelial β-adrenergic receptors, will inhibit milk ejection by rendering mammary myoepithelium inexcitable by oxytocin. In addition, vasoconstriction caused by catecholamines may decrease mammary blood flow thus decreasing the amount of oxytocin reaching the target cells.

Wagner and Fuchs[136] have demonstrated that alcohol will inhibit oxytocin release, and a significant reduction of the milk ejection reflex will result from the ingestion of large amounts of alcohol (1 to 2 g/kg).[137]

Summary

Lactation is influenced by any medication or drug that has an effect on prolactin secretion or oxytocin release. Frequently, the drug effect on lactation is coincidental to the intended therapeutic goal of the drug. For this reason, a knowledge of drug effect on lactation is important for physicians treating women who are breast-feeding. In general, most dopamine agonists will inhibit prolactin secretion while dopamine antagonists will stimulate prolactin secretion with corresponding effects on lactation.

Drugs can also be used intentionally to inhibit lactation in the puerperium. The most efficient of these is the ergot-derivative bromocriptine, which is now used clinically in doses of 2.5 mg twice a day for 14 days. The advantages of this drug over the hormone preparations that formerly were the preferred method of lactation suppression are that bromocriptine does not influence puerperal coagulation, is associated with only minimal rebound lactation when the drug is discontinued, and is effective even when used after lactation has been established.

Enhancement of lactation is occasionally needed for women who temporarily have had to discontinue lactation or who are having difficulty sustaining adequate milk production. Sulpiride and metoclopramide, which are dopamine antagonists, are both effective in enhancing lactation, but neither drug is currently approved for this use by the Food and Drug Administration. Until these drugs have been more thoroughly studied and approved for lactation therapy, oxytocin nasal spray can be utilized to enhance milk letdown and is often beneficial in treating lactation insufficiency.

REFERENCES

1. Knowles, J. A., 1965, Excretion of drugs in milk—A review, *J. Pediatr.* **66**:1068–1082.
2. Catz, C. S. and Giacoia, G. P., 1972, Drugs and breast milk, *Pediatr. Clin. North Am.* **19**:151–166.
3. O'Brien, T. E., 1974, Excretion of drugs in human milk, *Am. J. Hosp. Pharm.* **31**:844–854.
4. Vorherr, H., 1974, Drug excretion in breast milk, *Postgrad. Med.* **56**:97–177.
5. Anderson, P. O., 1977, Drugs and breast feeding: A review, *Drug Intell. Clin. Pharm.* **11**:208–222.
6. Loughnan, P. M., 1978, Digoxin excretion in human breast milk, *J. Pediatr.* **92**(6):1019–1020.
7. Polak, B. C. P., Wesseling, H., Herxheimer, A., and Meyler, L., 1972, Blood dyscrasias attributed to chloramphenicol, *Acta Med. Scand.* **192**:409–414.
8. Harris, R. C., Lucey, J. F., and Maclean, J. R., 1958, Kernicterus in premature infants associated with low concentrations of bilirubin in the plasma, *Pediatrics* **21**:875–880.
9. Aranda, J. V., Gorman, W., Gergsteinsson, H., and Gunn, T., 1977, Efficacy of caffeine in treatment of apnea in the low-birth-weight infant, *J. Pediatr.* **90**(3):467–472.
10. Loughnan, P. M., Greenwald, A., Purton, W. W., Aranda, J. V., Watters, G., and Neins, A. H., 1977, Pharmacokinetic observations of phenytoin disposition in the newborn and young infant, *Arch. Dis. Child.* **52**:302–309.
11. White, M., 1977, *Breast Feeding and Drugs in Human Milk*, La Leche League International, Inc., Franklin Park, Ill.
12. Anderson, P. O., 1979, Drugs and breast feeding, *Semin. Perinatol.* **3**:271–278.
13. Giacoia, G. P., and Catz, C. S., 1979, Drugs and pollutants in breast milk, *Clin. Perinatol.* **6**:181–196.
14. Lande, N. I., Rivlin, R. S., and Greentree, L. B., 1979, Update: Drugs in breast milk, *Med Lett. Drugs Ther.* **21**:21–24,
15. Wilson, J. T., Brown, R. D., Cherek, D. R., Dailey, J. W., Hilman, B., Jobe, P. C., Manno, B. R., Manno, J. E., Redetzki, H. M., and Stewart, J. J., 1980, Drug excretion in human breast milk: Principles, pharmacokinetics and projected consequences, *Clin. Pharmacokin.* **5**:1–66.
16. Kochenour, N. K. and Emery, M. G., 1981, Drugs in lactating women, *Obstet. Gynecol. Annu.* **10**:107–126.
17. Wilson, J. T., 1981, *Drugs in Breast Milk*, ADIS Press, New York.
18. Berlin, C. M., Jr., 1981, Pharmacologic consideration of drug use in lactating mother, *Obstet. Gynecol.* **58**:17S–23S.
19. Brown, R. D., 1981, Antimicrobials, in: *Drugs in Breast Milk* (J. T. Wilson ed.), ADIS Press, New York. p. 50–52.
20. Chyo, N., Sunada, H., and Nohara, S., 1962, Clinical studies of kanamycin in the field of obstetrics and gynecology, *Asian Med. J.* **5**:265–275.
21. Smith, J. A., Morgan, J. R., Rachlis, A. R., an Papsin, F. R., 1975, Clindamycin in human breast milk, *Can. Med. Assoc. J.* **112**:806.
22. Havelka, J., Hejzlar, M., Papov, V., Viktornova, J., and Prochazka, J., 1968, Excretion of chloramphenicol in human milk, *Chemotherapy* **13**:204–211.
23. Lande, N. I., Rivlin, R. S., and Greentree, L. B., 1975, Metronidazole, *Med. Lett. Drugs Ther.* **17**:53.
24. Gray, M. S., Kane, P. O., and Squires, S., 1961, Further observations on metronidazole (Flagyl), *Br. J. Vener. Dis.* **37**:278–279.
25. Beard, C. M., Noller, K. L., O'Fallon, W. M., Kurland, L. T., and Dockerty, M. B., 1979, Lack of evidence for cancer due to use of metronidazole, *N. Engl. J. Med.* **301**:519–522.
26. Posner, A. C., Prigot, A., and Konicoff, N. G., 1955, Further observations on the use of tetracycline hydrochloride in prophylaxis and treatment of obstetric infections, in: *Antibiotics Annual 1954–55* H. Welch and F. Marti-Ibanez, Medical Encyclopedia, Washington, D.C., p. 594–598.

27. Hawking, F. and Lawrence, J. S., 1950, *The Sulfonamides*, H. K. Lewis & Co., Ltd., London, pp. 95–96.
28. Sparr, R. A. and Pritchard, J. A., 1958, Maternal and newborn distribution and excretion of sulfamethoxypyridazine (Kynex), *Obstet. Gynecol.* **12**:131–134.
29. Hosbach, R. E. and Foster, R. B., 1967, Absence of nitrofurantoin from human milk, *JAMA* **202**:1057.
30. Varsano, I., Fischl, J., and Schochet, S. B., 1973, The excretion of orally ingested nitrofurantoin in human milk, *J. Pediatr.* **82**:886.
31. Berlin, C. M., Jr., Pascuzzi, M. J., and Yaffe, S. J., 1980, Excretion of salicylate in human milk, *Clin. Pharmacol. Ther.* **27**:245–246.
32. Erkkola, R. and Kanto, J., 1972, Diazepam and breast-feeding, *Lancet* **1**:1235–1236.
33. Patrick, M. J., Tilstone, W. J., and Reavy, P., 1972, Diazepam and breast-feeding, *Lancet* **1**:542–543.
34. Cole, A. P. and Hailey, D. M., 1975, Diazepam and active metabolite in breast milk and their transfer to the neonate, *Arch. Dis. Child.* **50**:741–742.
35. Schou, M. and Amidsen, A., 1973, Lithium and pregnancy. III. Lithium ingestion by children breast fed by women on lithium treatment, *Br. Med. J.* **2**:138.
36. Tunnessen, W. W. and Hertz, G. C., 1972, Toxic effects of lithium in newborn infants: A commentary, *J. Pediatr.* **81**:804–807.
37. Sykes, P. A. and Quarrie, J., 1976, Lithium carbonate and breast feeding, *Br. Med. J.* **2**:1299.
38. Berlin, C. M., Jr., 1981, Excretion of the methylxanthines in human milk, *Semin. Perinatol.* **5**:389–394.
39. Resman, B. H., Blumenthal, H. P., and Jusko, W. J., 1977, Breast milk distribution of theobromine from chocolate, *J. Pediatr.* **91**:477–480.
40. Yurchak, A. M. and Jusko, W. J., 1976, Theophylline secretion into breast milk, *Pediatrics* **75**:518–525.
41. Stec, G. P., Greenberger, P., Ruo, T. I., Henthorn, T., Morita, Y., Atkinson, A. J., Jr., and Patterson, R., 1982, Kinetics of theophylline transfer to breast milk, *Clin. Pharmacol. Ther.* **28**:404–408.
42. Aranda, J. V., 1976, Sitar, D. S., Parsons, W. D., Loughnan, P. M., and Neims, A. H., 1976, Pharmacokinetic aspects of theophylline in premature newborns, *N. Engl. J. Med.* **295**:413–417.
43. Lavovitz, E. and Spector, S., 1982, Placental theophylline transfer in pregnant asthmatics, *JAMA* **247**:786–788.
44. Jarboe, C. H., Cook, L. N., Malesic, I., and Fleischaker, J., 1981, Dyphylline elimination kinetics in lactating women: Blood to milk transfer, *J. Clin. Pharmacol.* **21**:405–410.
45. Levitan, A. A. and Manion, J. C., 1973, Propranolol therapy during pregnancy and lactation, *Am. J. Cardiol.* **32**:247.
46. Anderson, P. and Slater, F. J., 1976, Propranolol therapy during pregnancy and lactation, *Am. J. Cardiol.* **37**:325.
47. Bauer, J. H., Pape, B., Zajcek, J., and Groshong, T., 1979, Propranolol in human plasma and breast milk, *Am. J. Cardiol.* **43**:860–862.
48. Cruikshank, D. P., Varner, M. W., and Pitkin, R. M., 1982, Breast milk magnesium and calcium concentrations following magnesium sulfate treatment, *Am. J. Obstet. Gynecol.* **143**:685–688.
49. Healy, M., 1961, Suppressing lactation with oral diuretics, *Lancet* **1**:1353–1354.
50. Werthmann, M. W., Jr. and Krees, S. V., 1972, Excretion of chlorothiazide in human breast milk, *J. Pediatr.* **81**:781–783.
51. Mulley, B. A., Parr, G. D., Pau, W. K., Rye, R. M., Mould, J. J., and Siddle, N. C., 1978, Placental transfer of chlorthalidone and its elimination in maternal milk, *Eur. J. Clin. Pharmacol.* **13**:129–131.
52. Levy, M., Granit, L., and Laufer, N., 1977, Excretion of drugs in human milk, *New Engl. J. Med.* **297**:789.

53. Chan, V., Tse, T. F., and Wong, V., 1978, Transfer of digoxin across the placenta and into breast milk, *Br. J. Obstet. Gynaecol.* **85:**605.

54. Loughnan, P. M., 1978, Digoxin excretion in human breast milk, *J. Pediatr.* **92:**1019–1020.

55. Finley, J. P., Waxman, M. B., Wong, P. Y., and Lickrish, G. M., 1979, Digoxin excretion in human milk, *J. Pediatr.* **94:**339.

56. Buimovici-Klein, E., Hite, R. L., Byrne, T., and Cooper, L. Z., 1977, Isolation of rubella virus in milk after postpartum immunization, *J. Pediatr.* **91:**939–940.

57. Williams, R. H., Kay, G. A., and Jandorf, B. J., 1944, Thiouracil: Its absorption, distribution, and excretion, *J. Clin. Invest.* **23:**613–627.

58. Eckstein, H. and Jack, B., 1970, Breast feeding and anticoagulant therapy, *Lancet* **1:**672–673.

59. Orme, M. L'E., Lewis, P. J., de Swiet, M., Serlin, M. J., Sibeon, R., and Baty, J. D., 1977, May mothers given warfarin breast-feed their infants? *Br. Med. J.* **1:**1564–1565.

60. Cordello, H., 1973, The excretion of antiepileptic drugs in breast milk, *Weiner Klin. Wochenschrift.* **85:**695–697.

61. Mirkin, B. T., 1971, Diphenylhydantoin: Placental transport, fetal localization, neonatal metabolism and possible teratogenic effects, *J. Pediatr.* **78:**329–337.

62. Finch, E. and Lorber, J., 1954, Methemaglobinemia in the newborn probably due to phenytoin excreted in human milk, *J. Obstet. Gynaecol. Br. Emp.* **61:**833–834.

63. Pynnonen, K. J., Sillanpaa, M., and Erkkola, R., 1977, Carbamazepine: Placental transport, tissue concentrations in fetus and newborn, and level in milk, *Acta Pharmacol. Toxicol.* **41:**244–253.

64. Vagenakis, A. G., Abreau, C. M., and Bravorman, L. E., 1971, Duration of radioactivity in the milk of a nursing mother following TcM administration, *J. Nucl. Med.* **12:**188.

65. Miller, H. and Weetch, R. S., 1955, The excretion of radioactive iodine in human milk, *Lancet* **2:**1013.

66. Bland, E. P., Docker, M. F., Crawford, J. C., and Farr, R. F., 1969, Radioactive iodine uptake by thyroid of breast fed infants after maternal blood-volume measurements, *Lancet* **2:**1039–1040.

67. Berke, R. A., Hoops, E. C., Kereiakes, J. C., Saenger, E. L., 1973, Radiation does to breast feeding child after mother has TcM lung scan, *J. Nucl. Med.* **14:**51–52.

68. Wyburn, J. R., 1973, Human breast milk excretion of radionuclides following administration of radiopharmaceuticals, *J. Nucl. Med.* **14:**115–117.

69. O'Connell, M. E. A. and Sutton, H., 1976, Excretion of radioactivity in breast milk following TcM polyphosphate, *Br. J. Radiol.* **49:**377–379.

70. Ferguson, B. B., Wilson, D. J., and Schaffner, W., 1976, Determination of nicotine concentrations in human milk, *Am. J. Child.* **130:**837–839.

71. Martin, D. C., Martin, J. C., Streissgath, A. P., and Lund, C. A., 1978, Sucking frequency and amplitude in newborns as a function of maternal drinking and smoking, *Curr. Alcohol* **5:**359–366.

72. Redetzki, H. M., 1981, Alcohol, in: *Drugs in Breast Milk* J. (T. Wilson ed) ADIS Press, New York, p. 46–49.

73. Ouellette, E. M., Rosett, H. L., Rosman, N. P., and Weiner, L., 1977, Adverse effects on offspring of maternal alcohol abuse during pregnancy, *N. Engl. J. Med.* **297:**528–530.

74. Cobrinik, R. W., Hood, R. T., and Chusid, E., 1959, The effect of maternal narcotic addiction on the newborn infant, *Pediatrics* **24:**288–304.

75. Laug, E. P., Kunze, F. M., and Prickett, C. S., 1951, Occurrence of DDT in human fat and milk, *Arch. Ind. Hyg.* **3:**245–246.

76. Rogan, W. J., Bagniewski, A., and Damstra, T., 1980, Pollutants in breast milk, *N. Engl. J. Med.* **302:**1450–1453.

77. Manno, B. R., 1981, Insecticides, pollutants and toxins, in: *Drugs in Breast MIlk* (J. T. Wilson, ed.) ADIS Press, New York, p. 72–77.

78. Savage, E. D., 1977, National study to determine levels of chlorinated hydrocarbon insecticides in human milk: 1975–1976, and supplementary report to the national milk study: 1975–1976, National Technical Information Service, Springfield, Va., 1977.

79. *Action Levels for Poisonous or Deleterious Substances in Human Food and Animal Feed*, Food and Drug Administration, Washington, D.C., 1978.
80. Wickizer, T. M. and Brilliant, L. B., 1981, Testing for polychlorinated biphynels in human milk, *Pediatrics* **68:**411–415.
81. Hergenrather, J., Hlady, G., and Wallace, B., 1981, Pollutants in breast milk of vegetarians, *N. Engl. J. Med.* **304:**792.
82. Dickey, R. P. and Stone S. C., 1975, Drugs that effect the breast and lactation *Clin. Obstet. Gynecol.* **18:**95–111.
83. Dickey, R. P., 1979, Drugs affecting lactation, *Semin. Perinatol.* **3:**279–286.
84. Hull, V. J., 1981, The effects of hormonal contraceptives on lactation: Current findings, methodological considerations, and future priorities, *Stud. Fam. Plann.* **12:**134–155.
85. Buchanan, R., 1975, Breastfeeding, aid to infant health and fertility control, *Popul. Rep.* **J:**49–67.
86. Weinstein, D., Ben-David, M., and Polishuk, W. Z., 1976, Serum prolactin and the suppression of lactation, *Br. J. Obstet. Gynaecol.* **83:**679–682.
87. Morris, J. A., Creasy, R. K., and Hohe, P. T., 1970, Inhibition of puerperal lactation: Double blind comparison of chlorotrianisene, testosterone enanthate with estradiol valerate and placebo, *Obstet. Gynecol.* **36:**107–114.
88. Markin, K. E. and Wolst, M. D., 1960, A comparative controlled study of hormones used in the prevention of postpartum breast engorgement and lactation, *Am. J. Obstet. Gynecol.* **80:**128–137.
89. Daniel, D. G., Campbell, H., and Turnbull, A. C., 1976, Puerperal thromboembolism and suppression of lactation, *Lancet* **2:**287–289.
90. Jeffcoate, T. N. A., Miller, J., Roos, R. F., and Tindall, V. R., 1968, Puerperal tromboembolism in relation to the inhibition of lactation by estrogen therapy, *Br. Med. J.* **4:**19–25.
91. Zuckerman, H. and Carmel, S., 1973, The inhibition of lactation by clomiphene, *J. Obstet. Gynaecol. Br. Commonw.* **80:**827–823.
92. Turkington, R. W., 1972, Inhibition of prolactin secretion and successful therapy of the Forbes Albright syndrome with L-dopa, *J. Clin. Endocrinol. Metab.* **34:**306–311.
93. Canales, E. S., Soria, J., Zarate, A., Mason, M., and Molina, M., 1976, The influence of pyridoxine on prolactin secretion and milk production in women, *Br. J. Obstet. Gynaecol* **83:**387–388.
94. Delita, G., Masala, A., Alagna, S., and Devilla, L., 1976, Effect of pyridoxine on human hypophyseal trophic hormone release: A possible stimulation of hypothalamic dopaminergic pathway, *J. Clin. Endocrinol. Metab.* **42:**603–606.
95. Foukas, M. D., 1973, An antilactogenic effect of pyridoxine, *J. Obstet. Gynaecol. Br. Commonw.* **80:**718–720.
96. Marcus, R. G., 1975, Suppression of lactation with high doses of pyridoxine, *S. Afr. Med. J.* **49:**2155–2156.
97. MacDonald, H. N., Collins, Y. D., Tobin, M. J. W., and Wijayaratne, D. D., 1976, The failure of pyridoxine in suppression of puerperal lactation, *Br. J. Obstet. Gynaecol.* **83:**54–55.
98. DeWall, J. M., Steyn, A. F., Harms, J. H. K., Slabber, C. F., and Pannall, P. R., 1978, Failure of pyridoxine to suppress raised serum prolactin levels, *S. Afr. Med. J.* **53:**293–294.
99. Batta, S. F., Gagliano, P. G., and Martini, L., 1974, Effect of prostaglandins E1 and F2 on milk yield in lactating rats, *Proc. Soc. Exp. Biol. Med.* **146:**1003–1005.
100. Nasi, A., De Murtas, M., Parodo, G., and Faminiti, F., 1980, Inhibition of lactation by prostaglandin E2, *Obstet. Gynecol. Surv.* **35**619–620.
101. Crosignani, P. G., Lombroso, G. C., Caccamo, A., Resechini, E., and Peracchi, M., 1978, Suppression of puerperal lactation by metergoline, *Obstet. Gynecol.* **51:**113–115.
102. Delitala, G., Masala, A., Alagna, S., Devilla, L., Lodico, G., and Lotti, G., 1977, Metergoline in the inhibition of puerperal lactation, *Br. Med. J.* **1:**744–746.
103. Caballero, A., Sr., Palomo, A., Molina, C. E., Albarran, F. J., Caballero, A., Jr., and Mena, P., 1982, Metergoline as a lactation inhibitor, *J. Reprod. Med.* **27:**202–206.

104. Pasteels, J. L., Canquy, A., Frerotte, M., and Ectors, F., 1971, Inhibition of prolactin secretion by erocornine and 2-Br-α-ergocryptine: Direct action on the hypophysis *in vitro,* *Ann. Endocrol. (Paris)* **32:**188–192.

105. Floss, H. G., Cassady, J. M., and Robbers, J. E., 1973, Influence of ergot alkaloids on pituitary prolactin and prolactin-dependent processes, *J. Pharm. Sci.* **62:**699–715.

106. del Pozo, E., Brun del RE, R., and Hinselmann, M., 1975, Lack of effect of methyl ergonovine on postpartum lactation, *Am. J. Obstet. Gynecol.* **123:**845–846.

107. Brun del RE, R., del Pozo, E., de Grandi, P., Friesen, H., Hinselmann, M., and Wyss, H., 1973, Prolactin inhibition and suppression of puerperal lactation by br-ergocryptine (CB154), *Obstet. Gynecol.* **41:**884–890.

108. Rolland, R., DeJong, F. H., Schellekens, L. A., and Lequin, R. M., 1975, The role of prolactin in the restoration of ovarian function during the early post partum period in the human female. II. A study during inhibition of lactation by bromoergocryptine, *Clin Endocrinol.* **4:**27–38.

109. Dewhurst, C. J., Harrison, R. F., and Biswas, S., 1977, Inhibition of puerperal lactation, *Acta Obstet. Gynecol. Scand.* **56:**327–331.

110. Duchesne, C. and Leke, R., 1981, Bromocriptine mesylate for prevention of lactation, *Obstet. Gynecol.* **57:**464–467.

111. de Cecco, L., Venturini, P. L., Ragni, N., Rossato, P., Maganza, C., and Gaggero, G., 1979, Effect of lisuride on inhibition of lactation and serum prolactin, *Br. J. Obstet. Gynaecol.* **86:**905–908.

112. Nilson, P. A., Meling, A. B., and Abildgaard, U., 1976, Study of the suppression of lactation and the influence on blood clotting with bromocriptine (CB 154) (Parlodel): A double blind comparison with diethylstilbesterol, *Acta Obstet. Gynecol.* **55:**39–44.

113. Walker, S., Groom, G., Hibbard, B. M., Griffiths, K., and Davis, R. H., 1975, Controlled trial of bromocriptine, quinoestrol, and placebo in suppression of puerperal lactation, *Lancet* **2:**842–845.

114. Utian, W. H., Begg, G., Vinik, A. I., Paul, M., and Shuman, L., 1975, Effect of bromocriptine and chlorotrianisene on inhibition of lactation and serum prolactin. A comparative double-blind study, *Br. J. Obstet. Gynaecol.* **82:**755–759.

115. Boes, E. G. M., 1980, Inhibition of puerperal lactation. A comparative study of bromo-criptine and pyridoxine, *Afr. Med. J.* **57:**900–903.

116. Schwartz, D. J., Evans, P. C., Garcia, C. R., Rickels, K., and Fisher, E., 1973, A clinical study of lactation suppression, *Obstet. Gynecol.* **42:**599–606.

117. Lo Presto, B. and Caypinar, E. Y., 1959, Prevention of postpartum lactation by adminis-tration of deladumone during labor, *JAMA* **169:**250–252.

118. Kochenour, N. K., 1982, Lactation suppression, *Clin. Obstet. Gynecol.* **23:**1045–1059.

119. Sulman, F. G., 1970, *Hypothalamic Control of Lactation,* Springer Verlag, New York, p. 58–156.

120. Sherman, L. and Kolodny, H. O., 1971, The hypothalamus, brain catecholamines, and drug therapy for gigantism and acromegaly, *Lancet* **1:**682–685.

121. Nickerson, M. and Ruedy, J., 1975, Antihypertensive agents and the drug therapy of hypertension, in: *The Pharmacological Basis of Therapeutics,* 5th ed., (L. S. Goodman and A. Gilman, ed.) Macmillan Publishing Co., New York. pp. 708–709.

122. Aono, T., Shioji, T., Kinugasa, T., Onishi, T., and Kurachi, K., 1978, Clinical and endocrinological analysis of patients with galactorrhea and menstrual disorders due to sulpiride or metoclopramide, *J. Clin. Endocrinol. Metab.* **47:**675–680.

123. Aono, T., Shigi, T., Aki, T., Hirota, K., Nomura, K., and Kurachi, K., 1979, Augmentation of puerperal lactation by oral administration of sulpiride, *J. Clin Endocrinol. Metab.* **48:**478–482.

124. McNeilly, A. S., Thomer, M. O., Volans, G., and Besser, G. M., 1974, Metoclopramide and prolactin, *Br. Med. J.* **2:**729.

125. Delitalia, G., Masala, A., Alagna, S., and Devilla, L., 1976, Effect of metoclopramide on serum prolactin in humans, *Clin. Endocrinol.* **5:**731–734.

126. Sousa, P. S. R., 1975, Metoclopramide and breast feeding, *Br. Med. J.* **1:**512.

127. Tyson, J. E., Perez, A., and Zanartu, J., 1976, Human lactation response to oral thyrotrophin releasing hormone, *J. Clin. Endocrinol. Metab.* **43:**760–768.
128. Hall, D. M. D. and Kay, G., 1977, Effect of thyrotrophin-releasing factor on lactation, *Br. Med. J.* **1:**777.
129. Frantz, A. G., 1974, Prolactin secretion in physiologic and pathologic human conditions measured by bioassay and radioimmunoassay, in: *Lactogenic Hormones, Fetal Nutrition and Lactation* (J. B. Josimovich, M. Reynolds, and E. Cobo, eds.), Wiley, New York, p. 379.
130. Lucas, A., Drewett, R. B., and Mitchell, M. D., 1980, Breast-feeding and plasma oxytocin concentrations, *Br. Med. J.* **281:**834–835.
131. Ingerslev, M and Pinholt, K., 1962, Oxytocin treatment during the establishment of lactation, *Acta Obstet. Gynecol. Scand.* **41:**159–168.
132. Luhman, L., 1963, The effect of intranasal oxytocin on lactation, *Am. J. Obstet. Gynecol.* **21:**713–717.
133. Ruis, H., Rolland, R., Doesburg, W., Broeders, G., and Corbey, R., 1981, Oxytocin enhances onset of lactation among mothers delivery prematurely, *Br. Med. J.* **283:**340–342.
134. Newton, M. and Egli, G. E., 1958, The effect of intranasal administration of oxytocin on the let-down of milk in lactating women, *Am. J. Obstet. Gynecol.* **76:**103–107.
135. Huntingford, P. J., 1961, Intranasal use of synthetic oxytocin in management of breast-feeding, *Br. Med. J.* **1:**709–711.
136. Wagner, G. and Fuchs, A. R., 1968, Effect of ethanol on uterine activity during suckling in post partum women, *Acta Endocrinol.* **58:**133–141.
137. Cobo, E., 1973, Effect of different doses of ethanol on the milk ejecting reflex in lactating women, *Am. J. Obstet. Gynecol.* **115:**817–819.

14

Lactation and Contraception

James A. McGregor

> If a woman nurses her baby, she is permitted to use an anticonceptional device. The occurrence of a new pregnancy could place the baby in danger for lack of milk.
>
> *Talmud (Babt Yebamot, Fol 12B)*

Much controversy surrounds the theoretical and practical considerations of fertility control for lactating women.[1-3] The positive benefits of breast-feeding are increasingly promoted, often without mention of the complex interplay between lactation, fertility, and the individual woman's reproductive "life plan."[4,5] Because use of contraceptive devices and practices, other than condoms and abstinence, may affect the quality and adequacy of breast feeding, it is appropriate to review the interaction between these modern-day imperatives, breast-feeding and fertility control. In order to place these concerns in perspective, we will examine the length and degree of infertility associated with lactational amenorrhea and the proven and likely influences of different contraceptive formulations and devices on milk production and composition as well as their possible effects on the duration of lactation.

METHODOLOGIC CONCERNS

Winikoff has pointed out that studies of breast-feeding, like studies of human sexuality, are complicated by the intimate nature of this natural process which involves the cooperation of at least two individuals in a complex series of behaviors that must be repeated many times under widely varying circumstances.[6] Basic difficulties in the many observational studies of contraceptive usage during lactation stem from a number of sources including problems in measuring breast milk volume and quality, lack of an adequate

---

James A. McGregor • Department of Obstetrics and Gynecology, University of Colorado School of Medicine, Denver, Colorado 80262.

definition of the duration of "successful" lactation, and the use of differing parameters for the nursling's growth and development.[6,7,8] All these issues have been dealt with in unstandardized ways with varying periods of follow-up in widely differing populations. Even definitions of establishment and maintenance of lactation differ widely.[9] Further, the contraceptive agents being evaluated often differ from one study to another.[10] Finally, unless carefully controlled, psychological factors may have a profound effect on the outcome of an investigation[7] (see subsection entitled "Effect of Contraceptive Steroids on the Volume and Composition of Breast Milk"). Despite these difficulties, we will attempt to draw some useful guidelines for contraceptive practice during lactation.

THE EFFECTS OF LACTATION ON FERTILITY

Lactation is a physiologic process that has been long and widely understood to postpone subsequent childbearing.[11] Even though modern medical practitioners have tended to disregard this effect, it is now recognized that breast-feeding acts as a natural birth spacer, or as Short pointed out "Nature's own contraceptive." He commented further that, throughout the world, more births are prevented by lactation than by all other contraceptive practices combined.[12] In many parts of the developing world, prolonged lactation serves as the main limitation of population growth.[13-17] On the other hand, as we shall show in this section, for the individual woman, lactation offers unreliable protection from pregnancy.

Endocrine Basis of Lactational Amenorrhea

Prolactin secretion occurs in response to suckling and the plasma level of prolactin is related to the frequency and duration of suckling as well as the postpartum interval (see Chapter 4).[18-21] Most authorities believe that hyperprolactinemia, acting both at the level of the hypothalamus and on the ovaries, is itself responsible for the inhibition of ovarian function often observed during lactation.[22-23] For example, Delvoye and his colleagues, working in Zaire, observed on a population basis that menstruation did not reappear until plasma prolactin levels had dropped below an average value of 869 μU/ml (34 ng/ml).[21] Howie and McNeilly[22,23] hypothesized that increased prolactin levels induced by suckling interfere with the normal positive feedback effect of estrogen on the hypothalamus. This, in turn, leads to diminished GnRH production and loss of pulsatile LH secretion from the pituitary with inhibition of ovulation. Knobil and his associates have suggested that suckling may also have a direct inhibitory effect on the hypothalamic secretion of gonadotropins.[24] After weaning, there is a fall in prolactin concentrations, and ovulation generally occurs within 14 to 30 days. It is important to note that breast-feeding, even with high prolactin levels, does not invariably suppress ovulation so that ovulation and resumption of menses are not uncommon in breast-feeding women.[13-17,25] It is in fact quite possible for lactating women to become pregnant prior to the resumption of menstrual cycling.[10]

It has been suggested that the nutritional status of lactating mothers influences the maintenance of elevated prolactin levels and thus modulates their relative infertility. In a study of plasma prolactin levels in breast-feeding Gambian women, dietary supplementation of the mother was found to have no effect on the frequency of breast-feeding which occurred 10 to 16 times a day.[25,27] However, supplementation was associated with lower basal prolactin levels than in Gambian women not fed dietary supplements. This decreased prolactin level may explain the association between improved nutritional status and the trend toward reduction in the period of lactational amenorrhea noted by Delgado *et al.* in Guatemala.[28] If this formulation is correct, the antifertility effect of physiologic lactation may be a protective mechanism that, when food is less available, prevents a new pregnancy that could further embarrass the nutritional status of both the mother and the nursling. As teleologically attractive as this formulation may be, it is important to note that Bongaarts in a recent review showed that, in general, nutrition appears to have only marginal effects on fecundity.[29]

In any case, the period of lactational infertility varies greatly among individuals and is determined by many factors, including frequency and intensity of suckling, maternal nutrition, and likely other local or individual cultural, psychological, or sociological factors such as prohibition of coitus during lactation. In order to gain an understanding of the actual effects of lactation on fertility in both large groups and individuals, we must review some epidemiologic studies.

Conception and Lactation

The delayed occurrence of ovulation after childbirth has been documented in a variety of studies utilizing various techniques to examine the resumption of postpartum ovarian activity.[13-18,30] Most studies have been small and have utilized heterogeneous populations without true control groups. In a remarkable study that is not likely to be repeated, Perez and co-workers analyzed postpartum ovulation by means of monthly endometrial biopsies, basal body temperatures, vaginal cytology, and evaluation of cervical mucus in a group of 170 postpartum Chilean women.[31,32] Although adequate follow-up was not always available in this study, certain trends are clear. Among the 30 women who did not breast-feed, none appeared to ovulate before 36 days postpartum. But by 60 days postpartum, fully 84% appeared to have ovulated, reconfirming the importance of contraception in the puerperium for nonlactating women. In lactating mothers, increased intensity and length of feeding correlated with a decreased probability of ovulation for a given duration of lactation. During the first 9 postpartum weeks, totally nursing women were nearly completely infertile with a probability of only 0.01 of ovulating in the eighth postpartum week. The incidence of ovulation increased rapidly to a probability of 0.08 during the 11th week with roughly similar risk of ovulation during each succeeding week of total breast-feeding. Initial postpartum cycles appeared to be ovulatory in 78% of these women. There was a tendency for an anovulatory menstruation to precede ovulation when lactation was of long standing or when there was less dietary supplementation of the baby. Conversely, ovulation tended to precede the first menstruation where lactation was of shorter duration and infant feeding was supplemented. The earliest pregnancy in this study occurred in a woman practicing unsupplemented breast-feeding who appeared to ovulate 75 days postpartum.

In a similarly large study, Kamal and colleagues studied lactation and return of fertility during 290 lactational episodes among 120 poor urban Egyptian women.[33] They found maternal age and parity to be significantly associated with the duration of lactation as older and more parous women tended to breast-feed more successfully and for longer periods. Although the status of lactation and ovulation were less accurately studied, breast-feeding Egyptian women appeared to initiate menstruation rather promptly, with one-third reporting menstruation by 3 months postpartum and two-thirds reporting menstruation by 9 months postpartum. Kamal indicated that fully one-half of all patients became pregnant while lactating and half of these conceived prior to return of menses. This contrasts with the 3 to 8% of women who become pregnant prior to the return of menses reported in other studies.[10] Kamal and his colleagues also noted that pregnancy was a cause for the cessation of lactation in roughly one-third of women.[33] These findings reinforce the suggestions of others that lactation is an unreliable method of contraception for individual women. They also suggest that reliable contraception may reinforce lactation by decreasing the occurrence of pregnancy.

Summary

Studies among varied populations show a correlation between mean duration of lactation, lactational amenorrhea, and interpregnancy intervals.[10,15–17,20] Despite many contending factors, some generalizations can be made. Ovulation returns in nonlactating mothers within 1 to 3 months, whereas the return of ovarian activity and ovulation in lactating women occurs generally after the ninth postpartum week and nearly always by 18 months postpartum unless there is intercurrent disease. Pregnancy may occur in individual fully lactating women as early as 10 weeks postpartum. In long-term studies, as many as 50% of women become pregnant while still lactating, with 3 to 8% likely to become pregnant without ever resuming menstruation. In addition, the occurrence of pregnancy is a common factor in discontinuation of lactation.

CONTRACEPTION DURING LACTATION

Possible interactions between breast-feeding and contraceptive methods are complex and not likely to be completely understood in the near future. We often view such complex problems from the perspective of our culture and fail to comprehend the possibly mortal ramifications of inadequate lactation and fertility control. Despite its advantages, many Western women can afford to disdain breast-feeding as a form of infant nutrition without any perceptible damage to their newborns. Western woman may choose from a variety of contraceptive methods and technologies, and possibly seek an elective abortion if an unwanted pregnancy occurs. In the developing world, cessation or reduction of maternal milk supply, possibly induced by a contraceptive, may lead to increased disease and possible infant death. Moreover, pregnancy remains a major reason for weaning in most of the world where too short of an interpregnancy interval may displace the nursling and threaten his or her health. Suitable contraception may reinforce and extend lactation by helping to delay a subsequent pregnancy and therefore may be of importance for protection of the health of the mother and nursling as well as possible future pregnancies.

In choosing a contraceptive technique to be used during breast-feeding, its suitability for the individual and possible effects on lactation must be considered in addition to ability to prevent pregnancy. The use of various contraceptive methods in a particular culture must be understood. If contraceptive methods are to be optimally employed, there must be knowledge of the woman's individual circumstances as well as understanding of the possible effects on lactation and on the growth and development of the newborn. In this section, the advantages and disadvantages of the available methods of contraception will be discussed.

Abstinence

Abstention from intercourse is well known as the most effective contraceptive method, even though such restraint may not have great appeal in "modern society." Cultural, sociological, psychological, and even practical restraints against coitus during lactation in many parts of the world serve to delay subsequent conception and pregnancy until the present baby is safely weaned. Saucier has reviewed postpartum taboos against intercourse with lactating women around the world.[34] These constraints appear particularly powerful in societies where lactation may be an important condition for an infant's survival, such as in North and Saharan Africa, Melanesia, and Central America. Observations of Guatemalan Indians by Hinshaw and colleagues suggest that some of these Indians understand that coitus postpartum may ultimately impair milk production.[35] Hinshaw states, "the more anxious the parents are to keep the child alive," the more abstinence they practice.

Polygyny may facilitate prolonged abstention from coitus with lactating women in some cultures and reduce any sense of male deprivation.

Practical, situational difficulties may also interfere with the resumption of coitus postpartum in many parts of the world. Nag described difficulties in achieving sexual privacy in rural India.[36] Nineteenth-century Europeans may not have been much better off, as described by Knodel.[37] Sexuality in lactating postpartum women remains incompletely studied. Impression and anecdotes abound, such as Raphael's comment that some breast-feeding women may have reduced libido, "while others find the act of lactating so fulfilling that their fecundity is enhanced as their sexual role as female is heightened."[38] Men with hyperprolactinemia may complain of decreased libido as may occasional women with galactorrhea–amenorrhea. The hyperprolactinemia-induced reduction of circulating estrogen is often a cause of dysparunia because of inadequate vaginal lubrication. Such physiologically induced coital discomfort may be a powerful disincentive for intercourse. The sexual interest of the male partner may be decreased by confusion over the breast's nutritive and sexual functions. In any case, some couples' individual or cultural circumstances may lead to decreased coital frequency that may be adequate for nearly complete protection against conception during the amenorrheic portion of lactation. However, a recent survey suggests that American couples in general initiate intercourse several weeks postpartum; for such couples, abstinence or even *coitus interruptus* is either unrealistic or inadequate as a method of contraception.[39]

Barrier Methods

It seems unlikely that barrier methods, such as condoms, diaphragms, cervical caps, vaginal sponges, or even coitus interruptus, have any ill effect on lactation other than method failure and possible pregnancy. These methods would seem ideal in backing up the relative infertility of lactating women who are amenorrheic. The main drawbacks of barrier methods remain patient motivation and inherently higher risks of failure.

One note of caution should be added: Nonoxynol-9 is a detergent substance that is the spermicidal ingredient in most contraceptive foams, jellies and sponges. The agent has been shown to be absorbed through skin, with subsequent secretion in milk in both rats and rabbits where it was also identified in the serum of the pups.[40] The possibility that the agent is secreted in significant quantities in human breast milk has not been evaluated.

Rhythm or Natural Family Planning

Various forms of periodic abstinence are suitable contraception for many motivated couples. Since menstruation is one of the main signposts for timed abstinence, the possible lack of menses prior to the initial postpartum ovulation makes application of natural family planning methods problematic. Examination of cervical mucous changes and basal body temperature evaluation for prediction of ovulation remain to be established as effective contraceptive adjuncts in the lactating woman. Therefore, for the 3 to 8% of women who may become pregnant prior to any return of menstruation, the small but real risks of conception may be unacceptable.

Postpartum Sterilization

Postpartum sterilization is obviously a practical method of fertility control for women who have completed their families. The possibility that the surgery or general anesthesia may interfere with either the initiation of lactation or the complex behavioral interactions the baby and mother share to initiate successful lactation has only been preliminarily examined in a study of 36 women.[41] Women who were operated upon within 24 hr of delivery lactated as well as control patients. Women sterilized 4 to 6 days postpartum produced less milk for up to 2 weeks.[41] Although further studies are needed, it appears that maternal sterilization may be done prior to 4 days after birth with little effect on lactation. Regional or local anesthesia may be preferable. In any case, the postpartum period is also an ideal time for elective sterilization of the male partner with vasectomy.

Intrauterine Devices

The use of intrauterine devices (IUDs) to augment lactational infertility appeals to many because this relatively effective form of contraception has no obvious effect on milk quantity or quality. Several studies suggest actual enhancement of lactation associated with IUD usage, but these studies remain to be confirmed by other investigators.[42,43] Gomez-Rogers and co-workers found the "lactational half-life" (time when 50% of women stop lactating) was 7 months 21 days among women with postpartum IUD insertion.[42] The control group was imperfectly matched, but had a "lactational half-life" of 4 months and 21 days, which was a statistically significant difference. Hingorani and Umabai showed a trend toward more prolonged lactation in Indian women with postpartum IUDs, but the differences were not statistically significant.[43]

Some potential complications of postpartum IUD insertion have been described. Horne and Scott reported two women with galactorrhea mediated by increased prolactin levels coincidental with IUD insertion; the condition resolved promptly with IUD removal.[44] In another report, increased prolactin levels were found in nonlactating women with copper containing IUDs. However, more recent studies do not show any endocrinologic alterations in postpartum women wearing IUDs.[45-48] IUD insertion in the immediate postpartum period in lactating women has been thought to be followed by higher expulsion rates, perhaps because of the increased uterine contractions attendant on active suckling. For this reason, a working group from the International Planned Parenthood Association suggested an 8-week waiting period prior to postpartum IUD insertion in lactating women. Cole and colleagues recently re-examined this issue and could demonstrate no difference in the expulsion or perforation rates of IUDs between lactating and nonlactating women.[49] Although the optimal time for IUD insertion for postpartum women may be dictated by the woman's individual circumstance, it appears that the IUD as a contraceptive method does not interfere with lactation and may be considered on the basis of its own merits and disadvantages.

Steroid Contraceptives

The clinical availability of steroidal contraception in the early 1960s was promptly followed by recognition of several possible untoward effects on lactation. Because higher doses of estrogen were used to prevent lactation in non-breast-feeding women, there was concern that combination or sequential oral contraceptives might inhibit milk formation. Further concerns were that contraceptive steroids would alter the composition of the milk, pass through the milk and be absorbed by the infant, or simply interfere in a more general way with the well-being of the mother. We will review and put in perspective the available information on these points, which still remain the objects of controversy.

Within the last decade, more than 50 investigations and several broad-ranging reviews have been devoted to these questions.[7,10] Evaluation of our present knowledge remains difficult because of methodologic problems with many of the studies as well as the use of varying contraceptive formulations. In many cases, observed changes have been within the normal range, making it difficult to evaluate their significance. Few studies mention the actual efficacy of any contraceptive method in lactating women. In the last analysis, it is the growth and development of the infant and the overall health of the mother and family including the ability to space children appropriately, which are most important. If contraceptive steroids are to be used, they must be employed in ways that minimize any possible untoward effects on lactation or on infant and maternal health, as well as having the desired contraceptive effect.

Effect of Contraceptive Steroids on the Volume and Composition of Breast Milk

The constituents of estrogen–progestogen oral contraceptive formulations theoretically may influence the composition of breast milk either by altering overall maternal concentrations of different nutrients, thus changing the amounts of these substances presented to the breast, or by directly influencing the mechanisms of milk secretion. The nutritional relevance of any induced change must always be considered. Although numerous studies demonstrate alterations in bodily levels or metabolism of different vitamins, minerals, serum proteins, lipids, and other nutrients including glucose induced by oral contraceptive agents, to date, no oral contraceptive-induced change in human milk has been shown to consistently exceed the normal limits for unmedicated women.

Examination of the multiple studies addressing possible changes in breast milk composition points up the practical and analytical difficulties of such investigations. Pomerance was among the first to stress the importance of psychological influences in determining the outcome of investigations of human lactation suggesting that "what the mother thinks the pill will do" may be the controlling factor.[50] Zanartu *et al.* addressed the issue of motivation and the patient's support systems for breast-feeding.[51] He compared the lactational performance of motivated and educated breast-feeding women using the progestogen chloradionone diacetate (0.6 mg daily) with that of a group of unmotivated women who were using IUDs for postpartum contraception. The unmotivated, uneducated women rapidly stopped breast-feeding, with only 5% lactating 6 months postpartum. Fully 80% of the progestogen-treated group continued breast-feeding beyond 6 months postpartum, suggesting that either progestogen has a positive beneficial effect or that motivational factors overcome any deleterious effects of the contraceptive. In two other double-blind investigations in which 75 μg of mestronal and 2.5 mg of lynestenol were used, oral contraceptive administration was found to have no statistical effect on lactation performance among women who positively wanted to breast-feed, but significantly shortened the length of lactation in women not motivated for breast-feeding.[52,53] There is widespread medical and lay belief that any estrogen will "dry up breast milk." An investigation with a small number of mothers demonstrated that placebos are as effective as large doses of estrogen for elective lactation suppression in women who did not want to breast-feed.[54] These observations suggest that the expectation of suppressed lactation may lead to maternal presumption of inadequate lactation. It may be that maternal behavior is more important than direct effects of oral contraceptive agents on breast tissue.

Despite these behavioral problems, several trends have emerged. Nearly all investigators report that combined oral contraceptives containing 50 μg or more of ethinyl estradiol, or equivalent amounts of mestranol, appear to decrease the amount of milk produced and to shorten the duration of lactation in a dose-related way.[7,10,56] These effects appeared most marked in primiparous women whose experience and probably self-confidence were lacking. The estrogen component has been considered to be the main adverse ingredient, since large doses of estrogen inhibit the initiation of lactation.[55] However, studies of the effects of steroid contraceptives have not kept up with clinical practice. Combination estrogen–progestogen formulations now in general use contain considerably less estrogen than pills used in the majority of studies and very much less estrogen than was used for intentional suppression of lactation or in early combination birth control pills.

In a well-controlled study, Lönnerdal and his colleagues compared two low-dose combination oral contraceptives (250 μg *d*-norgestrel with 50 μg of ethinyl estradiol and 150 μg *d*-norgestrel with 30 μg of ethanyl estradiol) with a progestogen-only preparation (30 μg of *d*-norgestrel).[57] Their results illustrate the wide variability of milk composition and volume that occurs in normal women. While there were significant differences in albumin and lactoferrin concentrations in the milk of the medicated women, there was no difference in the lactose concentrations, and milk volumes tended to decrease only initially. Alterations in the composition of the milk of individual women fell within the normal range for well-nourished Swedish women, leading Lönnerdal to question the nutritional significance of any of these changes for mothers and their infants.

The relevance of the above studies for less well-nourished women and babies has not been established. Unwanted side effects of oral contraceptive steroids in certain populations in developing countries have been sufficiently severe that the term *contraceptive marasmus* has been coined to denote the morbid malnourished condition found in infants of mothers taking oral contraceptives.[58,59] In underdeveloped countries nursing infants likely have no safe alternatives to breast-feeding and may show decreased weight gain in mothers receiving relatively high-dose estrogen combined oral contraceptives.[58] In lactating Egyptian women, Kamal *et al.* showed that decreased infant weight gain was related to oral contraceptives. This group suggested that any drug-induced reduction of milk volume may have devastating effects among marginally nourished infants and infants who have no satisfactory substitute for breast-feeding.[33]

Although the effects of low-estrogen dosage birth control pills must be studied in more numerous settings with improved methodological approaches before we can come to a definitive conclusion, two studies suggest that steroid combinations currently in use do not adversely affect lactational performance.[57,60] Whether this conclusion can be applied to malnourished populations is not yet clear.

Secretion of Steroidal Contraceptive Agents in Breast Milk

It is accepted that nearly all substances taken by the mother during lactation can be transferred to some degree to the nursling through human milk. (see Chapter 13). Since Curtis' unique report in 1964 of a male infant with transient gynecomastia thought to be induced by breast milk transfer of oral contraceptive steroids, there has been much interest in measuring the transfer of steroids through breast milk.[61–63]

Studies by Nilsson and colleagues showed that an infant consuming an average of 600 ml of breast milk daily from a mother taking 50 μg ethinyl estradiol received roughly 10 ng of the agent each day or 0.02% of the maternal dose.[63] This amount of estrogen is comparable to the amount of estradiol consumed by a nursling from breast milk produced by mothers not taking oral contraceptives. For example, during the anovulatory period postpartum, it is estimated that the suckling infant receives from 3 to 6 ng of estradiol a day through milk.[64] After ovulation has returned to the lactating woman, the baby may receive 6 to 12 ng of estradiol from breast milk depending on the phase of the ovarian cycle.[51] The degree to which these adventitious and natural estrogens are absorbed and metabolized and any possible metabolic significance remains to be worked out in the suckling newborn.

Oral contraceptive progestogens such as megestrol acetate and *d*-norgestrel are found in breast milk at only 10 to 20% of maternal serum concentrations, presumably because binding to maternal serum protein substantially prevents transfer to the milk (see Chapter 13).[10] In one study, for example, Nilsson evaluated the nursling's absorption and metabolism of *d*-norgestrel when mothers took either 30 μg *d*-norgestrel alone or combined oral contraceptives containing 150 μg *d*-norgestrel with 30 μg ethinyl estradiol or 250 μg *d*-norgestrel along with 50 μg ethinyl estradiol.[65] The investigators estimated that the infants received 0.03 μg, 0.15 μg and 0.3 μg of *d*-norgestrel, respectively, per 600 ml daily breast milk feeding or roughly 1/1000 of the maternal dose. The infant's serum levels of progestogen approximated 1/50 to 1/100 of maternal blood levels when levels were detectable. This suggests that *d*-norgestrel is metabolized in the infant to some degree and is not accumulated. Comparable data were obtained in a similar study using megestrol acetate.[66]

In summary, the proportion of most oral steroid contraceptive formulations finding their way to breast milk is small and the reported side effects are minimal. If the principles of drug usage discussed in Chapter 13 are applied to the oral contraceptives, it seems unlikely that deleterious side effects of these amounts of steroid would result in any full-term healthy infant fully fed on breast milk containing these steroid dosages. More caution may be necessary in premature or other infants with, for example, liver disease, in which steroid metabolism might be compromised. Possible influences of endogenous and exogenous sex steroids in human milk on brain development and gender identification remain unknown, but sexual determination occurs before birth and gender identification is a complex process not likely to be altered by the small amounts of sex steroids found in milk.

Combined Estrogen–Progestogen Pills

Well over 40 investigations on the effects of combined birth control pills on lactation have been published in the last two decades.[10] Many of these studies are too small or too flawed to be authoritative. Some of the more reliable studies have been summarized in previous sections. Clear effects of high-dose estrogens on lactational performance have been documented. Although the low-dose combinations currently in use do not appear to have these side effects in well-nourished women, more studies are needed in underdeveloped countries before a similar conclusion can be firmly stated for malnourished women.

Progestogen-Only Contraception

Studies of progestogen-only contraception in lactating women are numerous but unfortunately individualistic in design. In general, the progestogen-only-based contraceptive formulations have the drawback of being somewhat less effective in preventing pregnancy and being more often associated with bleeding difficulties than are the combined oral contraceptive agents. However, these disadvantages may be less important in the breast-feeding woman who has reduced fertility and may have prolonged amen-orrhea in any case. When menstruation and full fertility return, more effective forms of contraception may be substituted.

Further differentiation among different progestogen-only formulations is difficult because the studies have not been comparable. However, it appears that 19-norprogestogens, such as norethynodrel, norethindrone, and quin-gestenol, have the potential of behaving more like combination estrogen–progestogen contraceptives, because they are partly metabolized to estrogen *in vivo*. However, there is presently no firm evidence that progestogen-only contraceptives presently available alter milk composition or volume in con-sistently deleterious ways.

Injectable progestogen contraceptive formulations such as medroxypro-gesterone have the advantage of relative ease of administration, efficacy, and possible endocrinologic reinforcement of breast-feeding with prolongation of lactation in many studies and no known effect on the fetus or newborn.[67] Enthusiasm for these preparations should be tempered by the variable length of the individual's induced infertility, possible irregular uterine bleeding, the continuing controversy over possible tumorigenicity, and the observation that medroxyprogesterone is secreted in relatively high amounts in breast milk. Saxena *et al.* demonstrated that medroxyprogesterone concentration in human milk approximates the mother's blood level.[68] These disadvantages may be compelling when alternative forms of contraception are available.

Strategies for the Use of Oral Contraceptive Agents during Lactation

If oral contraceptive agents are chosen, they should be initiated at the point when the woman has a realistic risk of unwanted conception. There is no need to initiate oral contraceptive agents prior to 2 weeks postpartum even in women who do not plan to breast-feed. Delaying initiation of oral contraceptives for at least this interval tends to bypass the period of high risk for postpartum thrombotic complications. For sexually active, fully lactating women, a low-dose (less than 50 μg of ethinyl estradiol or equivalent estrogen) combination oral contraceptive agent may be begun after the ninth postpartum week. Prior to 9 weeks, low-dose combination pills may be begun on an individual basis in women using supplementary feeding or planning to wean their infants rapidly. For women wishing to use oral contraceptive agents, an alternative strategy may be to use barrier methods, IUDs, abstinence, coitus interruptus and progestogen-only preparations to furnish contraception until the return of menstruation when low dosage combined oral contraception may be begun.

Summary of Contraceptive Usage in Lactation

Unsupplemented breast-feeding is the biological device for birth spacing in the human species, providing roughly 90% protection against conception until menstruation returns. The strategies for providing supplementary contraception may differ in this relatively infertile period until the return of menstruation, at which time more effective methods may be instituted. Properly chosen contraceptive methods may actually support and prolong lactation by preventing or delaying subsequent pregnancy. In situations where breast-feeding is the only secure source of infant nutrition and child spacing, ill-advised usage of fallible contraceptive methods and subsequent pregnancy may jeopardize the nutritional resources of the mother, the unborn baby, and the nursling by displacing the dependent infant from the nutritional superiority and relative sterility of its mother's breast.

Many studies suggest that nonlactating postpartum women commonly ovulate by the end of the sixth postpartum week and that lactating women are rarely fertile prior to completing the ninth postpartum week. These observations make the institution of a contraceptive method by the sixth week of great importance in nonlactating women, whereas breast-feeding women who are not giving their infants supplemental feedings should not require any contraceptive method until approximately the tenth week postpartum. The main imperative in birth control choice during lactation is that the agent, device, or practice interfere with lactation as little as possible, while supplying adequate protection. No method except high-dose estrogen-containing oral contraceptives need be entirely proscribed from use in breast-feeding women. Appropriate choice of any method should address the degree of the individual's need, motivation, and acceptance of that method. If a woman or couple uses a particular contraceptive method poorly or inconsistently, then pregnancy may occur even sooner than if the woman simply breast-feeds fully as long as possible.

A review of the salient features of the different birth control methods suggests that each has its appropriate use under certain circumstances. These methods, which have been described more fully above, are listed in summary form here.

1. Although not particularly effective in normally fertile couples, decreased coital frequency and coitus interruptus may offer adequate supplementary contraception for certain amenorrheic lactating women.
2. Barrier methods such as condoms, diaphragms, caps, sponges or other devices may be used throughout the period of lactation without known effects on milk composition or the duration of lactation and probably represent optimum protection in breast-feeding couples with the motivation and skills to properly employ them.
3. Natural family planning techniques have not been shown capable of predicting the onset of ovarian activity in the lactating woman and may, therefore, not be particularly useful prior to the onset of menses.

4. Female sterilization by tubal ligation is routinely done in the postpartum period and remains a useful contraceptive procedure for the individual who has completed her family. Male sterilization also offers advantages. Either of these procedures requires a highly individual decision that may presently be made without regard to lactation.

5. Intrauterine device contraception has the advantage of a one-time insertion and relatively high efficacy in poorly motivated individuals and seems unlikely to interfere with lactation in any way. Disadvantages of the IUD in any patient include possible perforation and pelvic infection leading to subfertility or infertility among other complications. For this reason, IUD usage necessitates competent patient education and provision for follow-up in case of difficulties.

6. Steroidal contraceptive agents remain as useful formulations for effective birth control in lactating women. Possible complications from oral contraceptive use are known but have a low incidence. The metabolic and medical consequences of passage of small amounts of oral contraceptive steroids to the nursing infant through breast milk remain incompletely studied but are probably minimal. Higher estrogen dose formulations appear to be associated with decreased milk production and should be avoided. It appears likely, but not well-substantiated, that lower-dose estrogen and progestogen preparations as well as progestogen-alone pills are not frequently associated with these unwanted effects.

It is apparent that prolonged unsupplemented breast-feeding, in addition to its other advantages, operates as the most important pregnancy spacer for the human species. However, for individual women, lactation is an unreliable contraceptive. Further, pregnancy may be an important cause of cessation of lactation even in women who are breast-feeding without infant food supplementation. Appropriate choices and timing of contraception in lactating women may serve to prolong lactation and allow individual women and their families better control of their reproductive futures.

REFERENCES

1. Breastfeeding and the Oral Contraceptive, Information Sheet No. 18, La Leche League International, November 1975.
2. Rosa, F. W., 1976 Resolving the "public health dilemma" of steroid contraception and its effects on lactation, *Am. J. Pediatr. Health* **66:**791–792.
3. Committee on Drugs, 1981, Breast feeding and contraception, *Pediatrics* **68:**138–139.
4. Hales, D. J., 1981, Promoting breastfeeding: Strategies for changing hospital policy, *Stud. Fam. Plann.* **12:**167–177.
5. Committee on Nutrition, 1980, Encouraging breast-feeding, *Pediatrics* **65:**657–658.
6. Winikoff, B., 1981, Issues in the design of breastfeeding research, *Stud. Fam. Plann.* **12:**177–184.
7. Hull, V. J., 1981, The effects of hormonal contraception on lactation: Current findings, methodologic considerations, and future priorities, *Stud. Fam. Plann.* **12:**134–155.

8. Coward, W. A., Whitehead, R. G., Sawyer, M. D., Prentice, A. M., and Evans, J., 1979, New methods for measuring milk intake in breast-fed babies, *Lancet* **2**:13–14.
9. Kader, M. M. A., Kamal, J., et al., 1969, Clinical biochemical and experimental studies on lactation, III. Biochemical changes induced in human milk by gestogens, *Am. J. Obstet. Gynecol.* **105**:978–85.
10. Breastfeeding, fertility and family planning, 1981, *Popul. Rep. Ser. J*(24), Nov–Dec.
11. Kolata, G. B., 1980, ¡Kung hunter-gatherers: Feminism, diet, and birth control, *Science* **185**:932–934.
12. Short, R. V., 1976, Lactation—the central control of reproduction, Ciba Symposia 45, *Human Lactation*, pp. 73–86.
13. Van Ginnekan, J. K., 1978, The impact of prolonged breast-feeding on birth intervals and on postpartum amenorrhea, In: *Nutrition and Human Reproduction* (W. H. Mosley, ed.), Plenum Press, New York, pp. 179–195.
14. Van Ginneken, J. K., 1977, The chance of conception during lactation, *J. Biosocial Sci. (Suppl.)* **4**:41–54.
15. Bonte, M. and Van Balen, H., 1969, Prolonged lactation and family spacing in Rwanda, *J. Biosocial Sci.* **1**:97–100.
16. Simpson-Herbert, M. and Huffman, S. L., 1981, The contraceptive effect of breast-feeding, *Stud. Fam. Plann.* **12**:125–133.
17. Breast-feeding—Aid to infant health and fertility control, 1975, *Popul. Rep., Ser. J* (4), July.
18. Tyson, J. E., Freedman, R. S., Pereza, A., Zacur, H. A., and Zanartu, J., 1976, Significance of the secretion of human prolactin and gonadotropin for puerperal lactational infertility, Ciba Symposia 45, *Human Lactation*, pp. 48–65.
19. Tyson, J. E., Carter, J. N., Anderassen, B., Huth, J., and Smith, B., 1978, Nursing-mediated prolactin and luteinizing hormone secretion during puerperal lactation, *Fertil. Steril.* **30**:154–159.
20. Delvoye, P. J., Delogne-Desroek, J., and Robyn, C., 1977, The influence of the frequency of nursing and of previous lactation experience on serum prolactin in nursing mothers, *J. Biosocial Sci.* **9**:447–451.
21. Delvoye, P., Demaego, M., Uwayitu-Nyampeta, A., and Robyn, C., 1978, Serum prolactin, gonadotropins and estriol in menstruating and amenorrheic mothers during the year's lactation, *Am. J. Obstet. Gynecol.* **130**:635–639.
22. Howie, P. W. and McNeilly, A. S., 1979, Lactational amenorrhea, prolactin and contraception, *Eur. J. Clin. Invest.* **9**:237–238.
23. NcNeilly, A. S., 1979, Effects of lactation on infertility, *Br. Med. Bull.* **35**:151–154.
24. Schallenberger, E., Richardson, D. W., and Knobil, E., 1981, The role of prolactin in the lactation amenorrhea of the rhesus monkey (*Macaca mulatta*), *Biol. Reprod.* **25**:370–374.
25. Giosiosa, R., 1956, Incidence of pregnancy during lactation in 500 cases, *Am. J. Obstet. Gynecol.* **70**:162–174.
26. Whitehead, R. G., Hutton, H., Müller, E., Rowland, M. G. M., Prentice, A. M., and Paul, A., 1978, Factors influencing lactational performance in rural Gambian mothers, *Lancet* **2**:178–181.
27. Lunn, P. G., Austin, S., Prentice, A. M., and Whitehead, R. G., Influence of maternal diet on plasma prolactin levels during lactation, *Lancet* **1**:623–625.
28. Delgado, H., Brineman, E., Lechtig, A., Bongaarts, J., Martorell, R., and Klein, R. E., 1979, Effect of maternal nutritional status and infant supplementation during lactation on postpartum amenorrhea, *Am. J. Obstet. Gynecol.* **135**:303–307.
29. Bongaarts, J., 1980, Does malnutrition affect fecundity: A summary of the evidence. *Science* **208**:564–569.
30. Berman, M. L., Hanson, K., and Hellman, I. L., 1972, Effect of breast-feeding on postpartum menstruation, ovulation, and pregnancy in Alaskan Eskimos, *Am. J. Obstet. Gynecol.* **114**:524–534.
31. Perez, A., Vela, P., Masnick, G. S., and Potter, R. G., 1971, Timing and sequence of resuming ovulation and menstruation after childbirth. *Popul. Stud.* **25**:491–500.

32. Perez, A., Vela, P., Masnick, G. S., and Potter, R. G., 1972, First ovulation after childbirth: The effect of breastfeeding, *Am. J. Obstet. Gynecol.* **114**:1041–1047.

33. Kamal, I., Hefnawi, F., Ghoneim, M., Talaat, M., Younis, N., Tagui, A., and Abdulla, M., 1969, Clinical, biochemical, and experimental studies on lactation, I. Lactational patterns in Egyptian women, *Am. J. Obstet. Gynecol.* **105**:314–323.

34. Saucier, J. F., 1972, Correlates of the long post-partum taboo: A cross-cultural study. *Curr. Anthropol.* **13**:238–245.

35. Hinshaw, R., Pyeati, P., and Habicht, J. P., 1972, Environmental effects on child spacing and population increases in highland Guatemala, *Curr. Anthropol.* **13**:216–220.

36. Nag, M., 1972, Sex, culture and human fertility: India and the United States, *Curr. Anthropol.* **13**:231–238.

37. Knodel, J., 1968, Infant mortality and fertility in three Bavarian villages: An analysis of family histories from the 19th century, *Popul. Stud.* **22**:297–310.

38. Raphael, D., 1972, Untitled letter, *Curr. Anthropol.* **13**:253.

39. Richardson, A. C., Lyon, J. B., Graham, E. E., and Williams, N. L., 1976, Decreasing postpartum sexual abstinence time, *Am. J. Obstet. Gynecol.* **126**:416–417.

40. Chrapil, M., Eskelson, C. D., Stiffel, U., Owen, J. A., and Droegemueller, W., 1980, Studies on nonoxynol-9, intravaginal absorption distribution, metabolism and excretion in rats and rabbits, *Contraception* **22**:325–336.

41. Dusitsin, N., Chompootaweep, S., and Tankeyoon, M., 1977, The effect of postpartum tubal ligation on breast-feeding. Presented at the 6th Asian Congress of Obstetrics and Gynecology, Bangkok, Thailand, Nov. 20–25, 1977. Cited in Breast-feeding, fertility and family planning, 1981, *Popul. Rep. Ser. J(24)*, Nov–Dec, p. J-551.

42. Gomez-Rogers, C., Ibarra Polo, A. A., Faundes, A., and Guiloff, E., 1967, Effect of the IUD and other contraceptive methods on lactation, in: *Proceedings of the 8th International Conference of the IPPF, International Planned Parenthood Federation*, London, Fanfare Press, London, p. 328–332.

43. Hingorani, V. and Umabai, G. R., 1970, Lactation and lactational amenorrhea with postpartum IUCD insertion, *J. Reprod. Fertil.* **23**:513–515.

44. Horne, H. W. and Scott, J. M., 1969, IUD insertion and galactorrhea, *Fertil. Steril.* **20**:400–404.

45. Hefnawi, F., Danoil, F., Badraovi, O., Elgaali, M. M., Abdel, M., Kader, M. M., Talaat, M., Aziz, A., and Bahgat, R., 1975, Effect of inert IUDs on lactation, in *Analysis of Intrauterine Contraception, Proceedings of the Third International Conference on Intrauterine Contraception, Cairo, Egypt, December 12–14, 1974* (F. Hefnawi and S. J. Siegel, eds.), North-Holland Publishing, Amsterdam, pp. 431–438.

46. Wenoff, M., Aubert, J. M., and Reyniak, J. V., 1979, Serum prolactin levels in short term and long term use of inert plastic and copper intrauterine devices, *Contraception* **19**:21–27.

47. Spellacy, W. N., and Buhi, W. C., 1979, A prospective study of plasma prolactin levels in women using the progesterone-releasing intrauterine device (P-IUD), *Contraception* **19**:91–94.

48. Badraovi, M. H., Hefnawi, F., Bahgat, R., Fawzi, G., El Gaali, O., Ismail, H., and Hegab, M., 1981, Contraception during lactation. Presented at the 10th World Congress of Fertility and Sterility, July 13, 1980, Madrid, Spain. Cited in Breast-feeding, fertility and family planning, 1981, *Popul. Rep. Ser. J(24)*, Nov–Dec., p. J551.

49. Cole, L. P., McCann, M. F., Higgins, J. E., and Waszak, U. S., 1981, Effects of breast-feeding on IUD performance. Presented at 109th Annual Meeting of the Public Health Association, Los Angeles, November 1–5, 1981. Cited in Breast-feeding, fertility and family planning, 1981, *Popul. Rep. Ser. J(24)*, Nov–Dec., p. J551.

50. Pomerance, J., 1972, Steroidal contraception and its effects on lactation are a public health dilemma, *Health Serv. Rep.* **87**:611–616.

51. Zanartu, J., Aquilera, E., and Munozpinto, G., 1976, Maintenance of lactation by means of continuous low dose progestogen given postpartum as a contraceptive, *Contraception* **13**:313–318.

52. Semm, K. and Dittmar, F. W., 1966, Postpartum ovulation: Inhibition and milk yield, *Curr. Therap. Res.* **8:**48–51.
53. Semm, K., 1966, Contraception and lactation, in: *Social and Medical Aspects of Oral Contraceptives* (M. N. G. Dukes, ed.), Excerpta Medica, Amsterdam, International Congress Series, No. 130, pp. 98–101.
54. Borglin, N. E., 1966, Discussion, in: *Social and Medical Aspects of Oral Contraception*, Organon Oss, The Netherlands, pp. 101–105.
55. Borglin, N. and Sandholm, L., 1971, Effect of oral contraceptives on lactation, *Fertil. Steril.* **22:**39–41.
56. Bernard, R. M., 1977, Studies on lactation and contraception in WHO's research programme, *J. Biosocial Sci. (Suppl.)* **4:**113–120.
57. Lönnerdal, B., Forsum, E., and Hambraeus, L., 1980, Effect of oral contraceptives on composition and volume of breast milk, *Am. J. Clin. Nutri.* **33:**816–824.
58. Mosley, W. H., Osteria, T., and Huffman, S. L., 1977, Interactions of contraception and breast-feeding in developing countries, *J. Biosocial Sci. (Suppl.)* **4:**93–111.
59. Moreley, D., 1973, *Pediatric Priorities in a Developing World*, Butterworths, London, p. 470.
60. Prema, K., 1981, Effect of hormonal contraceptives and IUDs on lactation and return of menstruation in lactating women, *Contraceptive Delivery Systems, 1981*. Cited in Breastfeeding, fertility and family planning, 1981, *Popul. Rep. Ser. J(24)*, Nov–Dec., p. J558.
61. Curtis, E. M., 1964, Oral contraceptive feminization of a normal male infant: Report of a case, *Obstet. Gynecol.* **23:**295–296.
62. Harforche, J. K., Appearance of contraceptive steroids in human milk: Effects on the child, *J. Biosocial Sci. (Suppl.)* **4:**165–179.
63. Nilsson, S., Nygren, K. and Johansson, E. D. B., 1979, Ethinyl estradiol in human milk and plasma after oral administration, *Contraception* **17:**131–139.
64. Nilsson, S., Nygren, K., and Johansson, E. D. B., 1978, Transfer of estradiol to human milk, *Am. J. Obstet. Gynecol.* **132:**653–657.
65. Nilsson, S., Nygren, K., and Johansson, E. D. B., 1977, d-Norgestrel concentrations in maternal plasma, milk and child plasma during administration of oral contraceptives to nursing women, *Am. J. Obstet. Gynecol.* **129:**179–184.
66. Nilsson, S., Nygren, K., and Johansson, E. D. B., 1977, Megestrol acetate concentrations in plasma and milk during administration of an oral contraceptive containing 4 mg megestrol acetate to nursing mothers, *Contraception* **16:**615–623.
67. Schwallie, P. C., 1981, The effect of depot-medroxy progesterone acetate on the fetus and nursing infant: A review, *Contraception* **23:**375–385.
68. Saxena, B. N., Shrimanker, K., and Grudzinskas, J. G., 1977, Levels of contraceptive steroids in breast milk and plasma of lactating women, *Contraception* **10:**605–613.

15

Pregnancy, Lactation, and Breast Cancer

Mary B. Mockus and Kathryn B. Horwitz

INTRODUCTION

Breast cancer accounts for 20% of all cancer deaths among women in the United States. This disease is the third leading cause of cancer deaths today, affecting in their lifetime, 1 out of every 13 women. When carcinoma of the breast is diagnosed in a pregnant or lactating woman, it is particularly tragic. Breast cancer coinciding with pregnancy or lactation occurs about once in every 1000 pregnancies, and represents 1% of total breast cancers. If only women of childbearing age are considered, then the reported frequencies of coincidence range from 7 to 14% of breast cancers.

A wide variety of factors influencing breast cancer risk have been studied, from the truly relevant to the bizarre, and the best available evidence indicates that pregnancy and lactation have neither a protective effect nor a predisposing influence upon the development of breast carcinoma. In this chapter, the epidemiology of breast cancer is discussed and related to breast-feeding; the relationship between endocrine status and breast cancer is summarized, with particular emphasis on the endocrine milieu of pregnancy and lactation; and data on the presence of viral particles in milk and a viral etiology of breast cancer are reviewed. Finally, the clinical picture, management, and prognosis of breast cancer in the pregnant or lactating woman are discussed.

EPIDEMIOLOGY

The goals of epidemiologic studies of cancer are to define the magnitude of the problem and to identify persons who are most at risk of developing the

Mary B. Mockus and Kathryn B. Horwitz • Departments of Medicine and Biochemistry, Biophysics, and Genetics, University of Colorado Health Sciences Center, Denver, Colorado 80262.

Table I. Breast Cancer Risk Factors

Factor	High risk	Low risk	Risk ratio[a]
Sex	F	M	99:1
Age	>40	<40	6
Race	White	Oriental	5
Genetic predisposition	Yes	No	9
Prolonged menstrual history			
Menarche	Early (<12)	Late	1.3
Menopause	Late (>50)	Early	1.5
Age at 1st birth	>34	<18	4
Parity	Nulliparous	Parous	3
Lactation	—	—	1
Previous breast disease	Yes	No	5
Endometrial cancer	Yes	No	2
Oophorectomy (<37)	No	Yes	3
Obesity	Yes	No	2
Obesity—diabetes—hypertension	Yes	No	3
Chronic psychological stress	Yes	No	2
Climate	Cold	Warm	1.5
Socioeconomic status	Affluent	Poor	2
Religion	Jewish	Non-Jewish	2

[a] The relative risk of developing breast cancer is expressed as the increase in risk relative to individuals not presenting with the characteristic described. For example, a female is 99 times more likely than a male to develop breast cancer, for a risk ratio of 99. (The computed relative risk is based on a review of the epidemiology of breast cancer by H.P. Leis, Jr. and A. Raciti, ref. 7.)

disease. A more fundamental goal is to discern a single cause of the disease by searching for a link among known risk factors. For breast cancer, this has proven to be a formidable task. A wealth of data have been amassed, but no clear relationships among the established risk factors have emerged. The variables related to increased breast cancer risk include a history of previous breast disease, genetic or hereditary factors, endocrine status, exogenous estrogen and oral contraceptive use, viral factors, radiation exposure, diet and obesity, geographical location, and socioeconomic status. In the last decade, the epidemiology of breast cancer as it relates to childbearing has received much attention,[1-6] and this chapter will concentrate primarily on these studies.

A compiled summary of risk factors in breast cancer is shown in Table I.[7] Many of the factors in this table suggest a relationship between the development of breast cancer and endocrine status.

Breast cancer occurs almost exclusively in women; cases in men account for only 1% of the total. An obvious difference between men and women is the degree of breast development, however, breast cancer risk is not correlated with breast size or tissue mass. The risk of developing this disease is influenced by ovarian function, parity, age at menarche, age at first birth, and age at menopause.[1-3] These factors are all related to the endocrine system, and suggest a role for the ovaries and the pituitary in the etiology of breast cancer. An early first pregnancy (<18 years) as compared to late (>34 years) decreases the risk of breast cancer fourfold.[4–8] At its 1980 meeting, the Multi-Disciplinary Project on Breast Cancer of the International Union Against Cancer recommended that, in the absence of any compelling reasons to the contrary, a woman should have her first child by the age of 25 years.[9] Unlike early first pregnancy, early menarche appears to increase breast cancer risk. The contradiction that early first pregnancy is protective while early menarche increases breast cancer risk may be resolved if other factors such as nutritional status and socioeconomic group are considered. Several studies have shown that diet, particularly a diet high in fats, increases the risk of breast cancer one- to eightfold.[10–12] In addition, nutritional status appears to influence the age of menarche, with overall good nutrition resulting in early menarche. Perhaps for these reasons, a higher socioeconomic status, a prerequisite of good nutrition, is related to increased breast cancer risk.[8]

Prolonged ovarian function, whether due to early menarche, late menopause, or both, has been associated with an increased breast cancer risk.[13] Factors that shorten the duration of ovarian function, such as oophorectomy and early menopause, decrease risk.[14,15] Repeated pregnancies lead to frequent interruptions in cyclic ovarian function and multiple parity has been associated with a decreased breast cancer risk in studies in many different populations.[1,15–17] Although multiparity implies an early age at first birth, even when this factor is removed there remains a protective effect of multiparity.[1] One explanation for these observations is Korenman's estrogen window hypothesis.[18] *In vivo* estrogens exert a proliferative influence on the breast, which may be opposed by endogenous progesterone. Korenman has postulated that the influence of estrogen, unopposed by progesterone, creates a favorable environment for tumor induction. There are two periods or windows, during a woman's life when this situation exists: from the onset of prepubertal changes to the establishment of regular, ovulatory cycles after the birth of the first child, and from the perimenopausal time through to menopause. Both of these windows are characterized by menstrual irregularities, usually manifest as long cycles that are luteally inadequate and/or anovulatory, with decreased progesterone secretion. If these windows are extended for any reason, as in women with an early menarche and/or late age at first birth, breast cancer risk increases as expected. Similarly, extension of the window due to late menopause is also associated with an increased risk, and shortening of the window by multiple pregnancies or early menopause decreases risk. While this hypothesis still requires rigorous testing, at this time it is consistent with the epidemiology of breast cancer.

In regularly cycling women, parenchyma proliferates, and DNA synthesis increases during the follicular phase.[13] In contrast, during the second half of pregnancy and throughout lactation, there is a reduction in mammary proliferative mitotic activity, and the rate of DNA synthesis is very low. This period of mitotic rest has led to the proposal that pregnancy, and especially lactation, may have a protective influence against breast cancer. This idea was first studied and proposed in 1926,[19] and received further support in the 1930s from Wainright.[20] Again in 1960 and 1964, a weak correlation was found between lactation and decreased breast cancer risk.[21,22] These studies were pursued because a protective effect of lactation would explain much of the epidemiologic data on breast cancer. For example, the incidence of breast cancer is lowest in those countries where breast-feeding is most common. Also, the effects of parity vs. nulliparity on breast cancer risk could be explained by the changes in the breast that occur during pregnancy and lactation. Finally, it is tempting to suggest that a breast that has lactated has undergone some absolute change that lowers breast cancer risk.

Unfortunately, more recent carefully controlled studies have failed to show that lactation has any protective effect.[4,16,23] MacMahon et al.[23] attempted to correlate lactation and breast cancer in seven different geographic areas, including areas of low, intermediate, and high breast cancer risk. Their large study did not reveal any protective effect of lactation on the development of breast cancer. Shapiro et al.[16] carried out a large, prospective study of over 20,000 women in New York City, and found no protective effect offered by short-term (6 months) or prolonged (up to 2 years) breast-feeding. It is difficult in any epidemiological study to consider one factor in a disease distinct from all others. However, both of these very large, well-controlled studies indicate that breast-feeding does not exert any protective influence against development of breast cancer. Consequently, while breast-feeding may be considered desirable for many reasons, a reduction in the risk of developing breast cancer appears not to be one of them.

STEROID HORMONES AND BREAST CANCER

In 1896, Beatson showed that metastic cancer regressed in a woman whose ovary was ablated.[24] This was the first demonstration of the relationship between a woman's endocrine status and breast cancer. Since this report, many endocrine therapies have been employed aimed at controlling breast tumor growth by alteration of the hormonal milieu.

Endocrine therapies generally take one of two forms; they are either ablative or additive. Ablative therapy involves surgical removal of the pituitary, ovaries and/or adrenals, with the goal of removing the sources of hormones (such as ovarian steroids or prolactin) which have been implicated in tumor induction, promotion and growth.[16,25–30] The goal of endocrine additive therapy is to achieve tumor regression through the administration of pharmacological doses of natural or synthetic hormones, including progestins, androgens, estrogens, and antiestrogens. The mechanisms of these pharmacologic hormone doses are unknown. It remains paradoxical that a hormone that stimulates tumor growth at physiological concentrations inhibits growth at pharmacological ones. Thus, while the rationale for treatment is empirical, endocrine therapies either ablative or additive are successful in 20 to 40% of breast cancer patients.[30]

Current research efforts are focusing on improving the response rate to endocrine therapies. Improved surgical techniques (for example, the transphenoidal approach for hypophysectomy) have been developed, a variety of new synthetic steroids and hormone antagonists exist, and chemical methods for endocrine organ ablation (aminoglutethemide)[31] are now available. The response rate to endocrine therapy is now approximately 80%,[32-40] due to our understanding of the basic mechanisms of action of both steroid and peptide hormones. The mammary gland, as a target tissue for these hormones, contains receptors for estrogens, androgens, progesterone, glucocorticoids, prolactin, and placental hormones.[30,41,42] The first step in the action of a steroid hormone is the specific binding of the hormone to cytoplasmic receptor proteins in the target cell. This binding activates the receptors, and translocation, the movement of receptor–hormone complexes from the cytoplasm to the nucleus, occurs next. The hormone–receptor complexes then bind to chromatin, and a series of events occurs, including increases in DNA, RNA, and protein synthesis. The result is a specific response, characteristic of the particular steroid hormone and target tissue.

This knowledge of steroid hormone mechanism of action has provided a means to preselect patients harboring tumors likely to respond to endocrine therapy.[30] Assays for steroid hormone receptors in breast tumor cytosols have shown that breast tumors may contain specific receptors for estrogens, androgens, progestins, and glucocorticoids.[42] If, for example, the presence of the estrogen receptor (ER+) in a tumor is used to preselect patients for endocrine therapy, the response rate to these therapies is increased from 20 to 40% to 55 to 60%.[30] Thus, by preselection of the patient population, women with tumors lacking steroid receptors are spared therapy, which is unlikely to give positive results, while therapy can be directed at patients whose tumors are most likely to respond. However, about 40 to 50% of patients with ER+ tumors fail to respond to endocrine therapies. Horwitz, *et al.*[43] proposed the use of progesterone receptors (PgR) as a marker, because the synthesis of PgR is estrogen dependent.[44] If the PgR in the breast were similarly controlled, then assaying breast tumor cytosols for PgR, a product of ER action, should identify most hormone responsive tumors. Assays have been developed to measure PgR in rat mammary tumors, in human breast cancer cells (MCF-7) in culture, and in human breast tumor biopsies,[45] and the dependence of PgR synthesis on estrogen stimulation has been demonstrated in these models.[45] In ER+ human breast tumors, 74% are PgR+.[46] Recent data show that if only those breast cancer patients with ER+, PgR+ tumors are selected for endocrine therapy, the response rate is increased to 75 to 80%,[32-40] while the response rate in ER+ but PgR− tumors is only 30%. Table II summarizes the results of the most recent clinical studies.

The mechanisms involved in the hormonal control of mammary tumor growth are not clearly understood. Normal mammary tissues contain steroid hormone and prolactin receptors in variable quantities. However, many breast tumors show marked increases in the levels of some of these receptors;[41] it is possible that the process of carcinogenesis may involve an

Table II. Response to Hormone Therapy as a Function of ER and PgR in 480 Cases

Series[a]	ER−, PgR−	ER−, PgR+	ER+, PgR−	ER+, PgR+
McGuire, 1978[30]	0/11	—	7/17	13/16
Bloom, 1980[32]	0/10	1/1	3/14	23/30
Matsumoto, 1980[124]	2/20	0/1	9/25	12/20
Brooks, 1980[34]	—	—	2/7	4/6
Dao, 1980[35]	2/28	—	18/31	10/13
Degenshein, 1980[36]	0/14	1/1	3/14	26/33
Manni, 1980[37]	0/2	—	3/5	15/24
Pertschuk, 1980[38]	0/8	—	4/10	9/14
Skinner, 1980[39]	3/30	2/3	2/6	9/12
Young, 1980[40]	2/9	1/2	3/14	20/29
Total	9/132(6.8%)	5/8(12.5%)	54/143(37.8%)	141/197(71.6%)

[a] The results of ten clinical studies are summarized. Hormone therapy in most cases was additive involving the administration of diethylstilbestrol, estradiol, tamoxifen, nafoxidine, or androgens, or ablative involving adrenalectomy, oophorectomy, and/or hypophysectomy. Response refers to decrease in the incidence, size, and associated symptoms of metastases.

unmasking or induction of some receptors, and cause the transformed cell to become sensitive to complex endocrine controls. How these complex changes relate to the endocrine milieu of the breast in pregnant or lactating women is unclear. In rats it has been shown that pregnancy stimulates the growth of 7,12-dimethylbenz(a)anthracene (DMBA)-induced mammary tumors.[47] Direct administration of progesterone to rats not only accelerates the growth of DMBA tumors, but also increases the rate of their appearance and overall number.[48,49] If estrogen is given together with progesterone, however, tumor regression results and there are decreases in tumor size and in the rate of tumor appearance.[50]

It is possible that the hormone sensitivity of the pregnant and lactating mammary gland may be altered by changes in receptor content. For instance, it has been demonstrated in rats that ER levels increase during pregnancy.[51] Although the rise in plasma estradiol levels during pregnancy is not as great as the increase in progesterone levels, this could partially be offset by an increase in estrogen receptors, rendering the mammary cells particularly sensitive to available estrogen. The higher levels of progesterone in pregnancy, then, may be accompanied by an increase in estrogen sensitivity and so human pregnancy may not necessarily parallel the endocrine status in the progesterone plus DMBA-treated rat. A careful examination of the steroid hormone receptor level in tumor biopsies from pregnant and lactating women is not yet available.

In addition to the changes in estrogen and progesterone levels during pregnancy, the changes in the levels of the placental and pituitary hormones, especially prolactin (Prl) must also be considered. Both serum Prl and placental lactogen increase steadily during pregnancy; Prl remains elevated during early lactation.[52] Thus, any influences of lactogenic hormones on the development and/or growth of mammary tumors may be exacerbated during the pregnant and lactating states.

Prolactin has been shown to increase ER levels in normal and malignant breast cells.[51,53] In addition, both normal and malignant tissues contain prolactin receptors. In general, the number of receptors in tumors is elevated compared with normal tissues, though the significance of this is unknown.[54]

In many clinical studies, attempts have been made to correlate serum Prl levels with breast cancer.[55-58] However, the results of these studies are so contradictory that the exact role of Prl in human breast cancer remains unclear. Women with galactorrhea induced by hyperprolactinemia are at no greater risk of developing breast cancer than other women.[57] Drugs that cause hypersecretion of prolactin such as reserpine and methyldopa are not associated with an increased incidence of breast cancer.[59-62] Furthermore, treatment with estrogens may cause remission of metastic breast cancer although Prl levels are increased two- to threefold.[55,63,64]

VIRUSES AND BREAST CANCER

A viral etiology for mammary cancer in the mouse has been well established, but there is no conclusive evidence for a similar etiology in human mammary cancer.

In the mouse, mammary tumor viral particles (MMTV) and viral-associated proteins have been identified.[65] MMTV is an Oncornavirus B; it is an RNA virus, contains reverse transciptase, and is the only oncornavirus associated with carcinoma.[66-70] MMTV may be transmitted through the milk or genetically transmitted. A number of studies have attempted to demonstrate similar viral particles in human tumors.[71,72] By electron microscopy, B-like particles have been seen in some human breast tumors and milk samples.[71,72] In some human breast cancers, particles have been found which are similar in size and shape to MMTV. They possess outer membranes and a central core consisting of a 70S RNA molecule complexed to an RNA-dependent DNA polymerase (reverse transcriptase).[67-70] Demonstrated partial homologies between RNAs of human breast tumors and MMTV RNA[71-73] have led to the suggestion that human tumors may contain proteins that are antigenically related to MMTV proteins. Antisera have been raised against MMTV proteins, and used as probes to search for related proteins in human breast cancer tissues. Indirect immunoperoxidase techniques have been successful in identifying an antigen in paraffin sections of human tumors that is immunologically related to the group-specific antigen, gp 52 of MMTV.[71,74] Both serological and cellular studies have demonstrated the existence of antibodies in human breast cancer patients that bind to murine cells producing MMTV.[75-77] The cellular immune response to gp 52 has been used to demonstrate that some human breast cancer patients have components present in their tumors that are immunologically related to gp 52, and that the inhibition of leukocyte migration of MMTV or gp 52 is correlated with the amount of gp-52-related component present.[77-83]

Additional studies have concentrated on the analysis of human milk samples to detect viral particles or activities. B-like particles have been isolated from human milk,[77–84] however, after careful study, only a very small proportion of these particles have actually been shown to possess membrane characteristics similar to B particles.[85] Furthermore, the breast cancer risks of the donors did not correlate with the presence of these B-like particles.[86] Some human milk has been found to contain DNA polymerase activity similar to the RNA-dependent DNA polymerase of MMTV[87–89] in its preference for Mg^{++} as a divalent cation, and in the synthesis of DNA with an oligo (dG)-poly(Cm) as primer-template.[89] In general, however, the MMTV-like DNA polymerase detected in milk has not been well characterized, and has not been demonstrated to be of viral origin at all.

A variety of molecular hybridization studies have been performed to detect any viral RNA and DNA sequence in human tumors.[68–71,90] Viral RNA sequences have been detected in a limited number of human tumors (about 30%), however, the presence of MMTV-like RNA does not correlate with the cellular immune response of the patients to MMTV proteins.[91] Furthermore, DNA–DNA hybridization studies have, at best, detected a few imperfect hybridizations between breast tumor DNA and cDNA probes of MMTV.[65,91]

It has been suggested that the antigenic cross reactivity between gp 52 and human breast cancer tissue is due to carbohydrate residues and is not specific for the amino acid sequence of any protein.[91] Recent work however[65] has shown that the deglycosylated protein is fully capable of crossreacting with anti-MMTV gp 52 antibody.

There is no evidence in humans to support the notion that any sort of breast cancer factor is transmitted through the milk.[92] Studies of women who were breast-fed compared with those who were not show no differences in breast cancer risk for these two groups.[93,94] In countries where the incidence of breast-feeding is high, the incidence of breast cancer is low,[95,96] another indication that milk transmission is unlikely. Furthermore, throughout the 1950s and 1960s, there was a decrease in breast-feeding while there was an increase in breast cancer.

In summary, it appears from the available scientific evidence that the etiology of human mammary cancer, if it is indeed viral at all, is not as straightforward as in certain strains of mice. If there is a human virus related to MMTV, it is probably not biologically similar. It is quite possible that the etiology of human mammary cancer involves the interaction of a variety of factors including viruses, and any one of these factors may be predominant in different ways at different stages during carcinogenesis.

PREGNANCY, LACTATION, AND BREAST CANCER: THE CLINICAL PICTURE

Any temporal relationship between breast cancer and pregnancy or lactation is now thought to be purely coincidental.[97] Pregnancy and lactation appear to have neither protective nor predisposing influences on the development of breast cancer. Quite simply, there is a probability that, among women who have breast cancer during their childbearing years, a proportion will be pregnant or lactating. In a series of 9003 patients in Philadelphia County reported by Mausner,[97] 73 of the patients were pregnant or lactating at the time of diagnosis. Although these women represent less than 1% of the total cases of breast cancer seen, they represent 11.3% of the women seen for breast cancer occurring during the childbearing years. Similar figures, ranging from 7 to 15%, have been reported in other large, clinical studies.[98–101]

The detection, diagnosis, and treatment of breast cancer during pregnancy and lactation is often delayed due to physician procrastination. This regrettable situation has been reported to result in delays in diagnosis and treatment of 11 to 15 months for the pregnant woman, compared to 6 to 7 months for her nonpregnant counterpart.[97,98,102–107] The physiologic changes of pregnancy certainly hamper detection of breast masses, and once detected, physicians will often attribute any abnormalities to the normal hypertrophy of the gland. Additional factors that contribute to delays in diagnosis and treatment are the reluctance of the physician to submit a pregnant woman to general anesthesia or radiographic procedures, for fear of damage to the fetus, or to surgery, for fear of uncontrollable bleeding or milk fistula occurring in the enlarged breast. In addition, nipple discharge, often a sign of breast cancer in the nonpregnant woman, is not a useful sign in the pregnant woman. Cancer should be considered when a cloudy, milky or bloody discharge is present in conjunction with a breast mass, and then the mass and not the discharge should be followed up vigorously.[97] Rosemond and Mier[103] recommend that the breasts be thoroughly examined at the initial and all subsequent prenatal and postpartum examinations. In addition, the patient should be instructed to examine her own breasts on a monthly basis. In lactating women, an interesting clinical situation reported by Goldsmith[108] has been called the "milk-rejection sign." In this report, infants were noted to abruptly and quite consistently reject the milk from one breast and not the other. In each of the six cases reported, the breast the infant rejected was later found to have a malignant tumor. Physician and patient awareness of this unusual sign may lead to earlier diagnosis and treatment of malignancies during lactation.

When breast masses are detected in a pregnant or lactating patient, simple needle aspiration or biopsy under local anesthesia on an outpatient basis may be used to distinguish benign lesions from solid tumors.[107]

The prognosis of the pregnant or lactating woman with breast cancer is the same as that of a nonpregnant woman when the two are matched by age and axillary node involvement. As summarized by Cheek in 1953,[109] earlier reports on the prognosis of the patient with breast cancer during pregnancy and lactation were very discouraging. More recent data has shown these earlier reports to have been overly pessimistic, and Costarides and

Table III. 5-year Survival of Pregnant or Lactating Patients
with Operable Breast Cancer

Series[a]	No. of patients	Survival (percent)
Early, 1969[118]	2	100
Horsley, 1969[100]	12	100
Peete, 1969[117]	14	64
Divitt, 1964[123]	19	58
Applewhite, 1973[98]	48	56
Mausner, 1969[97]	73	48
Bunker, 1963[122]	150	47
Holleb and Farro, 1962[120]	283	40
Rosemond, 1963[121]	77	33[b]
Treves and Holleb, 1958[99]	78	28

[a] The 5-year survival of patients who were diagnosed as having breast cancer during pregnancy, lactation, or up to 1 year postpartum.
[b] Twenty-four patients were actually followed; 8 survived.

Theofanides[110] have attributed their poor results to delay in diagnosis and treatment, which decreased the patients' chances of survival.

Table III summarizes the results of 756 reported cases of breast cancer coinciding with pregnancy or lactation. In the Philadelphia County series by Mausner[97] of 647 cases of breast cancer in nonpregnant women of child-bearing age, 62 patients survived 5 years. The 5-year survival in Table III ranged from 28 to 100%. This is similar to the 48% seen for nonpregnant women with node involvement.[97] The percentage of women with axillary node involvement was the same in the Philadelphia study for the pregnant and nonpregnant groups; however, it appears that once metastases have occurred, survival is poorer for the pregnant woman. This underscores the importance of early breast cancer detection and treatment when it coincides with pregnancy.

When a malignant tumor is detected in a pregnant or lactating woman, an immediate mastectomy is indicated. There has been one report[104] in the literature that recommends deferring surgery until after delivery if the cancer is not aggressive and the woman is in the third trimester. In other studies,[107] there was no benefit in waiting, and the current view is that surgery should be performed immediately regardless of the trimester of pregnancy. The use of radiotherapy and cytotoxic agents pose many obvious hazards to the fetus, and offer unclear benefits to the patient.

Although it was once controversial, it now appears on the basis of several recent clinical studies[104,111-114] that interruption of the pregnancy has no influence upon 5-year survival. Donegan[107] states that "therapeutic abortion for potentially undisseminated cases of breast cancer associated with pregnancy is no longer debated as an essential component of effective treatment; evidence is lacking that termination of pregnancy enhances curability." Thus, although theoretically it would seem advantageous to reverse the hormonal and physiologic changes of pregnancy, particularly the growth of the breast, clinically it does not appear that therapeutic abortion in any way increases the chances for survival.

Furthermore, there appears to be little danger to the fetus. In 1970, Potter and Schoeneman[115] reviewed four reported cases of breast cancer metastasizing to the placenta. In all four cases, however, the child was healthy.

The prognosis for patients with advanced and disseminated cancer is poor. Treatment includes discontinuation of the pregnancy, endocrine ablation, and/or cytotoxic chemotherapy. Effective palliation requires both surgical castration and therapeutic abortion in order to remove the source of placental hormones. In early, nondisseminated cases, prophylactic castration is recommended by Donegan[107] only if there is a recurrence and/or an estrogen receptor assay indicates that the tumor is estrogen responsive (ER+). This may be particularly important to the patient, as it appears that subsequent pregnancies do not decrease survival. Several large clinical studies have conclusively shown that pregnancy subsequent to treatment for breast cancer does not adversely influence the rate of recurrence or survival.[98,104,105,112,116] In fact, if anything, these studies have shown that pregnancy following treatment may enhance survival. If a woman desires to become pregnant following treatment, it is recommended that she wait 3 to 5 years, during which time the risk of recurrence is greatest. This is particularly important if axillary nodes were involved, as the risk of recurrence is consistently greater for this group. Thus, pregnancy is not harmful, but, if possible, should be avoided until the greatest risk of recurrence is past. A pregnancy is not, however, a guaranteed sign that treatment has been successful, and should not be seen as a test of the effectiveness of treatment.

In summary, with aggressive investigation of any breast masses, prompt diagnosis and treatment, the clinical course of the pregnant or lactating woman with breast cancer is likely to be the same as in her nonpregnant counterpart.

SUMMARY

The causes of breast cancer are unclear. Epidemiologic studies indicate that hormonal factors are important, and endocrine manipulations are an important part of breast cancer therapy. However, the hormonal changes that occur during pregnancy and lactation do not appear to influence the risk of developing breast cancer or the course of the disease once established.

A viral etiology in human breast cancer has not been clearly demonstrated. When recent advances in genetics and nucleic acids research are applied to this problem, a clear role for mammary tumor viruses may emerge.

The pregnant woman with breast cancer has the best chance of surviving to care for her baby if she is treated exactly like her nonpregnant counterpart. Similarly, the lactating woman should be treated promptly and assured that her chances of survival are in no way diminished by her recent pregnancy and lactation.

REFERENCES

1. MacMahon, B., Cole, P., and Lin, T. M., 1970, Age at first birth and breast cancer risk, *Bull. WHO* **43:**209–221.
2. Juret, P., Couette, J. E., Mandard, A. M., Carré, A., Delozier, T., Burne, D., and Vernhes, J. C., 1976, Age at menarche as a prognostic factor in human breast cancer, *Eur. J. Cancer* **12**(9):701–704.
3. Lilienfeld, A. M., Coombs, J., Bross, I. D. J., and Chamberlain, A., 1975, Marital and reproductive experience in a community-wide epidemiological study of breast cancer, *Johns Hopkins Med. J.* **136**(4):157–162.
4. MacMahon, B., Cole, P., and Brown, J., 1973, Etiology of human breast cancer: A review, *J. Natl. Cancer Inst.* **50:**21–42.
5. Sherman, B. M. and Korenman, S. G., 1974, Inadequate corpus luteum function: A pathophysiological interpretation of human breast cancer epidemology, *Cancer* **33:**1306–1312.
6. Stavraky, K. and Emmons, S. J., 1974, Breast cancer in premenopausal and postmenopausal women, *J. Natl. Cancer Inst.* **53**(2):647–654.
7. Leis, H. P., Jr. and Raciti, A., 1976, The search for women at high risk, in: *Risk Factors in Breast Cancer* (B. A. Stoll, ed.), Heinemann Medical Books, London p. 207–225.
8. Thomas, D. P. and Lilfienfeld, A. M., 1976, Geographic, reproductive and sociobiological factors, in: *Risk Factors in Breast Cancer* (B. A. Stoll, ed.), William Heinemann Medical Books, London p. 25–53.
9. Miller, A. B. and Bulbrook, R. D., 1980, The epidemiology and etiology of breast cancer, *N. Engl. J. Med.* **303**(2):1246–1248.
10. DeWaard, F., 1969, The epidemiology of breast cancer: Review and prospects, *Int. J. Cancer* **4:**577–586.
11. Diekamp, V., Bitran, J., and Ferguson, D. J., 1976, Breast cancer in young women, *J. Reprod. Med.* **17:**255–276.
12. Tannenbaum, A. and Silverstone, H. 1957, Nutrition and the genesis of tumours, in: *Cancer*, Volume 1 (R. W. Raven, ed.), Butterworths, London p. 306–334.
13. Vorherr, H. and Messer, R. H., 1978, Breast cancer: Potentially predisposing and protecting factors. Role of pregnancy, lactation and endocrine status, *Am. J. Obstet. Gynecol.* **130**(3):335–358.
14. Hirayama, T. and Wynder, E. L., 1962, A study of the epidemiology of cancer of the breast: The influence of hysterectomy, *Cancer* **15:**28–38.
15. Dunn, J. E., Jr., 1969, Epidemiology and possible identification of the high risk group that could develop cancer of the breast, *Cancer* **23:**775–780.
16. Shapiro, S., Strax, P., Venet, L., and Fink, R., 1968, The search for risk factors in breast cancer, *Am. J. Public Health* **58:**820–835.
17. Cole, P., 1980, Major aspects of the epidemiology of breast cancer, *Cancer* (Suppl.) **46:**865–867.
18. Korenman, S. G., 1980, Estrogen window hypothesis of the etiology of breast cancer, *Lancet* **1:**700–701.
19. Lane-Claypon, J. E., 1926, *A further Report on Cancer of the Breast with Special Reference to the Associated Antecedent Conditions*. Ministry of Health Reports on Public Health and Medical Subjects, MO 32, His Majesty's Stationery Office, London.
20. Wainwright, J. M., 1931, Comparison of conditions associated with breast cancer in Great Britain and America, *Am. J. Cancer*. **15:**2610.
21. Kamoi, M., 1960, Statistical study on relation between breast cancer and lactation period, 3. Study through relative liability, *Tohoku J. Exp. Med.* **72:**72–77.

22. Levin, M. L., Sheeke, P. R., Graham, S., and Glidewell, O., 1964, Lactation and menstrual function as related to cancer of the breast, *Am. J. Public Health.* **54:**580–587.
23. MacMahon, B., Lin, T. M., and Lowe, C. R., 1970, Lactation and cancer of the breast. A summary of an international study, *Bull WHO.* **42:**185–194.
24. Beatson, G. T., 1896, On the treatment of inoperable cases of carcinoma of the mamma: Suggestions for a new method of treatment with illustrative cases, *Lancet* **2:**104–162.
25. Huggins, C. and Bergenstal, D. M., 1952, Inhibition of human mammary and prostatic cancers by adrenalectomy, *Cancer Res.* **12:**134–141.
26. McGuire, W. L., Horwitz, K. B., and De la Garza, M., 1976, A biochemical basis for selecting endocrine therapy in human breast cancer, in: *Breast Cancer: Trends in Research and Treatment* (J. C. Heuson, W. H. Mattheim, and M. Rozencweig, eds.), Raven Press, New York, pp. 127–182.
27. Pearson, O. H. and Ray, B. S., 1960, Hypophysectomy in the treatment of metastatic mammary cancer, *Am. J. Surg.* **99:**544–552.
28. Jensen, E. V., Smith, S., and DeSombre, E. R., 1976, Hormone dependency in breast cancer, *J. Steroid Biochem.* **7:**911–917.
29. Minton, J. P. and Dickey, R. P., 1973, Levodopa test to predict response of carcinoma of the breast to surgical ablation of endocrine glands, *Surg. Gynecol. Obstet.* **136:**971–974.
30. McGuire, W. L. (ed.), 1978, *Hormones, Receptors and Breast Cancer*, Raven Press, New York.
31. Santen, R. J., Worgul, T. J., Samojlik, E., Interrante, A., Boucher, N. E., White, D. S., Smart, E., Cox, C., and Wells, S. A., 1981, A randomized trial comparing surgical adrenalectomy with aminoglutethimide plus hydrocortisone in women with advanced breast cancer, *N. Engl. J. Med.* **305**(10):545–551.
32. Bloom, N. D., Tobin, E. H., Schreibman, B., and Degenshein, G. A., 1980, The role of progesterone receptors in the management of advanced breast cancer, *Cancer* **45**(12):2992–2997.
33. McGuire, W. L., 1978, Hormone receptors: Their role in predicting prognosis and response to endocrine therapy, *Semin. Oncol.* **5**(4):428–433.
34. Brooks, S. C., Saunders, D. E., Singhakowinta, A., and Vaitkevicius, V. K., 1980, Relation of tumor content of estrogen and progesterone receptors with response of patient to endocrine therapy, *Cancer* **46:**2775–2778.
35. Dao, T. L. and Nemoto, T., 1980, Steroid receptors and response to endocrine ablations in women with metastatic cancer of the breast, *Cancer* **46:**2779–2782.
36. Degenshein, G. A., Bloom, N., and Tobin, E., 1980, The value of progesterone receptor assays in the management of advanced breast cancer, *Cancer* **46:**2789–2793.
37. Manni, A., Arafah, B. V., and Pearson, O., 1980, Estrogen and progesterone receptors in the prediction of response of breast cancer to endocrine therapy, *Cancer* **46:**2838–2841.
38. Pertschuk, L. P., Tobin, E. H., Gaetjens, E., Carter, A. C., Degenshein, G. A., Bloom, N. D., and Brigati, D. J., 1980, Histochemical assay of estrogen and progesterone receptors in breast cancer: Correlation with biochemical assays and patients response to endocrine therapies, *Cancer* **46:**2896–2901.
39. Skinner, L. G., Barnes, D. M., and Ribeiro, G. G., 1980, The clinical value of multiple steroid receptor assays in breast cancer management, *Cancer* **46:**2939–2945.
40. Young, P. C. M., Ehrlich, C. E., and Einhorn, L. H., 1980, Relationship between steroid receptors and response to endocrine therapy and cytotoxic chemotherapy in metastatic breast cancer, *Cancer* **46:**2961–2963.
41. DeSombre, E. R., Kledzik, G., Marshall, S., and Meites, J., 1976, Estrogen and prolactin receptor concentration in rat mammary tumors and response to endocrine ablation, *Cancer Res.* **36:**354–358.
42. Allegra, J. C., Lippman, M. E., Thompson, E. B., Simon, R., Barlock, A., Green, L., Huff, K., Hoan My T. Do, and Aitken, S. C., 1979, Distribution, frequency and quantitative analyses of estrogen, progesterone, androgen and glucocorticoid receptors in human breast cancer, *Cancer Res.* **39:**1447–1454.
43. Horwitz, K. B., McGuire, W. L., Pearson, O. H., and Segaloff, A., 1975, Predicting response to endocrine therapy in human breast cancer: A hypothesis, *Science* **189:**726–727.

44. Freifeld, M. L., Feil, P. D., and Bardin, C. W., 1974, The *in vivo* regulation of the progesterone receptor in guinea pig uterus: Dependence on estrogen and progesterone, *Steroids* **23**:93–103.
45. Horwitz, K. B. and McGuire, W. L., 1975, Specific progesterone receptors in human breast cancer, *Steroids* **25**:497–505.
46. McGuire, W. L., 1980, An update on estrogen and progesterone receptors in prognosis for primary and advanced breast cancer, in: *Hormones and Cancer* (S. Iacobelli, ed.), Raven Press, New York.
47. McCormick, G. M. and Moon, R. C., 1965, Effect of pregnancy and lactation on growth of mammary tumors induced by 7,12-Dimethylbenz (A) anthracene (DMBA), *Br. J. Cancer* **19**:160–166.
48. Huggins, C. and Yang, N. C., 1962, Induction and extinction of mammary cancer. A striking effect of hydrocarbons permits analysis of mechanisms of causes and cures of breast cancer, *Science* **137**:257–262.
49. Huggins, C., 1965, Two principles in endocrine therapy of cancers: Hormone deprival and hormone interference, *Cancer Res.* **25**:1163–1175.
50. McCormick, G. M. and Moon, R. C., 1973, Effect of increasing doses of estrogen and progesterone on mammary carcinogenesis in the rat, *Eur. J. Cancer.* **9**:483–486.
51. Witliff, J. L., Gardner, D. G., Battema, W. L., and Gilbert, P. J., 1972, Specific estrogen receptors in the neoplastic and lactating mammary gland of the rat, *Biochem. Biophys. Res. Commun.* **48**:119–125.
52. Speroff, L., 1981, The ovary, in: *Endocrinology and Metabolism* (P. Felig, J. D. Baxter, A. E. Broaders, and L. A. Frohman, eds.), Mcgraw-Hill Book Co., New York, p. 688.
53. Meites, J., Cassell, E. E., and Clark, J. H., 1971, Estrogen inhibition of mammary tumor growth in rats: counteraction by prolactin, *Proc. Soc. Exp. Biol. Med.* **137**:1225–1227.
54. Shiu, R. P. C., 1979, Prolactin receptors in human breast cancer cells in long-term tissue culture, *Cancer Res.* **39**:4381–4386.
55. Wilson, R. G., Forrest, A. P. M., Boyns, A. R., and Griffiths, K., 1973, Studies on human prolactin, in: *Human Prolactin, Proceedings of the International Symposium on Human Prolactin* (J. L. Pastells, C. Robyn, and F. J. G. Ebling, eds.), Brussels, pp. 11–23.
56. Boyns, A. R., Cole, E. N., Griffiths, K., Roberts, M. M., Buchan, R., Wilson, R. G., and Forrest, A. P. M., 1973, Plasma prolactin in breast cancer, *Eur. J. Cancer* **9**:99–102.
57. Dickey, R. P. and Minton, J. P., 1972, L-Dopa effect on prolactin, F.S.H. and L.H. in women with advanced breast cancer: A preliminary report, *Am. J. Obstet. Gynecol.* **114**:267–269.
58. Franks, S., Ralphs, D. N. L., Seagroatti, V., and Jacobs, H. S., 1974, Prolactin concentrations in patients with breast cancer, *Br. Med. J.* **4**:320–321.
59. Boston Collaborative Drug Surveillance Program, 1974, Reserpine and breast cancer, *Lancet* **2**:669–671.
60. Armstrong, B., Stevens, N., and Doll, R., 1974, Retrospective study of the association between use of ranwolfia derivatives and breast cancer in English women, *Lancet* **2**:672–675.
61. Heinomen, O. P., Shapiro, S., Tuominen, L., and Turunen, M. I., 1974, Reserpine use in relation to breast cancer, *Lancet* **2**:675–677.
62. Minton, J. P. and Dickey, R. P., 1972, Prolactin, FSH and LH in breast cancer: Effect of levodopa and oophorectomy, *Lancet* **1**:1069–1070.
63. L'Hermite, M., Robyn, C., Heuson, J. C., and Rozencweig, M., 1974, Letter: Breast cancer regression under estrogen therapy, *Br. Med. J.* **1**:390.
64. Wilson, R. G., Buchan, R., Roberts, M. M., Forrest, A. P. M., Boyns, A. R., Cole, E. N., and Griffith, K., 1974, Plasma prolactin and breast cancer, *Cancer* **33**:1325–1327.
65. Moore, D. H., Long, C. A., Vaidya, A. B., Sheffield, J. B., Dion, A. S., and Lasfargues, E. Y., 1979, Mammary tumors viruses, *Adv. Cancer Res.* **29**:347–417.
66. Dalton, A. J., Heine, V. J., and Melnick, J. L., 1975, Symposium: Characterization of oncornaviruses and related viruses—A report, *J. Natl. Cancer Inst.* **55**:941–942.

67. Moore, D. H., Charney, J., Kramarsky, B., Lasfargues, E. Y., Sarkar, N. H., Brennan, M. J., Burrows, J. H., Sirsat, S. M., Paymaster, J. C., and Vaidya, A. B., 1971, Search for a human breast cancer virus, *Nature (London)* **229:**611–614.
68. Gerard, G. F., Loewenstein, P. M., Green, M., and Rottman, F., 1975, Detection of reverse transcriptase in human breast tumours with poly(Cm)-oligo (dG), *Nature* **256:**140–143.
69. Axel, R., Gulati, S. C., and Spiegelman, S., 1972, Particles containing RNA-instructed DNA polynurase and virus-related RNA in human breast cancers, *Proc. Nat. Acad. Sci. USA* **69:**3133–3137.
70. Axel, R., Schlom, J., and Spiegelman, S., 1972, Presence in human breast cancer of RNA humologous to mouse mammary tumor virus RNA, *Nature (London)* **235:**32–36.
71. Spiegelman, S., Axel, R., and Schlom, J., 1972, Virus related RNA in human and mouse mammary tumors, *J. Natl. Cancer Inst.* **48:**1205–1211.
72. Mesa-Tejada, R., Keydar, I., Ramanrayanan, M., Ohno, T., Fenoglio, C., and Spiegelman, S., 1978, Detection in human breast carcinomas of an antigen immunologically related to a group specific antigen of mouse mammary tumor virus, *Proc. Nat. Acad. Sci. USA* **75:**1529–1533.
73. Vaidya, A. B., Black, M. M., Dion, A. S., and Moore, D. H., 1974, Homology between human breast tumor RNA and mouse mammary tumor virus genome, *Nature (London)* **249:**565–567.
74. Keydar, I., Mesa-Tejada, R., Ramanarayanan, M., Ohno, T., Fenoglio, C., and Spiegelman, S., 1978, Detection of viral proteins in mouse mammary tumors by immunoperoxidase staining of paraffin sections, *Proc. Nat. Acad. Sci. USA* **75:**1524–1528.
75. Bowen, J. M., Dmochowski, L., Miller, M. F., Priori, E. S., Seman, G., Dodson, M. L., and Maruyama, K., 1976, Implications of humoral antibody in mice and humans to breast tumor and mouse mammary tumor virus-associated antigens, *Cancer Res.* **36:**759–764.
76. Hoshino, M. and Dmochowski, L., 1973, Electron microscope study of antigens in cells of mouse mammary tumor cell lines by peroxidase-labeled antibodies in sera of mammary tumor bearing mice and of patients with breast cancer, *Cancer Res.* **33:**2551–2561.
77. Miller, M. F., Dmochowski, L., and Bowen, J. M., 1977, Immunoelectron microscope studies of antibodies in mouse sera directed against mouse mammary tumor virus, *Cancer Res.* **37:**2086–2091.
78. Priori, E. S., Anderson, D. E., Williams, W. C., and Dmochowski; L., 1972, Immunological studies on human breast carcinoma and mouse mammary tumors, *J. Natl. Cancer Inst.* **48:**1131–1135.
79. Black, M. M., 1977, Immunogenicity and MµMTV-like antigenicity of human breast cancer tissues, in: *Contemporary topics in immunology,* (M. G. Hanna Jr. and F. Rapp, eds.) Plenum Press, New York, p. 239–262.
80. Black, M. M., Moore, D. H., Shore, B., Zachrau, R. E., and Leis, H. P., Jr., 1974, Effect of murine milk samples and human breast tissues on human leukocyte migration indices, *Cancer Res.* **34:**1054–1060.
81. Black, M. M., Zachrau, R. E., Shore, B., Moore, D. H., and Leis, H. P., Jr., 1975, Prognostically favorable immunogens of human breast cancer tissue: Antigenic similarity to murine mammary tumor virus, *Cancer* **35:**121–128.
82. Black, M. M., Zachrau, R. E., Dion, A. S., Shore, B., Fine, D. L., Leis, H. P., Jr., and Williams, C. J., 1976, Biological considerations of tumor-specific and virus-associated antigens of human breast cancers, *Cancer Res.* **36:**4137–4142.
83. Black, M. M., Zachrau, R. E., and Shore, B., 1981, MµMTV-like characteristics of human breast carcinoma immunogens, in: *Bibliothica Haematologia* Vol. 43, (J. Clemmenson and D. S. Yohn, eds.), 559–564, Karger Co., New York.
84. Black, M. M., Zachrau, R. E., Shore, B., 1976, Biological considerations of tumor-specific and virus associated antigens of human breast cancers, *Cancer Res.* **36**(2 pt 2):769–774.
85. Zachrau, R. E., Black, M. M., Dion, A. S., Shore, B., Isac, M., Andrade, A. M., and Williams, C. J., 1976, Prognostically significant protein components of human breast cancer tissues, *Cancer Res.* **36:**3143–3146.

86. Sarkar, N. H. and Moore, D. H., 1972, Electron microscopy in mammary cancer research, *J. Natl. Cancer Inst.* **48:**1051–1058.

87. Sarkar, N. H. and Moore, D. H., 1972, On the possibility of a human breast cancer virus, *Nature (London)* **236:**103–106.

88. Schlom, J. and Spiegelman, S., 1971, Simultaneous detection of reverse transcriptase and high molecular weight RNA unique to oncogenic RNA virsus, *Science* **174:**840–843.

89. Dion, A. S., Vaidya, A. B., and Fout, G. S., 1974, Isolation and characterization of RNA-directed DNA polymerase from a B-type RNA tumor virus, *J. Virol.* **14:**40–46.

90. Schlom, J., Colcher, D., Spiegelman, S., Gillespie, S., and Gillespie, D., 1973, Quantitation of RNA tumor viruses and viruslike particles in human milk by hybridization to polyadenylic acid sequences, *Science* **179:**696–698.

91. Axel, R., Schlom, J., and Spiegelman, S., 1972, Evidence for translation of viral-specific RNA in cells of a mouse mammary carcinoma, *PNAS (USA)* **69:**535–538.

92. Fraumeni, J. F., Jr., and Miller, R. W., 1971, Breast cancer from breast-feeding, *Lancet* **2:**1196–1197.

93. Tokuhata, G. K., 1969, Morbidity and mortality among offspring of breast cancer mothers, *Am. J. Epidemiol.* **89:**139–153.

94. Anderson, D. E., 1975, Genetics and breast cancer, in: *Early Breast Cancer: Detection and Treatment* (H. S. Gallager, ed.), John Wiley, New York, p. 41–49.

95. Juret, P., 1981, Reproductive factors and the natural history of breast cancers. Reviews on endocrine-related cancer, *Cancer* **9:**29–35.

96. Dole, R., Muir, C., and Waterhouse, J. (eds.), 1970, *International Union Against Cancer (UICC), Cancer Incidence in Five Continents,* Volume 2, Springer-Verlag, Berlin.

97. Mausner, J. S., Shimkin, M. B., Moss, N. H., and Rosemond, G. P., 1969, Cancer of the breast in Philadelphia hospitals, 1951–1964, *Cancer* **231:**260–274.

98. Applewhite, R. R., Smith, L. R., and DiVincenti, F., 1973, Carcinoma of the breast associated with pregnancy and lactation, *Am. Surg.* **39:**101–104.

99. Treves, N., and Holleb, A. I., 1958, A report of 549 cases of breast cancer in women 35 years of age or younger, *Surg. Gynecol. Obstet.* **107:**271–283.

100. Horsley, J. S., III, Alrich, E. M., and Wright, C. B., 1969, Carcinoma of the breast in women 35 years of age or younger, *Annals Surg.* **169:**839–843.

101. Cancer Statistics: 25 year cancer survey, 1975, *American Cancer Society Professional Education Publication, Ca–A Cancer Journal for Clinicians* **25:**2.

102. Rosemond, G. P., and Mayer, W. P., 1971, Pregnancy and breast cancer, in: *Breast Cancer—Early and Late,* (M. D. Anderson Hospital) Year Book Medical, Chicago, pp. 227–235.

103. Rosemond, G. P., 1966, Management of patients with carcinoma of the breast in pregnancy, *Ann. N.Y. Acad. Sci.* **114:**851–856.

104. Peters, M. V., 1968, The effect of pregnancy in breast cancer, in: *Prognostic Factors in Breast Cancer* (A. P. M. Forrest and P. B. Kunkler, eds.), Williams and Wilkins Co., Baltimore, p. 65–80.

105. White, T. T. and White, W. C., 1956, Breast cancer and pregnancy: report of 39 cases followed five years, *Ann. Surg.* **144:**389–391.

106. Byrd, B. F., Jr., Bayer, D. S., Robertson, J. C., and Stephenson, S. E., Jr., 1962, Treatment of breast tumors associated with pregnancy and lactation, *Ann. Surg.* **155:**940–947.

107. Donegan, W. L., 1977, Breast cancer and pregnancy, *Obstet. Gynecol.* **50(2):**244–252.

108. Goldsmith, H. S., 1974, Milk-rejection sign of breast cancer, *Am. J. Surg.* **127:**280–281.

109. Cheek, J. H., 1953, Survey of current opinions concerning carcinoma of the breast occuring during pregnancy, *Arch. Surg.* **66:**664–668.

110. Costarides, J. and Theofanides, C., 1963, Carcinoma of the breast during pregnancy or lactation, *J. Int. Coll. Surg.* **40:**146–151.

111. Haagensen, C. D., 1967, Cancer of the breast in pregnancy and during lactation, *Am. J. Obstet. Gynecol.* **98:**141–149.

112. Rissanen, P. M., 1968, Carcinoma of the breast during pregnancy and lactation, *Br. J. Cancer.* **22:**663–668.

113. Helman, P. and Bennett, M. B., 1963, Breast cancer and pregnancy, *S. Afr. Med. J.* **37:**1236–1239.
114. Erwald, R., 1967, Mammary carcinoma and pregnancy, *Acta Obstet. Gynecol. Scand.* **46:**316–326.
115. Potter, J. F. and Schoeneman, M., 1970, Metastases of maternal cancer to the placenta and fetus, *Cancer* **25:**380–388.
116. Cheek, J. H., 1973, Cancer of the breast in pregnancy and lactation, *Am. J. Surg.* **126:**729–731.
117. Peete, C. H., Jr., Shimkin, M. B., and Moss, N. H., 1969, Cancer of the breast in pregnancy, *N. Carolina Med. J.* **27:**514–520.
118. Earley, T. K., Gallagher, J. Q., and Chapman, K. E., 1969, Carcinoma of the breast in women under thirty years of age, *Am. J. Surg.* **118:**832–834.
119. Haagensen, C. D., 1971, *Diseases of the breast,* W. B. Saunders Co., Philadelphia, p. 662.
120. Holleb, A. I. and Farrow, J. H., 1962, The regulation of carcinoma of the breast and pregnancy in 283 patients, *Surg. Gynecol. Obstet.* **115:**65–71.
121. Rosemond, G. P., 1963, Carcinoma of the breast during pregnancy, *Clin. Obstet. Gynecol.* **6:**994–1001.
122. Bunker, M. L. and Peters, M. V., 1963, Breast cancer associated with pregnancy or lactation, *Am. J. Obstet. Gynecol.* **85:**312–319.
123. Devitt, J. E., Beattie, W. G., and Stoddart, T. G., 1964, Carcinoma of the breast and pregnancy, *Can. J. Surg.* **7:**124–128.
124. Matsumoto, K. Ochi, H., Momura, Y. Takatani, O., Izuo, M., Okamoto, R., and Sugano, H., 1978, Progesterone and estrogene receptors in Japanese breast cancer, in: *Hormones, Receptors and Breast Cancer* (W. L. McGuire, ed.), Raven Press, New York, pp. 43–58.

Index